SPACE

First published in the UK by HarperCollins Children's Books in 2009

1 3 5 7 9 10 8 6 4 2

ISBN: 978-0-00-732745-4

A CIP catalogue record for this title is available from the British Library.

www.harpercollins.co.uk

THE MOON

The Moon is the only astronomical body other than Earth that human beings have ever set foot on. Like Earth, it is about 4.6 billion years old, though it does not support life of any kind.

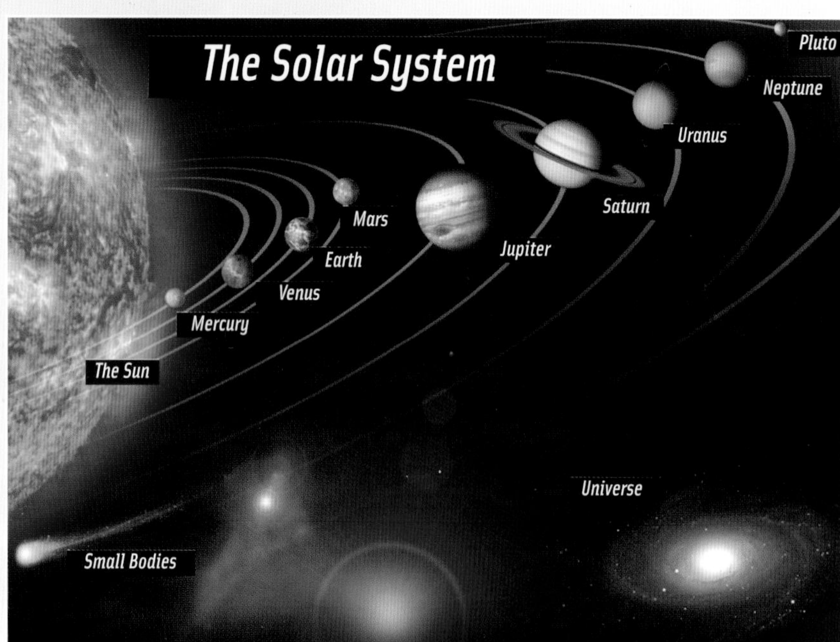

Many Moons

The Moon is Earth's only natural satellite and one of almost 140 moons orbiting planets in our solar system. Earth has only one moon, but some planets have many. Jupiter has 63!

The Moon is the brightest object in the night sky. Its light is reflected from the Sun - it doesn't give off any of its own.

As the Moon rotates around the Earth, it rotates around its own axis, so we always see the same side of the Moon.

Far side of the Moon contrasts with... the blighted near-side of the Moon

DID YOU KNOW?

The difference between a moon and a planet is that a planet orbits the Sun, while a moon orbits a planet.

On the Surface

Seen from Earth, the Moon's surface has both light and dark patches. The light areas are the highlands and are known as terrae (Latin for 'lands'). They are the original crust of the Moon, which has been shattered over time by asteroids, comets and meteoroids hitting the Moon. The dark areas are known as maria (Latin for 'seas'). They are craters that were once partly flooded by lava, which froze to form smooth rock.

Earth's Neighbour

The Sun's gravity acts on Earth and the Moon as if they were a single body with its centre about 1,000 miles beneath Earth's surface. This is called the barycentre and it is the point of balance between the heavy Earth and the lighter Moon. Because the Moon has less mass than Earth, its gravity is about ⅙ of that on Earth. This means that when astronauts visit the moon, their weight is also only ⅙ of that on Earth. The Moon is close enough to Earth that its gravitation pull creates tides in our seas.

Phases of the Moon

Depending on the positions in the sky of the Sun, Earth and Moon, and the amount of sunlight reaching the Moon, different parts of it are visible on Earth at different times of the month. These are known as the four phases of the Moon, which are new moon, first quarter, full moon and last quarter. When the Moon becomes more and more visible over a number of nights, it is said to be waxing. As less and less of it can be seen, it is waning.

When the Moon, Sun and Earth are in a straight line, an eclipse occurs. A lunar eclipse is when Earth gets between the Sun and the Moon and Earth's shadow falls on the Moon. This can only happen when the Moon is full. A solar eclipse is when the Moon gets between the Sun and Earth, and the Moon's shadow falls on Earth.

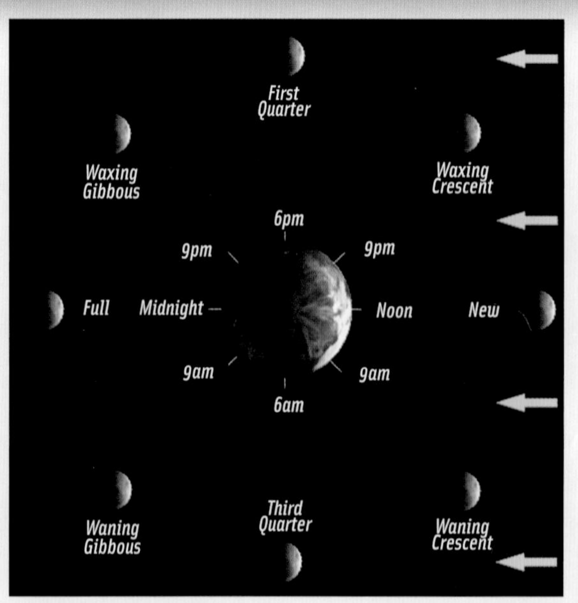

SOME POINTS TO COMPARE:

	Earth	**Moon**
DIAMETER	7,927 miles/12,756 kilometres	2,159 miles/3,476 kilometres
ROTATION (length of day)	23 hours, 56 mins	29.5 days
AVERAGE TEMPERATURE	15°C/59°F	Ranges from -173°C/-280°F to 127°C/260°F
ATMOSPHERE	Oxygen, nitrogen and argon, as well as water vapour, carbon dioxide and small amounts of other chemicals	Hydrogen and helium with some neon and argon
AVERAGE CRUST	6 miles/10 kilometres thick	43 miles/70 kilometres thick
CORE RADIUS	2,200 miles/3,500 kilometres	250 miles/400 kilometres

THE HISTORY OF OUR MOON

The Moon is an incredible 4.5 billion years old. There are several theories about how it was made, ranging from the scientific to the surreal!

Crash! One theory suggests the Moon is a result of a collision between Earth and another object

DID YOU KNOW?

We can see the Moon because it reflects light from the Sun. If the Sun wasn't there, we wouldn't be able to see the Moon at all.

On the Surface

The most popular theory is that the Moon was created when a huge object, the size of Mars, smashed into the Earth and blasted vaporized material into space. The material then fused together to form the Moon.

A little while later, the Moon became surrounded by a gigantic shell of molten rock called the lunar magma ocean. Crystals formed within the magma, creating a crust around the Moon called the anorthosite crust.

Over the next few billion years, it continued to evolve.

Moon Myths

In ancient times, some people thought that the Moon was a huge revolving bowl of fire. Others believed that it was a giant mirror that reflected the Earth. Some Greek philosophers thought that the Moon was a world similar to Earth, with the dark areas being seas and the bright regions being land.

Over time, lots of other myths about the Moon have materialised. One of the most well-known is that the Moon is made of cheese!

People have also believed that the Moon is a god or goddess, that there is a man who lives in the Moon and that people can turn into werewolves at a full moon.

Even to this day, many believe that the Moon has an effect on people's moods.

Artist's impression of a werewolf

Galileo

Italian astronomer Galileo, who lived from 1564 to 1642, was the first person to write a scientific description of the Moon, based on what he had observed through a telescope. His report contradicted the common belief that the Moon was smooth – he described it as rough and mountainous.

Galileo sparked a 350-year debate about the origins of holes on the Moon after describing a large crater in the central highlands.

Galileo

SCIENCE FICTION OR SCIENCE FACT?

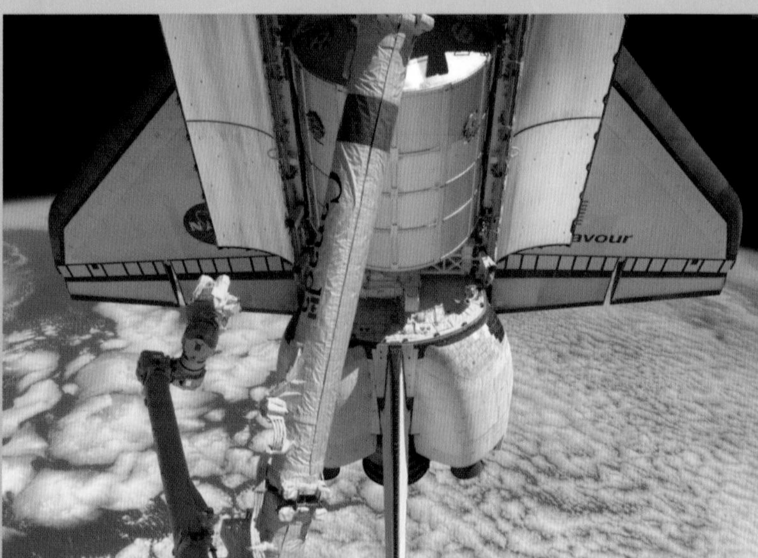

Space exploration has come a long way since writers first imagined...

What would you predict for the future of space exploration?

Many writers imagined what space travel might be like, and, in doing so, often predicted the future.

Jules Verne – In 1865, Jules Verne published *From the Earth to the Moon*, a novel about three men travelling into space. Although technically flawed, it was well researched and inspired scientists to look at his imagined methods of space flight. He accurately predicted the use of aluminium in building spacecraft and suggested Florida (now home of NASA's Kennedy Space Centre, America's 'gateway into space') as a perfect place to launch. The Apollo missions over 100 years later surprisingly resemble the one in his story!

HG Wells – In 1901, H G Wells' novel *The First Men in the Moon* told the story of two men who used an antigravity substance called 'cavorite' to propel them to the Moon.

Arthur C Clarke – Science fiction writer Arthur C Clarke predicted numerous inventions in his writing, including the concept of using rockets in orbit around Earth to relay radio communication, twelve years before the first satellite, *Sputnik 1*, was launched in 1957.

The 1920s to 1940s

Although people had always stared up at the stars and longed to visit them, it wasn't until the beginning of the 20th century that space travel began to seem a real possibility. The Wright Brothers built and flew the first aeroplane in 1903 and from then aviation developments moved incredibly quickly.

Rocket Power

Rockets work by burning chemical propellants and use the same basic principles as ancient fireworks! The first rockets were made in 10th century China and burned gunpowder, which was made from sulphur, charcoal and saltpetre. The sulphur and charcoal were the fuel and the saltpetre provided the oxygen. This mixture was known as black powder. Rockets were used for hundreds of years in firework displays, before their military use became common.

Early illustration of a Chinese rocket

The first British war rockets were built in the early 19th century by Sir William Congreve, who also used black powder to fuel them. They were used to carry explosives and could travel almost 2 miles/3 kilometres.

Sir William Congreve

Russian school teacher, Konstantin Tsiolkovsky, was the first person to calculate that if a rocket burns a liquid propellant, it can reach the high speeds needed to orbit Earth and operate in the vacuum of space. Robert Goddard launched the world's first liquid propelled rocket in 1926. The rocket flew at almost 60 miles/97 kilometres an hour and landed 184 feet/56 metres away.

Once the potential power of the rocket had been established, rocket research advanced in the US, USSR and Germany particularly.

The devastating V-2 Rocket

Wernher von Braun

Wernher von Braun was one of the most important developers at the beginning of space exploration. He was recruited by the German army when they began to investigate the possibility of using rockets as weapons in the 1930s. Von Braun led a team at a secret laboratory in Peenemünde, which spent between £1-2 billion on developing the V-2 missile. The V-2 flew over 3,500 miles per hour and could reach targets 500 miles away. Over 3,000 of them were fired during the Second World War.

When it became clear that Germany was not going to win the war, von Braun and 500 of his scientists surrendered to the US Army, taking all their knowledge and research with them. He worked for the US military for 15 years, later transferring to NASA where he eventually became Director of the Marshall Space Flight Centre and the chief architect on the Saturn V rocket that took Americans to the Moon.

Wernher von Braun

ANIMALS IN SPACE

Humans weren't the first Earthlings to travel into space...

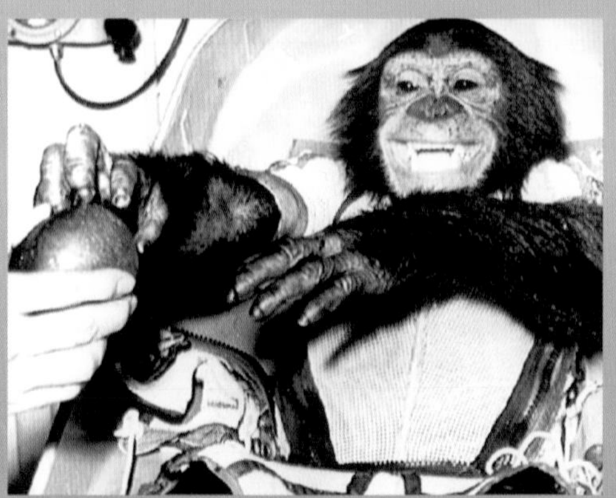

Ham claims his reward on his return to Earth!

Fruit flies – In 1947, the first living things to be launched into space were fruit flies! Scientists studied the effects of space travel on them, as genetically, fruit flies are much more similar to humans than you might think!

Monkeys – In 1948, Albert II, a Rhesus monkey, was sent into space in a specially adapted American V-2 rocket. It flew to 83 miles/134 kilometres above Earth.

Mice – Both the US and USSR sent many mice into space over the years.

Dogs – From 1951 onwards, Russia experimented with sending dogs into space. In 1957, space dog Laika became the first animal to orbit Earth in the *Sputnik 2* satellite.

Chimpanzees – In 1961, Ham was the first chimpanzee in space. He was followed 11 months later by Enos, who was the first chimpanzee to orbit Earth.

Cats – French scientists launched Felix, the first cat into space, in 1963.

All kinds of other creatures have travelled into space, including; turtles, worms, rabbits, spiders and even jellyfish!

The 1950s to 1960s

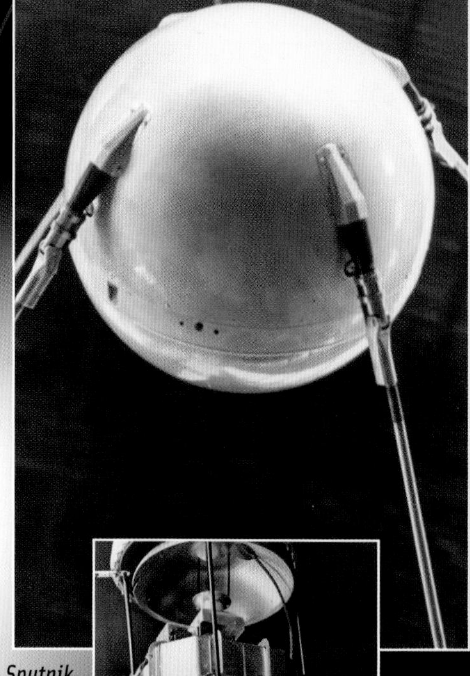

Sputnik

The 50s and 60s saw some major advances in aerospace exploration. The National Aeronautics and Space Administration (NASA) was formed in July 1958 as the agency responsible for the USA's public space programme, the first human was successfully sent to space and the Apollo Programme was launched.

The Space Age

The Space Age really began when the USSR launched their satellite, Sputnik I, into orbit in October 1957. The world's first satellite was about the size of a beach ball and weighed about 184 pounds/83 kilograms. It took around 98 minutes to orbit Earth. Only a month or so later, the Soviets launched Sputnik II. It was much bigger and even carried a dog, Laika, with it.

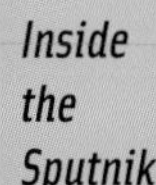

Inside the Sputnik

Russian Advances

Control panel from the Vostok 1

Russian Cosmonaut, Yuri Gagarin, became the first man in space on April 12th, 1961. Onboard a spacecraft named Vostok 1, Gagarin orbited the Earth on a mission that lasted just two hours. Vostok 1 had been designed to crash land, so Gagarin had to jump out of the spacecraft using a parachute before it hit the ground!

Two years later, Valentina Tereshkova became the first woman in space. She went on to become a very important member of the Russian Government and even had a crater on the Moon named after her.

First lady in space

Launching Vostok 1

The Huntsville Times

Man Enters Space

'So Close, Yet So Far,' Sighs Cape

U.S. Had Hoped For Own Launch

Hobbs Admits 1944 Slaying

Soviet Officer Orbits Globe In 5-Ton Ship

Maximum Height Reached Reported As 188 Miles

To Keep Up, U.S.A. Must Run Like Hell'

The space race begins...

John F. Kennedy

Race to the Moon

In 1963, the President of the USA, John F. Kennedy, announced to the world that Americans would land on the Moon before the end of the decade. America had fierce competition from the USSR and a race to be the first country to step foot on the Moon began.

Launching Surveyor 1

In 1966, NASA sent Surveyor 1, a robot spacecraft, to the Moon to ensure it could land without crashing in preparation for the mission.

Apollo 8 astronauts

The Apollo Programme

The Apollo Programme was designed to land humans on the Moon and bring them safely back to Earth.

From 1968, Apollo astronauts successfully tested out new spacecraft and journeyed to uncharted destinations.

SUPER SATELLITES

Sputnik was the first man-made satellite to orbit Earth, but there are now many hundreds of satellites and bits of space junk circling the planet. These satellites are indispensible in our daily lives. Here are just a few of the things they do for us:

Artist's picture of a satellite going off to orbit

Communications networks for telephones, radio and television.
Navigation systems for cars, aircraft and ships.
Provide data for weather and climate forecasting.
Scientific research – monitoring data about space, Earth and its atmosphere and even other planets and stars.
Observe Earth for military purposes – detecting the launch of missiles and military movement on land or sea.

Lunar Landing

With the words, "That's one small step for man, one giant leap for mankind," history was made when Neil Armstrong became the first person to set foot on the Moon on July 20th, 1969. Grainy black and white images of the event were broadcast to at least 600 million people on Earth.

The Apollo 11 crew

Apollo 11

Neil Armstrong, along with crew members Buzz Aldrin and Michael Collins, travelled to the Moon in Apollo 11. The spacecraft was made up of three parts: the Command Module (Columbia), the Service Module and the Lunar Module (Eagle).

Armstrong and Aldrin landed on the Moon in Eagle while Collins remained in Columbia, communicating with crews on Earth and photographing the Moon's surface. At the end of the mission, Armstrong and Aldrin rejoined Columbia, which was the only part of the spacecraft to return to Earth.

The Saturn V Rocket

The amazing Saturn V Rocket was used to launch Apollo 11 on its historic mission to the Moon.

The rocket was 111 metres/363 feet long. Before launch, it weighed more than 6 million pounds/2.7million kilograms and was capable of sending a spacecraft weighing over 100,000 pounds/45,000 kilograms to the Moon.

The rocket flew at 24,000 miles/38,500 kilometres per hour, the speed it needs to reach in order to fight against the gravitational pulls from Earth and the Sun. It could have gone faster, but it would have cost a lot more as it would have burned more fuel.

The rocket used an incredible 3,374,237 litres of propellant just to get it into orbit! Space is 50 miles/80 kilometres away, travelling straight up, but it only takes eight minutes to get there! The Moon is about 239,000 miles/385,000 kilometres from Earth.

Roll it out! - Saturn V being transported to its launch pad

DID YOU KNOW?

To travel the distance between Earth and the Moon by car would take 130 days!

MAN ON THE MOON

Neil Armstrong and Buzz Aldrin spent two and a half hours walking on the Moon's surface. This is what they did:

- Took photographs.
- Collected soil samples to take back to Earth.
- Conducted various exercises, including testing methods for moving around on the Moon.
- Spoke to the President, Richard Nixon, through a telephone-radio transmission.
- Planted an American flag.
- Unveiled the plaque with the President's signature on it.

Life in Space

Life in a spaceship or space station is very different to life on Earth!

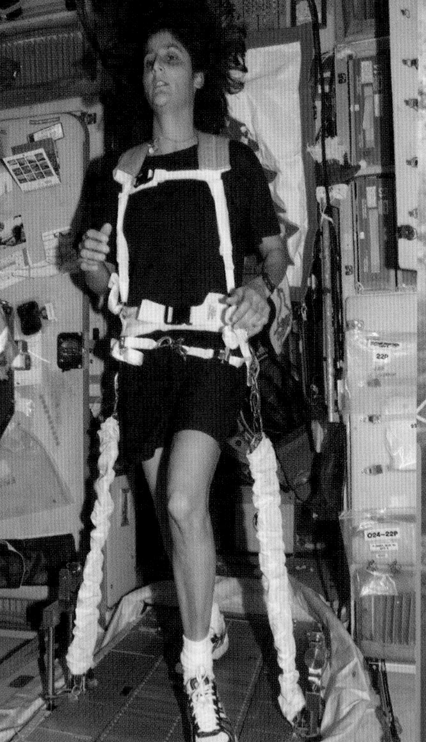

An astronaut exercises in space

Gravity

The gravity on Earth gives us weight and pulls us down. In space, the lack of gravity is very difficult on the human body. Our bones, muscles and organs have evolved with the force of gravity always on them, so prolonged periods without gravity cause the body to weaken.

DID YOU KNOW?

During the early space flights, astronauts wore special apparatus to collect their waste and bring it back to Earth to be analysed!

Food and Drink

Astronauts must make sure they have enough food to last the length of their mission. It has to be light, so it doesn't add too much weight to the spacecraft, and compact, so it doesn't take up too much space, and also remain edible for as long as possible.

One way to conserve weight for launch is to remove water from certain items of food, so many things are dehydrated. Water that has been produced by the spacecraft is then added to the food before it is eaten. The menus are carefully planned to make sure the astronauts get all the vitamins and minerals they need on their long voyage.

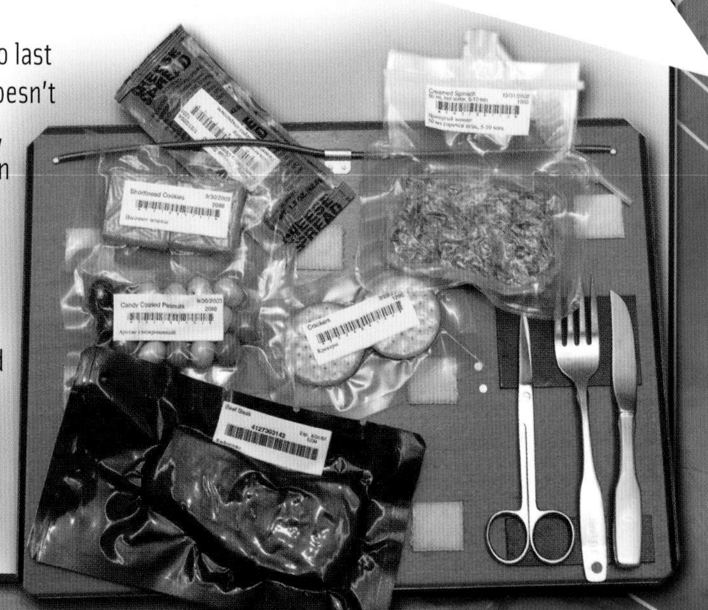

Astronauts unpack their special sleeping bags

Sleeping

To get any sleep in space, astronauts have to strap themselves into a chair, bunk bed, or sometimes even a sleeping bag attached to the wall!

THE INTERNATIONAL SPACE STATION (ISS)

The ISS is the largest artificial satellite orbiting Earth and is almost as big as an American football field. Due to its size and the number of reflective solar panels on it, it can actually be seen from Earth by the naked eye!

It is a joint project between the space agencies of the United States, Russia, Japan, Canada and Europe and has been visited by astronauts from sixteen different nations. Construction of the ISS began in 1998 and is scheduled for completion in 2011. The first astronauts to live there were Bill Shepherd, Yuri Gidzenko and Sergei Krikalev in 2000.

The ISS is used primarily for research and is helping scientists understand the effects of long-term space travel on the human body. The data they are gathering could make the colonisation of space a reality!

On the Moon

The crew of Apollo 11 left various items on the Moon including a replica gold olive branch – the traditional symbol of peace, a silicon disk containing goodwill messages from leaders around the world and a mission patch.

First Footprint

The surface of the Moon is rocky and powdery, similar to charcoal. When Neil Armstrong stepped out of Eagle he made the first ever footprint on the Moon. The prints from this first Moon landing will be there for a million years because there isn't any wind on the Moon to blow them away.

Space Science

Scientific instruments were left on the Moon by the crew of Apollo 11 and have also been left by subsequent crews. These include retroflectors which are still being used today in an ongoing experiment to measure the continually changing distance between Earth and the Moon. Lasers on Earth are aimed at a retroflector and the time delay for the reflected light to return is determined. From this, the exact distance to the Moon can be calculated.

Information from these experiments has shown that the Moon is moving away from the Earth at a rate of about 3.8 cm/1.5 inches every year.

Astronauts use Lunar Rovers to travel on the Moon

The McDonald Observatory, Texas, USA: Laser beams are regularly sent to the Moon from this research centre

CONSPIRACY THEORIES

Some people argue that the Apollo 11 Moon landing was faked, so that America could claim to have won the space race against the USSR! Here are some of their queries – and the reasons used as proof to show that it was not faked!

Could it have been filmed in a television studio? In the 1960s, special effects were really bad! It would also have been impossible to accurately predict what it would be like on the Moon, and subsequent missions would have shown the inconsistencies.

Why does the flag look like it's flying in the breeze, if there is no air on the Moon? The astronauts wanted to be sure when they took photos of the event, that the American flag would be clearly seen. As there is no air on the Moon, they knew the flag would droop down, so they put a pole through the top of it to make it stick out.

Why are there no stars visible in the background? The light from the sun shining off the Moon's surface is so bright that the camera can't capture anything in the distance. The same effect can be found in cities, where it is much harder to see the stars because of all the light from buildings.

The Apollo 11 mission cost billions of dollars and over 390,000 people were involved in making it happen. There have also been five subsequent journeys to the Moon. If the landings really were a hoax, surely someone would have admitted it by now!

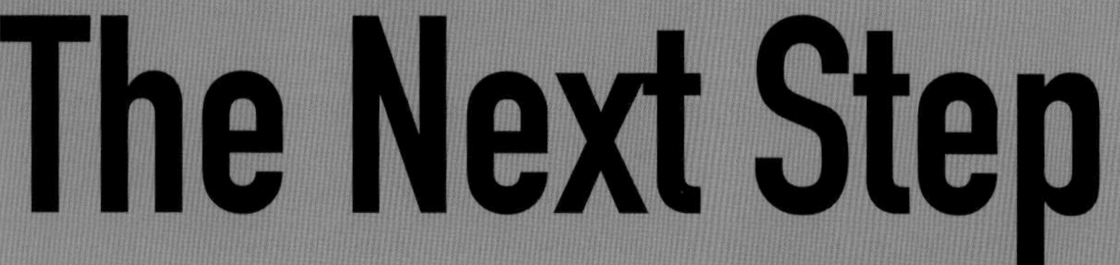

The Next Step

The last man to walk on the Moon was Eugene Cernan, Commander of Apollo 17, on December 18th, 1972. NASA cancelled three subsequent Apollo missions to make way for new developments such as the International Space Station. To this day, only 12 men have walked on the moon.

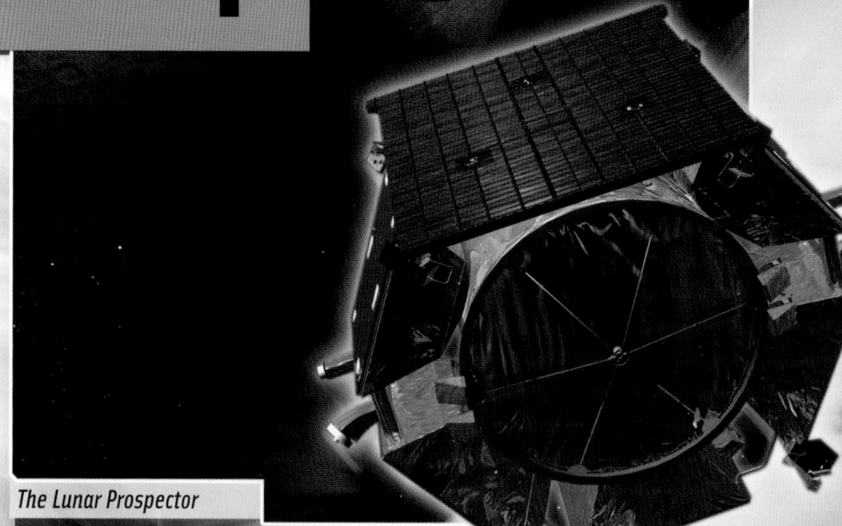

The Lunar Prospector

Back to the Moon

The USSR sent four Luna robot craft to the Moon after the Apollo missions. The last Luna returned to Earth in August 1976 with samples of lunar soil.

It wasn't until 1994 that the next spacecraft was sent to the Moon – the US's Clementine. Over a three month period, Clementine took more than 2 million pictures of the Moon and measured the height and depth of mountains and craters using a laser device.

The south pole of the Moon, as seen by Clementine

SMART-1

Between January 1998 and July 1999, the Lunar Prospector orbited the Moon. This US spacecraft mapped the surface composition of the Moon, measured its magnetic fields and found evidence of ice at the Moon's poles.

The European Space Agency launched SMART-1 in 2003, which orbited the Moon in 2004. The spacecraft investigated the origin of the Moon and surveyed the chemical elements of the Moon's surface.

In 2004, George Bush, the President of the United States of America, announced plans to build a new spacecraft and return to the Moon by 2020. China has also announced its intentions to put a man on the Moon by 2020 and India wants to do it by 2015.

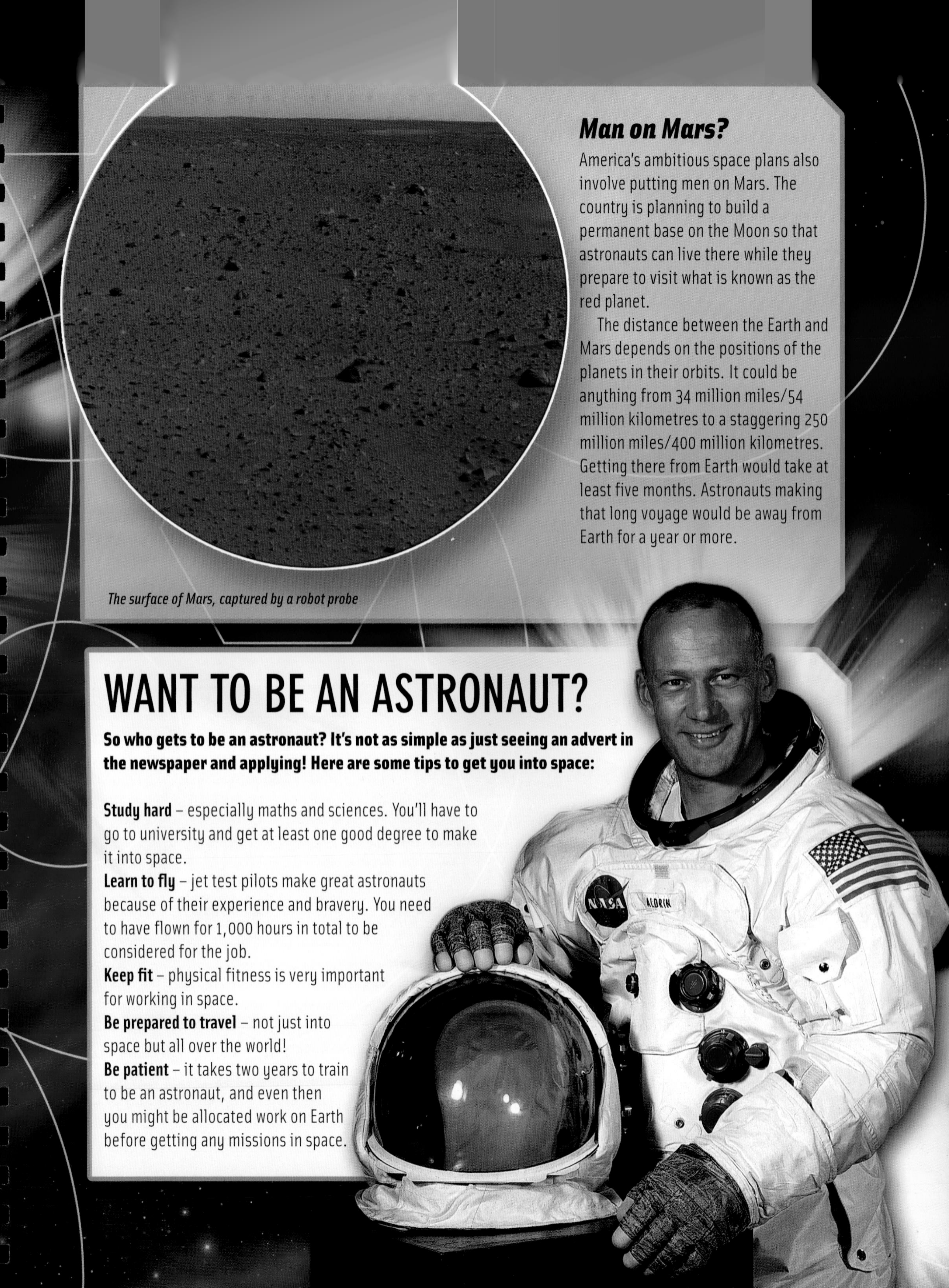

The surface of Mars, captured by a robot probe

Man on Mars?

America's ambitious space plans also involve putting men on Mars. The country is planning to build a permanent base on the Moon so that astronauts can live there while they prepare to visit what is known as the red planet.

The distance between the Earth and Mars depends on the positions of the planets in their orbits. It could be anything from 34 million miles/54 million kilometres to a staggering 250 million miles/400 million kilometres. Getting there from Earth would take at least five months. Astronauts making that long voyage would be away from Earth for a year or more.

WANT TO BE AN ASTRONAUT?

So who gets to be an astronaut? It's not as simple as just seeing an advert in the newspaper and applying! Here are some tips to get you into space:

Study hard – especially maths and sciences. You'll have to go to university and get at least one good degree to make it into space.

Learn to fly – jet test pilots make great astronauts because of their experience and bravery. You need to have flown for 1,000 hours in total to be considered for the job.

Keep fit – physical fitness is very important for working in space.

Be prepared to travel – not just into space but all over the world!

Be patient – it takes two years to train to be an astronaut, and even then you might be allocated work on Earth before getting any missions in space.

COLUMBIA MODULE AND SERVICE MODULE MODEL INSTRUCTIONS (DIFFICULTY RATING: EASY)

General instructions

Follow the instructions below carefully. Only press out each piece as you need it. Where necessary, fold along the marked creases. The models have been designed so that when you push the tabs through the appropriate slots, the tab ends should spring back, locking the part in place. Make sure that the coloured side is on the outside of the model and that all tabs are hidden on the inside of the model.

1 Slot **Part A** into **Part B** and push them both through **Part C** to form the Docking Probe.

2 Fasten the two ends of **Part D** together to form a cone shape.

3 Press the Docking Probe in place at the bottom of the cone, slotting the six tabs through the six slots.

4 **Parts E** and **F** form the Heat Shield. Work your way around the circle slotting the tabs into place – the outer piece will begin to bend into a flattened cone shape. Now fasten the two ends of **Part E** together.

5 Line up the seams and attach the heat shield to the part made previously.

6 To make the Service Module, bend **Part H**, the Deep Space Antenna, into shape and fasten it to **Part G**, the base of the Service Module, as shown.

7 Bend **Part I** into shape, as shown, and attach to **Part G** using the tabs.

8 **Parts J** and **K** form a Rocket Engine. Fasten the two pieces together as you bend them into a cone shape, then use the tabs to close the cone.

9 Connect the engine to the base of the Service Module (**Part I**).

10 Use the tabs to attach **Part M** to **Part L**, then line up the red dots and connect the walls of the Service Module to the base. Once you've connected all the base tabs, join the ends of the walls together to form a cylinder.

11 Fold **Part N** in half and fix it inside the cylinder, as shown on the opposite page.

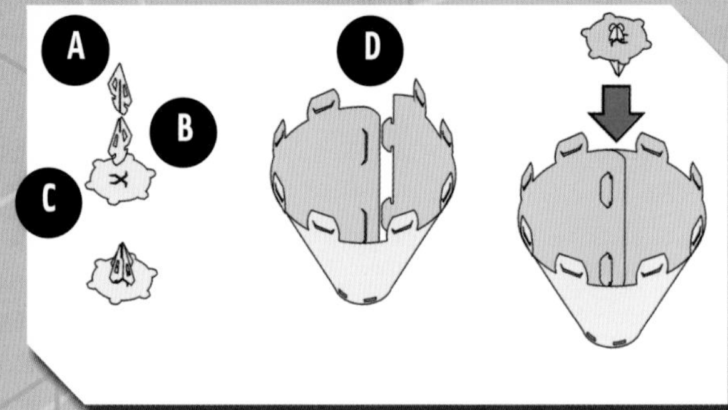

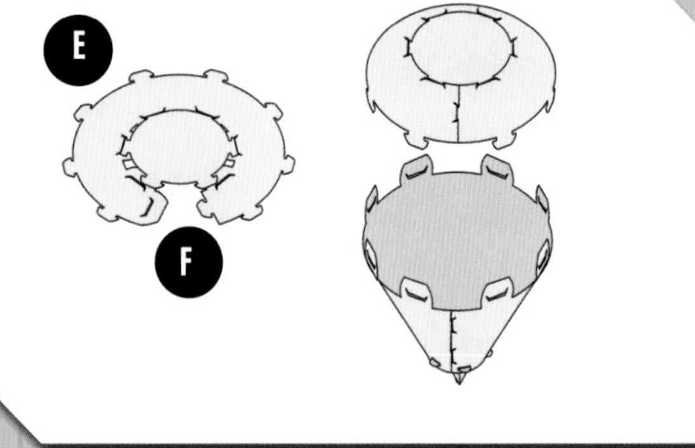

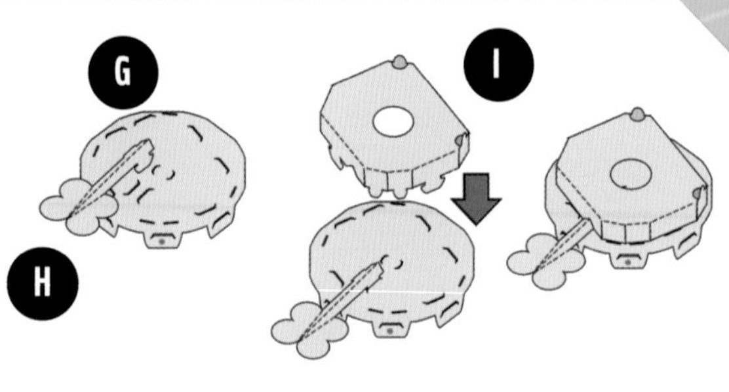

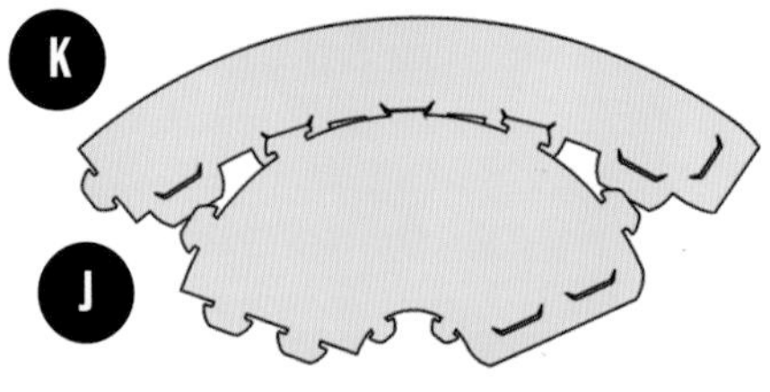

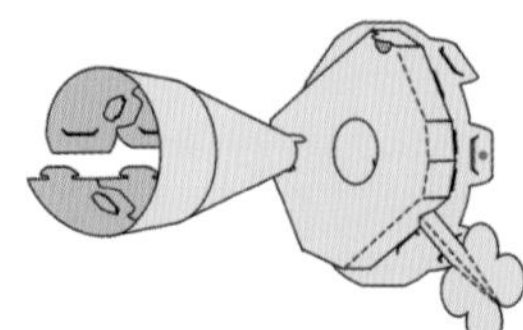

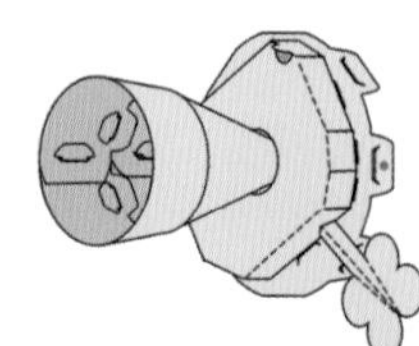

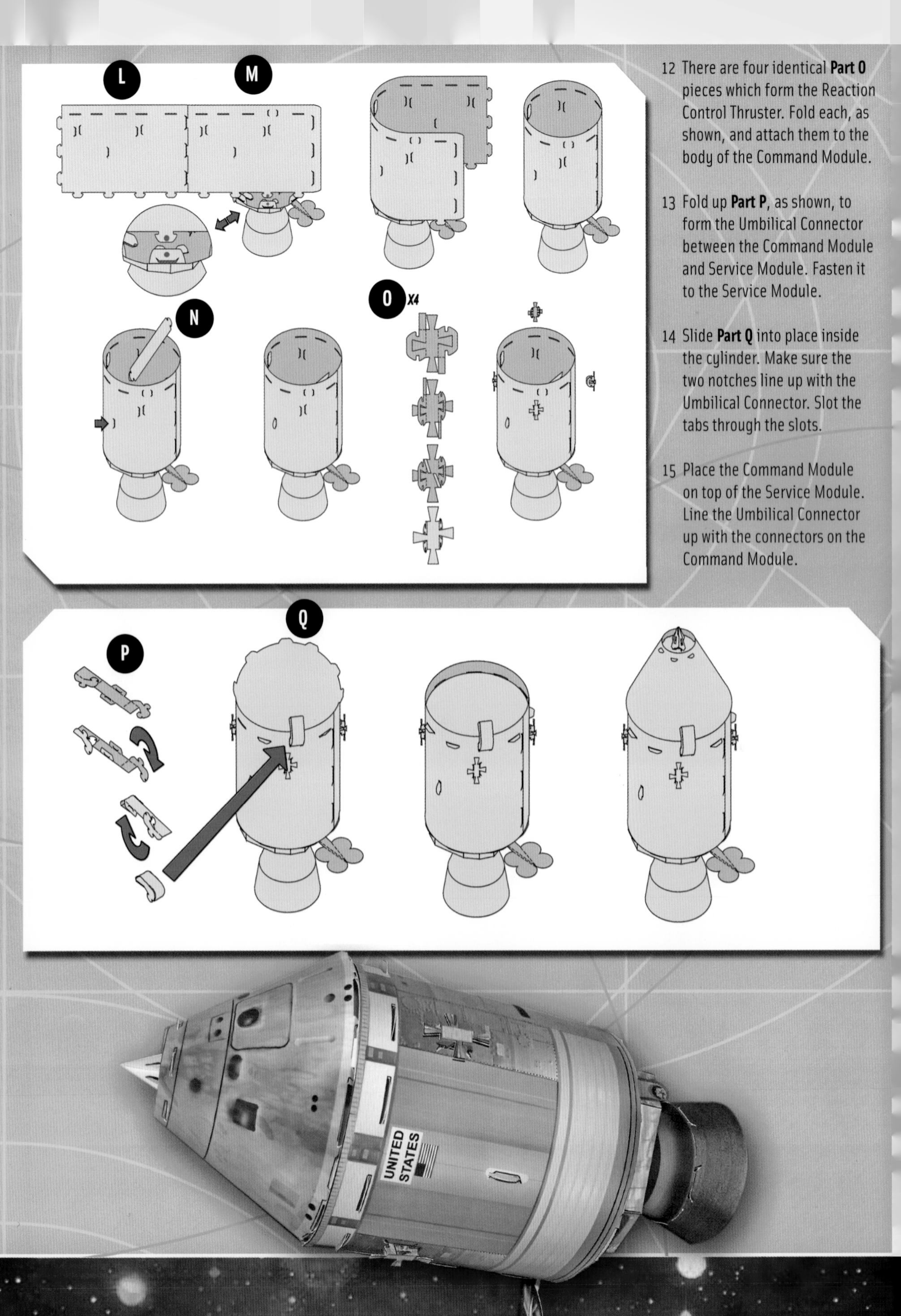

12 There are four identical **Part O** pieces which form the Reaction Control Thruster. Fold each, as shown, and attach them to the body of the Command Module.

13 Fold up **Part P**, as shown, to form the Umbilical Connector between the Command Module and Service Module. Fasten it to the Service Module.

14 Slide **Part Q** into place inside the cylinder. Make sure the two notches line up with the Umbilical Connector. Slot the tabs through the slots.

15 Place the Command Module on top of the Service Module. Line the Umbilical Connector up with the connectors on the Command Module.

SATURN V ROCKET MODEL INSTRUCTIONS
(DIFFICULTY RATING: MEDIUM)

General instructions

Follow the instructions below carefully. Only press out each piece as you need it. Where necessary, fold along the marked creases. The models have been designed so that when you push the tabs through the appropriate slots, the tab ends should spring back, locking the part in place. Make sure that the coloured side is on the outside of the model and that all tabs are hidden on the inside of the model.

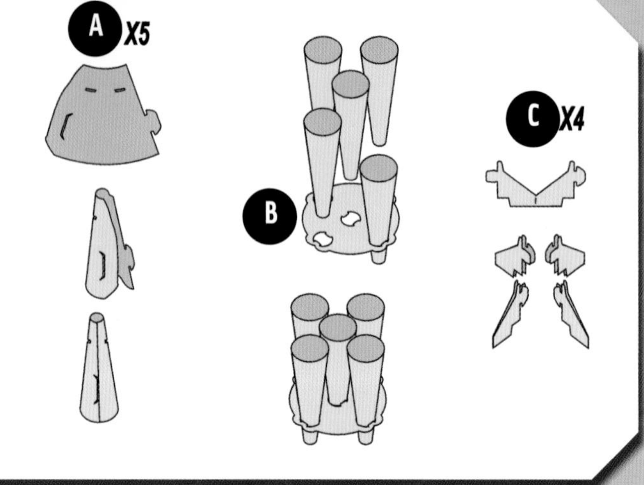

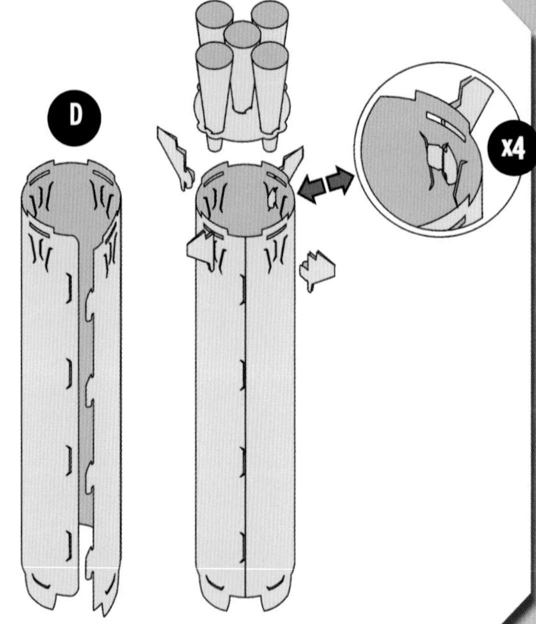

1 There are five identical **Part A** pieces, which form the five Saturn Engines. Fold each into a cone shape and fasten it shut.

2 Each engine has two locating slots near the narrow end. Push each engine into place in **Part B** (on the card sheet, you will find this piece in the centre of the **Part A** pieces) so that the slots lock into the notches.

3 Bend **Part D** into a cylinder and fasten it shut.

4 The four identical **Part C** pieces make the four rocket fins. Fold each one in half and attach it to the cylinder.

5 Flatten the two tabs that hold each fin in place so they rest against the walls of the cylinder, as shown. Push the engines inside the cylinder, using the tabs to fix them place.

6 The four identical **Part E** pieces form the Engine Cowlings. Slide one over each of the fins and fasten the ends to the cylinder.

7 Bend **Part F** into a cylinder and fasten it shut. Bend **Part G** into a partial cone, as shown on the opposite page, and fasten shut. Attach the two pieces together.

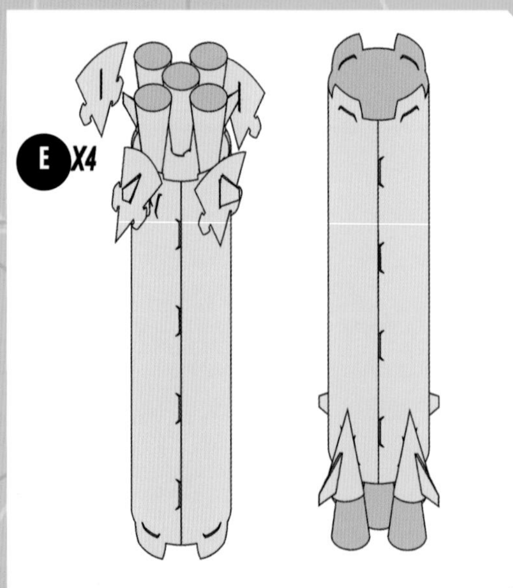

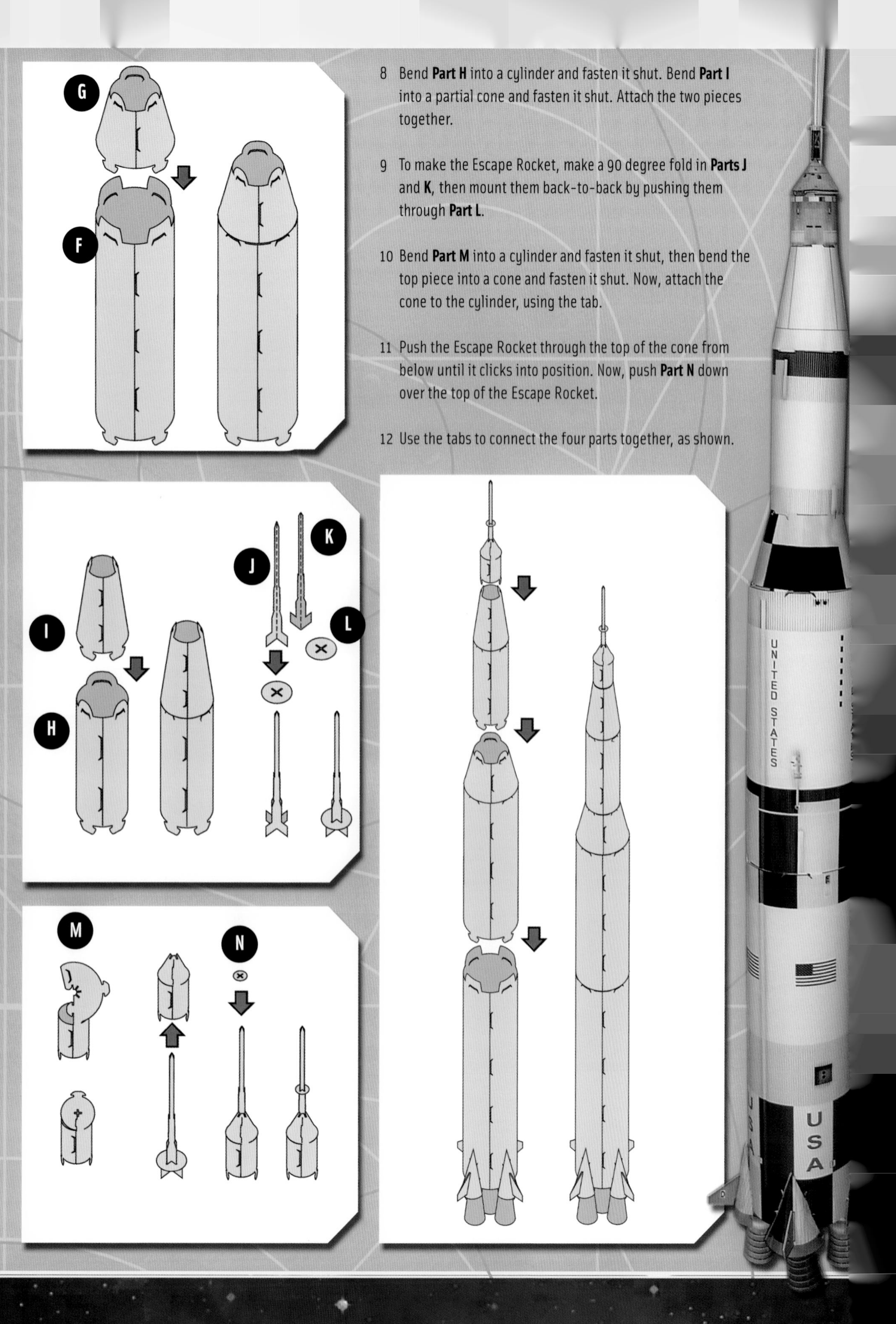

8 Bend **Part H** into a cylinder and fasten it shut. Bend **Part I** into a partial cone and fasten it shut. Attach the two pieces together.

9 To make the Escape Rocket, make a 90 degree fold in **Parts J** and **K**, then mount them back-to-back by pushing them through **Part L**.

10 Bend **Part M** into a cylinder and fasten it shut, then bend the top piece into a cone and fasten it shut. Now, attach the cone to the cylinder, using the tab.

11 Push the Escape Rocket through the top of the cone from below until it clicks into position. Now, push **Part N** down over the top of the Escape Rocket.

12 Use the tabs to connect the four parts together, as shown.

EAGLE LANDER AND LUNAR EXCURSION MODULE MODEL INSTRUCTIONS
(DIFFICULTY RATING: HARD)

General instructions

Follow the instructions below carefully. Only press out each piece as you need it. Where necessary, fold along the marked creases. The models have been designed so that when you push the tabs through the appropriate slots, the tab ends should spring back, locking the part in place. Make sure that the coloured side is on the outside of the model and that all tabs are hidden on the inside of the model.

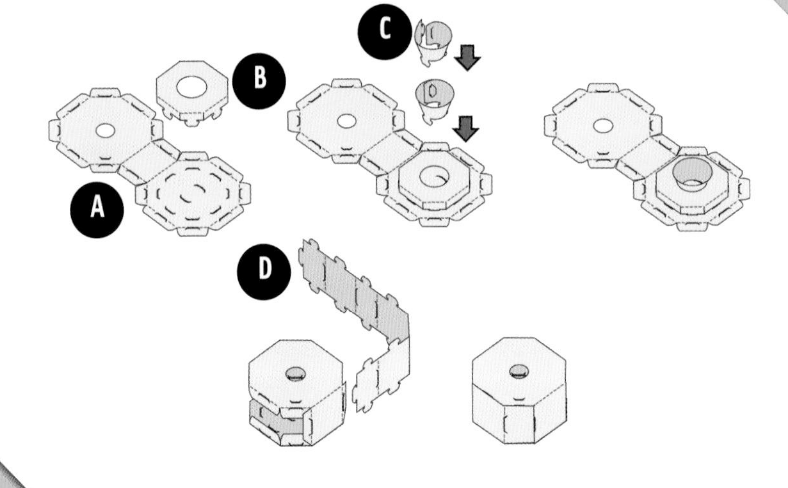

1 Bend **Part B** into place and use the tabs to attach it to the base of **Part A** to make the Descent Stage.

2 Bend **Part C**, the Descent Stage Rocket, into a partial cone and fasten the ends together. Use the tabs to attach it to the base of **Part A**.

3 Bend **Part A** into a box shape and attach **Part D** to form the side walls of the box.

4 There are four identical **Part E** pieces, which form the legs of the Lunar Excursion Module. Fold each one in half and attach them to the body of the Descent Stage, as shown below.

5 **Part F** is the ladder. Slide it over the Lunar Excursion Module, as shown, then bend it round and slot the tab in place. Finally, bend the handrails up, as shown below.

6 There are four identical **Part G** pieces, which are the feet. Push these into place, as shown below.

7 To make the Assent Stage, lay out **Part H** and bend up the front sections, as shown on the opposite page.

8 Wrap the side wall round, as shown, using the tabs to fix it in place.

9 Bend the Radar Antenna Dish into shape by tucking the tab through the slot and bending it flat, as shown.

10 Wrap the other side wall round, as shown. Fasten the sides as you go, then fasten the top.

11 Bend the front section of **Part H** into a box shape. Bend it downwards so it fastens into the front face of the assembly.

12 Fold the two Reaction Control Thrusters back on themselves, as shown on the right, and slot the ends into the slots on the Lunar Excursion Module body. Bend **Part I** into a box shape and attach it in place, as shown.

13 **Parts J** and **K** form the back section of the Lunar Excursion Module. Attach the two parts, as shown on the right, then bend the side walls into place, fastening the tabs as you go.

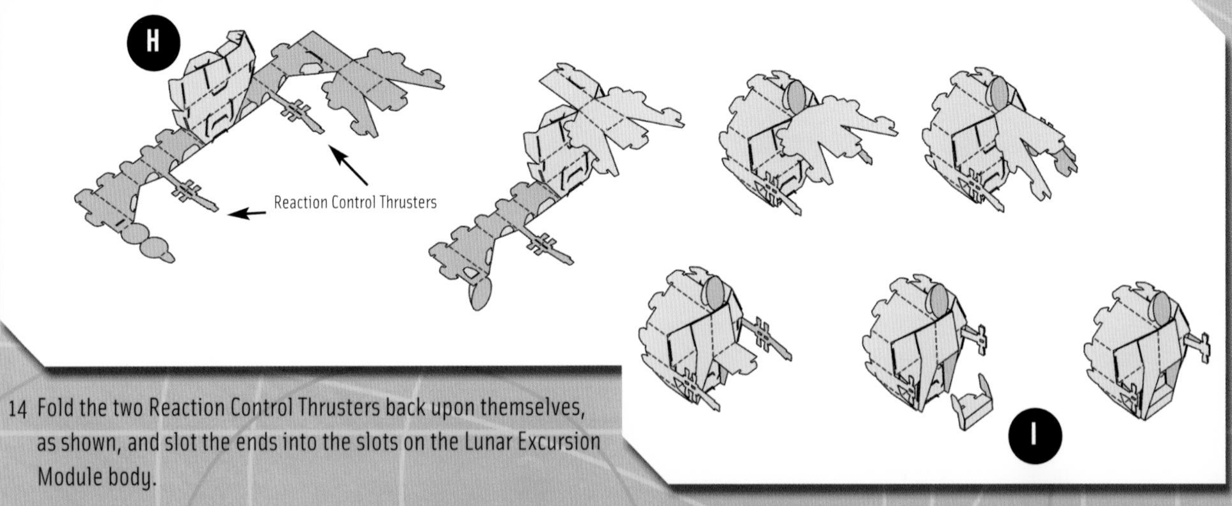

14 Fold the two Reaction Control Thrusters back upon themselves, as shown, and slot the ends into the slots on the Lunar Excursion Module body.

15 Fold **Part L** down the middle to form an antenna and attach it to **Part M**, as shown. Now, attach the back of the Lunar Excursion Module to **Part M**, making sure the Antenna is sticking out.

16 Partially fold **Part M** into shape to form the mid section of the Lunar Excursion Module, but don't attach the tabs just yet. Attach the front section of the Lunar Excursion Module.

17 Fasten the top and sides of the Lunar Excursion Module mid section together, but keep the bottom piece open.

18 **Part N** forms the cover for the Assent Propulsion Fuel Tank. Attach it to the side of the Lunar Excursion Module, as shown below, then bend the top and bottom panels into place and attach using the tabs.

19 Bend **Part P** into a tube to form the Docking Ring at one end and the Assent Engine at the other, as shown on the next page. Push **Part O** into the tube and locate the appropriate notches – this can be a bit fiddly and you may find it easier to use a pencil rather than your fingers.

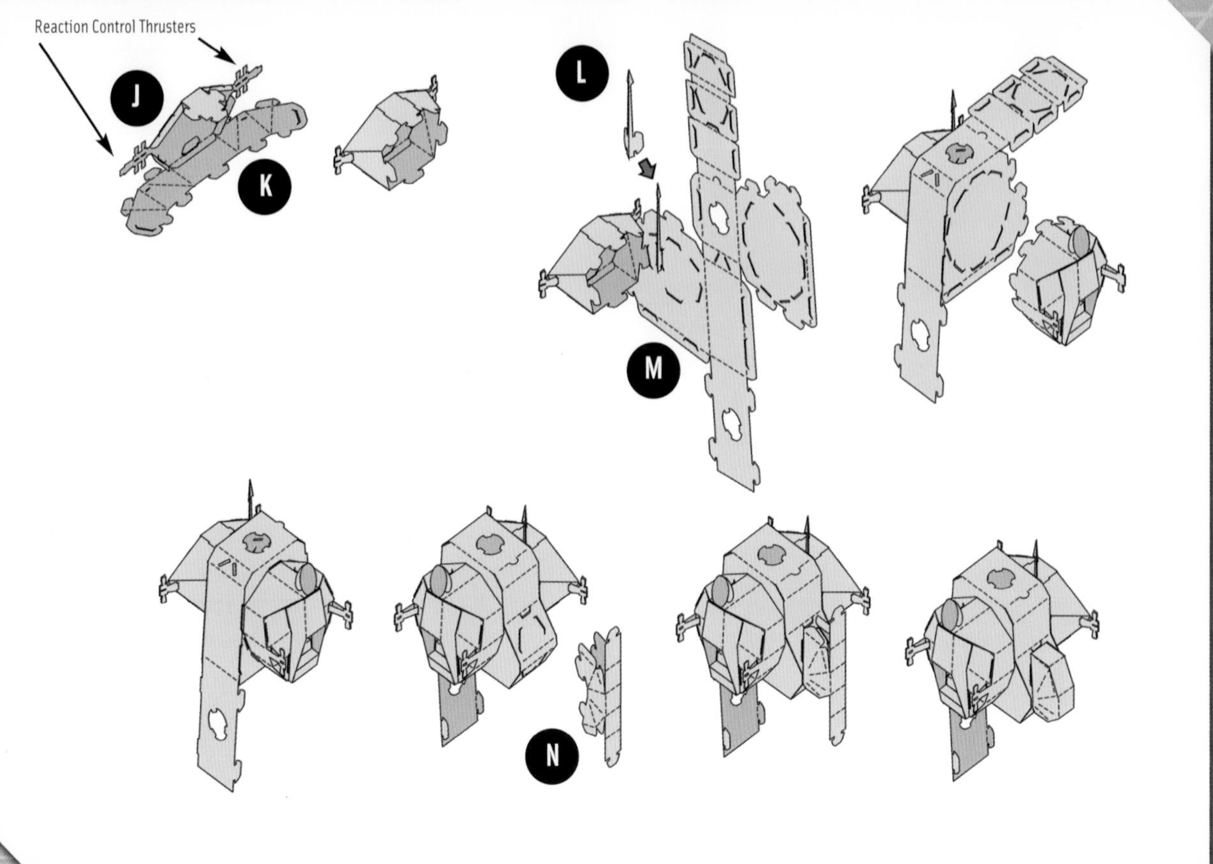

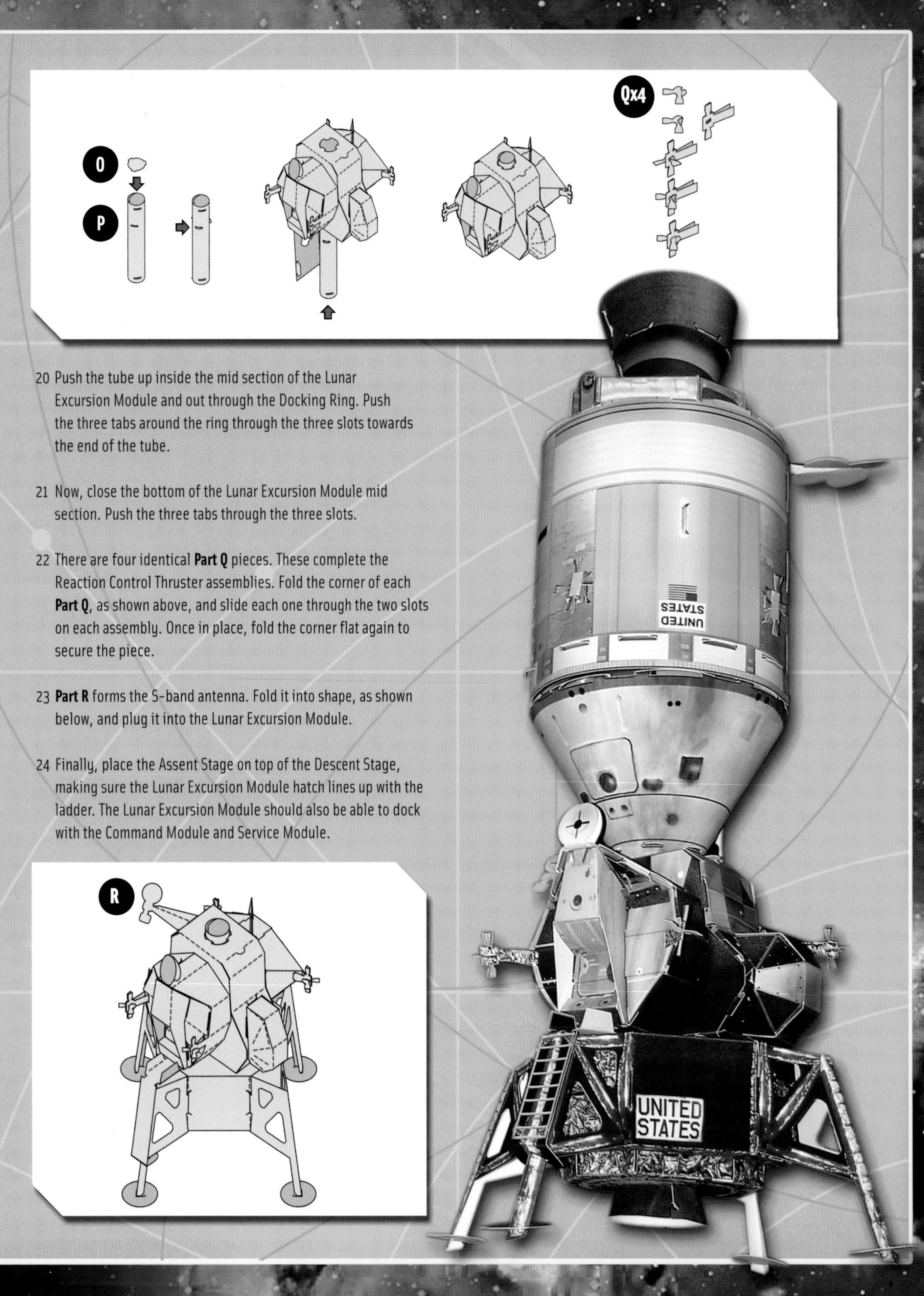

20 Push the tube up inside the mid section of the Lunar Excursion Module and out through the Docking Ring. Push the three tabs around the ring through the three slots towards the end of the tube.

21 Now, close the bottom of the Lunar Excursion Module mid section. Push the three tabs through the three slots.

22 There are four identical **Part Q** pieces. These complete the Reaction Control Thruster assemblies. Fold the corner of each **Part Q**, as shown above, and slide each one through the two slots on each assembly. Once in place, fold the corner flat again to secure the piece.

23 **Part R** forms the S-band antenna. Fold it into shape, as shown below, and plug it into the Lunar Excursion Module.

24 Finally, place the Assent Stage on top of the Descent Stage, making sure the Lunar Excursion Module hatch lines up with the ladder. The Lunar Excursion Module should also be able to dock with the Command Module and Service Module.

Columbia Module and Service Module pieces

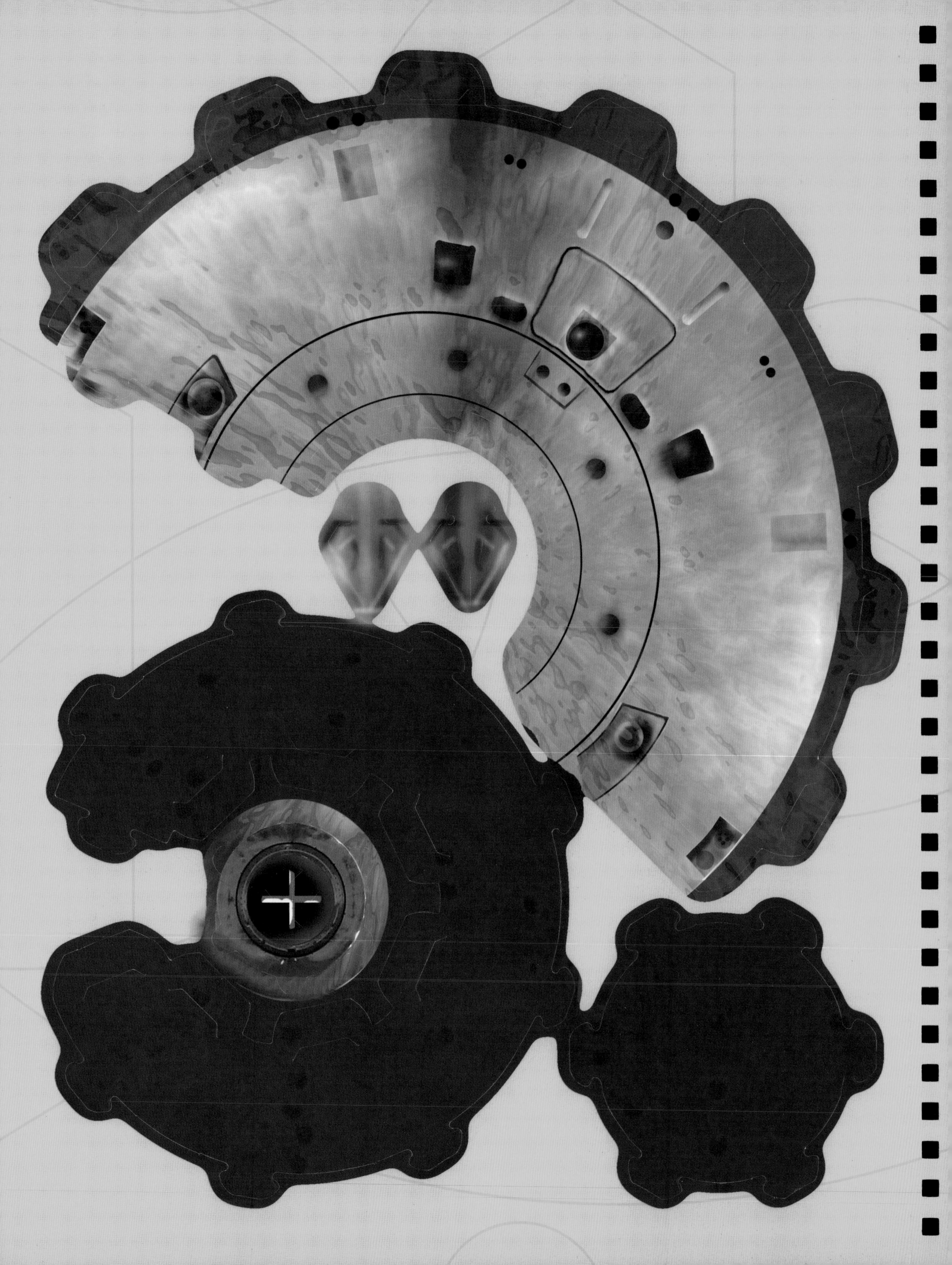

Columbia Module and Service Module pieces

Columbia Module and Service Module pieces

Columbia Module and Service Module pieces

M

UNITED STATES

UNITED STATES

L

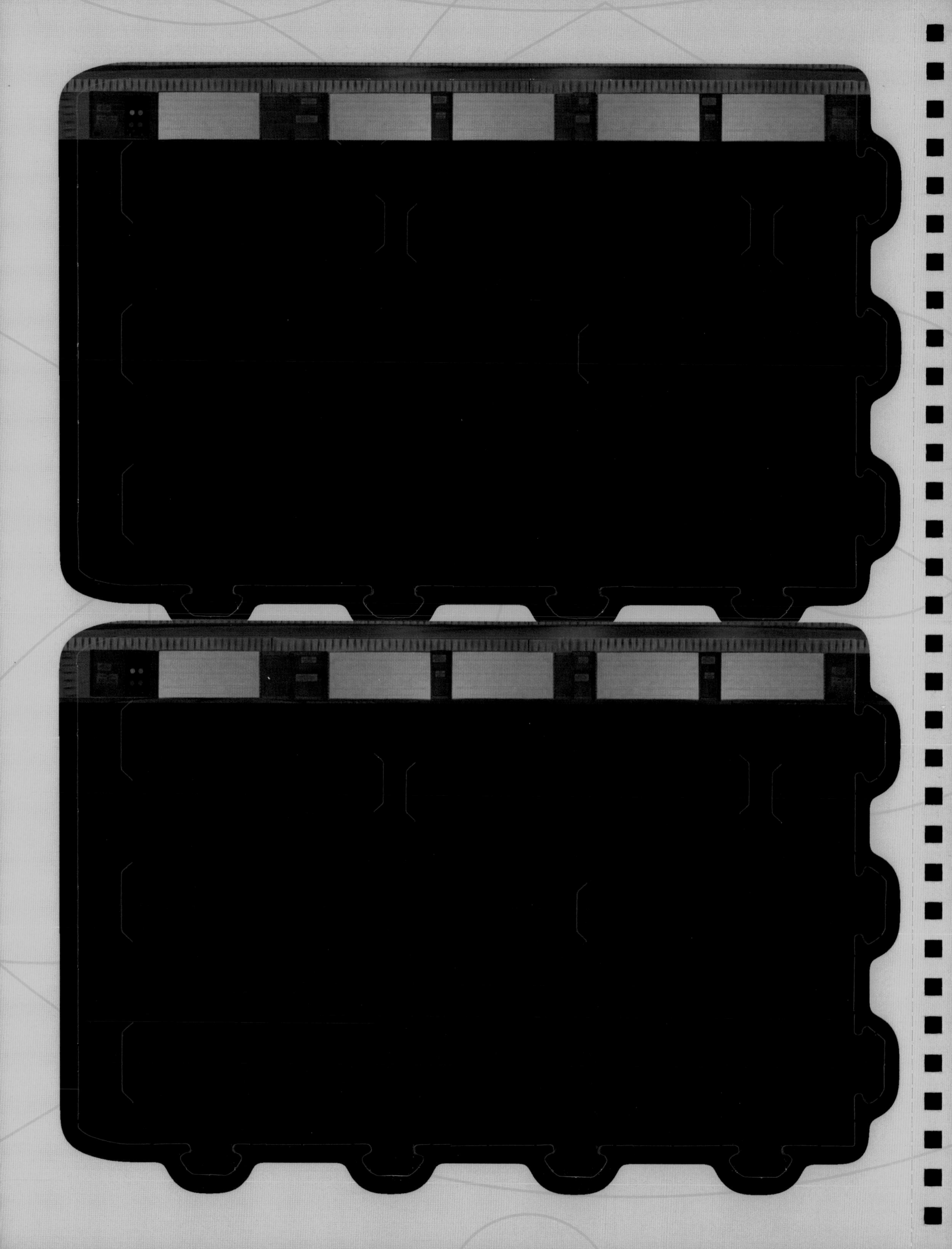

Saturn V Rocket pieces

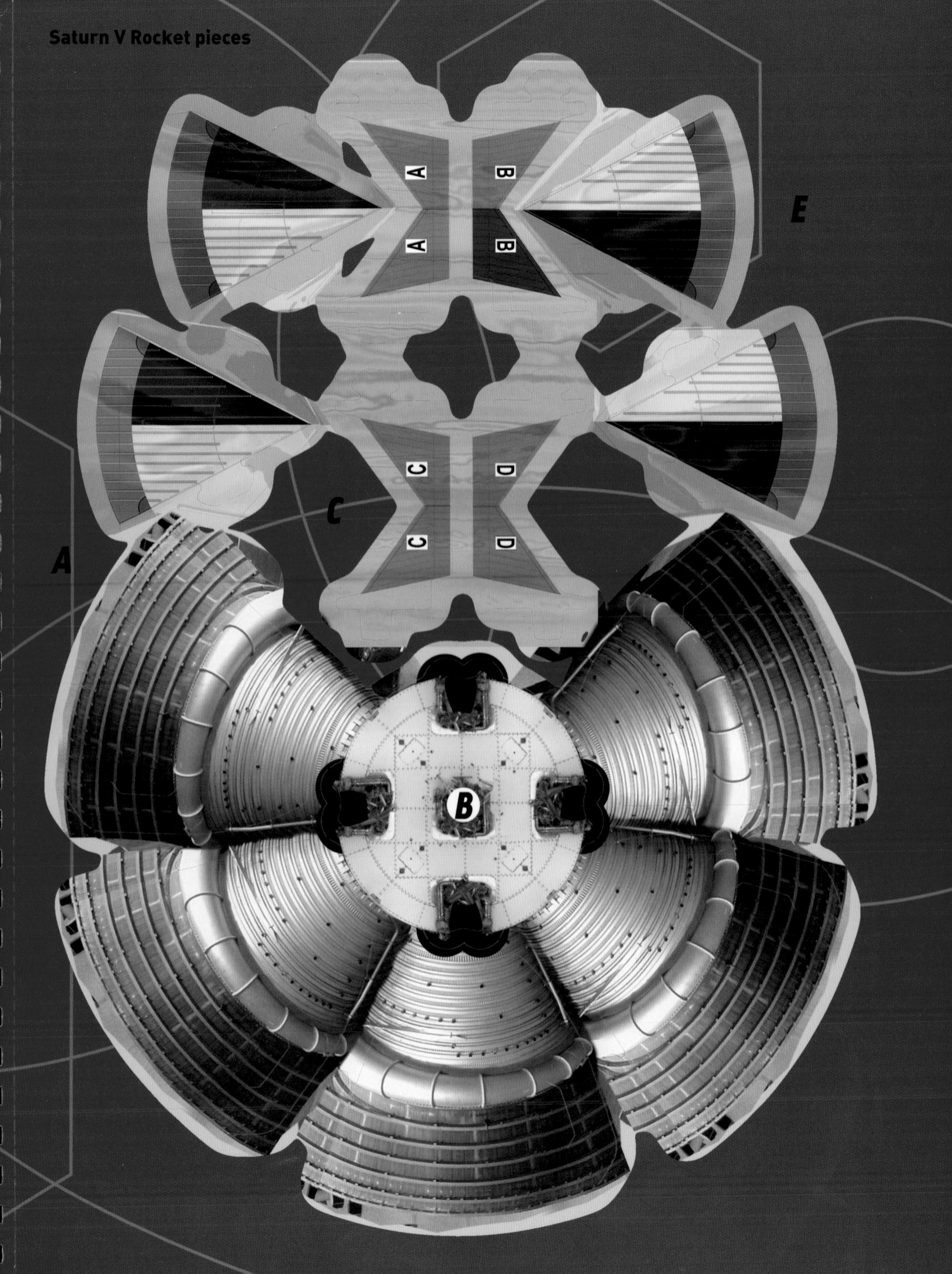

Saturn V Rocket pieces

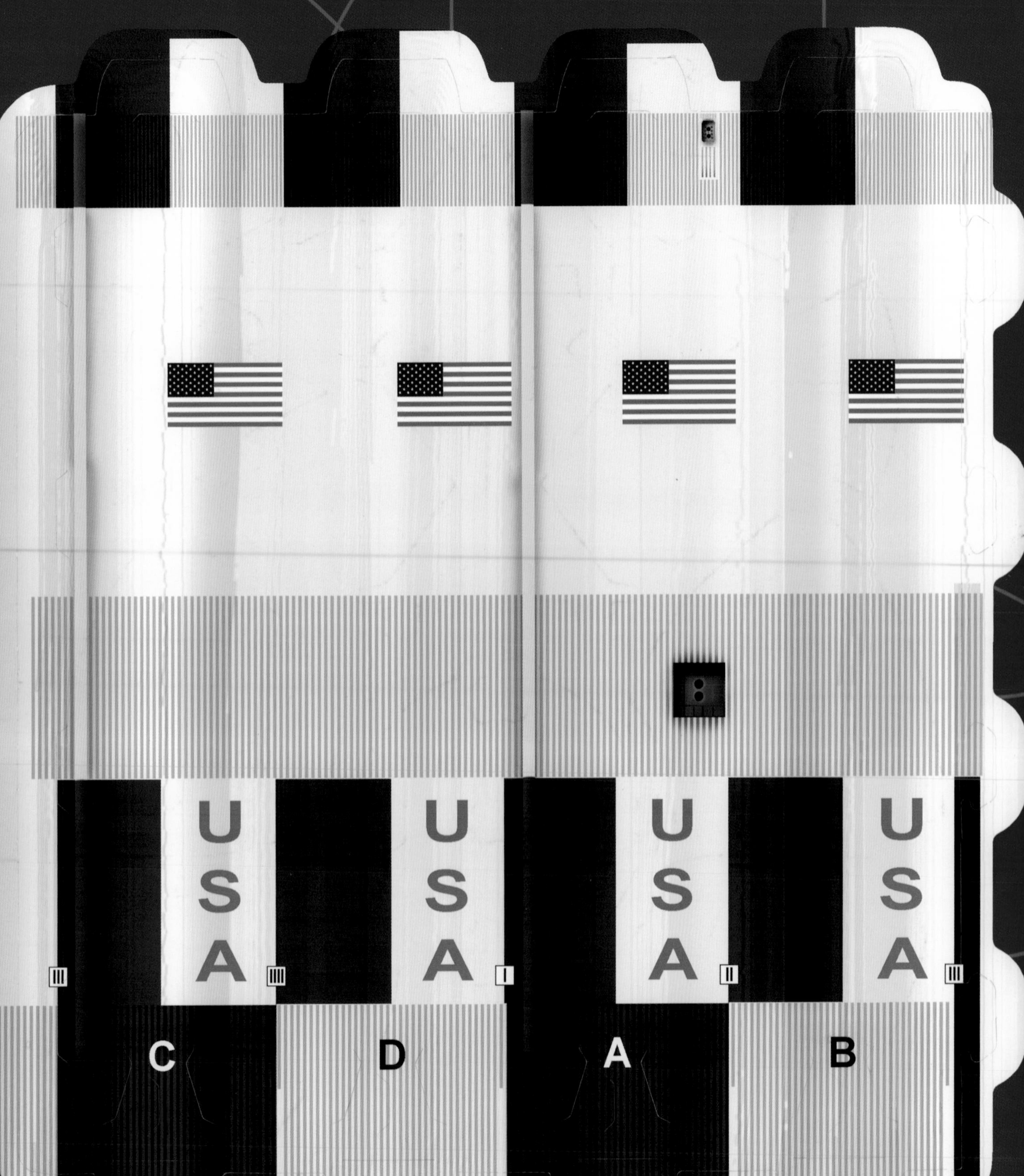

Saturn V Rocket pieces

G

F

UNITED STATES

UNITED STATES

UNITED STATES

UNITED STATES

Saturn V Rocket pieces

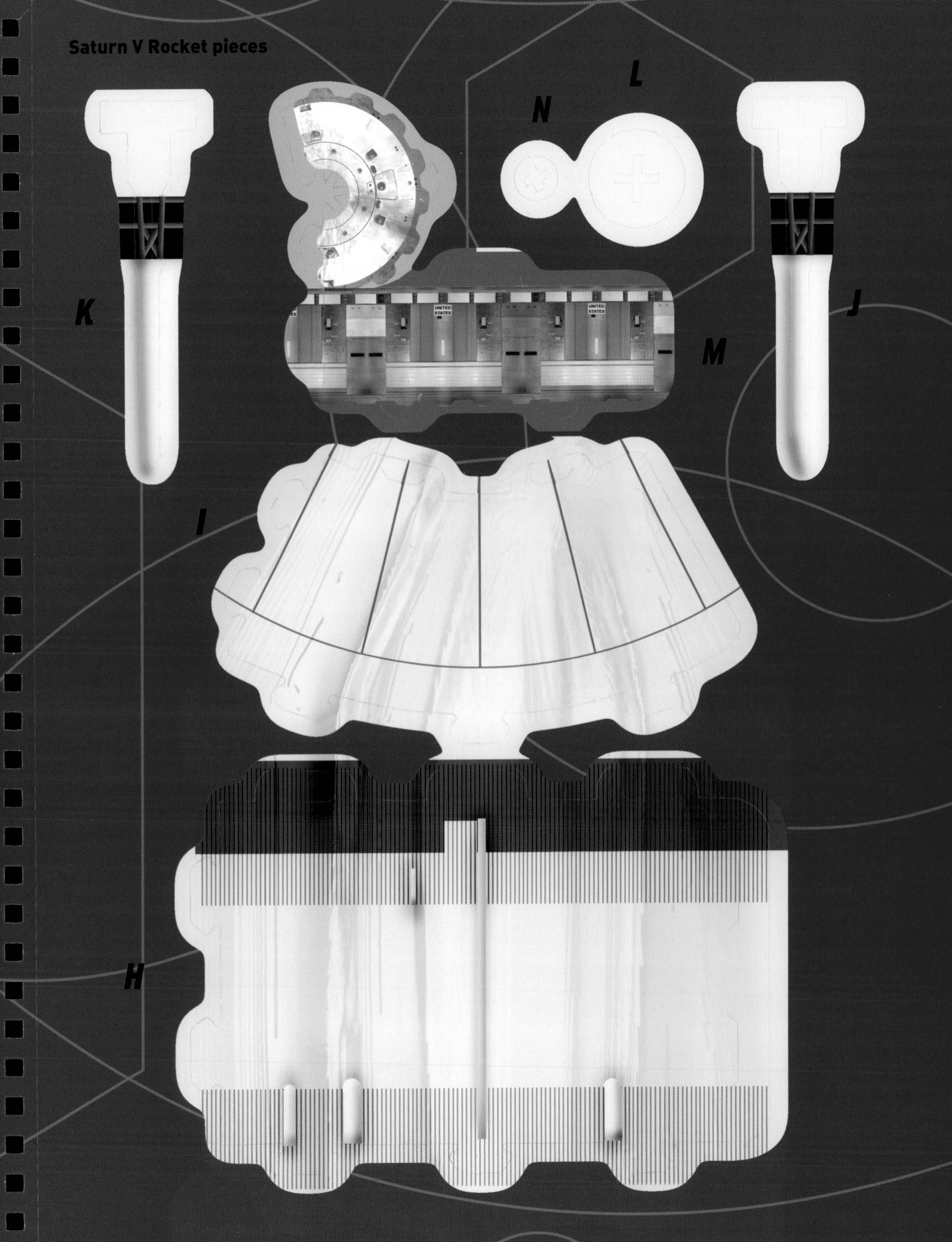

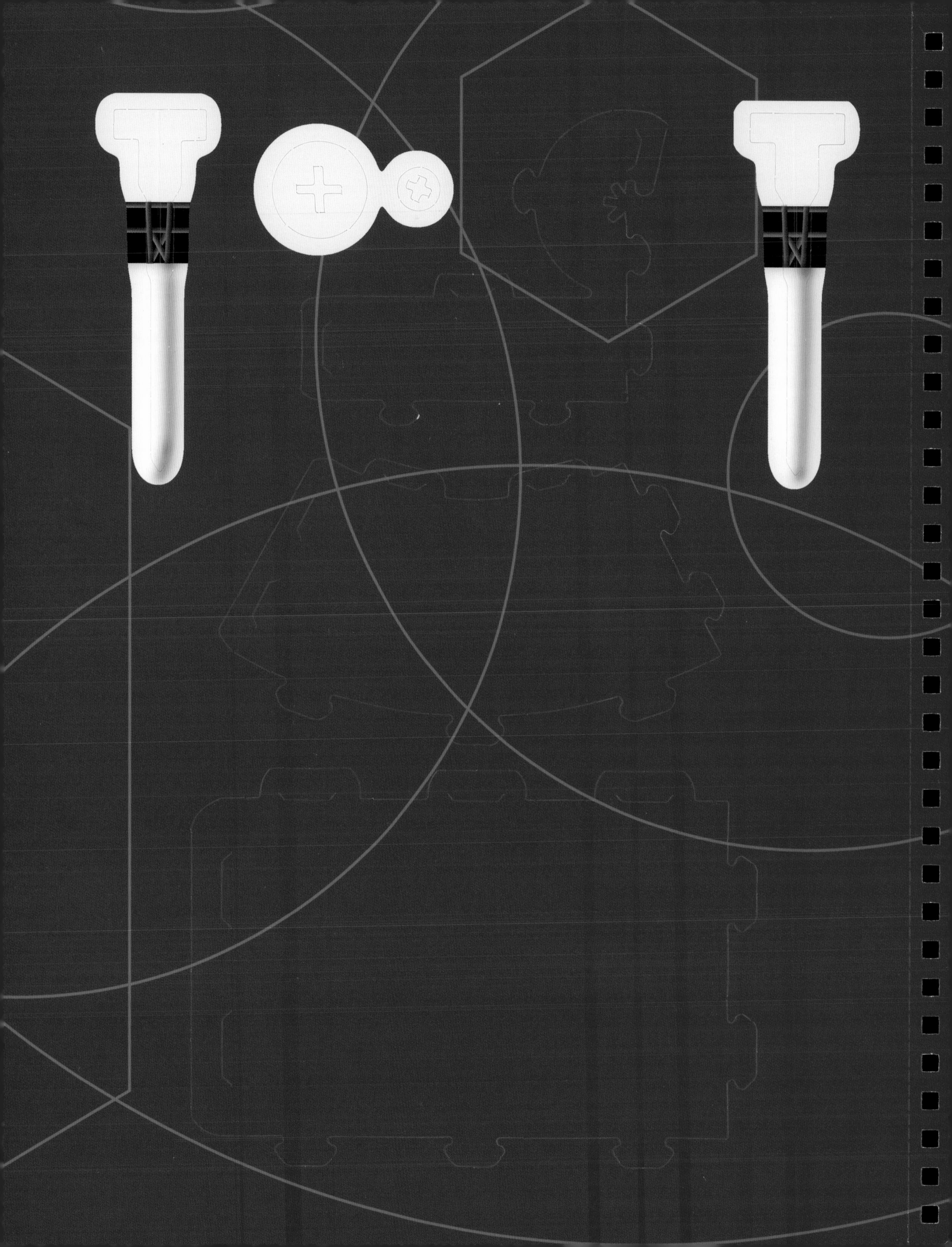

Eagle Lander and Lunar Excursion Module pieces

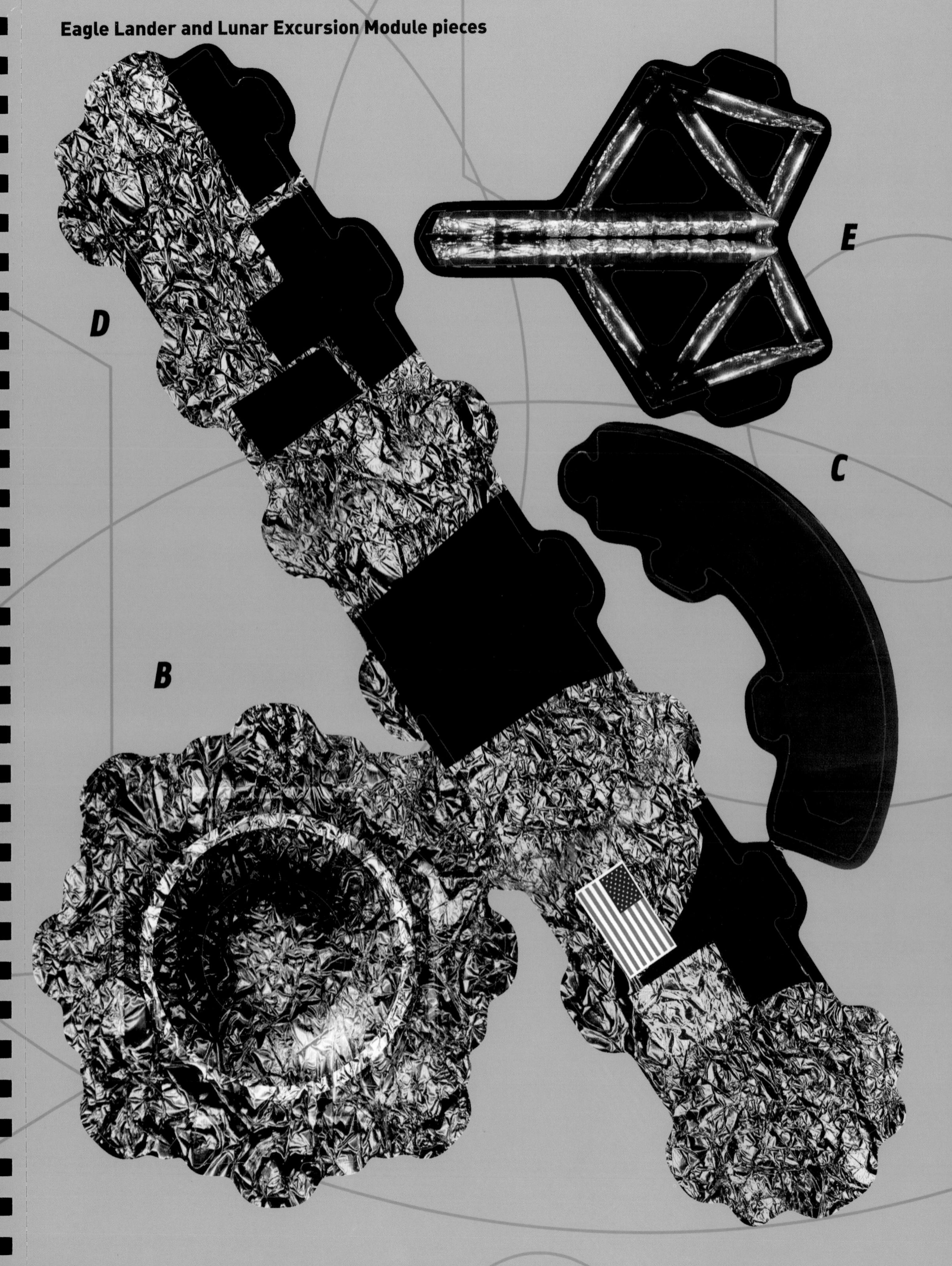

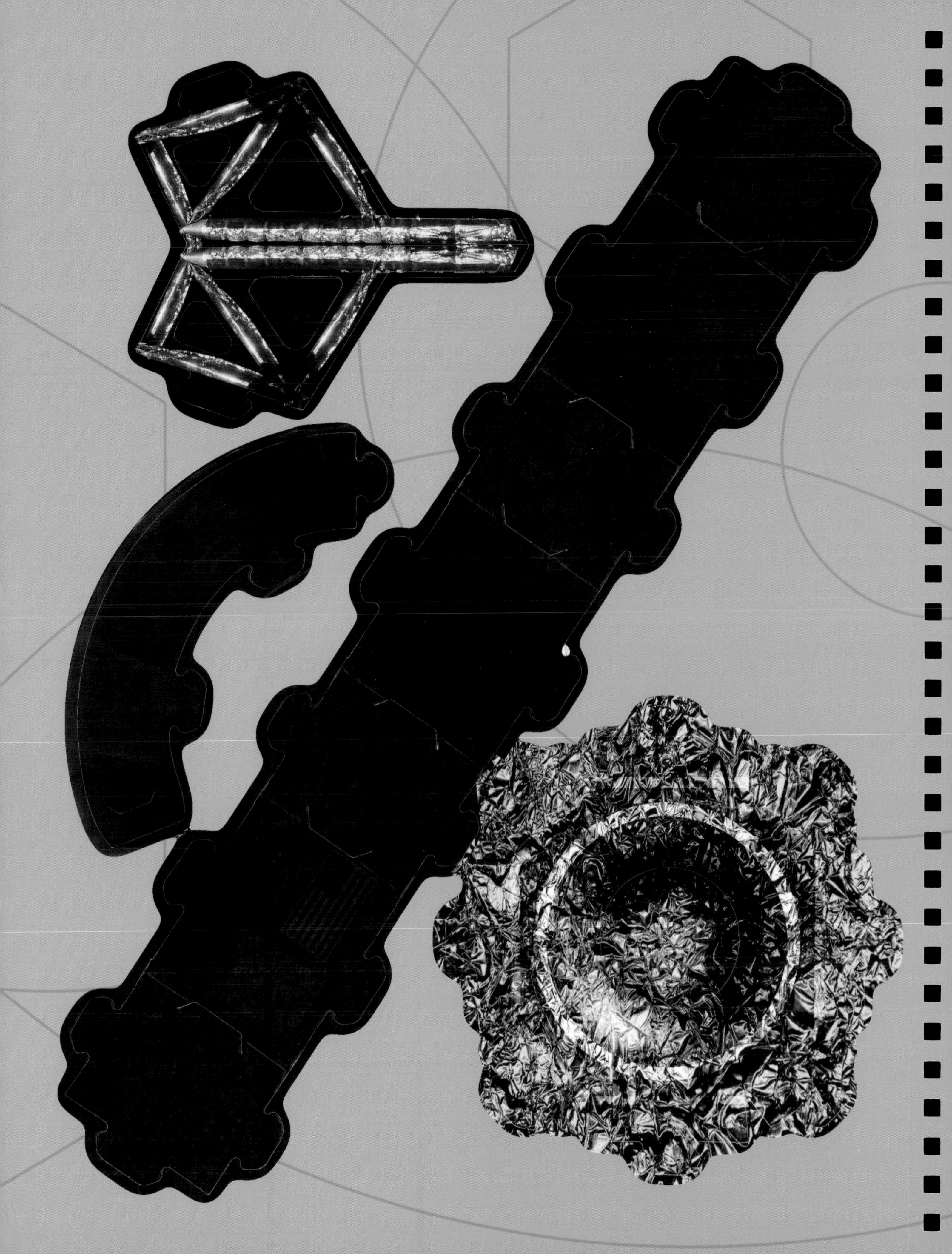

Eagle Lander and Lunar Excursion Module pieces

Eagle Lander and Lunar Excursion Module pieces

Eagle Lander and Lunar Excursion Module pieces

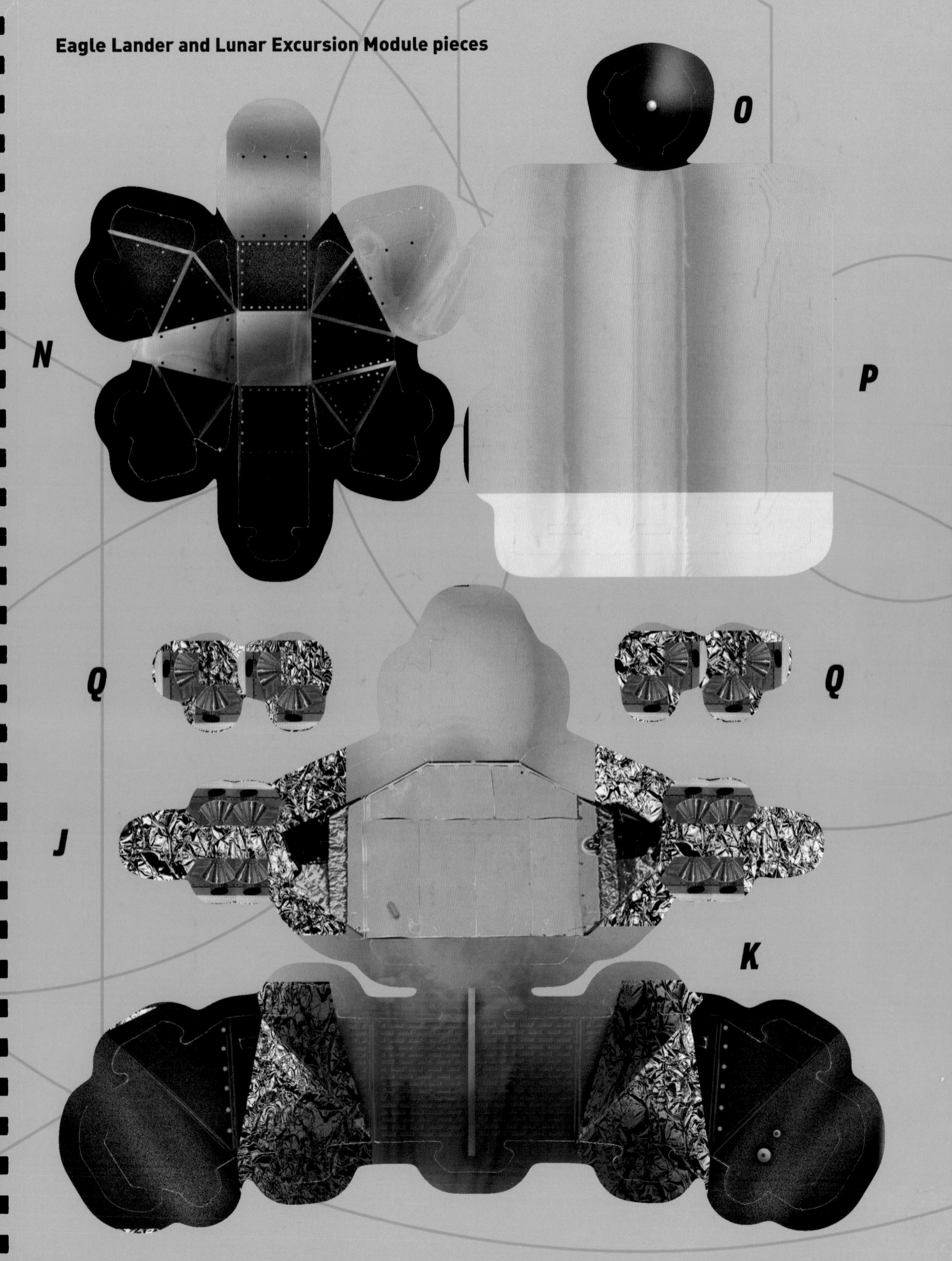

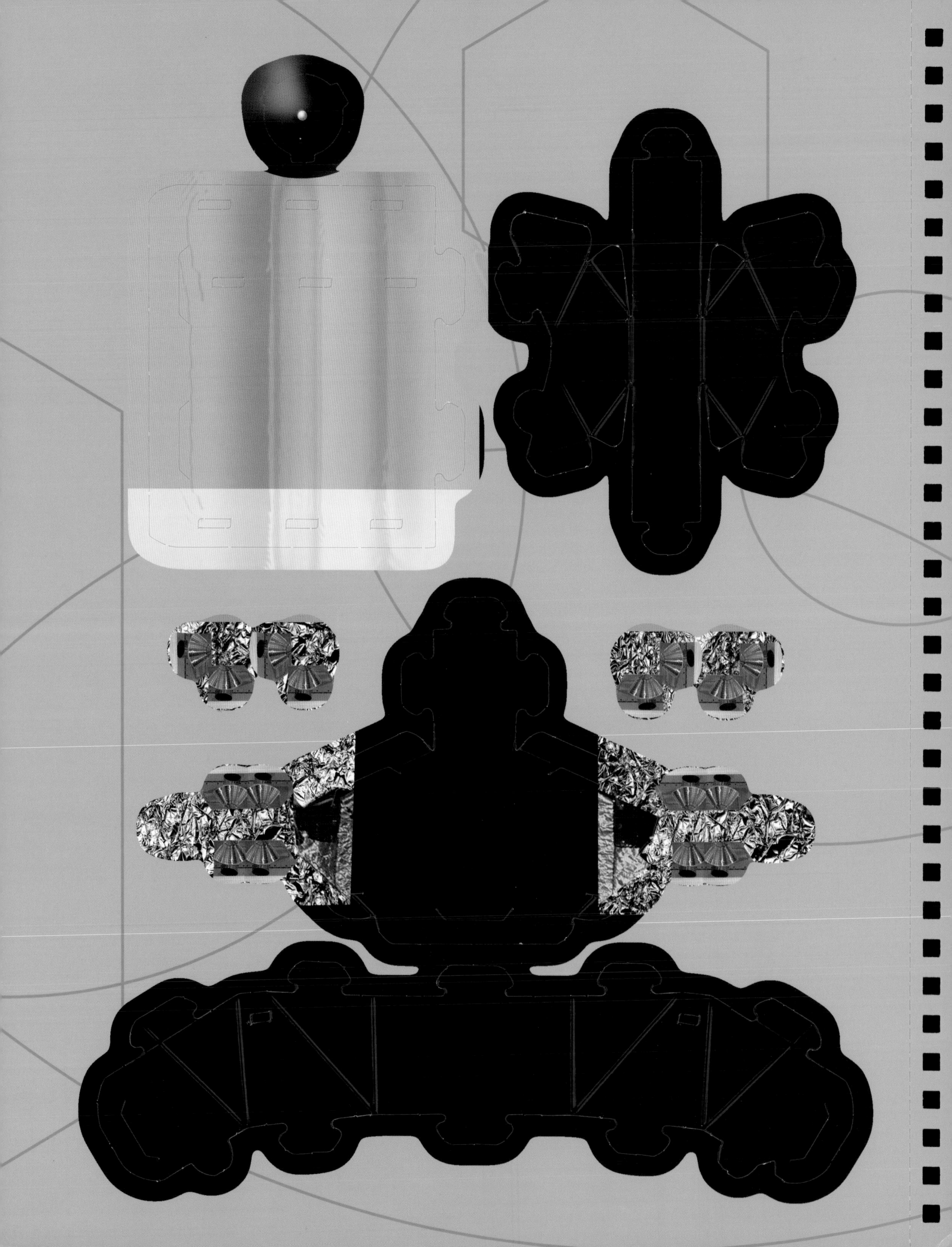

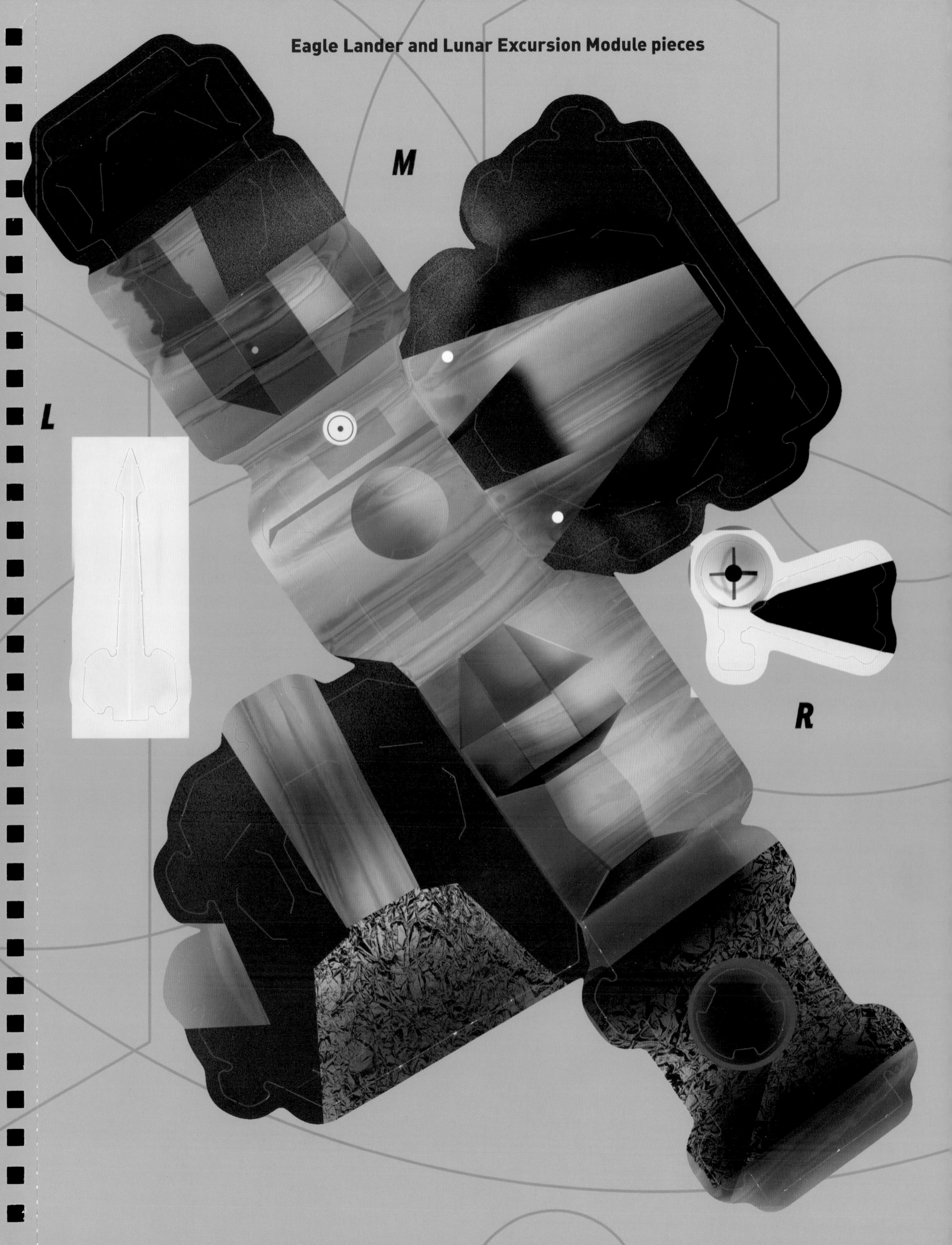
Eagle Lander and Lunar Excursion Module pieces
M
L
R

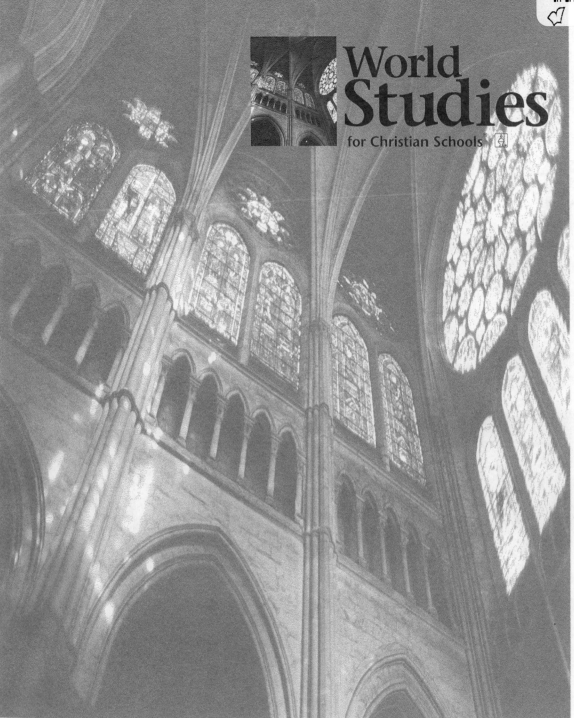

World Studies

for Christian Schools®

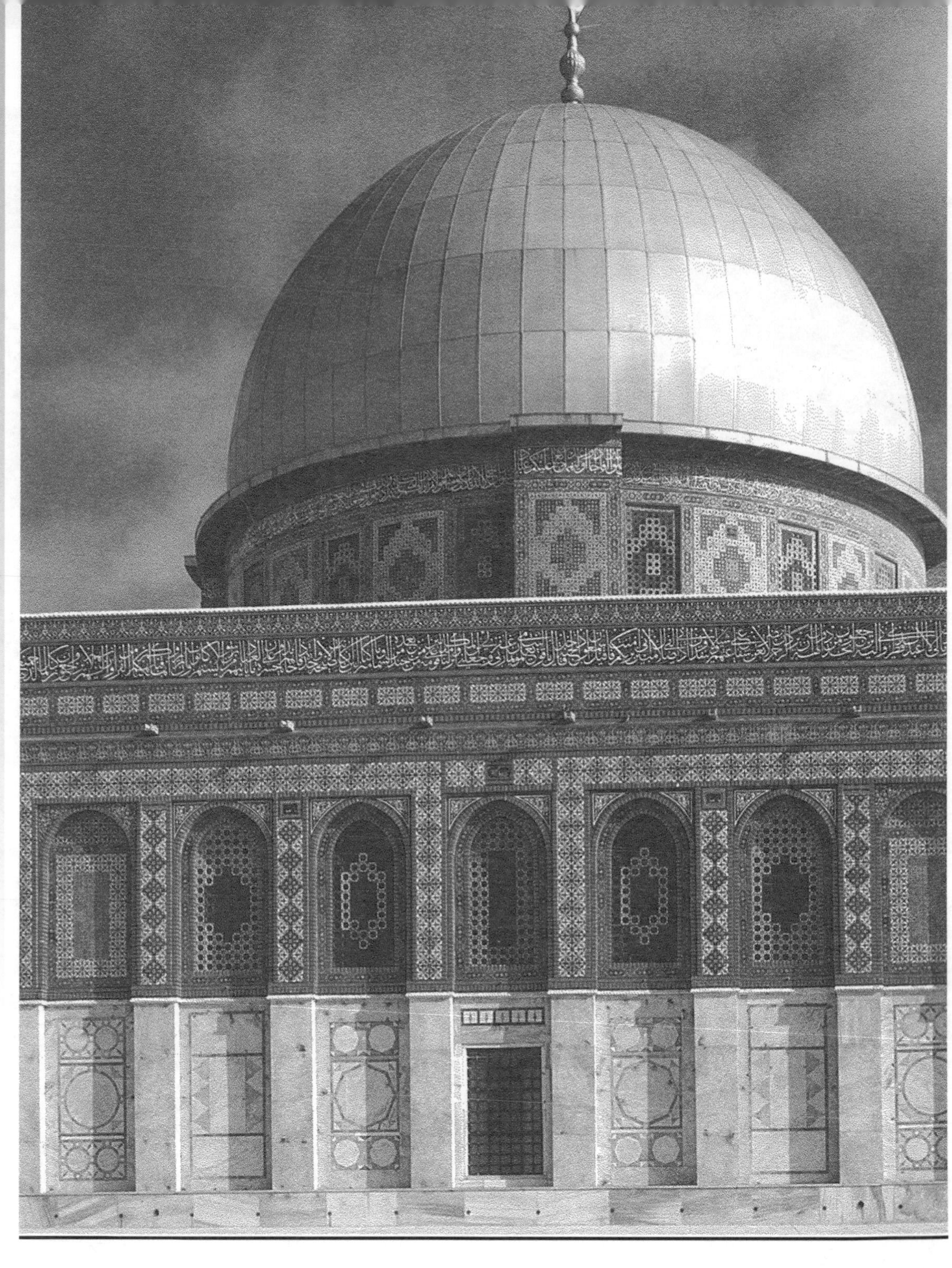

World Studies
for Christian Schools®

SECOND EDITION

Terri Koontz, B.S.
Mark Sidwell, Ph.D.
S. M. Bunker, M.A.

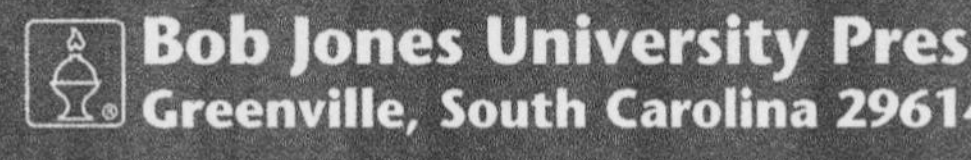

Bob Jones University Press
Greenville, South Carolina 29614

NOTE:
The fact that materials produced by other publishers are referred to in this volume does not constitute an endorsement by Bob Jones University Press of the content or theological position of materials produced by such publishers. The position of Bob Jones University Press, and the University itself, is well known. Any references and ancillary materials are listed as an aid to the student or the teacher and in an attempt to maintain the accepted standards of the publishing industry.

WORLD STUDIES for Christian Schools® Teacher's Edition
Second Edition

Terri Koontz, B.S.
Kirsten-Leeann Alexander, B.S.

Contributing Writers
S. M. Bunker
Lydia Gwaltney
Thomas Luttmann

Produced in cooperation with the Bob Jones University College of Arts and Science and Bob Jones Junior High.

Editor
Manda Kalagayan

Compositor
Nancy Lohr

Designer
Joyce Landis

ISBN 1-57924-235-9

15 14 13 12 11 10 9 8 7 6 5 4 3

Contents

vi

List of Settings Maps

vii

Act Three

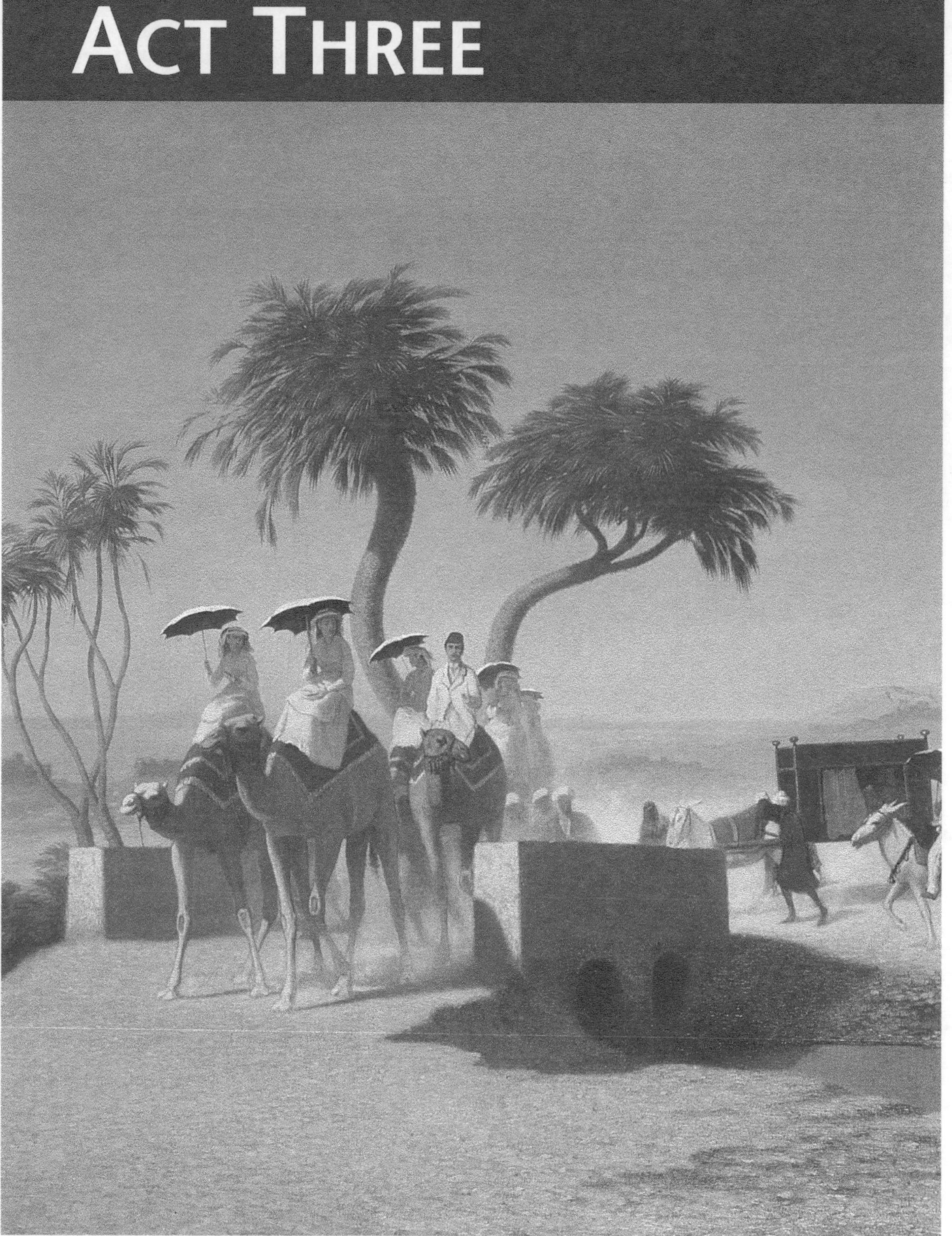

Chapter Eleven

The nineteenth century was Britain's century, a period dominated by Queen Victoria (1837-1901). The chapter focuses on Britain and her leadership in world affairs, particularly in industrialism and imperialism. The principles and movements presented in this chapter are basic to understanding the other chapters of the unit. Major movements covered in the chapter include revolution, industrialism, capitalism, socialism, communism, evolution, romanticism, realism, and impressionism.

Chapter Twelve

This chapter focuses on the rule of Britain in India. After the explorers found usable ports along India's coast, both France and Britain raced to settle there. Eventually, Britain gained control and ousted France. But Britain had problems keeping peace within India. The Sepoy Mutiny is an example of the type of problem Britain faced. At the same time, the British brought much improvement to India in the form of agriculture, industry, transportation, communication, and education. India was one of the first countries to be widely evangelized by missionaries such as William Carey and Hannah Marshman. This century was called the "Great Century of Christian Missions" because of its revivals and new missionary societies.

Act Three			
Chapter Title	**Main Concept**	**Pages**	**Time Frame**
11. European Transformation	As the middle class grew in England, Napoleon ruled France. New philosophies emerged in economics and science.	295-321	7-10 days
12. Raj India	Britain controlled India first through trade and then through politics, but India received her independence in 1947.	322-47	8 days
13. China and the West	The Manchu dynasty declined and fell when opium was introduced to the country, though the Boxers tried to stop the decline.	348-77	7-9 days
14. Colonial Africa	Exploration and slave trade opened Africa to missionaries and imperialists.	378-405	7-10 days
Feature: Music and Art in History	Music and art have changed most rapidly in the twentieth century.	406-13	1 day
Total Suggested Days			30-38 days (6-8 weeks)

CONQUESTS

1800 TO 1900

The challenges and accomplishments of Act Two will greatly affect the events of the nineteenth century played out in this act. European countries have lost some colonies but are still convinced that colonization is an important way to extend their influence and trading power. Colonization efforts in this century turn to more familiar territories—India, China, and Africa.

This act reveals the nineteenth century as a century of conquest over lands and people, natural laws, and energy. In this century Britain shines as a world leader in industrialism, imperialism, and missions.

New players come to the stage as the old rule of the aristocrats gives way to the rule of anyone who can rise from poverty to wealth. A new, powerful middle class awakens, looking for new things to buy and places to go. Britons, and Europeans in general, look increasingly to their exotic colonies to fill these needs.

This act uncovers internal friction in Europe over ideas and philosophies such as Marxism and evolution. It also displays struggles over the exploitation and division of India, China, and Africa as imperialism takes hold in Europe. By the end of this act, the stage will be set for conflicts on an unprecedented scale.

But as that main plot weaves its way through the century, other events show a greater hand directing history. Missionary efforts flourish as young men and women go out to all the world, taking the gospel to people who have never heard of Christ's great sacrifice.

Opening Photo—Empress Eugénie of France (wife of Napoleon III) visiting the pyramids

Chapter Thirteen

When the Manchu dynasty came to power in 1644, China had turned her back on the West. China's motivation behind this move was her pride, her attitude of superiority over other cultures. However, during the centuries covered by this unit, the West far surpassed China. In the 1800s Europeans arrived in China desiring to trade. The Chinese refused, but the Europeans forced their way in. This chapter recounts the history of China's relationship to the West. A special emphasis is given to missionary work, always a primary factor in European colonization.

Chapter Fourteen

Africa was the continent to suffer most from the imperialistic aims of Europe. This chapter covers the exploration, exploitation (through slavery), division, and evangelization of the continent. Africa presented a special challenge to Europeans because of its harsh climate, hostile people, wild animals, and exotic diseases. Many went to this continent for reasons that ranged from adventure to economics to missionary zeal.

Student Objectives
Students should be able to

1. Describe the lives of the middle class during the Victorian era.
2. Analyze how the Victorian decor reflected England's imperialism.
3. Assess the situation of poor people in the Victorian era.
4. Locate England on a map.
5. Read and create a supply and demand chart.
6. Explain the function and use of a political map.
7. Contrast parliamentary government and absolutism.
8. Name the leader of the French who was defeated at Waterloo.
9. Illustrate examples of newly formed countries.
10. Define *imperialism*.
11. Identify important inventions of this era.
12. Compare and contrast capitalism and socialism.
13. Describe communism and evaluate its flaws.
14. Critically evaluate the theory of evolution and its flaws.
15. Discuss changes in religion due to science in this era.
16. Distinguish between romantic, realistic, and impressionistic works of art and music.

Opening Photo—A colored lithograph of the opening of the Great Exhibition

The Victorian Era

Cut out examples from Victorian style magazines or Victorian books and make a bulletin board collage. You may want to have students contribute to this board.

Another idea would be to place pictures of inventors, philosophers, and other important people in the chapter and connect string between each person and the thing he represents or vice versa (e.g., pictures of the inventions).

CHAPTER 11

The Great Exhibition of the Works of Industry of All Nations opened in London on May 1, 1851. People came from around the world to visit the **Great Exhibition.** It was housed in a huge iron-and-glass structure called the **Crystal Palace,** built in London's Hyde Park. Nearly three hundred thousand panes of glass, held in place by more than five thousand iron columns and girders, enclosed the Crystal Palace's nearly one million square feet of floor space. Running the width of the building was a central vault high enough to cover the park's ancient elms. Inside, flowers and trees, fountains, and statues surrounded the exhibits. Joseph Paxton's design was a success.

On May 1, 1851, everything was ready for the opening except one finishing touch: the arrival of the queen. Promptly at noon **Queen Victoria,** dressed in pink brocade and wearing diamonds, arrived with her husband, **Prince Albert,** and two of their children. The excited crowd cheered their arrival. The people loved their queen and her family. She so characterized this age that it is often called the **Victorian Age.** Trumpet fanfares, speeches, dedicatory prayers, and a thousand-voice choir singing Handel's "Hallelujah Chorus" highlighted the day's opening ceremonies. For the next six months, more than six million people viewed the displays of over thirteen thousand exhibitors.

In addition to displaying the world's manufactured items, the Great Exhibition also underscored Great Britain's position in the world. She was the unchallenged leader in industry and commerce. Her factories produced the most advanced products available, while her ships ruled the sea routes of the world. In areas besides industry Britain was also first. The activities and culture of Britain influenced and characterized Europe in the nineteenth century.

A.D. 1750 - A.D. 1900

The First Fleet Arrives in Australia 1788

U.S. Revolutionary War 1776-81

1750

Age of Reason 1600-1800

Chapter 11 Lesson Plans			
Section Title	**Main Concept**	**Pages**	**Time Frame**
1. The Rise of the Middle Class **Settings: England*	As the middle class began to grow, people started to enjoy decoration, servants, and optimism.	294-301	2 days
2. Balancing Power	Europe was in a state of upheaval during the 1800s as a result of Napoleon's conquests and other revolts for independence.	302-6	1-2 days
3. The Age of Industrialism **Interpretations: Steel*	This was the time of many inventions; capitalism and socialism were the major economic philosophies.	307-12	1-2 days
4. Belief and Expression **Characterizations: Christian Orphanages*	The philosophies of evolution and the social gospel began in this time along with different artistic styles.	313-19	1-2 days
Total Suggested Days (including 1 day for review & 1 day for test)			7-10 days

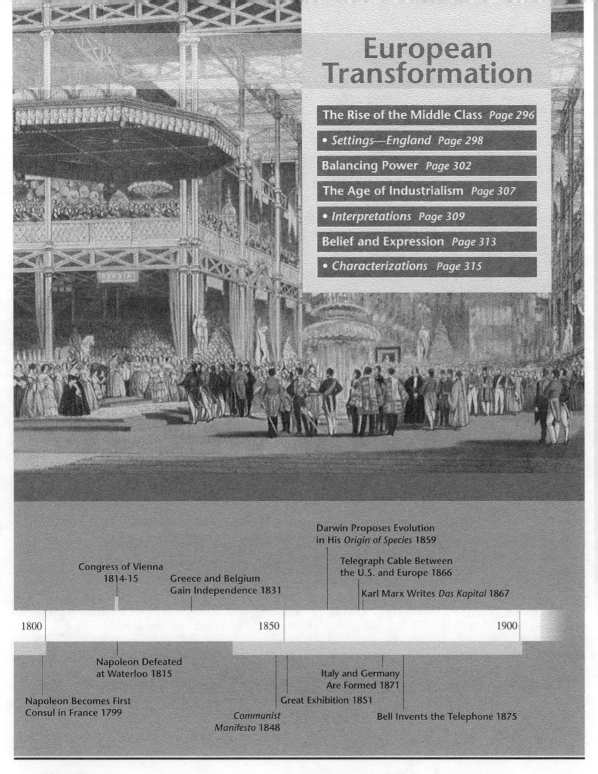

European Transformation

Napoleon Becomes First Consul in France 1799

Congress of Vienna 1814-15

Napoleon Defeated at Waterloo 1815

Greece and Belgium Gain Independence 1831

Communist Manifesto 1848

Great Exhibition 1851

Darwin Proposes Evolution in His *Origin of Species* 1859

Telegraph Cable Between the U.S. and Europe 1866

Karl Marx Writes *Das Kapital* 1867

Italy and Germany Are Formed 1871

Bell Invents the Telephone 1875

1800 1850 1900

Chapter Motivator

To introduce the chapter, tell your students that Britain will be the focal point. (Remind them that France was the emphasis of Chapter 9.) The nineteenth century was Britain's century. Thus, what occurred in England eventually affected the rest of the world. Use the following information to spark your students' interest as they prepare to study this chapter.

The Victorian era in England (1832-1914) was a time of great change. Some of the major changes are listed below. Present them to your students, with illustrations if possible:

- Men's clothing styles changed from knee pants to long pants.
- Travel developed from horse-drawn coach to train to automobile and from sailing ship to steam ship.
- Lighting changed from oil lamps to gas lights to electric lights.
- Communication changed from mail to telegraph to telephone.
- The middle class grew in size and influence.
- Portraiture changed from painting to photography; however, the subjects had to sit perfectly still for long periods of time in order for the process to work. That is why photographs from this time period often show people with unpleasant expressions on their faces.

I Timothy 6:17-18

The Bible often commands the Christian to do good. Much of the Victorian era is characterized by people helping other people. I Timothy 6:17-18 says, "Charge them that are rich in this world, that they be not highminded, nor trust in uncertain riches, but in the living God, who giveth us richly all things to enjoy; That they do good, that they be rich in good works, ready to distribute, willing to communicate." (BLM verse 11)

Materials

- BLM verse 11
- Victorian picture books
- SimCity 2000 computer software
- Map of Europe or England (BLM 11-1)
- *Teaching Transparencies* for use with *WORLD STUDIES for Christian Schools* (Second Edition)
- Poster board for chart
- Video about Napoleon
- Electricity experiment or telegraph experiment or directions and materials
- Items containing steel
- Guest speaker to discuss economics
- *LIFE SCIENCE for Christian Schools* (BJUP)
- Bibles for Bible study
- *Oliver Twist* video
- George Mueller's *Autobiography*
- Examples of classical, romantic, and impressionistic music
- Monet paintings

SECTION 1

Student Objectives
Students should be able to

1. Describe the lives of the middle class during the Victorian era.
2. Analyze how the Victorian decor reflected England's imperialism.
3. Assess the situation of poor people in the Victorian era.

Why Focus on England?—Although this chapter is about Europe in the nineteenth century, the focus is on the undisputed leader of that century—Great Britain. As Louis XIV and France molded the previous century, Victoria and Great Britain shaped the nineteenth century. The Great Exhibition of 1851 captures the spirit of this century at its midpoint and makes a unifying element of this chapter. More pictures of the Great Exhibition can be found in *Age of Progress,* S. C. Burchell, Time-Life, 1966.

Victoria and Albert—Queen Victoria was dedicated to Prince Albert. (Since he was not in line for the throne, he could not be called king.) Theirs seems to have been a very happy marriage and a model marriage for all of England. For the first time, the royal family was presented in portraits, not only formally but also informally in family settings with the children and parents playing together.

When Prince Albert died, Queen Victoria went into mourning from which she never emerged. She wore her mourning clothes until her death. Most widows during this time conformed to a set of rules for appropriate mourning. When a woman's husband died, she immediately had a black dress made and a heavy black crepe veil. She wore a black dress for a year and never appeared in public without her veil during that time. For the next six months to a year she wore lighter and lighter dresses from charcoal grey to dove grey or light purple.

Other ways to remember the dead were available. The flowers from the funeral could be dipped in wax and displayed. Those who could afford it had marble busts of the deceased made. People

The Rise of the Middle Class

The elevator, invented by Elisha Graves Otis, was one of many inventions demonstrated at the Great Exhibition.

Queen Victoria left her name and her values on a generation of Britishers and much of the world.

The nineteenth century saw the growth, both in numbers and importance, of the middle class. A class of merchants and manufacturers had existed in Europe since the late Middle Ages. However, during the Industrial Age this middle class gained new wealth and power in Europe, ranking next to nobles and landowners. Many members of the middle class had their start as poorer businessmen who had used new technology to make their businesses more efficient and productive. Through hard work and creativity, they had improved their businesses and gained wealth.

The Great Exhibition was a tribute to this new middle class, especially Britain's middle class. Many of the goods displayed had been made by the middle class and for the middle class. Whether they were new gadgets for the home or intricate machines for the factory, these goods symbolized the twofold focus of middle-class life: home and business.

Middle-Class Houses

Members of the middle class generally lived in the cities. They owned or rented large homes in the better sections of town. Often these houses were highly decorated, as if to show off the extent of their owners' newly gained wealth. The interior of these houses

SECTION 1

Materials

- Victorian picture books
- SimCity 2000 computer software

also showed the new wealth of the middle class. The main rule of Victorian decorating was to fill every bit of space. Heavy wooden furniture, covered with curves and carvings, had been turned out by machine rather than handcrafted. Bushy plants and feathers filled every corner, while ribbons, pictures, and fans hung on the papered walls. The wallpaper was also made by machine, not hand painted. The parlor had overstuffed furniture of heavy brocade, and ruffled pillows lay everywhere.

Other new items equipped the middle-class home. One was the special piece of furniture called a *whatnot*—a set of shelves just to hold knickknacks. Another was the piano, which up until this time had been in only a few homes. Now many middle-class homes had an upright piano, and evenings spent playing and singing were common. The coal that provided the power for new factories also heated houses in the nineteenth century. Rooms which had previously been heated by wood now used coal in newly invented coal stoves placed in each fireplace.

Middle-Class Lifestyles

Every middle-class family had servants—butlers, maids, grooms, washerwomen, and cooks. The lady of the house directed their activities. They kept busy cleaning and taking care of those large households. Their jobs became somewhat easier as new inventions entered the home. Iron stoves and wringer-style washers made cooking and laundering easier.

A very important servant in the house was the **governess.** Her job was to supervise the family's children. She saw to their discipline and early education. Often girls received all their education from their governess or a tutor, but boys usually went away to boarding school before their teen years, and then some went on to college. Boys were sent to school not to become scholars but only to become reasonably well educated. The most important part of school was meeting other young men of their social class and developing character. The boys who attended school together would be the men who later did business together.

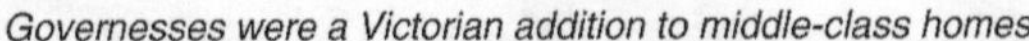

Governesses were a Victorian addition to middle-class homes.

planted weeping willows, made floral pictures of the deceased, and used the woven hair of the deceased to make watch fobs.

The New Rich Finding Their Way—For the first time in centuries people of low birth had the opportunity to substantially raise their economic and social position in life. The titled landowners felt their power and position threatened by these newcomers. However, many of the new rich remained near the cities in new suburbs.

The clutter that we have come to associate with Victorian decorating was a display of the quantity of things available to those who could afford them. Exotic items were especially popular, and many represented new places that the English were adding to their empire. It was popular to have furnishings from China, the Middle East, and India.

The royal family also greatly affected decor of the era. They decorated their Scottish hunting estate with plaid upholstery, so plaid became the rage. The royal family used garden statuary such as stags, so every garden had to have a statue.

Why Servants?—The employment of servants showed that the woman of the house was a "lady."

Rearing Victorian Children—Children were put on a pedestal in the home and had special rooms dedicated to them and their play. The "nursery" was a playroom and schoolroom usually near or connected to the sleeping areas of the children and the governess or nurse. In the seventeenth century, children had been treated as miniature adults, but in this century they were allowed more of a childhood. Daily clothes were designed for more comfort and freedom of movement.

Victorian Age girls from the middle and upper classes learned needlework, piano, singing, and drawing. Their main job in the future would be to run a home, so they were trained to do this and to be delightful hostesses.

In school the boys studied the classics, concentrating in Latin and Greek. Instruction would take around twenty hours a week. The rest of the time was for study, but

Victorian Decoration Exhibition—Bring to class picture books with examples of Victorian decoration, clothing, advertising, transportation, and inventions. Use them to introduce your students to Victorian culture. Your local library should have several books of this kind from which to choose. See the sources listed for this chapter in the Appendix.

because the classics tended to be unappealing, many boys spent another fifteen to twenty hours playing cricket. Unfortunately, this careless lifestyle produced a lax attitude toward time and money management.

Young clergymen were normally the teachers in the schools, but the discipline in the school was handled mostly by the older boys in what was called a monitorial system. The younger boys were servants to the older boys and were expected to respect and obey them. It was believed that this system trained men to be good rulers and leaders.

Student Objectives
Students should be able to

1. Locate England on a map.
2. Read and create a supply and demand chart.
3. Explain the function and use of a political map.

What's the Weather?—Share with the students the following comments about English weather. Roman historian Tacitus wrote, "Britain's sky is overcast, with continual rain and cloud."

England is a country with "no climate, only weather" according to some Englishmen.

European Unity—After many European countries, including England, relinquished or lost their imperial possessions, they began looking for other alliances that would help them in trade and power.

While regions of Europe seek autonomy (Scotland, the Basque region, South Tyrol), Europe as a whole has formed stronger ties through the EEC (European Economic Community) and later the EU (European Union). The introduction of a new standard European currency, the Euro, in 1999 and the complete changeover planned for 2002 may help to unify the continent even further.

SETTINGS—England

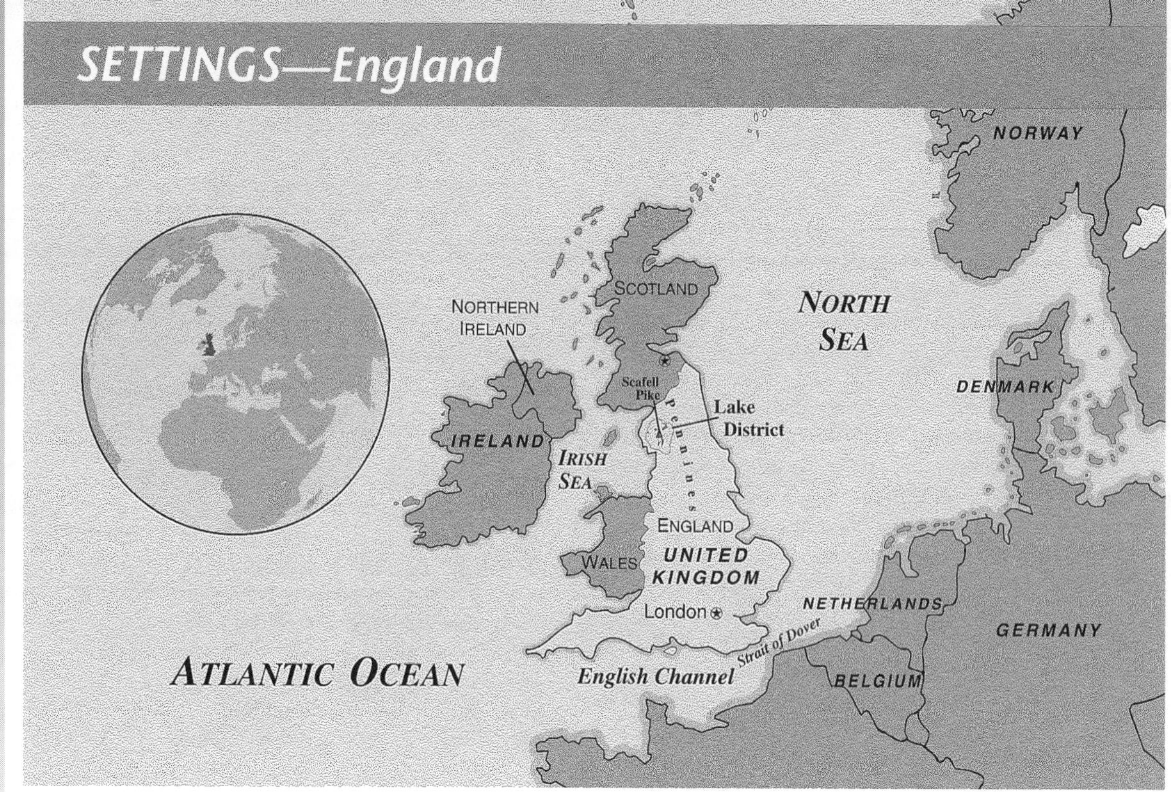

Location—England is the name of part of the United Kingdom located in the southern portion of Great Britain. The United Kingdom is located off the northwestern corner of Europe. England's borders include the Irish Sea and Wales in the west, Scotland in the north, the North Sea in the east, and the English Channel in the south.

Climate—All of Great Britain has a marine west coast climate. It is greatly affected by the water that surrounds it. Although it is only 360 miles from the southernmost part to the northern border, England has great variety in its weather. When snows blanket the mountain ranges of the north, palm trees still grow well in the south. The North Atlantic current of the Gulf Stream brings moist, warm air to the country and with it the constant potential for rain.

Topography—England is divided into three regions. The Pennines are a mountain range that runs from the Scottish border to the center of England. England's highest peak, Scafell Pike (3,210 ft.), is located west of the Pennines in the Cumbrian Mountains. Another feature of this area is the Lake District, which was immortalized by the Lake Poets of the 1800s. Fifteen beautiful lakes nestle down among the mountains. The next area is the Midlands. This is the fertile farmland of the country. The third region is the Southwest Peninsula. Another interesting topographical feature is the famous white chalk cliffs of Dover which line the coast of the Straits of Dover.

Natural Resources—The most important natural resource in England's early history was its fertile soil. Coal and iron ore deposits exist near the Pennines. Access to the rest of the world by water

Materials

- Map of Europe or England (BLM 11-1)
- Transparencies for Chapter 11

Map Activity—Use map 11-C from the Student Activities manual to reinforce the geography lesson.

Going Beyond—Read the Settings pages with your students and answer the questions. Use a political map of Europe to teach the function and use of a political map (TT 11-A). Political maps are best for showing country boundaries. Countries are often color coded to help delineate their territory. (This is especially useful when the country includes islands.) Usually political maps include country names, capitals, major cities, and major rivers.

Comparing Climates—"Foggy London Town" is not an unusual reference to that city. The United States has cities that are remembered by their weather. Ask the students if they know some. *(Chicago—The Windy City, San Fransciso—fog, Seattle—rain, Phoenix—always sunny)* Have students look at other areas on the same latitude as England. What climate do they have? (generally cool or cold) Have the students look at the climates of England and the Northwest coast of the United States. Why are their climates the same? *(Both have a marine west coast climate; the greatest factor is the effect of the ocean current on the weather.)*

has been especially important to trade throughout the British Isles.

Geography & Culture—England's green, fertile land attracted settlers to its shores. Evidence of human occupation of the island goes back to thousands of years before Christ. England came to the attention of the Romans during the Roman Empire and later to the Scandinavian Vikings.

The fact that England is an island has added to its appeal. Water access has made England a prime trading center for centuries. With the defeat of the Spanish Armada in 1588, England claimed control of the seas.

England's separation from the rest of Europe has allowed it to take a different path politically and culturally from much of the rest of Europe.

Settings Review

1. What geographical feature has a great impact on England's weather?
2. What mountain range runs through northern England?
3. What district was written about by a set of poets?
4. What are two features of England that attracted settlers to its shores?

Look at a world map for other countries that are geographically separate from their neighboring countries. Choose one of those countries and look in the encyclopedia to see whether its geographic isolation has caused that country to develop differently from the countries around it.

Although England is a relatively small country, its fertile land has allowed it to become a major force in world history.

Settings Review Answers

1. the North Atlantic current
2. the Pennines
3. the Lake District
4. green, fertile land and the fact that it is an island

Answers will vary. Choices may include Australia, Japan, Madagascar, and Iceland.

City Life for the Poor—Although conditions improved through the century, city life was very bad at the beginning of the 1800s, and improvements came slowly.

Infants were most susceptible to poor conditions. In lower income homes, sixty-two out of one hundred babies born died in infancy. Neglect was one of the main causes for death, but there were many illnesses that were also a problem. Whooping cough, diarrhea, smallpox, typhus, typhoid fever, and measles all were rampant in the close quarters of the poorer sections.

Many of these diseases were caused by poor sanitation. Water supplies were taken downstream from where sewage was dumped. There were so many dead in the cemeteries that extra dirt had to be brought in to cover the bodies buried over other bodies. Rain water leached down through these cemeteries into the ground water.

The stench from the cemeteries and general overcrowding caused them to be closed and new burial places to be opened outside of the city. This caused a burden on the poor, who had to find means to transport their deceased loved one the long distance out of town.

Tuberculosis and other lung diseases were the most feared by adults. Throughout the century it was estimated that one in six people died of TB. Occupational hazards also caused many lung problems. Black lung disease was common to miners, women in straw plaiting factories suffered lung problems from inhaling straw particles, and workers in textile factories also had lung trouble from inhaling fibers.

Middle-Class Optimism

The middle class was a group of people filled with optimism. They looked around them and saw how much life had changed during their century. They watched fast trains, steamships, iron stoves, and running water grow from being special to being commonplace. They saw improvements in living and working conditions, education, and health. These people overflowed with belief in their way of life, their culture. They desired to share their culture with others in the world whom they viewed as unfortunate and uncivilized.

Poverty in the Midst of Prosperity

In Mark 14:7 Jesus makes a sobering observation that is hard for many to accept: "For ye have the poor with you always." Chapter 9 described the poverty that many people in Europe suffered during the Industrial Revolution. In the 1800s the poor suffered in many of the same ways that they had a century earlier—families were crowded into one room, people lived in the streets, children worked long hours in dangerous conditions.

Poverty and its suffering have always existed. It should not surprise us, then, that in the era of Victorian optimism among the middle classes there was still great misery among the lower classes. But Jesus went on to say, "And whensoever ye will ye may do them good." Victorians took these words to heart. Many in the upper class believed that they were responsible to help change the conditions of the poor. There were some wealthy Englishmen with such a heart for the poor that they were willing to share their wealth to help relieve some of their suffering. What resulted was not a free handout but low-cost housing that met needs previously disregarded.

Rows of flats (apartment houses) built by rich men who charged nominal rentals sprang up to help provide the housing needs of the working class. They provided multiple bedrooms as well as a living area, indoor plumbing, and gas lighting. Low-cost houses that resembled the row houses of many cities in the United States today were also built. Working people could own a home with upstairs bedrooms, a kitchen, and two parlors. They even had a patch of yard to call their own.

Other philanthropists (wealthy people who give their resources to benefit humanity) such as **W. H. Lever**, founder of Lever Brothers,

London's streets teemed with poor people looking for a way to earn a living. This young girl is selling scarves.

SimCity 2000—If a computer is available to the students, use a simulation program such as SimCity 2000. This would be an ideal example of the different aspects of city planning. Such computer software is available from both retail and educational sources. Students will enjoy the challenge and variety that computer software provides.

Philanthropists set up factory towns such as New Lanark in Manchester, England, to meet the social and physical needs of their workers.

took his factory and workers out of the city and built the town of **Port Sunlight.** This model town included two styles of houses with three or four bedrooms in each. Every house had a back yard, but Lever insisted that the company maintain the front yard so that the entire town would be well kept. He also included in his town an art gallery and public gardens.

Through the efforts of these good people, conditions changed for some of the poor of England. As the middle class grew wealthier, the benefits spread to the lower classes in the form of jobs. The middle class could now afford to buy services and hire help, thus employing the lower classes and improving their conditions in this age of optimism.

Section Review

1. What jobs did the middle class hold?
2. What principle guided their tastes?
3. What musical instrument became a part of many middle-class homes?
4. What servant became especially important to middle-class children?
5. What attitude characterized the middle class?
6. Name the philanthropist who developed a model town. What was the town called?

Many wealthy people saw the poverty around them but did nothing to ease it. They knew what needed to be done but did not do it. Are we like that today? What are at least three things we know to do from God's Word but fail to do? How can we get the power to accomplish those things?

Providing Housing—Your students should understand that even with these efforts at providing housing, poverty and squalid conditions continued to exist.

Philanthropy Dissuaded—Another view of dealing with the poor said that improving squalid conditions would only encourage the poor to have more children, thereby worsening their financial situation. In other words, according to this view, helping the poor merely produced more poor.

Section Review Answers

1. merchandise and manufacturing
2. They wanted to fill every bit of space.
3. piano
4. governess
5. optimism
6. W. H. Lever; Port Sunlight

Answers will vary. Many times we are still like that today. Some things that we fail to do from God's Word include doing good to all men, being kind one to another, forgiving one another, treating all as equal in the sight of God, and giving up pride. We can pray for the Lord to change our outlook and attitude so that we can be better testimonies for Him. We can strive to help others in their plight. We can minister to people's hearts primarily.

Section 2

Student Objectives

Students should be able to

1. Contrast parliamentary government and absolutism.
2. Name the leader of the French who was defeated at Waterloo.
3. List examples of newly formed countries.
4. Define *imperialism*.

Laws and the Working Class—Laws that reduced the working day and increased wages created a new thing for the working class people—leisure time. For the first time in centuries, the working class's time was not filled with work alone. This leisure time, along with the added income to families from the working women, and the availability of train travel allowed working-class families to take trips to the sea or to their former homes in the country. If no such trip was possible, there was always time to play or watch a cricket or football game.

Better Economics for All—Although your students should know that conditions in England were severe for the poor in the early 1800s, your students need to see that as the middle class grew wealthy, wealth also spread to the lower levels of society. Jobs became available for the lower classes as servants, in factories, in shops, and so on. By the end of the century, even people at the bottom of the economic ladder made more money and had more prospects than ever before. This positive look to the future gave the lower classes reason to demand more say in government.

Votes for Men Only—For many years in the United States and England, men were allowed to vote only if they owned property. During the nineteenth century this stipulation was removed.

Balancing Power

In Chapter 9 you saw the power of the absolute rulers and the aristocracy of the eighteenth century. This system continued into the nineteenth century, but not without disruption. Revolutions in the United States and France challenged the rights of monarchy. The rise of the middle class encouraged the common man to demand more control of his destiny. Extreme contrast in wealth caused discontentment. Conflict in government caused unrest in much of Europe.

Parliamentary Government in Great Britain

One reason for Great Britain's strength in the nineteenth century was its stable government. Because England was ruled by a representative body, Parliament, and not an absolute king, the British people were more content than other Europeans. At the beginning of the century, few people had the right to vote. However, beginning in 1832, Parliament passed laws giving the right to vote to more and more people. These laws decreased the power of the king and upper class and increased that of the middle and lower classes. Britain's parliamentary government is much like the representative government of the United States. Changes can be made gradually and legally. Because the British followed this procedure, they escaped the disruptive revolts that plagued the rest of Europe.

By the end of the century, most men in Britain were permitted to vote. (Women did not get the vote until the twentieth century.) Because Parliament was elected by the people, it passed laws that the people wanted. Throughout the nineteenth century, the British Parliament often voted to aid the working poor. It passed laws to help women and children working in the mines and factories. It also tried to improve living conditions in the new industrial cities. By recognizing and responding to the need for changes and making them gradually, the British maintained governmental stability. This in turn encouraged business prosperity. This heritage of stability and prosperity made Queen Victoria's era one of greatness.

Disruption on the Continent

The power of the French king was broken by the French Revolution. The revolution went through four phases as it attempted to reorganize its government. When the third attempt at reorganization was overthrown by the army, conditions were right for **Napoleon Bonaparte** to come to power. In 1799, with the help of a

A romantic vision of Napoleon at Waterloo before his defeat

Section 2

Materials

- Poster board for chart
- Video about Napoleon

Government Chart—Start a chart (to be completed throughout the chapter) of all of the "isms" in the chapter (e.g., nationalism, imperialism, etc.). Include columns for the "ism," the definition, the name of the country or man most closely associated with the "ism" (one or more), and effects. Nine rows will be enough for all of the "isms" in the chapter. Encourage students to use this as a study guide (BLM 11-2).

Citizens wore the tricolors of France to display their nationalism and loyalty to the new government.

new constitution, he gave himself the title First Consul. In 1804 Napoleon proclaimed himself emperor of France, but his vision went far beyond France's boundaries. By 1812 he and his mighty armies had conquered much of Europe, making him the master of the continent. But his mastery was short-lived. By 1815 Napoleon was defeated and sent into exile. (See p. 304.)

With Napoleon gone, the leaders of Europe faced the problem of putting the Continent back together. For two years these leaders came together for meetings, called the **Congress of Vienna** (1814-15). **Prince Metternich** (MET ur nik) of Austria was the leading statesman at the Congress, and his ideas were very influential. The Congress faced three problems: (1) redrawing boundaries, (2) punishing France, and (3) putting kings back on their thrones. Their goal was to restore peace and security to Europe.

The leaders at the Congress feared the ideas spread by Napoleon's armies throughout Europe. France had been the home of ideas about man's natural rights. These ideas emphasized that all men had certain natural rights to freedom. The French expressed these ideas with the phrase "Liberty, Equality, Fraternity." Accepting these ideas, people demanded more liberty from their leaders. They also wanted equality of representation in government. Finally, the French promoted the idea of nationalism. **Nationalism** is intense devotion and loyalty to one's own people (or nationality). People who shared a common language and culture but lived under the rule of another country desired freedom to rule themselves. As hard as the Congress tried to restrain these ideas, it could not. Soon revolts broke out all over Europe.

Leading statesmen met at the Congress of Vienna to put Europe back together after Napoleon was defeated.

Napoleon Is Back?—Students may notice that the Battle of Waterloo, mentioned on the next page, occurred *after* the Congress of Vienna was in session and *after* Napoleon had supposedly been exiled. It is important for your students to know that less than a year after his exile to the island of Elba in 1814, Napoleon escaped and began his journey back to Paris. Along the way the French people greeted him with so much enthusiasm that King Louis XVIII left the city of Paris before Napoleon arrived.

Napoleon's return began a time known as the Hundred Days. Napoleon set himself up as the head of France, but the rest of Europe would not let him remain in that position after all the damage he had done before. Ever the aggressor, Napoleon marched to Belgium to defeat the Anglo-Prussian army. There "he met his Waterloo."

After his defeat Napoleon was exiled permanently to the island of St. Helena where he was held prisoner. There he died from the effects of what is now known as a gastric ulcer on May 21, 1821. The memory of his deeds remained a legend in France. The French government brought Napoleon's remains back to France in 1840.

Napoleon—Find a brief video that gives a good overview of the life and work of Napoleon Bonaparte. Your students will probably be very interested in this man and his military conquests and downfall.

Revolutions in Europe—The revolts mentioned here are covered in more detail in *World History for Christian Schools*. Here they are presented to show the spirit of the era rather than for factual mastery. A time line of the events of this century will help your students grasp the several cause-and-effect relationships present in this period.

Napoleon at Waterloo

You may have heard of someone "meeting his Waterloo." A person using this expression usually means that someone has suffered a major setback, a final defeat. The expression comes from the Battle of Waterloo, perhaps the most famous battle of all history. There France's emperor Napoleon met his final defeat.

In June of 1815, Napoleon's situation was desperate. Nearly every other country in Europe had allied itself against him. Napoleon decided that only a quick, decisive victory could save his throne. He quickly raised an army and marched north into Belgium. Opposing him were a Prussian army and a British army under the Duke of Wellington.

Napoleon knew his army was outnumbered by these combined forces. Therefore, he decided to try to divide the enemy forces, concentrate on one part and defeat it, and then turn and crush the rest. A large French force launched a surprise attack against the Prussians, sending them reeling away from the British. Napoleon assumed that he had shattered the Prussian forces and could now ignore them. This was a great mistake, for the Prussians were daunted but not destroyed.

Nonetheless, the French turned to crush the British. Wellington took up a strong defensive position near the Belgian village of Waterloo. He knew that his best chance lay in holding off the French until the Prussians could come to his aid. Napoleon was overconfident. He delayed the beginning of the attack for several hours, waiting for the ground to dry from recent thunderstorms. When he finally attacked, his maneuvers were not subtle; instead, he charged head-on into the British lines. He believed that the British would surely collapse in the face of a fierce attack.

The British held on, however. They bravely beat back attack after attack. As evening approached, the supposedly defeated Prussian army entered the eastern end of the battlefield. Caught between two armies, the French army collapsed and fell into a confused retreat. At Waterloo Napoleon lost not only a battle but also the war and his throne.

Nationalism and Revolution

The revolts came in three waves. The first wave hit in the 1820s. Most of these revolts were crushed, but in 1829 **Greece** gained its independence from the Ottoman Empire after ten years of fighting. Starting in 1830, a second wave of revolts occurred. In 1831 **Belgium** became independent from the Netherlands, but the Poles and Hungarians were crushed when they fought for independence. The last wave came in 1848. By this time, Europe's rulers knew they had to make changes or continue to risk revolt. The second half of the century was marked by a gradual movement away from absolutism.

Nationalism also encouraged the formation of two other nations during this century—**Italy** and **Germany.** For centuries these areas had been made up of many individual states, some ruled independently and some ruled by empires such as Austria. After years of trying, Italy and Germany were born in 1871.

Historic Expressions—You may want to discuss other history-related phrases used in conversation. Phrases include "sword of Damocles," "Pyrrhic victory," "crossed the Rubicon," and "Gordian knot."

CHARGED WITH ROMANCE

The Romantic movement produced many great poets. One of the most outstanding was Alfred, Lord Tennyson (TEN ih sun). An Englishman, he was proclaimed Britain's poet laureate (LOR ee it), the official poet of the king and queen.

In the following poem, Tennyson is telling the story of the Light Brigade that made a charge against the Russians in the Crimean War. The job of the Light Brigade was to retake guns at the end of a valley flanked by the enemy. Unfortunately, a badly worded command sent the brigade charging straight into the enemy's guns.

Look ahead to page 316 and read the paragraphs that deal with the Romantic movement. As you read the poem below, what Romantic themes do you see in it? What is your reaction to the poem? Do you think that was the reaction that Tennyson wanted?

The Charge of the Light Brigade

Half a league, half a league,
Half a league onward,
All in the valley of Death
Rode the six hundred.
"Forward, the Light Brigade!
Charge for the guns!" he said.
Into the valley of Death
Rode the six hundred.

"Forward, the Light Brigade!"
Was there a man dismayed?
Not tho' the soldier knew
Someone had blundered.
Theirs not to make reply,
Theirs not to reason why,
Theirs but to do and die.
Into the valley of Death
Rode the six hundred.

Cannon to the right of them,
Cannon to the left of them,
Cannon in front of them
Volleyed and thundered;
Stormed at with shot and shell,
Boldly they rode and well,
Into the jaws of Death,
Into the mouth of Hell
Rode the six hundred.

Flashed all their sabres bare,
Flashed as they turned in air
Sabring the gunners there,
Charging an army, while
All the world wondered.
Plunged in the battery-smoke
Right thro' the line they broke;
Cossack and Russian
Reeled from the sabre-stroke
Shattered and sundered.
Then they rode back, but not,
Not the six hundred.

Cannon to the right of them,
Cannon to the left of them,
Cannon in front of them
Volleyed and thundered;
Stormed at with shot and shell,
While horse and hero fell,
They that had fought so well
Came thro' the jaws of Death,
Back from the mouth of Hell,
All that was left of them,
Left of the six hundred.

When can their glory fade?
O the wild charge they made!
All the world wondered.
Honor the charge they made!
Honor the Light Brigade,
Noble six hundred!

The Charge of the Light Brigade—Students may wonder about the name "Light Brigade." A light brigade was literally that—the men used less weaponry and lighter horses. Heavy brigades used the heavy war horses pictured in many portraits of the era.

Of the 673 men in the brigade, 195 were present for the next charge. One hundred thirteen of those absent were dead, 134 were wounded. The reason so few were ready for the next charge was that 475 horses had been killed.

For Tennyson the nobility of the action was more important than the actual effect of the charge.

The *Charge of the Light Brigade*—After reading the poem, ask the students the following questions: Why does Tennyson use the description "valley of Death" in line 3? *(because their task will lead to certain death; because it is a valley)* What does the second stanza tell us about the men in the Light Brigade? *(They are brave in the face of certain doom; they do not question their orders.)*

Art for the *Light Brigade*—Have artistic students draw a picture of what they imagine the charge to have looked like according to the description in the poem. This might also be used as a project idea.

Imperialism—Imperialism will be a major theme throughout the rest of this unit and much more of the book. European dominance over other lands (whether in Asia, Africa, or the Americas) was a sign of true power in the nineteenth century. It was not until the middle of the twentieth century that many countries finally received their independence.

★★★★★★★★★★

For a color version of the map on this page, see page A7 in the Appendix.

Imperialism

The rulers of Europe were not concerned just with events on the continent during the nineteenth century. They were also interested in building empires, a movement called **imperialism.** The Americas, India, China, and Africa all contained areas that the European nations desired to control. Their motives were several. First they needed raw materials and markets to support their growing industries. Next they desired to share European culture with others whom they viewed as less civilized. This motive included the spreading of Christianity to lost people. A third reason was to appear powerful before other European nations. Unless a nation had colonies, it was considered weak. Toward the end of the century, the race for colonies reached a furious pace and was one of the major causes of World War I (1914-18). In later chapters we will look at how European nations treated their colonies.

Section Review

1. What type of government did Great Britain have?
2. What problems did the workers in the new cities have? How did Parliament help them?
3. What group tried to restore Europe to pre-Napoleonic conditions?
4. Although Napoleon was defeated, what ideas did he spread through Europe? What did this French influence promote in Europe?
5. Give two examples of unsuccessful nationalism.
6. Name two nations that gained independence in Europe in the 1800s.

In this chapter we see many revolutions occurring. Is revolting against government a proper response for a Christian? Support your answer with Scripture.

Unification—Discuss why it took so long for Italy and Germany to coalesce into unified countries. Reasons include geography, tradition, segments with powerful rulers, and loyalty to one's own section.

Section Review Answers

1. parliamentary
2. working conditions and living conditions; it passed laws to help people working in the mines and factories and improved living conditions
3. Congress of Vienna
4. Liberty, Equality, Fraternity; nationalism
5. the Poles and Hungarians
6. Greece and Belgium

Answers will vary. As Christians, we may not revolt against the government. Romans 13:1-2 says to "let every soul be subject unto the higher powers. For there is no power but of God: the powers that be are ordained of God. Whosoever therefore resisteth the power, resisteth the ordinance of God: and they that resist shall receive to themselves damnation." We must obey the government in all areas unless a law or policy specifically goes against the direct commands or principles of God. Even then we must accept the consequences. We never have a biblical justification for revolt. We must be a good testimony even in rejecting anti-biblical laws.

The Age of Industrialism

The Industrial Revolution began in the eighteenth century and was fully underway by the mid-nineteenth century. At the Great Exhibition many exhibits showed the results of new industries. Undoubtedly, Great Britain was the leader in manufacturing. But slowly the other nations of Europe, the United States, and Japan caught up.

Technology and Invention

The nineteenth century was the heyday of inventors, both European and American. Using new technologies and simple guesswork, they all had the same goal in mind: discover something new. The "new" might be an entirely new object or an improved version of an old one. From this attitude of discovery came such important inventions as the **steam locomotive,** electrical generators, the telephone, and the automobile.

The new inventions dramatically changed almost every aspect of life—especially transportation. The steam locomotive and iron rails improved land travel. Now, instead of walking or riding in bumpy carriages on dirt roads, people could travel on steam-powered trains. Some of these trains sped along at almost sixty miles per hour. In sea travel, steam engines replaced sails on ocean-going vessels. Gradually iron, which made the ship move faster and last longer, replaced wood in ships' hulls.

New inventions also affected communication. The **telegraph** allowed people to send messages quickly over great distances by wire instead of relying on the slower delivery by foot or horse. In 1866 an undersea telegraph cable was laid between Europe and North

New inventions such as the camera and the motor car brought change to the world.

SECTION 3

Student Objectives
Students should be able to

1. Identify important inventions of this era.
2. Compare and contrast capitalism and socialism.
3. Describe communism and evaluate its flaws.

Imperialism and Technology— The innovations in transportation and communication in Europe were not limited to Europe. Imperialists transferred them to portions of China, India, and Africa as they laid claim to those countries. In the next three chapters point out the technological advances that were transported.

SECTION 3

Materials

- Electricity experiment or telegraph experiment or directions and materials
- Items containing steel
- Guest speaker to discuss economics

Inventors—These inventors provide a good example of setting goals and striving to reach them. Read aloud Prov. 13:12, 19 and Phil. 3:13. Discuss goal setting in relation to these verses.

Communication—Ask your students to imagine life without modern communications. Have them write a one-paragraph description of the way their day would be changed without modern communications. Remind the students that today the means of communication are also changing with the growth of computer, Internet, and satellite technology.

Local Communication—Before the telephone became useful in every home, the penny-post expanded communication in London. For the first time poor people who had taken jobs in the city could easily correspond with their relatives in the country.

Typewriters and QWERTY—Early typewriters had the keys arranged alphabetically. It was so easy for typists to find the keys that they became very fast. However, frequently used letters placed close together on the keyboard jammed. In 1870 typewriter inventor Christopher Sholes came up with the QWERTY layout (named for the order of the keys on the left side of the top row of letters). This order separated frequently used letters so that the typist could be fast but the keys would not get jammed.

Today, as typewriters become obsolete and computers and word processors take over, the problem of key jamming is not a factor. Changing the keyboard has become a matter of discussion once again.

Women in the Workforce—The telephone service employed more and more women when women proved to be better at handling the exchanges than their male counterparts.

In the 1881 census in England, there were very few women in offices. Ten years later there were 18,000 women registered as office clerks (secretaries and typists).

Factory-Produced Goods—Remind the students of machine-made furnishings produced in this era. These furnishings could be made less expensively and so were available to more of the population. Other things that became available were ready-made clothing and shoes. At that time it was a sign of wealth to have clothing handmade for you by someone else; today handmade clothes are sometimes derided.

Alexander Graham Bell's telephone brought instant communication to people miles apart.

America. Near the end of the nineteenth century an American inventor named **Alexander Graham Bell** invented the **telephone.** Technological advances in printed communications resulted in larger printing presses run by steam engines. These presses turned out newspapers and books faster and more economically than before.

Two other important inventions for publishing, writing, and business were the **typewriter** and the camera. The typewriter produced easily readable, consistent text for business forms and correspondence. The science of **photography** added a new dimension to publishing. It also allowed families and historians to chronicle the events of life more accurately.

Two of the inventions mentioned above, the typewriter and the telephone, changed women's lives especially. Before this time, women worked outside the home only if they were poor or if their families were unable to support them. The jobs available to them were meager and unappealing. With the advent of the telephone and typewriter, women took a new place in the work force in offices and other businesses. People began to accept the idea of single women working outside the home.

As expected, technology especially affected the factories. Machines that made goods more quickly and efficiently were constantly being invented and improved. New processes for casting iron and smelting steel made these two metals much easier to produce. As a result, these metals became basic to many manufactured goods. Cast iron was used for everything from textile looms to garden fountains, while steel became as common in the kitchen as in the factory.

The invention of the camera allowed this young girl to keep a visual record of her first telephone call.

Science Projects—Either purchase a telegraph kit or an electric light kit from a local hobby store or find directions in a book of science projects and assemble the parts needed to construct it yourself. Set it up in class to explain how the technology works.

INTERPRETATIONS

Steel

In the mid-1800s men on both continents and England were racing to produce inexpensive steel. Prior to this time, cast iron, wrought iron, and brick were the building materials of choice, but their usage was limited. The inexpensive production of steel changed architecture, transportation, and daily life in the late 1800s.

With new means such as the Bessemer converter and the open-hearth method, steel producers could quickly separate the impurities in iron into a slag that was poured off and gases that blew away. The product of these processes was a material that could be poured, rolled, and shaped into many forms that were stronger than the iron from which they came.

The great strength of steel allowed the Firth of Forth Bridge to be built. For the first time a bridge spanned 1,710 feet between piers. Previously iron had spanned only 500-600 feet between piers and brickwork only about 300 feet. The Eiffel Tower, built for the Paris Exposition in 1889, was a miracle in technology, not only because of its maze of steel beams and wires but also because it was outfitted with electric lights.

Steel transformed transportation. Railroad tracks were smoother and engines finer. By the late 1800s France had nearly eleven thousand miles of railway. Trains traveled an amazing fifty miles an hour to rush the French from town to coast. In the late 1800s motor cars came on the scene, allowing personal mobility for the wealthy and soon for many more.

In daily life, steel was used for common household implements such as knives, but its most significant impact was as a sheathing for the transatlantic cable that allowed messages to be sent back and forth from continent to continent. The main copper wires in the cable were first surrounded by insulation and lastly surrounded by ten steel wires that were each insulated and protected by hemp. The steel wires formed a protection against the sea and the rocks.

The easy production of steel was one of the technological advances that revolutionized life in the 1800s and continues to allow comfort and facility in our lives today. Practically every building, every machine, and every vehicle that you use today contains steel components.

The open hearth method of steel production

The Firth of Forth

Steel Show and Tell—Have students bring in examples of items which contain steel. These should be extremely easy to find. Have them explain how the steel in each item aids in its use.

★★★★★★★★★★

For a color version of the graph on this page, see page A7 in the Appendix.

Understanding Economics— The concepts in this section are difficult but essential for your students to be acquainted with. Work through these concepts as a group, using the diagrams for visual reinforcement.

More on Capitalism—Capitalistic principles allow a product's price to be set as high as the market will bear. For example, a product that many people want but that is in low supply could be sold at a high price. On the other hand, a product that few people want but that is in large supply would have to be sold at a lower price. Of course, price includes the cost of production plus profit. When a product sells, it pays for its production and also gives the businessman a profit. Although the businessman might keep some profit for himself (thereby growing wealthier), he often puts much of it back into his business. With this capital investment he improves his machinery and production processes, and these improvements in turn increase his sales and his profits.

Striking Out Against Business— The strike was the most effective means that the labor classes had to influence their employers. In the 1800s strikes occurred across Europe and America, and the first labor unions were established.

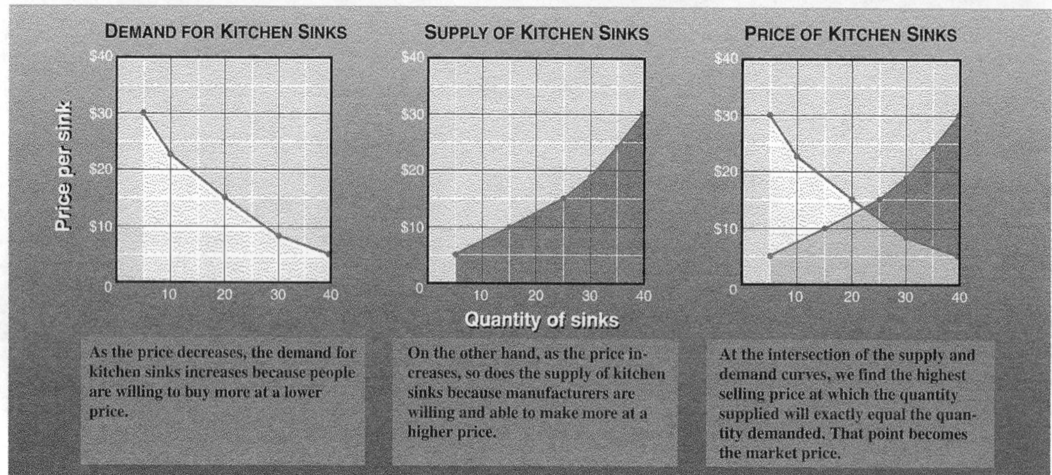

As the price decreases, the demand for kitchen sinks increases because people are willing to buy more at a lower price.

On the other hand, as the price increases, so does the supply of kitchen sinks because manufacturers are willing and able to make more at a higher price.

At the intersection of the supply and demand curves, we find the highest selling price at which the quantity supplied will exactly equal the quantity demanded. That point becomes the market price.

Managing Industrialism

Two major problems faced the early industrialists: production and marketing. **Production** includes designing or inventing new products. It also includes building machinery to produce them and finding raw materials. **Marketing** includes setting prices for the products and advertising them. The businessman must also find markets for his products and transport them there.

One answer to the problems of production and marketing was **capitalism.** In capitalism, all property (factory buildings and equipment) is owned privately by a businessman or group of businessmen. This property is known as *capital,* hence the name *capitalism.* Capitalism thrives on competition: businessmen trying to outdo each other with newer, better, or less expensive products.

In marketing, capitalism relies on **supply and demand.** Supply and demand deals with how much there is of a product and how many people want it or need it. The product's price depends on how much of a product is in supply as well as customers' demands for that product. The diagrams above show this principle at work.

Capitalism works best when there is **free trade,** trade between or within countries without taxes on goods. Great Britain led the free-trade movement by trading freely with her colonies. Britain's leadership in sea trade encouraged other nations to practice free trade. Gradually throughout the nineteenth century, more countries followed the principle of free trade.

Capitalism also discourages government interference. However, man's sinful, greedy nature often leads to unethical or unsafe practices in production and marketing. By the end of the century many governments passed regulations to protect owners, workers, and consumers.

Labor: Problems and Responses

In Chapter 9 you read about the working conditions and living conditions of factory workers. As industrialism grew, these problems worsened. They contributed to many of the revolts of the nineteenth century. The people desired better working environments and living conditions as well as political freedom. In some countries, such as Great Britain,

Economics—Ask your students to name a popular Christmas gift item. Use this item to talk about supply and demand. Copy the diagram from this page onto the chalkboard to help students work through this information. (TT 11-B)

governments passed bills in an attempt to improve the workers' lives. In many European countries, though, governments often did not respond to the workers' needs, and the workers did not wait for the slow process of lawmaking.

Because it seemed unlikely that some governments would ever change, many workers turned to the ideas of the socialists. **Socialism** is opposed to capitalism. The socialists encourage governmental control. They say that the government—not individuals—should own all business property. Socialists also believe that government can use this power for the good of society. The name *socialist* came from this emphasis on society or social good. According to this philosophy, workers benefit by sharing equally in the profits rather than by earning according to their labor.

One problem with this belief is best shown by illustration. A man who produced twenty pairs of shoes in a day was paid the same amount as a man who produced only ten pairs. The man who produced twenty pairs of shoes received no recognition or increased pay for his greater effort. Do you think he will want to continue producing twenty shoes a day?

Another problem of socialism is that it assumes government is capable of determining what should be produced. It is far from clear in socialist writings, however, how government is supposed to know how to make such decisions. Socialism ignores the limitations of human knowledge and assumes that government is not susceptible to the same evil excesses of which it accuses businessmen.

A socialist government is involved with society as well as with business. It seeks to provide services, such as welfare, housing, education, and health care. Heavy taxation pays for these programs. As one man said, "Taxation for social benefit is like getting a blood transfusion from your right arm to your left arm, and losing half the blood in the process." Although people receive many material benefits in a socialistic system, individual worth, achievement, and responsibility are valued little. Also, the resulting economic burden on the nation can be disastrous.

Karl Marx (1818-83) developed a philosophy called **Marxism.**

> "Philosophers have only sought to *interpret* the real world in various ways; the real point is to *change* society." Karl Marx

As the quotation above reveals, Marx wanted to change society. He felt that society's main problem was that the rich controlled the means of producing goods. Karl Marx wrote two books about his philosophy that have been used as guidebooks for other leaders: the *Communist Manifesto,* written with Friedrich Engels, and *Das Kapital* (DAHS kah-pee-TAHL). In these books Marx envisioned his philosophy helping the evolution of government to result in the perfect society—**Communism.** In Communism all people would share in labor and in the goods that resulted from that labor.

Marx promoted revolution as a means of overthrowing governments that oppressed the working class. Marx's philosophy was used by later Communist leaders to urge workers to rebel against their employers and rulers. Because the governments of Europe gradually responded to the needs of workers and made some reforms, Communism did not take over in Europe entirely. Only in Russia were the Communists successful in overthrowing the government (see pp. 448-49).

With a socialist economic system meeting the needs of the people and no private ownership of goods, Marx believed that people should be perfectly content. Unfortunately, Marx did not consider man's sin nature. In the early Christian communities of the New Testament, a type of communism was used. Acts 4:32-35 says,

Marx and Communism—Marx believed that government went through an evolution similar to the process Darwin thought animals had. He taught that economic systems had progressed from patrician/slave to lord/serf to employer/worker. These class struggles, Marx believed, would be ended if there were no private ownership of goods. Communism, with socialism as its economic base, would erase private ownership as well as meet the needs of all its people.

Marx's quotation is good evidence of the flaw in his philosophy. He did not consider *how* the change would be made and *what* would happen if anything other than his vision of a classless society arose. In the countries where communism has taken over, the class distinctions no longer are between the owners and the workers but rather between those who control the government and the rest of the population.

Economics Guest Speaker—A local Christian businessman may be able to present the topics of supply and demand clearly to your class and give students exposure to these concepts in the real world. In advance, carefully interview any speaker to check for appropriateness, clarity, and testimony. A special speaker must be more than an entertaining diversion for your students.

Germany and Communism— In the early 1900s, Germany went through a very difficult time of poverty. Chief minister Otto von Bismarck saw the importance of meeting the needs of the poor for food and housing. He installed social programs to better the physical lives of the lower classes. Bismarck desired the masses to see the state as a kind father who was to be defended and obeyed. But Bismarck's purpose was not altruistic. He saw that discontentment was drawing people to socialism and that the inductees into the army were in poor health. His programs settled unrest in Germany which might otherwise have led to revolution and communism. They also established Germany as having the strongest and best army in Europe.

Hunger and poverty sometimes motivated people to follow socialist revolutions. German expressionist artist Käthe Kollwitz caught this mood in her print Uprising, *1899. (Courtesy of Emery Bopp)*

> And the multitude of them that believed were of one heart and of one soul: neither said any of them that ought of the things which he possessed was his own; but they had all things common.
>
> And with great power gave the apostles witness of the resurrection of the Lord Jesus: and great grace was upon them all.
>
> Neither was there any among them that lacked: for as many as were possessors of lands or houses sold them, and brought the prices of the things that were sold,
>
> And laid them down at the apostles' feet: and distribution was made unto every man according as he had need.

Even in this Christian community where "great grace" was upon them, problems arose. Shortly after these verses, the pride and lies of Ananias and Sapphira were revealed (Acts 5:1-10) and the murmuring over the neglect of the widows began (Acts 6:1). There is little possibility of Marx's vision of Communism becoming a reality in this sinful world.

Section Review

1. What nation led industry in the nineteenth century?
2. List three inventions of this period.
3. What two problems faced nineteenth-century businessmen?
4. What two factors influence the setting of a price in capitalism? What type of trade makes capitalism work best?
5. How did many governments of Europe handle labor problems?
6. To what did workers turn when the governments did not respond quickly?

List four things that would hinder Communism from working in a society. Explain the effect of each item on your list.

Section Review Answers

1. Great Britain
2. steam locomotive, electrical generators, telephone, automobile, telegraph, typewriter, photography (any three)
3. production and marketing
4. supply and demand; free trade
5. did not respond
6. socialism

Answers will vary. Some things that would hinder communism from working in a society might include man's sin nature—he will not naturally share, and he is greedy; natural disaster—lack of goods from one area would severely decrease the amount of finished product from another; leaders in power—though everyone is supposed to be totally equal, some would be "more" equal than others; decreased motivation—everyone receives the same pay, so why work harder than the slowest person?

Belief and Expression

Accidents in the lab don't always bring disaster.

Science obviously held an important place at the Great Exhibition in 1851. The exhibits showed new scientific discoveries. Scientists of this century carried on the work begun in the Age of Reason. Many inventions at the Exhibition were the result of scientific study put to work on specific problems. But sometimes new inventions were merely side benefits of scientific research. An example of this was the development of synthetic dyes. While trying to find a new medicine, a young researcher accidentally discovered a substance that dyed cloth purple. Purple had always been the color of royalty and wealth because it was expensive to make from natural substances. With the discovery of the synthetic purple, which was cheap and easy to use, nearly everyone could afford purple cloth. Mauve (MOHV), a shade of purple, became so fashionable that the 1890s were called the "Mauve Decade."

Science and Evolution

The amazing achievements of science caused many people to look at science as the answer to all their problems. To them, scientifically "proving" something gave it a stamp of approval. Science is a useful tool; however, an undue emphasis on science is dangerous because a person may hold the results of science above the truth of Scripture.

This danger became reality with the work of **Charles Darwin.** Darwin struck at the root of Christian belief and biblical teaching with his theory of evolution. **Evolution** denied Creation by God's direct act. Evolutionists said that all creatures, including man, evolved from nonliving elements. They stated that simple life forms came from these basic elements; then the less complex animals evolved, and finally man appeared. According to Darwin, this process took hundreds of millions of years with improvements coming gradually as creatures adapted to their changing environments. With his theory, Darwin denied Scripture on two counts: first, he denied divine Creation (Gen. 1:1); second, by saying man evolved, he denied man's special creation after God's likeness and image (Gen. 1:26). Evolution was and is today a direct attack on God's sovereignty and power.

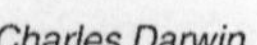

Charles Darwin

SECTION 4

Student Objectives
Students should be able to

1. Critically evaluate the theory of evolution and its flaws.
2. Discuss changes in religion due to science in this era.
3. Distinguish between romantic, realistic, and impressionistic works of art and music.

More on Evolution and Creation—The idea of evolution was not original to Darwin. For several hundred years, men of science had proposed that man and animals change over time. The newness of Darwin's theory was that it gave a reason or cause for the change—natural selection through survival of the fittest.

For more information on evolution and biblical Creationism, see *LIFE SCIENCE for Christian Schools 2nd Edition,* Chapters 9 and 10.

Making Mauve—In an attempt to create a synthetic drug for quinine, lab assistant William Henry Perkin performed an experiment on coal tar. The result was a black powder which did not seem too promising, but when Perkin added alcohol to the powder a deep purple mixture resulted. Artificial purple dye had been discovered. Now the color of kings, once obtained only from sea snails, could be had by all.

Lab assistant turned discoverer, Perkin soon set up a factory of his own and produced *mauvine.* Other men followed in his steps and created many other synthetic dyes to replace the once strictly organic colors.

SECTION 4

Materials

- *LIFE SCIENCE for Christian Schools* (BJUP)
- *Oliver Twist* video
- George Mueller's *Autobiography*
- Examples of classical, romantic, and impressionistic music
- Monet paintings

Evolution—Chapter 12 of *LIFE SCIENCE for Christian Schools* discusses in greater detail the evolutionary theories. Since your students should be studying these theories near the time you are teaching this chapter, a good discussion about the errors of evolution can occur. Students should be very active in this discussion since they already know about this subject.

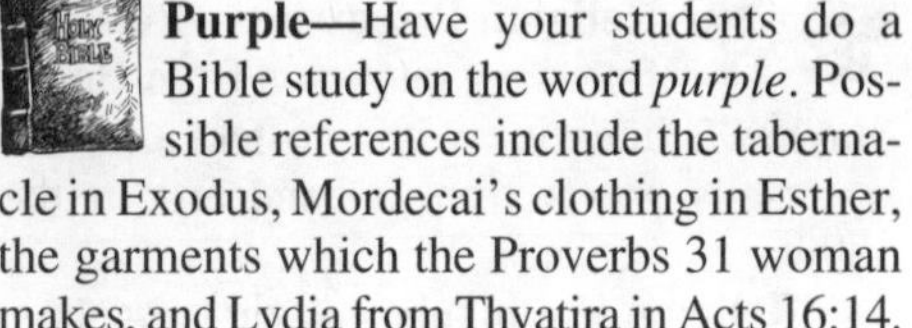

Purple—Have your students do a Bible study on the word *purple*. Possible references include the tabernacle in Exodus, Mordecai's clothing in Esther, the garments which the Proverbs 31 woman makes, and Lydia from Thyatira in Acts 16:14.

Higher Criticism—There are two forms of biblical criticism: higher and lower. Lower criticism is the legitimate attempt of scholars to determine how closely the Scriptures we have correspond to what the original authors wrote. Higher criticism, however, is the study of the history of the Bible. This also sounds like a legitimate, scholarly goal, but it has become a dangerous source of liberal thought.

When rationalism and deism became widely accepted in the eighteenth century (Chapter 9), some scholars began looking at the Bible in the light of these new philosophies. In fact, they had to either reexamine Scripture or give up their new way of thinking: deism and rationalism denied the possibility of revelation.

Unfortunately, higher criticism found many followers in Christianity. Scholars and religious leaders who had, perhaps, already begun to lose faith found in higher criticism reason to doubt the inspiration, and hence authority, of Scripture. Their lack of faith slowly filtered down to ordinary church members in major denominations and began to erode their faith. The present condition in most major denominations can be traced to the work of the higher critics, who robbed many theologians of their belief in the Bible as the Truth of God.

Charles Haddon Spurgeon—Spurgeon was born at Kelvedo, Essex, England, in 1834. When he was a teenager, he slipped into a Methodist church one night to find refuge from a snowstorm. That night he also found refuge from life's storms through salvation in Christ. He soon felt God's call to spread the gospel and preached his first sermon at the age of sixteen.

In 1854 Spurgeon became pastor of a church in London. His powerful preaching won so many converts that the church needed a new building within a year. Almost immediately construction was begun on the Metropolitan Tabernacle, a hall that seated six thousand and served as his pulpit for the rest of his life. While the Tabernacle was being built, Spurgeon preached at the Surrey Gardens Music Hall to

Charles Haddon Spurgeon

Science and Religion

The emphasis on science which had begun during the Age of Reason in the 1700s continued to greatly influence people's religious beliefs and actions. The ideas of evolution and the questioning of the power and existence of God shook the faith of many. Unbelieving theologians used scientific methods and principles to attack God's Word. They denied the inspiration of Scripture. Believers who were not fully grounded in the Word and unbelievers who had no foundation in Christ were often misled by the claims of "scholars" who questioned and denied Scripture. Many ideas of these nineteenth-century theologians are still alive today. Christians must study the Bible and become firmly rooted in the truth of Scripture so that they can use "the sword of the Spirit, which is the word of God" (Eph. 6:17) against these attacks.

The people who accepted Darwin's ideas believed that, with the proper external influences, man could still be made better. They believed the **social gospel,** which taught that people could be improved by changing their living conditions rather than by converting their souls. However, *true* improvement comes only from God's power and starts at salvation. Second Corinthians 5:17 tells us, "Therefore if any man be in Christ, he is a new creature: old things are passed away; behold, all things are become new." Despite the attempts at reform in the nineteenth century, poverty, disease, and crime remained. Once again this evidence shows the failure of man to permanently improve his external conditions without first improving his heart.

As in any age, the only true answer to society's problems is Christ. During the 1800s several revivals swept England and America. The preaching of **Charles H. Spurgeon** and **Dwight L. Moody** brought many people to the Savior. These new Christians wanted to help others by teaching them of Christ. Improved transportation allowed many to go to the mission fields of China, India, and Africa. (See "Fulfilling the Great Commission," on p. 250.)

Other believers stayed in Europe to establish ministries at home. These Christians helped people by pointing them to Christ's saving blood. The **Salvation Army,** the Young Men's Christian Association (YMCA), and the Young Women's Christian Association (YWCA) were started to meet both physical and spiritual needs. Orphanages, schools, hospitals, and Sunday schools provided for the poor and needy. The dedicated Christian men and women who ran these ministries touched many lives as they spread the love of God to those in need. Their works showed their faith by combining the Bible's commands to "preach the gospel" (Mark 16:15) and to "do good unto all men" (Gal. 6:10).

Religion Discussion—Read the following quotation from Henry Mayhew's interview with a coster (someone who sells goods from a handcart) in the 1800s.

"Religion is a regular puzzle to costers. They see people come out of church and chapel, and as they're mostly well-dressed, and there's very few of their own sort among the church-goers, the costers somehow mix up being religious with being respectable, and they have a queer sort of feeling about it. It's a mystery to them." (BLM 11-3)

Discuss how churches still have difficulty ministering to social and economic classes that are different. Ask the students how they think the problem occurs and what our response as Christians should be.

CHARACTERIZATIONS

Christian Orphanages: The Work of Thomas Barnardo and George Mueller

The plight of orphans in Victorian England was severe. Even orphanages built expressly to help such children were often managed by cruel, unconcerned people. Many Englishmen called attention to this unhappy situation and demanded changes. Christians especially felt compassion toward the orphans and tried to help them. They took seriously the word of Psalm 82:3, "Defend the poor and fatherless: do justice to the afflicted and needy."

One Christian man, Dr. Thomas Barnardo (1845-1905), devoted his life to building orphanages. Converted as a result of the Irish Revival of 1859, Dr. Barnardo wanted to be a medical missionary to China. However, health problems prevented his going. Instead, he became interested in the needs of orphans. In 1867 he opened his first home for them. Making his motto "no destitute child ever refused admission," Dr. Barnardo eventually helped over ten thousand orphans in his homes.

George Mueller

Unwanted and orphaned children were everywhere in England.

Perhaps even better known than Dr. Barnardo was George Mueller (1805-1898). Born in Prussia, Mueller was converted at the age of twenty and came to England to prepare for the mission field. While living in the city of Bristol, he became concerned about the orphans there. Believing himself to be led of God, Mueller built an orphanage. Mueller ran his home on faith. He had no governmental or even church funding. He simply prayed for God to supply his needs, and the Lord always did. Often, Mueller would go to bed not knowing where the next day's food would come from. Yet God graciously rewarded his faith and supplied his needs. As a result of God's faithful provision, thousands of orphans benefited from the work of George Mueller.

audiences of ten thousand people at a time.

Spurgeon's popularity spread quickly throughout England and beyond for a number of reasons. One was his dynamic preaching style. In contrast with many of the preachers of his time, Spurgeon preached lively sermons that incorporated interesting illustrations and humor with sound teaching of Scripture. He was one of the first preachers to take advantage of the communications revolution. Sermons he preached to his congregation at the Metropolitan Tabernacle in London were translated, printed, and sent all over the world within a few days. (His collected sermons fill more than fifty volumes.) Spurgeon also wrote extensively: books, tracts, pamphlets, and devotional booklets all came from his active pen. Many of those works are still in use today.

Although he was very popular and became a prominent figure in nineteenth-century Christianity, Spurgeon did not approve of the growing liberal trends he saw. He especially distrusted the increasingly popular scientific approach to biblical criticism which had come over to England with the higher-criticism movement of France and Germany. He recognized the danger of these attitudes toward God's Word, and in 1887 he left the Baptist Union because it was accepting liberal teachings.

Social Gospel—The Salvation Army, YMCA, and YWCA started well, but over the years they compromised scriptural principles and accepted many of the attitudes and actions of the social-gospel teachers. Today these organizations often offer little more than social help with no spiritual comfort for those to whom they minister. These organizations illustrate the dangers of compromise.

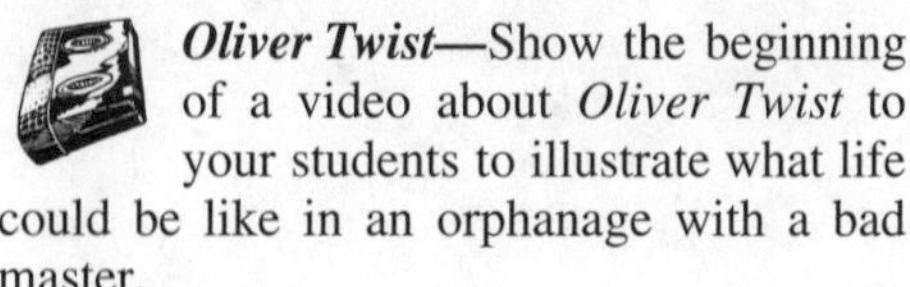

Oliver Twist—Show the beginning of a video about *Oliver Twist* to your students to illustrate what life could be like in an orphanage with a bad master.

Autobiography—Read portions of Mueller's *Autobiography* to your students.

Romanticism—The term *romanticism* did not refer to Rome as neoclassical art did but rather to Roman languages or vernacular. Romantic writers rejected Latin and wrote entirely in the vernacular of the western European countries. Nor did the romantic painters, composers, and authors seek to separate themselves from their work and present an objective view as in classical or neoclassical style. Instead they poured their emotions into their work in an effort to gain an equally emotional response from the viewer or listener.

The Hay Wain *by John Constable*

Changes in the Arts

The nineteenth century was an age of change, and the arts were no exception. Several styles of art appeared in the nineteenth century. **Romanticism** dominated the first half of the century. Several themes characterize romanticism: a desire to imitate the past, especially the medieval time with its higher call to chivalry; an emphasis on the mysterious and the supernatural; a love of freedom; nationalism; and nature. These themes also reflect the political ideas of the time. Romantic themes appeared in nineteenth-century literature as well, such as Sir Walter Scott's medieval story *Ivanhoe.*

Romantic paintings often are peaceful scenes of rural life or landscapes. Some artists also painted scenes from the revolutions. In music, composers reacted to the orderly, classical style by changing to the full, emotion-filled romantic style. **Ludwig van Beethoven** (BAY-TOH-vun) is perhaps the best-known composer of this age. He mixed classical and romantic elements in his works. The romantic composers **Johannes Brahms** and **Frédéric Chopin** (shoh PAN) used folksongs in their works, showing the influence of nationalism. This century was also the height of opera, a combination of music, drama, and literature. The leading opera composer, **Giuseppe Verdi,** lived at this time.

By midcentury, romanticism lost popularity to a new style: **realism.** Realism reacted against romanticism's dreamlike quality by emphasizing, as its name suggests, how life really is. In writing and painting, realists pictured everyday life in realistic detail. For example, the novelist **Charles Dickens** used realistic elements in his stories of working-class Englishmen. His books did much to publicize the horrible conditions of the lower classes. The new science of photography influenced realistic painters. They often tried to copy the precision of photographs.

By the end of the century a third style called **impressionism** (im PRESH uh NIZ um) emerged, continuing into the twentieth century. Impressionism differed from both romanticism and realism. The impressionists sought to capture the impression a scene made on one's mind. New scientific discoveries showed that the mind perceived images through light and color. Impressionist painters were less concerned with their subject matter than with

A Boat on the Shore *by Gustave Courbet (Metropolitan Museum of Art)*

Listening Activity—Play examples of classical music (Haydn, Mozart), romantic music (Chopin, Brahms), and impressionistic music (Debussy) for your class. Discuss the differences in the music and how each reflects the spirit of its age. Bring examples of neoclassical (David, Ingres) and romantic (Delacroix, Ryder) painting to show along with the music. Ask your students if they can detect a similarity in spirit between the music and the art of the same period. The following selections are found on the Listener's Choice recording available from BJU Press.

- "Clair de lune" (Debussy)
- "Le petit negre" (Debussy)

Two Views of London

Early Victorian author Jane Austen often showed London as a city where the rich rented homes in the winter so that they could be part of the round of social events held by the social elite. She said very little about the plight of the poor.

Dickens presented quite a different view of London in many of his books. His perspective dwells on the trials of the poor across England but especially in London. In the following excerpt from *Dombey and Son,* Chapter 33, Dickens gives us a glimpse of people who are migrating to London from the country.

> She often looked with compassion, at such a time, upon the stragglers who came wandering into London, by the great highway hard by, and who, footsore and weary, and gazing fearfully at the huge town before them, as if foreboding that their misery there would be but as a drop of water in the sea, or as a grain of sea-sand on the shore, went shrinking on, cowering before the angry weather, and looking as if the very elements rejected them. Day after day, such travellers crept past, but always, as she thought in one direction—always towards the town. Swallowed up in one phase or other of its immensity, towards which they seemed impelled by a desperate fascination, they never returned. Food for the hospitals, the churchyards, the prisons, the rivers, fever, madness, vice, and death—they passed on to the monster, roaring in the distance, and were lost.

High hopes for a new life were often dashed by the reality of a dirty, bustling city filled with many people and few jobs.

Jane Austen—Jane Austen's famous books include *Pride and Prejudice, Sense and Sensibility, Emma*, and *Persuasion*.

Dickens—Encourage your students to write in a realistic style a one-page paper on life in big cities today. Compare the finished papers to Charles Dickens's works.

Monet—Claude Monet was a famous impressionistic artist. His artwork is available in myriad forms today. Calendars, umbrellas, picture books, and journals are among the items that display his works.

the technical aspects of their work, especially light and color. By observing scenes at various hours, they saw how changes in light caused changes in color. They recorded these effects of light on their canvases. Each impressionistic painting captures a scene at a particular moment and often seems to lack purpose or substance. For these reasons impressionistic art was at first rejected by art critics.

In music, impressionism was displayed in shimmering music with no standard form. A leading impressionistic composer was **Claude Debussy** (duh BYOO see). Debussy rejected the emotionalism and form of the romantic composers. Instead of producing a connected work that builds emotion, the impressionist composer uses unconnected musical phrases to create a temporary mood. Debussy is so identified with the impressionist form that some argue that he is the only true impressionist composer.

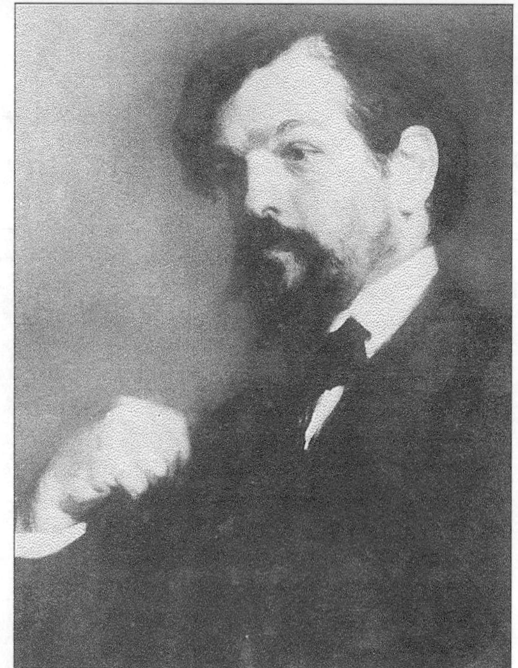

Claude Debussy was the inventor of impressionistic music.

House of Parliament—Sun Breaking Through the Fog, *Claude Monet*

Monet—Show your students a calendar or book with examples of Monet's impressionistic paintings. Discuss the artistic merit of Monet's work. Ask for a show of hands of which students like this style of art and which do not.

Section Review

1. How did many people look at science in the nineteenth century?
2. What most dangerous result of science came in this age?
3. In what two ways did Darwin deny Scripture?
4. What did the social gospel teach? What is really the only answer to man's problems?
5. How did the romantic composers react against classicism? Who was the best-known early romantic composer?
6. What two elements of painting did impressionistic artists concentrate on?

What are three things in this section that were affected by science? Why does science have such a strong effect on so many areas of life?

Spanning the Ages

The great advancement in technology in Great Britain would prepare her for the imperialism that was to come. Soon she would be using her immense power to influence and then control nations on most other continents. She needed raw materials to feed the growing industries in her own country, and she found these materials around the world.

Summary

Throughout the nineteenth century a growing middle class glowed with optimism. This optimism carried them to all corners of the world, where they shared their culture with others. The nineteenth century was Britain's great century. Britain led the world in manufacturing, trade, empire building, and society. The nineteenth century on the Continent was confronted by the ideas spread by Napoleon. One result of this confrontation was the formation of new nations—Greece, Belgium, Germany, and Italy. In industry and trade, the opposing systems of capitalism and socialism conflicted. Governments and businessmen learned to improve living conditions and working conditions at least slightly or face the threat of riots, revolts, and even Communism. In thought and religion, science became even more important. Darwin proposed his theory of evolution, while scholars attacked God's Word by using so-called "scientific" methods. But God sent revival through godly preachers, and many believers reached out to help those around them and give them the gospel. Many went to foreign mission fields. In art, three styles dominated the 1800s: romanticism, realism, and impressionism. These styles reflected the spirit of the age.

Section Review Answers

1. as the answer to all their problems
2. Darwin's theory of evolution
3. He denied divine Creation; he denied man's special creation after God's likeness and image.
4. that people could be improved by changing their living conditions rather than by converting their souls; salvation
5. They changed from the orderly, classical style to the full, emotion-filled romantic style; Ludwig van Beethoven.
6. light and color

Answers will vary. Belief in God and His Word, the view of how the world began, dyes and textiles, and so on were all affected by science. Science affects so many areas of life because it changes life, often creating an easier and more efficient lifestyle.

Chapter Review Idea

Play an inventors game based on the game of hangman. Divide the class into two teams. Using the model of an old telephone or car, students must add a feature when they incorrectly answer a question or do not answer at all. The first team with a finished invention loses.

Chapter Enrichment Activities

Devotionals—Throughout this week, use Spurgeon's works for class devotionals. The student text and teacher's text discuss Spurgeon. Reading Spurgeon while studying this chapter will help to put his work in perspective and also show the timelessness of scriptural teaching.

Victorian Culture—Have students create a notebook of Victorian culture, including clothing, advertisements, decoration, and at least one invention. Include a fifty-word report about Victorian culture.

Create-Your-Own—Creative students could create their own invention, presenting a diagram of its parts and a paragraph explaining its use. Extra credit may be given if they bring in a model of their invention.

Research Activity—Hundreds of inventions were developed during the nineteenth century. Have each student choose one invention or discovery and trace its development through history. Final reports should be mounted on construction paper and should include drawings, pictures, or photographs to illustrate the history of the invention. This activity may also be adapted for use as a group project.

CHAPTER REVIEW

People, Places, and Things to Know

Great Exhibition
Crystal Palace
Queen Victoria
Prince Albert
Victorian Age
governess
W. H. Lever
Port Sunlight
Napoleon Bonaparte
Congress of Vienna
Prince Metternich
nationalism
Greece
Belgium
Italy
Germany
imperialism
steam locomotive
telegraph
Alexander Graham Bell
telephone
typewriter
photography
production
marketing
capitalism
supply and demand
free trade
socialism
Karl Marx
Marxism
Communism
Charles Darwin
evolution
social gospel
Charles H. Spurgeon
Dwight L. Moody
Salvation Army
romanticism
Ludwig van Beethoven
Johannes Brahms
Frédéric Chopin
Guiseppe Verdi
realism
Charles Dickens
impressionism
Claude Debussy

Review Questions

Completion

Choose the appropriate word to complete these statements.

1. The nineteenth century was an age of (change, stagnation).
2. The nineteenth-century middle class was (optimistic, pessimistic).
3. The nineteenth century was a time of (peace, revolution)

Fill in the Blanks

Complete the statements by filling in the correct terms.

4. In the nineteenth century, carriages were replaced by (a) _____, sailing ships by (b) _____.
5. During most of the nineteenth century, the ruler of Great Britain was (a) _____, and her husband was (b) _____. During her reign the (c) _____, showing Great Britain as the leading industrial power, was held.

Chapter Review Answers

Completion

1. change
2. optimistic
3. revolution

Fill in the Blanks

4. (a) trains and/or automobiles
   (b) steam-ships
5. (a) Queen Victoria (b) Prince Albert
   (c) Great Exhibition

Matching

Match the following statements to the nineteenth-century movement each describes.

6. attempt to gain foreign territory
7. property is owned by the government
8. creatures came from nonliving elements
9. art style showing everyday life
10. extreme loyalty to one's own people
11. property is owned by individuals
12. all people share labor and goods
13. art style emphasizing nature and freedom
14. art style that captures the impression of a scene

(a) capitalism
(b) Communism
(c) evolution
(d) imperialism
(e) impressionism
(f) nationalism
(g) realism
(h) romanticism
(i) socialism

Connections

For each of the following pairs of items, write a sentence or two explaining the connection between them.

15. Italy / Germany
16. Spurgeon / Moody
17. Salvation Army / YMCA

Multiple Choice

Choose the man who is connected to each movement.

18. evolution: Napoleon, Darwin, Marx, Metternich
19. realism: Chopin, Darwin, Dickens, Verdi
20. romanticism: Beethoven, Haydn, Debussy, Bach
21. Communism: Darwin, Lever, Marx, Spurgeon

Think About It!

This chapter has shown some of the changes that occurred in Europe during the 1800s. Those changes were reflected by the three art styles: romanticism, realism, and impressionism. Write a one-paragraph essay that explains how art reflects the spirit of an era. Compare the three styles while telling what you know about the time.

Recipe: Scones— With tea the British generally have "biscuits" (cookies), pastry, or scones. Here is a traditional scone recipe.

Ingredients:
2 c. all-purpose flour
2 Tbsp. sugar
1 Tbsp. baking powder
1/2 tsp. salt
1/3 c. raisins, optional
6 Tbsp. margarine
1 egg, beaten
1/2 c. milk

Mix flour, sugar, baking powder, and salt. Using a pastry blender, cut in the margarine and raisins until thoroughly integrated with the dry ingredients. (This will make small raisin bits in each scone.) Make a well in the center and add the milk and egg. Handling the dough as little as possible, stir the milk in until the dough is completely moistened. Make tablespoon-sized dollops and drop on a lightly greased baking sheet. Bake at 400° for 15 minutes. Slice and place jam on each half. Top with whipped cream (or English clotted cream if available; this goes on before jam).

Matching

6. d
7. i
8. c
9. g
10. f
11. a
12. b
13. h
14. e

Connections

15. Both Italy and Germany formed unified countries in the 1800s.
16. Spurgeon and Moody were great preachers of the 1800s.
17. The Salvation Army and the YMCA were started to minister to souls and were used to help the less fortunate.

Multiple Choice

18. Darwin
19. Dickens
20. Beethoven
21. Marx

Think About It!

Answers will vary. Art reflects the thought of the people during an era. Romanticism was a reflection of the optimism that had come about with the rise of the middle class. Realism, a reaction to romanticism, tried to show how life really was for those not as prosperous as the middle and upper classes. Impressionism showed the new preference for emotion rather than orderliness.

Student Objectives
Students should be able to
1. Explain the reason for the East India Company's interest in India.
2. Summarize the course of the British takeover of India.
3. List reasons for the Sepoy Mutiny.
4. Define *raj*.
5. Locate South Asia on a map.
6. Use a vegetation map to identify types of vegetation in an area.
7. Correlate information on the vegetation map with other map types.
8. Define *sahib*.
9. Identify problems and opportunities that Britain encountered while ruling India.
10. Evaluate the results of bringing rubber and tea plantations to India.
11. Illustrate changes in agriculture, industry, transportation and communication, education, and society.
12. Define *babus, Sanskrit,* and *suttee*.
13. Assess reasons for missionaries to go to Raj India.
14. Identify early missionaries to India.
15. Appraise the situation of women in India before and after salvation.

Opening Photo—A view of the Ganges River showing ghats (steps) going down to the river

CHAPTER 12

The flow of Indian history has been periodically interrupted by invaders. The Aryans disrupted Indian life around 1500 B.C. A thousand years later, the Persians conquered them. Although Alexander the Great did not conquer India, he did threaten its borders in the fourth century B.C. Another thousand years passed before the coming of the Muslim Arabs. The Mongol Tamerlane invaded India around 1400, and the Mughuls (also of Mongol heritage) came to rule India in 1500. At the same time, Europeans landed in India. These new invaders were traders. The first one was the Portuguese Vasco da Gama. (See Chapter 6.)

After hesitant first encounters, the Portuguese established fortified factories along the western coast of India. The supreme sea power of the Portuguese, and eventually the Spanish, allowed them to monopolize European trade in India throughout the sixteenth century. But when the Spanish Armada was destroyed in 1588, the opportunity came for other European nations to establish control—first the Dutch, then the English, and finally the French.

A.D. 1750 - A.D. 1900

CHAPTER 12 LESSON PLANS			
Section Title	**Main Concept**	**Pages**	**Time Frame**
1. Expanding English Control **Settings: South Asia*	Britain took control of India over many years after fighting the French and taking control of the East India Company's holdings.	322-29	2 days
2. Establishing British Rule	As Britain gained control, separation between *sahibs* and Indians increased.	330-31	1 day
3. Effects on Indian Culture **Center Stage: Tea Time!*	British rule greatly affected many areas of Indian life.	332-39	2 days
4. Missionaries to India **Characterizations: Pandita Ramabai*	Missionaries to India had a difficult but rewarding work. Women's lives in India were changed for the first time.	340-45	1 day
Total Suggested Days (including 1 day for review & 1 day for test)			8 days

Raj India

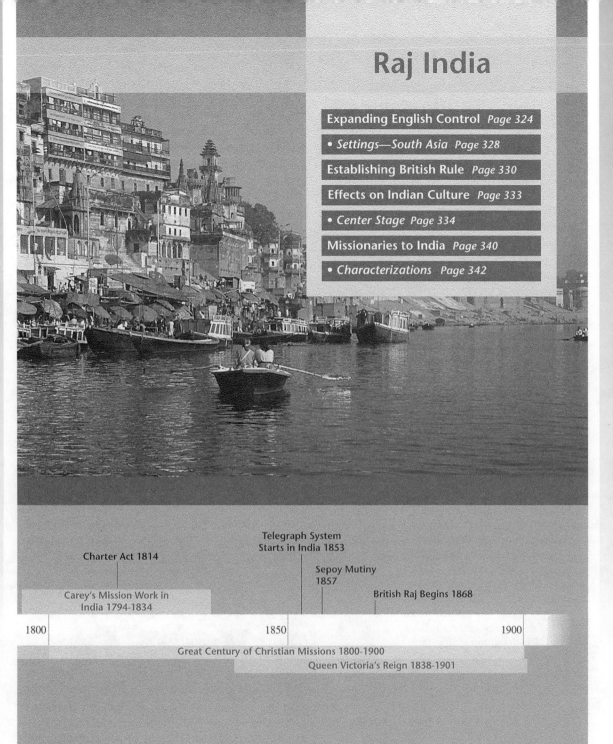

Telegraph System Starts in India 1853
Charter Act 1814
Sepoy Mutiny 1857
British Raj Begins 1868
Carey's Mission Work in India 1794-1834
1800
1850
1900
Great Century of Christian Missions 1800-1900
Queen Victoria's Reign 1838-1901

South Asia

Place a map of the countries of South Asia in the center of the board. Create enlarged cutaways of each country studied and write general information about the country inside or underneath it.

Another idea would be to print out some of Rudyard Kipling's sayings in different fonts using a computer and arrange them on the bulletin board.

Chapter Motivator

Review with your students the invaders and conquerors of India. This information is in the introduction. The students should be able to recall basic facts about each. Alexander the Great was a conqueror who established a huge empire from Egypt to India (TT 1-A). The Muslims took over much of India in their wars of conquest for their religion. Tamerlane conquered part of northwest India in 1400, and Akbar's peaceful empire included much of India (see p. 100, Chapter 4). Rival princes divided the territory into pieces, and England finally seized control (TT 12-A). Discuss how the English language helped to unify India.

Matthew 28:19-20

Much of the change in India during this time period came not only from economic and political factors but also from spiritual factors. Missionaries went and sacrificed much, sometimes even their lives, to reach the unsaved with the gospel of Christ. Matthew 28:19-20 says, "Go ye therefore, and teach all nations, baptizing them in the name of the Father, and of the Son, and of the Holy Ghost: Teaching them to observe all things whatsoever I have commanded you: and, lo, I am with you alway, even unto the end of the world. Amen." (BLM verse 12)

Materials

- Scripture verse (BLM verse 12)
- Wall map of South Asia (BLM 12-1)
- *Teaching Transparencies* for use with *World Studies for Christian Schools* (Second Edition)
- Pictures of Egypt's engineering feats and traditional India
- Tea, mug, sugar, cream, cookies
- *The Secret Garden* or *The Little Princess* by Frances Hodgson Burnett
- Indian cloth: madras, calico, or cotton
- Spices: pepper, saffron, cardamom, or cinnamon
- Bibles for Bible study
- *The Jungle Book* by Rudyard Kipling
- *Just-So Stories* by Rudyard Kipling
- Items for letter writing: paper, envelopes, stamps
- Guest speaker, an Indian or a missionary to India
- *With Daring Faith* by Rebecca Davis (BJUP)

Review—Review the empires your students learned in Chapter 4 as well as in Heritage Studies 6. Ask your students if they remember what they are. *(the Indus Valley civilization, the Aryans, the Gupta dynasty, the Mughuls)* Show the transparency for this chapter to illustrate the areas of empire (TP 12-A).

Section 1

Student Objectives
Students should be able to

1. Explain the reason for the East India Company's interest in India.
2. Summarize the course of the British takeover of India.
3. List reasons for the Sepoy Mutiny.
4. Define *raj*.

The French in India—Your students may remember that the French learned about and mingled with the natives in North America. They learned their ways and made good alliances. In the same way, the French learned and mingled with the Indians. This gave the French a sound advantage in India and North America that could have changed history.

In 1746 Joseph Françios Dupleix used what he knew about the Indians to set himself up as the *nawob* (prince) after he had defeated the local one. With the death of the enemy prince, Dupleix became *nizom* (king) of the area. If the king and queen of France had been able to take their eyes off France and see the control that was possible in India, they would have declared Dupleix the "Emperor of India" and put their military support behind him, and perhaps France would eventually have controlled all of India.

Remind your students that seemingly small decisions and missed opportunities can change the course of history.

Robert Clive—In 1725 Robert Clive was born into a somewhat poor British family. At the age of eighteen he began his career in India by signing on as a clerk with the East India Company. He arrived in India a poor young man dreaming of making a fortune, but the salaries of company employees were very low. They were expected to supplement their incomes by conducting business of their own with the natives.

During the French-British conflict for control of India, Clive gave up his job as a clerk and joined the army. He proved to be an excellent military leader, and when he went home to England in 1753 for a short visit, he found that he

Expanding English Control

The English came to trade and ended up ruling the country. They helped develop India by bringing Western culture and technology. The British contributed much to the people of India yet did not understand or appreciate native Indian culture. Throughout the years of their rule, occasional conflicts flared up because of these cultural differences. Eventually British rule ended when the Indians gained their independence in 1947.

The East India Company

The growth of English control in India was gradual, taking over 250 years. The first Englishmen to come to India were not even officials of the government. They represented the **East India Company,** a company chartered by Queen Elizabeth I in 1600. The company's main purpose was trade. The traders desired the cotton, silks, spices, drugs, and other goods from India as well as a place to sell English goods. When they finally arrived in India in 1608 with a letter from James I, the Indians were not impressed. For the next eleven years, the English tried to "impress" the Mughul emperors with their power by using well-armed ships to bombard ports and rival ships. Finally, in 1619, the Mughuls allowed the English to set up trading stations in Surat. Within a hundred years, the company had centers at **Bombay, Madras,** and **Calcutta.**

The India trade was profitable, and the company's business grew. A major problem, however, was the French, who also had trading posts in India. The French, who had made political agreements with several Indian princes, tried to harm British trade. In 1756 French and British rivalry erupted. The Seven Years' War broke out between these two nations in Europe and India. In the **Battle of Plassey** (PLAHS ee) in 1757, the British defeated a leading Indian prince. With only three thousand men, British commander **Robert Clive** (KLIVE) routed a disorganized Indian force of eighty thousand. The victory at Plassey broke

Prior to England's involvement, India was ruled by several princes who lived richly on the taxes of the people.

Section 1

Picture Analysis—Look at the elephant in the picture. Compare the size of his sawn-off tusks to the man's hand. These tusks are usually larger than most of us picture them. Can you tell why they had been sawn off? *(probably for protection from their sharp points)* Today taking tusks for ivory is illegal. The Indian elephant can be distinguished from the African elephant by the size of its ears (much smaller). Indian elephants are becoming more endangered as people take over jungle land. Have an interested student do research about Indian elephants. Have him report his information to the class.

France's strength in India. Within three years the French were completely defeated.

For the next hundred years, British trade with India grew. The East India Company opened more markets and added more territory to its holdings. The company's official reasons for annexing lands and exerting control over India were twofold. One was to protect its trade and employees from Indian violence. A second reason was to provide stable governments for the Indian frontiers, especially in the north. Many frontier areas had weak or lawless governments that hampered company trade and safety.

Although these reasons may be true in part, another major motive for the company's action was greed. The British traders desired to increase their company's income. In opportunistic moves they annexed one territory after another as weak Indian princes and warring Indian factions proved unable to control their lands and people. With the annexing of these lands came the monetary tribute normally paid to the prince. Indian silver poured into company coffers and eventually into England.

While their motives may not have been philanthropic, the East India Company did nothing to really harm life for the common people. The princes of the land did not care for the people. The people had no say in their government. In essence, the people just exchanged one absolute ruler for another.

Robert Clive used his victory at Plassey to influence British investors. As a result, he became wealthy at a young age.

The Black Hole of Calcutta

When war broke out between France and England in 1756, some Indian rulers tried to take advantage of the situation. One such leader seized the British-controlled city of Calcutta. Most of the British citizens escaped, but others could not make it out in time. The story reported to the British by the surviving British commander, John Holwell, was that the Indian commander ordered all the British prisoners to be placed in the city's fortress, in a cell called "the Black Hole."

The cell measured only about eighteen feet by fourteen feet—about the size of a large bedroom. Holwell said that 146 people, including one woman and about a dozen wounded officers, were crowded into the room. In the hot, humid climate of India with only one small window for air, many prisoners suffocated overnight. Only twenty-three survived the ordeal. Holwell himself lived only by staying near the window and sucking his shirt sleeve to relieve his thirst.

The incident horrified the British, who later recaptured Calcutta and drove the French completely out of India. The British used this atrocity to help justify their takeover of India.

was something of a national hero. Two years later he returned to India a wealthy commissioned officer in the Royal British Army.

Placed in command of the British forces, Clive recaptured Calcutta after the Black Hole incident. In the time between the taking of Calcutta and the Battle of Plassey, he blackmailed and overthrew a major Indian official, acquiring a fortune in money and property in the process. Many British fortunes were made in the same manner in the next few years. Paradoxically, as governor of India, Clive tried to battle the same type of corruption that had made him rich. But he lost the battle and was caught up in the corruption once again.

Clive returned to England in 1760 an extremely wealthy man. He purchased a controlling interest in the East India Company, bought his way into the House of Commons, and was made lord of one of the Irish territories. In 1764 he resumed a governorship in India and successfully defended the British rule of Bengal. He also struggled to maintain law and order and to control corruption among the British company officials and military.

Robert Clive retired to England after his second term as governor. A few years later, Parliament appointed a committee to investigate corruption in India, and Clive's early misconduct came to their attention. Many members of Parliament censured him for abusing his power and setting a bad example for fellow Englishmen in India. Eventually Parliament decided to overlook the offenses and passed a resolution commending the former governor for his service to the Crown. By his leadership, Clive had given England the basis for her empire in India. But the combined strain of the disgrace and poor health had evidently been too much for him. A year after the commendation from Parliament, Robert Clive took his own life.

Black Hole—When the British living in Calcutta realized that the Indian troops were coming, they rushed to boats to flee. Unfortunately, so many men fled first that they filled the boats. Their cowardice forced many women and children to stay behind. The

East India Company—Discuss with your students the motives behind the East India Company's expansion into India. Describe the results that took place. Ask the students how life may have been different for all involved if the company had been a philanthropic group.

The Black Hole—Read the box above and compare it to the supplementary information in the margin. Whose version do your students believe?

commander of Fort William was left with only 170 soldiers.

Records by Indian scholars reveal that only sixty-four people were imprisoned and of these only twenty-one survived until morning. They also record that the prince was unaware of the imprisonment until morning when the captives were released.

★★★★★★★★★★
For a color version of the map on this page, see page A8 in the Appendix.

Calming the Mutiny—To say the mutiny was stopped in a year overlooks what was a very bloody revolution. The British, who many times before were known for their temperate way of dealing with the Indian people, launched an all-out effort to eradicate dissension.

As Indians killed British missionaries, women, and children, the British burned whole villages and strapped mutineers to cannons before discharging the cannons. The main ruler of India was exiled and his children slain.

One of the things that Britain did to pacify India and avoid further mutiny was to reestablish and insure the reign of several princes and their heirs who vowed loyalty to the British.

The British had to deal with conflicts not only between themselves and the Indians, but also between Hindus and Muslims. Historically, the two groups have not cooperated. This conflict eventually resulted in the formation of independent Pakistan in 1947. Today violence continues in parts of India.

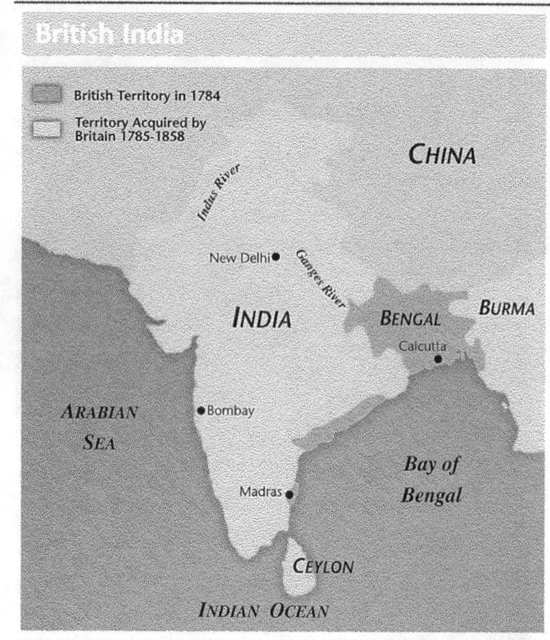

The British Government Takes Over

In 1858 the British government took final control of affairs in India. During the late 1700s and early 1800s, the government had been exerting more and more control over the activities of the East India Company. In 1814 the **Charter Act** gave the crown control over all that the company possessed. The final takeover came in response to an uprising of Indian soldiers, called **sepoys** (SEE POYZ).

The **Sepoy Mutiny** (1857-58) was the result of the Indians' fear and discontent about some of the changes the British were making in traditional Indian life. There was much worry within the ranks that the British were conspiring with the missionaries. The sepoys thought that the missionaries wanted to make them unclean so that they would be more willing to convert.

Each new incident seemed to support that belief. The British passed a **General Enlistment Act,** requiring troops to serve anywhere the British deemed necessary, even across the sea in Burma, where they would be forced to mingle with other castes. However, the match that ignited the fear and resentment came in the form of a new type of rifle. At that time, ammunition cartridges had to be opened before they were used. Usually the soldiers bit them open. The problems arose because the cartridges for the new rifle required greasing, and the sepoys believed that they were greased with either pork or beef fat. The Hindu soldiers were offended because the cow was sacred to them; the Muslim soldiers were offended because pork was considered unclean. Therefore, both factions of Indian soldiers were insulted by the new cartridges.

When they were commanded to load weapons, regiment after regiment of sepoys refused, and the British stripped them of their uniforms and pensions. The sepoys' once proud loyalty to the British was gone, and only hatred was left.

On Saturday, May 9, 1857, the mutiny became war in Meerut, India. Eighty-five sepoys there refused to use the weapons and were imprisoned. The next day they were freed by other rebellious soldiers, and the violence of the Sepoy Mutiny had begun. In the days that followed, both the Indians and the British massacred many innocent people.

Within a year the mutiny was stopped. Six months later Queen Victoria proclaimed India under control of the British crown rather than the East India Company. In the proclamation, the British government for the first time recognized the rights of a native people to have a voice in their own government. The document also committed the British government to protect the rights and beliefs of the Indian people and disclaimed any desire to extend British holdings in India.

Role-play—Two to three days ahead of time, assign students to play different parts of the Sepoy Mutiny. Assign them the following parts: a Parliament official, the officials of the East India Company, Hindu soldiers, Muslim soldiers, prison guards, Queen Victoria, and the new viceroy. The students must read the material in this section and be ready to act out their parts when their turn comes. It would be best to allow 10-15 minutes before class starts for them to practice role-playing. Allow them to dress up if they wish to do so.

Queen Victoria appointed a **viceroy** to rule India. The viceroy lived in splendor typical of past Indian emperors. He rode about the capital on a bejeweled elephant with many servants following. Official British rule is called the **British Raj** (RAHJ), from the Sanskrit word *raj,* meaning "ruler." Twenty years after the Sepoy Mutiny, the remaining independent princes pledged loyalty to the queen. In a grand ceremony Queen Victoria was proclaimed **Empress of India.** India was now part of the British Empire.

Queen Victoria, Empress of India, catches up on correspondence while attended by an Indian servant.

Company Control—Remind your students that the idea of "certain unalienable rights" had not arrived in India yet and still has not arrived in some countries around the world. Although some Indians saw a negative change in their economic status because of the English takeover, many later profited as the English brought jobs to the land.

Section Review

1. What first brought the English to India?
2. What major problem faced the English in India? How was the problem resolved?
3. Why did the East India Company take over land?
4. In what year did the British government take control of India? What caused the takeover?
5. What was British rule in India called?

What might have been different in India if the British had tried to adapt to the Indian culture rather than assume British cultural superiority?

The Sepoy Mutiny allowed England to take control of India and weaken the East India Company's influence.

Picture insight—Look at the picture of Queen Victoria. Notice she is sitting in the open air. India is generally a very warm country, yet at this time there would have been no air conditioning. Remind your students that they live in better conditions than did the queen of England a century and a half ago. Discuss changing technology and its effect on people. Surely Victoria's subjects thought that she lived in the lap of luxury as the queen, and she definitely had the best in art, decoration, service, clothing, and so on. However, her living conditions would make most modern-day students uncomfortable if not miserable. Ask the students to think of areas other than comfortable living conditions which have changed as well. *(medicine, food, transportation, etc.)*

Section Review Answers

1. trade
2. the French; at the Battle of Plassey, the French and Indians were defeated
3. to protect its trade and employees from Indian violence, to provide stable governments for the Indian frontiers, and to satisfy greed
4. 1858; the Sepoy Mutiny
5. the British Raj

Answers will vary. The Indians and British might not have had so much strife or fighting as they did. The Indians might have appreciated the advanced technology more if it had not been forced on them. Ultimately, British rule might have been much more tolerable, and the final division between India and Britain might have been more like the division that occurred between Canada and Britain.

Student Objectives

Students should be able to

1. Locate South Asia on a map.
2. Use a vegetation map to identify types of vegetation in an area.
3. Correlate information on the vegetation map with other map types.

Other Interesting Facts—The monsoons also bring great destruction when they come too early or bring too much water. Flooding and mudslides take their toll on the population.

Some areas would receive no rain if it were not for the monsoons. In some areas of the Thar Desert, less than two inches of rain falls per year. In contrast, the heaviest recorded rainfall in history occurred in the Indian city of Cherrapunji. From 1860 to 1861 that city received 1,042 inches of rain.

Approximately 21 percent of the world's population lives in South Asia. India ranks second (behind China) in the world in population. Pakistan ranks seventh and Bangladesh ranks ninth.

Hydroelectric power could be available from the many rivers flowing from the Himalayas, but that resource is hardly developed. The people still use oil lamps and cook using dung patties for fuel.

Remind your students that the Hindus regard the cow as sacred and do not eat its meat. For the most part Hindus are vegetarian. Unfortunately, because they will not kill cattle, cattle roam freely throughout Hindu lands. They are a huge nuisance in cities, where they eat from the trash and block traffic.

SETTINGS—South Asia

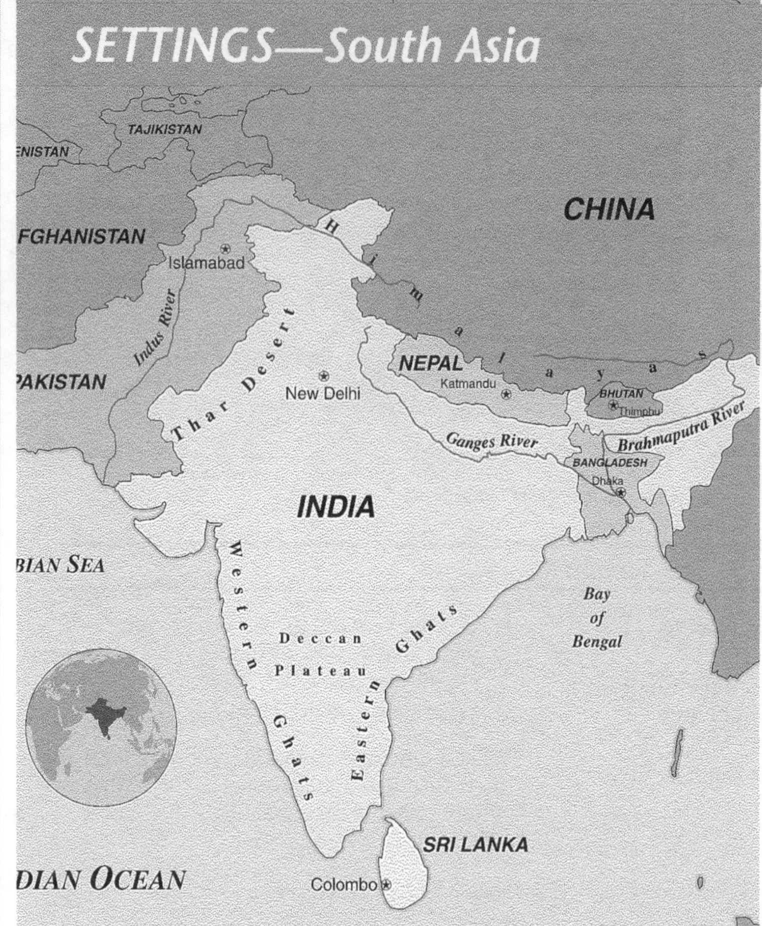

Location—This area is sometimes called the Indian subcontinent. It includes Pakistan, India, Nepal, Bhutan, Bangladesh (BAHNG gluh DESH), and the island of Sri Lanka (sree LAHNG-kuh), formerly known as Ceylon. The Arabian Sea lies to the west and the Bay of Bengal to the east.

Climate—The climate of the area can be divided into three basic types—tropical, dry, and temperate. The northeast ranges from tropical to subtropical (temperate). Moving west the moisture and elevation change, causing a steppe and desert climate similar to the Middle East. There is also a portion of steppe climate in the center of the lower peninsula. Two features of the South Asian climate especially affect the people. One is the monsoons. These shifting winds are responsible for bringing most of the area's rain, so when they are absent or late, great drought and famine result. Cyclones, called hurricanes in America, are also a yearly event and sometimes cause great destruction. In the extreme north of India and Pakistan, the climate is affected by the mountains.

Topography—South Asia is a land of high mountains and plateaus with fertile plains tucked between. The Himalaya Mountains stretch across the far north of the region. Two other ranges, called the Western and Eastern Ghats, run up the flanks of the Indian peninsula. Between the Ghats is the Deccan Plateau. Fertile plains run beside the Ganges, Brahmaputra, and Indus Rivers. To the east of the Indus River is the Thar Desert.

Natural Resources—The natural resource most used by the people is the fertile land. Most of South Asia's inhabitants are farmers. They rank first in the world's production of cashews, millet, peanuts, sesame seeds, and tea. Great reserves of ores and natural gas are available to the people of South Asia, yet these resources remain mostly underdeveloped. Hydroelectric power is also an

Materials

- Wall map of South Asia (BLM 12-1)
- Transparencies for Chapter 12

Map Activity—Use map 12-C from the Student Activities manual to reinforce the geography lesson.

Going Beyond—Read the Settings pages with your students and answer the questions. South Asia is a diverse area geographically. One of the results is a large diversity in vegetation. Teach your students to read a vegetation map (TT 12-B). Compare the information on the vegetation map with a climate map (TT Intro.-B). Ask students how vegetation reflects climate. *(more rain, more vegetation; cold climate, less vegetation)* Next have the students look at the relief map of Asia on page 611. Ask them if they see any relation between altitude and vegetation. *(Higher elevations tend to be drier.)* Finally, ask the students if they would expect to see the climate and vegetation affect population. *(Most will say yes.)* How do they expect it to affect population? Look at a population map to see whether their predictions are correct. (See *GEOGRAPHY for Christian Schools,* Second Edition, page 106.)

Monsoons—To explain how a monsoon develops. Use a diagram from a geography or science text (BLM 12-2).

underdeveloped resource that South Asians are hoping to utilize in the future. Many people of the region raise cattle and sheep. The cattle are raised for their milk or as beasts of burden in Hindu areas.

Geography & Culture—The Indus and Ganges River valleys provided the first homes for the ancient civilization of South Asia. The rivers supplied water, fish, and transportation. Although the Himalaya Mountains prevented invasion from the north, foreigners did come through the passes in the northwest to invade South Asia regularly throughout its history. Because desert and rough terrain lie south of the river valleys, invaders rarely penetrated farther south. The final invasion, the one that changed the area's history most, was the invasion by the Europeans from the waters of the Arabian Sea.

Settings Review

1. What countries are included in South Asia?
2. What climate feature brings yearly rains?
3. What mountain ranges run down the sides of the Indian peninsula?
4. What land feature prevented general invasion from the north?

Why are the resources of South Asia underdeveloped? What are some changes that could result from greater development of those resources?

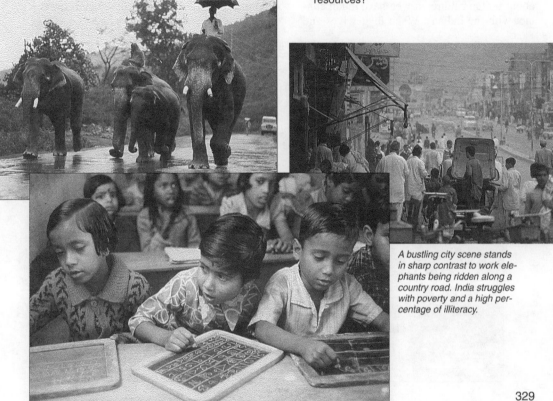

A bustling city scene stands in sharp contrast to work elephants being ridden along a country road. India struggles with poverty and a high percentage of illiteracy.

The Khyber Pass—One of the most strategically important locations in Indian history is the Khyber Pass. The pass is located on the border between Pakistan and Afghanistan. Through it runs one of the major routes to India from Central Asia.

The Khyber Pass has proved important for thousands of years. The Aryans used it when they invaded and overcame the Indus Valley civilization (see Heritage Studies 6). It was probably the route used by Alexander the Great when he conquered northern India in the fourth century B.C. The Mongols stormed through the Khyber during the twelfth century under Genghis Khan and again in the sixteenth century when the Mughuls established their empire. Later the Afghans used the pass to invade India. In 1839 the British drove the Afghans out of India and established a military post to guard the region. It is still guarded today by local Khyber tribesmen, who are paid by the government to continue policing the area.

Settings Review Answers

1. Pakistan, India, Nepal, Bhutan, Bangladesh, and Sri Lanka
2. monsoons
3. Western and Eastern Ghats
4. the Himalayan Mountains

Answers will vary. They may be underdeveloped because of their geographic isolation from the rest of Asia. Their strict adherence to tradition is also a deterrent to change. They have much undeveloped metal ore and natural gas that could greatly prosper India. They also have great need and potential for hydroelectric power. If they develop these resources, they could earn more money and raise their standard of living. They could have more benefit from the water products than from developing their mining potential.

SECTION 2

Student Objectives
Students should be able to

1. Define *sahib*.
2. Identify problems and opportunities that Britain encountered while ruling India.

"We"—Queen Victoria was known for always speaking of herself in the plural: "we do strictly charge" and "on pain of our highest displeasure." She continued to do this for the rest of "their" life.

Establishing British Rule

Even though the British were in control of India's government, changes in India did not occur immediately. The mutual distrust between the Indians and British continued. The segregation that resulted further complicated communication between the two cultures.

Problems

The British faced many problems in ruling India. The country was much larger than the British Isles and had several million inhabitants. These millions spoke over a hundred different languages and followed several different religions. The few thousand British officials in India often misunderstood their Indian subjects. Many had little desire to learn about Indian culture or even have much contact with the Indians. When their wives and children began joining them in India, the British officials cut themselves off from the Indians more and more and lived separate lives. Most white ***sahibs*** (SAH ibz; meaning "master" in Hindi) chose to have Indians as servants rather than as friends.

In an effort to avoid more strife, Queen Victoria announced "that none be in anywise favoured, none molested or disquieted, by reason of their religious faith or observances, but that all shall alike enjoy the equal and impartial protection of the law; and we do strictly charge and enjoin all those who may be in authority under us that they abstain from all interference with the religious belief or worship of any of our subjects on pain of our highest displeasure." This declaration greatly curtailed missionary activity and social efforts to protect women and children and outcastes.

Segregation and prejudice by the British toward the Indian people only heightened growing unrest that would eventually lead to Indian independence in 1947.

SECTION 2

Indian Servants—Direct each student to write a paragraph as if he or she were the servant of a powerful English ruler in India. What would a typical day be like?

Language Difficulties—The many languages in India not only made it difficult for the British but also affected the Indian interaction as a country. Discuss how a variety of languages and dialects tends to disunify a country. How did the British help unite India?

British Empire in 1914

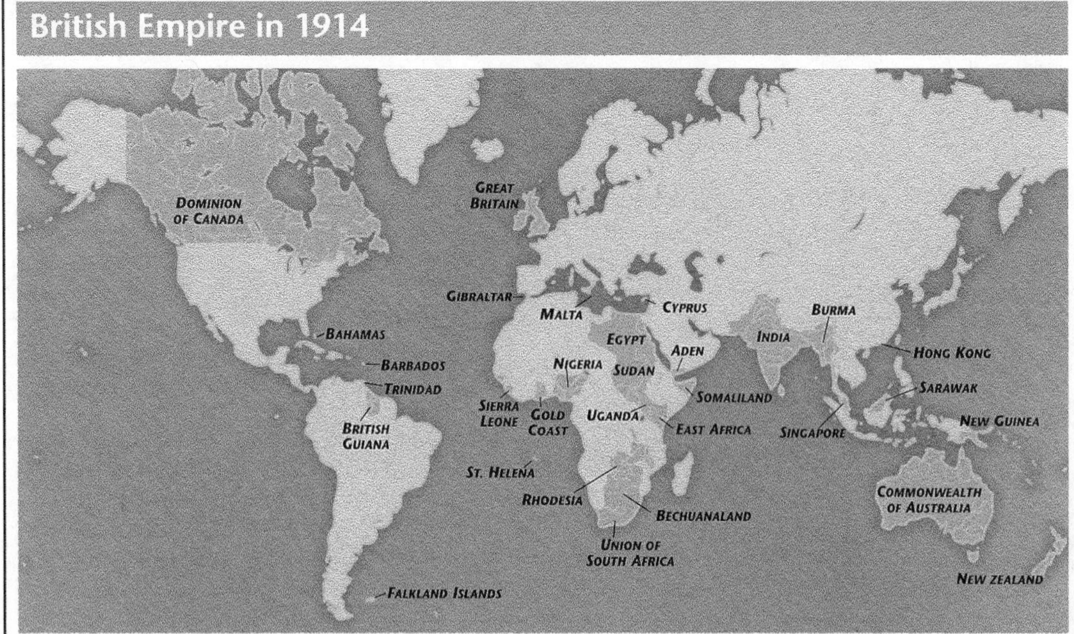

Empire—A famous saying during the time of the British Raj was "The sun never sets on the British Empire." The British controlled so much land that the sun was always up over some area that they ruled.

Opportunities

Despite its problems, India presented many opportunities for Britain. First it gave Britain economic advantages. India played a key role in the prosperity of the **British Empire,** which covered one-quarter of the globe in the nineteenth century. India's problems also gave the British an opportunity to help another people. They could apply the new learning and technology of Europe to an underdeveloped land. Agriculture, industry, transportation, and education improved under British rule. Most important, India presented a huge mission field. With the new policy of noninterference, the missionaries' focus changed to a less direct form of evangelism—meeting health and educational needs as a means to witness. The millions of Indians who worshiped false gods needed to hear the gospel. British missionaries eagerly took up Christ's Great Commission: "Go ye into all the world, and preach the gospel to every creature" (Mark 16:15).

Section Review

1. What attitude did the British have toward the Indians?
2. What does the word *sahib* mean?
3. List two things that the British gained from controlling India.
4. List three things that India gained through British control.

Describe both the cause and effect of Queen Victoria's edict (see page 330). In other words, why did she say it, and what resulted from it?

Speed Listing—Give students one minute to write down as many problems and opportunities the British had in India as they can. Answers should include the following:

Problems: larger country than England, many more people, many languages, several religions, misunderstood culture, and Indians as servants and white men as *sahibs*.

Opportunities: helping others; economic advantages; improved agriculture, industry, transportation, and education; and a new and large mission field.

Whoever has the most correct answers wins the contest. Have students write down all answers to use as a study guide.

Section Review Answers

1. distrust
2. master
3. economic advantages, opportunity to help others, opportunity to apply new learning and technology (any two)
4. improved learning and technology for agriculture, industry, transportation, and education; and missions

Queen Victoria wanted to end the strife and violence between the British and Indians. The Indians had been forced to turn to British ways, and Queen Victoria realized that this made them unhappy. Her statement hindered missionary activity because it would change the Indians' religion, and it hindered social activity such as protecting women. Eventually, the laws changing society were passed anyway.

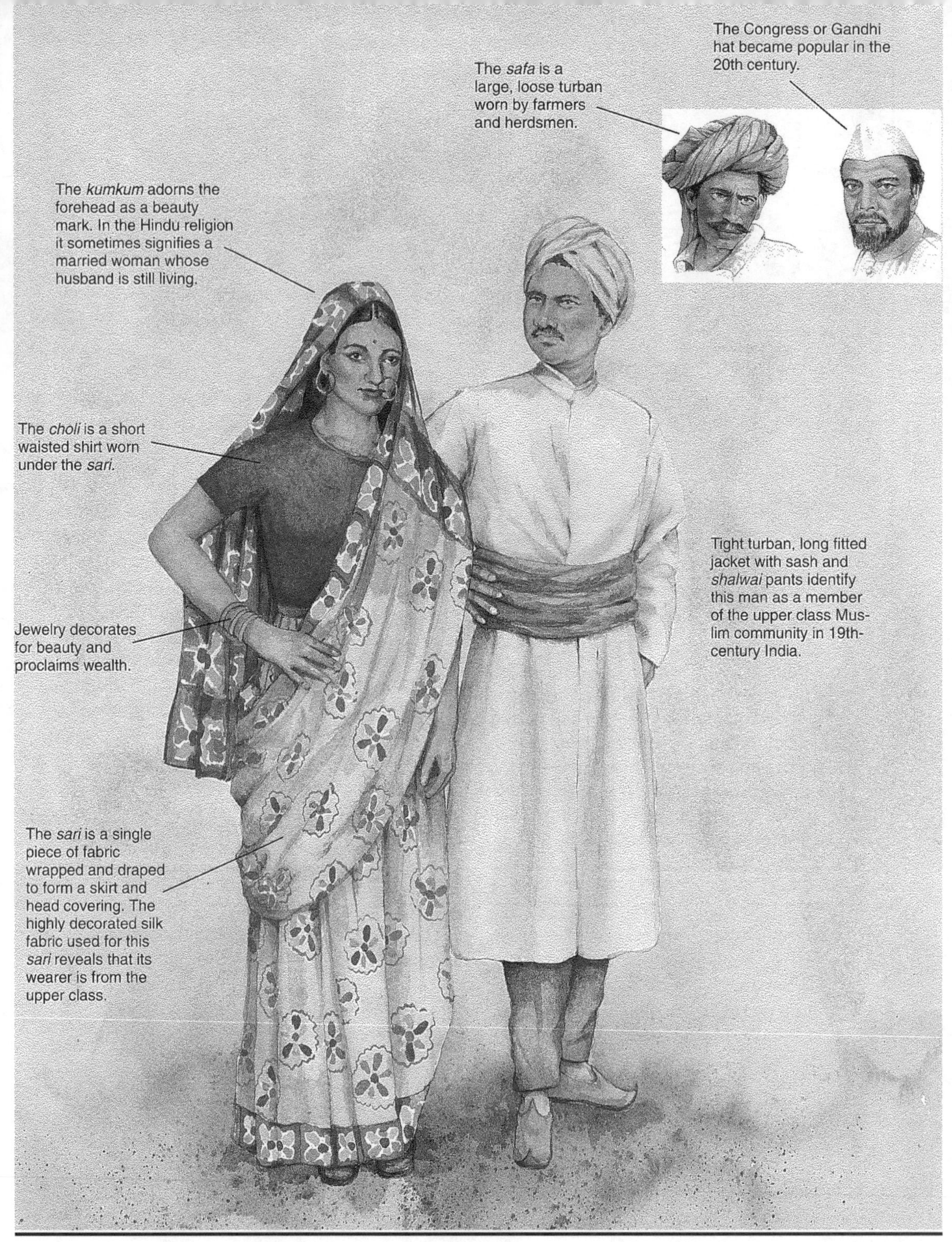

The Congress or Gandhi hat became popular in the 20th century.
The *safa* is a large, loose turban worn by farmers and herdsmen.
The *kumkum* adorns the forehead as a beauty mark. In the Hindu religion it sometimes signifies a married woman whose husband is still living.
The *choli* is a short waisted shirt worn under the *sari*.
Tight turban, long fitted jacket with sash and *shalwai* pants identify this man as a member of the upper class Muslim community in 19th-century India.
Jewelry decorates for beauty and proclaims wealth.
The *sari* is a single piece of fabric wrapped and draped to form a skirt and head covering. The highly decorated silk fabric used for this *sari* reveals that its wearer is from the upper class.

Traditional Clothing—Examine closely with your students the descriptions of traditional Indian clothing. If possible, bring an example of some to show or wear. If a student has access to Indian clothing, ask him to bring it in for the class to see.

Trends in Clothing—Discuss how clothing reflects our social status. Ask students if clothing can also reflect our spiritual status. Does it always accurately reflect our spiritual condition? Remind students that it is possible to dress right and still have a very wrong heart.

Effects on Indian Culture

British rule changed the Indian way of life. Some changes started on paper and took years to complete. Others occurred immediately. In the following sections we will look at the changes the British made in India and how these affected that country. The Indians did not always think these changes were improvements. The changes often seemed to threaten parts of traditional Indian culture and to ignore India's own heritage. Nevertheless, these changes eventually helped to make India a self-governing power in the modern world.

Agriculture

Over two-thirds of India's people were farmers. They used primitive farming methods, much like those used in Europe during the Middle Ages. These methods plus unpredictable **monsoons** (winds that bring rain during one season) made famine a constant threat. Despite these problems, the British did much to improve farming in India. They brought better equipment, fertilizer, new ideas in farm management, and agricultural research to Indian farmers. Slowly these improvements increased the amount of land farmed and food produced.

Although there are large cities in India, the majority of Indian people live in the country and are farmers.

The biggest farming improvement the British made was in building miles of irrigation canals. These canals brought water to dry areas, easing times of drought. Even with improved irrigation, though, famine remained a problem in India, as it still is today. To help people in times of famine, the British began an emergency relief plan. They moved food cross-country on railroads to the areas of worst famine. Although many were saved from starvation, in years of bad famine millions still died.

The British improved Indian farming not only to help the Indians but also to acquire India's agricultural products for trade. Indian cotton and jute supplied Britain's factories, and Indian spices filled Britain's shops. The British also developed the important tea industry of India, providing jobs for many Indians on large tea plantations. Soon India became a major supplier of this drink, which the British Empire made famous in both the Old and New Worlds. The British also brought the first rubber trees to the island of Ceylon (now Sri Lanka). The plant grew well, and Ceylon became a major rubber exporter. Thus the British not only helped India's food farming but also improved her production of other goods for export.

333

Section 3

Student Objectives
Students should be able to

1. Evaluate the results of bringing rubber and tea plantations to India.
2. Illustrate changes in agriculture, industry, transportation and communication, education, and society.
3. Define *babus, Sanskrit,* and *suttee*.

Threats to Modernization—One difficulty that the British encountered as they tried to modernize was rejection of the new ways and tools. One businessman saw the Indians carrying dirt for a railroad project in baskets on their head. In an attempt to help, he ordered wheelbarrows from England. He came to the project later and saw the Indians carrying the wheelbarrows on their heads with just a little dirt in each. When he asked them why they did not use it the way they should, they said they would not go against the way of their fathers. What had been good for their fathers was good enough for them, and they would not make themselves better than their fathers.

Monsoons—Monsoons are vital to the South Asian growing season. Without sufficient rain brought by the monsoons, crops die before harvest. Unfortunately, monsoons often bring too much rain and flooding occurs.

Section 3

Materials

- Pictures of Egypt's engineering feats and traditional India
- Tea, mug, sugar, cream, cookies
- Indian cloth: madras, cotton, or calico
- Spices: pepper, saffron, cardamom, or cinnamon
- Bibles for Bible study
- *The Jungle Book* by Rudyard Kipling
- *Just So Stories* by Rudyard Kipling
- *The Little Princess* or *The Secret Garden* by Frances Hodgson Burnett

Comparison and Review—The text states that "the biggest farming improvement the British made was . . . irrigation canals." Ask your students how this compares to ancient Egypt's system of canals and irrigation. The students will have learned about this in Heritage Studies 6. If they have a hard time remembering, have them look it up. Many interesting picture books show the splendors of ancient Egypt. Ask your students why it took India so long to use this idea. *(Answers may include the fact that India was relatively isolated, that Indians had no knowledge of this technology, or that they were so steeped in tradition that change was deemed bad.)* Also show pictures of traditional India.

Indian Agriculture—Discuss with your students the major industries of tea and rubber in India. Ask them to name things we use that include these two items. What would life be like today without them?

CENTER STAGE

"Take some more tea," the March Hare said to Alice, very earnestly.

Tea Time!

Once upon a time, long ago in ancient China, the servants of the Emperor Shen Nung were boiling water to purify it for drinking. A few leaves from a nearby bush fluttered into the water, turning it brown. The emperor tasted the brew and pronounced it delicious. And so, the legend states, tea was discovered.

Actually, we have no idea when or how tea was discovered, but it did originate in China. Tea drinking spread to Europe during the age of exploration. Traders carried back shiploads of tea from China. Tea was extremely expensive; only the rich could afford it at first. Gradually prices dropped, and by the eighteenth century tea had become the most popular drink in England. Enterprising businessmen opened "tea shops" all over England. Nobles, scholars, businessmen, and common people gathered in these shops for refreshment and companionship.

Tea rapidly became an important part of English life. Englishmen began to drink tea with all their meals. In fact, supper became "tea time"—a light meal often consisting of nothing more than tea and a pastry. Shops offered a variety of teas. One could buy strong teas, mild teas, scented teas, or spiced teas. Ladies bought elaborate tea sets of silver or china with which to serve their tea. Methods for brewing a perfect cup of tea were tried and refined. Only water remained a more popular beverage than tea. (The English drank their tea hot. Iced tea is an American invention—the result of a heat wave during the World's Fair of 1904 in St. Louis.)

One problem confronted the English tea merchants. China had a monopoly on tea production. This meant that all merchants had to buy tea from China at whatever price the Chinese asked. Then in the 1800s, someone discovered wild tea bushes growing in India. The English quickly took advantage of this discovery and built huge tea plantations. Today India and the nearby island of Sri Lanka produce most of the tea drunk in the West.

Tea must be hand-picked leaf by leaf.

Tea Party—To introduce the tea facet, have a "tea" for your class. Each student should bring a cup (you may need to remind them each day for several days in advance) and have volunteers bring cookies (called *biscuits* in Britain). Brew tea for them from several different blends, if you can, to offer them a choice. For a truly British tea, you should also supply sugar and cream. Seventh graders tend to enjoy tea with sugar but not with cream. As they have their tea, read aloud a portion of either *A Secret Garden* or *The Little Princess* by Frances Hodgson Burnett. (Both books are set during the time period being studied.)

Flag from 1900 representing the Importers of Indian Textiles

Industry

In Chapter 11 you learned that Britain was in the middle of the Age of Industrialism during the 1800s. In India the British found many of the raw materials their factories needed, especially cotton and jute. India also provided Britain with markets for her manufactured goods, such as woolens, clothing, and hardware. At first the British were content to obtain India's agricultural goods and sell British manufactured goods there. Not until the end of the nineteenth century did the British start industry to produce goods in India.

At that time in some of the larger Indian cities, British businessmen set up factories. Cotton mills, jute factories, and even some iron- and steelworks were built. They employed many Indians. The factories had some of the best British-made machinery and modern management. Although these factories were only the start of an industrial economy, they helped prepare India to enter the twentieth century.

Transportation and Communication

Perhaps the most important improvement the British made to India was the railroad system. Private companies and the British government laid several thousand miles of track and by 1900 had lines to most areas of India. Railroads made travel faster and more pleasant than walking or riding in oxcarts on dusty roads. The railroad also made the transportation of goods to market easier so that cotton and tea grown far inland could be shipped quickly to coastal ports. Likewise, goods brought into the country by boat could be sent inland to new markets. The railroad

Overcrowded trains transport travelers from the country to the city. If you have to sit on the roof, bring your own chair.

Other Industries—There were other industries as well in India. Until the discovery of chemical dyes, indigo (a plant from which a deep blue dye is made) plantations greatly increased. As the price of Chinese silk rose, India began to produce silk. During the American Civil War, India exported much cotton for Union textile factories.

Cloth—Bring to class samples of at least one type of cloth sought by the British in India (madras, calico, cotton) as well as samples of spices such as were found there by Vasco da Gama: pepper, saffron, cardamon, and cinnamon.

also played a major role in famine relief as supplies moved quickly to areas of need.

Although the railroad seemed one of the best British gifts to India, not all Indians liked it. Many complained that it disrupted family and village life by allowing family members to travel far away. Many more Indians complained that trains made them break the rules of their caste. The caste system taught that different castes should not mix. In a train car, however, it was impossible for them not to mix; the trains could not run a car for every different caste and subcaste. Nevertheless, many Indians rode the trains. They traveled in search of work or on visits to relatives or to make religious pilgrimages.

The British also improved communications in India. They set up a telegraph system that sent news quickly around the land. They also reorganized the postal system so that both government and personal mail moved faster. Although most Indians could not read or write, they did send letters. Whenever an Indian wanted to send a letter, he went to the **bazaar** (marketplace) and hired a letter-writer. This man knew how to write several languages, and for a fee he wrote down the sender's dictated letter. The sender then stamped the letter and mailed it through the new postal system.

Education

Before the coming of the British, few Indians had any formal schooling. Only those from the higher castes who could afford private teachers or schools received an education, and rarely were girls taught to read or write. The British government and missionaries set up schools to educate more Indians. In the cities and towns, grade schools taught grammar, mathematics, and science in the language of the people. They also taught English, because English was the official language of the government. Even with these new schools,

Letter-writers either wrote or read letters for paying customers anxious to hear from friends in other cities and villages.

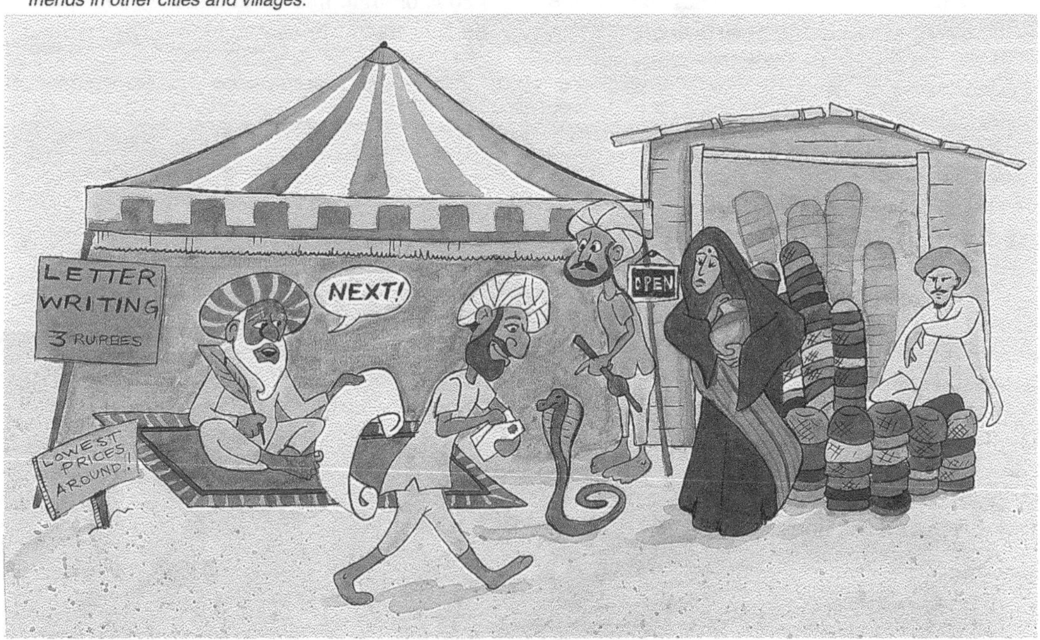

Caste System—Railroads brought trains, which mixed the castes. Review the caste system with your students. The castes in order included the Brahmans (priests), warriors and nobles, merchants, and servants. There were also the outcastes, not belonging to any class because of occupation or birth. Ask the students to describe how they would feel in each of these castes. Ask why some Indians did not like the railroads.

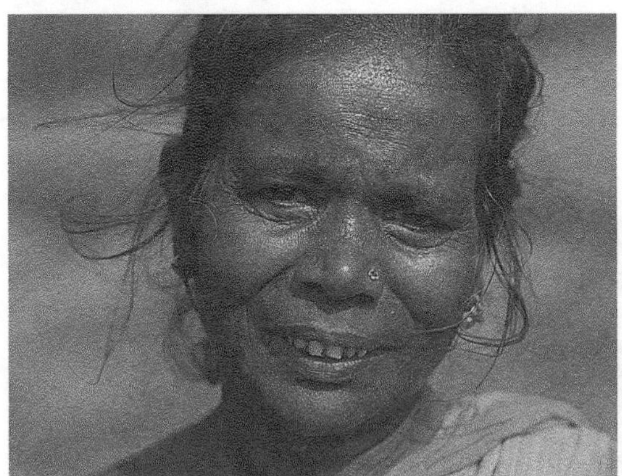

There was no place for a widow in Hindu society.

few Indian children were able to attend. Many of them needed to work to support their families. Others did not have the desire to learn. India remains to this day a highly illiterate country.

Some boys completed their grade-school classes and then went on to study at British universities in India. These educated Indians were called ***babus*** (BAH booz). A *babu* had an education similar to that of any young Englishman graduating from a British university. Because they knew English, *babus* usually held minor offices in the government of India or were lawyers for their people.

One problem with the British educational system in India was that it ignored India's native culture. The rich **Sanskrit** (ancient Indian language) literature and the accomplishments in mathematics and science of the Indian Golden Age were not taught. The British tried to replace Indian culture with their own culture. This effort eventually led to conflict between these two cultures.

Social Change

As British families and missionaries settled in India, they were shocked at the religious practices they saw. Many Hindu and Muslim practices show little regard for a person and his freedom. Gradually the British were able to outlaw certain abuses. Several laws especially helped the position of women, who were often considered of less worth than their husbands' livestock. One such law made ***suttee*** (suh TEE), or widow-burning, illegal. Because a woman was not allowed to remarry when her husband died, a higher caste woman might join her husband's burning body on the funeral pyre. Even though outlawed, the Hindu tradition of *suttee* was still followed by some women.

The British also helped widows by changing the law forbidding them to remarry. Widowhood was a great problem in India because a girl was often engaged in childhood. Even if her fiancé died before the wedding day, the girl was still considered a widow and forbidden

This girl paints a prayer in sand in front of her home to honor a Hindu deity.

Education for Women—One prominent Brahman during the British Raj period in India told a lady missionary that if she could teach his wife to read he would bring his cow to learn too, for women had no brain for such things, he thought.

Educated Indians—Educated young Indian men often found themselves placed in minor positions with no opportunity for promotion, much like the Creoles of Latin America. Higher job positions were allotted to British young men whether they were more qualified or not.

The *Vedas*—The Hindu holy writings, the Vedas, are written in Sanskrit. New Age philosophy is clearly seen in its teachings as the following verse suggests:

"As the web issues from the spider, as little sparks proceed from fire, so from the one Soul proceed all breathing animals, all worlds, all the gods, and all things" (II. I,20).

"A Woman's Place"—Discuss with your students the practice of suttee and the prohibition on remarriage even if a woman was not yet married to the man but simply his fiancée when he died. Discuss how the British attempted to correct these problems.

Stand Strong—The Indians' devotion to their false religions should be an example for us today in our devotion to Christ. Have students look up I Corinthians 16:13 to see the biblical command to stand and be strong. Galatians 5:1 tells us to "stand fast therefore in the liberty wherewith Christ hath made us free." Ephesians 6:13, Philippians 4:1, and I Thessalonians 3:8 are other verses on this topic.

Time Line—On the chalkboard draw a time line for students to fill in. Include the years 1600 (East India Company chartered), 1757 (Battle of Plassey), 1857 (Sepoy Mutiny), 1900 (railroads completed), and 1947 (independence). You may wish to extend the time line backward to include the invaders of India discussed in the introduction.

Women in India—Until Christianity was widely introduced and its influence felt in the twentieth century, women in India were under extreme hardship. Hinduism started with the veneration of women but over the centuries turned to the utter degradation of them while still espousing their supposed honor. The average age of marriage for a girl in British India was eight years old. Many were "married" even younger than that, some before their first birthday. If their boy husband died they were already a widow, confined to a life of seclusion. A woman was not supposed to say the name of her husband and was required to walk behind him when traveling. She must never sit while in the presence of a man, and she left the room if another man entered. She also would not eat until her husband had consumed his fill. At the turn of the century, only seven of every one thousand women could read and write, and these were mostly the "dancing girls" in the temples. Dancing girls were religious prostitutes who were married to the gods for a life of shame (though not looked upon as such by the native Indians).

An elephant salute honors the Prince of Wales during a trip to India in 1876. There was little mingling of the British and Indians.

ever to marry. She was confined to widow's quarters (separate rooms in the house) for the rest of her life. With the law changed, a widow could remarry. She might still lose her caste position if she remarried, but she was protected under the law. Although some Indians complained that the British were changing traditional Indian life, the British did much to help thousands of hopeless Indian women.

Section Review

1. What problems in farming faced the Indians?
2. What was the best farming improvement the British brought to India?
3. How did the British help in time of famine?
4. List three industries the British built in India.
5. Why was the railroad important in India? List two reasons that the Indians did not like the railroad.
6. What language did the British use in the Indian educational system? Why did this cause conflict between the two cultures?
7. List two laws that helped Indian women.

What were some of the pros and cons of the changes which the British brought to India? Were the changes good or bad, or were the changes a mixture of both? Explain your answer.

Section Review Answers

1. primitive methods and monsoons
2. irrigation canals
3. They built an emergency relief plan to transport food on railroads to the worst areas.
4. cotton mills, jute factories, and iron- and steelworks
5. It made travel more pleasant, transported food more quickly, and provided famine relief; it disrupted family and village life by allowing family members to travel far away, and by making them break the rules of the caste system.
6. English; it devalued the Indian language and culture
7. outlawed suttee, removed the prohibition against remarriage of a widow

Answers will vary. Pros may include more and better food, the growth of industry, better transportation and communication, better education, and laws to help women. Cons may include servitude to the British, breakup of the traditional family, and disregard of caste rules. This created a mixture of both bad and good. The changes would seem good to the Indians if they were willing to see the technological advancement offered them. The changes would seem bad to the Indians if their religious convictions pricked them too much.

RUDYARD KIPLING: SON OF INDIA

"Oh East is East, and West is West, and never the twain shall meet," wrote **Rudyard Kipling** (1865-1936). Yet in a sense East did meet West in the life of Kipling himself. Kipling was Western, being not only a British citizen but also a staunch defender against critics of the British Empire. But Kipling was also Eastern. He was born in Bombay, India, while his father was working there as an art teacher. Kipling spent the first six years of life in India, learning the native language thoroughly. Although his family moved back to Britain, Kipling later returned to India and worked there as a newspaper reporter from 1882 to 1889.

During this second period in India, Kipling began writing the stories and poems that earned him wealth and fame. Though he eventually returned to Britain, Kipling still made India the central theme of his work. His finest works, *Kim, The Jungle Book, The Light That Failed,* and others, are set in India. He understood Indian culture better than most Britons. He showed deep respect and sympathy for both the British soldiers in India and the native Indian people. His poem "Gunga Din," for example, tells how an Indian water boy saves the life of a British soldier at the cost of his own life. Kipling also believed that British rule was in the best interest of India, although he realized—as others did not—that such rule could not last forever.

In his poem "The White Man's Burden" he reveals his belief that British imperialism was a duty and an opportunity to help out those "less fortunate" countries and peoples. To properly carry out the duty required patience, sacrifice, and maturity. Yet Kipling also expressed the sense of superiority that native peoples resented in Europeans. Who, they wanted to know, asked the white man to take up this burden?

Rudyard Kipling

The White Man's Burden

Take up the White Man's burden—
Send forth the best ye breed—
Go bind your sons to exile
To serve your captives' need;
To wait in heavy harness,
On fluttered folk and wild—
Your new-caught, sullen peoples,
Half-devil and half-child.

Take up the White Man's burden—
In patience to abide,
To veil the threat of terror
And check the show of pride;
By open speech and simple,
An hundred times made plain,
To seek another's profit,
And work another's gain.
. . . .

Take up the White Man's burden—
Ye dare not stoop to less—
Nor call too loud on Freedom
To cloak your weariness;
By all ye cry or whisper,
By all ye leave or do,
The silent, sullen peoples
Shall weigh your Gods and you.

Take up the White Man's burden—
Have done with childish days—
The lightly proffered laurel,
The easy, ungrudged praise.
Comes now, to search your manhood
Through all the thankless years,
Cold, edged with dear-bought wisdom,
The judgment of your peers!

White Man's Burden—When the United States became involved in the Philippines, a U.S. newspaper said,

"We've taken up the White Man's burden of ebony and brown:
Now will you kindly tell us, Rudyard,
How we may put it down?"

The United States realized that it had taken on a grave responsibility.

The Jungle Book—Watch part of an old version or read sections from *The Jungle Book* by Rudyard Kipling. Many of your students may already have seen or read this and should be familiar with the story. You may wish to read part of the book each day that you are studying this chapter.

Just-So Stories—Read to your class from Rudyard Kipling's *Just-So Stories*. A few suggestions follow:

"How the Whale Got His Throat"
"How the Leopard Got His Spots"
"The Beginning of the Armadillos"
"The Cat That Walked by Himself"
"The Elephant's Child"

"The White Man's Burden"—Discuss with your students the British belief that their way of life was superior. Viewing other cultures in light of one's own and attempting to force one's culture on others is known as culturalism. Ask the students whether the white man had the right to think this was his burden. Ask why he might have felt compelled to make it his burden. *(Most students will answer negatively to the first part but will not realize that often they do the same thing in viewing others' culture. The white man may have felt compelled to bear this burden because the Europeans were farther advanced technologically and economically than the Indians and others. Often their burden was wrongly carried out but resulted from their correct desire to help others. But often the "others" did not want or accept their help.)*

SECTION 4

Student Objectives
Students should be able to

1. Assess reasons for missionaries to go to Raj India.
2. Identify early missionaries to India.
3. Appraise the situation of women in India before and after salvation.

Missionaries to India

All India is full of holy men stammering gospels in strange tongues; shaken and consumed in the fires of their own zeal; dreamers, babblers, and visionaries; as it has been from the beginning and will continue to the end.

—Rudyard Kipling, *Kim*

India under the British was still a land of many religions. Hinduism, Buddhism, Islam, and many variations of these bound the people in their sin. Their superstitions kept them in fear and ruled their daily actions. To these millions of lost people, Christian missionaries came with the burden of the truth of the gospel and the love of the Lord Jesus Christ. India presented a great field of opportunity for service to God, and in the early nineteenth century British Christians began the harvest.

Shiva, worshiped by Hindus as destroyer and restorer of worlds, is one of thousands of Hindu gods.

Early Missionary Endeavors

The first British missionaries, however, were not allowed into British territory because the East India Company did not want to disrupt relations with the Indians. They thought that the missionaries' message would anger the Indians and harm their trade. These men thought more of their own material gain than the spiritual condition of their neighbors. Proverbs 15:27 tells us, "He that is greedy of gain troubleth his own house." These men brought trouble to their neighbors as well as to themselves. Their greed kept the Indians from hearing the gospel message. Yet Christian missionaries willingly gave up all hope of gain to witness to the Indians. In the end these dedicated servants of God gained the riches of God's blessing, a much more valuable possession than material riches. As Proverbs 13:7 says, "There is that maketh himself rich, yet hath nothing: there is that maketh himself poor, yet hath great riches."

A statue of the god Nandi decorated for a festival

SECTION 4

Materials

- Items for letter writing: paper, envelopes, stamps
- Guest speaker, an Indian or a missionary to India
- *With Daring Faith* by Rebecca Davis (BJUP)

Letters—Have each student choose a missionary to write to. Either instruct the students to choose a missionary supported by their church or have the names and addresses of several missionaries on hand. Spend some time in class writing letters. Have students bring the paper, envelopes, and stamps for the letters. Collect them and send them out. Have the students read to the class any responses received.

Comparing Religions—Instruct the students to use pages 72-79 to make a chart to compare major religions. Columns should include Hinduism, Buddhism, Islam, and Christianity. Rows should be labeled with the following questions: Who is god? What is the result of sin? What is salvation? How is salvation obtained? (BLM 12-3)

William Carey labored for the Lord in India for forty years. He translated the Bible into Bengali and other Indian languages.

Even after being turned away by the company, one man, **William Carey,** was still convinced that God had called him to India. For forty years (1794-1834) this missionary to India labored with the people. He taught the natives the truths of God's Word and also translated the Scripture into the languages of India. Another missionary, **William Ward**, who worked with Carey was a printer by trade. He set the type and printed copies of the new translations. Without the help of this dedicated printer, the work in India would have been slow indeed. Carey and his coworkers saw Indians come to Christ, and many more heard the Word in their own language.

In 1813 the British government ordered the East India Company to allow missionaries into its territory. Now other British missionaries traveled to India. Like the Careys, they also found India a hard mission field. The bonds of caste and superstition held the people. The tropical heat and humidity were hard on the Europeans. Yet the missionaries worked faithfully, and slowly they reaped fruit for their labors. The poorer people often responded first to the truth of the gospel. They had no satisfaction from their caste and desired the freedom and peace of which the missionaries talked. The missionaries often concentrated their work among the poorer people. Sometimes they set up schools to teach the gospel along with reading and writing. The missionaries also witnessed faithfully to higher-caste Indians and eventually saw some of these come to the Lord.

Christian Indians such as these suffer persecution from Muslims and Hindus.

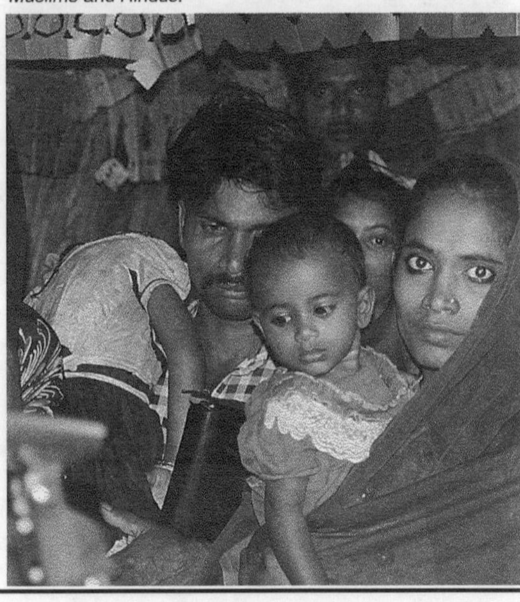

William Ward—Although Carey's is the name people remember, without the help of this printer, Carey's work would have been limited. This principle of service is important for your students to see: God uses all people and all types of work in His service. Encourage your students to be Christians first and businessmen, craftsmen, homemakers, or teachers second. As God used a printer in India (and many such Christians before and since), He uses men and women in all walks of life who are dedicated to Him.

Missions—Discuss with your students why missions made such an impact during this time. The Age of Exploration had opened up vast new territories with natives to evangelize. These natives may have seen the technological advancement of the conquering peoples and thought that their religion might be more advanced as well. The missionaries were a good testimony for the cause of Christ. Many people were praying and doing something (such as forming missionary societies) rather than waiting for someone else to do it. What things might make the gospel more effective in your culture? *(the testimony of Christians, prayer, and working for the Lord)*

Pandita Ramabai—Pandita Ramabai is a good example of a life committed to doing God's work. Any time a person is held up as an example, it is important to remind your students that the person highlighted has failings just as any other sinner saved by grace.

CHARACTERIZATIONS

Pandita Ramabai—A Woman of Faith

Hindu women had little hope of heaven. The Brahman priest said that a woman's hope lay in being a good wife to her husband so that she could serve him in heaven or in doing so much good during her current life that she would be born as a man in the next life. Missionaries had the gospel message for these hopeless hearts but had great difficulty getting that message to them. So it was that the Lord raised up Pandita Ramabai (RAH mah bye) to minister to the women of India.

Pandita did not quickly come to Christ. Born in the home of a prominent and open-minded Brahman, Pandita Ramabai had more freedom than many Indian women. Her father taught her and her mother to read Sanskrit writing. It was through her reading of the Hindu holy writings that she became dissatisfied with her religion and its hopelessness. She then began to study Christianity in India and later in England. Intellectually, Pandita decided that it was the best religion and that she should be baptized as a Christian. Ramabai later said,

> It was nobody's fault that I had not found Christ. He must have been preached to me from the beginning. My mind at that time had been too dull to grasp the teaching of the Holy Scriptures. The open Bible had been before me, but I had given much of my time to the study of other books about the Bible, and had not studied the Bible itself as I should have done. Hence my ignorance of many important doctrines taught in it. I gave up the study of other books about the Bible and took to reading the Bible regularly. I came to know, after eight years from the time of my baptism, that I had found the Christian religion, but I had not found Christ, who is the Life of the religion and "the Light of every man that cometh into the world." One thing I knew by this time, that I needed Christ, and not merely His religion.

Pandita Ramabai

Pandita and two workers with some of the children that she rescued during times of famine

Pandita saw her people as slaves to false religions.

Shortly after her true conversion, Pandita Ramabai started a faith mission for the girls and widows of India. In the spirit of George Mueller and Hudson Taylor, whose biographies she had read, Pandita and her helpers started a school and prayed for their needs to be met each day. When a great famine swept over India, Pandita went into the refugee camps and rescued widows and girls from certain death or abuse. Soon she had over a thousand women and girls at the mission. Providing for this many people during a time of great famine could have caused Pandita worry, but she said in her autobiography,

> I am spared all trouble and care, casting my burden upon the Lord. There are over 1,500 people living here; we are not rich, nor great, but we are happy, getting our daily bread directly from the loving hands of our Heavenly Father, having not a *pice* [a piece of money] over and above our daily necessities, having no banking account anywhere, no endowment or income from any earthly source, but depending altogether on our Father God; we have nothing to fear from anybody, nothing to lose, and nothing to regret. The Lord is our *inexhaustible treasure.*

Daily Pandita Ramabai and her helpers taught the women to read and write, showed them basic cleanliness, and encouraged them to learn a trade. But the most important thing the women learned was salvation through Jesus Christ. Several thousand Indian women came to Christ through Pandita Ramabai's ministry. Many of the women trained in her school became "Bible-women" who also took the gospel to the women of India.

Pandita saw the needs of her people and prayed that God would help others to see as well. She pleads with those who hear her story, "Dear brother and sister, whoever may happen to read this testimony, may you realize your responsibility to give the Gospel of Jesus Christ to my people in this land, and pray for them that they may each and all be cleansed from their filthiness and from all their idols, that they may find the true way of salvation."

Amy Carmichael—Amy Carmichael took upon herself the work of freeing the dancing girls from their shameful profession. She would stain her face and go into the temples to buy them. Often they did not cost anything, though sometimes they were quite expensive. On many occasions she tried to save them before they got to the temple. Mothers would give their daughters to the temple in payment of a vow, among other reasons.

Extra Reading—Read to your students the story of Amy Carmichael in *With Daring Faith* by Rebecca Davis (available through BJU Press).

Men, women, and children listen eagerly to a message from the gospel.

Ministering to the Women of India

A very fruitful field in India was in women's work. Most Indian women were not allowed to associate with any man outside their immediate family members. Thus, male missionaries could have no contact with them, but a woman could. The first woman missionary to India was **Hannah Marshman.** She went to the field with her husband, one of Carey's partners. After arriving in India, she became burdened for the women and saw the opportunity she had to work with them. She opened schools for poor Indian children and also for young women. Often the girls converted under her teaching went out to tell other women about Christ.

As the century went on, more single women came to the field. They were burdened for the many higher-caste wives and widows who were confined to their husbands' houses. Missionaries who came as teachers and nurses gained entrance to these women's quarters. They taught these lonely, lost women about the love of Christ. They brought divine healing to their souls as well as physical care to their bodies. Many Indian women came to know the love and joy of salvation because these missionaries took them the message.

The Great Century

The nineteenth century is often called the **"Great Century of Christian Missions."** Prompted by the revivals begun in England under John Wesley and George Whitefield, British Christians formed missionary societies to send missionaries to foreign fields. The **Baptist Missionary Society** sent out Carey and his partners. Many other societies from both Europe and America sent missionaries. Dedicated to the Lord and burdened to win others, these men and women went out motivated by Acts 1:8, "And ye shall be witnesses unto me both in Jerusalem, and in all Judaea, and in Samaria, and unto the uttermost part of the earth."

Millions in India have never heard the gospel of Christ. Will you take the message to them?

Women and Religion—The position of women in India still remains bleak. Contrast the poor treatment of women in India with the treatment of women in Christian countries. When a nation accepts Christianity, a change in the position of women is usually evident.

Women's Activity—Encourage the girls in your class to look for special opportunities for service that are more open to women than to men. Then encourage them to prepare the skills necessary for these fields of service. Discuss these opportunities in class. Perhaps they can choose one to research as a group. Help make arrangements for their activity.

India—Invite someone who has lived in India (perhaps a missionary) to speak to your class on life in that society.

Section Review

1. What religions did the people of India follow?
2. Why did the East India Company not allow missionaries into its territory?
3. Who was the first missionary to India?
4. How did Mrs. Marshman work with Indian women?
5. What did Christians do to prove that the nineteenth century was the "Great Century of Christian Missions"?

What do you think was different about the people or the era that caused so many to be interested in missions? What changes would have to occur in our world today to cause more missionaries to be sent out across the world? How could you make a difference?

Summary

India was an important part of the British Empire. The English first came to India around 1600 to trade under the leadership of the East India Company. For 250 years the East India Company increased its power in India. However, trouble arose between the British and the Indians, and in 1858 the British government took control of the country, which became a part of the empire. The British Raj ruled India for nearly a hundred years. During that time the British tried to help the Indians. They improved farming by teaching new methods, bringing new machinery, and building canals. They also brought some industry to India. To unite the country, the British built railroads and telegraph lines to all parts of the land. They increased education for more people, teaching mostly Western subjects, and also wrote laws to protect the people. The greatest contribution the British made to India was spreading the gospel. Many dedicated missionaries traveled to India and spent their lives telling the Indians about Christ. Despite these accomplishments, the British ignored India's long and fruitful heritage. They did not understand traditional Indian culture and often offended their Indian subjects. These two ways of life eventually clashed, and the Indians later gained their independence in 1947.

Spanning the Ages

The age of imperialism had grown greatly. Britain continued its technological advances in other countries as well as its own. Many times this imperialism provided raw materials with which to increase the mother country's industry. Britain and the rest of Europe did not stop with India. They went on to carve up China into "spheres of influence" and break up Africa on paper among themselves. Remind the students to look for more imperialist behavior in the next chapters. How did Europeans conflict as they claimed territory? What are these conflicts leading toward?

Section Review Answers

1. Hinduism, Buddhism, Islam, and variations of these
2. They thought it would harm their trade by angering the Indians.
3. William Carey
4. She opened schools for them.
5. formed missionary societies to send missionaries to foreign fields

Answers will vary. Technological advances were being made, and newly discovered lands were being conquered. People were curious about other peoples and cultures, even though they thought their own was best. People today would have to be more willing to go as missionaries or to send missionaries (i.e., be willing to pay for them) in order for more missionaries to be sent. The student could make a difference by being willing to go and by starting now to be a missionary in his own "Jerusalem."

Chapter Review Idea

The most ancient games still played today come from India. Parcheesi and chess are the two your students will be familiar with. Draw a large Parcheesi board on the board or overhead transparency and play with four teams. Use slips of paper to determine the number of spaces to move. Ask questions to review the chapter. If the student answers correctly, he may move forward that many spaces; if he does not, he loses his turn. Other rules of the game would apply as well, such as bumping another team's marker out of the spot if you just landed in the same spot.

Chapter Enrichment Activities

Trading Stations—Encourage your students to trace the forming of trading stations in India by the East India Company. They may write a report or give an oral report to the class, depending on how many respond.

Reading—Watch (or read) *The Secret Garden* by Frances Hodgson Burnett. The beginning of this story describes life in India; the rest of the book is life in England. Other good books would be some of Rudyard Kipling's stories, either *The Jungle Book* or *Kim*. Have the students write a 150-word book report about whichever book they choose. You may wish to do this in conjunction with the English teacher, with you grading the content and the English teacher grading the form.

Biography—Have students choose one missionary from the chapter and write a biographical sketch of him or her. This should include information about the missionary's childhood, the call to missions, where and when he or she served, and the effects of his or her ministry.

CHAPTER REVIEW

People, Places, and Terms to Know

East India Company
Bombay
Madras
Calcutta
Battle of Plassey
Robert Clive
Charter Act
sepoys
Sepoy Mutiny
General Enlistment Act
viceroy
British Raj
Empress of India
sahibs
British Empire
monsoons
bazaar
babus
Sanskrit
suttee
Rudyard Kipling
William Carey
William Ward
Hannah Marshman
"Great Century of Christian Missions"
Baptist Missionary Society

Review Questions

Map Analysis

Look at the map on page 326 and answer the following questions.

1. On which river is Calcutta located?
2. Which East India Company port is located on the Arabian Sea?
3. Near which East India Company port is Ceylon located?
4. Which Indian river flows into the Arabian Sea?

Completion

Complete the following statements.

5. In 1600 (a) ______, the English queen, granted a charter to the (b) ______ to trade in India.
6. For years England competed with (a) ______ for territory and trade until the Battle of (b) ______ gave England victory in India.
7. The East India Company expanded its territory until a group of Indian soldiers, called (a) ______, rose against them in the (b) ______.
8. The British government took control of India in the year (a) ______ and established official British rule called the (b) ______.

Chapter Review Answers

Map Analysis

1. Ganges River
2. Bombay
3. Madras
4. Indus River

Completion

5. (a) Elizabeth I (b) East India Company
6. (a) France (b) Plassey
7. (a) sepoys (b) Sepoy Mutiny
8. (a) 1858 (b) British Raj

Multiple Choice

Choose all the correct answers for each of the following questions.

9. Some of the problems the British faced in ruling India were
   (a) its size. (c) its poverty.
   (b) its languages. (d) its religions.
10. Britain made agricultural improvements in India. These included
    (a) irrigation canals. (c) improvement of the tea industry.
    (b) introduction of fertilizer. (d) redistribution of farmland.
11. India supplied Britain with certain raw materials. Among these were
    (a) wool. (c) timber.
    (b) cotton. (d) jute.

Definition

Define or explain each of these terms.

12. sepoys
13. viceroy
14. British Raj

Matching

Match these items.

15. Robert Clive	(a) missionary to India
16. Victoria	(b) educated Indian
17. William Carey	(c) Battle of Plassey
18. *babu*	(d) Empress of India

Think About It!

Remember that many of the chapters you are studying overlap chronologically. Add to the following list of major events in the history of British India at least seven other events from the past five chapters. Put these events in the proper order of occurrence. Use a separate sheet of paper and place them on a time line.

Battle of Plassey	Completion of India's railroad
William Carey in India	Sepoy Mutiny
Beginning of British Raj	Indian independence

Recipe: Spiced Rice—Lightly spiced, this rice recipe may be served with vegetables or split pea soup. Generally, Indians would not eat meat with their meals, but you could add chicken or other meat if you wish.

Ingredients:
4 Tbsp. water
1/8 tsp. tumeric powder
2 c. cooked rice
1/2 tsp. oil
1/2 tsp. mustard seed
1 small onion, chopped
dash ginger powder
1/8 tsp. ground cumin seed
1/4 tsp. coriander powder
1/2 tsp. chili powder
1 clove garlic, chopped
1/2 c. tomato, chopped
1/4 c. cilantro, chopped (optional)

Mix tumeric powder with water. Sprinkle over rice until rice is loose and slightly moist; put aside. Heat oil in pan and sauté mustard seeds until they begin to move in the pan. Add onion and remaining spices. After the onion is slightly softened, lightly sauté the garlic. Add the tomato and cilantro. Cook slightly until all ingredients and spices are well mixed. Add the tumeric-rice and heat thoroughly. Salt to taste. (courtesy of Darleen Gillette, retired missionary to India)

Multiple Choice

9. a, b, c, d
10. a, b, c
11. b, d

Definition

12. Indian soldiers under British command
13. ruler in place of the monarch
14. British rule in India

Matching

15. c
16. d
17. a
18. b

Think About It

Answers will vary. The proper order for those included is as follows:

1757—Battle of Plassey
1794-1834—William Carey in India
1857—Sepoy Mutiny
1858—Beginning of British Raj
1900—Completion of the railroad
1947—Indian independence

They should add at least seven other events from Chapters 7-11.

Student Objectives

Students should be able to

1. Define and describe the *Chung Kuo*.
2. Categorize specific inventions and characteristics of the Ming or Manchu dynasties.
3. Identify reasons for China's attitude of superiority.
4. Define *tribute* and *kowtow*.
5. Name the drug with which the British opened trade in China.
6. Analyze the effects of opium on a population and on individuals.
7. Describe the Opium Wars.
8. Locate Southeast Asia on a map.
9. Use a relief map to determine elevation.
10. Identify the first missionaries to China.
11. Evaluate Hudson Taylor's philosophy of becoming like the natives.
12. Describe the Taiping Rebellion and identify both its leader and the Manchu leader.
13. Analyze the decline of the Manchu dynasty.
14. Analyze the causes and effects of the Boxer Rebellion.
15. Identify the missionaries whose escape during the Boxer Rebellion was providential.

Opening Photo— The Lijiang River in China

CHAPTER 13

Sunday morning, August 23, 1868. The small mission station stood strangely silent. Smoke from smoldering piles of debris hung heavily in the summer air, already hot and humid hours before daybreak. As Hudson Taylor entered the house, he saw more destruction—broken furniture, burned books, ruined medical equipment and supplies, pieces of toys, and torn clothing. Leaving the house, he searched diligently until he found his wife and family. Injured and weary, they were with other missionaries at a neighbor's house. Hudson brought them home and waited. At dawn, the Chinese from the town returned and began to loot the station once more.

Unable to allow them to continue, Hudson climbed onto a broken chair and began to speak:

> *We were a party of strangers; we came from a distance to seek your good. Had we meant evil, should we have come unarmed? Or in such small numbers? Or with our women and children? Without provocation you have broken open our dwelling, plundered our property, wounded our persons, and tried to burn down our premises. And now you are back in your greed of plunder to do us more mischief.*
>
> *We are defenseless. We cannot withstand you. If we could, we would not. We are here for good, not for evil. . . . If you abuse us or kill us, we will not retaliate. But high Heaven will avenge. Our God, in whom we trust, is able to protect us and punish you, if you offend against Him.*

Hudson Taylor had come to China with a deep love for the millions of Chinese who had never heard the gospel. Under his ministry many Chinese found true salvation in the Lord Jesus Christ. However, many opposed him and his message.

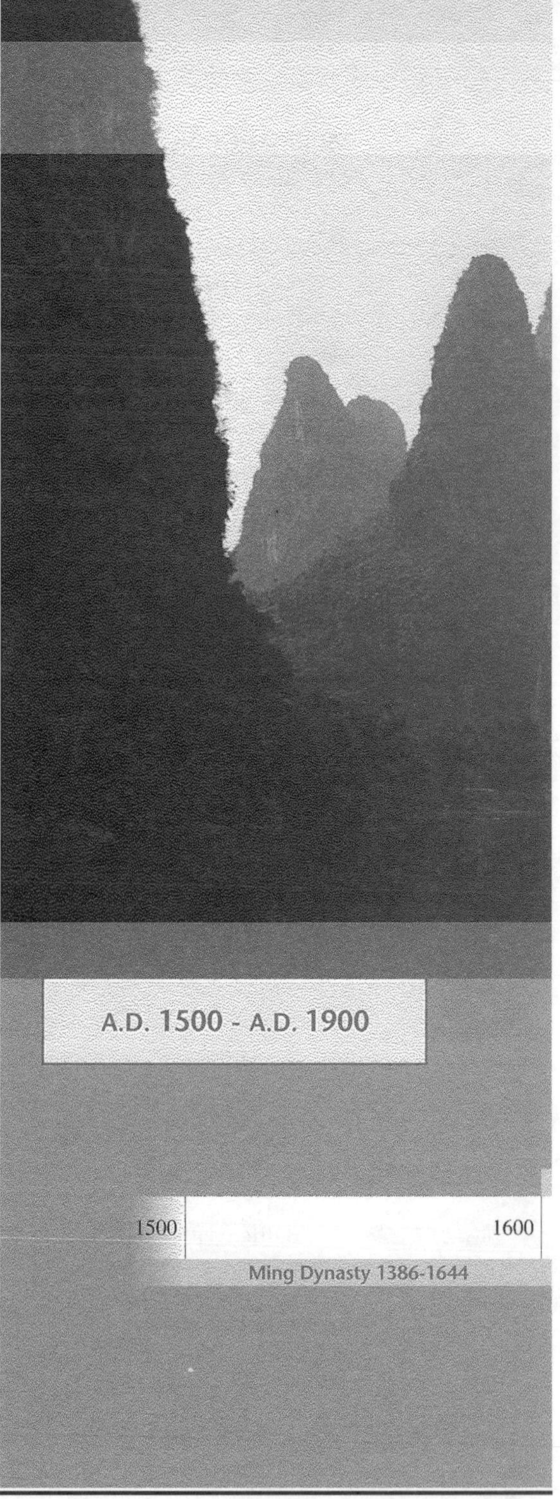

A.D. 1500 - A.D. 1900

Chapter 13 Lesson Plans			
Section Title	**Main Concept**	**Pages**	**Time Frame**
**Center Stage: Chinese Dynasties* 1. The Central Kingdom	Under the Ming and Manchu dynasties, the Chinese continued to view themselves as the superior Central Kingdom.	348-55	1-2 days
2. Western Trade **Settings: Southeast Asia* **Interpretations: Hong Kong*	The West (Great Britain) was finally able to increase trade in China through the exporting of the addictive drug opium.	356-61	1 day
3. Christian Missions	Robert Morrison and Hudson Taylor began to evangelize China.	362-65	1 day
4. Decline of the Manchu Dynasty **Backgrounds: The Opening of Japan*	The Manchu dynasty began to decline through internal weakness and external pressure.	366-70	1 day
5. The Boxer Rebellion	Political unrest culminated in the Boxer Rebellion that killed or expelled many foreigners.	371-75	1-2 days
Total Suggested Days (including 1 day for review & 1 day for test)			7-9 days

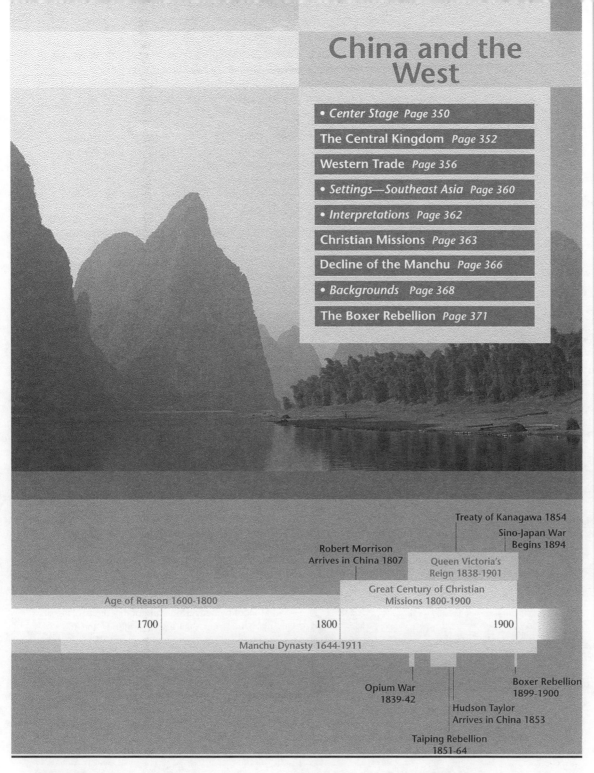

China and the West

Treaty of Kanagawa 1854
Sino-Japan War Begins 1894
Robert Morrison Arrives in China 1807
Queen Victoria's Reign 1838-1901
Great Century of Christian Missions 1800-1900
Age of Reason 1600-1800
1700
1800
1900
Manchu Dynasty 1644-1911
Opium War 1839-42
Boxer Rebellion 1899-1900
Hudson Taylor Arrives in China 1853
Taiping Rebellion 1851-64

Materials

- Scripture verse (BLM verse 13)
- Bibles for Bible study
- Concordances
- Guest speaker, a law enforcement officer
- Wall map of Asia or Southeast Asia (BLM 13-2)
- *Teaching Transparencies* for use with *World Studies for Christian Schools* (Second Edition)
- Periodical article about Hong Kong from July 1997
- Chopsticks
- Video about Hudson Taylor or the Goforths
- Biographies of famous missionaries to China

Decode the Message

Using a dictionary or other resource to find Chinese characters and their meanings. Draw Chinese characters that form a sentence on the bulletin board. In one corner put a key to the characters; have students solve the sentence. Place on your board pictures of Chinese hats, queues, vases, houses, and other items that represent China.

Chapter Motivator

Read with your students the story in this introduction. Discuss the story. Ask your students what they can tell about the attitudes of the Chinese and of Hudson Taylor. Share the following information.

God's servants often suffer persecution while doing His work. In Yangchow, where this incident occurred, the Chinese disliked the Taylors and their message. Note especially Taylor's attitude toward those who hated him. Hudson, Maria, and their family had to leave Yangchow for nearly three months while British and Chinese officials argued over the situation. Ask the students why government officials were involved. In what other countries did the government mediate between missionaries. Finally, on November 18, 1868, the Taylors returned to Yangchow to continue their work.

Isaiah 41:10

Missionaries to China one hundred years ago feared for their lives, yet they knew that God was in control. Some lost their lives for Christ's sake, and some survived miraculously. The Lord will always take care of and watch over His own. Isaiah 41:10 says, "Fear thou not; for I am with thee: be not dismayed; for I am thy God: I will strengthen thee; yea, I will help thee; yea, I will uphold thee with the right hand of my righteousness." (BLM verse 13)

Dynasties—You may review more about these dynasties in the sixth-grade Heritage Studies textbook.

Empress Dowager—Tz'u-hsi, born in 1835, was one of Chinese emperor Hsien-feng's sixty concubines. When she came to the court at the age of sixteen, she was in the lowest rank of concubines. While she was at court, she spent time learning Chinese history and the art of calligraphy.

In 1856, Hsien-feng made Tz'u-hsi a concubine of the second rank when she gave birth to the emperor's only male child. Six years later, Hsien-feng died, and his son became emperor. Another concubine named Tz'u-an was empress at the time of Hsien-feng's death, but Hsien-feng granted similar power to Tz'u-hsi because she was the mother of his son. Soon after Hsien-feng's death, an edict proclaimed both Tz'u-an and Tz'u-hsi Empress Dowagers of China. However, Tz'u-hsi exerted the main control over the kingdom, and Tz'u-an died in 1881.

In 1875, Tz'u-hsi's son died of smallpox. In a meeting to decide who would be the next emperor, Tz'u-hsi broke with traditional succession rules and chose her own three-year-old nephew Kuang-hsu. Tz'u-hsi adopted Kuang-hsu and then controlled him and all of China until his death on November 14, 1908. The Empress Dowager herself died the next day.

Tz'u-hsi had a terrible temper and lust for power. She supported and encouraged the Boxer Rebellion and made it difficult for China to accept Western influence peacefully. Her reign was marked by corruption.

CENTER STAGE

A Time Line of China's Past China has an ancient history that helps explain the people's feeling of superiority. China's history encompasses the rise and fall of several other empires. As you read the following time line, try to remember other empires that occurred during the same periods.

Chinese Dynasties

Xia, 2200-1766 B.C.—This legendary, ancient dynasty domesticated animals and wove silk.

Shang, 1766-1122 B.C.—This dynasty saw the widespread use of oracle bones. During this dynasty the Chinese also perfected the wheel for use on chariots and made bronze vessels.

Empress Dowager Tz'u-hsi ruled during the Manchu dynasty.

Chou (Zhou), 1122-221 B.C.—Iron casting was developed, and multiplication tables were recorded for the first time during this dynasty. During this time Confucius established his doctrines.

Chin (Qin), 221-206 B.C.—Many wonderful accomplishments occurred during this short dynasty. The Great Wall was begun. Improvements were made in roads and canals. A uniform writing system and standardized weights and measurements were established.

Han, 202 B.C.–A.D. 220—Four years of civil war preceded the Han dynasty. During this dynasty great technological developments occurred. Steel was manufactured, and the seismograph was invented.

Four centuries of war divided China into smaller kingdoms and dynasties. China was once again united in the Tang dynasty.

Tang, A.D. 618-906—The Tang dynasty claimed land stretching from Mongolia to Vietnam and from Korea to Iran. Great Chinese poets wrote, and craftsmen produced fine porcelain. A period of political division occurred between the Tang and Song dynasties.

Song (Sung), 960-1279—Movable type improved Chinese printing. The compass was invented but was used for fortunetelling. Paper money was developed but caused economic disaster.

Yuan (Mongol), 1279-1368—Kublai Khan came from the north and within a year conquered the Chinese. The Mongols adapted to the Chinese lifestyle.

Ming, 1368-1644—Rebels overthrew the weakened Mongol dynasty. Porcelain of this dynasty is famous. The Great Wall was extended, and the Imperial Palace was built.

Dynasties—Explain the dynastic cycle. The dynastic cycle describes a repeated pattern in Chinese history. Usually a family ruled as long as the people were satisfied with its rule and supported it. That rule could be very long or very short. As one family grew weaker, another family gained strength and support. When it grew strong enough, the new family took over from the old dynasty.

The Ming dynasty was weakened from within. While the Ming strength diminished, the Manchus were assimilating the Chinese culture. When the Ming cycle came to an end in 1644, the Manchus were able to step into power with little opposition because they were already so much like the Chinese.

Ancient China—When they see the long history of China, students may wonder why we do not generally study the rise and fall of each dynasty as we do the rise and fall of the Persians, Greeks, Romans, and so on. Remind students that China was isolated by its geographic position as well as by its own desire for solitude. For thousands of years traders exchanged goods with China, but China's silence on world matters and nonaggressive approach to Western countries made China easy to overlook.

Ask students how our study of Chinese history might have been different if China had been aggressive toward the West and claimed huge empires early in its history. What if Chinese armies had overthrown the Greeks and Romans? How would it have changed Western language? What other interests might have changed?

Manchu (Qing), 1644-1911—Chinese influence spread throughout the East. The Opium Wars, Taiping Rebellion, and Boxer Rebellion weakened the empire. European nations carved out holdings in the East. Empress Dowager Tz'u-hsi retained control of the dynasty and prevented the modernization of China.

(The next two entries will be discussed in greater detail in Chapter 17.)

Republic of China, 1911-1949—Revolutionary forces under the influence of Dr. Sun Yat-sen overthrew the Manchus. The Kuomintang party tried to unite China. Chiang Kai-shek took over the party after Sun Yat-sen died.

Communist China, 1949-present—The Communists, under Mao Zedong, defeated opposition forces. The Kuomintang government fled to Taiwan, where it established the Nationalist regime. The People's Republic of China established its capital in Peking, later called Beijing.

Geography helped isolate China from other cultures. In its thousands of years of history it has been ruled by foreigners only twice.

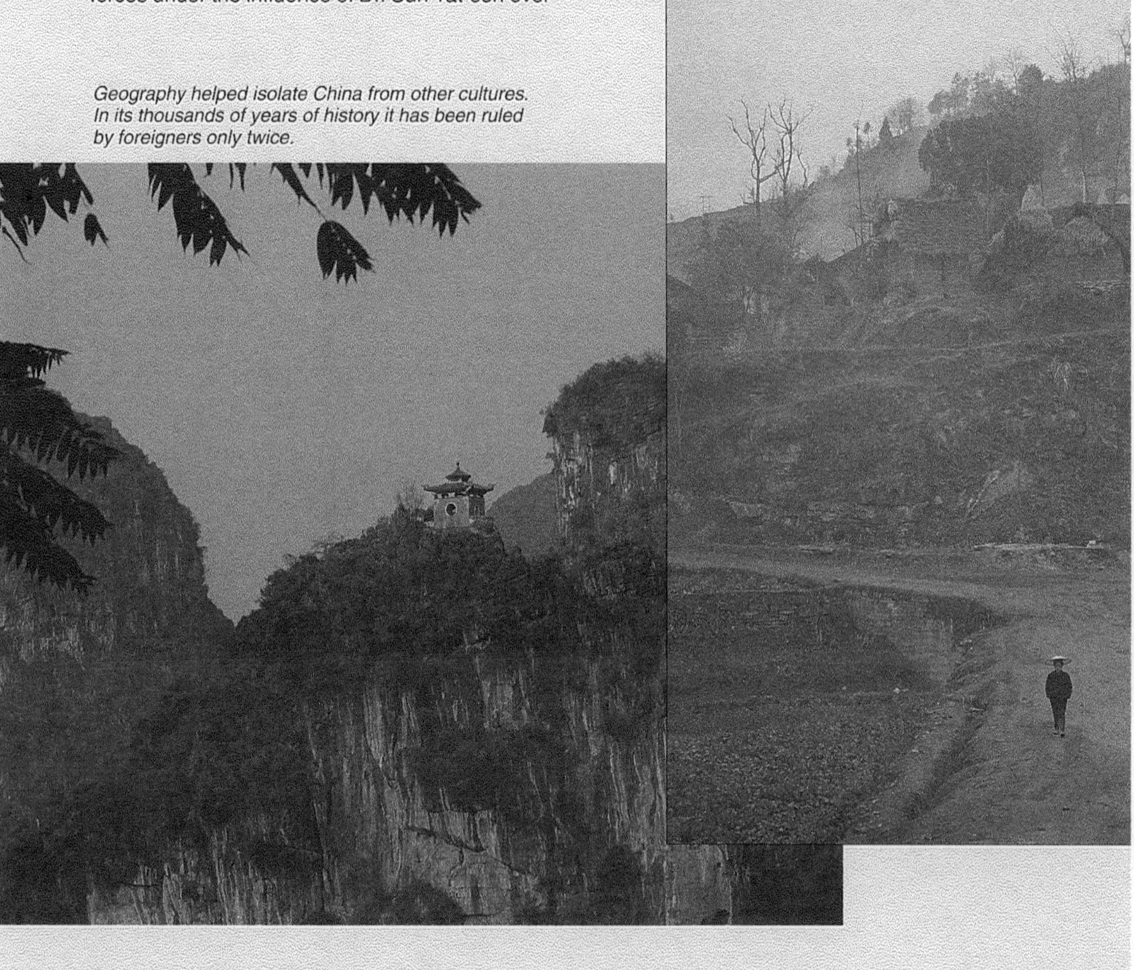

China and the West 351

SECTION 1

Student Objectives

Students should be able to

1. Define and describe the *Chung Kuo*.
2. Categorize specific inventions and characteristics of the Ming and Manchu dynasties.
3. Identify reasons for China's attitude of superiority.
4. Define *tribute* and *kowtow*.

Chinese Porcelain in America—More nineteenth-century Chinese porcelain is in America than in England today because America continued to import Chinese porcelain until the end of the nineteenth century.

At the time, porcelain was not considered very valuable compared to tea and silk from China. Crates containing porcelain goods were used as the bottom layer in the hold of a ship; tea and silk goods were placed on top where they would not get wet.

Chinese Names—Changes have occurred in Chinese names in the past twenty years. In 1979 China abandoned the Wade-Giles method of spelling Chinese words in English and began using the Pinyin method. Examples of words that have changed are listed below.

Wade-Giles	Pinyin
Chin dynasty	Qin dynasty
Peking	Beijing
Tz'u Hsi	Cixi
Canton	Quangzhou
Mao Tse-tung	Mao Zedong

The Central Kingdom

Historically, the Chinese called their land *Chung Kuo,* the **Central Kingdom.** For two thousand years China has existed as the central nation and great power in Asia. Its borders have changed, and one dynasty has overthrown another, but China has remained. Other empires that traded with the Chinese have come and gone. The Babylonians, the Persians, the Greeks, the Romans, all great at one time, have fallen, but China has carried on as a central power among the other Asian nations.

Reclaiming Chinese Rule

Chapter 4 introduced China during a time when it was ruled by a foreign power—the Mongols. Their rule was called the Yuan dynasty. The Chinese found it bearable only because Kublai Khan set up his palaces in China and relied on Chinese advisors. The Yuan dynasty did little to disrupt the flow of Chinese life. However, the relaxed life that the Mongols lived in China weakened their nomad-warrior ways. After a little over one hundred years, defiant Chinese forces overthrew the Mongols and established a new dynasty called the **Ming dynasty** (1386-1644).

The Ming dynasty reestablished native Chinese rule. In reaction to foreign rule, the new dynasty looked down on all foreigners, including European traders. Instead the Ming directed their attention to the internal problems and needs of China. This helped the dynasty establish an era of peace and prosperity.

The Ming concentrated on the arts, reconstruction, and exploration. Craftsmen perfected **porcelain** production, which helped to continue the demand for exports. The Ming took time to fix broken portions of the Great Wall and to extend it even further. They repaired roads and bridges and built the **Imperial City** in their capital city Peking (later called Beijing). They also began sending out **junks** (sailing vessels) to explore Southeast Asia and the Red Sea. But while the Ming directed their attention to the south and east, foreign invaders slowly took control of the Imperial City.

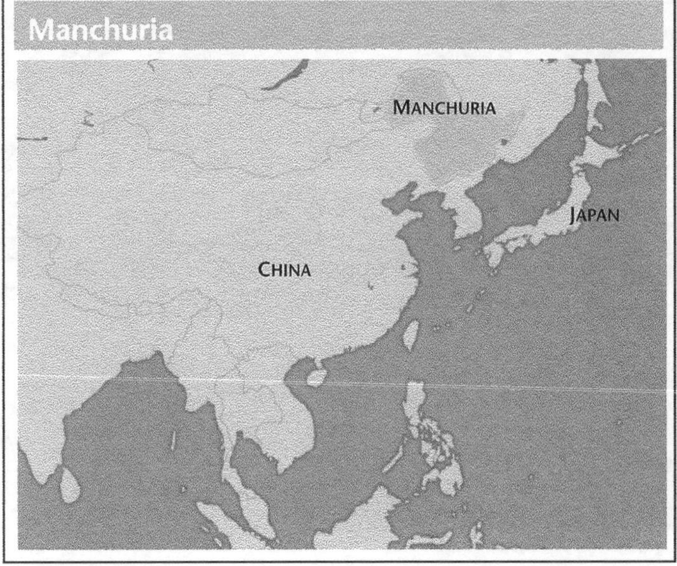

The Manchu Dynasty

In 1644 the **Manchu dynasty** took power from the failing Ming dynasty. The Manchus came from **Manchuria,** the region northeast of China. The Manchus came into China to help the Ming government defeat a group of rebels. Once invited into the country, however, the Manchus slowly took power from the weak Ming rulers. They established the second foreign dynasty to rule in Chinese history. The Manchu, or Qing, dynasty

SECTION 1

Materials

- Bibles for Bible study

Review—Review ancient Chinese history on pages 350-51 to refresh your students' memories about Chinese culture and accomplishments. Although the Chinese were superior when Europe was in its Dark Ages, the Chinese quickly fell behind as the West steamed ahead into the Industrial Age of the eighteenth and nineteenth centuries. China's feeling of superiority prompted it to close its doors to the West in 1644. It was this attitude that the West fought in trying to reopen China to trade in the nineteenth century.

ruled China from 1644 to 1911, when dynasty rule ended in China.

The Manchu rulers worked hard to build a good relationship with the people of their newly conquered empire. They knew that to stay in power and have a successful government, they needed the support of the people. The Manchus tried to become "Chinese" rather than making the Chinese become Manchurian. The Manchus allowed the Chinese to have a part in the government. At the higher levels of government, a Chinese and a Manchu often shared the same office. At the local level almost all government officials were Chinese.

Actually the Manchu government differed little from earlier dynastic governments. The emperor still held supreme power and could order any policy throughout the empire. Scholars received positions in government by doing well on civil service exams. Many Chinese scholars held important positions at the imperial court in Peking. Each level of government was responsible to the next higher level so that local governors had little control over their own affairs. In this way the Manchus successfully governed their Chinese subjects for nearly two centuries before discontent with their rule broke out.

A Chinese junk

This selection from a Chinese book on Europe gives an account of the Chinese opinion of Europeans.

In ancient times [Europe's] people hunted for a living, ate meat, and wore skins. Their customs were barbaric, and their spirit was wild and free. But during our own Shang period (2000 B.C.), Greece and other countries gradually came under the influence of the Orient. For the first time they began to till fields and manufacture products, build cities, and dig lakes. They began to do all kinds of things. Before long, writing and civilization began to flourish. Thus they became beautiful like the countries of the East.

(From Hsiao-fang hu-chai yü-ti ts'ung-ch'ao, *compiled by Wang Hsi-ch'i, published in 1891.)*

Chinese Superiority

Throughout their history the Chinese have had an attitude of superiority toward all other countries in the world. They called themselves the Central Kingdom because they considered themselves to be the center of the world. In many ways China truly was superior to other countries. For example, during the Dark Ages in Europe, China had a period of great achievement under the Tang and Sung dynasties. The Chinese invented printing, papermaking, gunpowder, and the compass. Before Europe entered the modern age, China was the most technologically advanced region in the world.

The Manchus continued to promote this attitude of superiority. They especially tried to keep China from having any contact with the West through trade. China closed all but one or two ports to Western trade during the eighteenth century.

However, this policy turned out to be a double-edged sword. It not only kept the West from receiving quantities of desirable Chinese

Chinese Proverbs and Curses—Chinese words of wisdom are often handed down in the form of proverbs.

- "Correct one's self, then correct others,"
- "To have a bad child is not as well as to have none,"
- "Great goodness and great wickedness, sooner or later, are sure to be rewarded."

Ask your students what other country that they have studied handed down words of wisdom in proverbs or sayings like these. *(Africa)* The following are examples or Chinese curses.

- "May the five thunders strike you dead!"
- "May your body be in one place and your head in another!"
- "May your bowels rot inch by inch!"

Chinese views—Read the box at the bottom of this page with your students. Encourage them to analyze Chinese views of foreigners. Why did they feel the way they did? Were they right? Eventually, China proved to be less powerful than Europe.

Superiority—Conduct a discussion about the feeling of superiority. Do all nations experience such feelings, in one way or another? Are older countries prouder? If yes, why? Do you think that they have a right to be? Ask the students to give examples of proud countries and then to compare those examples to their own patriotic feelings.

Cultural Confusion—The Chinese/British confusion over the meaning of Macartney's gifts is a cultural problem. This type of misunderstanding still occurs in the international business world today. Courses and seminars are available to instruct businessmen and businesswomen on acceptable behavior in foreign countries. Note the following guidelines.

- Never use your left hand to shake hands in the Middle East or South Asia.
- Do not talk about business during a meal while in South America.
- Some Asian cultures do not believe it is proper to say the word *no* or to disagree with someone, so businessmen must choose their words carefully when making business deals.

Macartney's refusal to kowtow was not appreciated by the emperor.

Macartney's Mission to China

In 1793 Great Britain decided to break through China's resistance to foreign trade. King George III sent a group to China led by Lord Macartney. Supposedly Macartney went to honor the Chinese emperor on his eighty-third birthday. In reality he planned to use this opportunity to negotiate a trade agreement with China.

Macartney came bearing numerous gifts to flatter the emperor. (The British government spent over seventy-five thousand pounds on the enterprise.) To the delight of Macartney, the Chinese welcomed him and his party warmly. The British were dismayed a bit, however, when the Chinese treated their gifts as "tribute," as though the British were submitting to the emperor as vassals. When meeting the emperor himself, Macartney created a stir when he refused to perform the customary kowtow. The emperor, however, allowed Macartney to bow as he would to his own king—kneeling on one knee.

Although Macartney was well treated and the Chinese proved gracious hosts, the mission failed. The Chinese emperor refused to recognize the group as anything more than tribute-bearers come to honor him on his birthday. The Chinese flatly denied any trade privileges. The emperor sent a letter to King George saying, "The Celestial Empire possesses all things in prolific abundance and lacks no product within its borders. There is therefore no need to import the manufactures of outside barbarians in exchange for our own products."

Then with condescending tone, he added, "It behooves you, O King, to respect my sentiments and to display even greater devotion and loyalty in future, so that, by perpetual submission to our Throne, you may secure peace and prosperity for your country thereafter."

Response to the Chinese—Have each student write a response to the king of China's letter to King George. Remind them that it needs to be in good taste and not insulting, yet firm on the British opinion of their own nation.

Draw Your Own—Take time to have each student draw a picture of a Chinese man and woman in traditional clothing. They may do this from pictures or descriptions in an encyclopedia or in other books.

goods but also kept the Chinese from receiving the new inventions and learning of the West. While the Western world moved rapidly into the modern age, the Chinese refused to change their traditional culture. Their pride in their traditional culture blinded them to the valuable achievements of other people. As individuals we must not let pride in our own abilities blind us to the wisdom and ability of others around us.

China's attitude of superiority was especially seen in its dealings with foreign ambassadors. When an ambassador from another land, whether it were Mongolia or Britain, came with a request, the Chinese official who greeted him demanded humble honor. This honor was given in the form of a **tribute,** usually money or goods, and the performance of the **kowtow.** The kowtow was performed by kneeling down and bowing one's forehead to the ground in a show of humility. The Chinese considered all foreigners "Outer Barbarians" and the tribute and kowtow only appropriate.

To those peoples living around China and having subordinate cultures, the kowtow was not offensive. Many of these areas owed their safety to China's good pleasure. However, to Europeans this practice was unthinkable, for they thought their own culture superior to the Chinese and regarded the Chinese as the barbarians. These two cultures were bound to clash, and as one might expect, it came in the area of trade.

Section Review

1. On which Chinese dynasty does this chapter focus?
2. What dynasty lost power at the beginning of this period?
3. How did the Manchurians successfully rule the Chinese?
4. What name for China showed her people's attitude of superiority?
5. How did the Chinese hurt themselves by their superior attitude?

Do you think that the British were right to refuse to kowtow? Explain your answer.

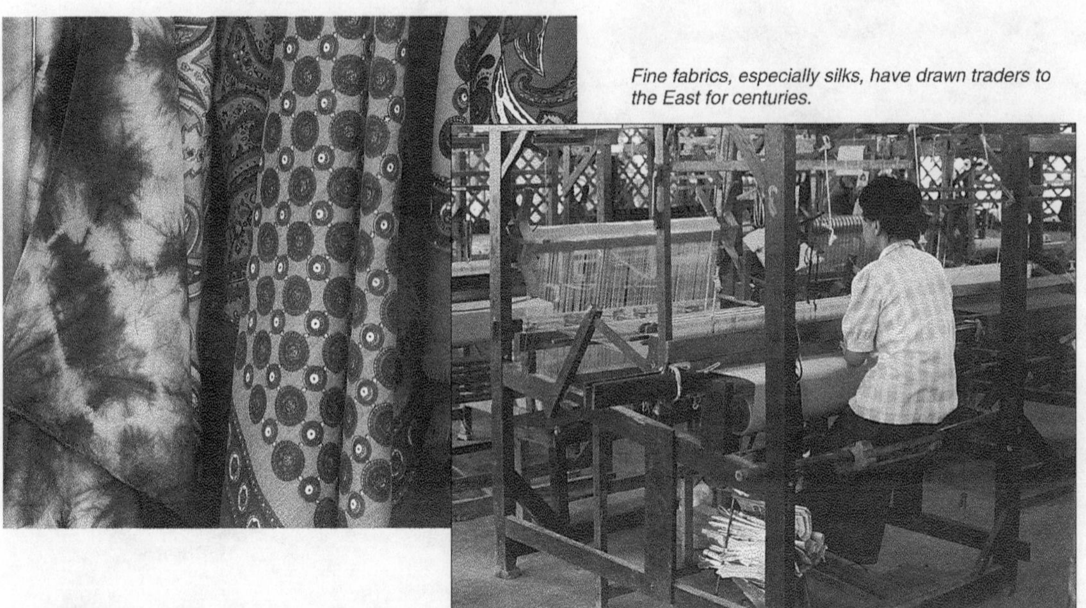

Fine fabrics, especially silks, have drawn traders to the East for centuries.

Pride—Conduct a class discussion on pride, beginning with its effects on national activities and attitudes. Then discuss the pitfalls awaiting individuals who consider themselves superior to others. The Bible has much to say about pride. In Philippians Paul warns Christians not to do things in vainglory, but to esteem others better than themselves (Phil. 2:3). In Proverbs we are told that a haughty spirit comes before a fall (Prov. 16:18). China's haughty spirit closed the nation to outside influences for centuries. In the same way, a person with a haughty spirit will be closed to influences, including the influence of the Holy Spirit. Other verses that may be of help to your students are Philippians 2:9-10, 3:7-8, 4:13; I Corinthians 10:31; and Psalm 84:11.

Section Review Answers

1. Manchu
2. Ming
3. They gained the support of the people by becoming "Chinese" instead of forcing the Chinese to become "Manchurian," and they allowed the Chinese to have a part in government.
4. Central Kingdom (or *chung kuo*)
5. It kept out the new inventions and learning of the West.

Answers will vary. The British may have been right not to kowtow to show that they believed their nation was at least as, if not more, powerful than China. Kowtowing was a symbol of utter humility which Britain certainly did not show to anyone at that time. The British may have been wrong in breaking tradition, fighting against the status quo, or showing their pride.

Section 2

Student Objectives
Students should be able to:

1. Name the drug with which the British opened trade in China.
2. Analyze the effects of opium on a population and on individuals.
3. Describe the Opium Wars.

History of the Poppy—Opium comes from the poppy flower. The poppy was grown long before opium became popular in the seventeenth century. Opium was previously used as a medicine, a poison, and a sleeping aid.

Narcotic—The definition of *narcotic* is "a drug that can dull one's senses, cause one to sleep, and become addicting."

Effects of Opium—Long-term use of opium weakens the mind and body. The longer a person uses opium, the more opium he needs to satisfy his desire. Once addicted to the drug, Chinese people did almost anything to get more. Addicts neglected business and sold things from their homes to get enough money to purchase the drug. When deprived of opium, users experienced agitation, restlessness, diarrhea, and disturbed sleep.

Sherlock Holmes—Opium use became a problem in nineteenth-century England. Sir Arthur Conan Doyle, author of the Sherlock Holmes stories, used his own experiences with opium in his stories. "The Man with the Twisted Lip" from *The Adventures of Sherlock Holmes* has several scenes that take place in the opium dens along the river in London.

Challenges to China: Western Trade

Ever since the Crusades, when Europeans were introduced to the luxuries of the Far East, they had wanted more. Explorers set out to find routes to these far-off lands. Nations set up trading companies to do business with the explorers. China, or Cathay, was one of the richest sources of these goods. Silks, spices, porcelain, and tea were in great demand in both European palaces and humble households. Following both land and sea routes, Europeans made long and hazardous journeys to the rich trading centers of the Central Kingdom.

Restrictions to Trade

Little did the early traders expect the first obstacle they met once safely in China: the Chinese did not really care to trade with them.

The beauty of the opium poppy masks the sorrow that addiction to opium and heroin causes.

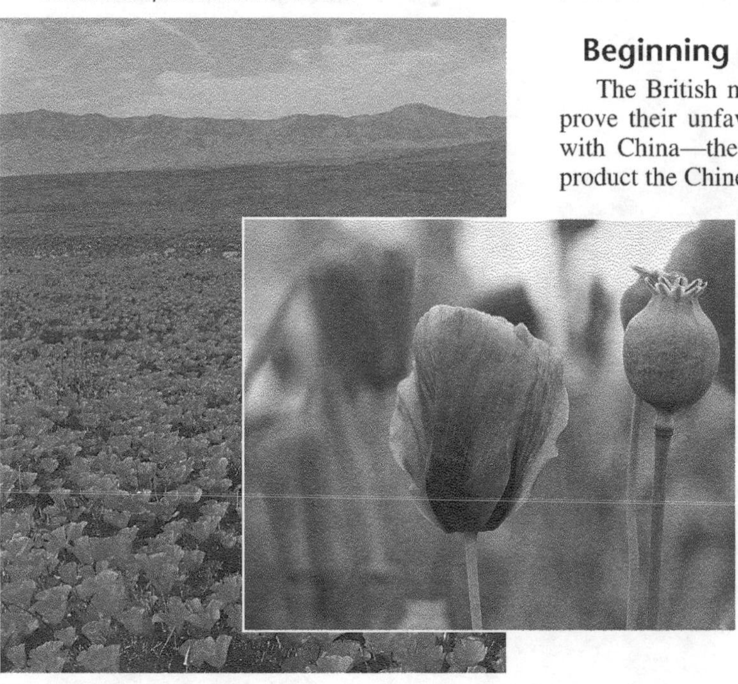

The goods of the West—woolens, metals, and some machinery—had little appeal to the Chinese. They considered themselves well supplied with all their daily needs and desires. The Chinese saw no need to grant the foreigners unlimited trading rights. In fact, they looked at trade as a privilege that could be taken away at any time.

During the eighteenth century, foreign traders were mostly limited to the port of **Canton**, the foreign trading center. The British controlled most of this trade. Their merchants lived in a specific section of the town and traded only through authorized Chinese agents. These agents set prices as high as they liked and could refuse to trade at any time. They also collected the high taxes on goods. Some of this money never showed up in the imperial treasury but stayed in the agents' pockets.

Beginning of the Opium Trade

The British merchants knew how to improve their unfavorable trading relationship with China—they simply needed to find a product the Chinese wanted. They found that product growing in India: **opium.** Opium is an addictive narcotic drug. Although sometimes used to treat disease, opium is also used as a drug that changes the user's state of mind. Usually this change brings about a false feeling of happiness and peace. Opium users desire this feeling because they believe they are escaping from their

Section 2

Materials

- Concordances
- Guest speaker, a law enforcement officer

Opium—This section deals with drugs and the correct foundation for Christian young people on this critical topic. The key to rejecting psychotropic (mind-altering) drugs is to have one's mind firmly fixed on Christ Jesus. As a class activity, use a concordance to have a Bible study on the word *mind*. Discuss the uses and effects of opium (BLM 13-1).

problems. However, this feeling is only temporary and solves no problems. Once the drug has worn off, the person still has his problems. Opium, or any other narcotic drug, is not the source of peace or answer to one's problems. The Bible tells us that salvation through Christ is the only source of peace. "And the peace of God, which passeth all understanding, shall keep your hearts and minds through Christ Jesus" (Phil. 4:7). The Christian does not need drugs to deal with his problems and should not use them for this purpose. As Philippians 4:7 promises, Christ will keep the believer's heart *and* mind.

Negotiations between Europeans and Chinese officials did little to open trade to the West.

Opium had been used in China for several centuries before the British came, mostly to treat illness. When the British began importing large amounts of the drug, the Chinese began to use opium for its narcotic (mind-changing) effect. As more people became addicted to opium, the demand for it grew. To meet the demand, the British imported more and more opium. By selling this drug, the British slowly began to make more profit on their exports to China than they spent on their imports of Chinese luxury goods. From the mid-1700s to the mid-1800s, the exporting of opium by Britain to China skyrocketed. The British went from bringing in about four hundred chests (one hundred kilograms or approximately forty-five pounds each) in 1736 to thirty thousand chests in 1850.

Chinese Response to the Opium Trade

As the opium trade grew, the Chinese government took action to stop it. Opium addiction produced many problems, especially idleness and poor production. These twin problems produced much poverty among the Chinese people. Another problem was that the Chinese people were spending more money on drugs than they were receiving from trade. This imbalance was draining China's silver reserves. (For a time the Chinese government discussed planting their own opium in China

Smoking Opium—The Chinese smoked opium in its liquid form, made by boiling the solid form. The liquid drug resembled dark molasses. Chinese smokers used a smoking pipe with a small oil lamp on top and always reclined while smoking the pipe. Stores that sold opium provided specially made platforms where patrons could smoke their purchases.

Chinese Phrases About Opium—A person who had smoked opium for many years was often referred to as "having three heads" because his shoulders became unnaturally raised, as if constantly shrugging. The Chinese term for smokers, who became very thin and bony, was "opium devils." A nineteenth-century Chinese phrase, "opium shops are more numerous than rice-shops," reflects the widespread use of opium.

Other Drugs—By now most of your students are very aware of many illegal drugs. This is as it should be, for the Bible tells us that although we are to be harmless as doves, we are to be wise as serpents (Matt. 10:16). But unfortunately, many times students are not wise; they just have some knowledge. This knowledge is not always accurate. By discussing other drugs with your students, you will give them a clearer picture of drugs and their effects, not only on the drug user, but also on his family and friends and on society as a whole. Take time to talk about this vital issue and offer your counsel for any questions at any other time.

Law Enforcement—As time allows, ask a law enforcement officer to come speak to your class on illegal drugs. He may speak on the types, effects, and punishments for dealers as well as other topics.

Alcohol and Opium—The British fully realized the harm they were causing by introducing opium into China. People from Britain who visited China saw that the effects of drinking alcohol were different from the effects of smoking opium. In their view, opium users in China were worse off than British drinkers because opium users almost always became addicted to the drug and neglected all other pursuits to satisfy their addiction.

Opium Users—In a public announcement issued in 1839, Imperial High Commissioner Lin observed the widespread use of opium; he noted that men and women, slaves and gentry used opium.

The harbor of Canton was filled with foreign trading ships ready to load goods from their respective trading houses. What foreign countries are represented by the flags?

to keep the money in the country.) The emperor ordered all opium sales to stop and made it illegal to import. However, the greed of both British and Chinese merchants caused them to keep up the trade, usually by smuggling the drug in along the coast.

Finally, the Chinese emperor appointed **Lin Tse-hsü** as his High Commissioner. Lin Tse-hsü took a message of prohibition and enforcement to the British. On March 10, 1839, Lin came to Canton to confront British traders with a question: "How dare you bring your country's vile opium into China, cheating and harming our people?" Then he made two demands. First, the British traders were to hand over all their unsold opium. Second, the British were to stop the import of opium into China. "If you continue, the opium will be confiscated, and those involved will be decapitated," said Lin.

Lin Tse-hsü gave the British two weeks to comply with the proclamation. The British had heard proclamations before and assumed that Lin was as corrupt as other politicians had been. Imagine their surprise when Lin ordered all transport to and from Canton to stop and ordered Chinese troops to surround the thirteen foreign factories (trade houses) in Canton. He then ordered all of the Chinese workers out of the factory and forbade the sale of food to those inside. The British trading houses became prisons.

At this point, Captain Charles Elliot, the English Superintendent of Trade, made a decision that affected British/Chinese negotiations later. Rather than tell the British merchants to turn their opium supply over to the Chinese directly, Elliot had them turn it over to him. This made the opium property of the British government. Then Elliot gave Lin access to the opium.

With the opium now in Lin's hands, Elliot once again expected Lin to be as corrupt as his predecessors. Lin surprised the British

Comparison—Have the students compare and contrast drinking alcohol and using a mind-altering drug such as opium. Is one morally worse than the other? Are the effects different? Alcohol use is a vital issue (probably even more so than drug use among Christian students) that needs to be discussed. The students need to have a correct and informed belief about alcohol and its consumption. You may also wish to discuss the errors of the social-drinking philosophy.

Reasons for Exploration and Imperialism—Have students review reasons for exploration. How do these reasons compare to the reason for imperialism? *(Reasons for both include money, land, religious freedom, and adventure.)*

once more by having two huge pools dug. He then had the water salted, the opium poured in, and lime added. This decomposed the opium. When the twenty-three day process was over, Lin had channels opened from the pools to the ocean and let the tide carry the residue out to sea.

Feeling that he had achieved a victory over the British, Lin presented a document for Captain Elliot to sign. It was an agreement that the British would honor Chinese regulations. Elliot refused to sign. He sent a letter to England and waited for a response.

The response came in the summer. The British blockaded (blocked trade from entering the harbor of) Canton and then went north to capture the city of Tinghai. The Emperor, angry with Lin for the situation, appointed a new negotiator, Ch'i-shan. When Ch'i-shan went onboard a British ship and saw the weapons, he quickly realized that the Chinese were outgunned. To prevent a total takeover, Ch'i-shan suggested that the Emperor adopt a policy of appeasement (to satisfy or calm) toward the British.

The Chinese offered to return to their former trading policy and to pay the British a small sum of money for their inconvenience. But the British saw the opportunity for gaining much more control in China. Since Captain Elliot had had all the opium turned over to the British government, the British now demanded to be paid for the "British" opium that had been destroyed. They also insisted that they be given the city of Hong Kong and access to other ports of trade.

The Chinese refused, and war broke out. Called the **Opium War,** the fighting lasted three years (1839-42). British military power proved superior, and the Chinese were defeated. The peace treaty, the **Treaty of Nanking,** signed at the end of the war ended hostility and gave in to the British demands.

A second opium war a few years later resulted in more open ports. At that time inland China was also opened for the first time to both trade and travel by foreigners. Through these wars the Western nations forced China to open. Although the Europeans obtained the trade rights they desired, they did not encourage good relations between China and the West. Resentment against the foreigners grew and led to many problems in China.

Severe Punishment for Opium Dealers—A 1729 Chinese edict against opium stated that all owners of opium stores would be strangled, while their employees would receive as punishment one hundred lashes with the bamboo, a three-month imprisonment, and banishment. However, addicts were not punished. American laws tend to deal harshly with the user, but the dealer often is not caught.

Section Review

1. What goods of the Far East did Europeans want? Why did the Chinese refuse to grant unlimited trading?
2. What European nation controlled much of the China trade?
3. How did Chinese agents cheat the European traders?
4. What trade item did the English introduce to solve their trade problem?
5. What wars were caused by the British "solution"?

How did the Chinese feel about foreign powers before the British came to China? List at least three ways that the British increased the Chinese hatred of foreigners.

Economics—Conduct a discussion about trade. Ask the students if they can give any examples of trade practices today that are similar to those of Britain with China during this period.

Section Review Answers

1. silks, spices, porcelain, and tea; they felt they had all they needed and that trade was a privilege to the foreigners
2. Great Britain
3. They set high prices and pocketed tax money.
4. opium
5. the Opium Wars

The Chinese felt that all foreigners were "outer barbarians" who came to bring tribute to them. The Chinese believed that China was the center of the world; therefore, it must have been the most powerful nation as well. The British increased Chinese hatred of foreigners by selling addictive opium, by disobeying the government, and by forcing China to open.

Student Objectives
Students should be able to:
1. Locate Southeast Asia on a map.
2. Use a relief map to determine elevation.

Asia—Remind your students of Asia's divisions. Generally we refer to South Asia, Southeast Asia, and East Asia. Usually we do not call Russia "northern Asia," although technically it is and may be referred to as such. Western Asia is the Middle East; hence, Jews are classified as an oriental people. Asian customs are found throughout all these lands.

SETTINGS—Southeast Asia

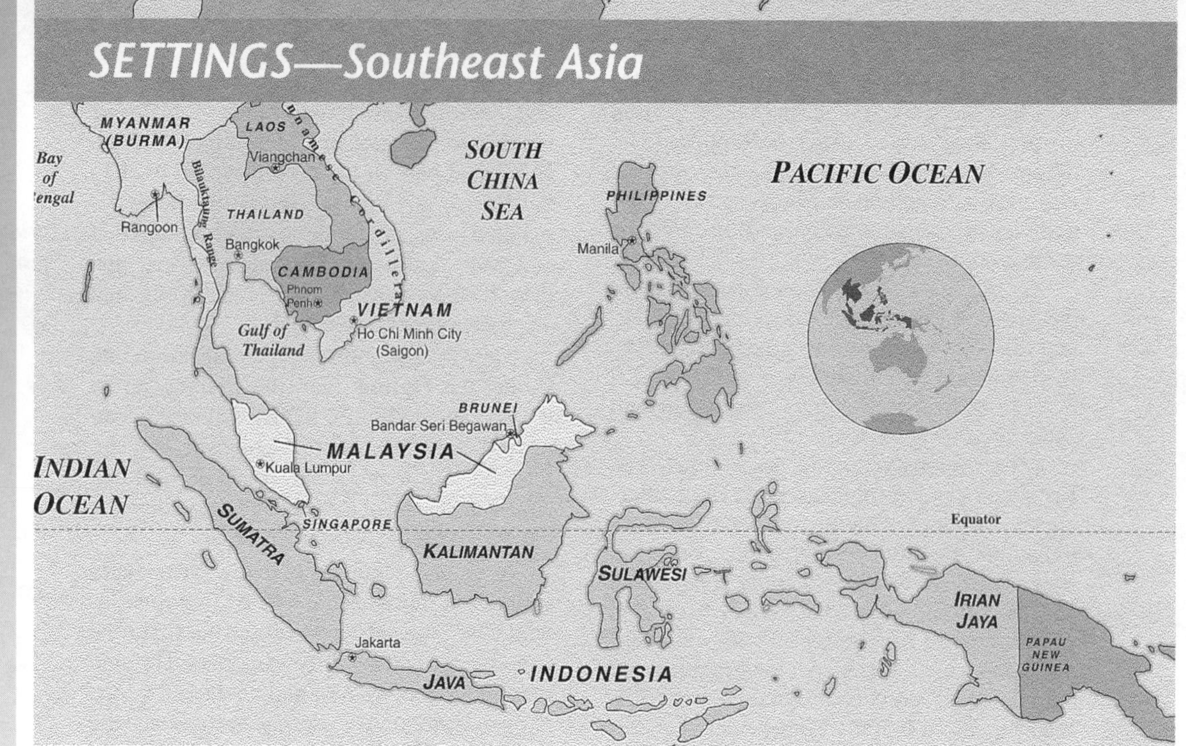

Location—The majority of the region called Southeast Asia lies between the tropic of Cancer and the equator. The region is bordered by China in the north, the Bay of Bengal and the Indian Ocean in the west and south, and the Pacific Ocean in the east. Southeast Asia includes Myanmar, Thailand, Laos, Vietnam, Cambodia, Malaysia, Singapore, the islands of Indonesia, and the Philippines.

Climate—Unlike most regions of its size, Southeast Asia has a fairly uniform climate. The region's climate is tropical. Rain forest (tropical wet) climate occurs in all the islands and up both coasts of the mainland. Savanna (tropical wet and dry) climate occurs between the **cordilleras** (parallel mountain ranges). Rain occurs an average of two hundred days per year, and the region receives approximately eighty inches of rain per year. Areas of humid subtropical climate are found in the north along with the highland climate in the higher elevations.

Topography—Thailand's long peninsula and the islands of Southeast Asia are known as the Malay Peninsula and the Malay **Archipelago** (a large cluster of islands). The Malay Archipelago is part of the **"Ring of Fire"**—the area in the Pacific known for volcanic and seismic (earthquake) activity. The Annamese Cordillera, Bilauktaung Range, and Arakan Range divide the fertile regions of the mainland. Few of the mountains in these ranges reach over ten thousand feet.

Natural Resources—Southeast Asia supplies most of the world's teakwood. Teakwood is a very hard, dense wood used for building ships and furniture. Mahogany, rubber, and ebony trees are also abundant. The rivers of the mainland and Malay Archipelago are used in hydroelectric production. The region also has deposits of coal, oil, and tin.

Materials

- Wall map of Asia or Southeast Asia (BLM 13-2)
- Transparencies for Chapter 13

Map Activity—Use map 13-C from the Activities Manual to reinforce the geography lesson.

Going Beyond—Read the Settings pages on Southeast Asia with your students and answer the questions. Use a relief map of Asia (TT 13-A) to teach the students to read and understand relief maps. Let the students examine the map for a few moments and then ask what they think the colors on the map signify. *(brown—mountains or high elevation; lighter brown—lower elevation; green—flatland close to sea level)* Discuss the topographical factors that led to China's isolation.

Ring of Fire—Using a map of the Pacific region, point out the perimeter of the Ring of Fire (BLM 13-3).

Geography & Culture—The Chinese greatly affected the eastern mainland of Southeast Asia, especially Vietnam. The Chinese brought information about fertilizers and other rice-growing techniques to the area. Rice farms in Vietnam are very productive. However, plowing is still done with water buffalo, and planting is done by hand.

Traders from the Arabian Peninsula came to the Malay Peninsula and Archipelago. Their contact brought not only trade but also the religion of Islam, which has become dominant in the region. Buddhism and Hinduism were brought to Southeast Asia from China and India.

Much of the region was divided by imperial powers in the eighteenth and nineteenth centuries. Imperialists introduced new technology, products, and ethnic diversity. Since the breakup of imperialist control, Southeast Asia has had to deal with self-government and ethnic conflict.

Settings Review

1. What type of climate is most widespread in Southeast Asia?
2. What is a term used for parallel mountain ranges?
3. What is an archipelago?
4. What Pacific area of high volcanic and earthquake activity is the Malay Peninsula a part of?

Remembering what you read about climate and rainfall in Southeast Asia, give one practical reason that Southeast Asian farmers would prefer to plant by hand and use water buffalos.

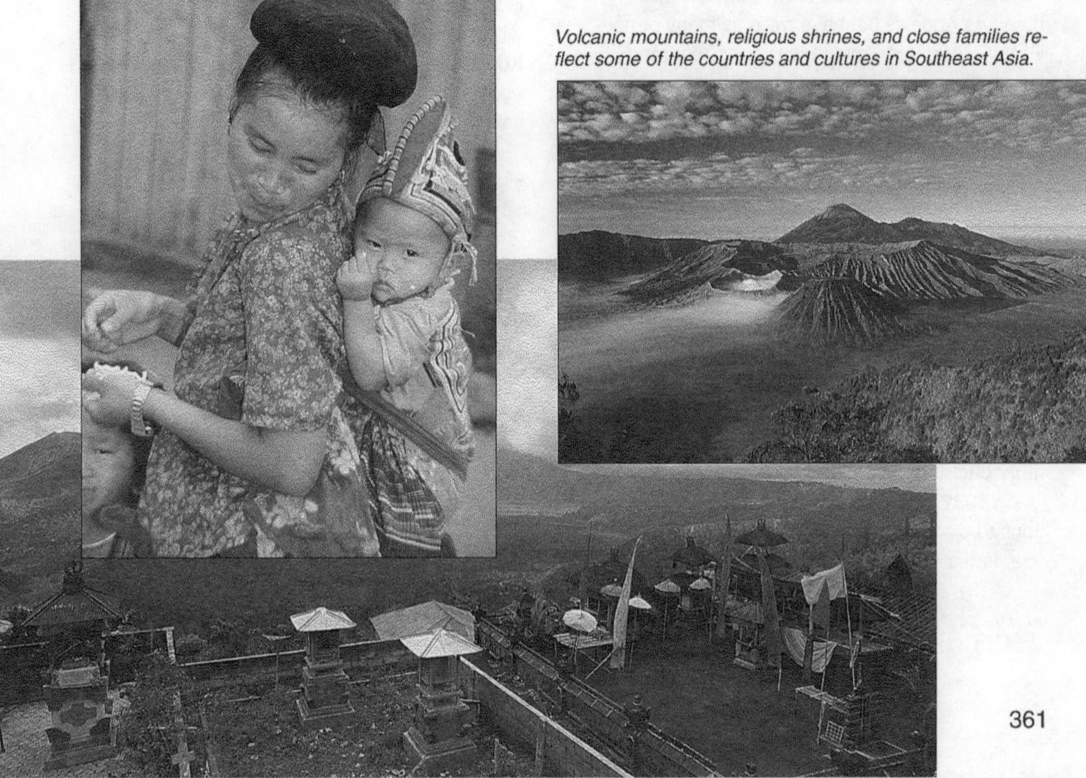

Volcanic mountains, religious shrines, and close families reflect some of the countries and cultures in Southeast Asia.

361

Settings Review Answers

1. tropical
2. cordilleras
3. a large cluster of islands
4. "Ring of Fire"

Answers will vary. Modern machines would probably not work or would become stuck in the standing water of Southeast Asia.

SECTION 3

Student Objectives
Students should be able to

1. Identify the first missionaries to China.
2. Evaluate Hudson Taylor's philosophy of becoming like the natives.

INTERPRETATIONS

British Control of Hong Kong

When the British and Chinese sealed the Treaty of Nanking, Hong Kong became the first portion of China owned by the British Empire. By 1860 further treaties gave England possession of Kowloon Peninsula, but Britain needed more mainland territory to keep Hong Kong self-sufficient. In 1898 Britain signed a ninety-nine-year lease with China for the New Territories. It is the end of this lease that has caused upheaval for Hong Kong.

Britain leased the New Territories to help support the growing population in Hong Kong. The empty island that Captain Elliot declared would be free of tariffs (trade taxes) soon became filled with more people than Hong Kong's resources could support. If you have ever been to Los Angeles, California, you know how crowded that city is. Hong Kong and its surrounding territories have almost one hundred fewer square miles than Los Angeles but have twice as many people. Today, Hong Kong must pipe water from mainland China, buy all its food from other countries, and import all its raw materials for industry.

Despite these seeming handicaps, Hong Kong

- ranks in the top ten countries for average household income.
- is the world's busiest container port.
- operates one of the world's largest gold bullion markets.
- has two of the world's top ten billionaires.

Seeing these statistics should help you understand why England would want to retain control of Hong Kong and why China would want the territory back.

In 1982 China and England began negotiations to discuss the ending of the ninety-nine-year lease. The **Sino-British Joint Declaration** (*Sino* is another word for China) signed in 1984 stated that England would give up all control of Hong Kong, Kowloon, and the New Territories with the guarantee that China would allow Hong Kong to retain control of its own government and economy for the next fifty years. This policy is called "one country, two systems."

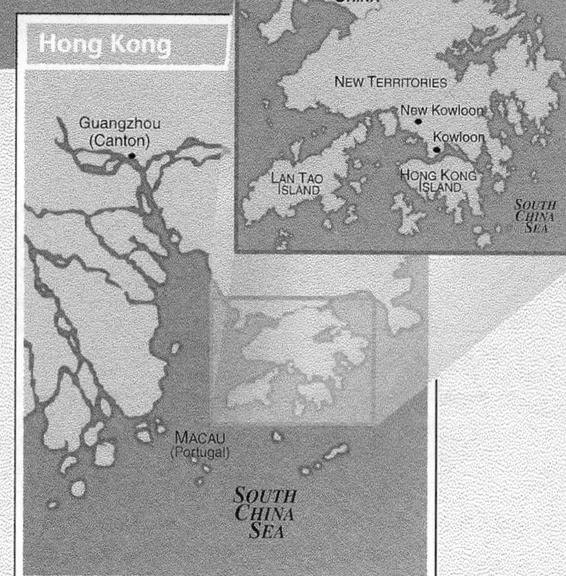

Much to China's dismay, Britain boosted Hong Kong's democracy during the thirteen years before 1997 to prepare it for self-rule. Britain turned more and more power over to the Hong Kong people by adding more natives of Hong Kong to the Legislative Council (the governing body of Hong Kong). China argued that the new government was not part of the agreement and vowed to replace the Legislative Council in 1997.

The impact of the Chinese takeover of Hong Kong will be closely analyzed over the next several years. It will also affect the return of Macau (a Portuguese holding) to Chinese control in 1999 and further attempts by China to control Taiwan.

SECTION 3

Materials

- Periodical article about Hong Kong from July 1997
- Chopsticks

Hong Kong—Look in periodicals from July 1997 to read accounts of the return of Hong Kong to China. Students will find many different opinions portrayed by the authors as to whether this was a good thing. Discuss any changes that have occurred in Hong Kong since China regained control, especially economic changes. If anything is currently in world news about the situation, discuss it with your students.

Challenges to China: Christian Missions

The treaties made after the Opium Wars encouraged both Western traders and Western missionaries to come to China. Few missionaries had come before that time. The earliest was **Robert Morrison,** who arrived in China in 1807. Although he worked for many years, he saw few converts. The strong power of Confucianism, Taoism, Buddhism, and ancestor worship bound many Chinese in their sins.

Hudson Taylor used new methods to bring the gospel to the Chinese people.

Morrison's greatest contribution to Chinese missions was a Chinese translation of the Bible and several books on Chinese language and grammar. His faithful work in this difficult language helped later missionaries learn Chinese.

Soon other missionaries came to China, sent out by the same missionary societies that had sent men and women to India. These missionaries usually settled in the ports opened up by the treaties. They lived in special sections of the towns reserved for foreigners. From there they preached, taught, and gave medical care to many Chinese. They aided the Chinese during times of famine and treated many opium addicts. The missionaries also ministered to the many foreign traders and their families in China.

Hudson Taylor

One young English missionary came to China from England with a great burden for the Chinese people. After a six-month ocean voyage, **Hudson Taylor** settled in at the mission compound in 1853. Taylor spent many hours learning to speak and read Chinese. He also accompanied other missionaries on preaching tours. As he went out among the Chinese people, Taylor became aware that the people immediately rejected him because of his European clothing. He did not want the Chinese to reject Christianity simply because they thought it was a Western idea. He began to pray for wisdom to know how to reach the people. After reading I Corinthians 9:22 where Paul says he was "made all things to all men," Hudson Taylor decided to give up his Western attire to look more Chinese. He wrote the following letter to his sister Amelia about the results of his decision.

"Where Have You Been?"—A Chinese convert asked Hudson Taylor how long his people had known the truth. Taylor replied that people in England had known the gospel for hundreds of years. The Chinese man was shocked. He could not believe that the English had not brought the Word to China sooner. He told Hudson Taylor that his father had searched for the truth for twenty years and died without it. Ask your students to make the application for themselves: What does this story say to Christians about witnessing?

Translation—Using the bulletin board suggested at the beginning of this chapter or making up your own key, provide a sentence for the students to translate. Direct them to translate the sentence. Discuss the immense amount of time required in actual translation work. Point out that Morrison and other translators did not necessarily have a key or a dictionary.

For the Record—In the days before tape recorders and television cameras, people relied on pen and paper to record their activities, thoughts, and feelings in journals and letters. Although we can record our lives on tape, keeping a written record is not just a thing of the past. Thankfully, we have these records from which to study history.

China Inland Mission—*The Lord Stood By Me,* compiled by the China Inland Mission, relates stories of care and protection by God. The following story entitled "Dead End," by Dora J. Hatton, is one example:

"When our district in West Yunnan was invaded by the Japanese, we hid in a number of different places to avoid capture by the enemy. On several occasions the Lord had wonderfully preserved us and had used apparent calamities to keep us from falling into Japanese hands.

"At one time we were making an attempt to cross the river to safety on the Chinese side. The Chinese general had arranged to send a military escort to meet us at the city of Pingka. Without this escort no one was permitted to cross the Salween River. Just as we planned to set out for Pingka, our little daughter became seriously ill, and we knew she could not be moved for at least two months. We wondered what our waiting escort would think when we failed to arrive. A few days later we heard that the Japanese had made a raid upon Pingka on that very day and had prevented our escort from crossing the river to meet us. Had we gone into the city as planned it would have been to find not our Chinese military escort, but hundreds of Japanese soldiers waiting for us.

We began then to wonder if the Lord really wanted us to leave Japanese-occupied territory. Perhaps He still had a work for us to do there, so we prayed that if we should leave for the Chinese side, He would do something to thrust us out. Otherwise we were willing to stay. Some time later the Japanese found out where we were and sent a letter ordering our return to a city where they were stationed. This would mean internment for us, and perhaps worse. We had

Hai-Yen City, August 28, 1855

My Dear Amelia—By way of surprise I mean to write you a letter—for I know you have never received one before from a man with a long tail and a shaven head! But lest your head should be bewildered with conjectures, I had better tell you at once that on Thursday last at 11 P.M. I resigned my locks to the barber, dyed my hair a good black, and in the morning had a proper *queue* [long braided pigtail] plaited in with my own, and a quantity of heavy silk to lengthen it out according to Chinese custom. Then, in Chinese dress, I set out with Dr. Parker, accompanying him about a hundred miles on his way to Ning-po. This journey we made an occasion for evangelistic work, and now that I am returning alone I hope to have even better facilities for book-distribution and preaching.

But I have not commenced the recital of my tribulations, and as there is some doubt as to whether they will all go into a single letter, the sooner I begin the better.

First, then, it is a very sore thing to have one's head shaved for the first time, especially if the skin is irritable with prickly heat. And I can assure you that the subsequent application of hair-dye for five or six hours does not do much to soothe the irritation. But when it comes to combing out the remaining hair which has been allowed to grow longer than usual, the climax is reached! But there are no gains without pains, and certainly if suffering for a thing makes it dearer, I shall regard my *queue* when I attain one with no small amount of pride and affection.

Secondly, . . . you no longer wonder that many Chinese in the employ of Europeans wear foreign shoes and stockings as soon as they can get them. For native socks are made of calico and of course are not elastic . . . and average toes decidedly object to be squeezed out of shape, nor do one's heels appreciate their low position in perfectly flat-soled heels. Next come the breeches—but oh, what unheard-of garments! Mine are two feet too wide for me around the waist, which amplitude is laid in a fold in front, and kept in place by a strong girdle. The legs are short not coming much below the knee, and wide in proportion with the waist measurement. Tucked into the long, white socks, they have a bloomer-like fulness capable, as Dr. Parker remarked, of storing a fortnight's provisions! No shirt is worn. But a white washing-jacket, with sleeves as wide as ladies affected twenty years ago, supplies its place. And over all goes a heavy silk gown of some rich or delicate colour, with sleeves equally wide and reaching some twelve or fifteen inches beyond the tips of one's fingers—folded back of course when the hands are in use. Unfortunately no cap or hat is used at this season of the year, except on state occasions, which is trying as the sun is awfully hot.

Wednesday, August 29

While still with Dr. Parker on the way to Hwang-chow Bay I was frequently recognized as a foreigner, because of having to speak to him in English, but to-day in going about Hai-yen City no one even guessed that such a being was near. It was not until I began to distribute books and see patients that I became known. Then of course my men were asked where I came from, and the news soon spread. Dressed in this way one is not so much respected at first sight as one might be in foreign clothing. But a little medical work soon puts that all right, and it is evidently to be one's chief help for the interior. Women and children, it seems to me, manifest more readiness to come for medical aid now than they did before . . . and in this way, too, I think the native costume will be of service

Writing—Have the students practice their personal writing skills by writing a journal entry or letter about an activity or idea that means much to them. The following list provides possible topics:

- Salvation experience
- Meeting a stranger
- Visiting relatives
- Going on a trip
- Witnessing to someone
- Participating in a church service
- Playing in a ball game
- Playing a musical instrument
- Recalling a special family activity

Taylor knew that his decision would be unpopular with the other missionaries. They would not agree with him. Yet he knew God had led him in making the decision. He wrote in his journal at this time, "And why should a foreign aspect be given to Christianity? . . . It is not the denationalization but the Christianization of these people we seek."

As he thought of "a million a month dying without God," Taylor's burden soon turned to China's interior, where most Europeans did not go. Acting on faith that God would supply his needs, Taylor began the **China Inland Mission** (C.I.M.) with a handful of dedicated men and women. Most C.I.M. missionaries followed Taylor's example of wearing Chinese clothing, eating with chopsticks, and using Chinese manners.

Many Chinese Christians today meet in house churches to avoid persecution.

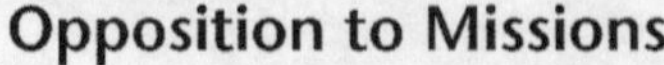

Opposition to Missions

The Chinese did not always kindly receive Hudson Taylor and the other missionaries. The incident told about at the beginning of this chapter shows the opposition they sometimes faced. Against these threats, the missionaries tried to show the Chinese that they loved them and that God loved them even more. Often their testimony in returning good for evil won them a hearing and then converts among the people. However, opposition to them and to God's Word continued.

Section Review

1. Who was the first Christian missionary to China?
2. What was his greatest accomplishment there?
3. How did Hudson Taylor's method of reaching the Chinese differ from the methods of other missionaries?
4. How did the missionaries respond to the hatred manifested by some Chinese?

Why do you think that Hudson Taylor's decision to dress like the Chinese made such an impact on his ministry?

already been warned that the Japanese were regarding us as spies for the Chinese government. . . . Our tribal friends knew how dangerous our position would be if we were taken by the Japanese. They agreed to help us flee in the opposite direction.

On that first day we had to travel twenty-five miles. After walking twenty miles we came to a place where three paths branched out ahead. Our Lisu friends were bewildered. The regular path they knew well, but on that day we had traveled by a little-used road in order to avoid meeting the Japanese. They examined those three paths and decided to take the most clearly defined of the three. We walked along that path for an hour when it suddenly faded into nothing. It was only a goat track leading to good pasture! It was already getting dark and there was no chance of reaching the city that night. We were very disappointed and concerned, and the Lisu Christians who felt responsible for the mistake were down hearted. My husband said, "Don't feel upset about this. All the way along the road today I have felt a burden of prayer about this journey. Perhaps this very mistake is the Lord's answer to prayer." And so it proved to be. On that day the Japanese had entered the city we were bound for! Finding shelter that night in a mountain hut far off the beaten track, we were delivered again from capture.

Chopsticks—Practice eating a meal with chopsticks. These are usually available at any specialty store or supermarket. This can be done in conjunction with the recipe preparation at the end of the chapter.

Section Review Answers

1. Robert Morrison
2. Chinese translation of the Bible and several books on Chinese language and grammar
3. He dressed and became as much like the natives as he could.
4. tried to show their love and God's love

Answers will vary. Hudson Taylor was able to reach more Chinese by dressing like them. They did not want to accept any foreigners or foreign ideas, so Taylor made himself seem as Chinese as possible. Not only would the Chinese not be distracted by his clothing, but some would realize his great care and concern to do this for them.

SECTION 4

Student Objectives
Students should be able to

1. Describe the Taiping Rebellion and identify both its leader and the Manchu leader.
2. Analyze the decline of the Manchu dynasty.

Reaction to Foreign Influence—Defeat in war, and the resulting increase in foreign influence combined with famine and high taxes to set the stage for the Boxer Rebellion. Never pleased with the presence of foreigners, many Chinese resented even more the growing foreign power in government and influence in culture. They hated and feared the change they saw coming.

There had been opposition to foreign incursions since China opened her doors to the West. Of course, the Chinese attitude of superiority motivated some of the opposition, but often the foreigners earned Chinese disapproval. The Portuguese, for instance, were the first Europeans to settle in China, establishing trading centers on the coast. Much of their time, however, they spent looting cities and villages rather than trading with them. They were eventually driven out of China. A group of Dutch traders was also expelled because of misdeeds.

The Chinese also resisted attempts at modernization. Often the resentment was greatest in rural, more conservative areas. One incident illustrates the extent of the reaction against modernization. The British built a railroad line across a particular province. The local people were opposed to the railroad because they thought that violating the beauty of the land brought bad luck. There was so much protest that the government finally purchased the railroad line, had it dismantled, and shipped it to Taiwan, where it was thrown into a lake.

The Decline of the Manchu Dynasty

Throughout the nineteenth century, the Manchu rulers were losing power in China. Several conditions in China showed that the Manchus were coming to the end of their dynastic cycle and that a change in government would soon take place. Had the Manchus accepted the changing times and worked with the new conditions, their fall might have been stopped. However, they were unwilling to change and clung to the old traditions of their culture. They believed their way to be superior to any other way.

Weakness Inside China

Throughout China the people rebelled and revolted to show their discontent with the Manchu government. The heavy taxation and government corruption especially angered the people. Another major problem was famine. China's population had grown greatly during this time, but the amount of farmland had not increased. Sometimes crops did not produce enough for a peasant to pay taxes and feed his family. Hungry and angry peasants often willingly joined leaders in rebelling against the government.

One rebellious uprising was initiated by a frustrated student, **Hung Hsiu-chuan.** Hung was a gifted student and desired to go into government service. He studied hard and could have passed any government exam except that, along with the test, the officials in charge expected to be bribed. Hung, whose poor family was loyal to the old Ming dynasty, saw his failure directly attached to the corrupt Manchu dynasty.

Shortly after Hung realized that his dream to become a government scholar would not come true, he became seriously ill. In a delirious (hallucinating) fever, Hung saw himself in the "Thirty-third Heaven." There he was met by a man called the Venerable in Years (*venerable* means "revered" or "respected"). The Venerable in Years gave Hung a sword and told him to exterminate the demon-worshipers who had rebelled against the Venerable in Years. With the help of the Venerable in Years's son, Hung saw himself doing battle against demon forces. When the battle was over, the Venerable in Years told Hung to return to earth and be encouraged, "for you are my son."

When Hung recovered from his fever, he was a new man with a purpose. He felt called to relieve the people's distress—the oppression

Historically, wealthy aristocratic families lived off the taxes of poor farmers. Undependable annual rains made famine a regular event but affected the farmers the most.

SECTION 4

Materials

- Transparencies for Chapter 13

Close to Christianity?—Compare Hung's vision to Christianity. What are some similar points? *(The Lord does battle against the powers of Satan; Hung became a child of God, etc.)* What are some very different points? *(Hung became the younger brother of Christ; he made a new testament of his revelations and referred to the actual New Testament as the "Former Testament.")* How do we know that Hung's "religion" was wrong? *(He added to the Scripture; he valued his own ideas and his supposed revelation above Christ.)*

Charles Gordon received the Yellow Riding Jacket of the Imperial Army in honor of his leadership during the Taiping Rebellion.

of the Manchus. Shortly after this change, Hung came in contact with a Chinese Christian who shared with Hung a Chinese Bible. Hung began reading the Old Testament and believed it confirmed his vision. He felt that he had met with God and that God had chosen him for a son.

Hung wanted to know more about the Christian religion. The missionaries he met saw the falsehood in Hung's vision. When they pointed it out, Hung left them and produced his own doctrines. He formed a cult called the God Worshipper's Society. In Hung's cult, God was the Father, Christ was the Son and Elder Brother, and Hung was the Younger Brother. He renamed the New Testament the Former Testament and called his own "revelations" the New Testament.

Encouraged by the weakness that was evident in Manchurian dealings with the British during the first Opium War and frustrated by government response to the famine of 1849-50, people began to flock to Hung's new religion and cause. By 1851 Hung had a ten-thousand-man army that was discontent and desired revenge on the Manchurians. The rebels cut off their pigtails and wore their hair loose in open rebellion to the Manchu.

The **Taiping** (ty PING) **Rebellion** lasted from 1851 to 1864. It has been estimated that in the prolonged fighting twenty to thirty million people lost their lives. Finally, corruption of the rebellion's leadership caused dissatisfaction with the Taiping cause. Hung committed suicide in June 1864, before his besieged capital, Nanking, fell into Imperial Army control.

Another character in the sequence of events surrounding the Taiping Rebellion was **Charles Gordon**, also known as "Chinese Gordon." A British officer, Gordon was given command of the "Ever Victorious Army" of the Manchus. Gordon's discipline and strategy helped lead the army to victory over the rebels.

Gordon made a good impression on the Chinese. Commander Li of the Imperial Army wrote in his diary of Gordon, "[He is] a direct blessing from Heaven. . . . He is superior in manner and bearing to any of the foreigners I have come into contact with and does not show outwardly that conceit which makes most of them repugnant in my sight." For his leadership, Empress Tz'u-hsi awarded Gordon the Yellow Riding Jacket, the highest order of the empire.

The End of the Taiping Rebellion—The city of Nanking was besieged for several years. Just before it was taken, Hung tried to encourage his starving troops. He said, "I have at my command an angelic host of a million strong: how then could one hundred thousand or so of these unholy Imperialists enter the city?" When the people begged for food, Hung told them to eat "sweet dew"—grass. He broke his pearl necklaces and threw the pearls to his troops. The men cried because they could not eat the pearls, nor could they buy food with them. When the city was taken on July 19, 1864, General Tseng reported that "not a single rebel surrendered. Many buried themselves alive rather than be taken." The body of Hung, the Heavenly King of the Heavenly Kingdom of Great Peace, was found lying in the sewer.

Character—What characteristics of Gordon were greatly admired by the Chinese? *(good discipline and strategy, not arrogant)* Why was he so well liked by people who typically hated foreigners? *(They were impressed that he did not force Western values on them.)* What do you think are the pros and cons of his position?

BACKGROUNDS

The Opening of Japan

On July 8, 1853, the Japanese people near the city of Yedo (modern Tokyo) were busy about their daily tasks. Fishing boats bobbed up and down off the coast as their crews hauled in catches of fish, crabs, oysters, and other seafoods. Life in Japan had changed little in the past two hundred years. In the 1600s, the ruler of Japan, the shogun, had decreed that no foreigners would be allowed into Japan and that no Japanese could leave the islands.

That morning, however, the course of Japanese history changed dramatically. On the horizon appeared several huge, black ships. They drew near to the harbor, then stopped and anchored off the coast. When Japanese officials sailed out to investigate, they found that the vessels were American warships. The commander, Commodore Matthew Perry, informed the shogun that he had been sent by the government of the United States to open trade relations with Japan. He would return the next year, Perry said, for the Japanese answer.

Perry did return as promised—with an even larger fleet. Some Japanese officials urged the shogun to drive out these "barbarians" and preserve Japan's isolation. Others realized that resistance would be difficult, if not impossible. Some even welcomed the Americans eagerly and greeted the opening of trade with the rest of the world. Faced with the American show of strength, the shogun gave in. By the Treaty of Kanagawa (1854) the United States received the desired trading privileges, and two hundred years of Japanese isolation came to an end. Unlike China, Japan accepted many Western ways. Soon the Japanese adopted Western styles in government, war, industry—even in fashion and diet. Within a few years Japan had become the most prosperous and powerful nation in Asia. It even joined the ranks of the Europeans in laying claim to portions of China. Perry's mission had an additional effect: Christian missionaries entered Japan and carried the gospel to many lost people who had never heard of Christ.

Japanese boats paddle out to investigate the black ships anchored in the harbor.

Japan's Continued Westernization—Remind students to look in Chapter 17 for the later effects of Japanese Westernization.

Pressures from Outside China

As foreign nations saw the Manchu dynasty weakening, they decided to take advantage of China. As you read in the Backgrounds page (p. 368), when Japan ended its years of isolation from the West, it began to modernize in many ways. One of the ways it modernized was in its military machinery and techniques. This gave Japan an advantage over China when Japan decided to seize control of Korea.

For years Korea had been under moderate Chinese control. In 1876 Japan forced a treaty of independence on Korea. China immediately began to maneuver to retain control. When a Korean secret society rebelled against the pro-Chinese king, he called for China to send troops to help. The Japanese also sent troops, and in 1894 the **Sino-Japan War** began. The result of this war was the resounding defeat of Chinese land and sea forces and humiliation for the Manchu government. In the peace agreement, Korea was left to Japanese influence, and Japan received Taiwan as well as other territories. Fearing that Japan would seek control of more Chinese territory, European countries with interest in China sought ways to claim territory for themselves and establish **spheres of influence** in China.

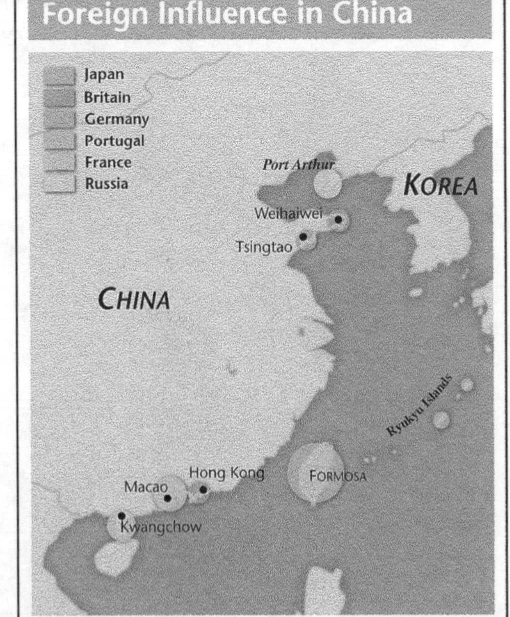

Like children eyeing a huge melon, each nation demanded a "slice" of China. Britain, France, Germany, and Russia all chose areas they wished to control. The desire to establish such spheres of influence led to rivalry not only with China but also among the negotiators. The weak Manchu government had little say in these decisions except to give away land. It seemed that China would be carved up and given to the Europeans, but the tensions displayed in China would soon erupt on a larger scale with the outbreak of World War I.

The actions of these nations plus the weaknesses of the Manchu rulers increased the people's resentment toward foreigners and their own discontent with the government. The pot of Chinese unrest was beginning to boil.

Uncle Sam holds back European powers in order to encourage free trade.

Sino-Japanese War—The group that led the rebellion was the Tonghak Society. When Japan and China both came "to the rescue," Japan attacked the palace at Seoul and replaced the royal family with a new government. The Korean government repudiated its former treaties with China and asked for Japanese assistance in removing Chinese troops. Pushed out of Pyongyang, the Chinese also lost at the Battle of the Yalu River. The Japanese then captured Port Arthur and won the Battle of Weihaiwei. China was forced to surrender and gave much land to the Japanese, though not as much as the Japanese wanted.

****

For a color version of the map on this page, see page A8 in the Appendix.

Foreign Influence—Look at the map on this page (or use TT 13-B) and discuss the various foreign influences in China. Ask your students questions that will help them review the material.

A Look at the Future—Glance ahead at Chapter 17. There you will find more about Japan and her interests in Russia and China. You will see how she became involved in World War II and was eventually defeated. Keep this in mind as you finish this chapter.

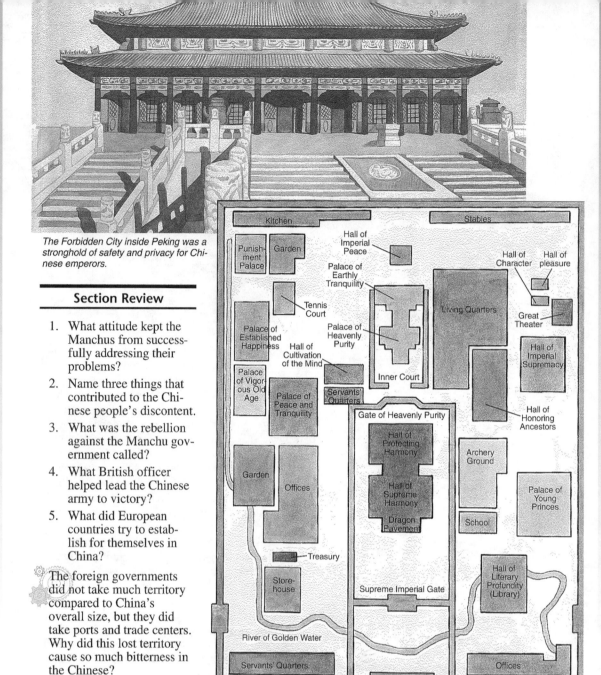

The Forbidden City inside Peking was a stronghold of safety and privacy for Chinese emperors.

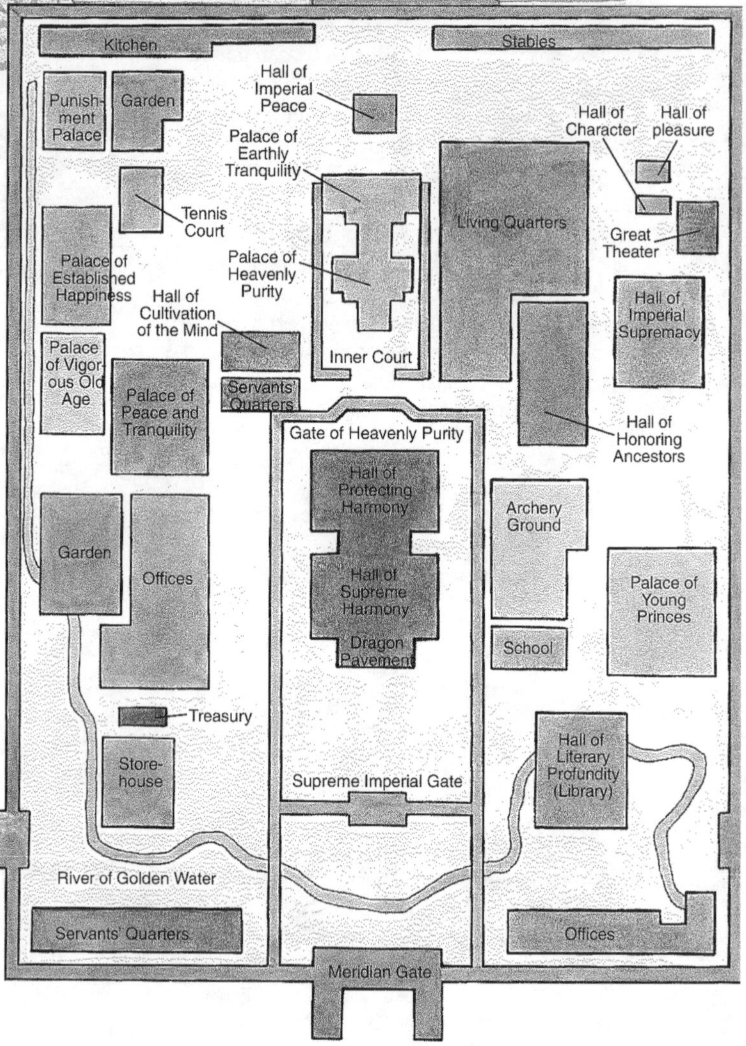

Kitchen
Stables
Hall of Imperial Peace
Punishment Palace
Garden
Palace of Earthly Tranquility
Hall of Character
Hall of pleasure
Tennis Court
Living Quarters
Great Theater
Palace of Established Happiness
Palace of Heavenly Purity
Hall of Cultivation of the Mind
Hall of Imperial Supremacy
Palace of Vigorous Old Age
Inner Court
Servants' Quarters
Palace of Peace and Tranquility
Gate of Heavenly Purity
Hall of Honoring Ancestors
Hall of Protecting Harmony
Archery Ground
Garden
Offices
Hall of Supreme Harmony
Palace of Young Princes
Dragon Pavement
School
Treasury
Hall of Literary Profundity (Library)
Store-house
Supreme Imperial Gate
River of Golden Water
Servants' Quarters
Offices
Meridian Gate

Section Review

1. What attitude kept the Manchus from successfully addressing their problems?
2. Name three things that contributed to the Chinese people's discontent.
3. What was the rebellion against the Manchu government called?
4. What British officer helped lead the Chinese army to victory?
5. What did European countries try to establish for themselves in China?

The foreign governments did not take much territory compared to China's overall size, but they did take ports and trade centers. Why did this lost territory cause so much bitterness in the Chinese?

370

Section Review Answers

1. unwillingness to change and belief in their superiority
2. heavy taxation, government corruption, and famine
3. Taiping Rebellion
4. Charles Gordon
5. spheres of influence

Answers will vary. China would have lost much profit if foreigners took over her trade centers. Control of the seas through ports and control of the trade centers would account for most of China's economic dealings. She no longer had control over her own country.

The Boxer Rebellion

In 1899 the pot of unrest boiled over when the **Boxer Rebellion** broke out. The Boxers were members of a secret society officially named the *Society of Righteous and Harmonious Fists*. The Europeans nicknamed the organization Boxers because the martial arts they practiced looked like shadowboxing. The society was anti-Manchu in the beginning, but they saw alliance with the Imperial government as a way to achieve their goals. They took on the slogan "Support the Qing [Manchu dynasty] and exterminate foreigners." Impressed by the society's claim of mystical powers and immunity to foreign weapons, Empress Dowager Tz'u-hsi encouraged the Imperial government not to attempt to restrain the movement.

Attacks on Foreigners

In the early months of 1900, the Boxers began by attacking missionaries and other foreigners in northern China. Many missionaries were aware of their danger but feared that leaving the mission would be more dangerous than staying. No missionaries were safe in areas where the Boxers were present, and many missionaries were killed. About 250 foreigners died in the attacks.

Canadian missionary **Jonathan Goforth** and his wife and children, along with other missionary families, began their escape on June 28, 1900, from Chang Te. They faced a journey of about twenty-four days through territory overrun with Boxers.

The Chinese Christians at their mission urged them to go. They knew that the Boxers had a special hatred for Chinese converts to Christianity. (They believed these Christians had denied traditional Chinese culture and heritage.) However, the Chinese Christians also knew that they could blend into their villages or hide in the countryside as the foreigners could not.

The Boxers killed many Christian missionaries in their attempt to rid China of foreign influence.

SECTION 5

Student Objectives

Students should be able to

1. Analyze the causes and effects of the Boxer Rebellion.
2. Identify the missionaries whose escape during the Boxer Rebellion was providential.

The Boxer Rebellion—The Boxers began in the early 1700s in rural China. They were a semi-religious group that practiced traditional Chinese calisthenics, which they believed helped them to develop supernatural powers. They taught a combination of Confucian, Taoist, and Buddhist thought.

The rebels had the support of many conservative members of the Chinese government and had allied themselves against the common foreign enemy. The Empress Dowager replied on June 18, 1900, by ordering all foreigners killed and declaring war on the invading nations. Many Europeans died before they could take refuge.

All over northern China, the Boxers slaughtered every European they could find and every Chinese Christian they could identify. Finally, in August, a relief force of twenty thousand soldiers crushed the Boxer force in Peking, breaking the siege and forcing the empress to flee. Other Chinese officials reorganized the government and arranged the settlement with the foreign powers.

Another result of the settlement was that the Empress Dowager agreed to initiate reforms in education, trade, and the military, and to begin the process of replacing the monarchy with a constitutional government.

Tz'u-hsi's Charm—The Empress Dowager could be very charming. In December of 1898, less than two years before the Boxer Rebellion, Tz'u-hsi invited the wives of foreign diplomats to the Forbidden City. She received them graciously and presented a large pearl ring to each lady. As they sipped tea, Tz'u-hsi pronounced "One family, all one family."

SECTION 5

Materials

- Video about Hudson Taylor or the Goforths
- Biographies of famous missionaries to China
- Bibles for Bible study

Taylor and Goforth—Show your students a video on Hudson Taylor or Jonathan Goforth. More than one good version of their lives exists. These will be of interest to your students. You will probably be able to find more on Taylor than on Goforth.

Jonathan and Rosalind Goforth—Jonathan and Rosalind Goforth met while working at the Toronto Mission Union. Rosalind had recently prayed that the Lord would lead her to a man who was totally committed to God and His work. Early in 1885 Jonathan was introduced to her as "our city missionary" at a mission meeting. When Jonathan was called out of the meeting, Rosalind slipped to his seat and examined his Bible. She noted the worn and marked pages and decided that this was the man she wanted to marry.

That fall Jonathan asked Rosalind to be his wife and go with him to China. Then he asked her to promise that she would always allow him to put God and His work first. She said yes to both questions.

Chosen By God—Before he died, Rosalind Bell-Smith's father had asked that she attend an art school in England. Because of this request, Rosalind's mother was very upset when Rosalind announced her plans to marry Jonathan Goforth and go to China as a missionary. After several weeks of separation, Rosalind returned home and showed her mother John 15:16, "Ye have not chosen me, but I have chosen you, and ordained you, that ye should go and bring forth fruit." Rosalind's mother embraced her and said, "O my child, I can fight against you, but I dare not fight against God." From then on, Mrs. Bell-Smith supported Rosalind and Jonathan.

Christians Under Suspicion—The Chinese people often regarded missionaries with great suspicion. Rosalind Goforth records a time when the Chinese thought that she and her family were drinking the blood of children they had murdered. Actually, they were drinking raspberry vinegar! The Boxers, who hated Christianity, also hated the Western ways the missionaries brought with them and encouraged rumors about the missionaries to scare the Chinese people and keep them from the gospel.

But He Passing Through the Midst of Them Went on His Way

Rosalind Goforth recalls the missionaries' flight from China in her book, *How I Know God Answers Prayer.* Several times along their journey, angry villagers gathered around their carts and shouted and threw things at them. One of the worst of these events came on July 8.

> After prayer we all got on our carts, and one by one passed out into the densely crowded street. As we approached the city gate we could see that the road was black with crowds awaiting us. I had just remarked to my husband on how well we were getting through the crowds, when our carts passed through the gates. My husband turned pale as he pointed to a group of several hundred men, fully armed, awaiting us. They waited till all the carts had passed through the gate, then hurled down upon us a shower of stones, at the same time rushing forward and maiming or killing some of the animals. Mr. Goforth jumped down from our cart and cried to them, "Take everything, but don't kill." His only answer was a blow. The confusion that followed was so great it would be impossible to describe the escape of each one in detail. . . . But I must give the details of Mr. Goforth's experience.
>
> One man struck him a blow on the neck with a great sword wielded with two hands. "Somehow" the blunt edge of the sword struck his neck; the blow left a wide mark almost around his neck, but did no further harm. Had the sharp edge struck his neck he would certainly have been beheaded!

In Another's Shoes—After the students have read this excerpt from Rosalind Goforth and the earlier one from Hudson Taylor, have them write a one-page paper on how it would feel to be a missionary. Encourage the students to imagine the new and sometimes frightening things they might encounter in a foreign place. Have them describe how they would reach out to people on the mission field.

His thick helmet was cut almost to pieces, one blow cutting through the leather lining *just over the temple,* but without even scratching the skin!

Again he was felled to the ground, with a fearful sword cut, which entered the bone of the skull behind and almost cleft it in two. As he fell he seemed to hear distinctly a voice saying, "Fear not, they are praying for you." Rising from this blow, he was again struck down by a club. As he was falling almost unconscious to the ground he saw a horse coming at full speed toward him; when he became conscious again he found the horse had tripped and fallen (on level ground) so near that its tail almost touched him. The animal, kicking furiously, had served as a barrier between him and his assailants. While dazed and not knowing what to do, a man came up as if to strike but whispered, "Leave the carts." By that time the onlookers began to rush forward to get the loot, but the attacking party felt the things were theirs, so desisted in their attack upon us in order to secure their booty.

At that point the missionaries slipped through the crowd to safety. This was only one incident on the missionaries' trip to the sea and safety. Many times along the way God used Chinese Christians and miraculous intervention to spare their lives. Within two years after their terrifying flight, the Goforths returned to China and their mission. The Boxer Rebellion was the first of many persecutions that the Chinese Christians would experience.

The Goforths and other missionaries experienced a miracle of God's love and protection in their lives. Yet the truth is that God was just as concerned for those missionaries who died; they were just as much under His love and protection, but God chose to glorify Himself in their deaths rather than in their deliverance.

Hebrews 11:32-35a illustrates this point. The writer speaks of those who were triumphant in victory in this world.

> And what shall I more say? for the time would fail me to tell of Gedeon, and of Barak, and of Samson, and of Jephthae; of David also and Samuel, and of the prophets: who through faith subdued kingdoms, wrought righteousness, obtained promises, stopped the mouths of lions, quenched the violence of fire, escaped the edge of the sword, out of weakness were made strong, waxed valiant in fight, turned to flight the armies of the aliens. Women received their dead raised to life again.

But in 11:35b-38 the epistle goes on to describe those who were triumphant in death.

> And others were tortured, not accepting deliverance; that they might obtain a better resurrection: and others had trial of cruel mockings and scourgings, yea, moreover of bonds and imprisonment: they were stoned, they were sawn asunder, were tempted, were slain with the sword: they wandered about in sheepskins and goatskins; being destitute, afflicted, tormented; (of whom the world was not worthy:) they wandered in deserts, and in mountains, and in dens and caves of the earth.

It is always difficult to understand why good people suffer. One of the ways that God works in lives is by teaching His children to trust Him. God in His sovereignty works out His will.

Return to China—In 1901, Jonathan Goforth returned to China. The following summer, his wife and their five children spent two months traveling from Canada to China. Delays and sickness marked the trip. Three of the five children caught whooping cough. When the Goforths finally arrived in Shanghai, a telegram informed them that Jonathan Goforth was in Changte (over a thousand miles away) with typhoid. After several harrowing weeks of traveling toward Changte and wondering how Mr. Goforth fared, Mrs. Goforth and the children met him in Tientsin for a happy reunion.

Chinese Christianity Continued—Though the Boxer Rebellion struck a strong blow to missionary efforts in China, it did not stop the spread of the gospel. Many missionaries returned soon after the rebellion, and revivals sprung up across the country. The Chinese were impressed with the Christians because most did not request indemnities for the death and destruction caused by the Boxers.

Many Chinese accepted Christ after witnessing the great courage and faith of the persecuted believers during the Boxer Rebellion.

Martyred Missionaries—At least 125 missionaries and 40 missionary children were killed during the Boxer Rebellion in 1900. Over 50 missionaries from the China Inland Mission lost their lives during that year. The mission had not lost any members in the thirty-three years it had existed before the Boxer Rebellion.

Persecution—Remind the students that American Christians do not face the kind of persecution that Christians in many other countries have faced in the past and still face today. When Christians were persecuted in Scripture, what were the results? Were they weakened or strengthened? Have the students give examples from the Bible.

Good Governor Tuang—Some of the Chinese officials actually helped missionaries escape during the Boxer Rebellion. Governor Tuang of the province of Shen-si issued a statement protecting foreigners in his province, in violation of the Empress Dowager's edict. Nearly one hundred foreigners escaped the country because of Tuang's kindness.

Chinese Christians—Missionaries were not the only Christians to suffer persecution during the Boxer Rebellion. Chinese converts were targets as well. The Boxers cruelly tortured and killed fellow Chinese who believed in the gospel. One Chinese pastor suffered great torment when he would not deny Christ. The Boxers cut off his lips, ears, and eyebrows, then extracted his heart.

Chinese Evangelist Chang—Chinese martyr Chang Shen gave his life to save fifty other Christians. Chang had lived a wicked life before his salvation, stealing and gambling. He was saved when he went to a missionary hospital searching for medical help for his blindness. There he received spiritual sight, and afterwards he became an evangelist. When the Boxers came to the town where Chang was preaching, fellow Christians sent the evangelist to the hills for protection. However, when Chang learned that the Boxers were about to kill fifty Christians unless the believers identified Chang's hiding place, he went voluntarily to the Boxers. The soldiers asked him to deny Christ and worship at the local temple; Chang refused. The Boxers executed Chang but were so afraid that his ghost would return to haunt them that they quickly left the area without killing any other Christians.

This copy of a painting by Sgt. John Clymer shows marines fighting Chinese Boxers outside the Peking Legation Quarter. (National Archives)

Foreign Governments Respond

To protect their citizens in China, foreign nations sent in troops. The troops were occupied mainly with trying to retake Peking. On June 20, 1900, the Boxers had attacked the **Legation Quarter** (embassies) of the main foreign powers. The legations were located just inside the wall of the Imperial City. From June 20 to August 14, hundreds of foreigners and thousands of Chinese Christians were held under siege by the Boxers. By the time international troops broke through the siege, hundreds of captives were dead, many were injured, and all were undernourished.

After defeating the Boxers at Peking, the Europeans demanded apologies and money payments from the Chinese government. Too weak politically to argue, the Manchus agreed. The Russians, Germans, Japanese, English, Americans, and French each won concessions. The Chinese paid indemnities (reimbursements) that totaled approximately sixty-five million dollars to the foreign governments. The United States gave its share of the money to a special fund that Chinese students could use for education in America. Using this money, thousands of Chinese were educated in the United States over a period of almost fifty years. The Communist takeover of China ended this arrangement.

Hardly ten years after the end of the Boxer Rebellion, the Manchu dynasty fell to a new Chinese government. (See Chapter 17.) The new government was not a dynasty headed by

Why Chinese?—Why would the Americans use the money China paid for damages to educate Chinese in this country? *(America may have wanted the Chinese to see that the Western world was not so bad after all and that one could receive a beneficial education from it. China was not nearly as technologically advanced as the West at this time, so this would give a glimpse of the benefits of advancement.)* Would you have used the money that way? *(Answers will vary. The students might not because of anger with China, or they might for the reasons listed above.)*

an emperor, but a republic headed by a president. The Manchus had tried hard to preserve ancient Chinese culture. However, their inability to deal with the problems of a changing world resulted in much of that traditional culture being destroyed. Even with their new government, the Chinese did not have peace. Within forty years China would be controlled by a Communist government.

Spanning the Ages

Europe's influence, particularly that of Great Britain, continued to grow. Not only did she control India, but now she controlled much of Chinese trade as well. In the next chapter you will see how Europe also became involved in Africa. All these chapters could be grouped under the heading of imperialism.

Section Review

1. What group led a rebellion against foreigners?
2. Why did the rebels especially hate the Chinese Christians?
3. What city did the Boxers beseige?
4. What did the United States do with its share of the indemnity?
5. What type of government finally came to China in the twentieth century?

In Rosalind Goforth's account of their flight, find at least two incidents that show God's miraculous protection of Mr. Goforth. Then find two Scripture verses in which God promises protection to His children.

Summary

For centuries the Chinese were confident in their superiority. Their power and dominance in the East were undisputed. In 1644 the Manchu dynasty came to power in China, and the Chinese world was shaken. For the next two hundred fifty years, China faced the challenges of the modern Western world. Holding on to their attitude of superiority, the Chinese refused to recognize the abilities of other nations. To Europeans this attitude was highly offensive. They made every effort to break down China's obstinate position. The Europeans desired China's luxury goods. Having no goods of their own worthy of Chinese purchase, the Europeans began trading in opium. Thousands of Chinese became addicted to this drug. Although the Chinese outlawed its import, the Europeans still brought it to China. Finally war broke out. As a result of the Opium Wars, more ports and inland China were opened for trade and travel. In response to these openings, traders and missionaries poured into China. The Christian missionaries tried to show the Chinese God's love and salvation through Jesus Christ. Despite their efforts, antiforeign feelings grew until the Boxer Rebellion broke out in 1899. The rebellion was finally put down by European forces. Internal and external pressures weakened the Manchu government so much that it fell in 1911.

Section Review Answers

1. Boxers (Society of Righteous and Harmonious Fists)
2. They thought they had denied traditional Chinese culture and heritage.
3. Peking (the Legation Quarter)
4. set up a fund for Chinese students to be educated in America
5. republic or communist

Answers will vary. The blunt edge of the sword hit his neck rather than the sharp edge; his helmet was cut through, but no skin was scratched; a horse protected him when it fell and kicked wildly at his assailants (any two). Psalm 17:7, Isaiah 41:10, Matthew 28:20, and Luke 10:19 are some verses among others which speak of God's protection. *[Of course, we are still to be careful; some use Luke 10:19 as an excuse for reckless behavior.]*

Chapter Review Idea

Play the Boxing Game. Divide the class into two teams. One person from each team will come up and sit or stand on either side of a desk or table. Each player will clench his fist. The teacher will ask a question, and the one who hits the desk first with his fist gets to answer the question. If he answers the question correctly, his team receives one point. If he answers incorrectly or does not answer within ten seconds, his team loses one point and the other team gets a chance to answer. If the default team answers correctly, they score one point. If not, they lose nothing. Repeat this until all members of both teams have had a turn. The team with the most points at the end is the winner.

Chapter Enrichment Activities

Biographies—Your students might enjoy reading more about missionaries in China. Suggest biographies about Hudson Taylor, Jonathan and Rosalind Goforth, Gladys Aylward, Isobel Kuhn, and Pearl S. Buck.

Calligraphy—Review the origin and use of calligraphy from Heritage Studies 6. Encourage the students to practice writing some on their own or in class.

CHAPTER REVIEW

People, Places, and Things to Know

Central Kingdom
Ming dynasty
porcelain
Imperial City
junks
Manchu dynasty
Manchuria
tribute
kowtow
Canton
opium
Lin Tze-hsü
Opium War
Treaty of Nanking
cordilleras
archipelago
"Ring of Fire"
Sino-British Joint Declaration
Robert Morrison
Hudson Taylor
China Inland Mission
Hung Hsiu-chuan
Taiping Rebellion
Charles Gordon
Sino-Japan War
spheres of influence
Boxer Rebellion
Jonathan Goforth
Legation Quarter

Review Questions

Matching

Match these missionaries with the statement(s) that apply to them.

Robert Morrison   Hudson Taylor   Jonathan Goforth

1. Translated the Bible into Chinese
2. Successfully escaped the Boxers
3. Wore Chinese dress and adopted Chinese customs
4. Started the China Inland Mission
5. One of the earliest missionaries to China
6. Wrote books on the Chinese language and grammar

Short Answer

Write a one- or two-sentence explanation of the following terms.

7. Manchu dynasty
8. spheres of influence
9. Taiping Rebellion
10. Treaty of Nanking

Chapter Review Answers

Matching

1. Robert Morrison
2. Jonathan Goforth
3. Hudson Taylor
4. Hudson Taylor
5. Robert Morrison
6. Robert Morrison

Short Answer

7. The Manchu dynasty took power from the fading Ming government. The Manchus began to decline at the end of the 1800s.
8. The Western powers wanted to divide China into spheres of influence, with each country controlling its own part.
9. The Taiping Rebellion was started and led by Hung Hsiu-chuan once he realized the government corruption. Charles Gordon led the Manchu forces against Hung and won.
10. The Treaty of Nanking giving in to British trade demands was signed at the end of the Opium Wars.

Connections

For each of the following pairs of items, write a sentence or two explaining the connection between them.

11. kowtow / tribute
12. silk / porcelain

Short Answer

Answer the following questions about the first Opium War.

13. When did the war occur, and what two nations fought in it?
14. What was the cause of the war?
15. What was one result of the war?

Think About It!

The British ignored the Chinese rejection of trade and imported opium to get around the rejection. Sometimes, as Christians, we try to maneuver around the authority over us when they reject our requests. Talk to your parents about how to appeal to authority and how to handle rejection. Write out three Scripture verses that deal with authority. Explain one of them in a paragraph.

Recipe: Egg Foo Yung—This tasty recipe is typical of Chinese cooking then and now.

Ingredients:
4 eggs, well beaten
1 one-lb. can of bean sprouts, drained
1/3 c. diced green onions
1 tsp. salt
1/4 tsp. pepper
1 c. cooked poultry
3 Tbsp. oil

Sauté onions and bean sprouts, add chicken; put aside. Beat eggs and mix with cooled vegetables. Heat 1 Tbsp. oil in skillet. Shape mixture into patties (about 1/4 cup each) and fry; turn only once. Cook until set and lightly browned. Serve with Egg Foo Yung sauce.

Ingredients:
1 Tbsp. cornstarch
2 Tbsp. soy sauce
1 c. chicken broth

Combine all ingredients in saucepan. Cook over low heat until thick, stirring constantly.

Connections

11. The Chinese emperors expected all "outer barbarians" (foreigners) to perform the kowtow and bring tribute to them.
12. Silk and porcelain, whose origins were in China, were highly prized by Europeans.

Short Answer

13. 1839-42; Great Britain and China
14. The Chinese refused to pay for the British opium they had destroyed.
15. China gave in to Great Britain, China was forced to open, and resentment against foreigners grew in China. (any one)

Think About It!

Answers will vary.

Student Objectives
Students should be able to

1. Assess the reasons that people would become involved in slave trade.
2. Describe the slave trade.
3. Define *abolition*.
4. Identify the country created specifically for freed slaves.
5. Describe difficulties in exploring Africa.
6. List at least four geographic findings of these explorations.
7. Locate Southern Africa on a map.
8. Identify each continent and subcontinent.
9. List at least four contributions Europeans made to Africans.
10. Evaluate the results of Moffat's and Livingstone's work in Africa on the future of Africa.
11. Analyze Leopold's reasons for taking the Belgian Congo.
12. Describe the partitioning of Africa.
13. Predict Africa's future in the twenty-first century based on imperialism.

Opening Photo— Zebras drinking at a watering hole

CHAPTER 14

The natives of Ujiji . . . hurry up by the hundreds to ask what it all means, this fusillading [shooting], shouting, and blowing of horns, and flag-flying. There are Yambos (How do you do's) shouted out to me by the dozen; and delighted Arabs have run up breathlessly to shake my hand, and ask anxiously where I came from. But I have no patience with them; the expedition goes far too slow; I should like to settle the vexed question by one personal view. Where is he? Has he fled? Suddenly a man, a black man at my elbow, shouts in English, "How do you do, sir?"—"Hallo! who . . . are you?"—"I am the servant of Dr. Livingstone," he says; but, before I can ask any more questions, he is running like a madman towards the town.

We have at last entered the town. The expedition comes to a halt; the journey is ended for a time; but I alone have a few more steps to make. There is a group of the most respectable Arabs; and, as I come nearer, I see the white face of an old man among them. He has a cap with a gold band around it; his dress is a short jacket of red blanket-cloth; and his pants—well, I didn't observe. I am shaking hands with him. We raise our hats; and I say, "Dr. Livingstone, I presume?" and he says, "Yes. Finis coronat opus." [Latin for "The end crowns the work."]

With these famous words, Henry M. Stanley met David Livingstone deep in the heart of Africa. Livingstone had spent over thirty years in Africa as a missionary, explorer, and representative of the British government. Like other Europeans who traveled in Africa in the nineteenth century, Livingstone gave the world much of its knowledge of Africa's interior.

A.D. 1750 - A.D. 1950

1750 — 1800

Age of Reason 1600-1800

Slave Trade Outlawed in Great Britain 1772

Chapter 14 Lesson Plans			
Section Title	**Main Concept**	**Pages**	**Time Frame**
1. Africans Enslaved **Center Stage: The Source of the Nile*	The beginnings of European and American dealings with Africa revolved mostly around the slave trade.	378-85	1-2 days
2. Africa Explored **Settings: Southern Africa*	Though it had many dangers, Africa drew many explorers.	386-91	2 days
3. Africa Evangelized **Backgrounds: Fighting Malaria*	Africa was opened to missionaries during this time, the most famous of whom was David Livingstone.	392-97	1-2 days
4. Africa Divided **Analysis: The Suez Canal*	At the height of their imperialism, European powers divided up Africa among themselves.	397-404	1-2 days
Total Suggested Days (including 1 day for review & 1 day for test)			7-10 days

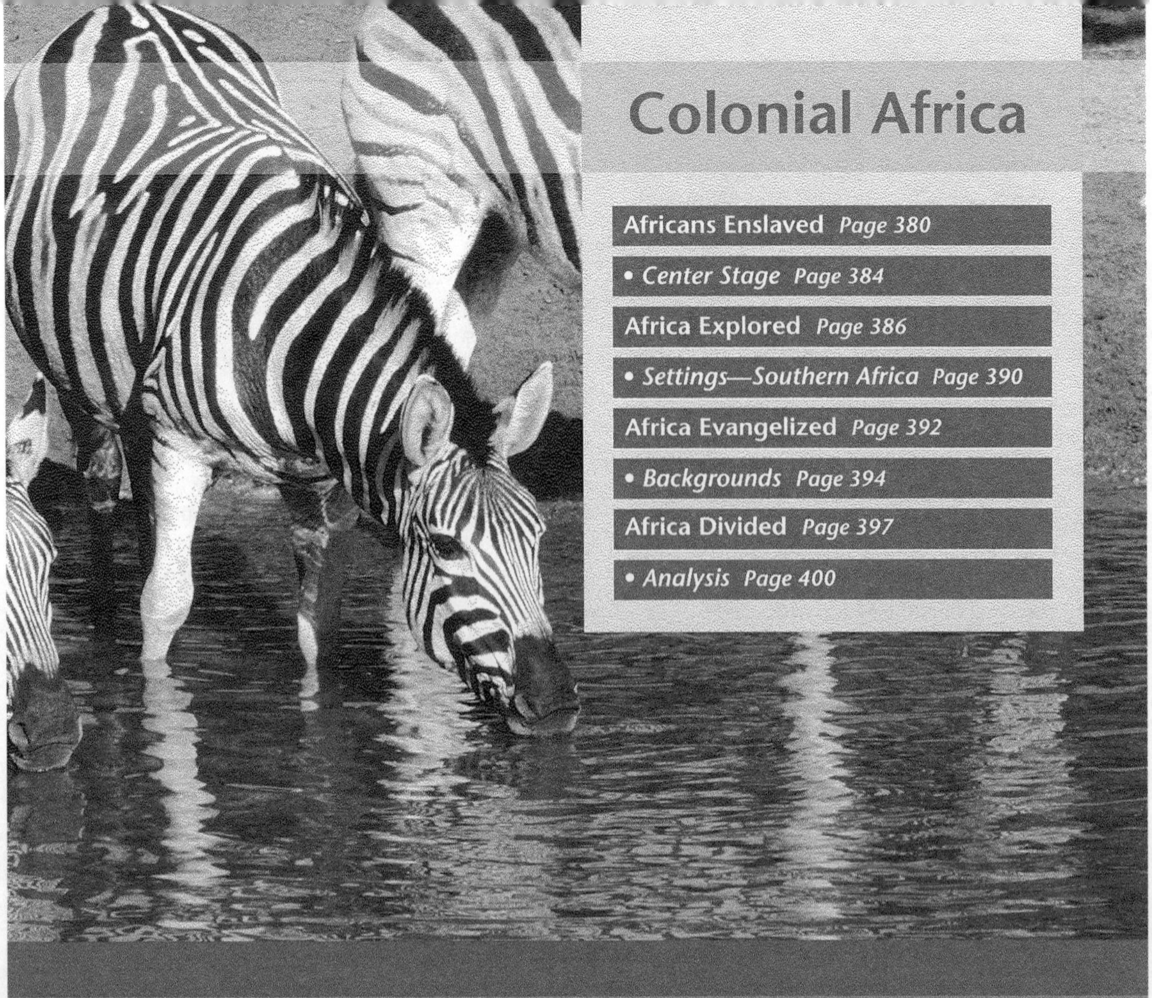

Colonial Africa

Slavery Abolished in the British Empire 1833

David Livingstone in Africa 1840-73

The Berlin Act 1884

Boxer Rebellion 1899-1900

British Control of the Suez Canal 1875-1956

1850 1900 1950

Robert Moffat in South Africa 1817-70

Queen Victoria's Reign 1838-1901

Great Trek Begins 1836

Liberia Founded 1821

People's Republic of South Africa 1909

Boer War 1899-1902

Materials

- Scripture verses (BLM verse 14)
- *The Slave Dancer: a Novel* by Paula Fox
- Lists of directions to follow and lists of items to find on a scavenger hunt
- Wall map of Southern Africa (BLM 14-2)
- *Teaching Transparencies* for use with *WORLD STUDIES for Christian Schools* (Second Edition)
- Guest speaker, a missionary (or a missionary letter)
- Biographical accounts of missionaries to Africa (available through BJUP)
- Bibles for Bible study
- Video on a missionary to Africa
- Pictures of missionaries to Africa
- Gospel tracts for visitation
- Large map of America

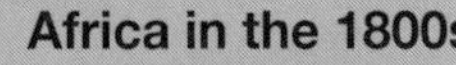

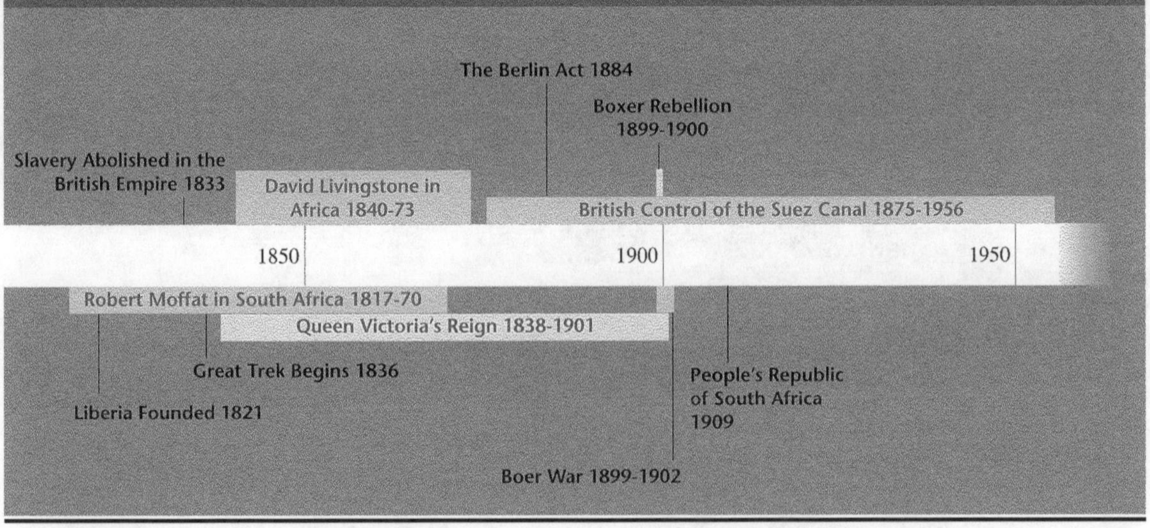

Africa in the 1800s

Use pictures of Africans, animals and nature, and maps to cover all the sections of this chapter. Or use pictures and sayings of David Livingstone and other famous missionaries to Africa, to create a bulletin board emphasizing missions.

Chapter Motivator

Review some of the material on explorers found in Chapter 6. Using a map of the world to illustrate, show your students that by this time most of the rest of the world had been explored by Europeans; the interior of Africa was the last great unknown. The explorers studied in this chapter were part of the last great age of exploration. To help the students visualize the immensity of the job, call their attention to the size of the continent of Africa in comparison to North America. Read to your students the opening story about David Livingstone and Henry Stanley. Discuss with your class the reasons for European interest in Africa.

Romans 10:13-15

These verses are at the end of the third section, which is called Africa Evangelized. Emphasize to your students the importance of missions and God's command for missions. We are to go to all the ends of the earth to preach the gospel to every creature. Romans 10:13-15 says, "For whosoever shall call upon the name of the Lord shall be saved. How then shall they call on him in whom they have not believed? and how shall they believe in him of whom they have not heard? and how shall they hear without a preacher? And how shall they preach, except they be sent? as it is written, How beautiful are the feet of them that preach the gospel of peace, and bring glad tidings of good things!" (BLM verse 14)

SECTION 1

Student Objectives
Students should be able to

1. Assess the reasons that people would become involved in slave trade.
2. Describe the slave trade.
3. Define *abolition*.
4. Identify the country created specifically for freed slaves.

The History of Slave Trade— Slavery has been practiced for thousands of years. (Farmers who went to war in ancient times enslaved their prisoners of war.) The Bible talks about slaves in the ancient times of the Old Testament. There were many slaves in both Greece and Rome in the Classical Period. Many times slaves were criminals or people who could not repay their debts. *Manumission*, or the freeing of a slave, was practiced as well. Typically, loyal slaves would be freed upon their master's death. The Middle Ages saw the decline of slavery and the beginnings of feudalism, but some slavery was still practiced around the Mediterranean where the newly discovered sugar was being grown. For the most part, these plantations used Russian slaves. Slavery grew as exploration increased. Though illegal in all the world, slavery is still practiced in some parts of Africa, Asia, and South America.

Livingstone and the Slave Trade— One of David Livingstone's lifelong goals was to end the slave trade. Above his tomb in Westminster Abbey in London, England, these words are inscribed: "All I can say in my solitude is, may Heaven's rich blessing come down on every one—American, English, Turk—who will help to heal this Open Sore of the World [the slave trade]." Livingstone wrote these words in a letter exactly one year before he died.

Africans Enslaved

In Chapter 6 we learned about the first explorers who sailed around Africa. Although their goal was to find routes to the East, they set up a few trading ports along the African coast. They traded European goods for the wealth of Africa-gold, spices, ivory, and ebony. However, what they desired most was slaves, black Africans captured and sold into bondage by other Africans. For centuries Africans had taken captives in war and made them slaves. These slaves were bought and sold throughout the continent. The Europeans discovered that they could also buy slaves for yards of cloth, pieces of gold, or colored glass beads. From these beginnings grew what was to become a horrible worldwide trade in human beings, the **slave trade.**

Growth of the Slave Trade

Before 1600 only about two thousand slaves were taken from Africa each year. One hundred eighty years later this figure had climbed to over seventy thousand slaves per year. The major reason for this growth was the settlement of the Americas. Throughout South America, the Caribbean, and North America, large plantations were built. These plantations needed laborers. Most of the native Indian population had been killed or forced to move when the settlers came. Europeans did not want to do heavy work in the hot, tropical climate. They felt that they were unsuited to it since they were from more moderate climates. When Indians were no longer available, Africans seemed the best solution to many Europeans.

This diagram shows how slaves were to be placed into slave ships. In these horrible conditions, many slaves died before they reached their destination.

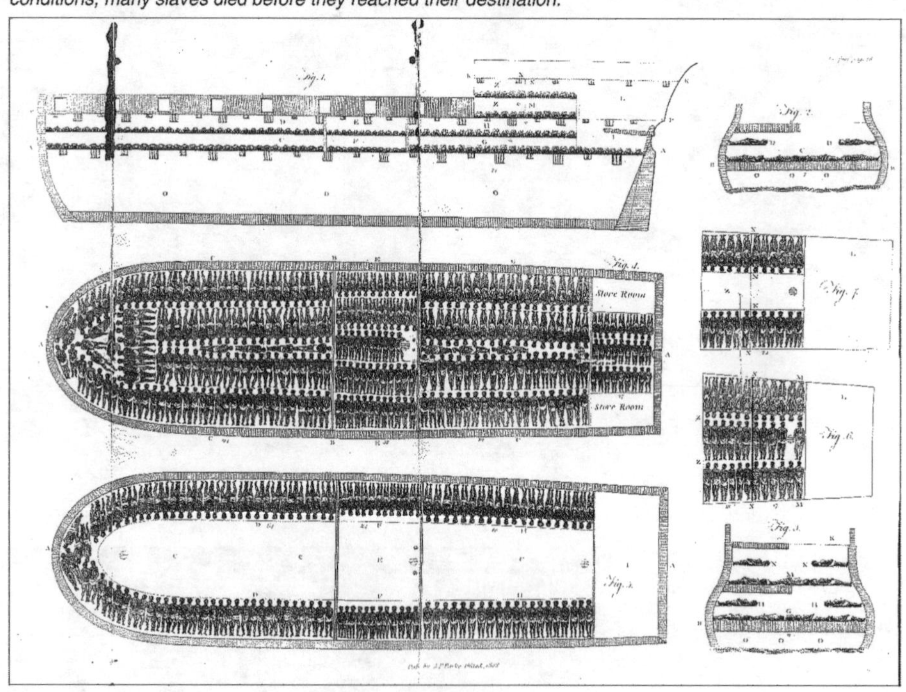

Materials

- *The Slave Dancer: a Novel* by Paula Fox

***The Slave Dancer: a Novel*—**Encourage the students to read (or take time to read aloud) *The Slave Dancer: a Novel* by Paula Fox. This story is about a thirteen-year-old boy who is kidnapped by the crew of a ship bound for Africa. He discovers to his horror that he is on a slave ship and his job is to play music for the exercise periods of the human cargo.

Reasons for Slavery—Ask your students to analyze how people might justify slavery. What reasons would they give? *(need for workers, tradition, inferior people, and so on)* Europeans soon began to view the African as less than a person, another justification for their evil practice. Ask your students to give present-day examples of this type of thinking. *(There is still slavery in parts of the world. People may look down their noses at poor or homeless people.)* Ask your students to suggest ways to combat partiality in our society.

After all, they said, Africans were used to the hot climate and hard work. With this as one excuse, the Europeans lulled themselves into believing that the slave trade was a respectable alternative to working the fields and mines themselves.

European slavers (mostly from Britain, France, and Portugal) anchored their ships off the western coast of Africa to pick up their human cargoes. African traders brought slaves from the interior to the coast. Held captive by chains, ropes, or yokes, slaves had often been forced to walk many miles to the coast. After the harsh treatment on the land journey, their sea voyage was no better. The traders crammed the slaves into their ships, which had decks too low to stand between and were often too crowded to move in. Each slave was chained to the ship to prevent his escape. For two months they lived—or died—in these hot, filthy quarters. At times they were allowed fresh air and exercise above deck, but in poor weather they were kept below with no fresh air. It is no wonder that many of these men, women, and children died before reaching their new home.

Opposition to the Slave Trade

As the eighteenth century wore on, more Europeans became aware of the atrocities of the slave trade. They began to speak out against this trade that caused so much human suffering. Much of this opposition resulted from the Wesleyan revivals in England. As people accepted the gospel, they became concerned about the conditions of these human beings. The movement to help other people, which characterized Europe at this time, began to reach out to Africa.

Attempts to end slavery began in Great Britain. This movement to abolish slavery is called **abolition.** Many heated debates occurred in Parliament between those who profited from the slave trade and those who saw it as a wicked practice. Many British had grown wealthy from the slave trade. Their greed kept them from admitting the evils of slave trading. Finally in 1772 slavery in Great Britain was outlawed. In 1807 Parliament outlawed the slave trade and in 1833 abolished slavery in the British Empire. Other nations followed Britain's lead in abolishing slavery and the slave trade. The slavery that had existed for centuries and whose evils had been magnified under European trade was by those same hands removed. By 1880 the slave trade was officially ended throughout the world.

President James Monroe and the American Colonization Society devised a plan for starting a free African state called Liberia.

Founding Liberia

Americans would finally resolve the issue of slavery at the end of the Civil War in 1865. But in 1816, United States president James Monroe and the American Colonization Society had a goal of finding a homeland for freed slaves. The plan was to start a country where

Earning Freedom from Slavery—Seventy-nine of the slaves who went to Liberia in 1842 had literally earned their freedom. One slaveowner, John McDonogh, set up a system for his slaves to work their way to freedom over a period of fifteen years. He paid his slaves for work done on Saturday afternoons; McDonogh allowed them to use this money to purchase Saturday morning freedom, then Fridays, then Thursdays, and so on. After fifteen years, the Blacks had "purchased" every day of the week.

After McDonogh's slaves were free, he expected them to emigrate to Liberia. He taught them to read and write as preparation for their freedom in Liberia. He even trained them in fields such as carpentry, blacksmithing, and spinning.

Many of the former slaves wrote letters to McDonogh from Liberia. McDonogh had sent his slave Washington Watts McDonogh to college to train as a missionary. Washington did become a missionary once he arrived in Liberia, and he wrote his former master with reports of his work.

Abolition—Discuss with your students the advantages and disadvantages of the abolition movement in Europe. People realized that Africans were human beings as much as anyone else and that they were being severely mistreated. Slaves were eventually freed in Europe and the Americas. Men whose profits had been from the slave trade lost much wealth when their trade came to an end.

Religion in Liberia—The Liberian settlement had many churches and church schools. Methodists, Episcopals, Presbyterians, Lutherans, African Methodist Episcopals, and Baptists all established churches in Liberia.

Haiti—Haiti is part of the island of Hispaniola. (The Dominican Republic makes up the other part.) Columbus discovered gold here in his explorations, causing a rush of settlers who killed off most of the Indians and brought slaves from Africa. Eventually the French took over the western side of Hispaniola, but the slaves revolted during the French Revolution. Napoleon sent troops to restore order, but so many of them died of yellow fever that the slaves were able to hold their own. They proclaimed their land the independent country of Haiti in 1804. Many dictators have ruled Haiti since that time, and the U.S. sends in troops to restore order when necessary.

Shops and stalls line the bustling streets of Liberia's coastal capital, Monrovia.

the former slaves would be not only free but also self-ruled. To meet their goal, the society purchased land along the west coast of Africa. This land, **Liberia,** would become home to thousands of resettled slaves.

The history of Liberia began in 1821 when a shipload of freed black slaves from the United States landed on Providence Island off the coast of West Africa. Early settlement was difficult. Most of the first 114 settlers died from disease. The next group of settlers fared better and established a permanent settlement. About 6,000 freed slaves were eventually resettled in Liberia. Those early settlers established Monrovia, which in 1847 became the capital of the independent Republic of Liberia. (The name *Liberia* comes from the Latin word for "free," and Monrovia was named in honor of President Monroe.) Liberia was the only black African republic in Africa for over one hundred years. (It is the second oldest independent black African republic. Haiti is the first.)

There are two main groups of people living in Liberia: the Americo-Liberians, whose ancestors came from America, and the tribal people, whose ancestors were African. Even today many of Liberia's government officials and their other leaders come from the Americo-Liberian group; however, a revolt in 1980 brought the indigenous Africans into power. Most Americo-Liberians live in Monrovia or other coastal cities, speak English (the official language), and have a westernized culture. Most of the tribal people (over 90 percent of the population) live in rural areas.

Newly Formed Liberia—Direct each student to write a one-page essay on what life would have been like for a newly freed slave in Liberia. Each student should write an account of his first week in the new country, the adventures, sights, and sounds, as well as the culture of the new land. The students may wish to read their essays in class.

About sixteen different tribes are represented in Liberia, each with its own language, customs, and religion. Although roads and schools are bringing gradual change, most tribes preserve the traditional ways of life. It is not unusual for extended families to live together, even in the urban areas. A relatively small number of Europeans, Americans, and Asians live in the country as well. They often serve as businessmen, teachers, and engineers, but they cannot become citizens or own land. Black ancestry is a requirement of Liberian citizenship, and only citizens may own land. This policy was instituted to ensure that Africans would retain control of the republic that was established especially for them.

Section Review

1. When did Europeans begin the slave trade?
2. In what country did the movement to help the slaves begin?
3. Why did some people want to continue the slave trade?
4. By what year did the slave trade officially end?
5. Where did the United States resettle freed slaves?

The former slaves who went to Liberia had either been born in America or been in America for several years. The area in which they settled was not only already claimed by indigenous tribes but was also wilderness. There were British and French colonies on either side of the region. Review this information and the section on Liberia. In a paragraph or two, discuss the advantages and disadvantages possible settlers would have had to consider before deciding to immigrate.

Looking over Monrovia from a hilltop above the city

A New Life—Compare and contrast a black person's life in Africa with life in the United States after emancipation. Discuss politics, religion, culture, society, and so forth in your comparison.

Section Review Answers

1. before 1600 *[Students will have to remember that European slave trading began during exploration of Africa in the 1400s and 1500s.]*
2. Great Britain
3. greed caused by wealth
4. 1880
5. Liberia

Answers will vary. Advantages may include having a land of their own, ruling that land, returning to their homeland, and having "civilized" European colonies on each side of them.

Disadvantages may include learning a different culture, encountering unfriendly tribespeople, carving growth out of wilderness, having to create their own government, and leaving their families.

Niger River Exploration—The Nile River certainly was not Africa's only river of mystery. Europeans were also interested in following the course of the Niger River in West Africa. One of the greatest figures connected with the history of the river's exploration is Mungo Park.

Park was born in Scotland in 1771, was educated as a surgeon, and served on a vessel as a medical officer. Because of his superior work in the East Indies, he won the support of the Africa Association in England to explore the river. There was certainly enough interest to support the exploration. River systems were the keys to Africa's interior—and the resources it held. Until this time, the Niger River had been thought to be more than one river because of its many tributaries. Park started off in 1795 to settle the issue.

The expedition began at the mouth of the Gambia River and headed inland to intersect with the Niger. Park traveled two hundred miles before reaching the British trading station of Pisania. The next leg of the journey was filled with danger. Park and his men caught a fever, and soon afterward Park was captured and imprisoned by an Arab chief. After four months, he escaped. Dedicated to his mission, Park continued toward the Niger with only a horse and a compass. Finally, a lack of supplies forced him to turn back. Again sick with a fever, Park survived only with the aid of a slave trader. Back in England, he published an account of the expedition.

Mungo Park was not finished with the Niger River though. Two years later he was asked to lead a second expedition to the Niger. The expedition began with forty men, but by the time it reached Bamako (Mali), only eleven remained. After passing through Ségue, the party lost contact with the outside world. Rumors circulated that Park and his men had met with disaster. Six years later in 1812, the suspicions were confirmed. The expedition had reached the rapids at Bussa (Nigeria) where it was attacked by natives. Park drowned in the attack.

The mystery of the Niger River remained until 1830. In that year two English brothers, Richard and John Lander, sailed down the Niger all the way to the Atlantic.

CENTER STAGE

Discovering the Source of the Nile

The ancient Egyptians knew where the Nile ended, but they did not know where it began. Finding "the source of the Nile" was not simply a matter of following the river upstream. Difficult obstacles such as swift cataracts (falls or rapids), rugged mountains, and dense jungles hampered would-be explorers. The Romans were halted by one of these obstacles when the emperor Nero sent an expedition southward to find the source of the Nile. The expedition was stopped when it confronted a huge, impassable swamp in the Sudan region. Around the same time, a Greek explorer said that he had found the source of the Nile. The river began, he said, from two lakes near a mountain range called the "Mountains of the Moon" (now the Ruwenzori Mountains).

Stories like those of the Greek explorer spurred further interest in the river. Little by little, explorers learned more about the Nile. They discovered that two great rivers joined to form the Nile. Explorers found the smaller of these two rivers, called the Blue Nile (because of its clearer waters), easier to explore. In the 1600s a Spanish missionary first discovered the source of the Blue Nile in the highlands of Ethiopia. The larger branch, called the White Nile, proved more difficult. The rough, dense jungle of mountainous central Africa hid its source.

Sir Richard Burton dressed in costume to blend in with the native people as he traveled.

The Course of the Nile

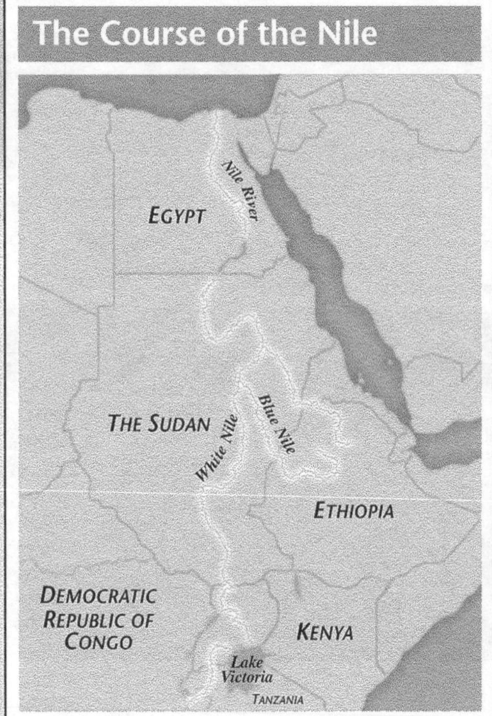

British explorer Sir Richard Burton (1821-90) was in the front rank of men who risked their lives to discover the secrets of unknown lands. Burton, although rather eccentric all his life, was a man of great intelligence. He also had a natural talent for languages and had learned six before he was eighteen years old. At the age of twenty-one he made his first trip to an exotic land, arriving in India as an army officer. His keen mind soon earned him a position in British Intelligence. On his assignments Burton often disguised himself as an Indian, using walnut juice to stain his face. His fluency in Indian languages further disguised his identity. He later did the same type of undercover work in Arabia and

Chapter 14

Africa. But Burton had one great goal shared by explorers for centuries—to find the source of the Nile River.

In 1855, with a fellow officer named John Speke, Burton made his first attempt to penetrate the African interior. Turned back by a native ambush, the two did not try again until 1858. Striking inland from Zanzibar, the explorers constantly faced obstacles that ranged from malaria to hills so steep that pack animals died trying to climb them. At last they reached the shores of Lake Tanganyika, then pressed on to find an even larger lake. By this time, both men were terribly ill but determined to continue their search. Burton finally had to stop and wait while Speke, who recovered more quickly, pushed on to discover **Lake Victoria.** He was convinced that he had found the source of the Nile. Burton, however, wanted more proof; the two men quarreled and eventually separated.

This bust of John Speke is done in Roman style except for the Scottish plaid on the toga.

Speke returned to England first. He had agreed to wait until Burton arrived to publicize their findings, but Burton reached England to find that Speke had already reported that he "saw that old father Nile without any doubt rises in [Lake] Victoria." (He named the lake "Victoria" in honor of the queen of England.) Speke took full credit for their discoveries. After years of quarreling in print and in person, the two men agreed to meet in a public debate to settle the issue. As he waited for the debate to begin, Burton was informed that Speke had died of a gunshot wound on a hunting trip the day before. Although officials concluded that Speke had shot himself accidentally, some historians believe that he committed suicide, driven by guilt over his injustice to Burton so many years before.

Burton and Speke were only partly right in claiming to have found the Nile's source. Although Lake Victoria is the greatest source of the Nile, it is not the most distant. It took later explorers to find that a river called the Kagera flows into the lake. That river is fed by another river, the **Ruvironza,** that flows north from Burundi. The Ruvironza River is now considered to be the farthest source of the Nile. Starting from the Ruvironza, the Nile measures 4,145 miles long, making it the longest river in the world.

Colonial Africa 385

SECTION 2

Student Objectives
Students should be able to

1. Describe difficulties in exploring Africa.
2. List at least four geographic findings of these explorations.

Conservation of Man or Beast?—A problem that faced Africans in the past as well as today is the conservation of African animals, plants, and forests in light of the growing human population. Balancing the needs of man and animal is very difficult. Examples are not just confined to our decade. In 1963, a group of Masai tribal people wrote to a government official complaining about elephants running through their farmland.

Nkongi Figures—Many of the people within and around the Congo Basin create Nkongi figures. Made out of wood, horn, ivory, or calabash, these little human figures are used to represent past leaders. Often the posture and expression a Nkongi is given shows how that leader was viewed by his people. A hole in the stomach of the figure is filled with sacred items and the opening is sealed off with a shell or a mirror. The people of the Congo believe that evil spirits can live in the Nkongi once this ritual has been performed.

The Nkongi figures are primarily objects of worship, but they also provide a history of the tribe. Whenever the people settle a legal dispute, they pound a sharp object into the Nkongi. Soon the figure is covered with nails and spikes that remind the people of what legal actions have transpired.

Unfortunately, the history of the people of the Congo has been filled with conflict and bloodshed. Unless they turn to Christ, violence will continue to plague the region.

Africa Explored

Much of Europe's knowledge of Africa came from brave explorers of the continent. Fascinated by the secrets of Africa, these men and women set out on long, hard trips to discover what lay beyond the coastline.

The Delight and Danger of Exploration

The explorers invaded Africa from all sides in many different manners. Some rode south across the burning Sahara on camels. Others traveled as far as they could by canoe or steamship up rivers and streams. They were curious to know where the mighty rivers—the Nile, Niger, Zambezi, and Congo—flowed. They wanted to study the deserts and jungles and to meet the people of Africa. Some desired fame or wealth. Some desired to hunt big game. Some desired to share the gospel with the millions of lost Africans. All the explorers desired the thrill of discovery, of seeing something first. And all of them desired adventure, which they found abundant in Africa.

Explorers faced many hardships on their way to adventure. There were no roads for them to take and often not even trails. The

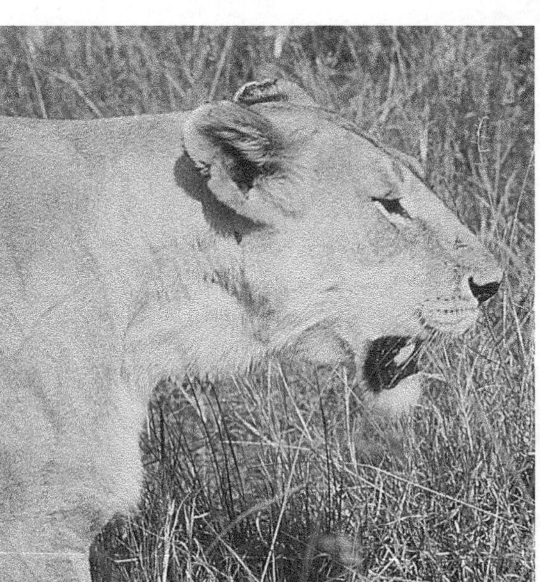

Adventure and discovery for explorers included the wild animals of Africa.

Materials

- Lists of directions to follow and lists of items to find on a scavenger hunt

Alexandrine Tinné

Not all the explorers of Africa were men. Alexandrine Tinné (1839-69), a Dutch woman, explored both the Nile and Sahara regions of Africa. She used her large inheritance to satisfy her own curiosity about the "dark continent." Miss Tinné was a beautiful, intelligent woman. She knew several languages and was an accomplished horsewoman as well. Above all, she possessed the combined qualities of courage and tenacity.

Accompanied by her mother and several scientists, Miss Tinné first traveled down the Nile in 1863. The expedition proved successful in acquiring scientific information, but Miss Tinné's mother and two of the scientists died. Undaunted, she prepared another expedition across the Sahara. On the journey, she took two large iron tanks of water. The Muslim natives in the party, thinking that the tanks contained gold, attacked Miss Tinné. They slashed her with their sabers, cutting off her hand so that she could not use her revolver. The attackers fled, leaving her to bleed to death. She perished, alone, on the desert.

Hungry Hippos—Lions weren't the only dangerous animals missionaries faced in Africa. In his book "Missionary Labours and Scenes in Southern Africa" (1852), Robert Moffat describes an encounter with an angry hippopotamus. As he traveled down an African river one day, a hippopotamus (or "sea cow," as he described it) rose from the water and charged Moffat's canoe. A fellow traveler hit the snorting beast with a stone as it neared the boat. Then the hippo turned and chased two men who, although they were on horseback, barely made it up the bank of the river.

Hippopotamuses are usually timid and gentle animals, but they can become violent when irritated. A hippo literally bit an African native in two after the man, who was hunting for hippos, tried to shoot the animal.

The word "hippopotamus" comes from two Greek words: *hippo* meaning "horse" and *potamos* meaning "river."

rugged terrain of mountains, swamps, waterfalls, and deserts made traveling tiresome and dangerous. Wild animals also posed a constant threat to their safety. Often their hired guides deserted them or led them the wrong way. There was also the threat of unfriendly tribes who practiced cannibalism. If they considered the white man their enemy, they would kill and eat him.

The biggest danger for the explorers, however, was disease. Many unknown tropical viruses and infections attacked the white man. Medical science learned much about these diseases and their treatment from the explorers, but many explorers suffered or died first. An ever-present problem was lack of food. Supplies often went bad, ran out, or were stolen. Game and fruit were not always plentiful. Despite these hardships, the explorers went on, many of them echoing Henry Stanley's words: "I can die, but I will not go back."

Results of Exploration

The explorers sent or brought home reports of their work. With each report, the map of Africa grew more detailed. Throughout the nineteenth century **cartographers** (map makers) slowly filled in the continent with rivers, mountains, plains, and deserts. In western Africa the explorers charted the course of the **Niger River** (NYE jur). In central Africa they found the source of the **Congo River.** In southern and eastern Africa they discovered the **Zambezi River** (zam BEE zee) with the

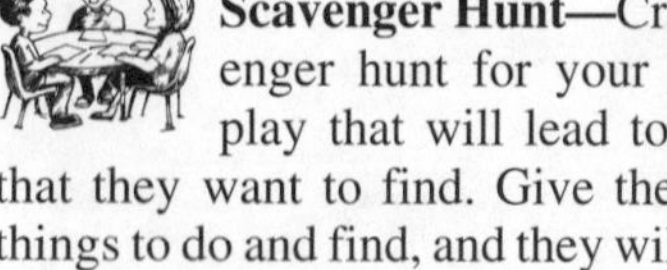

Scavenger Hunt—Create a scavenger hunt for your students to play that will lead to something that they want to find. Give them a list of things to do and find, and they will "explore" until they find it. As time allows, give them hunts with increasingly difficult directions.

"I Will Not Go Back"—What made the explorers so determined to explore Africa when so many difficulties were involved? Why could they say like Stanley, "I can die, but I will not go back"? *(The thrill of discovery at this time was strong, as was the power and prestige that came from finding something for the first time. Many were willing to die for this thrill. Likewise, missionary explorers were determined to take the gospel to people no matter what the cost.)*

Map Study—Using the map on the next page, find all the bodies of water that are listed on this page and the next (BLM 14-1). Encourage students to notice other rivers and lakes that are not mentioned on this page.

Other Animals—Cheetahs, hyenas, jackals, leopards, and lions prey on such animals as the antelope, gnu, and buffalo. Baboons, chimpanzees, and monkeys live in Africa. Crocodiles, flamingos, pelicans, and storks live in or near water. Some endangered species in Africa include the white rhinoceros, the gorilla, and the elephant. It is illegal to hunt these animals in most African countries. Illegal hunting is called poaching.

Lions, Elephants, and Lemurs—Some of the strangest animals found in Africa live on the islands of Madagascar and Comoros. Lemurs are long-tailed mammals with fluffy fur. Beyond that, it is difficult to describe them. There are sixteen species of lemurs with varying traits. Some look like monkeys; some look like squirrels; some resemble mice. The smallest lemurs measure about twelve inches long, while the largest are about forty-eight inches long. Sifakas are one of the monkey-like varieties of lemurs. With powerful hind legs, sifakas can spring from tree to tree, covering twenty feet in one leap! Another variety of lemur, the aye-aye, is a nocturnal creature. Bat-like ears help it listen for grubs underneath the bark of trees. To reach these tasty treats, the aye-aye uses its powerful incisors. These teeth can also cut holes into coconuts.

Perhaps the most well known type of lemur is the ring-tailed lemur. These lemurs have a distinctive long tail with alternating bands of black and white fur. Unlike other lemurs, ring-tailed lemurs spend much of their time on the ground.

magnificent **Victoria Falls** (named for Queen Victoria of Great Britain), **Lake Nyasa** (NYAH sah), and **Lake Tanganyika** (TAN gun YEE kuh). The search for the source of the Nile River was a most intriguing as well as time-consuming hunt.

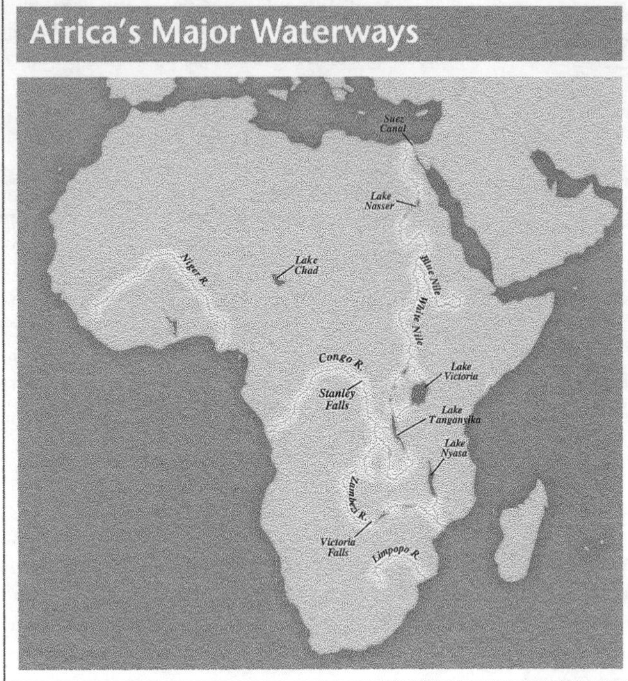

In Africa's interior the explorers saw many strange plants and animals for the first time. Zebras, giraffes, and rhinoceroses (which had at one time been mistaken for unicorns) were just a few of the animals unfamiliar to the explorers. Often the explorers found unusual plants with fruits and nuts, which they ate when their food ran out. The continent contained a vast field of study for botanists (scientists who study plants) and zoologists (scientists who study animals). The explorers made detailed descriptions of plants and animals to send back to Europe. Even today Africa remains a favorite place of study for many scientists.

The explorers also met many different African tribes. Each tribe had its distinctive customs even though most had similar traditional cultures. The explorers recorded in writing and drawings tribal clothing, houses, ceremonies, and art. A constant fear to any explorer was whether a new tribe he met would be friendly or savage. Some chiefs welcomed the white men, while others attacked them.

The explorers brought valuable information to Africa as well as taking it from Africa. They brought their heritage of Western ideas and technology. The explorers exposed the Africans to Western politics, economics, education, science, and medicine. This exposure to Western culture came mostly through teaching the Africans to read and write. First, African languages had to be written out and then Western works translated into them. It was slow work but one that had a great impact on African culture.

The explorers also helped to end the slave trade. They saw the harsh treatment of the slave dealers, and their reports to home spurred on those who fought to abolish the trade. Many explorers believed the way to end the slave trade was to increase the trade in other goods. Most African traders desired European goods and sold slaves to get them. If African resources in gold, diamonds, tin,

Animals and the Zoo—Have your student(s) name all of the typically African animals they can think of. As time permits, visit the zoo to see many of these animals.

Languages—If you or one of your students knows a foreign language that the rest of the class does not know, have him speak a sentence at a time to the class. The class should write down what they hear. This is much the same way that African languages were written down. Have the students try to figure out what he said. He may help them by pointing or acting, just as the Africans may have done to help Europeans learn the language. Later, the student should tell the others what he said.

and agricultural products were developed, the explorers said, then these would replace slaves as the most desired product of Africa. European businessmen soon saw the truth of this observation and began to develop some of Africa's resources. When the slave trade was abolished, these resources were developed even more.

Section Review

1. List four reasons that explorers went to Africa.
2. List four discoveries about Africa made by the explorers.
3. What did the explorers fear most about meeting new tribes?
4. How did Western culture come to African tribes?
5. What did the explorers suggest could replace the slave trade?

How did the Industrial Revolution help make exploration possible?

"I just love exploring! Don't you?"

Section Review Answers

1. curiosity, study, meet new peoples, fame, wealth, hunting, missions, discovery, adventure (any four)
2. Niger River, Congo River, Zambezi River, Victoria Falls, Lake Nyasa, Lake Tanganyika (any four)
3. that they would be savage
4. through explorers
5. trade in other goods such as gold, diamonds, and tin

Answers will vary. The Industrial Revolution contributed new technology and increased curiosity and thought. With new ships, explorers were able to sail ever farther than before. Other machines made production of needed goods possible.

Student Objectives

Students should be able to

1. Locate Southern Africa on a map.
2. Identify each continent and subcontinent.

Interesting Geographic Facts— The world's fourth largest island, Madagascar, is part of Africa. It lies to the southeast of the mainland.

The only lake that is bigger than Lake Victoria is Lake Superior in the United States.

Most parts of Africa stay around the same temperature all year long. The biggest temperature changes are actually from day to night, and for this reason night is called "the winter of the tropics."

Africa's Stars— In 1867 a farmer's son found "a pretty pebble" along the banks of the Orange River in South Africa. That pebble turned out to be one of Africa's stars—a diamond. The diamond industry did not begin to boom in South Africa until another discovery was made two years later. A shepherd found an eighty-four-carat diamond by the Orange River. News quickly spread to Europe, and the rush began.

The grand prize of Africa's diamond fields was found in 1905. Uncut the diamond weighed 3,106 carats. (1 carat=200 milligrams) It became known as the Cullinan diamond, named for Sir Thomas Cullinan, who discovered the mine in which the diamond was found. The diamond was presented to the reigning monarch of England, Edward VII. Dutch diamond cutters cut the stone into nine large stones and ninety-seven smaller ones. The largest one was named the Star of Africa. It continues to be the largest cut diamond in the world, weighing 530 carats. This pear-shaped gem is now set in the English scepter as part of the crown jewels.

SETTINGS—Southern Africa

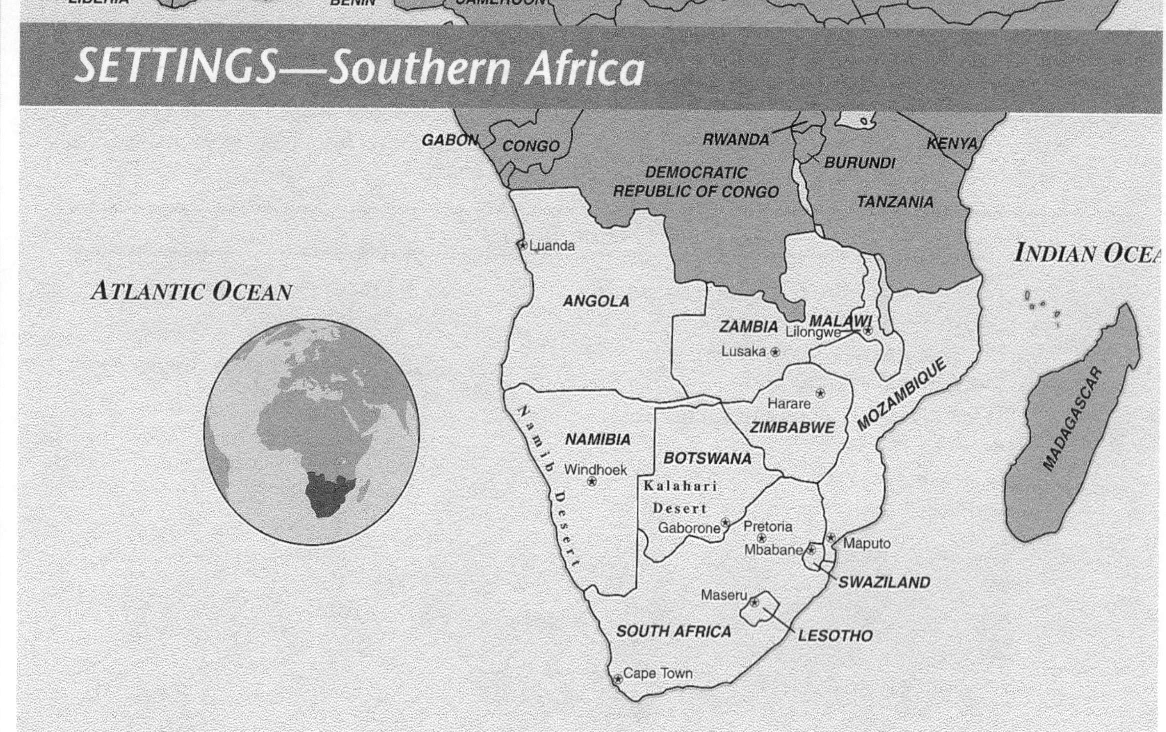

Location—This African region lies below the equator and includes Angola, Zambia, Malawi, Mozambique, Zimbabwe, Namibia, Botswana, Lesotho, Swaziland, and South Africa. The region is south of Tanzania and the Democratic Republic of Congo. The Atlantic and Indian Oceans form Southern Africa's western and eastern borders.

Climate—There are several climate areas in Southern Africa. Much of the northern portion of the region is savannah. Here great herds of animals migrate with the rainy season and the dry season. South of the savannah is a broad band of semiarid steppe climate, which along the west coast turns into desert. The harsh desert softens around Cape Town, South Africa, where a mediterranean climate takes over. Rains are much more consistent on the east side of South Africa, including Lesotho and Swaziland. This portion is the only humid area in the region.

Topography—There is a narrow coastal plain around this region. It averages about twenty miles wide with the exception of the large plain in Mozambique. From this plain the land rises sharply to the inland plateau. Because of this sharp rise, most rivers are navigable for only a few miles. The **Namib Desert** lies along the west coast of Namibia. Great fogs roll in off the ocean, bringing the only source of water to desert plants and animals. In the southern interior lies the **Kalahari Desert,** which, although it receives little rain, has many rivers running through it that support wildlife.

Natural Resources—Southern Africa is rich in mineral resources. It ranks among the top world producers of gold, chrome, antimony, manganese, bauxite, phosphate, asbestos, iron ore, and copper. Nearly all the world's diamonds are mined in Southern Africa.

Materials

- Wall map of Southern Africa (BLM 14-2)
- Transparencies for Chapter 14

Map Activity— Use map 14-C from the Activities Manual to reinforce the geography lesson.

Going Beyond— Read the Settings pages on Southern Africa with your students and answer the questions. Southern Africa was isolated from Northern Africa by the great Sahara for many years.

Use a world map (TT 14-A) to teach your students the continents and subcontinents. They should be able to locate and identify each one. You will want to take time to identify the Asian and European parts of Russia. Russia is divided at the Ural Mountains.

Geography & Culture—For years climate and topography hindered inland exploration. In this region, only South Africa has a climate that Europeans found hospitable. As a result, this area was settled early and came under European domination. Europeans' ignorance of tribal boundary lines when dividing other Southern African countries caused much internal strife for those countries. In spite of the great resources of the region, many countries are trapped in poverty because of unstable governments. Many areas remain unsettled and underdeveloped even today.

Settings Review

1. What climate region is home to many animals?
2. What two deserts are located in Southern Africa?
3. How are the deserts different?
4. This region is almost the world's sole source of what gem?

Name one way that an unstable government would keep a land underdeveloped and poor. Explain your answer.

This South African woman's wealth is in her neck rings, while this farmer seeks prosperity in a good harvest. Modern South African cities, such as Johannesburg, are changing the traditional agrarian lifestyle of some African people.

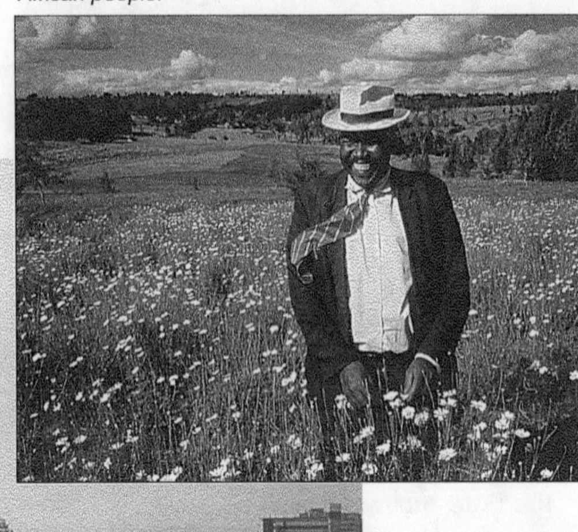

Neck Rings—Neck rings worn by the Ndebele (UN duh BEL uh) people of South Africa are called *iindzelas*. They are used to show wealth and status. The brass and copper rings can weigh as much as twenty pounds. Sometimes the rings are also worn on the ankles and arms.

The Ndebele are not the only people who wear neck rings. The Padaung women of Burma wear several neck rings that reach heights of one foot or more. The first rings are worked onto the neck when girls are only five years old. More rings are added periodically. Many assume that the rings cause the neck to stretch. However, the weight of the rings is actually pushing the collarbone and ribs down to give the appearance of a long neck.

Settings Review Answers

1. savannah
2. Namib and Kalahari
3. The Namib Desert receives its only water from great fogs rolling in off the ocean; the Kalahari, though it has little rain, has abundant rivers running through it.
4. the diamond

Answers will vary. An unstable government would devote its time to gaining power and fighting its enemies. No time would be available to develop resources. Instead of improving farming techniques and resource cultivation, the government would spend its time on its own greedy purposes.

SECTION 3

Student Objectives
Students should be able to

1. List at least four contributions Europeans made to Africans.
2. Evaluate the results of Moffat's and Livingstone's work in Africa on the future of Africa.

Missionary Mary Slessor— Mary Slessor is another missionary to Africa the students might like to study. Born in Scotland, Mary worked in a factory during her girlhood. She loved to read, and a Bible and a church publication were all she could find. The church publication always had an article on missions in Africa, and Mary cut out and saved each article and the accompanying map. She read about the coastal district of Calabar in West Africa, and eventually a missionary to Calabar spoke at a mission club Mary attended. Mary decided to go to Calabar as a missionary.

Twenty-eight-year-old Mary Slessor traveled to Calabar in 1876, where she taught day school at the Scottish mission. After twelve years in Africa, the mission finally allowed Slessor to travel to the north to minister to the Okoyong people. No European had ever been to this area north of Calabar.

The Okoyong practiced twin murder (killing all twins born to an Okoyong woman) and witchcraft. The people often got drunk and had gunfights. Though Slessor was small and alone, the Okoyong respected her and listened to her. She lived as the natives did—she ate their food, walked barefoot, did not wear a hat, and kept her hair short. She opened two schools and taught the tribal children to read. She adopted many of the orphaned and abandoned native children as her foster children.

In 1891, Mary took a furlough in England. While there, she visited the main mission board and asked for their permission to marry Charles Morrison, a missionary teacher at the Calabar mission. Morrison's health was poor, and the mission board was afraid he would suffer illness if he went to the land of the Okoyongs.

Africa Evangelized

The most important gift brought to Africa by the explorers was the gospel. Many of the explorers were really missionaries who explored new territory in their work. Other missionaries followed the routes of the explorers to reach the tribes of interior Africa for Christ.

The Gospel to Africa

Many contributions made by westerners to Africa—written languages, abolition of slave trade, and better medical care—came from the work of missionaries. They set up schools and hospitals. They learned strange languages so that they could teach the people of God's love from the Bible in their own tongues. They saw many leave their worship of idols and evil spirits and come to a knowledge of salvation through the Lord Jesus Christ.

Robert Moffat

Robert Moffat was born in Scotland in 1795. His parents were diligent, thrifty, and religious. His mother would gather the children together on winter evenings to teach them to sew and knit—the boys too. While they were busy practicing, Moffat's mother would read stories from the church papers about missionaries to Greenland and Labrador. God used both these early sewing lessons and the inspirational stories in the life of Robert Moffat.

In 1816, when Robert was eighteen, he took a job as a gardener in London. Just as his parents had taught him, Robert continued to read his Bible faithfully. It was at this time that the Lord brought Robert into contact with a group of Methodists who had been saved under the preaching of John Wesley. After Robert attended several Methodist meetings, he began to wonder whether he was truly converted. He asked a question that often confronts children born in a religious home. He wondered how he could have a conversion experience like the ones he read in the Bible when he had never been a great sinner. (He even considered doing great sins so that he could repent and be saved.)

This question burned in Moffat's heart and caused him to read the Bible even more. "One evening while poring over the Epistle to the Romans, I could not help wondering over a number of passages which I had read many times before. They appeared altogether different. I exclaimed with a heart nearly broken: 'Can it be possible that I have never understood what I have been reading?' turning from

Robert Moffat

Materials

- Guest speaker, a missionary (or a missionary letter)
- Biographical accounts of missionaries to Africa (available through BJUP)
- Bibles for Bible study
- Video on a missionary to Africa
- Pictures of missionaries to Africa
- Gospel tracts for visitation

Missionary—Bring in a missionary to Africa as a guest speaker for your students. Have him describe some of the sights, sounds, and peoples of Africa.

Reading—If a guest speaker is not available, read to your students some short biographical accounts of missionaries to Africa. (Some are included in the margins.) Most Christian libraries and bookstores will have books that give short accounts of many missionaries' lives. (Biographies of Livingstone and Slessor are available through BJUP as well as many other biographies of missionaries to other parts of the world.)

Moffat's homestead shows his efforts at cultivating fruit trees and vegetables native to Europe.

one passage to another, each sending a renovation of light into my darkened soul. The Book of God, the precious undying Bible, seemed to be laid open, and I saw what God had done for the sinner. I felt that, being justified by faith, I had peace with God through the Lord Jesus Christ."

Later that year after his conversion, Moffat was walking across a bridge and saw a sign posted that advertised a missionary meeting. As he stood and read, he "resolved to go to sea again and get landed on some island or foreign shore where [he] might teach poor heathen to know [the] Savior." In 1817 Robert Moffat landed on that shore, South Africa, to begin his ministry.

In the early years especially, life in Africa was difficult. Moffat often went without much food and drank brackish (salty) water. When he lived in one African village, he had to be careful at night because wandering village cows would come into his hut.

In spite of uncomfortable conditions, Moffat tried to keep himself neat. The sewing he had learned from his mother helped him keep his clothes in good repair. Another trick he learned from her did not help, however. He had watched his mother sometimes fold a shirt and slap it with a flat board to get the wrinkles out. Without a board available, Moffat used a smooth piece of granite. After slapping his shirt smooth, he picked it up and found that he had worn holes the size of his finger into it. At the end of his first year, Moffat came back to Capetown with all his shirt sleeves cut off.

Two years after Moffat came to South Africa, his sweetheart, Mary Smith, made the harrowing voyage from England to Capetown. After much prayer, she had decided to give up the comforts of England and home to join Moffat on the mission field. They were married on December 27, 1819.

During Moffat's fifty-three years in South Africa, he took the gospel to many tribes and established a mission that became a way station for later missionaries. He taught other missionaries to grow foods in the African soil and become self-sufficient in the harsh land. He established friendships with several tribal leaders and did much to bring peace to the area. Moffat also translated the Bible, *Pilgrim's Progress,* and a hymnal into one of the African dialects. Several of Moffat's sons and grandsons became leaders in South African politics. His daughter, Mary, married David Livingstone.

When the board asked Slessor if she would move back to Calabar if she married, she said no. Her mission was to the Okoyongs, and she would not leave them for any reason. Permission to marry was denied.

When Great Britain set up the Niger Coast Protectorate in 1889, the British government made Mary Slessor the vice-consul to the Okoyong people and told her to handle disputes as she saw fit. Mary worked slowly but surely to bring law and order to the area. She was not afraid of the tribesmen and often boxed their ears or took their gin and guns from them! She trusted the Lord and fearlessly spread His gospel to the natives of West Africa for thirty-eight years.

Sharing the Gospel—The Bible says in many places that we are to proclaim the gospel to the whole world. Each student should find and write at least five verses that show this. Discuss the verses in class.

Old-fashioned Ironing—Using an old t-shirt or other old shirt, have students practice ironing Robert Moffat's way. Point out that although it takes a long time, it does accomplish the purpose.

Livingstone and Malaria—The London Missionary Society originally wanted to send David Livingstone to the West Indies, but Livingstone wanted to use his medical skills in a place that desperately needed them. Medical practices were already set up in the West Indies.

Because of Livingstone's missionary work and exploration of Africa, people often forget that he was a physician. His medical work and experimentation with quinine helped other missionaries to survive in the African climate. Livingstone administered quinine as soon as symptoms of the fever showed, instead of waiting until it was too late to do any good as other physicians did.

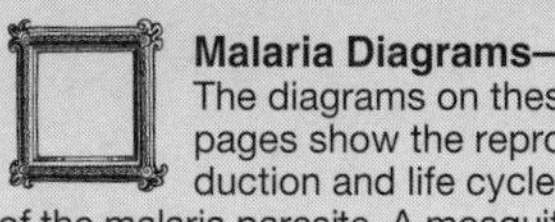

Malaria Diagrams—The diagrams on these pages show the reproduction and life cycle of the malaria parasite. A mosquito carries the malaria parasite after it sucks the blood of a human who has the disease. The top circle in the diagram shows the sexual reproduction of the malaria parasite that occurs in the mosquito's stomach. The bottom circle shows asexual reproduction, which occurs in the mosquito's body cavity. After the parasite reproduces in the mosquito's stomach or body, it migrates to the salivary gland and the mosquito injects it into another human.

BACKGROUNDS

Fighting Malaria

Malaria sickened and killed many explorers and missionaries, as well as natives, in Africa during the 1800s. Even in modern times, as many as one million people die annually as a result of malarial infection.

In ancient Italy the people found that if they lived in a swampy area they sometimes developed fevers. They went so far as to name the fever diseases *mal aria*—"bad air." For centuries, people believed that the fever (and many other diseases) came from the air. Their belief seemed to be supported by the fact that when they drained swampy areas, the incidence of malaria decreased. It would be years before they would find the true cause.

In 1880 a French physician found the cause of malaria. Charles Laveran discovered a **parasite** (an organism that grows in or feeds on another organism without contributing anything to it) in the blood of someone infected with the disease. Dr. Laveran knew that the parasite was making the victim sick, but how did the parasite get into the bloodstream? In 1897 a British doctor, Ronald Ross, discovered the same parasite in mosquitoes. The connection had been made. Dr. Ross was sure that the malaria parasite was transmitted to humans by the bite of the mosquito.

If the mosquito is sucking blood out of your arm, how does a parasite get into you? Does it swim "upstream"? No. Before it sucks, the mosquito injects you with a fluid to deaden the area

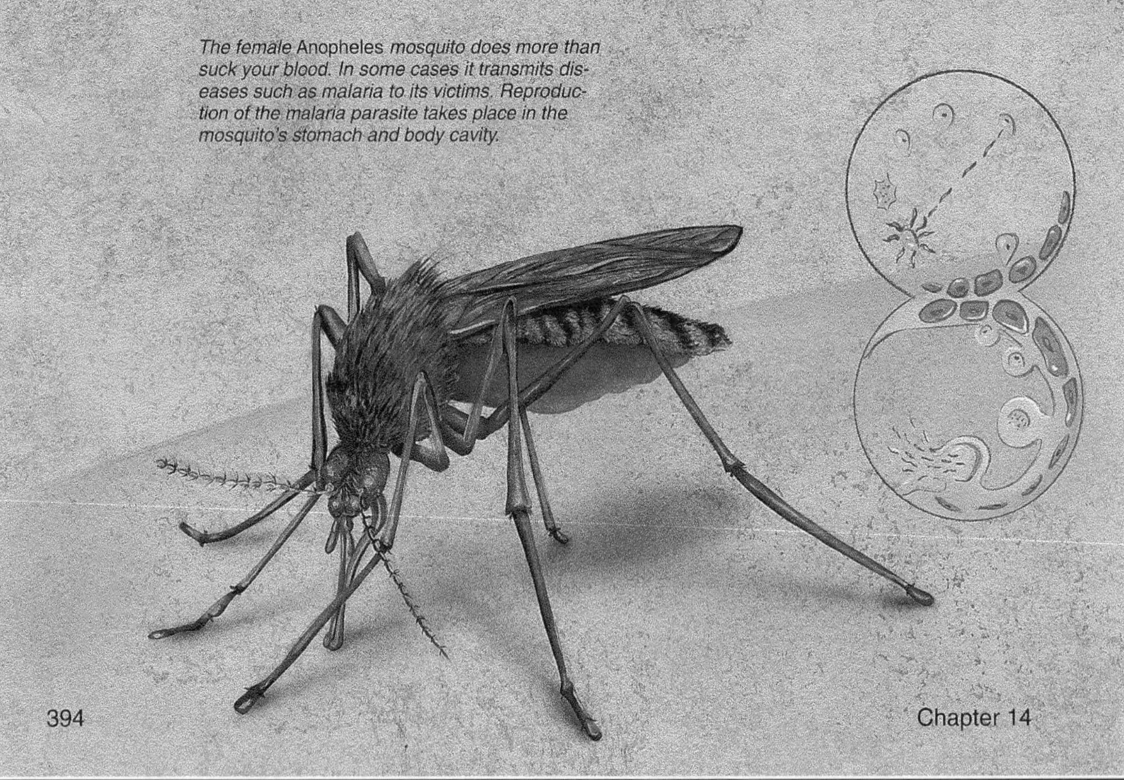

The female Anopheles *mosquito does more than suck your blood. In some cases it transmits diseases such as malaria to its victims. Reproduction of the malaria parasite takes place in the mosquito's stomach and body cavity.*

Mosquito Bites—Do not allow your students to become overly concerned about getting bitten by mosqitos. It is good to encourage them to apply insect repellant or to use other suitable deterrents. They may also be interested in learning about Lyme disease—a disease one receives from deer ticks, usually in forests or high grassy areas. Have them look up encyclopedia or Internet entries on mosquitos and ticks to find out other information about them.

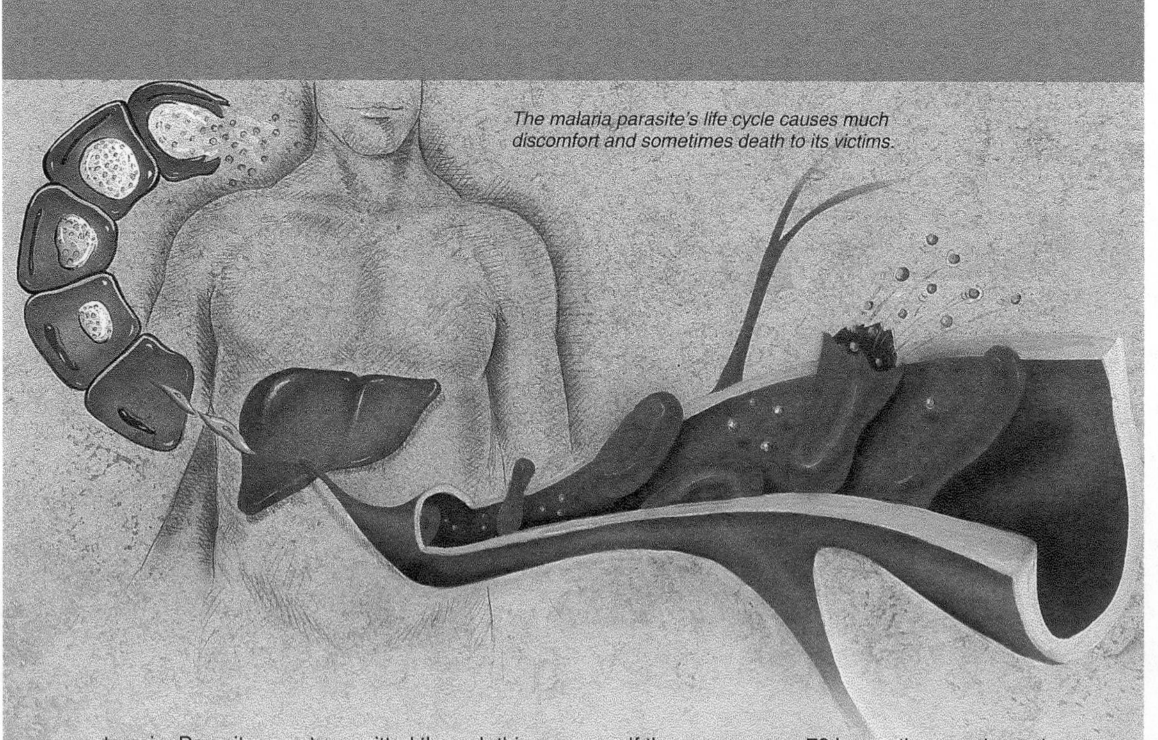

The malaria parasite's life cycle causes much discomfort and sometimes death to its victims.

to pain. Parasites are transmitted through this fluid. It is not until the mosquito has already begun sucking that your body's defenses react to the fluid and you feel the need to scratch. Then you see the fat, red-bellied thief on your arm. By that time, the microscopic parasites have flowed down the tubelike mouth of the mosquito into your blood.

Once in your bloodstream, the parasite continues its growth in stages. One stage develops inside your red blood cells. When mature, the parasites burst through the cells. The breaking of these cells (and your body's response to it) throws your body thermostat off, and you come down with chills and fevers.

Doctors can tell what kind of malaria parasite you have been infected with by timing the intervals between "attacks" of chills and fevers. If the attacks occur every 48 hours, then you have the *Plasmodium vivax, falciparum,* or *ovale* parasite. If they occur every 72 hours, then you have the *Plasmodium malariae.* "So what?" you might be saying. But the timing of the intervals allows doctors to administer the drug that is most effective on the specific parasite. Identification could be a matter of life or death—yours or the parasite's.

Even though doctors did not know until after 1880 how malaria was caused or what transmitted it, they did have a treatment that helped the symptoms long before that. When the Spanish Jesuits came to South America, the natives shared with them a cure for the fevers. The Indians knew that when the bark of the cinchona (sin KONE nuh) tree was boiled, it produced a liquid that helped the fevers. The medicine that resulted is called **quinine.** Every well-prepared explorer or missionary of the 1800s had a stock of quinine with him. Today most malaria cases are treated with synthetic drugs.

More on Malaria—The malaria protozoan spends two-thirds of its life cycle in the blood cells of its victim. After initially reproducing in the stomach of the mosquito, *Plasmodia* are released into a human host through the mosquito's saliva. Once in the human the *Plasmodia* travel to the liver and enter the liver cells where they multiply. The cells burst, and each *Plasmodium* invades a red blood cell where it multiplies again. The blood cell bursts and releases more *Plasmodia.* The rupturing of the blood cells produces the attack of malaria experienced by the victim. In this attack the victim develops chills, fever, nausea and headache. The attacks occur every forty-eight to seventy-two hours depending on the species of protozoan. In three of the four species, the attacks continue until they weaken and stop, whether treated or not. In two species the victim recovers only to experience relapses later. The most serious infection from one species almost always results in death.

Malaria is treatable now and can even be prevented. People who knew they would be traveling in areas of anopheles mosquitos used to take the drug chloroquine prior to their trip. However, today the disease has become more resistant and responds only to Fansidar and other more costly drugs.

The best prevention for malaria is to exterminate mosquitos. In the 1960s DDT and other insecticides were used against them with great success. Once mosquito populations were down, however, the effort was discontinued. When the mosquito population rose again, researchers discovered that some species had developed a resistance to the insecticides. Thus, malaria continues to be a problem in Africa and other areas.

Stanley and Livingstone—Orphaned as a baby, Stanley journeyed to America at age fifteen. During the Civil War he joined first the Confederate Army, then the Union side after Yankee troops captured him. Soon the Union Army discharged him, and he went into the navy, from which he eventually deserted.

After his war experiences, Stanley obtained a position at the *New York Herald*. In 1869 the manager of the paper sent Stanley to Africa to find Livingstone, though Stanley believed Livingstone was dead.

Stanley had never been to Africa before, and troubles abounded on the journey to Ujiji. Fever, desertion, and battles with the natives plagued the expedition, but Stanley pressed on. Finally, in November 1871, Stanley found Livingstone at Ujiji.

While Stanley was brave and adventurous, he could also be arrogant and overbearing. He went to Africa assuming that even if Livingstone were alive he would be a sour, quick-tempered, possibly demented man, completely changed after having experienced deprivation for so long. Stanley had even heard reports that Livingstone had married an African princess. However, Stanley reported that none of the reports were true; Livingstone was a kind, quiet gentleman, full of wisdom and not married to an African princess!

Livingstone refused to return to England with Stanley because he wanted to finish his work in Africa, although he did travel with Stanley to Unyanyembe to pick up supplies.

Livingstone's Monogram—In 1958, Quentin Keynes found what is believed to be David Livingstone's monogram, carved into a baobab tree in Shiramba, Mozambique. The monogram is done in the characteristic style seen in Livingstone's letters. An entry from Livingstone's diary suggests that he carved the monogram in 1858, one hundred years before its discovery by Keynes. The Shiramba baobab is now a Mozambique national historical monument.

David Livingstone

The most famous missionary to Africa in the nineteenth century was **David Livingstone** (1813-73) from Scotland. He arrived in South Africa in 1840 and served on the continent until his death in 1873. His few return trips to Great Britain allowed him to set before Europe the need for missionaries in Africa. His chief aim in life lay in telling Africans about Jesus Christ.

Livingstone was also one of the greatest explorers of Africa. Desiring to take the gospel to all men, he ventured far inland to places no white man had ever seen. He once wrote to his father, "I am a missionary, heart and soul. God had an only Son, and He was a missionary and a physician. A poor, poor imitation of Him I am, or wish to be. In this service I hope to live, in it I wish to die." Wherever Livingstone went, he preached Christ to the natives, in both word and deed. He followed the Zambezi River, discovered Victoria Falls, and later traveled around the great lakes of eastern Africa. It was on the shore of Lake Tanganyika that **Henry Stanley** found him and where he later died. His faithful native companions buried his heart in Africa, where it had always been. Then they embalmed his body and carried it to the coast. It was shipped to England and buried in Westminster Abbey.

David Livingstone

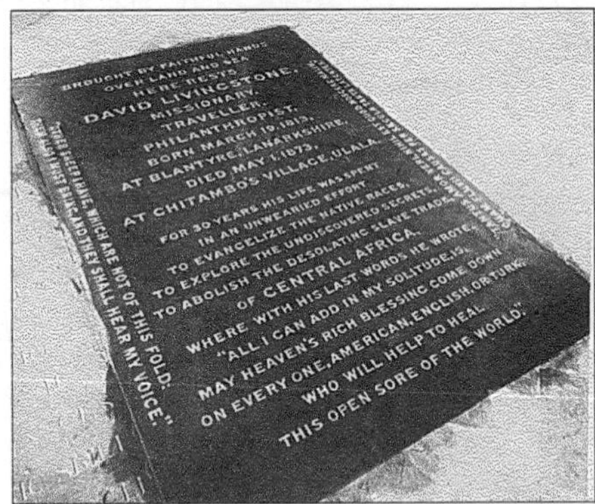

This stone in Westminster Abbey marks David Livingstone's burial site.

In response to David Livingstone's plea for workers, many other missionaries took up the work in Africa. The missionary societies that sent men and women to India and China soon saw the need of Africa and sent missionaries there too. New societies began with the main object of reaching the lost of Africa. These men and women trusted God to keep them from hostile Africans, wild beasts, disease, harsh conditions, and loneliness while they worked for Him. These missionaries heard and responded to the message of Romans 10:13-15:

> "For whosoever shall call upon the name of the Lord shall be saved. How then shall they call on him in whom they have not believed? and how shall they believe in him of whom they have not heard? and how shall they hear without a preacher? And how shall they preach, except they be sent? as it is written, How beautiful are the feet of them that preach the gospel of peace, and bring glad tidings of good things!"

Many lives were changed by God's grace because of the willingness of these missionaries to go to Africa and their selflessness in staying there to tell of Christ Jesus.

Missionary story—Show a video about a missionary to Africa. Your church library or any Christian bookstore should have a good selection of such videos.

Missionaries—Show your students pictures of famous missionaries to Africa. (Look for pictures in Sunday school materials or other books.) Use each one as you talk about that missionary.

Visitation—Take your student(s) on visitation around the neighborhood. Pass out gospel tracts or invite people to church. Special activities at the church are usually a good motivation for children to attend.

Livingstone's faithful African friend, Susi, waits with Livingstone's body after the long trip from Africa.

Livingstone and the Lion—In early 1844, Livingstone, sometimes called "the Lion of Africa," encountered a real lion in Mabotsa, Africa. Livingstone was with a hunting party, searching for lions that had been stalking the cattle. A lion attacked Livingstone and two other men before the party finally killed it. Livingstone suffered a broken bone in his shoulder and spent several weeks recovering from the incident. For the rest of his life, Livingstone fired his gun from his left shoulder, supporting the gun with his right hand and arm because his left arm was too weak to steady the rifle.

Mary Moffat—David Livingstone married Mary Moffat, the daughter of missionaries Robert and Mary Moffat. Mary was born in Africa and knew well the life of a missionary. After Livingstone's encounter with the lion in Mabotsa, he stayed with the Moffats for several weeks while he recovered. He was thirty, and Mary was twenty-three. Not even a year before, he had written to a friend that he was too busy to think of marriage. But by the next summer, he was engaged to Mary Moffat. After their marriage, Livingstone often referred affectionately to his wife as "my rib."

The Livingstones had three sons and three daughters.

No Sacrifice—David Livingstone said of his service for the Lord, "I never made a sacrifice. Of this we ought not to talk when we remember the great sacrifice which He made who left His Father's throne on high to give Himself for us."

Section Review

1. What was the most important gift the Africans received from the Europeans?
2. List four other contributions Europeans made to Africa.
3. Who was the most famous missionary to Africa in the 1800s?
4. Why did he explore as well as preach?
5. What was the attitude of missionaries going to Africa?

Someone once said, "A man's life is more than the measure of his days." In what way did Livingstone's life continue to affect the world after his death?

Africa Divided

In the second half of the nineteenth century, Europe turned its eyes toward Africa. As they had in India and the Far East, the land-hungry European nations carved up Africa and added the pieces to their growing empires. This rush for territory in Africa was known as **the Scramble.** Colonial expansion in Africa is one example (China was another) of European imperialism in the nineteenth century.

Europe's Big Appetite

The European imperialists needed colonies for trade and raw materials for their new factories built during the Industrial Revolution. They also needed new markets in which to sell their manufactured goods. Their crowded population needed new territory to overflow into. Africa, with its untouched mineral and agricultural resources, presented a valuable source of materials, offered opportunities for

SECTION 4

Student Objectives
Students should be able to

1. Analyze Leopold's reasons for taking the Belgian Congo.
2. Describe the partitioning of Africa.
3. Predict Africa's future in the twenty-first century based on imperialism.

Section Review Answers

1. the gospel
2. written languages, abolition of slave trade, better medical care, schools, hospitals (any four)
3. David Livingstone
4. because of his desire to take the gospel to all men
5. trust, willingness, and selflessness

Answers will vary. His life encouraged other missionaries to go to the field. He is a constant reminder of what a person who is sold out for Christ can do. His discoveries of geographic features and of isolated peoples opened new frontiers for future explorers and missionaries.

Materials

- Transparencies for Chapter 14
- Large map of America

The "Free" State—The Congo Free State was so named not because the people were free, but in reference to free trade for European merchants.

Leopold II—Leopold II was the absolute ruler of the Congo Free State. The country was essentially his own property to do with as he willed. Though Leopold claimed to be a philanthropist, he actually used the land and its people to his own advantage, stripping the land of its resources and forcing the people to work for him.

According to a report by the Official Commission of Inquiry that investigated the situation in the Congo in 1905, natives were required to travel away from their homes to gather rubber for two weeks at a time, with only a few days at home between trips. Beatings and mutilations were common if the natives refused to leave their homes to work in the forests. Witnesses reported that the minor officials and African soldiers instituted by Leopold were at the center of the violence, frequently committing murder and theft.

Stanley Again—Henry M. Stanley, the same man who went to Africa to find David Livingstone in 1869, was employed by Leopold II to explore the Congo ten years later.

new markets, and provided new frontiers for adventurous colonists.

For years some European nations had maintained colonies in Africa, but in the mid-nineteenth century, other countries increased their involvement in Africa. France began taking over areas in northern Africa. Then Britain added to its territory by taking control of Egypt (which was having financial problems) to protect the **Suez Canal.** Most of these territories were on the coastline, but it was the actions of **King Leopold II** of Belgium and **Otto von Bismarck** of Germany that did much to cause the Scramble.

Belgium Takes a Colony

Leopold had tried using his family fortune to purchase existing, undeveloped colonies from Portugal, France, and Britain. He told the British ambassador, Saville Lumley, that Belgium needed "a safety valve for her surplus energies." Leopold's idea was rejected by his own cabinet. Each country he approached rejected his proposal.

King Leopold hid selfish plans under the guise of humanitarianism.

But events were taking place that would help Leopold come up with another plan. David Livingstone's journal had been published. His plea had been "to heal the open sore of Africa" from its slave trade and spiritual darkness. Livingstone had suggested that honest trade would make up for lost profit of the slave trade. Verney Cameron, an explorer, had just returned from the Congo with reports of "unspeakable riches." But the governments that already had colonies were unwilling to pay for further exploration. Leopold decided to act.

He hosted a convention of explorers in 1876 and offered to help pay to "open to civilization the only part of our globe where it has yet to penetrate, to pierce the darkness which envelops whole populations." Leopold encouraged investment by other countries into what would be called the **International African Association** (IAA), but he retained control of the organization as president.

The world saw Leopold as the leader of the crusade against slavery. The fact that he used his own money was called "the greatest humanitarian work of his time." Leopold had finally gotten his "slice" of Africa. By 1882 Leopold owned the company that resulted from the IAA. The other European nations were becoming nervous.

What the investors in the IAA later found was that, far from humanitarian work, Leopold encouraged the harsh treatment and torture of African workers (slaves) on his plantations. Leopold's detestable actions caused an outcry that persuaded the Belgian government to take control of the territory themselves in 1884. The territory in the interior of Africa along the Congo River was called the **Belgian Congo.**

Imperialism Review—Review what you have already learned about imperialism in other explored lands. Have the students name as many lands as they can that were taken over by a European power and name that power. You may wish to make a chart listing the possessions of each European country mentioned.

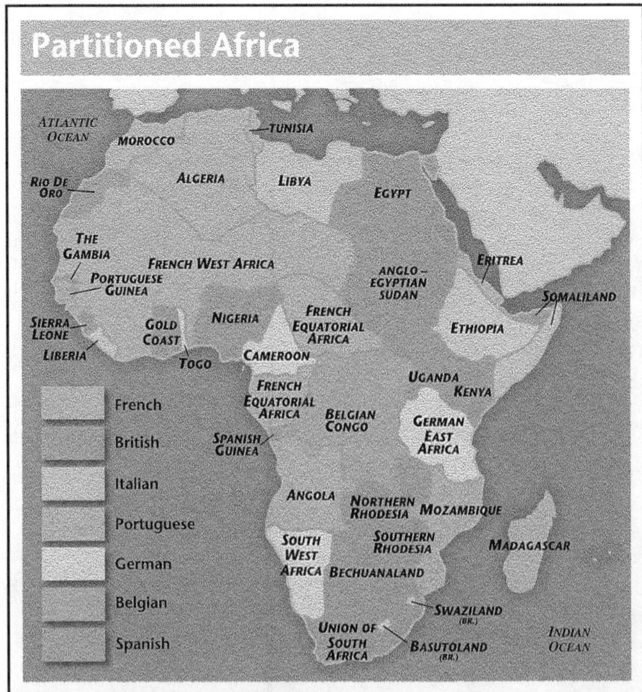

Partitioned Africa

Germany Joins In

In 1884 Germany, still a young nation, became interested in forming colonies. Otto von Bismarck, the German chancellor, chose colonies that would be politically beneficial. Bismarck made choices that would show preference to France by supporting its bids for territory in West Africa and Egypt. At the same time Germany's colonies greatly inconvenienced British commerce. In this way, Bismarck hoped to make Britain fall in line with German desires.

Germany made several claims in early 1884. It established protectorates over Togoland and Cameroon in West Africa. It then took Zanzibar in East Africa as a protectorate. Bismarck scared the rest of Europe by showing that any country with enough power to defend its claims could establish territory without actually occupying it.

The Scramble was well under way in 1884 when European leaders met at Berlin, Germany. The purpose of their meeting, the **Berlin Conference,** was to set down rules for claiming Africa. The result of the meeting was the **Berlin Act.** This act set the ground rules for claiming territory. Before any country could claim a territory, that country was required to inform the other European countries of its claim. If any other country had a claim to that territory, the countries must then negotiate boundaries. In this way the European powers hoped to avoid military conflict in Africa and Europe. The act also established the Niger River and the Congo River as free-navigation areas no matter who controlled the riverbanks.

With the rules set down, the race was on. Following Germany's lead of claiming land without occupying it, European nations began dividing up Africa on paper. If they had any claim to a region, they took a map of the area and drew in boundaries to their colony. This dividing process is called **partitioning.** Every European nation began taking more of Africa. Portugal, France, and Britain expanded existing colonies into the interior of Africa. They staked their territories based on treaties with African kings, but often the African leaders did not fully understand what the treaties meant. The division of land by these treaties caused many problems in the twentieth century when the African nations claimed their independence. By 1914 there was little of Africa that had not been claimed by a European empire.

★★★★★★★★★★

For a color version of the map on this page, see page A8 in the Appendix.

Otto von Bismarck—Bismarck believed in using force and might to achieve one's goals. He united Germany into one country. He was a prince and a lawyer who became a legislator and ambassador. He became prime minister of Prussia and secretary of foreign affairs in 1862.

Bismarck fought three wars on his way to creating a united Germany: the Danish-Prussian War, the Seven Weeks' War (against Austria), and the Franco-Prussian War. As a result of these conflicts, the Prussian king, William I, was crowned emperor of Germany, and Bismarck became the chancellor.

Partitioning—Use a historical map of Africa (TT 14-B) to show the partitioning of Africa.

Have the students divide land among themselves using a large map of America. They may "claim" the land if they have relatives there or other priority interests. Once the land is divided, discuss the difficulty of their taking control of that land just because they divided it up on paper. This will illustrate how difficult it was for many countries to control their holdings in Africa.

The Man for the Job—Ferdinand de Lesseps was the right person in the right place at the right time. Born in Versailles, France, Lesseps was raised in Egypt. His father was the French consul-general to Egypt.

While in Egypt, Lessep's father was influential in bringing Mohammed Ali to power. Meanwhile, young Lesseps became friends with the Egyptian ruler's son. He taught the youth how to ride a horse and also secretly brought him his favorite food, macaroni.

Later in life, Lesseps was appointed vice-consul to Alexandria. Upon arriving there, his ship was quarantined. Lesseps had to spend several days onboard. While he was waiting, he received a package of books from the French consul. The package contained a copy of La Pere's report of the proposed Suez Canal. Lesseps read the report, and his imagination was stirred. From that point on, he devoted time to studying the subject.

While in France a few years later, Lesseps received news that Mohammed Ali had died. Ali's son and successor was Said Pasha, the same boy Lesseps had played with as a youth. Said soon sent a message to Lesseps requesting his presence in Egypt.

Upon arriving in Egypt, Lesseps rekindled his friendship with Said. He also won the respect of many other Egyptians with his charm and superb horsemanship. He was truly the right man to build the Suez Canal.

ANALYSIS

The Suez Canal

Since the days of the pharaohs, men had dreamed of a waterway connecting the Mediterranean Sea to the Gulf of Suez. Egyptian legend says that a canal that connected the Nile to the Bitter Seas was actually built in 1500 B.C. by the ruler Sesostris. At that time the Bitter Seas were connected to the Red Sea, so the shallow canal made travel between the Mediterranean and the Red Sea possible.

For the next two thousand years, the Canal of the Pharaohs was opened or closed according to the whim of the current ruler. One ruler would have the canal filled with sand, and another would have it re-excavated. During the Roman occupation of Egypt, the canal was reopened under the name Canal of Trajan (the Roman emperor). The canal helped Rome to trade with more nations, manage its empire, and transport exotic circus animals from Africa and Asia to Rome.

After explorers such as da Gama (1498) opened the route to India by sailing around Africa, other European traders began thinking about getting to the East faster so that they could better compete with Portugal. They realized that a canal from the Mediterranean to the Red Sea would shorten the trip to the Far East by thousands of miles. But the Ottoman Empire effectively blocked any attempts by Europeans to reopen the Canal of the Pharaohs.

Napoleon was the first man in modern times to attempt to build a canal. He led an expedition into Egypt in 1798 and afterwards ordered a survey of the area. After a year, Napoleon's surveyor, Jacques-Marie Le Pere, came back with the report that the Red Sea was thirty-two feet higher than the Mediterranean. This difference he said would have to be fixed by building a series of locks (otherwise the Red Sea would flood Egypt).

It is a good thing that Napoleon never got a chance to build, because locks were unnecessary. Le Pere's calculations were wrong. The Red Sea and Mediterranean Sea are almost identical in height, with seasonal variations making the Mediterranean higher in the summer and the Red Sea higher in the winter. A canal could be

Suez Canal

Port Said
Ismalia
Lake Timsah
MEDITERRANEAN SEA
Suez
RED SEA

Suez Canal
Freshwater Canal
Cairo to Palestine RR

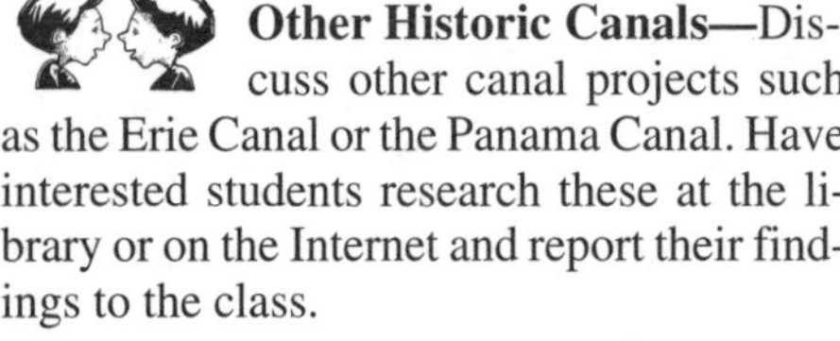

Other Historic Canals—Discuss other canal projects such as the Erie Canal or the Panama Canal. Have interested students research these at the library or on the Internet and report their findings to the class.

Field Trip—Visit a local canal or lock site that supports water trade.

built without the extra expense of locks. But it was still several years before anyone would begin construction.

Much wrangling went on among France, Austria, England, and three separate viceroys of Egypt before Viceroy Said Pasha (sah-EED PAH-sha) gave permission for **Ferdinand de Lesseps,** a former French diplomat, to build a canal. De Lesseps had formed a relationship with Said during his years of service in Egypt. On November 15, 1854, de Lesseps presented his plans to the viceroy and received the following response: "I am convinced; I accept your plan; we will concern ourselves during the rest of our expedition as to the means of carrying it out. You may regard the matter as settled, and trust to me."

Conflict and confusion continued within France, Austria, Egypt, and Britain even as a French construction company finally began work in 1859. Ten years later the Suez Canal opened for traffic. About one hundred miles long, the canal runs from Port Said (a man-made port) on the Mediterranean coast down to the city of Suez on the Gulf of Suez.

In 1875 the British bought out the Egyptian share of the canal and became partners with the French. The two managed the operation of the canal until 1956. In that year, the Egyptian government seized control and began collecting tolls from ships passing through the canal. From 1957 to 1967 Egypt collected as much as $227 million a year in tolls.

In 1967 Israel invaded Egypt, and the Suez Canal was closed. For the next seven years, all the ships that had once transported oil from Arabia through the canal had to make the long trip around Africa's tip as in da Gama's day. When the conflict was finally ended, the canal was out-of-date. During the war years, new oil tankers had been built that needed deeper channels. The old canal was too shallow. Egypt was faced with the daunting job of not only removing war debris from the canal but also digging to widen and deepen it. The improved Suez Canal was re-opened in 1979.

Colonial Africa 401

A Fruitful Defeat—Although the Afrikaners lost the Boer War, they actually experienced gain as a result. The British approved of white control over the black majority because the British wanted to use the blacks as cheap labor to work in the gold mines of the Transvaal.

British Concentration Camps—In December of 1900, General Kitchner, commander-in-chief of the British forces in South Africa, ordered his troops to clear the countryside and take the people who lived there to holding camps. He wanted to stop guerrilla warfare and thought that wasting the land where the guerrillas hid would stop them from fighting. The British rounded up Boer women and children, burned their houses, and took them to concentration camps after burning their farms. Most of the refugees were women and children; the men were away fighting.

Although the British concentration camps were set up as holding camps and not death camps like those of World War II, problems did arise and conditions worsened as the war went on. Supply shortages, severe winter weather, sickness, and poor nutrition combined to produce an estimated death toll of twenty thousand. Before the war, the Boer population had been around one hundred thousand. Children were especially susceptible to the diseases that swept through the camps.

Covered wagons and oxen teams transported Boer families into Southern Africa's interior.

Conflicts

The desire for colonies inevitably led to conflict. One conflict occurred in South Africa. The Dutch, who were called **Boers,** had first settled on the Cape of Good Hope in the seventeenth century. When the British took over **Cape Colony** in the nineteenth century, the Boers decided to move northward. This movement is known as the **Great Trek.** The Boer Great Trek was much like the westward movement in the United States, as families packed their belongings into covered wagons and set out to find new lands. Later in the century, conflict broke out again when gold and diamonds were discovered in the Boer lands. The British wanted some of this wealth, but the Boers refused. In 1899 war broke out. The **Boer War** lasted for three years. Expert Boer marksmen and horsemen defended their lands until the British defeated them in 1902. To bind up the wounds created by the fighting, the British gave the Boers an equal say in government. In 1909 the people of South Africa formed the **Union of South Africa.**

Jealousies grew between other European nations. The French, who controlled most of North Africa, resented Britain's control of Egypt. The British, who hoped to rule land stretching from Egypt to South Africa, were stopped when the Germans obtained land in central East Africa. The Italians struggled against all the other powers to obtain a small piece of the continent. Many of these problems in Africa and other regions touched by imperialism contributed to the outbreak of World War I in 1914.

Effect of Imperialism on Africa

Conflict also arose between the Europeans and the Africans. The Europeans usually obtained land by superior military force or by signing treaties with tribal chiefs. The Europeans ignored tribal identities and land ownership while carving out areas suitable to their own needs. Often enemy tribes were put in the same parcel, or a tribe was divided between two competing European rulers. Sometimes the Europeans treated their African subjects harshly. Rarely did the Africans have a voice in government.

Some Europeans hoped to help Africa and brought many gifts to them. We have already talked about these in the chapter: the gospel, written languages, new technology, trade, and Western learning. These gifts were often only side effects of European rule. The Europeans desired Africa mainly to help themselves in industrial development and political superiority. However, the Europeans also prepared Africa to enter the modern world one day.

The Dutch?—List all the names you can think of for the Dutch. *(Dutch, Boers, Netherlanders, Afrikaners, etc.)* List the two common names for their homeland. *(Holland [which is actually part of the country as England is part of Great Britain] or the Netherlands)* Name the country's two capitals. *(Amsterdam and The Hague)* The word *Dutch* originally meant "German," and the Dutch are a Germanic people. *Netherlands* means "low lands," which explains why the area is called the Low Countries. Today Belgium and Luxembourg join the Netherlands to form the Low Countries, also called Benelux.

European influence greatly changed African culture. The abundance of Western knowledge and technology encouraged Africa to become part of the world around it. But European ignorance of African history and traditions caused the Africans to resent European rule. By 1914 the Europeans had given Africa both the tools and the reasons for throwing off foreign rule. In the twentieth century, Africa would demand independence. Chapter 19 will address some of the conflicts Africa faced in the twentieth century.

"Be Prepared"—One of the English national heroes who emerged from the Boer War was Major Robert Baden-Powell. The Boers had brought the cities Kimberley and Ladysmith under their control, but the city of Mafeking remained firm under Baden-Powell. From October 12, 1899, till May 17, 1900, he held off a much larger Boer force. On the 217th day, the siege was finally lifted.

After the war, Baden-Powell served as a constable in South Africa. He finally returned to England to serve as inspector general of the cavalry. During that time he heard that his textbook *Aids to Scouting* was being used to train boys. To further this effort, Baden-Powell decided to open a trial camp on Brownsea Island in Dorset County, England. Thus in 1907 the Boy Scout movement was started. Soon troops were forming all across England.

In 1910, Baden-Powell and his sister Agnes formed the Girl Guides. To reach boys under the age of 11, Baden-Powell formed the Cub Scouts in 1916. At the first Boy Scout Jamboree in 1920, Baden-Powell was named Chief Scout of the World. Today the Boy Scouts exist in ninety-seven nations and are still known for their motto, "Be Prepared."

Section Review

1. What was the rush for territory in Africa called?
2. What was the purpose of the Berlin Conference?
3. What term is used to describe the division of land?
4. What two nations desired land in Southern Africa? What conflict resulted from this desire? What new nation was born from the conflict?
5. How did the Europeans violate tribal organization?
6. What gifts did the Europeans bring to Africa? Why did the Africans resent the Europeans?

Could Europeans have established colonies in Africa while maintaining good relations with the African people? Explain your answer.

Spanning the Ages

The race for colonies contributed to the outbreak of World War I. Nationalism became a large factor in many countries. Remind your students of the greed of these nations to devour the land of others. They will see its effect in the last unit of this book.

Summary

Europeans had their first contact with interior Africa in the seventeenth century. The explorers who sailed along the African coast traded goods for slaves brought from the interior. From these beginnings the slave trade grew until slaves became the most important African export. The slave trade was a horrible abuse of human beings that was finally made illegal in the late 1800s. The explorers and missionaries who traveled into interior Africa provided a major voice against the slave trade. Discovering much of the beauty and wealth of Africa, as well as the horrors of the slave trade, they encouraged Europeans to develop other African resources. The Europeans took their advice and began to develop Africa. The Europeans brought many gifts to the Africans, but they also began to claim land there. The Europeans' desires for land led to conflicts with the Africans and with each other. Eventually these conflicts led to African movements for independence in the twentieth century.

Section Review Answers

1. the Scramble
2. to set down rules for claiming Africa
3. partitioning
4. Holland or the Netherlands (Dutch) and Britain; Boer War; the Union of South Africa
5. Sometimes enemy tribes were put together in a parcel or one tribe were split between countries.
6. the gospel, written languages, new technology, trade, and Western learning; because they ignored tribal identities and divisions, treated subjects harshly, and gave them no voice in government

Answers will vary. Europeans might have been able to maintain good relations with the African people by not selling them into slavery, not partitioning their land, and not forcing European culture on them. Acquaintanceship rather than imperialism might have been the only way to do this. Because Europe was very imperialistic at this time, this might not have been possible.

Chapter Review Idea

Divide the class into three groups: the elephants, tigers, and lions. Have one representative at a time from each group go to the chalkboard. One should be on the left, one in the middle, and one on the right. Ask a review question. Whoever finishes writing on the chalkboard first with the correct and legible answer receives a point for his team. Repeat this until every student has had a turn.

Chapter Enrichment Activities

Research—Have students choose one from the following list of geographic features and write a one- to two-paragraph report: Victoria Falls, Cape of Good Hope, Lake Tanganyika, Congo Basin, sources of the Nile, Sahara Desert, Red Sea, Eastern highlands, Kalahari Desert, West Africa, or Madagascar. They should include information on the exploration, vegetation, and animal life of the area.

Engineering—Encourage the students to build a canal between two bodies of water (they may use bowls or other objects to make these). For an extra challenge, the students could attempt to build their canal between two uneven bodies of water (i.e., where one body of water is higher than the other, like the Panama Canal).

CHAPTER REVIEW

People, Places, and Things to Know

slave trade	Victoria Falls	David Livingstone	Berlin Conference
abolition	Lake Nyasa	Henry Stanley	Berlin Act
Liberia	Lake Tanganyika	the Scramble	partitioning
Lake Victoria	Namib Desert	Suez Canal	Ferdinand de Lesseps
Ruvironza River	Kalahari Desert	King Leopold II	Boers
cartographers	Robert Moffat	Otto von Bismarck	Cape Colony
Niger River	malaria	International African Association	Great Trek
Congo River	parasite		Boer War
Zambezi River	quinine	Belgian Congo	Union of South Africa

Review Questions

Listing

Make lists for the following.

1. The explorers in Africa met many hardships. How many can you list?
2. The explorers in Africa found the sources of a number of rivers and discovered many lakes. Name three African rivers and three African lakes.

True/False

Identify each of these statements as either true or false.

3. Europeans were the first to enslave the Africans.
4. By 1780 about seventy thousand African people were taken into slavery each year.
5. Africans helped capture fellow Africans to sell as slaves.
6. Explorers and missionaries helped end slavery.

Matching

Match the following items.

7. Berlin Conference	(a) dividing land on paper
8. Great Trek	(b) did away with slavery
9. abolition	(c) rule of one nation over another
10. imperialism	(d) the movement of Boers inland
11. partitioning	(e) decided rules for dividing Africa

Chapter Review Answers

Listing

1. no roads, rugged terrain, wild animals, desertion of hired guides, unfriendly tribes who practiced cannibalism, and disease (Answers will vary.)
2. Rivers: Nile, Niger, Congo, Zambezi, Limpopo (any three); Lakes: Nyasa, Tanganyika, Nasser, Chad, Victoria (any three)

True/False

3. false
4. true
5. true
6. true

Matching

7. e
8. d
9. b
10. c
11. a

Fill in the Blank

Write the word or words that correctly complete the sentence.

12. The source of the Nile River is the ______ River.
13. Stanley found Livingstone on the shore of ______.
14. Diamonds and gold were found in ______.
15. King Leopold II of Belgium bought ______ as a personal colony.
16. The British took control of ______ because of Egypt's financial problems.
17. When Livingstone discovered these falls, he named them ______ in honor of the queen of Great Britain.
18. The Boers first settled in ______.

Think About It!

Compare the exploration and colonization that took place in Africa in the 1800s to the exploration and colonization that took place in the New World during the 1500s. (Think about factors that led up to each exploration and conditions that made exploration possible.)

Recipe: Banana Fritters—This is a tasty and common dish in West Africa.

Ingredients:
$1\frac{1}{2}$ c. flour
6 Tbsp. sugar
3 eggs
1 c. milk
4-5 medium-sized ripe bananas
vegetable oil
confectioner's sugar

Stir together flour and sugar and, with a wire whisk, beat in eggs one at a time. Keep whisking and add the milk in 1/3-cup doses. Stir until batter is smooth and elastic. Peel and chop the bananas and mash with a fork to a smooth purée. Mix with batter and let sit for 30 minutes at room temperature. Pour about 2 inches of oil into an electric frying pan and heat to 375°. Ladle about 1/4 cup of batter into oil for each fritter. You can cook only two or three at a time since they will expand slightly. Turn once or twice with a slotted spoon for about three minutes or until golden brown. Drain on paper towels. While still warm, sprinkle with confectioner's sugar and serve.

Fill in the Blank

12. Ruvironza
13. Lake Tanganyika
14. South Africa
15. the Belgian Congo
16. the Suez Canal
17. Victoria Falls
18. the Cape of Good Hope (Cape Colony)

Think About It!

Exploration of both Africa and the New World began as a search for a shorter route to the East. Better ships, compasses, and astrolabes were invented to aid exploration. Curiosity and desire for wealth, fame, and adventure, along with a desire to bring the gospel, brought explorers to these lands. In both places, European colonies claimed land in their ever-growing imperialistic tendencies and so colonized most of Latin America and Africa.

Music and Art in History

Art and music are important mirrors that reveal how people are affected by and view the world around them. Many artists and composers with their various styles have already been discussed in previous chapters. Seeing those styles in the broader view of the panorama of history should help you understand them better and perhaps grasp the sequence of history more fully.

Virtually no music but some art from the years before Christ has survived to this day. Art pieces that remain are durable pieces, sculpted from or painted on stone or rock. Much of the art preserved from early civilizations records religious activities as in Mayan ruins or political figures as in Egyptian ruins. Rather than revealing the common people's preoccupation with these things, the art probably reveals that kings and temple leaders could afford to commission artists to create art for them.

The art also reveals the thoughts of the people. In Egypt, the art done on the interior walls of the pyramids looks strange to us with its half profile, half full front poses. But it was important to the Egyptians to show the whole person in the painting because they believed that only the things in the painting would be with the deceased person in the afterlife. If an arm was missing because it was hidden from view, then that person would be missing an arm after death.

406

UNIT THREE FEATURE

Draw Yourself—Encourage your students to draw a picture of themselves in some daily event before they read this feature. Is the picture happy or sad? How does it represent their lives? What is their main focus in life? School? Home? Church? Friends? Sports? Whether the pictures accurately represent the students' faces or not, do they show their feelings or mood? If they do, then the students can begin to understand how art and music reflect the moods of the artist and composer and the times in which they lived.

Styles—Bring in a tape or CD and play songs of various styles for your students. (*Listener's Choice* and *The Best of Leonard Bernstein,* available from BJU Press, include helpful examples.) Allow them to guess the style. Tell them the correct style if they cannot determine it. Do the same with pictures of artwork.

Pre-Renaissance Art

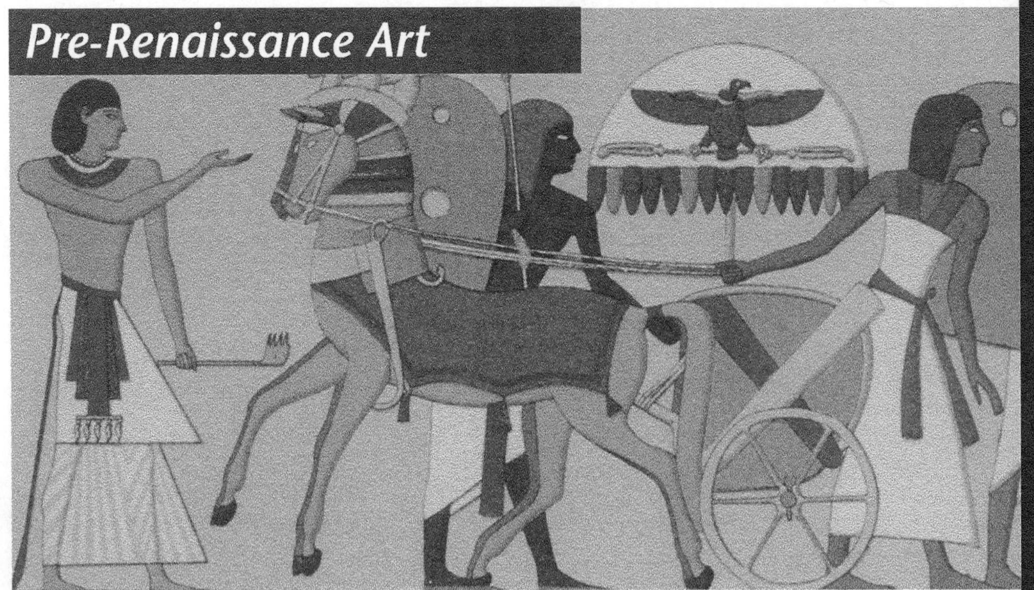

An Egyptian officer directs slaves and soldiers as they prepare a chariot for battle.

In most early civilizations there is a general absence of art for pure enjoyment except in the form of decorated objects for everyday usage. Pottery bowls reveal the common person's desire to beautify his world with art, but the lack of permanent art by the common man suggests that life then revolved around functional activities. Not only was there less leisure time for creative endeavors, but there were fewer resources available for art.

Architectural remains from the late B.C. years and early A.D. years seem to indicate that the Greeks and Romans felt good about themselves. They saw themselves as having knowledge and worth. Their sculpture reveals that they studied the human form as well as the world around them. They also had money left over after buying staple goods so that they could decorate with artwork. The remains of many homes have floor mosaics and wall frescos (pictures painted in wet plaster). Archaeological records also reveal that the Romans surrounded themselves with finely painted and glazed pottery and kept their oils, wines, and perfumes in beautiful bottles of colored glass.

Meanwhile, art in China seemed to expand from stone religious and political images to delicately painted silk banners. These silk banners honored people and illustrated proverbs. In China the interest in painting continued for the next several hundred years and reached its height during the T'ang dynasty. Portraits of emperors and courtiers were mingled with masterful landscapes and still lifes. Later, paintings decorated the walls of most temples and many homes.

As the Roman Empire waned, the center of Western art shifted to the Byzantine Empire. With Constantine's declaration that Christianity be made the official religion of the empire, religious art flourished. Elaborate mosaics depicted saints from the Bible and from church tradition. Iconography came to its height during the Byzantine Empire (500-1500) when

Music and Art in History 407

works of art served as tools for worship in the Orthodox Church (see pages 464-65). Byzantine icons look strangely flat when compared with the three-dimensional work of the Romans. Again, the art reveals the beliefs of the people. Icons represented celestial beings; these saints and Bible characters were not intended to look like regular people. Their eyes were often painted looking upward to draw the viewer to thoughts of heaven. Their physical features were unrealistic so that no viewer would mistake them for mere humans.

During the Byzantine Empire, Islam began to spread around the Mediterranean Sea. Islam prohibited the representation of people or animals because such representation was considered idolatry. Islamic decoration was very geometric and abstract with intertwining vines and flowers or repeated shapes.

Near the end of the Byzantine Empire, the Persians to the east came under the influence of the Mongols after years of Islamic control. The Mongol ruler Tamerlane brought Chinese influence to the art of Persia. Miniature paintings recorded historical events against highly stylized Asian backgrounds. Texts that recorded Persian history and told stories about the gods of the land were dotted with full-color illustrations.

While Europe wallowed in the Dark Ages, small groups of Irish monks kept the Scriptures safe by laboriously copying them by hand. While they copied, they illustrated Bible stories in the margins. The *Book of Kells* is one of the most beautifully illustrated manuscripts from this time period. What the pictures lack in perspective and accuracy is made up in gold-leaf highlights.

During the Renaissance, rich patrons began to support individual artists instead of artist guilds. With this change, artists became very competitive. The rise in towns gave middle-class people extra money with which to commission family portraits and other works commemorating their success. Finally, with the invention of the printing press, artist's etchings, such as those Dürer produced, could be mass-produced for books.

Before continuing the history of art, let's look back at music history to see how the two came together in their growth and development.

An early Chinese landscape shows a peaceful dwelling nestled at the base of the mountains.

Pre-Renaissance Music

*An older David receives inspiration for his psalms (*King David Playing the Harp, *Vouet, Bob Jones University Collection).*

Music has been part of man's development for thousands of years. Genesis 4:21 proclaims that Cain's descendant Jubal "was the father of all such as handle the harp and organ." Every culture since that time has sung and played folk music. Unlike art, singing does not require extra money or equipment. Music, however, is not something that can be preserved in stone.

Until the beginning of musical notation, musical pieces were passed from person to person and from generation to generation. Sometimes the songs were poems set to music. They often recorded stirring historical or political events. A few of these "songs" live on through their words even though the tunes are lost forever.

The Bible records many songs in the book of Psalms. The word *psalm* means "song" or "hymn." These Bible songs record great victories in battle, trials of sorrow, and praises to God. When God saved the children of Israel from death at the hands of pursuing Egyptians, the Bible records in Exodus 15:1 that "then sang Moses and the children of Israel this song unto the Lord, and spake, saying, I will sing unto the Lord, for he hath triumphed gloriously: the horse and his rider hath he thrown into the sea."

The music that the people of Israel sang would probably have sounded unusual to Western ears. The music that dominated the countries in the Middle East and across Asia featured rhythms and note patterns that were very different from European music. Even today, some Asian music sounds unusual to Western ears.

For over two thousand years, music has been performed by Chinese instrumental groups for religious and political events. Traditionally, Chinese musicians play a melody line with no harmony. In Japan, court music also flourished beginning in the 700s. Japanese theater productions were almost always accompanied by music in song or orchestra.

In other parts of Asia, musical form is dominated by religion. In India, note patterns called *ragas* are played according to the time of the day or the celestial significance of the notes. The musician uses the *raga* pattern as a starting point and then improvises the rest of the piece around the *raga.* In contrast, in the

Muslim countries of the Middle East, music is not allowed in religious worship at all, so it is used for entertainment only. The *muezzins* (criers) call Muslims to worship from the tops of minarets with a singsong call to prayer, but it is not normally considered "music."

Even the ancient Greeks emphasized music, saying it was the foundation of an ideal society. During great feasts, warrior chiefs hired men such as the famous Greek poet Homer to sing. Epic poems, such as *The Iliad* and *The Odyssey,* were divided into sections, which made it possible for the immense poems to be sung over a period of several days. In exchange for a meal or lodging, traveling singers brought information and entertainment to villages and towns. The tradition of the traveling minstrel, or *troubadour,* continued for centuries.

Music in Europe changed during the medieval years. The development of a musical notation system allowed music to be written and preserved for generations to come. But later innovations and philosophies caused the most dramatic change. Music and art started a journey which took them beyond the realm of religion and the wealthy into the homes and hearts of the common people.

Music and Art Since the Renaissance

The Renaissance revived Roman humanism. People considered themselves to be God's finest creation. Artists studied anatomy and reveled in the beauty of all that was man's to subdue. The backgrounds of paintings were now filled with mountains, trees, and rivers. By the end of the Renaissance, men had been to the ends of the earth. They were beginning to understand more fully the laws of science, and they had discovered more of the workings of the body. They no longer looked with such longing at eternity in heaven but looked for ways to make heaven on earth.

The Renaissance not only changed man's view of life but also brought new technology that changed the production of music and art forever. The invention of the printing press provided the written word for all to read in their own language. Soon the written word included verses of hymns and etchings of art. Reformers such as Luther used the printing press to put new hymnbooks into the hands of converts who were eager to sing God's praise. The effect of the Reformation on music continued through the baroque period (1600-1750) as great composers such as Bach and Handel set passages of Scripture to music.

Music in the 1700s continued its transformation with the development of orchestras, which delighted music enthusiasts. Court composers such as Haydn regularly wrote new music for kings and queens. The elegant upper class spent their evenings attending concerts and fancy balls.

In art, neoclassicism rejected the frills of the baroque style and went back to the ideals of Greek and Roman history to remind people of their noble heritage. As the nineteenth century approached, people saw that they knew many things that the Greeks and Romans never knew. They had seen more of the world than those other cultures ever imagined. Thus, romantic artists left the cold formalism of neoclassicism and showed exotic places and events such as Eugène Delacroix's *Lion Hunt.*

Reason, in the 1700s, taught people that they could know everything and did not need God to be involved in their daily lives; but without God, mankind fell into despair. Upheavals occurred as the agricultural revolution began to tear away at traditional farming society. People whose families had worked for generations as farmers were jobless. The Industrial Revolution of the 1800s further wore away the foundation of agricultural society. Displaced people crowded the cities. Discontented people overthrew governments.

Throughout the 1800s, romantic music masked social and political upheaval. Symphonic poems by Bedřich Smetana and Antonín Dvořák stirred nationalist pride as they wove their music around common folksongs.

In the 1800s the development and factory production of the piano allowed middle-class

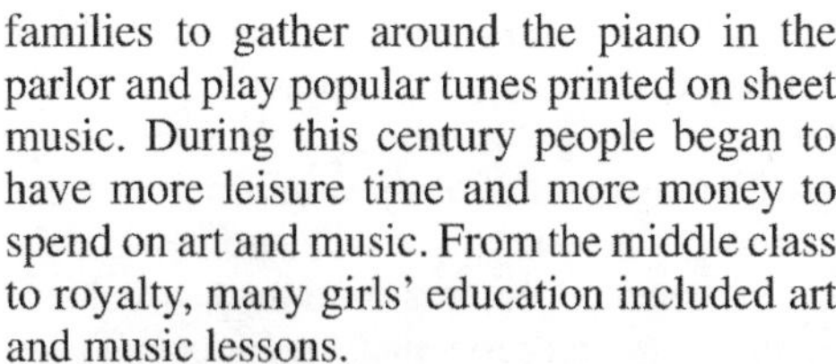

families to gather around the piano in the parlor and play popular tunes printed on sheet music. During this century people began to have more leisure time and more money to spend on art and music. From the middle class to royalty, many girls' education included art and music lessons.

In contrast to the consistent, romantic style of music during the 1800s, art went through a quick succession of styles as artists had more time to experiment. Artists began to paint for art's sake, not just to please an audience.

Romantic style art continued in the early 1800s with artists such as John Constable, but some painters were not content showing lovely landscapes or faraway places. Life was so much more than that. These painters were realists. They thought that the everyday events were significant enough to be depicted in art. Gustave Courbet painted the burial of an ordinary villager; Rosa Bonheur depicted a common horse fair in remarkable size and detail. In 1814 Francisco de Goya's painting *The Third of May* showed the reality of the Spanish revolution in stark colors and horrifying detail.

Toward the end of the 1800s, painters questioned their methods of painting. What was the purpose of doing sketches of nature and then bringing them indoors to a studio and painting in unnatural lighting? The newly invented camera showed the effects of light on a scene. That was what they wanted to paint! The impressionists were intrigued by light and color.

Starry Night, *a painting by post-impressionist Vincent Van Gogh, shows the transition from impressionism to fauvism.*

Music and Art in History 411

They tried to capture an impression of what the eye sees. The famous impressionist Claude Monet did several paintings of the same scene at different times of day and in different light just to see how the light affected color.

In America, painters continued in realism, ignoring the impressionists of Europe. These expressive realist painters such as Thomas Eakins, African American painter Henry Tanner, and self-taught Winslow Homer realistically recorded everyday events in America. Their paintings told stories about life in the emerging nation.

The impressionist painters of Europe influenced young composer and pianist Claude Debussy. Debussy changed his style of composing to capture the impression of a moment through his music. He deliberately ignored some of the standard harmonic rules of the classics and chose chords for their beauty rather than for their "correctness." His efforts greatly affected the composers of the twentieth century.

Change in the Twentieth Century

The twentieth century has been a century of rapid change. Communication, through the telephone, radio, television, and recording technology, has made the world a smaller place. Rapid change has also occurred in the arts as the pendulum of style swings rapidly from strict form to rejection of form.

When science and liberal philosophy shook church doctrine in the early 1900s, artists began to question the rules of art even more. A group of artists that European critics called *Fauves* ("wild beasts") painted in a style that was wild and free. They used intense colors and stressed design over perspective. Henri Matisse was the leader of this group with his brightly colored paintings. His paper cut-out piece entitled "The Knife Thrower" gives the minimum of detail in the intense squiggle that represents the knife thrower and the calm female form that awaits the throw against a quiet wallpaper of leaves. This style opened the way for nonobjective art and cubism.

In 1909 Wassily Kandinsky initiated nonobjective art by painting to express mood without any recognizable shapes. He felt that color and line by themselves could represent the inner emotion of the painter. His nonobjective art freed artists from having to express themselves using objects from nature.

Around the same time, Pablo Picasso left his realistic style and pushed the boundaries of art with cubism. After all, if Albert Einstein's theory of relativity was true and the laws of nature could be questioned, perhaps the laws of art and music could also be questioned. Instead of portraying a picture of a moment, Picasso showed several views of an object or event at the same time.

Debussy's earlier push against classic rules inspired composer Arnold Schönberg in the early 1900s to experiment with twelve-note scales and strange mathematical combinations of notes. Similar in style to Schönberg's works, Igor Stravinsky's ballet *The Rite of Spring* sounded primitive and barbaric to listeners in 1913, but it proved that modern sounds had a place in acceptable music.

Even as society questioned absolute rules and chose instead to do whatever brought immediate happiness, some musicians of the mid-1900s felt that even the definition of music was too confining. Composer John Cage defined music as any collection of sounds. His composition *Imaginary Landscape* featured

Will Henry Stevens, 1881-1949, untitled ["Abstraction: Primordial Forms"], 1940, Greenville County Museum of Art, Greenville, SC, Gift of Janet S. McDowell

two performers changing the volume and station settings on twelve radios. In contrast, other musicians anchored their music in ethnic heritage by once again using folksongs in new pieces. Appeal to the common man helps make composer Aaron Copland's music, such as *Appalachian Spring,* easy to listen to.

In the art world, Dadaism and surrealism wanted to sweep away the pain and devastation of civilization. These two art forms not only rejected rules but also inserted fantasy into their art. Mérat Oppenheim's fur-covered cup and saucer, which obviously could not be used for beverages, and Salvador Dali's *Persistence of Memory,* which features melting watches, are examples of Dadaism and surrealism, respectively.

Rather than desiring to do away with modern civilization, the American regionalists Grant Wood and Edward Hopper painted very realistic pictures to capture feelings about America. Wood's painting *American Gothic* reminded people during the depression of their roots in family and farm. Hopper's *Night Cafe* showed the loneliness of a city despite thousands of people living there.

After World War II a new art movement gained immediate recognition. Abstract expressionism showed the feelings of the painter—not in the subject painted but by the way the paint was applied and by the colors that the artist used. Jackson Pollack's enormous splattered canvases are an example of this movement. Once again, this art revealed a continued push toward freedom from rules and constraint.

The history of music and art provides another record of man's experiences in life. It exposes man's emotions of optimism or pessimism. It uncovers man's spirit by showing the god he worships. It reveals his relationships to the authority placed over him. Be aware of the art and music around you. How does it reflect the feelings of the people of your world?

Music and Art in History 413

Act Four

Chapter Fifteen

This chapter continues European history from Chapter 11. Imperialism and extreme nationalism had set the stage for the coming of the world wars. World War I brought great political as well as geographic change. The Great Depression affected the whole world with its devastation; and in the wake of depression, Fascism rose. The arts showed the low spirit of the age. Hitler launched another world war, even more devastating than the first, but lost. Europe started on the long, hard road to recovery. One result of this chaos is that many Europeans have turned cold to religion, yet some are still living for Christ.

Chapter Sixteen

During World War I, Russians became very dissatisfied with the leadership of the czar and violently changed their government to Communist rule. Leaders such as Lenin, Stalin, Khrushchev, Brezhnev, and Gorbachev ruled the nation, each having a different way of governing. The Soviets took over many countries through military force, but they also fought a Cold War with those whom they did not want to fight physically. One of the greatest and saddest problems of the Communist government was its policy of atheism. The Soviet Union collapsed in 1989.

Chapter Seventeen

This chapter focuses on Japan and China. In the twentieth century, the Chinese threw off the bonds of imperialism and, after a short time of republican government, came under the bonds of Communism. The people suffered economically, culturally, and spiritually under China's isolationism. Changes in political policy eventually opened China's doors to trade. China's growing economic power has made it a powerful force in Asia.

By adopting Western culture and technology early in the 1900s, Japan became a serious threat to China and the world. The Japanese attack on Pearl Harbor in World War II brought Japan world attention. It was no longer a tiny island nation, but a force to be contended with. The end of the war subdued Japan's military power, and Japan changed its focus to building its economy.

Act Four			
Chapter Title	**Main Concept**	**Pages**	**Time Frame**
15. A New Political Order in Europe	Nationalism led to two world wars. The depression caused economic upheaval in the world.	416-45	9-10 days
16. Red Menace in Russia	Communism changed under each leader, but this political system was doomed to fail.	446-73	8-11 days
17. Divisions in Modern Asia	China and Japan are representative of Asia, though very diverse in economic and political policy.	474-503	7-9 days
Feature: Canada	Canada has both English and French heritage and influence.	504-11	1 day
18. Realignment in the Middle East	The Middle East is known for oil, Judaism, and militant Islam. Constant strife is evident among many factions.	512-45	7-9 days
19. Africa Redrawn	The four sections of Africa represent the problems of oppression and violence, tyranny, racial prejudice, and tribal warfare.	546-75	8-10 days
20. The Changing Face of Latin America	Many rulers and totalitarian rule characterize most of Latin America, but a portion of the region is peaceful.	576-601	7-8 days
Total Suggested Days			47-58 days (10-11 weeks)

CONFLICTS

1900 TO Present

As Act Three closed, events set the stage for conflict. The first conflict of Act Four is described as a "war to end all wars." But its benefits are limited. An uneasy peace holds Europe together while the United States slowly builds a reputation for power and prosperity. Soon Europe is again at war, and all the world is drawn into the fray.

When World War II ends, two new giants, the United States and the Soviet Union, stand facing each other across an "iron curtain," waiting for any hint of aggression. Communism and capitalism war for the minds of new nations in Africa, Asia, and South America. Struggles result that change the balance of power. South American countries develop for themselves and not for European mother countries. African nations free themselves from the domination of Europe. Many of these countries find new oppression as powerful men and their ideas strive for control.

When the iron curtain collapses, glimpses of the Soviet Union show the weakened state of Communism in Europe. The inevitable breakup of the Soviet Union causes confusion, poverty, and more conflict in Europe. The ripples are felt around the world.

Japan and China become the first of several Asian countries to gain economic strength and, with it, political power. Europe moves toward unifying into one powerful economic and political bloc. The nations of Africa and Latin America cautiously embrace democratic government. Yet war and conflict do not cease. Violence is as natural to humanity as eating and drinking. There can be no peace on earth until the Prince of Peace reigns.

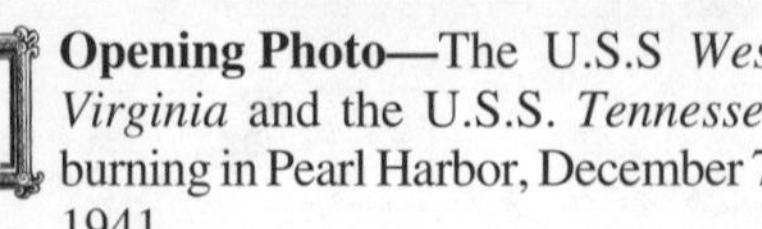

Opening Photo—The U.S.S *West Virginia* and the U.S.S. *Tennessee* burning in Pearl Harbor, December 7, 1941

Chapter Eighteen

This chapter focuses on the Middle East's relationship to the world today as represented by the countries of Turkey, Iran, Saudi Arabia, Israel, and Iraq. Turkey represents modernization and adoption of Western ways in the Middle East. Iran and Saudi Arabia represent Middle Eastern countries that are embracing traditional Islam and rejecting many Western ways. Since gaining statehood in 1948, Israel has sought to maintain independence and peace. Today the Middle East suffers from constant warfare and violence.

Chapter Nineteen

This chapter focuses on Africa by exploring one country in each of the four regions of Africa. Algeria in Saharan Africa suffered a bloody battle for independence from France and eventually was decolonized. In West Africa, Ghana was ruled by a dictator who had formerly been a Marxist. South Africa's controversial policy of apartheid no longer exists, but the nation still faces many challenges. Pan-Africanism and second-independence movements have been revolutionizing Africa as natives of some countries wish to show national pride or imitate other countries of the world. The struggle in Rwanda in East Africa portrays tribalism, a constant source of conflict in Africa. A look at the churches in Africa concludes this chapter on modern Africa.

Chapter Twenty

Latin America also faced great struggles during the twentieth century. The Mexican government changed hands often because rulers sought power, wealth, or social changes. Argentina suffered under many leaders and high inflation, with the most popular government being that of the Peróns. One bright spot in this area (and the world) is Costa Rica. This country would not allow totalitarianism to take over. Today Costa Rica enjoys a peaceful society in the midst of chaos. Catholicism is predominant in Latin America, but the Charismatic movement and Pentecostalism are growing.

Student Objectives

Students should be able to

1. Describe the events leading to World War I.
2. List the members of the Central Powers and Allied Powers of World War I.
3. Summarize the results of World War I.
4. Locate the Balkans on a map.
5. Read an import/export map.
6. Define *fascism*.
7. Match each Fascist leader with his country.
8. Analyze the problem of "German Christians."
9. Categorize artists and authors and their works.
10. Distinguish expressionist, cubist, and surrealist art.
11. List the members of the Axis Powers and Allies of World War II.
12. Describe the course of World War II.
13. Define the German terms *blitzkrieg* and *Luftwaffe*.
14. Evaluate the effects of the Holocaust on the formation of the Jewish nation.
15. Determine the causes of specified problems in Europe after World War II.
16. Name the economic community in Europe.
17. Analyze the problems of the World Council of Churches.
18. Name the well-known Ulster evangelist of the 1920s.

Opening Photo—World War II posters; Allied poster ("Victory of the United Nations is today certain!") and German poster ("New Europe is invincible!")

CHAPTER 15

At the conclusion of Sir Arthur Conan Doyle's story "His Last Bow," Sherlock Holmes and Dr. Watson are preparing to turn their prisoner, a captured German spy named Von Bork, over to Scotland Yard. It is August 2, 1914. Holmes looks eastward to the sea and says, "There's an east wind coming, Watson."

"I think not, Holmes," replies Watson. "It is very warm."

"Good old Watson!" cries Holmes. "You are the one fixed point in a changing age. There's an east wind coming all the same, such a wind as never blew on England yet. It will be cold and bitter, Watson, and a good many of us may wither before its blast. But it's God's own wind none the less, and a cleaner, better, stronger land will lie in the sunshine when the storm has cleared."

The storm Sherlock Holmes referred to was World War I. That conflict was indeed a cold and bitter wind upon all Europe. And it was God's own wind, for God controls the affairs of men and directs nations as He chooses. But Europe was not cleaner, better, and stronger for it. World War I brought the old order of Europe crashing down. From that wreckage came hope as democracy rose from the rubble. But also from that storm came a new and terrible challenge—cruel and bloody dictators. The twentieth century in Europe was to see the clash of democracy and dictatorship with the continent itself as the winner's prize.

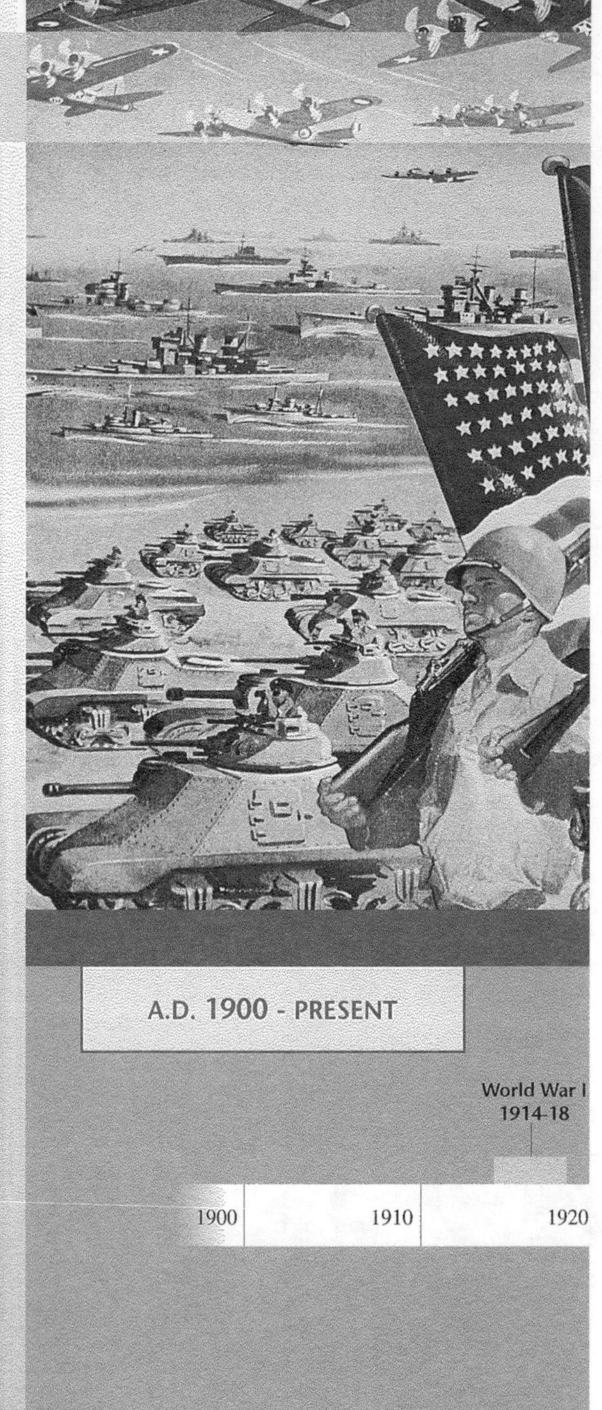

Chapter 15 Lesson Plans			
Section Title	**Main Concept**	**Pages**	**Time Frame**
1. The Old Order Passes **Settings: The Balkans*	Nationalism and alliances set the stage for a world war.	416-23	2 days
2. Despair and Dictators	Fascism arose, and a feeling of hopelessness between the wars was evident in the arts and literature of the day.	424-28	1-2 days
3. Democracy vs. the Dictators **Characterizations: Churchill*	Hitler's demands for land started a conflict that would set the stage for World War II.	429-35	2 days
4. Democracy Triumphant but Tried	The economic revival in Europe strengthened the democratic nations. Unrest remained, however, in regions such as the Balkans.	436-39	1 day
5. Religion in Modern Europe **Backgrounds: The Irish Problem*	Modern Europe cooled toward religion; the ecumenical movement attempted to bring churches together.	440-43	1 day
Total Suggested Days (including 1 day for review & 1 day for test)			9-10 days

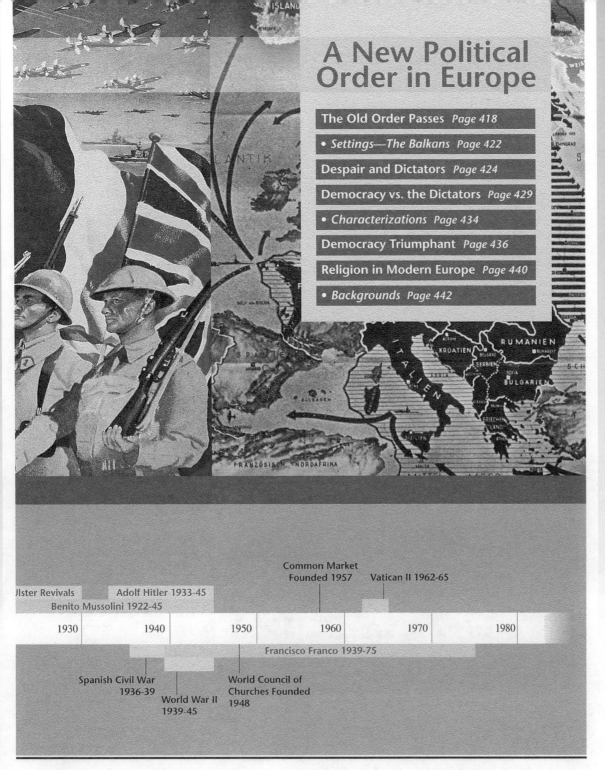

A New Political Order in Europe

Ulster Revivals

Adolf Hitler 1933-45

Benito Mussolini 1922-45

Common Market Founded 1957

Vatican II 1962-65

1930 | 1940 | 1950 | 1960 | 1970 | 1980

Francisco Franco 1939-75

Spanish Civil War 1936-39

World War II 1939-45

World Council of Churches Founded 1948

Materials

- Scripture verse (BLM verse 15)
- Wall map of the world or Europe and Japan
- *Teaching Transparencies* for use with *WORLD STUDIES for Christian Schools* (Second Edition)
- Recordings of World War I and II songs
- Wall map of Europe or the Balkans (BLM 15-1)
- Chart of countries and important terms and facts that go with each
- Recordings of music by Stravinsky or Schönberg
- Short video on World War I, World War II, or the Depression
- Guest speakers to speak on the Depression or World War II
- Recording of one of Churchill's speeches
- Currency from other countries
- *Faith of Our Fathers: Scenes from Church History* (BJUP)
- *Number the Stars* by Lois Lowry and *Molly Learns a Lesson* by Valerie Tripp

World Wars

Create a bulletin board that focuses on one of the topics covered in the chapter—World War I, the Depression, or World War II. You may wish to use pictures of such things as the Dust Bowl, battle scenes, and/or concentration camps. Flags, propaganda, airplanes, or other 3-D material will add interest to your board.

A movable chart bulletin board would also be good. Cut strips of paper and write the names of countries, leaders, and political leanings. Mount a pocket holder for the strips of paper and use them to fill in the chart throughout the chapter.

Chapter Motivator

Review the wars your students have studied in world history up to this point. You may want to have a world map or globe to show where each took place. Ask the following questions. Have you ever seen two students fighting? Why were they doing that? *(to gain control, to show that one was stronger than the other)* What might make you join one side or the other? *(peer pressure, friendships, thinking that one side is right, knowing who might win, or trying to help the underdog)* Discuss with the students the fact that Europe was going through a time of bullying each other as shown by four things: nationalism (to prove itself better than others), militarism (to prove its strength), imperialism (to build empires), and alliance (loyalty to other nations). Explain each one in terms of bullies on a playground, each one trying to gain the upper hand.

Proverbs 16:18

Extreme nationalism opened the door for both World Wars. Stress to your students that this wrong form of pride can lead only to disaster. As Proverbs 16:18 says, "Pride goeth before destruction, and an haughty spirit before a fall." (BLM verse 15)

Section 1

Student Objectives
Students should be able to

1. Describe the events leading to World War I.
2. List the members of the Central Powers and Allied Powers of World War I.
3. Summarize the results of World War I.

"Modern War"—The American Civil War has been called the first "modern war." But it was not until World War I that many other countries experienced the horrors of the modern battlefield. With telegraphy for quick communication as well as railroads and trucks for rapid transport, the pace of battle greatly increased. Automatic weapons appeared for the first time, enabling a single gunner to fire hundreds of rounds of ammunition per minute. Hand grenades and observation balloons used on Civil War battlefields also found service in Europe during World War I. Probably the most devastating Civil War tactic used during the Great War was trench warfare.

The Old Order Passes: World War I

Have you ever seen a fight about to break out? Two enemies approach each other, maybe in a vacant lot, each cautiously eyeing the other. Perhaps the friends of each fighter spread out behind their man, watching what the other side will do. When one fighter thinks he has the advantage, he lashes out, trying to win quickly. The other hits him back, his friends join in, and soon an all-out battle breaks loose.

Before World War I, Europe was like a group of wary fighters looking each other over. Germany was the strong man, with the best army in Europe. Its leader, Kaiser **Wilhelm II,** was ready to take on all comers to show the world that Germans were the most powerful people in Europe. Russia, under Czar Nicholas II, was huge but slow. It took a long time to get Russia going, but once it started—it fought like a bear. The Austro-Hungarian Empire had a big reputation, but the empire had stumbled in some smaller fights. Some European nations began to think the empire was not as tough as it used to be. Austria-Hungary depended on its ally Germany for help.

France was something like a kid who was always getting his nose bloodied (by Germany usually) and always coming back for more. But now the French had learned to get friends on their side. France had lined up Russia in particular. Italy went from one side to the other, depending on who it thought would offer the best deal for helping. Great Britain stood on the other side of the English Channel. With its powerful navy for protection, Britain claimed not did not care who was boss in Europe. But it watched closely to see who was becoming dangerously powerful.

Kaiser Wilhelm II

The little countries of Europe varied in their attitudes. Belgium and the Netherlands just tried to stay out of everybody's way. But in the Balkans, some small nations were placing a chip on their shoulders and daring the big powers to knock it off. These little nations—Serbia, Bulgaria, Romania, Greece, and others—had recently become independent of the Turkish Ottoman Empire. Most of the Balkan people

Section 1

Materials

- Wall map of the world or Europe and Japan
- Transparencies for Chapter 15
- Recordings of World War I and II songs

Role-play—After the Chapter Motivator discussion, divide the students into groups representing the alliances. Seat those from Central Powers heritage on one side of the room and those from Allied Powers heritage on the other. Seat those remaining in the middle as neutral countries or the United States. Go through the following list of events which sparked World War I and have one person or team role-play each country:

June 28, 1914—Archduke Francis Ferdinand from Austria-Hungary was assassinated in Sarajevo, Bosnia, by a Serbian nationalist.

July 5, 1914—Germany gives a "blank check" to Austria-Hungary.

July 23, 1914—Austria-Hungary demands an apology from Serbia.

July 25, 1914—Serbia refuses to comply completely with Austro-Hungarian demands.

July 25, 1914—Mobilization begins.

July 28, 1914—Austria-Hungary declares war on Serbia.

July 29, 1914—Russia begins to mobilize.

August 1, 1914—Germany declares war on Russia.

August 2, 1914—Germany gives an ultimatum demanding that Belgium allow German troops to march through. Belgium is neutral and refuses.

August 3, 1914—Germany declares war on France.

August 4, 1914—Germany invades Belgium. Europe is outraged.

August 4, 1914—Britain declares war on Germany.

The New York Times.

THE WEATHER
Local showers today; Tuesday, fair; fresh, shifting winds, becoming northwest.

NEW YORK, MONDAY, JUNE 29, 1914.—EIGHTEEN PAGES. ONE CENT

FEDERALS DESERT AGUASCALIENTES

Town South of Zacatecas Evacuated by Huerta's Forces, but Villa Turns Back.

IS CAMPAIGN ABANDONED?

Border Hears His Ammunition Is Exhausted — Row with Carranza Will Not Down.

ENVOYS WAIT ON CARRANZA

Propose Pan-American Memorial to Columbus

A splendid tomb topped by a great light is proposed to be erected in Santo Domingo, in the Caribbean Sea, by subscriptions from peoples of all lands. See NEXT SUNDAY'S TIMES.

OUR GUNS FIRE ON SANTO DOMINGO

Few Shots from the Machias Stop Bombardment of Puerto Plata by President Bordas.

HEIR TO AUSTRIA'S THRONE IS SLAIN WITH HIS WIFE BY A BOSNIAN YOUTH TO AVENGE SEIZURE OF HIS COUNTRY

Francis Ferdinand Shot During State Visit to Sarajevo.

TWO ATTACKS IN A DAY

Archduke Saves His Life First Time by Knocking Aside a Bomb Hurled at Auto.

SLAIN IN SECOND ATTEMPT

Lad Dashes at Car as the Royal Couple Return from Town Hall and Kills Both of Them.

LAID TO A SERVIAN PLOT

Heir Warned Not to Go to Bos-

Archduke Francis Ferdinand and his Consort the Duchess of Hohenberg

Slain by Assassin's Bullets.

The New York Times *announces the assassination of Archduke Francis Ferdinand and his wife, the event that touched off World War I.*

were Slavs, and they wanted other Slavs to be free too. But many of their fellow Slavs lived in Austria-Hungary, and the Austro-Hungarians wanted to expand their empire into the territory where the Turks had moved out. The Austrians hesitated, though, because the Russians were also Slavs. The Russians made it clear that they did not want their "little brothers" in the Balkans being pushed around.

By 1914, all Europe was lined up into two camps. On one side were Germany and Austria-Hungary. Italy said it would go along with them, but when war came, it did not. On the other side were France, Russia, and eventually Great Britain. In the middle of them all were the Balkans, "the powder keg of Europe." The danger with a keg of gunpowder is that just a spark can set it off.

The spark came on June 28, 1914. A Serbian terrorist assassinated Archduke **Francis Ferdinand,** the heir to the Austro-Hungarian throne. Austria-Hungary declared war on Serbia. Russia declared war on Austria-Hungary to protect Serbia. Germany declared war on Russia to keep its promise to Austria-Hungary. France came to the aid of Russia and went to war with Germany. Germany invaded Belgium to find an easier path into France. Great Britain declared war on Germany to protect Belgium. Shortly thereafter, the Ottoman Empire and Bulgaria joined Germany and Austria-Hungary. They became known as the **Central Powers.** Italy eventually joined the other side, which became known as the **Allies.** The conflict known as **World War I** engulfed Europe.

Balance of Power—The assassination of Archduke Ferdinand was not the sole cause of World War I. Rivalries and strife had been brewing in Europe for many years. As long as there was a balance of power in Europe, tensions and conflicts remained submerged. By 1914 the search for a balance of power had led to the alliance of two groups: Germany, Austria-Hungary, and Italy in the Triple Alliance; and France, Russia, and Great Britain in the Triple Entente. In effect, these countries had already "chosen up sides" before war threatened. The assassination in Sarajevo was the spark that lit the fuse of the European "powder keg."

Russian Strategy—In the battle between the Russians and the Germans at Tannenberg, the Germans knew the Russian plans because the Russians sent them over their radios uncoded. The Germans simply translated them.

Keeping Time—Throughout the chapter, record events on a time line.

Entrance to War—Using the chalkboard or overhead, draw a rough sketch of the countries of Europe. Explain the chronology of each country's entrance into the war again, this time lecturing and coloring each country as it joins the war. Color the Central Power countries one color and the Allied countries another. (TT 15-1) (Transparency 11-A can also be used.)

Trench Warfare—Trench warfare gave the defender the advantage. By providing a strong position against which the offensive army could not advance without great cost in lives, trenches allowed defenders to hold a line for long periods of time. For that reason, battles in the trenches could last for weeks and even months. Trenches began as small holes shoveled out by soldiers to escape enemy fire. The dugout was large enough only for the soldier and his gear. Later the dugouts were enlarged to form foxholes, which were deep enough for a man to stand in without being seen by the enemy. Foxholes were joined by small crawl spaces to form trenches. Some of these trenches were set up quickly in the heat of battle and were intended only for temporary use. Other trench systems were surveyed, designed, and dug by army engineers. Many had wooden floors to minimize the problem of mud.

The trenches were dug in a zigzag pattern for extra protection. This arrangement kept the enemy from using the deadly tactic of gaining access to a trench and raking its length with a machine gun.

Soldiers lived in the trenches for weeks at a time. They faced extreme hardships. They had to endure frigid, wet winters. Illness and disease were common. Men in the trenches also faced daily bombardments by enemy shells and raids from enemy scouting parties. Trench warfare proved to be a costly way to do battle—costly in human lives. By World War II, improved offensive weapons made trenches less useful.

German troops in full battle regalia, including gas masks, strike a pose, and Allied troops march in silhouette against the sky.

At first, everyone thought it would be a brief war, although each side thought it would be the one to win. But it did not work that way. After some early German successes, both sides began to dig trenches. They strung barbed wire in front of their lines. Artillery and machine guns protected their positions. Between the two armies was a muddy, bloody "no man's land." Each side hurled its men forward in waves, trying to break through the enemy's lines. Neither succeeded; men just died. For over four years, the nations of Europe tore at each other.

But a change took place as the war went on. At first, it was hard to tell just whose side was right. But soon it became apparent that this was more than just a fight for who would dominate Europe. The Central Powers consisted of nations built on military power and ruled by leaders who said their authority was not to be questioned. On the other side were France and Great Britain, democratic nations. Russia was originally a militaristic empire too, but in the middle of the war the Russian people overthrew the czar and Russia became a republic—for a while. When the United States joined the Allies in April 1917, President **Woodrow Wilson** told the American Congress, "The world must be made safe for democracy."

Wilson's dream seemed to come true. In 1918 the Allies won. Kaiser Wilhelm II fled, and Germany established the Weimar Republic. The Allies broke Austria-Hungary into several smaller nations, each with a chance to rule itself. Parts of the old Russian Empire

World War I—Write the following statement from a newspaper on the board: "As World War I rages on, many at home are giving all they can to help the war effort." Ask your students what is wrong with this headline. *(World War II had not happened yet, so World War I was not known as the first world war. It was generally called The Great War during the war. It could not have been called World War I until World War II commenced.)*

Optimism—Discuss with your students the optimism at the end of World War I. What reasons were there for this optimism? *(Imperialism was beginning to wane, authoritarian governments were put down, men would no longer have to go to war, democracy was made more "safe," etc.)*

Weapons of War—Refer to page 430 to discuss weapons used in World War I. Especially note the differences in the planes.

were freed too. Poland, for example, became an independent nation for the first time since 1795. In a thanksgiving sermon for the end of the war in Washington, D.C., African American pastor Francis Grimké said, "There are to be no more kaisers; no more czars; no more emperors with autocratic powers. The reign of the people has come—the reign of the common people. It is wonderful when you think of it!"

Section Review

1. What event sparked World War I?
2. What four countries made up the Central Powers?
3. Why did Woodrow Wilson say he wanted the United States to fight in World War I?
4. What was the name given to the government of Germany after the war?

How could a war make the world "safe for democracy"?

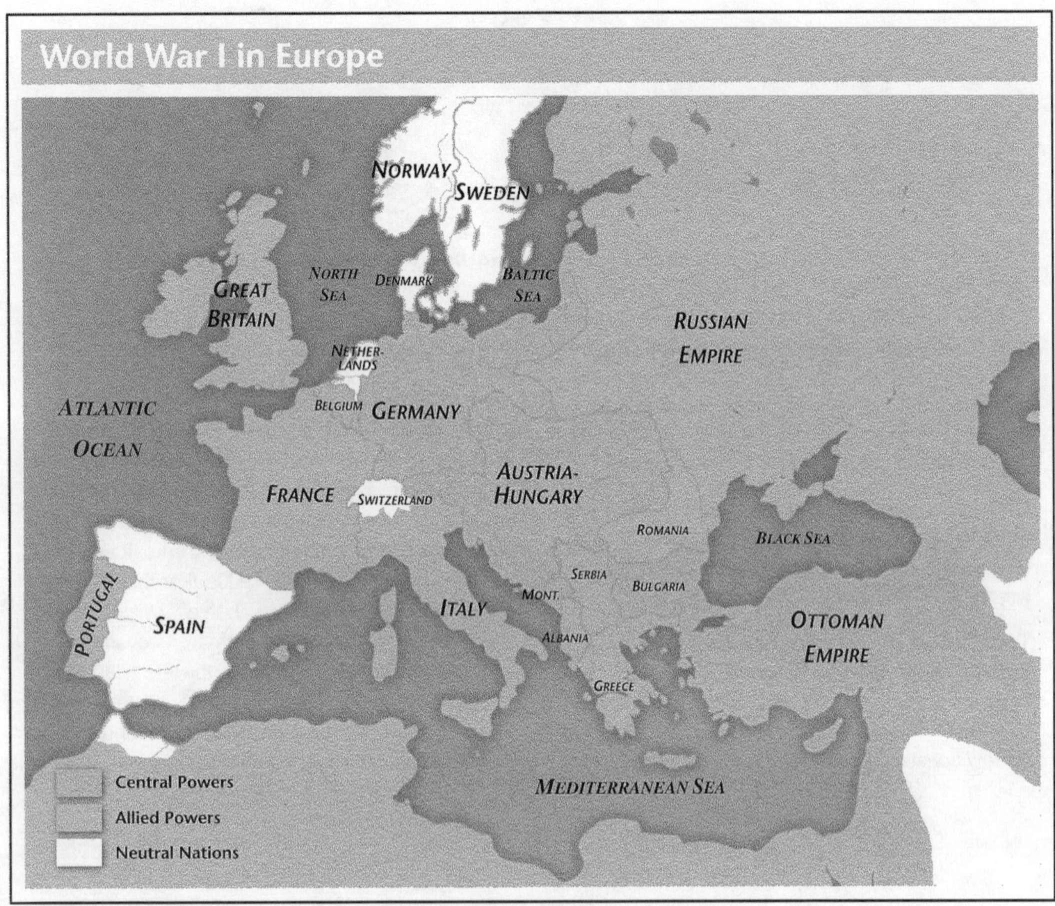

Did You Know?—In 1911 Marshal Ferdinand Foch said, "Airplanes are interesting toys, but they have no military value."

Ace Pilots—The men who did the flying in World War I attracted more attention than the planes they flew. The skillful flyers who had shot down at least five enemy aircraft were called "aces." These flyers were knighted and honored, sometimes posthumously, for their spectacular feats. Some of the men who became heroes in the air were still teenagers; many more of them died before they were twenty-one. Each country had its most famous ace, the most famous of whom was Germany's Red Baron. His real name was Manfred von Richtofen; and when he was finally shot down in April 1918, he had downed at least eighty Allied planes.

****

For a color version of the map on this page, see page A9 in the Appendix.

World War I Planes—In World War I, planes were initially used for reconnaissance. They could fly high above enemy lines to map enemy movement just as the observation balloons had in the American Civil War. However, the potential for using the airplane as a weapon was quickly discovered. While observing the movement below, pilots began to see how easy it would be to bomb the troops they saw. Pilots began carrying bombs at their feet. When they were over enemy lines, they would reach down, pick up a bomb, and drop it over the side of the plane. By World War II, technicians had developed methods for suspending the bombs below the plane's fuselage. The pilots dropped the bombs by triggering a mechanism from the cockpit.

Dogfights—Dogfights occurred when two or more planes from opposing sides met in the air. Early in the war when planes met, pilots actually shot at each other with handguns. By 1915, the Germans had developed a machine gun that was mounted in front of the pilot and was timed to fire between the propeller blades (Fokker E-111 Eindecker, page 430). This gave the Germans a distinct advantage over

Music of World War I or II—Bring to class a recording of World War I or II songs such as "Over There" or "It's a Long Way to Tipperary." Have students explain how these songs represent the spirit of the age.

Section Review Answers

1. the assassination of Archduke Francis Ferdinand by a Serb on June 28, 1914
2. Ottoman Empire, Bulgaria, Germany, and Austria-Hungary
3. to keep the world safe for democracy
4. Weimar Republic

Answers will vary. Although his strategy seemed paradoxical, Wilson wanted war to keep the relatively peaceful governmental system of democracy. He wanted to fight authoritarian regimes, and he wanted the rest of the world to experience the blessings of democracy. The result of winning a war against tyranny would be to bring democracy into those countries which were formerly led by dictators.

the French, who were slower to develop the same technology. The French did devise a front-mounted machine gun, but rather than timing the shots, they grooved the propeller blades so that the bullets would be deflected. Unfortunately, shooting off the tips of propeller blades was a common problem for the French until they developed the technology to synchronize their gunfire with the blades.

Student Objectives

Students should be able to

1. Locate the Balkans on a map of the world.
2. Read an import/export map.

The Balkans Today—Much of the Balkans was united into a single country called Yugoslavia at the end of World War I, but this political entity broke apart with the fall of communism. The countries that remain were once the republics of Yugoslavia: Croatia, Bosnia and Herzegovina, Slovenia, and Macedonia. Confusion reigns supreme today as extremist factions (especially Serbian) fight to win control over Croatia and Serbia. United Nations forces sent peacekeepers to the area, but they were pulled out when they were attacked and a few killed. The UN again sent troops into this "powder keg."

You may sometimes see Yugoslavia divided into two parts today. These parts are Serbia and Montenegro. In 1992 the UN revoked its recognition of Yugoslavia as a country. So UN member countries refer to the area as Serbia\Montenegro.

SETTINGS—The Balkans

Location—The Balkan Peninsula is located in southeastern Europe. It lies south of the Danube and Sava Rivers. It is made up of Albania, Bosnia and Herzegovina, Bulgaria, Croatia, Greece, Macedonia, Romania, Slovenia, and Yugoslavia—as well as a small piece of Turkey. On the east are the Black and Aegean Seas. On the west and south are the Adriatic, Ionian, and Mediterranean Seas.

Climate—The climate is moderate; most of the region has a mediterranean climate. Temperatures range from 28°F to 70°F. Rainfall averages between 15 and 47 inches.

Topography—The word *Balkans* comes from a Turkish word meaning "forested mountain." This description fits the peninsula, which is mountainous. A few river valleys cut the mountains, and a narrow coastal plain meets the water.

Natural Resources—The area does not contain an abundance of natural resources. Some minerals, such as coal, uranium, and iron ore, are found. However, the most important resource is oil.

Geography & Culture—Because it is at the crossroads between Asia and Europe, the Balkan Peninsula has been invaded many times throughout history. As a result, its culture is a mixture of East and West. In the late Middle Ages the Balkans came under the control of the Ottoman Turks. It was not until the 1800s and early 1900s that these areas became free from the Turks. Then after World War II the Soviet Union imposed Communist governments on these nations. It was not until the late 1980s and early 1990s that the Balkans threw off this yoke. Most of the people in the Balkans belong to an ethnic group known as the Slavs.

Materials

- Wall map of Europe or the Balkans (BLM 15-1)
- Transparencies for Chapter 15

Map activity—Use map 15-C from the Student Activities manual to reinforce the geography lesson.

Going Beyond—Read the Settings pages on the Balkans with your students and answer the questions. The Balkans have always been a hotbed of political fervor. World War I began here, and today it is the source of conflict between ethnic groups. Have your students find any current information on the Balkans or events that have occurred since the printing of this textbook.

Imports and Exports—Use a land-use map of Europe to teach your students about imports and exports in Europe. Remind your students that Germany needed more agricultural land to be self-sufficient and took over the Sudetenland. Also, show how Germany's supply of iron and coal helped it produce war machinery (TT 15-2).

Settings Review

1. What seas lie to the east of the Balkan Peninsula?
2. What is the origin of the name *Balkans?*
3. What is the most important natural resource of the region?
4. Who took control of the Balkans in the Middle Ages? Who took control after World War II?

Why would mountainous terrain like that in the Balkans tend to create disunity in a region? What other factors could cause disunity?

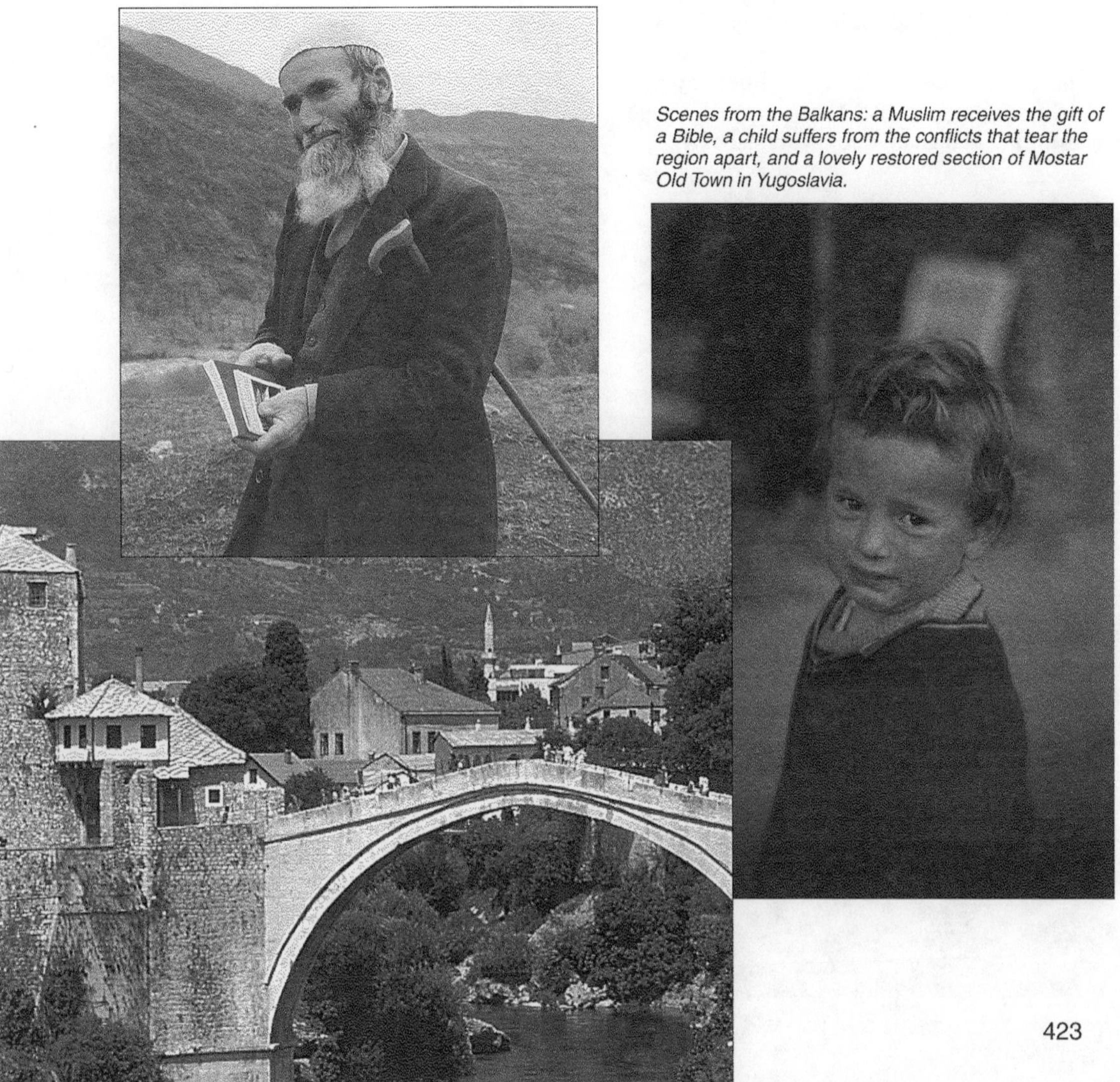

Scenes from the Balkans: a Muslim receives the gift of a Bible, a child suffers from the conflicts that tear the region apart, and a lovely restored section of Mostar Old Town in Yugoslavia.

423

Settings Review Answers

1. Black and Aegean
2. Turkish word meaning "forested mountains"
3. oil
4. Ottoman Turks; Communists (or Soviet Union)

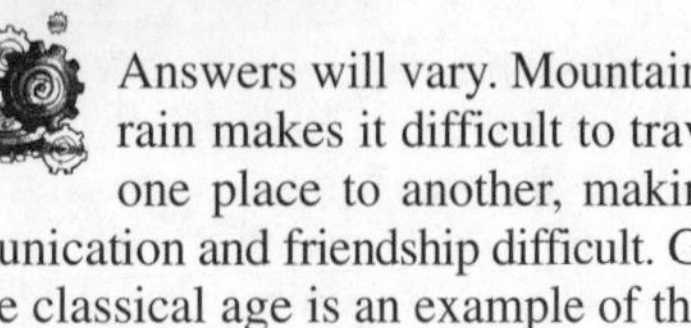

Answers will vary. Mountainous terrain makes it difficult to travel from one place to another, making communication and friendship difficult. Greece in the classical age is an example of this and is in this Balkan area. Differences in religion, culture, and language could also contribute to disunity.

SECTION 2

Student Objectives

Students should be able to

1. Define *fascism*.
2. Match each Fascist leader with his country.
3. Analyze the problem of "German Christians."
4. Categorize artists and authors and their works.
5. Distinguish expressionist, cubist, and surrealist art.

Did You Know?—On October 16, 1929, economist Irving Fisher said, "Stocks have reached what looks like a permanently high plateau."

Who Owes Whom?—The entire world felt the effects of the Great Depression. When its stock market crashed on October 29, 1929, the United States could no longer afford to send loans to Germany. Germany could not afford to pay the reparations (costs of the war) that the Allies had demanded by the Treaty of Versailles, and Europe could not afford to pay off its debts to the United States. This vicious cycle propelled the Depression far into the 1930s, especially for Germany.

The Law to End War—In 1928 an agreement called the Kellogg-Briand Pact was made between many nations to outlaw war as a means of settling disputes between nations. It did not have any penalties for repudiation and, like the League of Nations, it had no power to enforce its mission.

Washington Conference—Another agreement of this time was reached at the Washington Conference in 1921-22. The United States, Great Britain, Japan, France, and Italy agreed to a partial disarmament by limiting the number of new ships they would construct. This agreement was only partially successful because only large warships were included, not smaller ones such as submarines, which were highly destructive in World War II.

Despair and Dictators: Between the Wars

The hopes of peace did not last. Four years of bloody fighting had tired out the democratic nations of Europe. Many men had died in the trenches; the war had snuffed out a whole generation of Europeans. Germany's struggling new Weimar Republic had to pay huge debts to the victorious Allies. Then in the late 1920s the **Great Depression** hit, one of the most terrible economic downturns in history. All around the world, large companies went out of business. Millions of people lost their jobs. Many governments could not pay their debts. Economic bad times created greater suffering and greater political instability.

Rise of the Dictators

As a result of these conditions, dictators arose. A **dictator** is a ruler something like the absolutist monarchs discussed in Chapter 9. But a dictator has even greater power. His word is law, and with a word he can sentence people to prison or death. In the 1920s and 1930s, with powerful armies and secret police to support them, the dictators became major leaders in Europe.

In Russia the Communists toppled the young republic and established a dictatorship. (This revolution is discussed in the next chapter.) In Italy in 1923 **Benito Mussolini** and his gang of followers, called Fascists, frightened the king into making Mussolini the Italian leader. Mussolini, in fact, took the title *Il Duce* (DOO chay)—"the Leader." Throughout Europe, struggling young republics gave way before military "strong men" who ruled with an iron hand. Most of these rulers were Fascists.

Fascists basically believed in glorifying the state. Although people might own property, they had to be willing to let the state use their property however the nation's leaders

Adolf Hitler of Germany (left) and Benito Mussolini of Italy (right) were the most prominent in a wave of dictators who took power in Europe between the two world wars.

SECTION 2

Materials

- Chart of countries and important terms and facts that go with each
- Recordings of music by Stravinsky or Schönberg

Charting—Create a chart on the overhead or the chalkboard showing Russia, Italy, Germany, and the Western nations between the wars. Include important terms (e.g., Fascism), leaders, and national organizations. Add a small chart of the arts: the categories, the artists and authors, and their works (BLM 15-2).

wished. Because they stressed national power, Fascists tried to make their nations financially independent. Because they stressed national glory, Fascists tried to build strong armies and dreamed of military conquest. All the rights of the people—freedoms of speech, of religion, of the press—were subject to the whims of the state. Mussolini and his Italian Fascists were the first to gain power in Europe. But the worst of these Fascists were the Nazis of Germany. And the worst of the Nazis was their leader, **Adolf Hitler.**

Hitler was born in Austria in 1889. He dreamed of becoming a painter, but he lacked the talent. He stayed for a time in Vienna, hoping to profit from living in that great center of art and culture. But all he did was starve. He also learned to hate anyone more successful than he was because he thought they kept his talent from being discovered. Most of all he irrationally hated the Jews.

Hitler served as a courier in the German army in World War I. He was in a military hospital when the war ended, recovering from an attack by poison gas. With his eyes bandaged, Hitler heard the news that Germany had surrendered. He wept and blamed the "traitors" (Jews, Communists, and other "disloyal" Germans) who had stabbed Germany in the back. Hitler later wrote,

> The more I tried to achieve clarity on the monstrous event in this hour, the more the shame of indignation and disgrace burned my brow. What was all the pain in my eyes compared to this misery?
>
> There followed terrible days and even worse nights—I knew that all was lost. Only fools, liars and criminals could hope in the mercy of the enemy. In these nights hatred grew in me, hatred for those responsible for this deed.
>
> In the days that followed, my own fate became known to me. . . .
>
> I . . . decided to go into politics.

The face of evil: Adolf Hitler

Hitler joined a tiny political party called the National Socialist Workers' Party, or **Nazi Party** for short. Hitler practiced speaking until he could hold people spellbound with his words. Powerfully, Hitler preached hate and revenge.

Hitler and the Nazis got their chance when the depression hit in the late 1920s. Millions of Germans were out of work and were willing to listen to anyone who promised them help. Others feared the Communists and thought that the Nazis might help protect Germany. Many Germans thought their country had been wronged by the Allies and heeded this man who promised them revenge. Finally, in 1932 the Nazis became the largest party in the German legislature. The following year Hitler became chancellor of Germany and had the legislature pass a law making him dictator of Germany.

Fascism—The word *fascism* comes from the ancient Roman symbol of power, the *fasces* (a bundle of rods bound around an ax). Mussolini wanted to restore the glory of ancient Rome to Italy.

Hitler was a socialist in belief; he was not a proponent of nationalizing industries, but he said, "Our socialism reaches much deeper. It does not change the external order of things, it orders solely the relationship of man to the state. . . . Then what does property and income count for? Why should we need to socialize the banks and the factories? We are socializing the people."

Nazism—Hitler's basic idea was to promote a German "master race" of tall, strong, blond-haired men and women to rule the world.

What Makes a Hitler?—Have each student take out a piece of paper and write at least five to ten contributing factors to Hitler's evil. Why was he the way he was? Give a few examples such as disbelief in God, racism, and pride. Remind your students that God is in control of affairs and knew of Hitler's doings. Why might God allow the things Hitler did to happen? What did the world know as a result of Hitler's madness?

Aryans and the Swastika in History—Remind your students that the term *Aryan* was the name for early invaders of India. The swastika, which Hitler borrowed, was an Aryan sign of good luck. However, under Hitler's rule the connotation of this symbol began to represent the white, Germanic race. The swastika became the symbol of Nazism. Today the swastika is generally recognized as a symbol of radical white supremacist groups.

Adolf Hitler became ***der Führer*** (FY*OO*R ur; "the Leader"). He began to rebuild the army. This act created pride in the nation and put many workers back on the job building equipment for the army. He built a great highway system and sponsored colorful rallies and special holidays. Hitler encouraged Germans to look up to him, even to worship him. Children in Nazi orphanages offered blessings to him before they ate:

> O Führer, my Führer, sent to me by God,
> Protect and maintain my life,
> Thou who has served Germany in its hour
> of need.
> I thank thee now for my daily bread.
> Oh! Stay with me, Oh! Never leave me,
> Führer, my Führer, my faith and my light.

A group called the **"German Christians"** arose. They claimed to serve Christ and Adolf Hitler at the same time. "The Swastika on our breasts, and the Cross in our hearts" was their motto. But Hitler would not settle for divided loyalties. As a Nazi prosecutor said, "Christianity and we National Socialists have one thing in common, and one thing only: we claim the whole man." The German Christians eventually found, as Jesus said, that they could not serve two masters (Matt. 6:24). Some followed Christ and paid the price. Others sold out their Lord as Judas did and embraced the Nazis.

Hopelessness in the Democracies: The Arts and Culture Between the Wars

While the Fascists were growing in power across Europe, the Communists in the Soviet Union to the east appeared as yet another threat. The democracies meanwhile seemed buried in hopelessness and helplessness. The Great Depression in the 1930s threw millions out of work. The leaders of the democratic nations seemed colorless, unheroic, and unable to confront the might of these foes. Even in countries such as Great Britain and France,

Hitler stands in the middle of his cheering followers after one of his speeches, dwarfed by the trappings of his militaristic Nazi regime.

German Christians—From what you know of German Christians, create another group with a paradoxical name, such as Communist Christians or Worldly Christians. Write ten sentences on what the group would be like. What is its philosophy? What are its priorities? Where might you find people today striving to fit this lifestyle?

some politicians began claiming that their nations should also follow the Fascist or Communist way.

This sense of hopelessness was reflected in the arts between the wars. No longer did men write, as Robert Browning had written in 1841, "God's in His heaven— / All's right with the world." Many writers, painters, and sculptors were not even sure there was a God, let alone whether He was in heaven. And they felt certain that all was not right with the world. The terrible destruction of World War I and the rise of dictatorships caused many Europeans to lose hope in the future.

One example of this sense of drift was a group of writers known as the **"Lost Generation."** Most of these were Americans living in Europe, usually in Paris. Their nickname came from an American living in Paris who wrote to novelist **Ernest Hemingway,** telling him and others who had fought in World War I, "You are a lost generation." Hemingway used the line at the beginning of his novel *The Sun Also Rises.* He adopted a pessimistic view of the brutality of life. Other writers shared this outlook, such as novelist F. Scott Fitzgerald and poet E. E. Cummings. The "Lost Generation" also found sympathy among German writers such as **Erich Maria Remarque.** His popular novel *All Quiet on the Western Front* portrayed the senselessness the Lost Generation felt about the war.

Guitar *by Pablo Picasso, (Museum of Modern Art, New York)*

Tools and Fruit of Production *by Strzeminski is an example of Surrealist art.*

Styles in painting began to emphasize man's inner turmoil and to focus less on outward reality. A style known as **expressionism** became popular. Expressionist painters concentrated on representing their feelings about the objects they painted and not the object itself. **Cubist** painters tried to capture objects by presenting several views of an object at once. **Pablo Picasso** of Spain was the best-known cubist painter. **Surrealist** painters were perhaps most extreme. They painted regular objects but placed them in bizarre, unrealistic settings or distorted them. In the paintings of **Salvador Dali,** for example, watches melted and dripped off the edges of tables and trees like chocolate bars left lying in the sun.

Music also reflected a sense of discontent with the past. Composers began to alter the traditional tonal or key system. (Traditional Western music has an eight-tone scale, or key,

Functionalism—Another type of art during this period was functionalism in architecture. This was a plain rather than ornamental style for buildings. The idea was that the form and appearance of the building would reflect the purpose for which the building was used. "Form follows function" was the motto of functionalist architects.

The Lost Generation—Have each student write a five-line poem or prose work that includes elements of the Lost Generation (e.g., pessimism, senselessness of war, brutality of life). Have students then take the same work and make it into a work of hope as exemplified by T. S. Eliot's later works.

T. S. Eliot—Eliot's poem "The Journey of the Magi" compares his salvation experience to the journey of the wise men. This portion of the first stanza speaks of Eliot's condition before his salvation.

A cold coming we had of it,
Just the worst time of the year
For a journey, and such a long
journey:
The ways deep and the
weather sharp,
The very dead of winter.

This portion of the second stanza speaks of the hill of Calvary, death, the grave, and empty grave clothes.

Then at dawn we came down
to a temperate valley,
Wet, below the snow line,
smelling of vegetation;
With a running stream and a
watermill beating the darkness,
And three trees on the low sky,
And an old white horse galloped
away in the meadow.
Then we came to a tavern with
vine-leaves over the lintel,
Six hands at an open door
dicing for pieces of silver,
And feet kicking the empty
wineskins.

This portion of the last stanza tells of the new birth, the death of the old nature, and the struggle to live in a world of sin.

This: were we led all that way for
Birth or Death? There was a
Birth, certainly,
We had evidence and no doubt.
I had seen birth and death,
But had thought they were different; that Birth was
Hard and bitter agony for us,
like Death, our death.
We returned to our places, these
Kingdoms,
But no longer at ease here, in
old dispensation,
With an alien people clutching
their gods.
I should be glad of another
death.

T. S. Eliot

called an octave.) **Igor Stravinsky** (struh VIN skee) wrote pieces using several keys at once. These works sound harsh and dissonant to our ears. **Arnold Schönberg** (SHURN burg) wrote music with no fixed key. His pieces also sound very harsh and strange to our ears.

But the era was not devoid of hope, as illustrated by the career of poet **T. S. Eliot.** Born in St. Louis, he moved to England when he was in his twenties and became a leading poet. At first, Eliot also was one of the Lost Generation who felt despair about the future. His early poems are full of doubt, fear, and hopelessness. In one of his most famous poems, "The Hollow Men," he likens modern man to dry scarecrows whose voices are like "rats' feet over broken glass / In our dry cellar." At the conclusion of that poem, he says despairingly, *"This is the way the world ends / Not with a bang but a whimper."*

But in the late 1920s, Eliot suddenly announced to the world that he was embracing Christianity. His poems began to breathe hope instead of despair. His "Journey of the Magi" is the narrative of one of the wise men who journeyed to discover the Christ child—and the salvation He would bring. Eliot also offered a Christian response to the dictatorships that were spreading across Europe. He wrote a play, *Murder in the Cathedral,* about English Archbishop Thomas à Becket, who died for opposing the policies of King Henry II. Those living in the days of Hitler and Mussolini, with their policies of iron and fear, must have pondered Becket's words at the climax of the play—

It is the just man who
Like a bold lion, should be without fear.
I am here.
No traitor to the King. I am a priest,
A Christian, saved by the blood of Christ,
Ready to suffer with my blood.

Dictators could not answer that kind of faith.

Section Review

1. Who was the leader of the Fascists in Italy?
2. What was the Fascist party called in Germany? Who was its leader?
3. What does *der Führer* mean?
4. Who popularized the phrase "the Lost Generation"? In what novel did he use the phrase?
5. What German novel portrayed the senselessness of war? Who wrote it?
6. What leading poet turned his back on hopelessness and embraced Christianity?

What was the motto of the German Christians? Why would following this motto be difficult for a true Christian?

Stravinsky and Schönberg—Bring in some recordings of music by Stravinsky or Schönberg to play for your students. Most of them probably will not have heard much of this type of music before. Listen to other twentieth-century music available through BJUP on the following CDs: *Best of Leonard Bernstein* (BLB) and *Listener's Choice* (LC).

BLB—Polka from *The Age of Gold* (Dmitri Shostakovich)

BLB—March and Finale from *Peter and the Wolf* (Sergei Prokofiev)

BLB—*Greensleeves Fantasia* (Ralph Vaughan Williams)

BLB—Hoe-Down from *Rodeo* (Aaron Copland)

LC—Chaconne from *Suite No. 1 in E-flat, Op. 28a* (Gustav Holst)

LC—*One Hundred Fiftieth Psalm* (Howard Hanson)

Section Review Answers

1. Benito Mussolini
2. Nazi; Adolf Hitler
3. the leader
4. Ernest Hemingway; *The Sun Also Rises*
5. *All Quiet on the Western Front;* Erich Maria Remarque
6. T. S. Eliot

Answers will vary. The motto of German Christians was "the swastika on our breasts, and the Cross in our hearts." True Christians would have a hard time following this motto because a true Christian's first allegiance is to God, not to the social agenda of a political entity.

Democracy vs. the Dictators: World War II

Some had called World War I "the war to end all wars." Yet only a little more than twenty years later, Europe was again plunged into war. Hitler's dreams of dominance turned into a nightmare for the peoples of Europe.

Prelude to War

Europe looked on and wondered as Hitler rebuilt Germany. He began a series of "bloodless conquests" that increased his prestige and Germany's power. After World War I, for example, the Allies had required Germany to keep all military forces out of the **Rhineland,** a section of Germany next to France. In 1936 Hitler sent his army into the Rhineland. France and Great Britain did nothing.

In 1938 Germany annexed the German-speaking nation of Austria. This act was also a violation of a treaty, but no one did anything. In 1938 at a conference in Munich, Germany, Hitler convinced France and Britain to let him have the **Sudetenland** (soo-DATE-en-land), a German-speaking section of Czechoslovakia. Then after he had that territory, Hitler went ahead and took all of Czechoslovakia. He had gained huge tracts of territory without firing a shot. Hitler held the French and British in contempt. "Our enemies are little worms," he said. "I saw them at Munich."

Meanwhile, a civil war had broken out in Spain in 1936. A Spanish general, **Francisco Franco,** led the Fascist side against the Loyalists (a mixture of anti-Fascists including the Communists). Hitler and Mussolini sent troops and equipment to help Franco. With the aid of German and Italian soldiers, tanks, and planes, the Spanish general won the war in 1939. Fascism seemed on the verge of taking over Europe. More than that, in the Spanish civil war Europe saw what would be called the "dress rehearsal" for World War II.

Adolf Hitler was not satisfied. He wanted more power. He surprised the world by making a treaty with the Communist Soviet Union, his hated enemy. A secret part of that treaty was that Germany and the Soviet Union would split Poland between them if war came. With no fear of Communist attack, Hitler had a green light to launch his war.

Francisco Franco, leader of the Spanish Fascists and dictator of Spain

Section 3

Student Objectives
Students should be able to

1. List the members of the Axis Powers and the Allies of World War II.
2. Describe the course of World War II.
3. Define the German terms *blitzkrieg* and *Luftwaffe*.
4. Evaluate the effects of the Holocaust on the formation of the Jewish nation.

Appeasement—Giving in to Hitler's demands was called appeasement. Most of Europe thought that if they gave Hitler Austria and the Sudetenland, he would be happy and not bother them anymore. They were wrong.

Francisco Franco—Not only was Mussolini called *Il Duce* and Hitler called *Der Fürher,* both meaning "the leader," but Franco was called *El Caudillo,* meaning the same thing. Although Spain was officially neutral in World War II, Franco did send volunteers to help Germany.

Section 3

Materials

- Short video on World War I, World War II, or the Depression
- Guest speakers, people who remember the Depression or World War II
- Transparencies for Chapter 15
- Recording of one of Churchill's speeches

World War I, World War II, or the Depression—Watch a short video on World War I, the Depression, or World War II. The Holocaust is an especially interesting (and heart-wrenching) part of this era's history. Make sure that the material is previewed in order not to offend this age group by its graphic nature or violence.

Guest Speaker—Have one or more of the students schedule a time to bring in a guest speaker who will tell about his or her involvement in the Depression or World War II. (These testimonials take longer than you might expect. Do not try to limit the speaker to five or ten minutes.)

The *Lusitania*—One powerful "weapon" of war which the Germans employed was unrestricted submarine warfare. The most memorable example of this was the attack on the ocean liner *Lusitania*. The *Lusitania* was carrying passengers to Great Britain when she was attacked by a German U-boat *(untersee boat)*. One hundred twenty-eight Americans were killed in the attack. The Germans had placed an advertisement in the newspaper the morning of the ship's departure warning all those traveling aboard this Allied nation's ship. However, this seemingly unprovoked attack helped sway American opinion to favor entering the war on the side of the Allies.

Gas Warfare—Gas warfare began in World War I. A cloud of the chlorine gas surprised and greatly injured the Allied forces at Ypres (EE prah). From that point, chemical warfare has grown in quantity and complexity. Chemical and biological weapons are a threat in modern warfare.

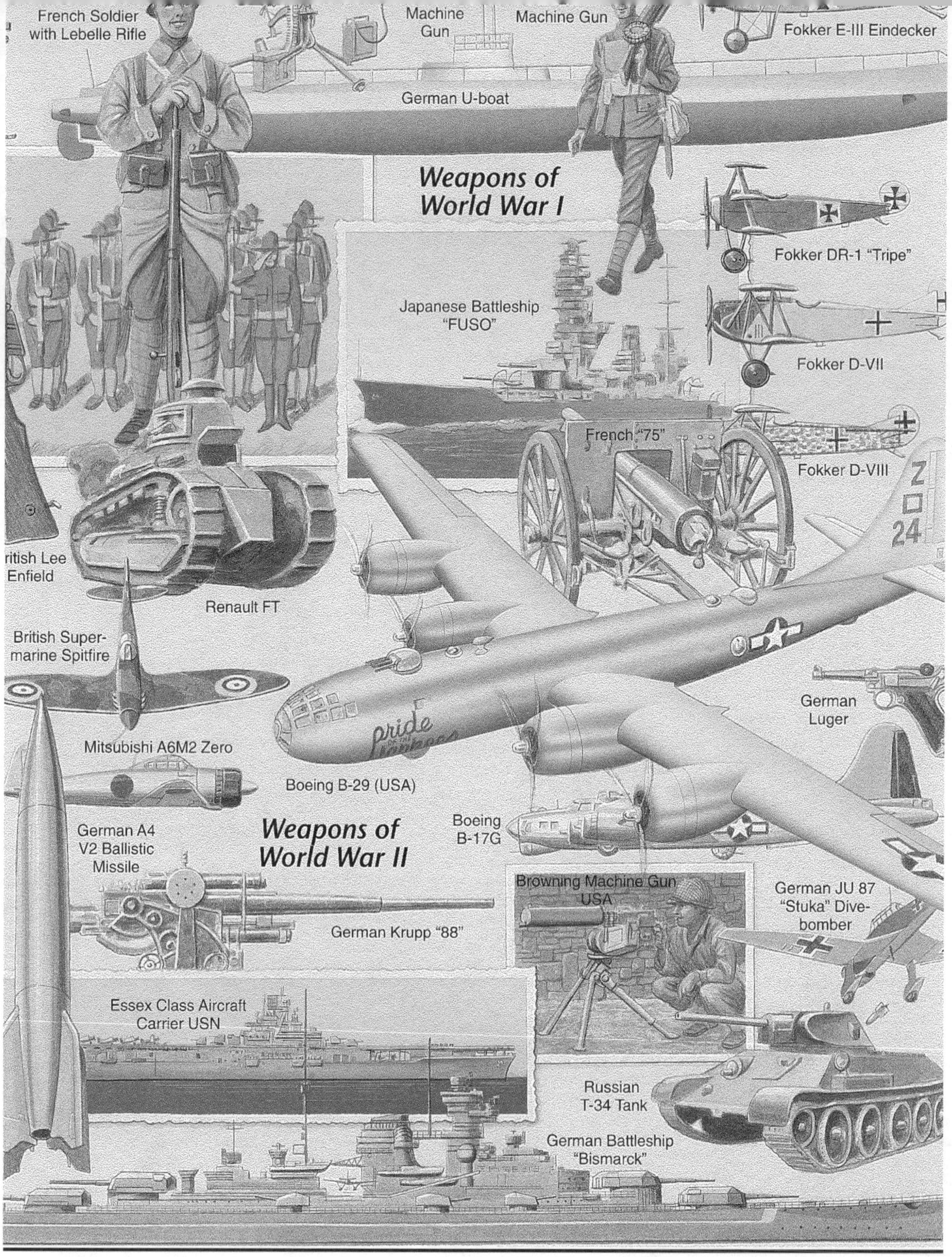

Ships of War—Make models of famous ships or aircraft from World War I or World War II. Research the story behind the ship or aircraft and write a half-page report about it.

The Coming of War

World War II began on September 1, 1939, when Hitler sent his forces crashing into Poland. This time the British and French did not back down. They came to the defense of Poland and declared war on Germany. But the help of France and Britain was not enough to save Poland. The German army developed a new type of warfare, **blitzkrieg** ("lightning war"). Using fighters and bombers, armored tanks and trucks, Hitler's forces overwhelmed opponents with dazzling speed and relentless pressure. Poland collapsed in less than five weeks.

Then Hitler turned west. His forces conquered Denmark effortlessly. Then a daring operation by sea and air brought Norway under Nazi rule. Finally, the armored divisions of Germany swept across the Low Countries, smashed the armies of France, and sent the British army reeling. France surrendered on June 22, 1940, only six weeks after Hitler's invasion. Mussolini brought Italy into the war on Germany's side. Germany, Italy, and Japan joined together as the **Axis Powers.** Adolf

The Low Countries—The Low Countries include Belgium, the Netherlands, and Luxembourg. Together these countries are also known as Benelux.

Axis and Allies—The Axis Powers were Germany, Japan, and Italy. The major Allies were Britain, France, and eventually Russia and the United States.

Rescue by Night—One of the most famous stories of World War II is the rescue at Dunkirk. The Germans had forced the Allied armies to the French coast at Dunkirk. To rescue these soldiers, thousands of British ships and small boats made numerous trips across the English Channel during the night to bring the troops to safety. Over 300,000 soldiers were saved through the efforts of the British navy, civilian fishermen, and boaters.

★★★★★★★★★★

For a color version of the map on this page, see page A9 in the Appendix.

Pictures of Wars—Have students bring in pictures of life and warfare during World War I and World War II (preferably in Europe). They may find these photos in encyclopedias, books, or personal resources. After researching the origin of the picture, have each student briefly state what his/her picture is about while showing it to the class.

Axis and Allies—List on the chalkboard or the overhead the countries of the Axis Powers and the Allies. In one column write the name of the country, in another the name of the leader of that country. Discuss how these countries hoped to benefit from their alliances.

Show a map of the Axis and Allied Powers during World War II (TT 15-1).

Resisting the Enemy—Many people joined the armed forces to fight against the Germans during World War II. Many others who would not admit defeat joined the Resistance, living in German-occupied countries. These brave resisters risked their lives to blow up ammunition dumps, to destroy railroads and bridges, to sabotage factories, and to send valuable information about the Germans to the Allies. Not all those in the Resistance were adults. Many young people also helped the Resistance. One example is a young deaf and dumb French boy named Pierre who lived in the Normandy village of Calvados. One night he saw a parachute land in the nearby woods. Going to the landing place, he discovered the parachutist was an American airman. Pierre led the man to his aunt's house and helped his aunt hide the man for about a week before the Resistance was able to get him back to England.

Perhaps the most unusual resistance group was made up of boys from the Aalburg Cathedral School in Denmark. In 1941 eleven boys formed what they called the "Churchill Club." Their purpose was to do anything possible to make things difficult for the Germans in Denmark. One of their first acts was to publish, using a toy printing press, a newsletter encouraging people to join the Resistance. They also succeeded at stealing guns from careless German soldiers. When at restaurants, the soldiers often left their guns and ammunition belts at the cloakroom. When no one was looking, the boys took them and hid them in the cathedral crypt.

Another Aalburg victory occurred unexpectedly. One day two boys were walking up a long hill when a German truck loaded with straw drove slowly by. The boys jumped into the back of the truck to hitch a ride. As they made themselves comfortable, they discovered that the straw was concealing a load of explosives. With matches they set the straw on fire and quickly jumped off the truck. A short while later they saw the truck explode.

In May 1942 the Germans caught the two boys and placed them in prison. However, a friend smuggled a metal file to them with which they filed through the bars

Hitler was the master of Europe. Or almost the master.

Still defiant was Great Britain. Between the Nazi forces in France and the British homeland lay the English Channel, protected by Britain's mighty navy. Hitler tried to bring down the British by sending his **Luftwaffe** (air force) to bomb the British into submission. British prime minister **Winston Churchill** vowed, "We shall fight on the landing grounds, we shall fight in the fields and in the streets, we shall fight in the hills; we shall never surrender." The **RAF** (Royal Air Force) of Britain fought back and cut the Luftwaffe to pieces. Britain had fought off the Nazis.

Frustrated because he could not defeat the British, Hitler turned on the Soviet Union, ignoring his treaty with the Communists. The invasion commenced on June 22, 1941. As in Poland and France, the German blitzkrieg devastated the surprised Soviets. The Soviet Union seemed on the verge of collapse. Hitler's dream of conquering the world seemed possible.

Driven to extremes by shortages resulting from the war, French farm women pull the plow themselves to prepare their fields.

Hitler looks on the wreckage of his German Empire. He had said his Third Reich would last a thousand years. It lasted only twelve.

Then the tide turned against the Nazis. A freezing Russian winter stopped the Nazi blitzkrieg. Even the fuel in their tanks froze in the frigid weather. Meanwhile, Germany's ally Japan attacked the American naval base at Pearl Harbor, Hawaii, on December 7, 1941. (For Japan's role in World War II, see pp. 483-85.) Now the United States again threw its might in against the Germans.

Slowly the Russians began to turn back the Nazi forces in the east. In the west, the United States and Britain began to chip away at the Axis empire. They landed in North Africa in 1942, then in Sicily in 1943, and then on the mainland of Italy two months later. Finally, on June 6, 1944, known as **D-day,** a huge Allied force landed in France and shattered Germany's

Resisting the Enemy—After reading the Resisting the Enemy section above, discuss with your students how to resist the enemy of all Christians: Satan. First Peter 5:8-9 tells Christians that they too have an enemy who is seeking to destroy them and whom they must "resist stedfast in the faith." The Bible gives the Christian many weapons and tactics to use against the Devil.

defenses. Like a vise, the Allied forces crushed the Axis nations between them. Italian rebels shot Mussolini and hung his body up in a gas station. Hitler shot himself in his bunker under the ruins of Berlin rather than surrender. On May 8, 1945, the war in Europe ended.

Peace came but at a great cost. Including the deaths in the fighting in Asia, over fifty million soldiers and civilians died in the war. But even these figures were not the end of the horror. As the Allied forces moved into Germany, they found death camps where the Nazis had slaughtered peoples they considered inferior—Slavs, the physically and mentally handicapped, and especially Jews. It is estimated that six million Jews died in the Nazi death camps. This horrendous slaughter has become known as the **Holocaust.**

Section Review

1. What country had to sacrifice territory as a result of the Munich Conference?
2. Who was the leader of the Fascists in the Spanish Civil War?
3. What country made a treaty with Hitler that gave him freedom to launch his war?
4. The invasion of what country sparked World War II?
5. What does *blitzkrieg* mean? Why was it a good description for how the Germans fought?
6. How did Mussolini and Hitler die?
7. What is the name we give to Hitler's slaughter of the Jews?

If you had been a political leader in Great Britain in the 1930s, what would you have advised the nation to do about Hitler's expansion? What arguments would you have used?

Two emaciated survivors from a German concentration camp gaze blankly at the camera. Millions did not survive.

on their cell window. Instead of escaping, they remained in prison, but every night they would sneak out, leaving dummies in their beds. For two months they carried out acts of sabotage. At dawn they returned to the prison to spend the day. Finally the Germans caught them and placed them in a more secure prison.

The Aalburg boys were only a few of the many Dutch, Norwegian, Yugoslavian, and Czech young people who risked their lives in the Resistance. They fought against an enemy who had taken their land and their freedom. They used many tactics in their special undercover warfare. Those who were caught were often tortured by the Nazis, who tried to get information from them. If they survived the torture and were under sixteen, they were placed in prison. Those over sixteen were usually executed.

The Holocaust—Hitler hated the Jews and blamed Germany's problems on them. During the war, millions of Jews were taken from their homes and sent to concentration camps. There they were fed little and made to work under horrible conditions. Many died of disease and starvation. The dead were put in mass graves or simply added to piles of unburied bodies. Many others were put to death by the Germans. Using huge gas chambers, the Nazis murdered hundreds of Jews at a time and then burned their bodies. The Germans used these methods to kill several million Jews.

Section Review Answers

1. Czechoslovakia
2. Francisco Franco
3. the Soviet Union
4. Poland
5. lightning war; Hitler's forces speedily crushed his opponents
6. Mussolini was shot and hung in a gas station; Hitler committed suicide in his bunker in Berlin.
7. the Holocaust

Answers will vary. The memory of World War I was still fresh enough to make most of Europe want to stay away from strife as much as possible. Hitler, however, had a bad reputation already and was making more and more claims on land. Appeasement never satisfies the greedy. As Churchill advised, the wise thing would have been to take action against Hitler or at least not give in to his demands. Aggression in the past has almost always led to more aggression, but the rest of Europe would not accept this truth.

Special Award—On April 9, 1963, Churchill became the first honorary American citizen.

CHARACTERIZATIONS

Winston Churchill

Winston Churchill at times wanted to be a soldier, sometimes a writer, and sometimes a statesman. He eventually did all three, and did them very well.

Born in 1874, Churchill graduated from Britain's leading military school and joined the army. He soon found himself in exotic places. He fought against a Muslim uprising in Sudan in 1898. There he came under fire in one of the last great cavalry charges in history. Afterwards, he wrote a history of the campaign, *The River War,* one of the first of many books he was to write. Soon afterwards he was in South Africa covering the Boer War as a newspaper correspondent. During the fighting he was captured by the Boers. Churchill escaped and daringly made his way back to British lines. The dramatic account he wrote of his escape made him famous in Britain.

Churchill began a spectacular rise in politics. When World War I broke out, he was head of the British navy. But he risked his career supporting a dangerous attack on the Ottoman Empire. The British hoped the attack by the army and navy would knock the Turks out of the war. But the attack failed, and Churchill was blamed and forced to resign as head of the navy.

Churchill's rise turned suddenly into a devastating fall. He wrote an excellent history of World War I, *The World Crisis,* but his political career went up and down. He was even voted out of Parliament for a time. When a group of British politicians visited the Soviet Union in 1932, Soviet dictator Joseph Stalin asked about several leading British politicians. "What about Churchill?" he said.

"Churchill?" replied one visitor with a laugh. "Oh, he's *finished.*"

In the 1930s Churchill stood on the fringes of politics. As the dictators rose to power on the Continent, he sounded warnings. At first, he was ignored by those who feared another war. But as Hitler became more powerful, more people began to listen to Churchill. After the Munich agreement sacrificed Czechoslovakia to Germany, Churchill declared, "And do not suppose that this is the end. This is only the beginning of the reckoning. This is only the first sip, the first foretaste of a bitter cup."

When war broke out, the British government made Churchill the prime minister. He knew the difficult job that lay ahead and told the people, "I have nothing to offer but blood, toil, tears, and sweat." His eloquence became a rallying point for the British. U.S. president John F. Kennedy later said, "He mobilized the English language and sent it into battle." On one occasion, for example,

Churchill surveys the rubble from a German bombing raid on London.

Listening to the Past—Play a recording of one of Churchill's speeches. What was it about his speeches that inspired his audiences? *(his excellent command of the English language, his ardent patriotism, etc.)*

What Makes a Man Great?—Discuss aspects of Churchill's life that make him one of the most influential men in history. *(tenacity, patriotism, etc.)*

Churchill treads the deck of a warship in preparation for a wartime meeting with President Franklin Roosevelt.

Churchill said, "We have not entered this war for profit or expansion, but only for honour and to do our duty in defending the right." In one of his most famous speeches, Churchill urged, "Let us therefore brace ourselves to our duties, and so bear ourselves that, if the British Empire and its Commonwealth last for a thousand years, men will say, 'This was their finest hour.' "

Just after the defeat of Nazi Germany, Churchill was surprisingly defeated for reelection. But he did not allow defeat to silence him. Before the war, he warned the world of Nazi tyranny. After the war, he warned of the equal danger of Communist tyranny. In a famous speech in Fulton, Missouri, in 1946 Churchill solemnly announced, "From Stettin in the Baltic to Trieste in the Adriatic, an iron curtain has descended across the Continent." Soon the phrase "iron curtain" was on everyone's lips. For millions of people Churchill had perfectly pictured the boundary between freedom and Communist slavery.

In 1951 Churchill returned to power as prime minister of Britain. He served until 1954 when poor health forced him to retire. Meanwhile, he had written a six-volume work, *The History of the Second World War,* which won him the Nobel prize for literature. The Queen of England knighted him, making him "Sir" Winston Churchill, and the United States made him an honorary American citizen. When he died in 1965, the British prime minister said, "The words and deeds of Winston Churchill will form part of the rich heritage of our nation and of our time for as long as history comes to be written and to be read."

Section 4

Student Objectives
Students should be able to

1. Determine the causes of specified problems in Europe after World War II.
2. Name the economic community in Europe.

The Marshall Plan—This successful plan was introduced by U.S. Secretary of State George C. Marshall. Speaking at Harvard's commencement in 1947, he said, "Europe's requirements for the next three or four years of foreign food and other essential products—principally from America—are so much greater than her present ability to pay that she must have substantial additional help or face economic, social, and political deterioration of very grave character." Europe was given loans and many outright grants with which to rebuild her economy. Though this helped many countries, it heightened the Cold War because the Soviet Union did not want to disclose her economic reports to America, a requirement for receiving aid.

Berlin Airlift—Berlin had been divided among the four victors of World War II; however, it was located in the heart of Soviet-controlled East Germany, and the Soviets decided to block access. In a major undertaking, the Americans and British airlifted over two million tons of food in almost a year's time. The blockade was eventually lifted, but this became another tension in the Cold War.

Democracy Triumphant but Tried

The war was over, but there was enormous rebuilding to do. The United States helped Europe through the **Marshall Plan.** Named for the American secretary of state, the Marshall Plan poured $12 billion into Europe to help the continent rebuild. However, the great European powers, France and Great Britain, were no longer as mighty as in the past. They lost their overseas empires and found themselves taking a back seat in world affairs to the United States and the Soviet Union.

King Juan Carlos of Spain reviews his troops. The king used his personal popularity to keep the army from toppling Spain's fragile young democracy.

Europe faced danger from the Communist Soviet Union. At the end of World War II, the Soviet armies stayed in the Eastern European countries they had invaded in order to attack Hitler. Countries such as Poland, Hungary, and Czechoslovakia fell under Communist dictatorships. Germany was split in two, and East Germany became a Communist state.

But **West Germany** was free. Aided by Western powers such as the United States, West Germany began to recover from the devastation of the war. Within ten years it had become a major economic power and a firm supporter of Western Europe against Communism.

Furthermore, Fascism began to die out in Europe. The last stronghold of Fascism was Spain under Francisco Franco. Franco himself had no desire to change, but he also knew he could not live forever. Instead, he decided to restore the Spanish monarchy. Franco declared that at his death Prince Juan Carlos, grandson of the last king of Spain, would become king.

When Franco died in 1975, King **Juan Carlos** declared that Spain would now become a democracy. But only with difficulty did he lead the nation away from dictatorship. Many of Franco's former followers resisted the move. The army, always Franco's main support, began plotting to overthrow the government.

On February 23, 1981, two hundred military policemen broke into a meeting of the Spanish legislature. One attacker fired his gun into the ceiling as the leader of the force declared that the army was taking control. The rebels held the legislators and other high

Section 4

Materials

- Currency from other countries

Economic Opinion—Ask your students the following questions. Would you have wanted to give aid to Europe after the wars? Why or why not? If you were to give aid, what kind of aid would you give and how would you give it? If you would not give any aid, what would you do instead to help Europe get back on its feet? Would you keep all resources here and practice a policy of isolation? When the discussion is over, ask how many would choose each option.

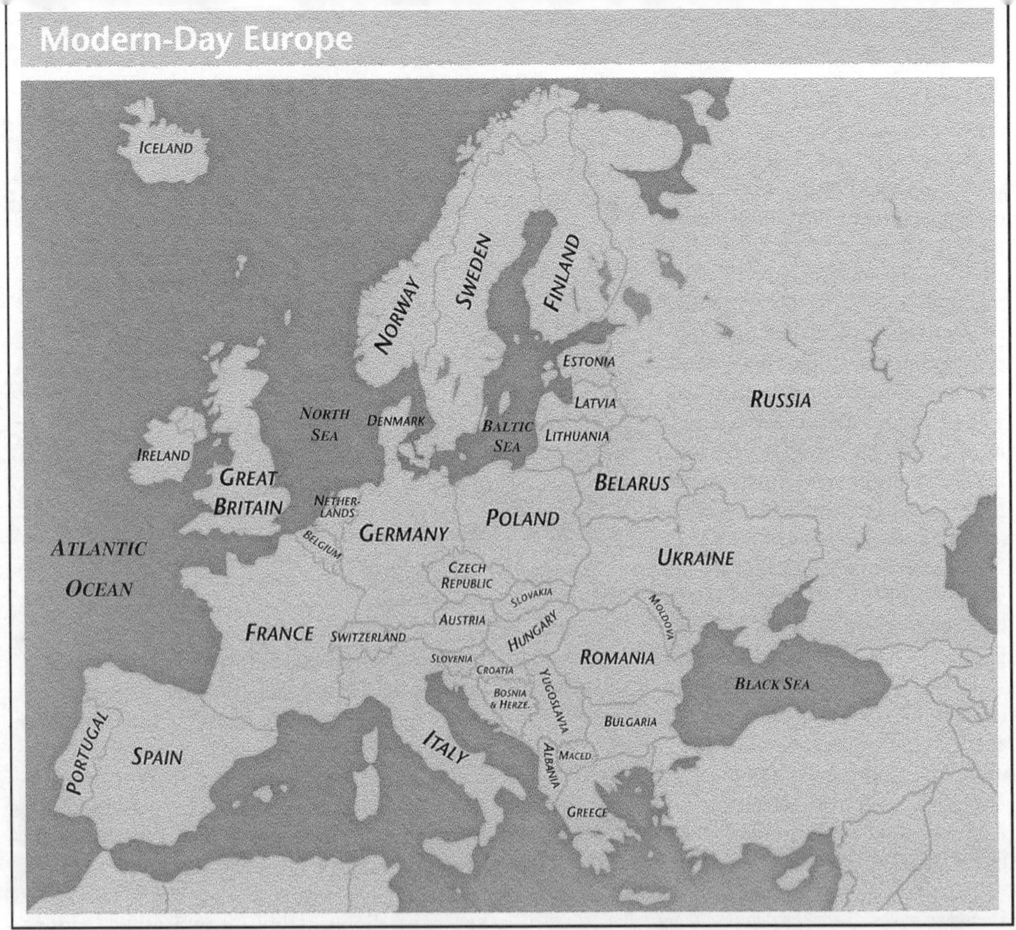

Spain—Under Franco, Spain reached one of the highest rates of economic growth in the world. In 1982, Spain elected a leftist government, the first one since Franco. Spain joined the European Community in 1986 and hosted the Olympics in 1992, the same year in which they celebrated the 500th anniversary of Columbus's discovery of the New World.

government officials hostage. The leader allegedly said that if the government forces tried to force their way in, he would block the doors with the bodies of the legislators.

Army officers began cautiously moving forward with their plot. One colonel declared a military emergency in the province of Valencia. In Madrid the army seized the television and radio stations. Spain teetered on the brink.

King Juan Carlos would have none of it. He told his advisers the plotters would have to shoot him if they wanted to seize power. He called leading generals on the phone and said that he was throwing his authority against the plot. The king went on television while the rebels were still holding the legislature captive. There would be no revolution, he declared. "The crown, symbol of the nation's permanence and unity, cannot tolerate, under any form, the action or attitude of those who seek by force to interrupt the democratic process."

The revolt collapsed. The government arrested and tried thirty-two military officers who had been involved in the plot. It was a turning point for Spain. Rather than return to the dictatorship of Franco, Spain would move

Juan Carlos—Ask your students why Juan Carlos was able to defeat those who wanted to overthrow his government. Analyze his statement that the crown cannot tolerate anything that interrupts the democratic process.

The European Community— The purpose of the European Community was to lift trade restrictions on steel and coal between member countries. Since its inception, the ECSC (European Coal and Steel Community) has merged with the EEC (European Economic Community) and Euratom (European Atomic Energy Community) to create a European Community. Member countries include France, Germany, Belgium, Italy, Luxembourg, the Netherlands, Denmark, Ireland, the United Kingdom, Greece, Portugal, and Spain.

The EFTA—The European Free Trade Agreement includes Austria, Finland, Iceland, Liechtenstein, Norway, Sweden, and Switzerland. Together the EFTA and the EEC make up the European Union.

forward into the ranks of the Western democracies.

Spain symbolized the changes taking place in Europe. Those parts of the continent not under Communist rule began to put away conflicts of the past and try to work together. In 1957 the Western European powers established the European Economic Community, better known as the **Common Market.** The Common Market was an economic agreement. The nations involved eliminated many trade restrictions and worked together to enrich the member nations.

A house wrecked by fighting reflects the destructive forces unleashed in the Balkans at the end of the twentieth century.

The Common Market's success caused some Europeans to dream of what Churchill had once called "a kind of United States of Europe." One step toward achieving this dream was the founding of the **European Union (EU)** in 1994 to draw Europe together not only economically but also politically. When Communism collapsed in Eastern Europe in the late 1980s (see the next chapter), Europe greeted its greatest opportunity in centuries to reshape the continent in peace and unity.

But Europe was still plagued by disagreements. The European nations argued over basic questions, such as whether to have a single currency for the whole continent. Some matters were more significant. With the collapse of Communism in Eastern Europe, the Balkans again became a powder keg. Freed from Communism, some Balkan states simply replaced Communist dictatorships with other kinds of dictatorships. The Balkan nations fought wars and civil wars. People fled in fear from their homes, seeking refuge from the fighting. Many civilians were killed in the fighting or brutally murdered by enemy troops. Problems great and small still stand in the way of the dream of a "United States of Europe."

Canadian soldiers serve as peacekeepers in the war-torn country of Bosnia.

Money Matters—Ask students to compare Europe to the United States of America. How would converting to one economic unit (currency) such as the Euro be valuable to the Europeans? How might it hinder them? Have students give examples of what America might be like if each state had different currency, languages, and customs. Ask if there are any examples of this in America, past and present. *(Examples might be currency before the states joined together, accents [such as from the South, New England, New York, the West, etc.], drinking hot tea [North] or sweet tea [South], etc.)*

Bring in some currency from different countries, preferably European. Distribute a piece or two to each student. Give each a card on which an item of trade is written. Have the students trade their money for desired items. It will soon become difficult and will probably change to a bartering system: trading item for item.

The United Nations

After World War I, the nations of the world formed the League of Nations. This organization was to provide a place where nations could talk through their differences in a civilized manner. Unfortunately, "uncivilized" aggressors such as Germany, Italy, and Japan simply ignored the League and launched brutal plans of conquest. Since members of the League of Nations were not willing to go to war to protect their members, the League collapsed.

During World War II, the Allied Powers often referred to themselves as "the United Nations," that is, united against the Axis Powers. After the war, the victorious powers formed a new organization dedicated to preserving world peace. Founded on April 25, 1945, in San Francisco, the organization took the name **United Nations (UN).**

Headquartered in New York, the UN has tried to preserve peace through discussion and debate. Virtually every nation in the world is represented in its General Assembly. On some occasions when discussion has failed, the UN, unlike the League of Nations, has even used military action. In the 1950s the United Nations defended South Korea from invasion by Communist North Korea, and in the 1990s the UN helped free Kuwait after it was invaded by neighboring Iraq. At other times, the UN has created "peacekeeping" forces made up of soldiers from the armies of its members. UN peacekeepers travel to troubled areas of the world and try—with varying degrees of success—to maintain peace.

The United Nations has had its share of failures. Member nations are often more concerned (sometimes rightly) with their own good than what the UN considers the good of the whole. The most powerful nations can usually ignore the United Nations whenever they wish. Some dictatorships have used the UN to cover their cruelty; their UN ambassadors speak of freedom and human rights while the government back home practices oppression. The UN has accomplished some good, but it has not been the instrument of world peace that its founders dreamed it would be.

UNITED
HE UNITED NATIONS FIGHT FOR FREEDOM

The League of Nations—Wilson wanted to create an organization which would consist of countries that would work together instead of fight. The League of Nations was created as the result of Wilson's Fourteen Points and was the hope for a brighter tomorrow when people would work out their differences by communication rather than by war.

Ironically, the United States did not join Wilson's international organization. This, and the fact that the League could not enforce its recommendations, caused the League to be almost powerless in world affairs.

United Nations—In 1942 Churchill suggested to Franklin D. Roosevelt that the name "United Nations" be used instead of "Associated Powers," the proposed name for the free nations in league against the Axis. Churchill took the name from a poem by Lord Byron:

> Thou fatal Waterloo.
> Millions of tongues record thee, and anew
> Their children's lips shall echo them, and say—
> 'Here, where the sword the united nations drew,
> Our countrymen were warring on that day!'
> And this is much, and which will not pass away.

Section Review

1. Through what plan did the United States give Europe billions of dollars to rebuild after World War II?
2. Who transformed Spain from a dictatorship into a democracy?
3. What is the name for the agreement that broke down trade barriers in Western Europe?
4. What region of Europe was a center of revolution and warfare in the late twentieth century?

Do you think the idea of a United States of Europe is a good one? Why or why not?

Section Review Answers

1. Marshall Plan
2. King Juan Carlos
3. Common Market (or European Economic Community)
4. the Balkans

Answers will vary. The United States of Europe could work if everyone could agree on how to do things. The introduction of the European common unit as the currency in all of Europe has met some resistance. Though the countries in Europe are relatively small, there are still many cultural differences in upbringing and economic background. Europe will have to work hard to make the United States of Europe a reality. Another problem some have with the idea is that it may lead to a one-world order.

SECTION 5

Student Objectives
Students should be able to

1. Analyze the problems of the World Council of Churches.
2. Name the well-known Ulster evangelist of the 1920s.

Major Religions in Europe— Catholicism is the largest religion in Europe, though many no longer claim to adhere to its tenets. Protestantism and Orthodoxy are about the same in number, with Judaism and Islam appearing in the more Asian sections of Europe. Judaism is still strong in Western Europe as well.

Secularism—Secularism was philosophized by Thomas Hobbes, who said that life is a "ceaseless search for power." Secularism originally meant separating religion from politics.

World Council of Churches— More than 400 million members belong to the churches that are part of the World Council of Churches. In recent times not only Protestant, Anglican, Old Catholic, and Orthodox churches (as well as Catholic) but also Muslim and Buddhist groups have been welcomed into discussions.

Vatican II—Some issues resolved in the Vatican II Council were celebrating the mass in the vernacular (native language), bringing back the emphasis on the Bible as supremely important, allowing lay people rights as the "people of God," and recognizing that the church is in the world and thus must be cordial to non-Catholics.

The council also condemned anti-Semitism and upheld the liberty of individual conscience. However, the council did not make any change to Catholic doctrine.

Religion in Modern Europe

The victory of democracies over dictatorships in Europe has been a noble one. But not all trends in modern European history are positive. One dismaying characteristic has been the decline of religious faith in Europe. There has been a great falling away from the teachings of the Bible, even from simple matters such as church attendance. In England, for example, church attendance plummeted after World War I.

France is yet another example of religious decline. In 1900 some 97 percent of the population claimed to be adherents of the Roman Catholic Church. By the end of the twentieth century that percentage had shrunk to 68.5 percent. Even within this group, a large number (4.5 million) were "disaffiliated." They had been born and baptized into the Catholic Church, but they had repudiated that bond. One-third of French Catholics did not practice their faith at all. Only about one in five Frenchmen attended church at least once a week.

The Cathedral of Chartes reflects the past glories of French Catholicism but masks its contemporary decline.

In European countries, the drop in Christian profession was not because Europeans were converting to Islam or some other religion. People simply ceased to regard religion as important. Europe was dominated by **secularism.** This means simply that people were concerned about the affairs of this life. They seldom bothered to think about heaven or God at all.

Some Christian leaders tried to rouse interest in the church by urging Christians to unite. They led an **ecumenical movement** to try to bring all the churches of the world together. (The word *ecumenical* means simply "worldwide." Today the term normally refers to efforts to bring all Christians together.) In 1948 many Protestant and Eastern Orthodox churches formed the **World Council of Churches** as a means of bringing churches together. In the 1960s the Catholic Church held a council called **Vatican II** to discuss reform. One major change was allowing Catholics to discuss possible union with other churches.

In trying to bring people together, the ecumenical leaders downplayed biblical doctrine because, they said, "doctrine divides." They failed to understand that the Scriptures' doctrines are the basis of the Christian faith. The apostle Paul stated that the Bible is a source for doctrine, which he said is necessary in order for Christians to "be throughly furnished unto all good works" (II Tim. 3:17). Paul also said that without the biblical teaching of the

SECTION 5

Materials

- *Faith of Our Fathers: Scenes from Church History* (BJUP)

Report—Have students choose one of the following topics and submit a seventy-five-word paper about it.

1. Choose a spiritual revival in another country and compare it to the revival in Northern Ireland.
2. Write at least three ways that a country which is cold to the Lord might experience a revival. See II Chronicles 7:14.
3. Suggest five ways to ease the tensions in areas that have much religious strife.

Collect the papers and grade them or have each student read his aloud.

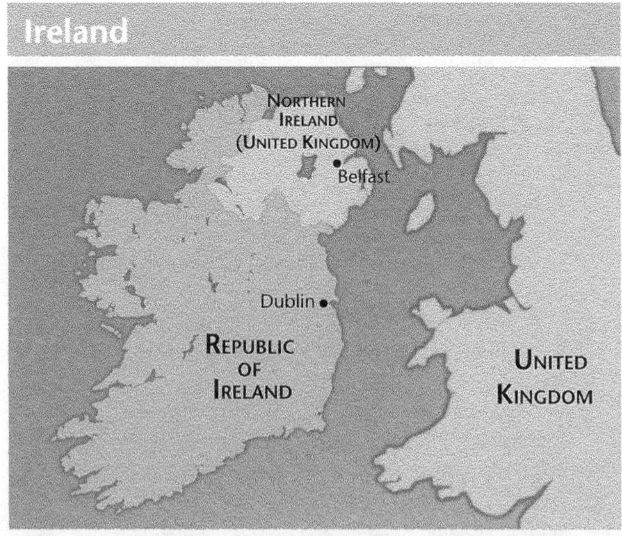

Evangelist W. P. Nicholson

resurrection "we are of all men most miserable" (I Cor. 15:19). The apostle John warned that anyone who did not hold proper doctrine about Jesus Christ could not be a Christian, and real Christians were to have nothing to do with such false teachers (II John 7-11). Christians cannot de-emphasize the Bible's teachings even to achieve unity.

Not all the history of Christianity in modern Europe is dark. In the 1920s, for example, the British province of Northern Ireland (also called Ulster) experienced a widespread revival. An Ulster evangelist named **W. P. Nicholson** preached with great power across the province. "Some fool wrote in the newspapers objecting to me talking about Christ as if He was my next door neighbour," Nicholson said in one meeting. "He is far nearer to me than my next door neighbour. He is in my heart." He preached as though Christ were in his heart, and he urged his hearers to open their hearts to Christ too. Thousands heard him, and numbers were converted under his blunt, direct preaching.

The Ulster revival is all the more remarkable because Northern Ireland was in the midst of major unrest over the separation of Ulster from the southern part of Ireland. (See p. 442.) Many times the crowds in Nicholson's services would hear gunfire outside.

****
For a color version of the map on this page, see page A10 in the Appendix.

Religions in Europe

Country	Religions
Ireland	Roman Catholic (93%) Anglican (3%)
United Kingdom	Anglican, Roman Catholic, other Christian, Muslim
France	Roman Catholic (90%)
Germany	Protestant (45%) Roman Catholic (37%)
Netherlands	Roman Catholic (34%) Protestant (25%)
Greece	Greek Orthodox (98%)
Italy	Roman Catholic (98%)
Spain	Roman Catholic (99%)

Religion Today—Copy the religion chart in the margin above to show to your students on the overhead projector. Discuss why certain countries are dominated by certain religions (BLM 15-3).

***Faith of Our Fathers*—**Read aloud to your students some stories about this time period. *Faith of Our Fathers: Scenes from Church History* includes "I Shook Hands with Hitler" by Edith S. Long, "E. J. Poole-Connor: A Lifetime of Faithful Service" by Mark Sidwell, and "Duncan Campbell and the Lewis Revival" by Christa G. Habegger.

Ulster—Review the map above to aid this discussion (BLM 15-4).

Peace in Ireland?—In May 1998, Britain voted on a peace plan. The Catholic minority in Ireland would be protected. Sinn Fein (pronounced SHIN FANE), the political arm of the Irish Republican Army (IRA), conceded to a ceasefire. Northern Ireland retained freedom to make its own decisions. The nationalists (those who want to unite with Ireland) and the unionists (those who want to remain British) reached a compromise that will create government jobs for former terrorists who have been released from prison. Ian Paisley, leader of the Democratic Unionist Party, and his party are not happy with the negotiations, for they fear Ireland will be reunited under a future vote in Ulster. They also resent the fact that former terrorists could have places in government.

BACKGROUNDS

The Irish Problem

The greed of a twelfth-century English king started more than eight hundred years of strife for England. King Henry II (1154-89) seized control of the neighboring island of Ireland and claimed it as an English possession. Understandably, the Irish did not appreciate this conquest, and they resisted. In the centuries that followed, numerous English kings sent forces into Ireland to put down rebellions and establish royal authority.

King James I (1603-25) tried to solve the Irish problem in a different manner. Just before James's reign, the divisions deepened between England and Ireland. England embraced the Protestant Reformation while Ireland remained steadfastly Roman Catholic. King James decided to settle thousands of Scottish and English Protestants in the northern part of Ireland. He thought that such settlements would make the population more loyal to the crown. Instead, the conflict worsened. The new settlers were loyal, but the native Irish resisted the English even more.

The native people of southern Ireland wanted "home rule"—the right to rule themselves free of English control. Northern Ireland, however, remained loyal to Britain. In 1921 the twenty counties of southern Ireland won their independence and became the Irish Free State (later the Republic of Ireland). The six counties of northern Ireland, also known as Ulster, became the province of Northern Ireland within the British Commonwealth.

Today the Protestant majority of Northern Ireland still wishes to remain joined to Britain. However, a large Roman Catholic minority in Ulster and the Catholic majority in the Republic of Ireland desire a united Irish state independent of Britain. Violence often erupts between these groups—especially in Ulster. Fighting still goes on to determine the future of Ireland, over eight hundred years since the conflict began.

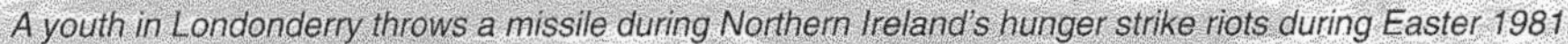

A youth in Londonderry throws a missile during Northern Ireland's hunger strike riots during Easter 1981.

Strife in Ireland—If Ireland is in the news, have your students bring in newspaper or magazine articles telling the latest developments. The students could give oral reports on their articles or post them on a current-events bulletin board.

442 Chapter 15

Those who rode streetcars to the services would sometimes lie on the floor to avoid stray bullets that flew through the windows. Despite the danger, they came, and God's Spirit moved among them.

But revivals like that in Northern Ireland have become rarer in Europe over the years. Christian faith is by no means dead in Europe, but it is certainly embraced by fewer people than it was in the past. Perhaps Europe should heed the message that Christ gave to the church at Sardis:

> Be watchful, and strengthen the things which remain, that are ready to die: for I have not found thy works perfect before God. Remember therefore how thou hast received and heard, and hold fast, and repent. If therefore thou shalt not watch, I will come on thee as a thief, and thou shalt not know what hour I will come upon thee (Rev. 3:2-3).

Spanning the Ages

World War I was a time for the creation of a new threat: communism. Inspired by Karl Marx's writings, extremists in Russia plotted to overthrow the incompetent czar and set up their own government. The most radical of these groups, the Bolsheviks, finally gained control and made Russia into a massive nation that swallowed up many surrounding republics. By the time of World War II, this giant was becoming powerful in world affairs. Though a part of the Allies, the Soviet Union began a Cold War with the Western powers after World War II was over. In the next chapter, we will study the formation of Communist Russia and its ultimate fall.

Section Review

1. What is secularism?
2. What organization founded in 1948 claims to be dedicated to furthering Christian unity?
3. In what part of Europe was there a notable revival in the 1920s? What minister led this revival?

Read all of Christ's message to the church at Sardis (Rev. 3:1-6). In what ways would these be appropriate verses to apply to modern Europe?

Summary

At the beginning of the twentieth century, Europe was divided into rival camps. Conflict in and over the Balkan Peninsula eventually sparked World War I. That war did not solve Europe's problems, however. After the war, Communist dictators and Fascist dictators (notably Benito Mussolini and Adolf Hitler) threatened the free nations of Europe. Hitler eventually sparked a second world war, which ended in the destruction of Nazi Germany, Fascist Italy, and Japan. Europe rebuilt after the war, and the remaining Fascist and Communist states in Europe eventually collapsed. Europe achieved some economic unity and dreamed of political unity. Unfortunately, more troubles in the Balkans unsettled the continent. Also Europe turned its back on its rich spiritual heritage and became increasingly secular in its outlook.

Section Review Answers

1. being concerned about the affairs of this life rather than heaven or God
2. World Council of Churches
3. Northern Ireland or Ulster; W. P. Nicholson

In the 1800s Europe was the center of religious truth in the world. England sent out thousands of missionaries during that century. Like Sardis, Europe should remember, repent, and return to godly living.

Chapter Review Idea

Have students bring in small index cards or small blank pieces of paper on which to write the terms from this chapter. Have them write the term on one side and the definition on the other. These may be used as a study tool for the quiz and/or test.

Chapter Enrichment Activities

Book Report—Have your students read one of the following books and write a book report on it, or read a small portion each day in class. *Number the Stars* by Lois Lowry is about a young girl in Copenhagen during World War II. *Molly Learns a Lesson* and other Molly books by Valerie Tripp (part of the American Girls Series) are fictional stories about growing up during World War II.

Further readings include *A Bell for Adano* by John Hesey, *Storm Warning* by Jack Higgins, and *I Never Left Home* by Bob Hope.

CHAPTER REVIEW

People, Places, and Things to Know

Wilhelm II	*der Führer*	T. S. Eliot	Marshall Plan
Francis Ferdinand	"German Christians"	Rhineland	West Germany
Central Powers	"Lost Generation"	Sudetenland	Juan Carlos
Allies	Ernest Hemingway	Francisco Franco	Common Market
World War I	Erich Maria Remarque	World War II	European Union (EU)
Woodrow Wilson	expressionism	blitzkrieg	United Nations (UN)
Great Depression	cubism	Axis Powers	secularism
dictator	Pablo Picasso	Luftwaffe	ecumenical movement
Benito Mussolini	surrealism	Winston Churchill	World Council of Churches
Fascists	Salvador Dali	RAF	Vatican II
Adolf Hitler	Igor Stravinsky	D-day	W. P. Nicholson
Nazi Party	Arnold Schönberg	Holocaust	

Review Questions

Relations

Choose which of the items in the following lists are least related to the others and explain how the other three are related.

1. (a) Winston Churchill
   (b) Francisco Franco
   (c) Adolf Hitler
   (d) Benito Mussolini

2. (a) F. Scott Fitzgerald
   (b) Ernest Hemingway
   (c) W. P. Nicholson
   (d) Erich Maria Remarque

3. (a) cubism
   (b) expressionism
   (c) Nazism
   (d) surrealism

4. (a) Austria-Hungary
   (b) Germany
   (c) Ottoman Empire
   (d) United States

Chapter Review Answers

Relations

1. Winston Churchill; Franco, Hitler, and Mussolini were fascist leaders
2. W. P. Nicholson; Fitzgerald, Hemingway, and Remarque were writers
3. Nazism; cubism, expressionism and surrealism are styles of art
4. United States; Austria-Hungary, Germany, and the Ottoman Empire were part of the Central Powers

Matching

Match the following people to the quotation that best fits each.

Winston Churchill	Ernest Hemingway	Juan Carlos
T. S. Eliot	Adolf Hitler	Woodrow Wilson

5. "Only fools, liars and criminals could hope in the mercy of the enemy."
6. "I have nothing to offer but blood, toil, tears, and sweat."
7. "This is the way the world ends / Not with a bang but a whimper."
8. "The world must be made safe for democracy."
9. "The crown . . . cannot tolerate . . . the action or attitude of those who seek by force to interrupt the democratic process."
10. "You are a lost generation."

Identify

Name the country described by each of the following phrases.

11. World War II began when Germany invaded this country.
12. The king of this nation crushed a rebellion by appearing on television.
13. The Munich Conference took the Sudetenland from this country and gave it to Germany.
14. Most of the American writers of "the Lost Generation" lived in this country for a time.
15. After World War II, this country was split into two parts, one part under Communist rule and the other part under democratic rule.
16. This nation had the first Fascist government in Europe.

Think About It!

Think about Robert Browning's words "God's in His heaven— / All's right with the world." Do you agree or disagree with his statement? Why?

Recipe: Poor Man's Cake—This recipe was developed during the Depression when people could no longer afford the eggs and milk that normally went into a cake.

Ingredients:
- 1 c. water
- 2 c. raisins
- 1 c. brown sugar
- 1/3 c. oil
- 1/2 t. cinnamon
- 1/2 t. allspice
- 1/2 t. salt
- 1/8 t. nutmeg
- 2 c. flour
- 1 tsp. baking powder
- 1 tsp. baking soda
- 1 c. nuts

Boil water, raisins, brown sugar, oil, cinnamon, allspice, salt, and nutmeg. Cool. Blend together the flour, baking powder, and baking soda; stir into raisin mixture until smooth. Add nuts. Bake in a greased 7-inch tube pan 1 hour at 325 degrees.

Matching

5. Adolf Hitler
6. Winston Churchill
7. T. S. Eliot
8. Woodrow Wilson
9. Juan Carlos
10. Ernest Hemingway

Identify

11. Poland
12. Spain
13. Czechoslovakia
14. France
15. Germany
16. Italy

Think About It!

Answers will vary. The student should realize that since "God's in His heaven," He is ultimately in control and "all's right with the world." He is the one we need to trust to take care of us in this world. Some students may say that the world is Satan's domain and that since many are not Christians, Satan is working his plan of deceit upon them. In this scenario, all is not right with the world.

Student Objectives
Students should be able to

1. List the reasons for the formation of the Soviet Union.
2. Explain the changes in Lenin's economic policies.
3. Locate Russia on a map.
4. Analyze and create a bar graph.
5. Evaluate the effects of Stalin's policies.
6. Describe Russia's involvement in World War II.
7. Define the term *Cold War*.
8. Identify the two Communist leaders of the USSR after Stalin.
9. Compare and contrast the Soviet Union under the earlier and later Communist leaders.
10. Define the term *détente*.
11. Recall the title for the head of the Eastern Orthodox Church.
12. Assess the religious situation in Russia during Communism.
13. Evaluate the positions of the registered and unregistered churches.
14. Define the terms *perestroika* and *glasnost*.
15. Analyze the reasons for the fall of Communism.

Opening Photo—
The Kremlin in Moscow

CHAPTER 16

John Reed, American reporter and Communist, walks along the streets of St. Petersburg, Russia, on November 7, 1917. The city, now going by its Russian name of "Petrograd," is in turmoil. The emperor, Czar Nicholas II, has been deposed and imprisoned somewhere. Russia's fragile new democratic "Provisional Government" fights for its life. World War I rages, but the German army to the west is only one problem facing Russia. Other factions are struggling to seize power. Later, Reed will set down his impressions of these momentous events in his book *Ten Days That Shook the World*.

On this day Reed tours the confused city. He goes to the Winter Palace, formerly the czar's home and now the headquarters of Aleksandr Kerensky, head of the Provisional Government. Reed walks in past the guards. Soldiers and sailors mill around, arguing with each other and ignoring their officers. One officer approaches Reed. "I am very anxious to go away from Russia," he says to the reporter. "I have made up my mind to join the American army. Would you please go to your Consul and make arrangements? I will give you my address."

It is rumored that the Communists, the most extreme political group, are going to seize power. Reed hears about a dramatic meeting of the Petrograd Soviet (a workers' organization). In that meeting the Communist leader, Lenin, has announced that the Provisional Government is doomed. As night falls, guns boom in the darkness. The revolutionaries occupy government offices, and Kerensky flees the city. Petrograd is in Communist hands. Eventually, all of Russia will be.

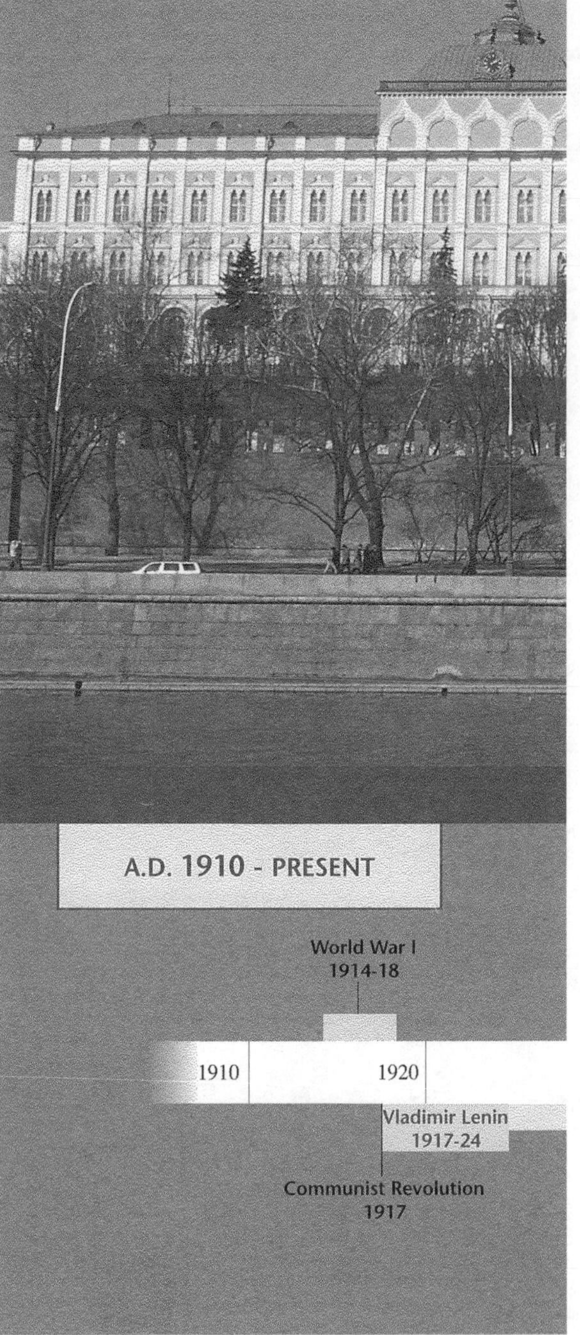

Chapter 16 Lesson Plans			
Section Title	**Main Concept**	**Pages**	**Time Frame**
1. Lenin and the Revolution **Settings: Russia*	The czar was overthrown, and the Communists, led by Vladimir Lenin, took over Russia, creating the Union of Soviet Socialist Republics.	446-53	2 days
2. Stalin and the "Age of Terror"	Joseph Stalin made suffering the way of life in the USSR through his cruelty. Russia was able to turn back the Germans in World War II.	454-57	1-2 days
3. The Cold War	After World War II, the Cold War was fought between the Communists and the free world until the fall of the Soviet Empire.	458-62	1-2 days
4. Religion in the Soviet Union **Backgrounds: Orthodox Church*	Officially atheist, the Communist government greatly persecuted religion.	463-67	1 day
5. Decline and Fall **Characterizations: Sakharov*	In 1989, Russian Communism fell under Gorbachev's policies of *perestroika* and *glasnost*.	468-71	1-2 days
Total Suggested Days (including 1 day for review & 1 day for test)			8-11 days

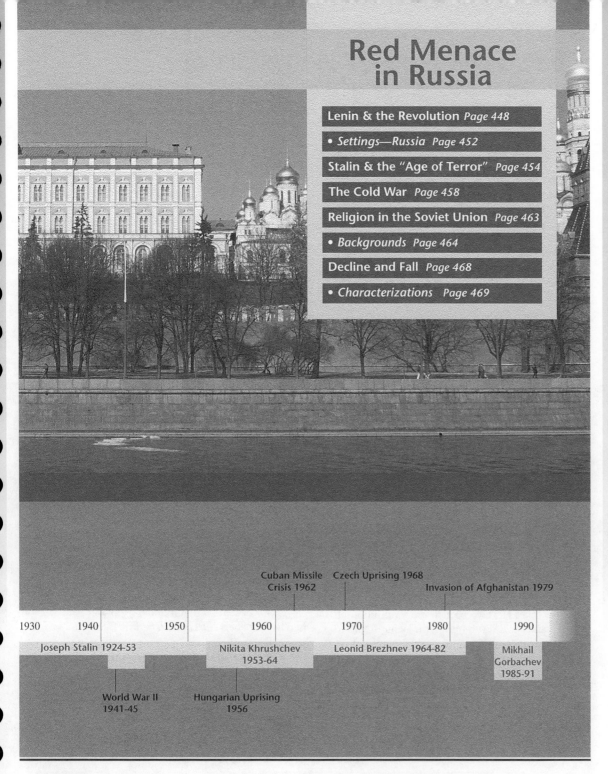

Red Menace in Russia

1930 1940 1950 1960 1970 1980 1990

Joseph Stalin 1924-53
World War II 1941-45
Nikita Khrushchev 1953-64
Hungarian Uprising 1956
Cuban Missile Crisis 1962
Leonid Brezhnev 1964-82
Czech Uprising 1968
Invasion of Afghanistan 1979
Mikhail Gorbachev 1985-91

Materials

- Scripture verse (BLM verse 16)
- Pictures of Red Square and the Kremlin
- *Teaching Transparencies* for use with *WORLD STUDIES for Christian Schools* (Second Edition)
- Wall map of Russia (BLM 16-1)
- Calculators
- *The Leningrad Symphony* by Dmitri Shostakovich
- *Coming Out of the Ice* by Victor Herman
- Bibles
- Religion chart
- Pictures of Orthodox churches and icons
- *Three Generations of Suffering* and/or *Testament from Prison* by Georgi Vins
- Video on the fall of Soviet Communism
- Periodical articles on the fall of Communism in any Eastern Bloc country

The Harvest Is Plenteous

Draw a Soviet hammer-and-sickle flag as a background for your board. Create a missions board by showing a sickle cutting wheat and by placing Matthew 9:37b on the board: "The harvest truly is plenteous, but the labourers are few." Talk about how missions has a new foothold in Russia (though the Orthodox Church is trying to force it out) and ask your students what they can do to help.

Chapter Motivator

Review the Mongol Empire of the Golden Horde in Russia (Chapter 4). Look back at Chapter 15. The Bolshevik Revolution of 1917 brought about change in Russia. Later, the Soviet Union had to withdraw from World War I because of problems at home. Ask your students what they have heard about Soviet Communism. (They are too young to remember it.) Name missionaries to the former Soviet Union and pray for them. Encourage your students to bring in missionary prayer cards to add to your bulletin board.

Psalm 33:10, 12*a*

Marxist Communism has failed in many ways. Economically, former Communist countries are in serious upheaval. Standards of living are much below those of the West. But more than anything else, the policy of atheism has hurt the former Communist countries. The Bible says in Psalm 33:10 and 12*a*, "The Lord bringeth the counsel of the heathen to nought: he maketh the devices of the people of none effect. . . . Blessed is the nation whose God is the Lord." (BLM verse 16)

SECTION 1

Student Objectives
Students should be able to

1. List the reasons for the formation of the Soviet Union.
2. Explain the changes in Lenin's economic policies.

The Puzzle of Russia's Identity—Russia's concept of itself has been complicated over the centuries by many factors. A fundamental dilemma has been a very simple question: Is Russia European or Asian? Over the centuries Russia's identity has been clouded by conquest and assimilation of its neighbors into Russia. Many non-Russians have been part of its elite over the centuries.

For centuries Russians have had an uncanny ability to borrow technology from foreigners. Peter I brought in Baltic Germans to carry out his reforms and hired foreigners to build his navy. Czars in the eighteenth and nineteenth centuries hired Germans to do their explorations. The ruling family of the czars, the Romanovs, were by the eighteenth century ethnically German. Italian architects, along with some other foreigners, constructed the Kremlin and most of the new capital, St. Petersburg. The degree to which the Russian language has many English, French, and German words reveals a general willingness to borrow from other nations.

This process of borrowing from other cultures not only has made the concept of Russian identity ambiguous but also has had a profound political consequence. Since there was no core culture that bound Russia to her conquered neighbors in czarist and Communist days, the Russian rulers have relied on force to keep the nation or empire together. By the 1980s, ethnic nationalism in various Soviet republics overwhelmed the Communist rule and the Soviet empire collapsed.

Lenin and the Communist Revolution

Reed goes on to write, "So. Lenin and the Petrograd workers had decided on insurrection, the Petrograd Soviet had overthrown the Provisional Government. . . . Now there was all great Russia to win—and then the world! Would Russia follow and rise? And the world—what of it? Would the peoples answer and rise, a red world-tide?"

Three years later, John Reed died of typhus, and the revolutionary government buried him with great honors in Red Square in Moscow. Seventy years later, the "red world-tide" Reed described would ebb. The Soviet Union was born just after the turn of the twentieth century; it died just before the turn of the twenty-first.

Students are often confused that the Communist Revolution is sometimes called "the October Revolution" since it occurred on November 7, 1917. The cause of this confusion is calendars. The czars (emperors) of Russia had refused to join the nations of Europe in adopting the Gregorian calendar (devised by Pope Gregory XIII in 1582). They followed the old Julian calendar (devised by Julius Caesar), which ran eleven days behind the Gregorian. The Communists changed the country over to the Gregorian calendar. This change might have been hard for some people to get used to, but it was actually one of the mildest changes the Communists made.

Lenin addresses the masses, attempting to rally them to revolution. Joseph Stalin stands directly behind Lenin.

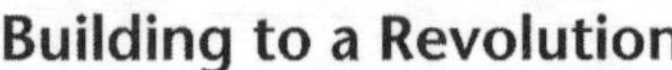

Building to a Revolution

The name of the leader of the Communist Revolution, **Vladimir Ilich Lenin,** was actually fake. He had been born Vladimir Ilich Ulyanov in 1870 but took the name Lenin to protect himself from the czar's secret police. He came from a well-to-do family but one with a streak of revolutionary fervor. His brother joined a plot against Czar Alexander III. Lenin's brother was then caught, arrested, and hanged.

Lenin became a revolutionary too, but he had little success. Eventually he was forced to leave Russia and live in Europe, where he might have lived for the rest of his life had it not been for World War I. Russia was not ready

SECTION 1

Materials

- Pictures of Red Square and the Kremlin

Calendar Days—Write some dates on the chalkboard or the overhead using today's calendar system. Ask your students to change them to the Julian calendar as mentioned in the section. *(Example: June 9, 1922, would be May 29, 1922, and December 16, 1947, would be December 5, 1947.)* Some sources say that there is a twelve-day difference.

448 Chapter 16

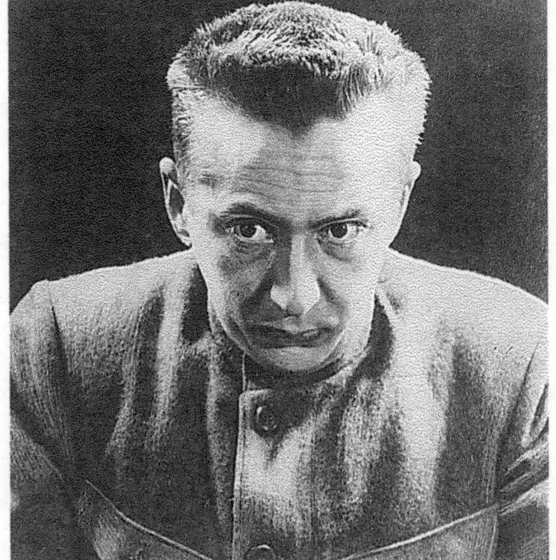

Aleksandr Kerensky

for war, and the Germans inflicted grave defeats on the Russians. The people were starving from shortages of food. The poorly equipped, poorly led Russian soldiers were dying for a cause they no longer cared about. Czar Nicholas II was incompetent. In March 1917 the Russian people overthrew the czar. The new **Provisional Government,** led by **Aleksandr Kerensky,** promised freedom and relief.

Kerensky did not take Russia out of the war, however. Germany therefore smuggled Lenin back into the country, hoping that he would stir up trouble and weaken Russia even more. The war was not going any better for Kerensky than it had for Nicholas II. The Russian people began to listen to Lenin's slogan of "Peace, Land, Bread."

Lenin finally succeeded, and the Communist Revolution toppled the Provisional Government. Other factions fought for control of Russia too. For two years Russia fought a bloody civil war. The Communists finally defeated all their opponents and imposed their rule. In the mid-1920s Communist Russia officially took the name **Union of Soviet Socialist Republics (USSR)**, or **Soviet Union** for short.

After the Communist Revolution, outside powers intervened to help the anti-Communist forces. Here Japanese soldiers march beneath the flags of the nations that tried, in vain, to halt the revolution.

Union of Soviet Socialist Republics—The former USSR was made up of the following countries: Armenia, Azerbaijan, Belarus, Estonia, Georgia, Kazakhstan, Kyrgyzstan, Latvia, Lithuania, Moldova, Russia, Tajikistan, Turkmenistan, Ukraine, and Uzbekistan.

Karl Marx—Communism received its foundations from the teachings and writings of Karl Marx, the German socialist. According to him, all cultures go through five stages, the last of which is the coveted communism, where all live together and share labor and wealth. Of course, the Soviet Union never did become truly communistic by this definition.

Bolsheviks or Communists?—The Bolshevik branch of the socialists in Russia was the one that finally won power in the civil war. The name "Bolshevik" was changed in March 1918 to "Communist." Other common names used to describe Russia are "Marxist," "socialist," and "soviet."

Soviets (Workers)—*Soviet* means "group of workers." Ask your students to list some ways in which employers are able to make their employees want to work hard. *(good pay, benefits, good working conditions, shared philosophy and goals)* What would make them not want to work hard? *(little pay, poor environment, lack of incentive or motivation, harsh conditions)*

Lenin and Kerensky—Have the students look at the pictures of Lenin and Kerensky on these pages for at least thirty seconds each. Then have them describe what they think each man must have been like based on these pictures. Their descriptions can be oral or written. Encourage students to share their observations with the class.

Vladimir Ilich Lenin—After Lenin's brother was executed as a state criminal, it was Alexander Kerensky's own father, Lenin's principal, who wrote a letter to get Lenin into a university. Lenin had graduated first in his class, and though expelled from the university, he eventually took first place in every bar examination and finally became a lawyer. The unfairness of law to the lower classes taught him to hate the idea of social classes. The revolution he started became something he did not want, however, as the government took dictatorial control and became corrupt.

Nature of Soviet Communism

In Chapter 11 we studied about socialism, including the Marxist and Communist forms. You will recall that Karl Marx taught that the root of society's problems was the unequal distribution of wealth. The rich controlled the means of producing goods and kept the profits while the laborers who did all the work received little. Marx believed that eventually the workers would rise up against the rich. They would institute a government in which there would be no classes. All men would be equal. No one would actually own anything, but everybody would share with anyone who was in need.

Lenin added a twist to Marx's ideas. The Russian revolutionary did not think that revolution would arise naturally. Instead, revolutionaries might use violence, as Lenin did, to spur the revolution along. Once his revolution had been brought to its bloody climax, Lenin was ready to impose his Communist state.

There was no room for individual freedom or private ownership of property. The people, in whose name the revolution had been made, actually had little power. The government ran the businesses and paid the workers. The people had to obey the government's orders and accept the Communist philosophy or risk punishment. The people became little better than slaves to their Communist leaders. Lenin promised "Peace, Land, Bread," but he gave the people little of these.

Lenin at first tried to establish pure Communism with what he called **"War Communism."** The Communists took over all

****
For a color version of the map on this page, see page A10 in the Appendix.

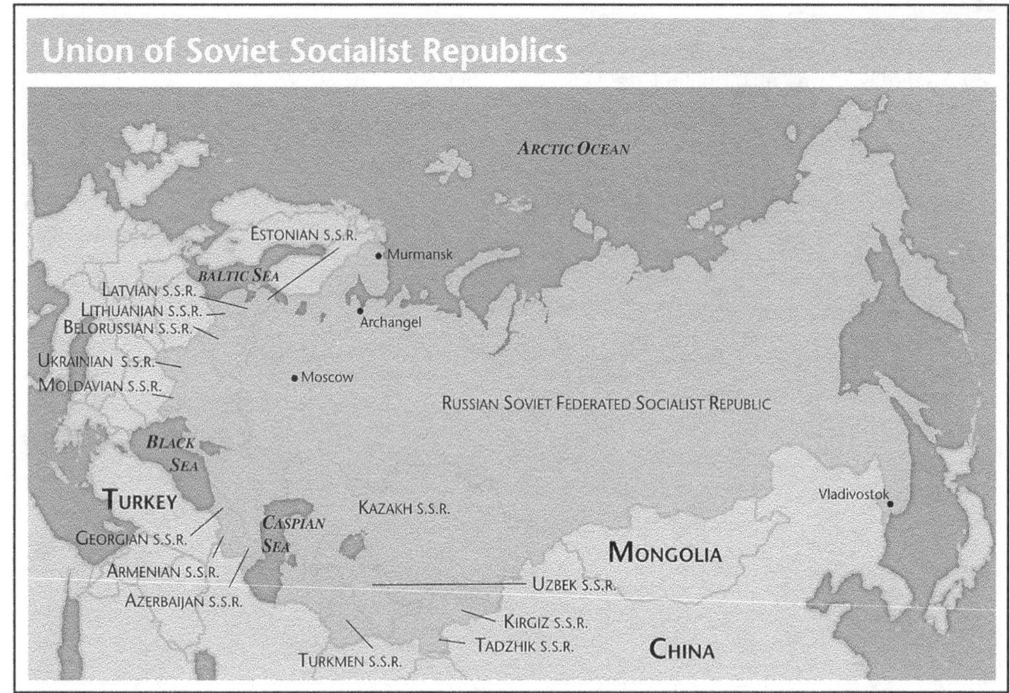

Red Square—Bring in pictures of Red Square and the Kremlin to show your students. Without telling what the pictures are of, but mentioning that they have to do with Russia, have each student write out a description of his picture. Let the students read their descriptions; then tell them the place of the picture.

A variation of this activity for larger classes would be to have two of each picture and let the students find the person with the matching picture. The pair can then describe the picture together.

Home School Activity Home schoolers may wish to go the library or use the Internet to find pictures of Moscow, including the Kremlin and Red Square. Look for architectural elements borrowed from other countries and regions.

Lenin's tomb in Moscow where the embalmed remains of Lenin are still on public display.

Red Square and Moscow— Moscow is built in the shape of a wheel with the busiest part at the center near the Kremlin. The Kremlin is a walled fortress housing the government of Russia and formerly of the Soviet Union. Cathedrals, palaces, and government buildings lie inside its nearly 1½ miles of walls.

Just outside the Kremlin's walls lies Red Square, a large plaza. The department store GUM (pronounced *goom,* initials standing for state department store), pictured on page 453, is across from the Kremlin. St. Basil's Cathedral, the beautiful onion-domed orthodox church, is also there (pictured on page 463 and on the cover).

businesses, took control of all private property, and seized all the food for distribution. The nation nearly starved. Lenin then announced the **"New Economic Policy."** This was really old capitalism in disguise. Farmers could sell some of their produce, and merchants could make profits from their goods. The government invited foreign investment in Russian industry. Under this plan, the Soviet Union began to recover.

Lenin intended for the New Economic Policy to be only temporary, but he never had a chance to change it. He survived an assassination attempt in August 1918 but never fully recovered. His health steadily declined, especially after a series of strokes beginning in 1922. The last two years of his life Lenin spent as an invalid waited on by a huge team of doctors and nurses. He died on January 21, 1924. His body was laid in public view in a glass case in a mausoleum (MAW suh LEE um; a large building housing a tomb) in Moscow's Red Square. Lenin was gone, but his revolution went on.

Section Review

1. Who was the leader of the Provisional Government, which the Communists overthrew?
2. How did Lenin get back into Russia after World War I began?
3. What idea did Lenin add to the theories of Karl Marx?
4. What was Lenin's name for the pure form of Communism he first tried to impose? When it failed, what policy did he replace it with?

Why would the slogan "Peace, Land, Bread" have appealed to the Russian people in 1917?

Section Review Answers

1. Alexander Kerensky
2. The Germans smuggled him into the country to undermine the Russian war effort.
3. that violent revolution could speed the creation of the classless society
4. War Communism; New Economic Policy

Answers will vary. The people were poor, hungry, and tired of war. The slogan would have therefore appealed to those seeking solutions for these problems. There could also be an appeal to greed, especially with the promise of land. However, the promise of land also seemed to promise political reform from the authoritarian czarist state.

Student Objectives
Students should be able to

1. Locate Russia on a map.
2. Analyze and create a bar graph.

The CIS Today—In 1991, two republics of the Soviet Union, Georgia and Lithuania, declared their independence from the crumbling empire. Soon every other republic except Russia followed.

The member nations of the loose confederation called the Commonwealth of Independent States include Armenia, Belarus, Kazakhstan, Kyrgyzstan, Russia, Tajikistan, Turkmenistan, Ukraine, and Uzbekistan. The headquarters for the CIS are in Minsk, Belarus. Two countries which were originally members of the CIS, Azerbaijan and Moldova, pulled out of the organization within two years. Four of the republics, Georgia, Estonia, Latvia, and Lithuania, never joined.

SETTINGS—Russia

Location—Russia occupies the eastern part of Europe and all of the northern part of the Asian continent. It is bordered in the west by Norway, Finland, Estonia, Latvia, Lithuania, Belarus, and Ukraine. A piece of western Russia, Kaliningrad, is separated from the rest of the country and is wedged between Lithuania and Poland against the Baltic Sea. In the south are Georgia, Azerbaijan, Kazakhstan, China, Mongolia, and North Korea. The northern and eastern sides are bordered by water.

Climate—The climate of Russia varies from icy in the north to dry in the south. In the land between, the climate is mostly highland or snowy. The European section of Russia has mostly a humid continental climate, and the Asian section has mainly a subpolar climate. Along its northern border, Russia has a polar (tundra) climate, and along the southern border it has a semiarid (steppe) climate. Temperatures throughout Russia vary from between -33° and 10°F in the winter to between 30° and 80°F in the summer.

Topography—Most of Russia is on a plateau. Much of the plateau consists of steppes (grassy plains), thick forests, and high mountain ranges in the central and eastern parts. Many rivers flow through the land. The Ural Mountains cut through the country. They divide European Russia from Asian Russia. The Caucasus Mountains separate Russia from Georgia and Azerbaijan and have been a hiding place for rebellious factions throughout history.

Natural Resources—The abundant farmland of Russia has some of the richest soil in the world. Thick forests provide wood. The many rivers are a

Materials

- Transparencies for Chapter 16
- Wall map of Russia (BLM 16-1)

Map Activity—Use map 16-C from the Student Activities manual to reinforce the geography lesson.

Going Beyond—Read the Settings pages on Russia and answer the questions. Use a map of Europe and Asia (TT 20-B) to show the modern countries of the CIS. Using a map of the former USSR, have your students find each of the former republics. (TT 16-A) Note which other countries they are near, and predict what kind of culture, language, and religion each has.

Show your students a bar graph (TT 16-B). Discuss how a bar graph is a visual representation of information. A bar graph is best used with specific numbers. Have the students create their own bar graph for page length of sections in this chapter. Then have the students estimate, based on their graph, which section would require the most study time.

source, largely untapped, of hydroelectric power. Almost every mineral needed for industry is found in quantity. The only exception is tin.

Geography & Culture—Even though much of Russia is on the Asian continent, this nation's culture is mainly European. The European part of Russia was more favorable to settlement and development, and European Russia is far more heavily populated than the Asian part. The regions near the Baltic and Black Seas have become agricultural and industrial because the favorable climate and topography have made transportation possible. In contrast, the Asian section (Siberia) has a cold climate that is unfavorable for agriculture, industry, or stable transportation facilities.

The desire to escape the cold has shaped Russia's history. For many years, Russia had no warm-water ports; all of its seaports were frozen during the winter months. Therefore, Russia constantly pushed toward the Baltic Sea in the east and the Mediterranean Sea in the south. The Russians reached the Baltic finally but have never succeeded in getting a port on the Mediterranean.

Settings Review

1. What kind of climate is generally found in the European section of Russia? What kind of climate is generally found in the Asian section?
2. What mostly untapped source of electricity is abundant in Russia?
3. What is the only important mineral for industry that Russia does *not* possess in sufficient quantity?

Why would the cold climate of Siberia make it less suitable for settlement?

Scenes from modern Russia: a shopping mall in Moscow (top right), the Russian countryside (bottom right), and St. Basil's Cathedral in Moscow (left)

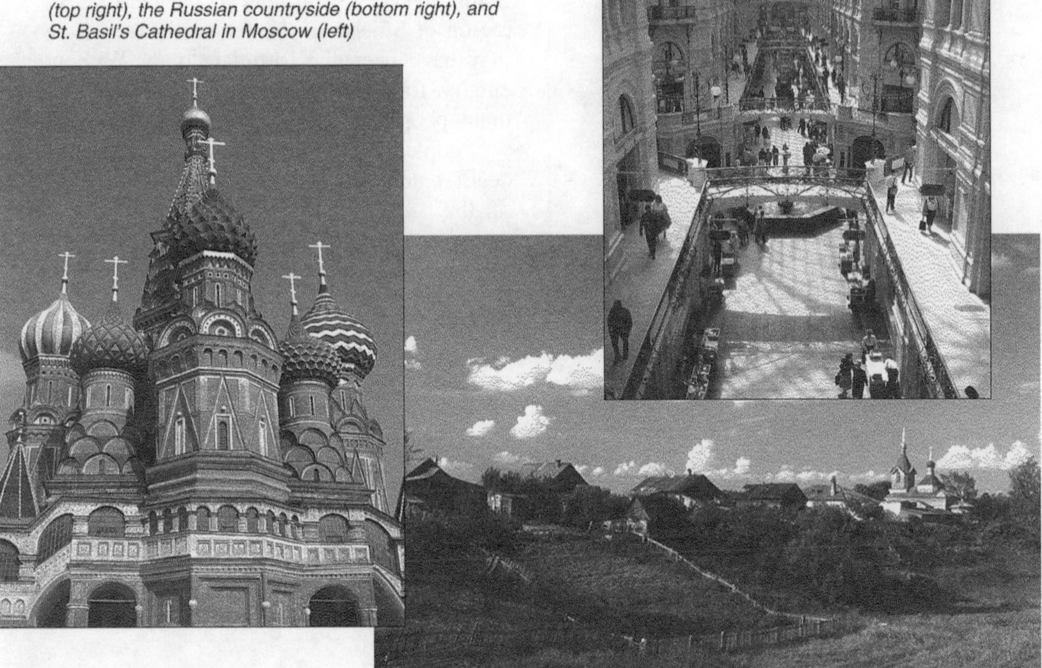

Settings Review Answers

1. humid continental; subpolar
2. rivers
3. tin

Answers will vary. The most obvious reason is that people are less likely to want to live in a cold area such as Siberia. The climate also makes it difficult to build up industry and agriculture and to develop a transportation system.

Section 2

Student Objectives
Students should be able to

1. Evaluate the effects of Stalin's policies.
2. Describe Russia's involvement in World War II.

Stalin's Mother—Stalin's mother wanted him to be a priest, but her efforts were of no avail. Stalin was arrested many times for revolutionary activities, though his frequent and easy escapes led some to think he was a spy for the czar.

Stalin and the "Age of Terror"

Lenin's successor was **Joseph Stalin.** He was born Josef Dzhugashvili but, like Lenin, took a false name for safety. He chose Stalin because it means "man of steel." Stalin liked the tough sound of the name. He would prove, at any rate, that he had a heart of steel, for Joseph Stalin became one of the cruelest dictators in history.

Industrialization and Collectivization

Because the Soviet Union was far behind Europe in industry, Stalin began to build modern factories. Under his **Five-Year Plans** (beginning in 1928), Stalin directed factories to produce goods for industry, agriculture, and the military. Factories made few consumer goods. Many people went without household goods and new clothing as factories followed Stalin's, not the people's, desires. Not only did people miss owning luxuries; often they could not find decent shoes or clothing to buy.

Joseph Stalin

The suffering caused by Stalin's plan of industrialization, however, was nothing compared to the suffering caused by his agricultural policies. Stalin sought to collectivize the farms of the USSR. **Collectivization** meant taking the land from owners of all farms and joining it into large farms run by the government. Communist officials then assigned farmers to work the new farms and ordered them to turn the harvest over to the government. The government paid the farmers low wages, with which they purchased food and goods in the government-run stores.

Many farmers fought collectivization. They slaughtered their animals and dumped out their milk rather than give it to the government. Some held huge feasts to wolf down their food before the Communists could get it. Stalin sent many farmers to the cold, harsh region of Siberia in the far northeast. These may have been the fortunate ones. Without enough food to go around, Stalin simply let many people starve.

People died of starvation, but courts gave death sentences to those who tried to steal food off the collective farms. Sometimes if someone showed no sign of starvation, officials assumed he was stealing food. They would beat him to find out where he was hiding it. In desperation, a few Soviets resorted to cannibalism but were put to death when the Communists discovered what they were doing. Hatred of Stalin was almost as great as fear of the Soviet dictator. An American visiting Soviet farms in the late 1930s saw a grave marked, "I love Stalin. Bury him here as soon as possible."

Section 2

Materials

- Calculators
- *The Leningrad Symphony* by Dmitri Shostakovich
- *Coming Out of the Ice* by Victor Herman

Collectivization—Have your students write down one parent's occupation. All such jobs will be collectivized in the area (i.e., if the student's father is a shoemaker, all shoemakers in the area will be collectivized). Remember that the government not only collectivizes each occupation but also pays low wages. A person does not make more money for working harder. Everyone makes the same. Each student should answer the following questions:

1. Would your parent work harder or less hard in this situation?
2. Your parent no longer can order the material he needs to do his job. The government does this for him. What will your parent do if there is too much material? not enough?
3. What if your parent does not have enough income to feed the family because he does not have enough material for his occupation?
4. The government realizes that your family and all others in the same occupation are not making ends meet. It allows them to work up to ten hours a week for themselves, not the government. How would this help your family's income?

Two scenes reflecting the changes Stalin brought to the Soviet Union: peasants joining a collective farm and the Bereznikovsky chemical factory

The collectivized farms were a failure. Whatever farmers grew went to the state. With little reward for success, workers did not put out their best efforts. The most productive farming took place on tiny plots of land given to the peasants to grow what they wanted. On these plots, farmers could keep all they grew. In 1938 these private plots were 4 percent of Soviet farmland, but they provided 20 percent of its produce.

Purges

Stalin cruelly disposed of all opposition to his rule. To do this he used the secret police and fixed trials. The secret police watched the people and tortured those they arrested in order to get "confessions." In the schools and local meeting places, government officials taught the people to report any antigovernment attitudes or actions, such as hiding food. Neighbors turned in neighbors to the Communists. Even children, prodded by their teachers, accused their own parents.

Stalin trusted no one. In the 1930s he began a series of **purges** to eliminate anyone he thought might be disloyal. The secret police arrested loyal Communists. Special courts accused the astonished officials of all sorts of fictitious crimes against the state. In almost every case the verdict was guilty and the punishment either imprisonment or death. Stalin swept away political officials, military officers, and anyone else he thought could be a threat to his power, even writers, artists, and actors. Membership in the Communist Party could be more a danger than a protection. In 1934 nearly two thousand delegates attended a major Communist Party assembly. Within five years, over half of these had been shot on Stalin's orders.

A prosecutor reads the verdicts in a Stalinist trial.

Stalin's Purges—Under Stalin, the Communist regime became so repressive that everyone was afraid of him. He had his best friend murdered, and his wife committed suicide. In the beginning years of his leadership, he used a voluntary system of collectivization of agriculture. When this did not work, he forced the farmers into collectivization. The kulaks who refused were killed or deported as a way to rid Russia of them and served as a threat to any others who might get in Stalin's way.

In Stalin's purges, he went so far as to require quotas: a certain percentage of citizens had to be arrested in each sector. By the time of his death, the people so feared him that they could not even help him. He had a stroke in the morning, but the soldiers were too afraid to wake him without being summoned once they realized he was not up at his usual time. The government officials who came for a meeting took one look at him and turned around and went home. They did not want to be accused of anything. The doctors who were called in were afraid to work with him for fear of another "Doctor's Purge," such as the one that had recently happened. In the end, Stalin's plan backfired.

Taking Control—Discuss with your students Stalin's control over Russia. How do leaders such as Stalin and Hitler maintain control? *(fear, loyalty of people near them, apathy of the masses)* What would have to occur in a democratic republic such as the United States for such a powerful leader to seize control? How can it be prevented?

The War in Russia—In "Operation Barbarossa," Hitler attacked Stalin's ill-prepared army. Stalin was warned by anti-Nazi soldiers of Hitler's plans, but he turned a deaf ear. He could not allow himself to believe that anyone would break his word to him.

The great problem with the siege on Leningrad was the lack of food. The warehouses storing large supplies of food were burned. Many people starved to death. There was no electricity in the winter of 1941 either. Death became a common occurrence. The "ice road" across Lake Ladoga was the real help in bringing food and supplies. Without the brave-hearted men driving supply trucks under air attack, certainly all the people would have starved. By the second winter of the siege, supplies were much more readily available.

The Leningrad Symphony—While rehearsing Shostakovich's symphony, one of the trumpet players stopped playing. When asked why, he said that he did not have the strength to play. Shostakovich said that he must play "for the people." The trumpeter continued playing through the rest of the rehearsal.

At the end of the first performance, while the audience applauded, a young girl came to the director's podium and presented Shostakovich with a bouquet of flowers. The audience then burst into tears and shouts because no fresh flowers were available in the city. The flowers encouraged the orchestra and the audience alike with the thought that they indeed would find a way to outlast the siege.

World War II

Yet there was also a source of suffering for the Soviet people that was not Stalin's doing, at least directly. As we learned in the last chapter, Adolf Hitler desired to launch a war of conquest, and he made a treaty with Stalin in 1939. Germany and the Soviet Union agreed not to attack each other, and they agreed to split Poland between them when the war broke out.

Neither dictator intended to keep this bargain, but Hitler broke it first. In June 1941 Nazi Germany attacked the Soviet Union. At first, the Germans won devastating victories over the surprised Soviet army. Some citizens even welcomed the Nazis as liberators from the oppression of Stalin.

Hitler, however, hated the Russian people as an "inferior race." Therefore, German soldiers treated the people with great cruelty. The people rallied against the invaders. Many practiced a **"scorched-earth" policy.** As they retreated, the Soviet people burned food, crops, homes—anything that the Germans might be able to use.

The people suffered terribly from the fighting. The Germans surrounded Leningrad (formerly St. Petersburg). For 880 days, the Germans encircled the city. Inside, thousands of people died each day from starvation. Many just collapsed quietly and died at their jobs or in the streets. Starvation killed a million people. But the citizens of Leningrad held on. Despite the German siege, composer Dmitri Shostakovich worked on what would become his Seventh, or "Leningrad," Symphony. After writing the first two movements, the composer went on the radio to announce he had finished them. "Why do I tell you this?" he asked. "I tell you this so that those Leningraders who are now listening to me shall know that the life of our city is going on normally." Finally, in the spring of 1944, the Soviets broke the siege of Leningrad.

The United States and Great Britain poured supplies into the Soviet Union to help the Soviets defeat Germany. The people, although they hated Stalin, rallied to defend their homeland. The turning point was the **Battle of Stalingrad,** fought from July 1942 to February 1943. Germans and Soviets fought ferociously for the city, reducing Stalingrad to a heap of rubble. The new factories Stalin had built for his Five-Year Plans became blood-drenched battlefields. The fighting was incredibly fierce. A German officer wrote,

> We have fought fifteen days for a single house, with mortars, grenades, machine guns, and bayonets. By the third day fifty-four German corpses lay strewn in the cellars, on the landings and the staircases. . . . There is a ceaseless struggle from noon to night. From story to story, faces black with sweat, we bombard each other with grenades in the middle of explosions, clouds of dust and smoke, [and] heaps of mortar. . . . Ask any soldier what half an hour of hand-to-hand struggle means in such a fight. And imagine

A Russian commander urges his troops forward against the invading Germans.

Math—Have your students use calculators to figure out how many years and months (days are already given) Nazi soldiers besieged Leningrad. *(880 days=2.4 years or 28.9 months. Altogether the siege lasted 2 years, 4 months, and 27 days.)*

Leningrad Symphony—Bring in a recording of Dmitri Shostakovich's *Leningrad Symphony* to play for your students. Other good examples of Rusian music would be *Peter and the Wolf* by Prokofiev or works by Rimsky-Korsakov.

Coming Out of the Ice—Read to your class portions of the autobiography *Coming Out of the Ice* by Victor Herman (New York: Harcourt Brace Jovanovich, 1979). Be sure your students understand the context of the story: Stalin's policy was to slaughter or imprison anyone who was even suspected of being an "enemy of the people." Many thousands of Russians were exiled to Siberia, a land where snow lies on the ground up to six months each year and temperatures remain below zero much of the time. For any who were ill or weak, exile to Siberia amounted to a death sentence. Many of those who survived considered the prison camps a fate worse than death.

At the same time Stalin was imposing his economic and agricultural policies on the people, he was recruiting American aid in modernizing Russia's industry. Many American companies sent employees to live in Russia and teach American technology to the Russians. Engineers helped with building roads, dams, and power plants. Mechanics and factory managers helped establish automobile and heavy-equipment plants. Victor Herman's father went to Russia as an employee of the Ford Motor Company and took

Soviet troops hug the ground in the middle of the rubble of Stalingrad.

> Stalingrad: eighty days and eighty nights of hand-to-hand struggles. . . . Stalingrad is no longer a town. By day it is an enormous cloud of burning, blinding smoke; it is a vast furnace, lit by the reflections of the flames. And when the night arrives, one of those scorching, howling, bleeding nights, the dogs plunge into the Volga [River] and swim desperately to gain the other bank. The nights of Stalingrad are a terror for them. Animals flee this hell; the hardest stones cannot bear it for long; only men endure.

The battle ended with the death or surrender of over two hundred thousand German soldiers. After Stalingrad, the Soviet army slowly became stronger, and the German army gradually became weaker. Finally, in 1945, Soviet troops moved into Berlin itself, and Hitler committed suicide.

The Soviet Union had won a great victory but at great cost. Estimates are that seven million soldiers and seven million civilians died in the war. The war did not change Stalin's nature. He quickly moved to enslave Eastern Europe. He forced Poland, Czechoslovakia, East Germany, and other nations to accept Communist governments. Stalin did not even spare his own suffering people. When Soviet soldiers returned from German prison camps after World War II, Stalin feared that they might have picked up "dangerous ideas" during their imprisonment. So he sent them straight to Communist prison camps in Siberia.

How many people died under Stalin's reign of terror? In 1991 the Soviet secret police estimated that 42 million citizens died by execution or starvation or died in prison between 1928 and 1952. This huge number does not even count the millions of Soviet soldiers and civilians who died in World War II. Historians rightly consider Nazi dictator Adolf Hitler a monster. But even Hitler did not slaughter as many people as the bloody-handed Joseph Stalin. "A single death is a tragedy," Stalin once said coldly. "A million deaths is a statistic." If so, he was an expert in statistics.

Stalin's Son—Stalin had a son named Jacob who tried to commit suicide in his twenties. When this did not work, Stalin called him a weakling. He would not even exchange prisoners for his son when his son was a prisoner of war in World War II.

Section Review

1. What does *Stalin* mean?
2. What was Stalin's name for his plans to improve Soviet industry?
3. What is meant by the "collectivization" of agriculture?
4. During World War II, what Soviet city was the site of a lengthy German siege?
5. What battle was the turning point of the war for the Soviet Union?
6. What did Stalin do in Eastern Europe after World War II?

Why were the private plots of Soviet citizens, which were only 4 percent of Soviet farmland, able to provide 20 percent of the nation's produce?

his family with him. Victor was not allowed to leave Russia for forty-five years, and spent much of that time in exile in Siberia. *Coming Out of the Ice* is the story of his time in Russia. Be sure to preview any material you plan to read to the class.

Section Review Answers

1. "man of steel"
2. Five-Year Plans
3. Collectivization means taking the land from farm owners, joining the land into large government-owned farms, and assigning farmers to work the land for the government.
4. Leningrad (St. Petersburg)
5. the Battle of Stalingrad
6. He forced Communist governments on the nations of that region and brought them under Soviet domination.

Answers will vary. People naturally work harder when they profit directly from the work. In the collective farms, a worker received the same pay no matter how hard he worked. With the private plots, the harder a person worked, the more he had to eat or trade. People would therefore do their best to get all the produce they could out of their small plots.

SECTION 3

Student Objectives
Students should be able to

1. Define the term *Cold War*.
2. Identify the two Communist leaders of the USSR after Stalin.
3. Compare and contrast the Soviet Union under the earlier and later Communist leaders.
4. Define the term *détente*.

Europe and the Cold War Map—The Warsaw Pact was forced to disband after the fall of Communism. Three of the countries that had belonged to the Warsaw Pact (Hungary, Poland, and the Czech Republic) joined NATO.

****

For a color version of the map on this page, see page A11 in the Appendix.

The Cold War and the Communist State

Before Stalin died in 1953, he began what has been called the **Cold War.** A "hot war" is one in which two sides fight openly against each other. World War II was a hot war. The phrase "Cold War" refers to a period of competition between the Communist world and the free world. Sometimes it broke out into a hot war, as in the Vietnam War. Usually, though, the two sides—led by the Soviet Union and the United States—competed behind the scenes. The Soviet Union sought to expand its power and spread Communism around the world. It sought to avoid an open war with the United States and other free nations. A Cold War seemed safer because by the 1950s both the U.S. and the USSR had nuclear weapons that could destroy each other. Indeed some people feared that at any time the tension between the free world and the Communist world might explode into a horrible nuclear war.

The leaders of the Soviet Union after Stalin, therefore, wanted to expand Communism's influence without provoking a war. The leaders of the free world sought to contain Communist growth, also without sparking a war. This tense Cold War continued from

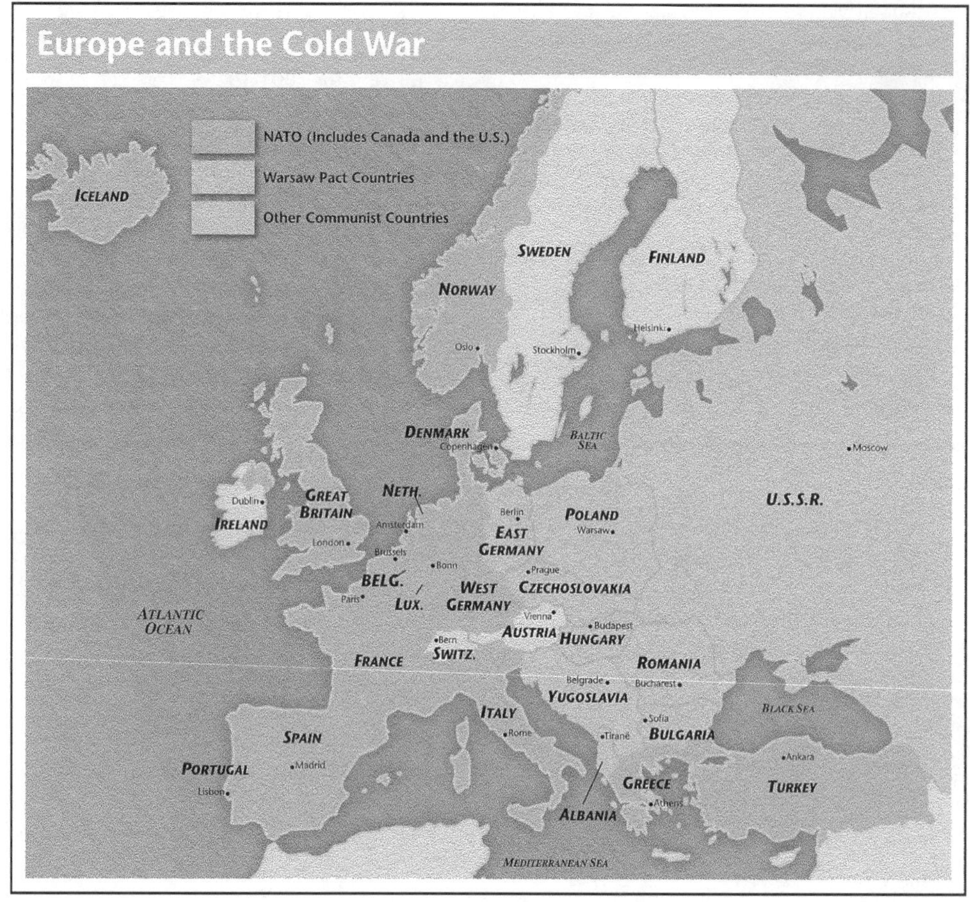

SECTION 3

Materials

- Bibles

The Cold War—Discuss with your students ways in which one can fight without physical force. These could include using words to tear down a reputation, gossiping, building military might to prove superiority, ignoring others, and so on. Mention to your students that wrong words are spoken frequently in today's circles and ought not to be. Have a sword drill with your class with the following verses: Leviticus 19:16; Psalm 15:1-3; and Proverbs 10:19; 11:13; 18:8; 26:20.

Europe and the Cold War—Look at the map above. Each student should list the countries that belong to NATO and the countries that belong to the Warsaw Pact. Compare each group of countries in modern-day events. What typifies each group in areas such as economics, military strength, and religious views?

Lands and Peoples—Use the book *Lands and Peoples, Special Edition: The Changing Face of Europe* (1996) to see a brief overview of Communism since World War II. It includes a multipage chart of events in all Communist countries since Communism began. It is printed by Grolier, Inc. and can probably be found in the reference section of the public library.

shortly after the end of World War II until the collapse of the Soviet Union in the 1980s.

Khrushchev

Replacing Stalin as Soviet dictator was **Nikita Khrushchev** (KROOSH chef). He surprised the world by announcing a policy of **"de-Stalinization."** Stalin had gone too far, Khrushchev said, in his policies of terror and repression. He would allow more openness in Soviet society. Symbolically, Soviet officials took Stalin's body from its place next to Lenin's and buried it under tons of concrete. The government freed many prisoners from Stalin's prison camps. One prisoner was writer **Aleksandr Solzhenitsyn** (SOLE zhuh NEET sin). The Soviet government not only released him but allowed him to publish a novel, *One Day in the Life of Ivan Denisovich,* that was harshly critical of the labor camps. The book won international acclaim and seemed to prove that a change was taking place in the USSR.

A man burns a picture of Lenin during the 1956 uprising in Hungary. The Soviets ruthlessly crushed the Hungarians.

Nikita Khrushchev

Khrushchev also announced a policy of **"peaceful coexistence"** with the nations of the free world. Instead of military competition, he said, the two sides would get along with each other and compete economically. The Soviet leader was so sure of the superiority of the Communist system that he told the West, "We will bury you."

But Khrushchev's reforms had their limits. When he took power, he quickly had the head of Stalin's secret police arrested and executed. Then Khrushchev made one of his own followers the leader of the secret police. He did make less use of prison camps than Stalin had, but under his leadership the Soviets began treating **dissidents** (people who criticized the Soviet government) as being mentally ill. Instead of being sent to Siberia, dissidents found themselves in mental hospitals where "psychiatric treatment" was the punishment instead of hard labor. Khrushchev may not have been as bad as Stalin—but then very few men in history have been as cruel as Joseph Stalin.

Nikita Khrushchev—Born a peasant, Khrushchev lived in an *izba* like other peasants. Izbas are one-room cottages with wooden or mud walls. After farming for a while, the family moved and became miners. After Khrushchev joined the Communist Party, he was made the administrator of one of the mines, but while he was doing this, his wife died in a great famine in the area. During his time in the Ukraine, he was so mean and ruthless that he was known as the "Scourge of the Ukraine."

"We Will Bury You"—Ask your students what they think of Khrushchev's statement to the West: "We will bury you." Was he intending to fight the West and force them into the Communist camp? Or was he intending merely to show how Russia's socialism (the economic arm of Communism) would far outdo the West's capitalism? Could he have meant both?

The U-2 Incident and the Bay of Pigs—In 1960, an American spy plane flown by Francis Gary Powers was shot down over the Soviet Union. Powers was then forced to admit that he was a spy. When Eisenhower refused to apologize for the incident, Khrushchev canceled the next scheduled meeting with the president.

Before the Cuban missile crisis in 1962, Kennedy sent anti-Castro Cubans to incite a civil war in Cuba in 1961. The United States trained and equipped the Cubans but did not commit any U.S. troops to the endeavor. The civil war did not start, and within a short time, the anti-Castro Cubans were shot or arrested. Many blame the failure of the anti-Castro movement on poor planning. The situation led to greater tension between the United States and the Soviet Union.

Russia and Chess—Russians excel at the game of chess; over the decades Russia has produced numerous world champions. Russia even claims to have invented the game. While most historians believe chess began in India around A.D. 600, archaeologists during the Soviet era claimed that animal figurines discovered in Uzbekistan in 1972 dating back to the second century A.D. were chess pieces. Experts do agree, however, that Russia played a critical role in the development of chess. Around 1500 Russia helped establish the modern form of chess, and after 1920 the Soviet government was instrumental in standardizing modern chess by displacing various other forms.

Why did chess become so popular in Russia? One reason is that after 1920 the Soviet government promoted it as a means of showing that the Soviet Union could compete with the West. Soviets also believed that chess was an excellent incentive for individual self-improvement, which was important for making Communism work. Others argued that chess promoted military training, literacy, and general social discipline. There was another reason that chess caught on in the Soviet Union. A. F. Il'in-Zhenevsky was a very good chess player and a leading Communist who was influential in the promotion of chess. He was the leader of the Soviet military training

At the United Nations during the Cuban missile crisis, the Soviet ambassador (left) protests, saying, "I am not in an American courtroom, sir. Therefore, I do not wish to answer questions put to me in the fashion in which a prosecutor puts questions." American ambassador Adlai Stevenson (right) replies, "You are in the courtroom of world opinion right now."

Neither did Khrushchev lighten the Soviet rule in countries under his control. As mentioned before, at the end of World War II, Stalin had forced Communist governments on Eastern Europe. In 1956 the people of Hungary tried to throw off Soviet domination. Hungarian rebels broadcast radio messages to the West begging for help. No help came as Khrushchev sent in the army and crushed the uprising.

The Soviets also sought to expand their power under Khrushchev. They won an enormous victory in 1959 when the island of Cuba came under the rule of a Communist dictator, Fidel Castro. Now Communism was fewer than a hundred miles off the coast of the United States. But Cuba also turned out to be Khrushchev's undoing. In 1962 he decided to strengthen his position by placing nuclear missiles in Cuba. The United States, under President John F. Kennedy, would not tolerate this threat. The U.S. put a naval blockade around Cuba and demanded that the Soviets remove the missiles. In this **Cuban missile crisis,** the world teetered on the brink of nuclear war. But Khrushchev knew his nuclear arsenal was not as big as Kennedy's, and he backed down.

The humiliation of the Cuban missile crisis angered many Communist leaders. They began plotting to get rid of Khrushchev. Finally, in 1964 the Communist Party announced that Khrushchev had "retired" for "health reasons." In reality, he was sent to live in exile until his death in 1971. Even then, he remained proud of the changes he claimed to have brought to the Soviet Union. After his fall he wrote, "They were able to get rid of me simply by voting. Stalin would have had them all arrested."

Leonid Brezhnev (left) appears with President Richard Nixon of the United States (right).

What If?—What would have happened if the Soviet Union had won the standoff in the Cuban missile crisis? How would the world have changed? Would Communism have fallen so easily? Would America and the Soviet Union have launched a war? Each student should write a paragraph on the possibilities that such a turn of events could have brought.

Fearful of democracy, the Soviet Union sent its forces into Czechoslovakia to crush a Czech reform movement in 1968.

Brezhnev

Eventually succeeding Khrushchev was his former assistant **Leonid Brezhnev** (BREZH nef). Like Khrushchev he said that the Soviet Union saw no reason to continue the Cold War. Instead of "peaceful coexistence," Brezhnev announced his support of a policy of **détente** (day TAHNT), from a French word referring to the relaxing of tensions. Many people in the West took him at his word.

Détente was not for regions under Soviet control, however. In 1968 Czechoslovakia, like Hungary in 1956, tried to reform the Communist system. And like Khrushchev, Brezhnev sent in the army to crush the movement. Under Brezhnev, the Communists promoted and supported revolutions in Asia, Africa, and Latin America. They helped the Communist forces in Vietnam (discussed in the next chapter). Some leaders in the West began to warn that détente was just a smokescreen to hide Soviet expansion.

Brezhnev was one of the Communist leaders who felt humiliated by the Cuban missile crisis. He was determined that nothing like that would happen again. He oversaw a great buildup of Soviet military forces and built an arsenal of nuclear weapons that could match that of the United States. The Soviet Union geared its whole economy toward supporting its military forces. The result was a powerful army.

The result was also a stagnant economy. Stores contained very few goods and only a poor quality of food. When goods were available, people would stand in line for hours to buy basic items such as flour or sugar. The state-run factories were inefficient and poorly

The Soviet Union maintained its military power by devoting much of its economy to building weaponry at the expense of the citizens' need for food and clothing.

organization, and from it he recruited leading Russian players for a Russian championship tournament in 1920. A few years later the state created an organization to promote the game.

For much of the twentieth century, state patronage of chess has succeeded. Great chess players received privileges that other Soviet citizens did not enjoy. The Soviet Union also basked in the prestige from championships in international competition. Recent world champions have been Karpov and Kasparov. The Soviets received a blow in 1972, however, when American Bobby Fischer won the world championship. Russian chess players continue to play a role as celebrities in their society, in much the same way that professional sports figures do in the West.

Military Might—Discuss with your students whether it is important for a country to build up its military. Should there be armed forces at all? *(Anwers will vary; probably yes for protection.)* Should the army be a country's total focus? *(Answers will vary; probably not because God talks about doing many other things in this life.)* What is a good balance between military strength and providing for the people of one's nation? *(Answers will vary; probably having a military to protect the nation but using it sparingly.)*

Afghanistan—The Soviets and Afghans enjoyed increased trade in the 1970s, but this was a ploy for the Soviets to build up forces on the border. In 1979 Russia invaded Afghanistan, a staunchly Muslim country. Some reasons suggested for this untimely invasion include Russia's desire to have secure borders; hard-liners in the Politburo who wanted to expand; fear that the leader of Afghanistan, Hafizullah Amin, would be overthrown by anti-Marxist, conservative Muslims (which would draw away some Soviet Muslims); and Russia's need to make its presence felt in Southwest Asia.

The invasion hardened Cold War tensions as well as changed policies in public relations on both sides. The USSR had no choice but to start to change after this show of force failed.

Other Leaders—Other leaders of Russia between Brezhnev and Gorbachev include Yuri Andropov (former ambassador to Hungary and KGB chairman) and Konstantin Chernenko (a peasant from Siberia and Brezhnev's choice to succeed him).

Soviet troops in Afghanistan, which became to the Soviets a problem as great as Vietnam had been for the United States

managed. The products they turned out were often shoddy. Workers gave little effort to earn the nearly worthless Soviet money. One worker said, "We pretend to work, and they pretend to pay us."

Shortly before he died in 1982, Brezhnev launched the Soviet Union into one of its biggest disasters. In 1979 he invaded the neighboring nation of Afghanistan to prop up its Communist government. The Afghan people fought back. Brezhnev had spent billions on building the Soviet army. But this expensive army proved unable to crush the Afghans. Although few observers realized it, the Soviet empire was beginning to fall apart.

Section Review

1. What is the phrase describing the period of competition between the Communist world and the free world from the end of World War II to the 1980s?
2. What author did Khrushchev release from a Soviet labor camp? What book did that author write describing life in such camps?
3. In what Eastern European nation did Khrushchev crush a democratic uprising in the 1950s? In what Eastern European nation did Brezhnev crush a similar movement in the 1960s?
4. What island nearly became the cause of war between the United States and the USSR? What Soviet act on this island sparked this crisis?
5. What neighboring nation did the Soviet Union invade in 1979?

Why would Khrushchev be proud that his followers had voted him out and that he had not had them arrested as Stalin would have done?

Christian Perspective—What is wrong with the worker's statement, "We pretend to work, and they pretend to pay us"? Do you see any antibiblical theme in his claim? *(Though it is easy to see why one would feel this way, as Christians we are to always do our best for God's glory.)* What should the motto have been for Christians in the Soviet Union?

Apply this principle to your schoolwork. Do you do nothing or give just a half-hearted effort on your work, both in school and out? What should your attitude and effort be?

Section Review Answers

1. the Cold War
2. Alexander Solzhenitsyn; *One Day in the Life of Ivan Denisovich*
3. Hungary; Czechoslovakia
4. Cuba; placing nuclear missiles on the island
5. Afghanistan

Answers will vary. The fact that Khrushchev's opponents were able to vote him out indicated to Khrushchev that the Soviet Union had moved away from the terror and cruel dictatorship of Stalin. He would see this as an accomplishment of his period of rule.

Religion in the Soviet Union

The Communists were officially atheists. **Atheism** (from the Greek meaning "no God") is the belief that God does not exist. In 1913 Lenin wrote, "Every religious idea, every idea of God, even flirting with the idea of God, is unutterable vileness." The Communists thought that religion was a drug that leaders used to keep people quiet. Therefore, they sought to destroy religion. They closed most churches and persecuted Christians. Jews and Muslims also suffered under Communist rule. Leaders of the Orthodox Church were arrested for opposing the state.

The Communists forced over fifty thousand churches to close their doors. They turned some churches into museums or factories. Sometimes they were more subtle. In later years, the Soviet television network would broadcast its most popular programs on Easter Sunday to lure people away from attending church.

The Russian Orthodox Church built beautiful cathedrals, which the Soviets often turned into factories or museums.

General Persecution

The Soviet constitution promised citizens "the right to profess . . . any religion." But the government did everything it could to discourage religion. To oppose the churches, the Communists set up the League of the Militant Godless. This atheistic group claimed five million members at its height.

Even the **Russian Orthodox Church** was not spared. The Orthodox Church had been the state church of Russia for centuries. The czars had permitted almost no other groups to exist, and most Russians belonged to the Orthodox Church. The Communists, however, sought to control or crush it. They defaced **icons,** the pictures of Christ and saints used in worship in Orthodox churches. They stripped jewels and gold off the icons to pay for building factories. The wooden icons themselves were burned as firewood.

SECTION 4

Student Objectives
Students should be able to

1. Recall the title for the head of the Eastern Orthodox Church.
2. Assess the religious situation in Russia during Communism.
3. Evaluate the positions of the registered and unregistered churches.

Religion in Some Former Communist Countries—Although the official religion of the Soviet Union was atheism, other religions abounded, predominantly Russian (Eastern) Orthodoxy and Islam. These religious differences cause some strife today in the CIS and surrounding nations.

Religions in Former Communist Countries

Country	Religions
Bosnia Herzegovina	Muslim (40%), Orthodox (31%), Catholic (15%)
Bulgaria	Bulgarian Orthodox (85%), Muslim (13%)
Croatia	Catholic (76%), Orthodox (11%)
Czech Rep.	Atheist (39.8%), Catholic (39.2%), Protestant (4%), Orthodox (3%)
Hungary	Catholic (67.5%), Calvinist (20%), Lutheran (5%)
Poland	Catholic (95%)
Romania	Romanian Orthodox (70%), Catholic (6%), Protestant (6%)
Slovakia	Catholic (60%), Protestant (8%)
Slovenia	Catholic (96%)
Yugoslavia	Orthodox (65%), Muslim (19%), Catholic (4%)

SECTION 4

Materials

- Bibles
- Religion chart
- Pictures of Orthodox churches and icons
- *Three Generations of Suffering* and/or *Testament from Prison* by Georgi Vins

Atheism—Have your students look up Psalm 53:1: "The fool hath said in his heart, There is no God." Ask your student what God calls atheists. (*fools*) What is the end of the atheist? (*certain destruction forever in hell*)

Religions in Former Communist Countries—Copy the chart from the margin onto the chalkboard or the overhead projector. Ask the students which countries they think would have the most religious conflict. (those with Muslim and Catholic groups) You may want to discuss some of the problems in Bosnia and Yugoslavia (BLM 16-2).

BACKGROUNDS

The Orthodox Church

Christians in the Americas and Western Europe often think of Christianity in terms of Protestantism and Roman Catholicism. We have already seen, however, that there have been other churches within Christendom (the Christian world). We studied the Nestorian Church in Chapter 4 (pp. 95-96). We also mentioned the Coptic Church in Egypt (p. 114; see also p. 569) and the Ethiopian Church (p. 114; see also p. 569). Another important and influential section of Christendom is the Orthodox Church. It is still the most important Christian group in Eastern Europe and Russia.

The Orthodox Church is often called by other names. Sometimes it is called the Eastern Orthodox Church as opposed to the "Western" Roman Catholic Church. Sometimes it is called the Greek

Russian icon, Madonna and Child, *17th Century (Bob Jones University Collection)*

Orthodox Church because its headquarters for many centuries was in the Greek-speaking Byzantine (BIZ un TEEN) Empire. It also goes by the name of the different countries in which it is located. One of the largest segments of the Orthodox Church is the Russian Orthodox Church.

During the Middle Ages, the church in Western Europe and the church in Eastern Europe began to drift apart. The church in the West became known as the Roman Catholic Church. It used primarily Latin in its services and was led by the pope. The church in the East used primarily Greek. It had no single leader but a group of patriarchs. The most important of these patriarchs was the **patriarch of Constantinople,** the capital of the Byzantine Empire. The Western and Eastern churches often clashed. Finally in 1054 the pope and the patriarch of Constantinople declared each other "outside of the church." From that date the Roman Catholic Church and the Orthodox Church were considered officially separate.

Despite its arguments with the popes, the Orthodox Church did not differ greatly from the Roman Catholic Church. It stressed tradition and formal worship. Bishops and monks were the

464 Chapter 16

Art—Bring pictures of Orthodox churches and icons to show your students. St. Basil's in Moscow, pictured on page 463, is the most well known Orthodox cathedral. Its many colored onion domes are its most recognizable architectural feature. You should be able to find several old paintings of saints and other religious figures since much medieval art is from the Orthodox Church in Russia. Almost any book or poster board would also show this type of art, so you might want to collaborate with the art teacher on this activity.

spiritual leaders of the church. The Orthodox Church is distinct in its use of icons to aid worship. Icons are pictures of God or Christ or the saints. Orthodox worshipers are supposed to focus their attention on these pictures to help them imagine the real person they represent. Some other Christians believe that this practice leads to idolatry as people begin to treat the picture as though it were an object to be worshiped.

The Orthodox Church never underwent a reform like the Protestant Reformation. One leader, Patriarch **Cyril Lucar** of Constantinople, tried to introduce Protestant reforms in the 1600s. His efforts failed, however, and the church rejected his teaching. Therefore, the Orthodox Church is still generally characterized by the formalism and traditionalism that Protestants reject in Roman Catholicism.

In 988 Grand Prince Vladimir of Kiev announced that he was converting to the Orthodox faith. This event is said to mark the conversion of Russia. Vladimir ordered mass baptisms of his subjects. Soon Orthodox priests and missionaries began to spread out all over Russia, and almost all Russians became members of the Orthodox Church. After Constantinople fell to the Ottoman Turks in 1453, Russia became the main center of Orthodoxy.

The Orthodox Church, however, has always suffered from the control of political leaders. The patriarch of Moscow was the leader of the church. But the famous Russian leader Czar Peter the Great did away with the office of patriarch of Moscow in the 1700s. In its place he created the **Holy Synod,** which made the Orthodox Church virtually a department of the Russian government.

When the Communists took power, they cut off government support of the Orthodox Church. The church in turn opposed the government. The ruling council of the Orthodox Church restored the office of patriarch of Moscow as the church's leader. The new patriarch, Tikhon, denounced the Communist government. He was finally arrested but was released after reversing himself and declaring himself loyal to the Communist state. From that time, most church leaders tried to work with the Communists. The fall of Communism in the Soviet Union brought new freedom to the Orthodox. However, Orthodox Church leaders have used their new influence with the government of Russia to try to keep Christian missionaries out of their land.

Cyril Lucar, patriarch of Constantinople (1620-38)

Red Menace in Russia 465

Testimony from Prison—This is a firsthand account of the life of a man who went to prison for serving the Lord as a pastor. (Another testimony from a political prisoner is included on Appendix page A4.)

"In the fifties the state had very tight control over religion. Churches that did not follow the government regulations were closed. In 1961, children were prohibited from services. Parents sought for a way around this. Guards were placed at the doors to keep children out. A letter was sent to regional church leaders to [encourage unity]. This caused contention among believers. A letter was sent to all Baptist preachers to support separation and to have a day of prayer and fasting. I got this letter in 1962, and it caused many difficulties. The KGB came to my house very quickly. Believers were asked to petition the government about a meeting. The government invited only those in favor with it. This meeting declared real believers to be enemies of the state. The KGB asked me to denounce these enemies. I said that I didn't support the men, but the Scripture. They scheduled a court case for me. On October 2, 1962, I was arrested. After a year I received a sentence of three years (instead of the usual five). I was released early under Brezhnev, but he was even harder than Khrushchev. I was free for about one year. I was arrested again by the KGB because my movement for religious freedom had set off a chain reaction. Then I was free until 1974, when I received a five-year sentence. Four hundred men were arrested at that time. Arrests grew. They told me they would lengthen my sentence if I preached in prison. I said since I no longer had a church or family, then that was the only reason I was in prison.

Prison conditions were bad; the purpose was not to contain, but to make prisoners terminally sick. The Lord preserved me even with the bad food. Even now I have no medical problems. Still they pressured me not to preach. I am glad to have suffered for Christ, because it was a great spiritual school. The other prisoners could not understand why I was in prison or why I continued to preach. . . . They eventually had me sing my religious songs every day to the new convicts.

Stalin, who had once studied for the Russian Orthodox priesthood, was one of the worst persecutors. He killed or imprisoned countless religious leaders and lay Christians. Only during World War II did he become more tolerant. Because of the Nazi invasion, Stalin rallied Christians to his side by allowing them more freedom. Khrushchev, despite his policy of "de-Stalinization," was almost as bad as Stalin. In fact, some of the most concentrated persecution of Christians took place under his rule in the 1950s. Khrushchev routinely tore down churches for government building programs. This oppression took place while Khrushchev was announcing Soviet reforms to the rest of the world.

A Russian Mennonite family poses in 1929 in China, where they had fled to escape Communist persecution.

The Example of the Russian Baptists

The troubles of Christians in the Soviet Union are illustrated by the story of the Russian Baptists. In the 1800s the czars had allowed some German Mennonites to settle in Russia. These were descendants of the Anabaptists of the Reformation. To attract these farmers to his country, the czar allowed them to practice their own religion instead of Russian Orthodoxy. In the mid-1800s some of these Mennonites were influenced by the **Stundist revival.** The name of this revival comes from the German word *stunde,* meaning "hour." Much of the revival took the form of special hours of Bible study and prayer. Many people were converted and many Christians spiritually strengthened through these hours of study and prayer. The czar also allowed some German Baptist missionaries and English missionaries to work among the immigrants. These believers often considered themselves both Mennonites and Baptists because both groups practiced the baptism of adults by immersion.

After several years, the czar began to worry about the growth of the Russian Baptist movement, and he began to persecute its followers. The czar was especially angry that some native Russians were turning to the gospel from the deadness of Russian Orthodoxy. The Russian Revolution at first brought relief to these Christians. The Soviet government needed all the help it could get, and it allowed some freedom of religion. The Communists even allowed missionaries into the country. Once their control was firm, though, the Communists began to crack down on all Baptists and

Connections—Share with your students some stories of Russian Christians who were persecuted for their faith under Communism. You can find a good example of this in Georgi Vins's books *Three Generations of Suffering* (London: Hodden and Stoughten, 1976) and *Testament from Prison* (Elgin, Ill.: D.C. Cook Publishing Co., 1975), as well as in the additional information in the margin and on Appendix page A4.

other Protestants. Many Baptist leaders died in prison camps.

During World War II, when he was trying to win over the churches to his side, Stalin encouraged these different Protestant groups to form the **Union of Evangelical Christians—Baptists** (1944). Later Khrushchev's government demanded that this group follow certain guidelines. They were to limit evangelism, for example, and not to baptize anyone under the age of thirty. These requirements split the Baptists. One portion wanted to go along with the government. The Communists recognized their organization, and they became known as the **"registered churches."**

Members of an unregistered church meet in the woods for worship.

Others would not sacrifice their beliefs in this way. They became known as the **"unregistered churches"** and began to meet illegally. The Communists treated the unregistered churches harshly. Their leaders were arrested and imprisoned. Ministers found themselves in jail cells with murderers and rapists. The registered churches did not suffer so harshly. Yet even they faced constant government regulation and interference with their churches. The two groups opposed each other. The registered churches thought the unregistered churches were making trouble when they did not have to. The unregistered churches thought the registered churches were compromising the gospel.

The collapse of the Soviet Union brought relief to both the registered and the unregistered churches. Baptists now number somewhere between two and three million, although that is still a small portion of the population. The two groups nonetheless still suffer division over the bitterness of past conflicts.

They called me Father Alexei. . . . The Psalmist said, 'It is good for me to be afflicted.' [Ps. 119:71] You lose your fear of going to prison."

Registered vs. Unregistered— Tell your students that most Fundamentalist churches in Russia today are unregistered. However, missionaries must register in order to enter the country. This causes some tension between missionaries and national pastors of unregistered churches.

Adult Baptism— Russian Baptists still believe today that one cannot be truly saved and therefore baptized until he is at least twelve years old. They feel he cannot understand the great gift of salvation before this age. Therefore Christian visitors saved at a young age often avoid telling how old they were at their conversion.

Section Review

1. What is the official religious belief of Communism?
2. What was the state church of Russia?
3. Among what religious-ethnic group did the Russian Baptists originate?
4. What was the difference between the "registered" and the "unregistered" Baptist churches?

Which policy do you think was more biblical in its relationship to the Soviet government, that of the registered or the unregistered churches? (Consider Acts 5:29 and Romans 13:1 as you answer.)

Section Review Answers

1. atheism
2. Russian Orthodox Church
3. German-speaking Mennonites (from the Anabaptists)
4. Most registered churches cooperated with the Soviet government and submitted to government regulation of their practices; unregistered churches refused to follow regulations they thought limited the practice of their faith.

Answers will vary. On the one hand, Romans 13:1 tells Christians to obey the leaders that God sets over them. In that light the registered churches appear more obedient. In Acts 5:29, however, Peter said that Christians must obey God even if human authorities command something else. In that light the unregistered churches appear more obedient. The answer should center on whether cooperating with the Soviet government compromised the Christian faith. If it was a compromise, then the unregistered churches were likely right. If it was not a compromise, then the registered churches may have been right.

SECTION 5

Student Objectives
Students should be able to

1. Define the terms *perestroika* and *glasnost*.
2. Analyze the reasons for the fall of Communism.

Gorbachev's Failures—Certainly one of the remarkable figures in recent Russian history was Gorbachev. He left an important record of change during his six and a half years as leader of the Soviet Union. In 1988, because of his reforms, he enjoyed an 80 percent approval rating, but that figure dropped to 10 percent in 1990 and to 3 percent by December 1991 when the Soviet Union collapsed. Even today in Russia he remains a very unpopular figure. Why, despite all the dramatic economic and political reforms that he brought and which the people supported, did he become so unpopular?

A fundamental mistake that Gorbachev made was that he greatly misunderstood the seriousness of the Soviet Union's problems and the radical reforms that would be required. In short, he thought that maintaining the old Communist state and making some modest changes would be sufficient. He had wrong priorities with his reform efforts, placing political over economic changes. Economic reforms that would have made the quality of life better for the citizens would have made him more popular. Gorbachev also misunderstood the deep nationalism of the people in the various republics that had been controlled by the Soviet Union for so long. Once reforms were underway, he made the mistake of trying to keep Communist party stalwarts satisfied. Furthermore, Gorbachev himself found it difficult to give up his Communist ideology. Again he apparently thought that Communism could be reformed and made to work better. Finally, he failed to let the people vote on the reforms. If he had and the people had voted overwhelmingly for them, which was likely to happen, he would have had a mandate from the people.

Decline and Fall of the Soviet Empire

After Brezhnev died, the weaknesses in the Soviet Union began to appear. The two leaders who followed him were aged and died after brief terms in office. The war in Afghanistan was going badly. The Afghan people, supported by the United States, were fighting back against the Soviet army. The Soviet forces could hold the main Afghan cities but could not conquer the countryside. The Soviet people were sick of the war and tired of a Communist economy, which could not provide them with decent food and clothing.

Gorbachev

At this point, in 1985, the Communists chose a new leader. **Mikhail Gorbachev** (GOR buh CHAWF) was much younger than Brezhnev and his successors. He announced that he wanted better relations with the free world. More important, he seemed to have energy and a vision for reforming the Soviet system that earlier leaders had lacked.

Two Russian terms sum up Gorbachev's efforts at reform. First, he called for ***perestroika*** (PEHR ih STROY kuh), which means "restructuring." Gorbachev wanted to fix the Soviet economy. By improved technology and increased productivity, he would improve the quality and output of Soviet industry. He promised to reduce government interference and eliminate corruption. He even allowed some capitalistic practices, as Lenin had done with his New Economic Policy. These small changes, however, could not cover up the fact that the economy of the Soviet Union was a wreck.

The more important term associated with Gorbachev's reform was ***glasnost*** (GLAHS nust), which means "openness." He wanted to allow more freedom and give people more say in the government. The government relaxed some of the restrictions on churches and released many prisoners. Gorbachev pulled the troops out of Afghanistan and ended that unpopular war. However, Gorbachev said plainly that the nation would not abandon Communism. The Soviet Union remained a military dictatorship with power in the hands of the Communist Party.

Gorbachev found that *glasnost* was hard to control. Having tasted a little freedom, the people wanted more. The first break came in Eastern Europe in 1989. When Gorbachev began withdrawing Soviet troops from that region, the nations of Eastern Europe began throwing off their Communist governments. East Germany got rid of its Communist leaders and reunited with West Germany. Other nations, such as Poland, Hungary, and Czechoslovakia, became free for the first time in years.

Unrest spread to the Soviet Union itself. Some reformers were elected to the legislature while protesters called for more changes. Sections of the Soviet Union, such as Ukraine, declared their independence. Unable to maintain control of the country, Gorbachev resigned on Christmas Day 1991. A few days later, the Soviet Union officially broke into a confederation of independent states binding themselves loosely as the "Commonwealth of Independent States" (CIS). The Soviet Union was dead.

Mikhail Gorbachev

SECTION 5

Materials

- Transparencies for Chapter 16
- Video on the fall of Soviet Communism
- Periodical articles on the fall of Communism in any Eastern Bloc country

Old USSR/New CIS—Use a map of Russia to review with your students the old USSR. (See the map on page 450.)

Fall of Communism—Show your students a video about the fall of Soviet Communism. This should be available in the library or from a mail order catalog. A video on the reunification of Germany may be more readily available than one on the Soviet Union. If possible, the video should include other aspects of the former USSR as well, such as geographic features and differing cultures.

Another exciting video, *The Printing*, is offered by Unusual Films, the film division of Bob Jones University. Your church may have a copy, or you can find this film listed in the BJUP catalog.

Popular Music in Russia—Use the following information about music in modern Russia to discuss the problems of rock music. Also discuss how music reflects a society's culture.

One of the ironies about reform in the former Soviet Union and in Russia during the 1980s and the 1990s was that with freedom also came decadent Western, mostly American, popular culture. In a strange twist, the old atheistic Communist system rejected rock music as too lewd. The Soviets con-

CHARACTERIZATIONS

Andrei Sakharov

In the Soviet Union, one of the most dangerous labels to wear was "dissident." The secret police watched and harassed dissidents. Some vanished, never to be seen again. One famous dissident was a man who had been one of the Soviet Union's heroes, Andrei Sakharov (uhn-DRAY SAHK-uh-rawf).

Sakharov was a brilliant scientist. He graduated from college during World War II but was kept out of the army to conduct scientific research for the government. Sakharov is best known for helping the Soviets develop the hydrogen bomb in the 1950s. But he also made several breakthroughs for peaceful uses of nuclear power.

The bomb he had helped create started Sakharov on the path to dissidence. He protested to Khrushchev against unnecessary nuclear tests. He feared these tests needlessly endangered people's lives and health. From this protest, he went to asking for greater freedom of speech. The government removed him from his top-secret work and revoked his special status as a scientist. Losing his special privileges made Sakharov realize what drab and dreary lives most Soviet citizens led.

Persecution only made him speak out more. He called for greater religious liberty and defended others who had spoken out and been imprisoned. The secret police began to watch him and to compile files of information that could be used against him. He enjoyed little protection. After Sakharov criticized activities of the USSR's Arab allies, Arab terrorists broke into his apartment. They held him, his wife, and his stepson hostage for over an hour. "Do you want to kill us?" Sakharov's wife asked. "We can do worse things than kill you," they replied. After the terrorists left without doing anything, the scientist reported this incident to the police. They were not interested.

Andrei Sakharov with his granddaughter Anya

All that saved Sakharov was that he was well known outside the Soviet Union. The Communists feared that if something happened to him it would harm the USSR's image abroad. But when Sakharov criticized the Soviet invasion of Afghanistan in 1979, that was too much. He was exiled to the industrial city of Gorky. There he was constantly watched by secret police outside his apartment. He went on hunger strikes to protest government policies and his treatment. Fearing that he might die, the Communists put him in the hospital and force-fed him.

When demanding reform, Sakharov had called for *glasnost,* "openness." In 1986 Mikhail Gorbachev, an advocate of *glasnost,* allowed the dissident scientist to return from exile. Sakharov continued to call for reform. In 1989 he was chosen to serve in a new Soviet legislature. On December 12, 1989, he publicly demanded an end to Communist rule. Two days later he died of natural causes. But two years later his demand became reality as the Communist government dissolved. It was the bravery of men and women such as Andrei Sakharov that helped bring an end to the Communist dictatorship.

That would have given him greater political authority.

Still, despite his failures, Gorbachev did succeed in dismantling the Soviet Union and ending Communist rule there and in Eastern Europe. In the end, that is what the people wanted. While he may have been unpopular at home, his efforts were often highly regarded in the West.

Privileges of the Few—Very few enjoy the privileges of the elite in Russia. Besides top government officials, other elites in Russia include sports figures, chess players, and scientists. Government officials were given special privileges including being able to shop in stores which accepted only foreign money, special departments at GUM (the state department store), vacation homes, camps for children, special food, housing (including *dachas,* small summer villas in rural areas), telephones, and special waiting rooms at plane and train stations.

Modern Moscow—Moscow today is a highly commercialized, Westernized society. It is so different from the more isolated rest of Russia that many people consider it almost another country. Over 60 percent of all foreign investment in Russia has been in Moscow, leaving the rest of the nation to forge ahead on its own. And this prosperity exists only in downtown Moscow. On the outskirts of the city are many miles of housing developments where the people have not yet felt the good aspects of capitalism, only the bad. Older people in particular want to go back to Communism because at least everyone was equally poor, and most did not have to beg for food.

Modern Russia—Although Moscow and other large cities may be feeling the effects of modernization, most of the rest of Russian towns and communities are not. As you drive through the countryside in Russia today, you will often see grandmothers wearing *babushkas* (head scarves) and old-fashioned skirts, gathering hay with a pitchfork in a field, their husbands in suspenders beside them. Americans may view this as quaint or cute, but to many Russians living this backward life, it is drudgery.

demned rock music in the press and tried to suppress it by arresting performers and concert organizers. When those efforts failed, they tried to co-opt with state-sponsored and then state-controlled music. Despite those efforts, underground or illegal rock bands thrived in the former Soviet Union.

When Gorbachev came to power, rock music was one of the first areas to enjoy new freedom. Rock music was officially accepted. Now Russian rock music has to compete with that from Western countries. Underground rock music had thrived with its message of resistance to Communism, but in the 1990s it was primarily concerned with commercial success, as in America.

It certainly is a rebuke to Westerners, especially American Christians, that the old Communists, who were atheists, saw Western rock music as dangerous. For spiritual reasons, Americans need to see its danger.

Finding a solution—Half of your class should write specific questions dealing with problems facing countries of the former USSR. The other half should formulate answers, either together or individually. A sample question is "Russia's money is worth very little. What should she do about this?" *(She should pattern her economy after free-world nations and allow capitalism, but not corruption, to take over. She should develop a system of trade in which she exports more than she imports so that her money would be of more value.)* Of course, this is idealistic, but the students should have to think hard about real problems in the world today. Have them predict the future of the CIS in the next ten years.

★★★★★★★★★★
For a color version of the map on this page, see page A12 in the Appendix.

How long will it be before the living standard of rural Russia rises?

Russia in the 1990s: The Bad News—In the post-Communist era, a new group emerged behind the scenes to dominate Russia—the new oligarchs. They were particularly instrumental in Yeltsin's successful presidential campaign in 1996. During the chaotic time after the fall of the Soviet Union in 1991, these oligarchs made fortunes in banking, industry, and the media. With their alliance with Yeltsin they obtained positions in the government and of course had access to Russia's great resources. If anyone wanted a license or permission to operate a business, the oligarchs demanded bribes. These new oligarchs were particularly hated by the Russian people, not so much for their wealth, but for the fact that much of their wealth left the country. Some experts have concluded that as much as $300 billion found its way overseas (in foreign bank accounts, for example).

Quality of life was troubling too for the post-Communist world. Poverty rapidly increased. Life expectancy for men fell quickly. The murder rate was two times that of the United States. Many policemen were corrupt; thus, personal security firms were the fastest growing service industry in the country.

Russians no longer have a rosy view of the promise of private enterprise or freedom. Observers point out that Russia in its present state is not a democracy, only that it has some democratic features. Elements of oligarchy and authoritarianism remain. For centuries, Russia was isolated and ruled by dictators, both the czars and the Communists. The political culture will take time to change.

Russia in the 1990s: the Good News—Clearly since 1991 Russia has rejected its absolutist past. Even in the past there were revolts against authoritarianism. Peter the Great and Catherine the Great encountered resistance, and in the nineteenth century there was a re-

Aftermath

The events of 1991 did not solve the region's problems. The new states simply divided the Soviet Union's economic and political problems among themselves. Russia, the largest and strongest of these states by far, dominated the Commonwealth. Some extremists proclaimed that Russia should rebuild its empire and bring the new nations back under its control.

Still, there were certainly changes for the better. In 1993 Russia had its first free election since 1917. The Communist Party still existed, but it was now only one party among several. Russia and the other new states had imperfect democracies, but they were nonetheless democracies. This was more than Russia had enjoyed under either the czars or the Communists. Still it would take time to develop an informed and intelligent electorate. Until the people were ready to bear the responsibility of governing themselves, their democracy would be fragile.

The future of Russia and the other nations that made up the Soviet Union is unclear. They may fall back into dictatorships, perhaps even Communist ones. Communism, after all, continues to exist in China. But the "red worldtide" that John Reed had portrayed in *Ten Days That Shook the World* had not swept the world. Instead, it had been swept away.

Commonwealth of Independent States

470 Chapter 16

Did You Know?—In 1983, a Columbia University professor of political science said, "The Soviet Union is not now nor will it be during the next decade in the throes of a systemic crisis, for it boasts enormous unused reserves of political and social stability that suffice to endure the deepest difficulties."

Discuss with your students the reasons that the professor may have made this statement. *(Reasons will vary. Even though Westerners do not agree generally with the political philosophy of communism, it had dominated every part of life in the Soviet Union for over sixty years by the time this statement was made. Control by the government was so tight that no revolution was thought possible.)*

The Mafia in Russia—Since the Iron Curtain has fallen, the Mafia in Russia has become very large. Merchants must pay protection money. Vices of every kind are brought in and encouraged by the Mafia. Tourists are especially susceptible to Mafia victimization. One mission group stayed in a hotel in Moscow and woke up the next morning without their money. Someone had come in during the night and taken it while the missionaries were asleep.

Discuss with your students how the fall of such a seemingly terrible political system can result in many other problems instead of creating a much better society. *(New freedom without responsibility leads to disaster; they have never had this type of freedom before; atheism resulted in moral guidelines; etc.)*

Factory workers in the former Soviet Union symbolize the transition from a Communist to a capitalist economy.

Section Review

1. What Soviet leader took power in 1985?
2. What is the meaning of *perestroika?* of *glasnost?*
3. When the Soviet Union dissolved, what confederation took its place? What nation dominated this confederation?

Why would a concept like *glasnost* be difficult for a government to control?

Summary

In *Russia and the Independent States,* Daniel C. Diller recounts a popular joke from the last days of the Soviet Union. A train is traveling across the USSR. Among the many passengers, in a special compartment, are Lenin, Stalin, Khrushchev, Brezhnev, and Gorbachev. Suddenly, the engine breaks down and the train comes to a halt. Lenin says he will take care of it, and he goes to the engine and lectures the engineer on the principles of Marxism and the importance of duty to the Soviet Union. The train still doesn't go, so Stalin goes to the engine and shoots the engineer. Still the train doesn't move, so Khrushchev says, "We must not hold the engineer's past mistakes against him." He proceeds to the engine and props up the engineer's body at the controls. When this doesn't help, Brezhnev suggests they close the blinds and pretend the train is moving. This they proceed to do, remarking about how quiet the ride is. Finally, Gorbachev gets out, climbs on top of the train, and announces, "Look, everybody, the train is not moving!" The passengers are delighted to have a leader so honest.

The train, however, still doesn't go anywhere.

volt against Nicholas I. During the Cold War period, dissidents often challenged the Soviet system. The events of the 1990s could be seen as the fruition of that legacy. With Yeltsin's election to another term as president, all segments of Russian society had accepted democracy as the way to power.

There are other hopeful signs. Russia has become more and more an urban nation. Change came dramatically for Moscow, and perhaps the rest of Russia will change as well. Russia's literacy rate was an incredible 99 percent, and that offered hope that over time a well-informed citizenry through a free press could make democracy work better. About 80 percent of the Russian economy is in private hands. Russia also has abundant natural resources.

Since 1991 Russia has suffered from unrealistic expectations at home and abroad. Events in Russia since the fall of Communism must be put in perspective. As recently as the late nineteenth century, monarchy, not democracy, was common for most European countries. Even the United States did not develop an effective democracy with a strong two-party system until about sixty years after its founding. As the communist generation passes in Russia, perhaps those who have known only democracy will make it work more successfully.

Spanning the Ages

Communism began to take hold in other areas as well. After World War II, China fell to the forces of communism and began to spread its new philosophy to other Asian nations. In the next chapter we will learn about China under communism and Japan, a threatening country until the end of World War II, under capitalism. The immense differences in the nations today speak well for the plight of communism and the power of capitalism.

Section Review Answers

1. Mikhail Gorbachev
2. *Perestroika* means "restructuring." *Glasnost* means "openness."
3. Commonwealth of Independent States (CIS); Russia

Answers will vary. Freedom by its very nature is hard to control. The USSR had so little experience with responsible government that the people did not know the disciplines needed to maintain freedom. Furthermore, the Soviets had limited freedom for so long that people pressed immediately for all the liberties that citizens enjoy in countries such as the United States.

Summary—Read the Summary aloud with your students in preparation for answering the Think About It question on page 473.

Chapter Review Idea

Play the Communist Game. Divide the class into three groups: ordinary citizens, KGB spies, and anti-government dissidents. Give each student a slip of paper telling him which group he is in. He must not give any indication of his group to anyone else. The teacher will ask each student one question. The student will have thirty seconds to answer the question stereotypically of his group. For example, if you ask the question "In what year was the Communist (or Bolshevik) Revolution?" the student who is a citizen should answer something to the effect that in 1917 the czar's reign was overthrown by Communists offering peace, land, and bread. The KGB spy could answer the same thing or accuse someone of something. For example, he might say, "The czar had friends, who are obviously in this room right now." The dissident would answer that the rightful government was overthrown in 1917. At the end of the questions, each person is to write down who belongs to which group. If he gets *his own* group completely correct, he stays alive. Otherwise, he dies. If anyone from another group gets a different group completely correct, that entire found group dies, even if a student in that group got his own group completely correct. Each student must use a strategy so that his own group can tell he belongs, but other groups cannot. As time permits, you may redistribute the papers to those who are still alive until you have only one person left living. This is the new Communist leader.

CHAPTER REVIEW

People, Places, and Things to Know

Vladimir Ilich Lenin
Provisional Government
Aleksandr Kerensky
Union of Soviet Socialist Republics (USSR)
Soviet Union
War Communism
New Economic Policy
Joseph Stalin
Five-Year Plans
collectivization
purges
"scorched-earth" policy
Battle of Stalingrad
Cold War
Nikita Khrushchev
de-Stalinization
Aleksandr Solzhenitsyn
peaceful coexistence
dissidents
Cuban missile crisis
Leonid Brezhnev
détente
atheism
Russian Orthodox Church
icons
patriarch of Constantinople
Cyril Lucar
Holy Synod
Stundist revival
Union of Evangelical Christians—Baptists
"registered churches"
"unregistered churches"
Mikhail Gorbachev
perestroika
glasnost

Review Questions

Matching

Match the Soviet leader with the term most closely associated with him. Answers may be used more than once.

1. collectivization
2. de-Stalinization
3. détente
4. Five-Year Plans
5. *glasnost*
6. New Economic Policy
7. peaceful coexistence
8. *perestroika*
9. treaty with Hitler
10. War Communism

(a) Lenin
(b) Stalin
(c) Khrushchev
(d) Brezhnev
(e) Gorbachev

Chronology

Put the following events in their proper chronological order from earliest to latest.

11. The Battle of Stalingrad takes place.
12. Cuba turns Communist.
13. Czar Nicholas II is overthrown.

CHAPTER REVIEW ANSWERS

Matching

1. b
2. c
3. d
4. b
5. e
6. a
7. c
8. e
9. b
10. a

Chronology

14. German Mennonites settle in Russia.
25. World War I begins.
13. Czar Nicholas II is overthrown.
19. The Provisional Government is overthrown.
18. Lenin dies.
16. Hitler invades the USSR.
11. The Battle of Stalingrad takes place.
24. Uprising in Hungary is crushed.
12. Cuba turns Communist.
22. The Cuban missile crisis takes place.
17. Khrushchev falls from power.
23. Uprising in Czechoslovakia is crushed.
20. The Soviet Union invades Afghanistan.
15. Gorbachev becomes the Soviet leader.
21. The Soviet Union is dissolved.

14. German Mennonites settle in Russia.
15. Gorbachev becomes the Soviet leader.
16. Hitler invades the USSR.
17. Khrushchev falls from power.
18. Lenin dies.
19. The Provisional Government is overthrown.
20. The Soviet Union invades Afghanistan.
21. The Soviet Union is dissolved.
22. The Cuban missile crisis takes place.
23. Uprising in Czechoslovakia is crushed.
24. Uprising in Hungary is crushed.
25. World War I begins.

True or False?

Which of these statements are true and which are false?

26. Communism teaches that society should have no classes.
27. Communism teaches that people should own their own property.
28. Communism teaches children to honor their parents more than their country.
29. Communism is officially atheistic in belief.
30. Communism is based on the teaching of Karl Marx.

Think About It!

Read the chapter summary on page 471. In a paragraph or two, describe how this story summarizes the history of the Soviet Union. Explain how its portrayal of the five leaders reflects the actions and character of each leader.

Chapter Enrichment Activities

Research—Take or send your students to the public library. Have each one find an article written during the years 1989-91 and describing the fall of Communism (this could be in any newly freed country such as East Germany, Poland, or Romania). He should read the article and write a brief report on his findings and a bibliographic entry.

Hands-On Activity: Dill—Bring in some dill for your students (preferably fresh) and have them eat it on everything in their lunch that day. Western Russians use this spice for all dishes from salads to meats to pastas. Compare its taste to other dill tastes such as pickles.

Recipe: Beets with Dill—

Ingredients:
1 can beets
dill weed

Chop beets finely. Sprinkle dill weed on top. Serve warm as an appetizer.

True or False?

26. True
27. False
28. False
29. True
30. True

Think About It!

Answers will vary. None of the leaders actually did anything about the problems facing the Soviet Union. Lenin, in lecturing the engineer, reflects the idea that Communism could be made to work if everyone just believed in it. Stalin, in shooting the engineer, believed that force and terror could make the system work. Khrushchev, in propping up the engineer's body, thought that relieving the terror could make the system work. Brezhnev, in closing the blinds, simply ignored the fact that the system was not working. Gorbachev, by announcing the train was not moving, showed that he realized the system was not working—but he still did not have a way of making it work. (The students may show a great range of answers to this question. The point is understanding how each leader ruled and that the Communist system did not work.)

Student Objectives
Students should be able to
1. Identify the twentieth-century nationalist leaders of China.
2. Illustrate the Three Principles of the People by giving an example of each.
3. Summarize the struggle between Chiang Kai-shek and Mao Zedong.
4. Identify the first twentieth-century communist leader of China.
5. Evaluate Ghandi's policy for becoming independent from Britain.
6. Define the term *westernizing*.
7. Describe World War II in the Pacific.
8. Locate Asia on a map.
9. Analyze and create pie graphs.
10. Recognize the proper names for the two countries of China.
11. Identify the second twentieth-century communist leader of China.
12. Evaluate China's response to the call for democracy at Tiananmen Square.
13. Describe in their own words the problems in Korea and Vietnam.
14. Contrast Japan before and after World War II.
15. Describe religion in China before and after communism.

Opening Photo—
Three pagodas and a reflecting pool

A Moment in Time
Use the idea of a clock to write dates on the bulletin board. Start with 1911 in the one o'clock position: the beginning of the Chinese republic led by Sun Yat-sen. Add Chiang Kai-shek, Mao Zedong, and Deng Xiaoping for China. Add the Tiananmen Square incident of 1989 and any present developments in China. In a different color, place Japan's wars of aggression, Emperor Hirohito, World War II (with V-J Day), and present developments in Japan. Add the Korean and Vietnam Conflicts.

CHAPTER 17

Asia is huge. It is larger than any other continent (over seventeen million square miles). Over three billion people (more than half of the world's population) live there. Trying to study such an enormous region in a single chapter is rather like trying to stuff a tablecloth into a napkin holder. Because Asia has that much land and that many people, you can imagine the variety of cultures, and conflicts, the continent of Asia might have. For this reason, we study Russia and the Middle East individually even though they are part of Asia.

One way to approach Asia in the twentieth century is to look at the parallel history of two of its major countries, China and Japan. Those two nations have dominated events in the continent and have drastically affected their neighbors—including each other.

As important as China and Japan are to Asian history, there is much more involved than just those two nations. We will touch on other countries, notably India, and look at the history of Christianity in modern Asia. We will seek to understand the conditions of life in this land that is home to over half the people in the world.

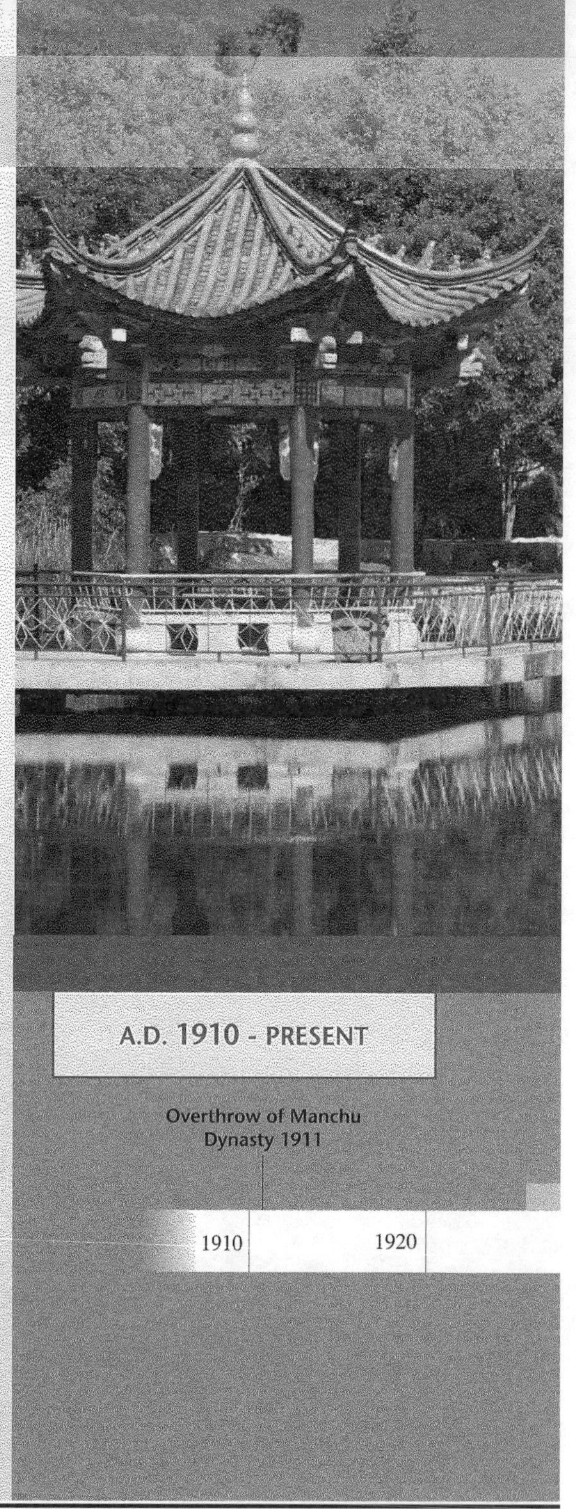

A.D. 1910 - PRESENT

Overthrow of Manchu Dynasty 1911

1910 1920

Chapter 17 Lesson Plans			
Section Title	**Main Concept**	**Pages**	**Time Frame**
1. The Scholar and the Samurai **Interpretations: Gandhi* **Settings: Japan*	China and Japan are representative of Asian countries in the twentieth century.	474-85	2-3 days
2. The Communist and Capitalist **Analysis: Nintendo*	Communism and suffering have taken over China and other southeast Asian countries. Japan and other capitalist societies are prospering.	486-95	2-3 days
3. Christianity in Asia **Characterizations: John Sung*	Christianity represents a very small portion of religion in Asia today.	496-501	1 day
Total Suggested Days (including 1 day for review & 1 day for test)			7-9 days

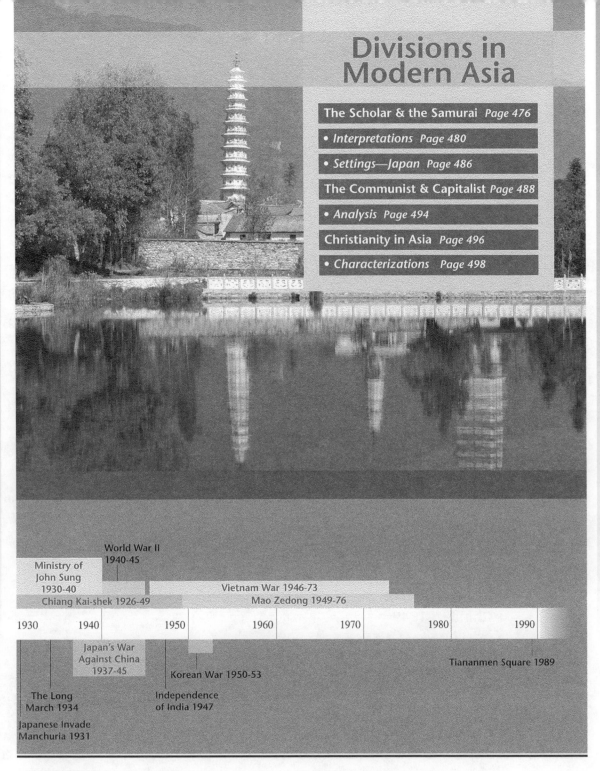

Divisions in Modern Asia

Ministry of John Sung 1930-40

World War II 1940-45

Vietnam War 1946-73

Chiang Kai-shek 1926-49

Mao Zedong 1949-76

1930 1940 1950 1960 1970 1980 1990

Japan's War Against China 1937-45

Korean War 1950-53

Tiananmen Square 1989

The Long March 1934

Independence of India 1947

Japanese Invade Manchuria 1931

Chapter Motivator

Review Chapter 13 with your students. Chapter 17 starts where Chapter 13 leaves off, right after the Boxer Rebellion. You will review Japan from Chapter 15 later in this chapter. Take a poll in your class. Ask who would rather read and study and who would rather play sports. Then place them in the categories of China and Japan respectively. Tell them that this is because China was led by a class of scholars and Japan was led by a class of samurai (fighters).

Ask your students if they have a Nintendo system and what they like about it. Ask them to name some other electronic items that Japan produces. Why do so many electronic items come from Japan? *(Because of its unconditional surrender at the end of World War II, Japan had to convert its military plants to commercial plants that produced electronic goods.)*

Ask your students to list some hardships or inconveniences that missionaries going to Asia might encounter. Remind them, of course, that the benefits far outweigh the inconveniences. Later in this chapter you will use prayer cards and pray for specific missionaries.

II Timothy 3:12

The Bible says that if you are a true Christian you will be persecuted. Persecution comes in different forms, but the most obvious is physical violence. II Timothy 3:12 says, "Yea, and all that will live godly in Christ Jesus shall suffer persecution." Paul responds correctly to persecution in II Corinthians 12:10 when he says, "Therefore I take pleasure in infirmities, in reproaches, in necessities, in persecutions, in distresses for Christ's sake: for when I am weak, then am I strong." (BLM verse 17)

Materials

- Scripture verse (BLM verse 17)
- Chinese food
- Bibles for Bible study
- Wall map of Asia and Japan (BLM 17-1)
- *Teaching Transparencies* for use with *WORLD STUDIES for Christian Schools* (Second Edition)
- Periodical articles relating to Tiananmen Square
- Pictures of Asia
- Guest speaker, a veteran of the Korean or Vietnam Conflict
- Video of China or Japan
- Nintendo (optional)
- Prayer cards for missionaries to Asia

SECTION 1

Student Objectives
Students should be able to

1. Identify the twentieth-century nationalist leaders of China.
2. Illustrate the Three Principles of the People by giving an example of each.
3. Summarize the struggle between Chiang Kai-shek and Mao Zedong.
4. Identify the first twentieth-century Communist leader of China.
5. Evaluate Ghandi's policy for becoming independent from Britain.
6. Define the term *westernizing*.
7. Describe World War II in the Pacific.

Countries of Asia—Besides China and Japan, the other countries of Asia are India, Pakistan, Bangladesh, Nepal, Bhutan, Sri Lanka, Maldives, Myanmar (formerly Burma), Vietnam, Laos, Cambodia, Thailand, Malaysia, Singapore, Brunei, Indonesia, Philippines, Mongolia, Taiwan, North Korea, South Korea, and a large portion of Russia.

Chinese Peasants—Peasants in Chinese history did not have a happy lot in life. Those who owned land usually did not have enough on which to make a living. Those who did not own land worked in a feudalistic-type system for a landlord, who required them to give between 30 and 60 percent of their produce in payment for land use. In some cases, peasant families were so poor that they sold their children into slavery to get the needed money.

Today, in a somewhat capitalistic system, farmers meet quotas for their group farm (collective) and for the government, and then they may keep or sell all that is left over. Though the peasants' standard of living has risen since the communist takeover, they are still very poor.

The Scholar and the Samurai

Since the time of the philosopher Confucius, the Chinese have given a special place of honor to scholars. It was the scholars who studied and preserved Chinese tradition. Chinese empires might rise and fall, but the scholar

Confucius

class endured. Japan, on the other hand, has honored its class of warriors, the samurai. Japan has had a long line of emperors, but from the Middle Ages until the 1800s, the real ruling power was the shogun. This "great general" (which is what *shogun* means) ruled the nation like a samurai chief. Of course, there were warriors in China and scholars in Japan. But the image of the Chinese scholar and the Japanese warrior helps us understand the history of Asia in the first half of the twentieth century.

China to 1949

As we noted in Chapter 13, in the early 1900s China faced several enormous problems. European countries wanting to trade with China had forced their way into the country. The snobbish manners of these foreigners angered the Chinese, and the foreigners forced their laws and customs on some parts of China. Because they had shunned the ideas of Europe, the Chinese lacked the weapons, machinery, and other technology that could have helped them defend their country.

The Chinese people hated not only Europeans but also their own rulers. The Chinese detested the Manchu leaders who controlled the country. Landlords and the government heavily taxed the poor peasants. The rich and powerful, both Chinese and foreign, lived in luxury while millions of poor Chinese suffered terrible hardships. This discontent finally exploded in revolution.

Sun Yat-sen

In 1911 the Chinese arose in revolt against the Manchu government. **Sun Yat-sen** led the

Sun Yat-sen

SECTION 1

Materials

- Chinese food
- Bibles for Bible study

Assignment Suggestion—If you would like to break Section 1 into two sections to assign for homework, this could best be done between the sections on China and Japan. The section on China ends on page 479 and corresponds to questions 1-3. The section on Japan starts on page 482 and corresponds to questions 4-7 and the Think About It question. The Interpretations section on Gandhi may be read with either assignment.

Food—Sometime during the chapter (if your school, budget, and class size permit) have a Chinese (or other Asian country's) food day. Try to include only traditional foods such as rice and steamed vegetables (stir-fry food), or if you just want a fun activity, get all types from a local Oriental restaurant.

Oriental Restaurant—Eat at an Oriental restaurant. Take the opportunity to talk to the workers or owners. Have them describe the foods they eat and what changes they make in their recipes to make the foods more appealing to Westerners.

movement to form a Chinese republic. Although born in China, Sun had a Western education. As a teenager, he went to school in Hawaii. Later, he studied medicine and became a doctor. As a highly educated man, Sun represented in many ways the class of Chinese scholars.

Sun developed a plan for reforming China called the **Three Principles of the People.** The first principle was nationalism. Sun believed that the Chinese should rule themselves. This meant he opposed not only foreign power in China but also the Manchus because the Manchus were from Manchuria and not considered native Chinese. His second principle was democracy. Sun wanted China to have a constitutional government in which all Chinese were considered equal. His third principle was livelihood. Sun and his followers sought to provide every Chinese man with the means to support himself and his family. To further his ideas, Sun founded the **Kuomintang** (KWOH min TAHNG), or Nationalist Party.

The Manchu dynasty ended, but Sun's hopes for a Chinese government that would solve the country's problems were not fulfilled. Strife and rebellion in China grew. China suffered under a system similar to feudalism in Europe in the Middle Ages. Military leaders known as **warlords** ruled the different regions of China. These warlords raised and paid their own armies. Anyone who would lead China had to persuade at least some of the warlords to support him. The division of China among the warlords made some fear that the country would break apart.

Chiang Kai-shek

When Sun Yat-sen died, **Chiang Kai-shek** (CHANG KYE-SHEK) took over as leader of the Kuomintang. Chiang had been leader of Sun's military school. He followed Sun in seeking to establish a stable government in China, and he managed to become president. Chiang faced many obstacles to solving China's problems. One problem was the warlords, but an even greater problem was the Communists.

While Chiang tried to gain control of the large and unhappy country, Communists began to spread their teachings. These Communists

Chiang Kai-shek

Chinese Names—Chinese names start with the last name (the family or surname), so in the name Chiang Kai-shek, Chiang is his last name. Refer to the margin note on page 352 to remind the students of the change in the English spellings of Chinese words.

The Empress Dowager—The Empress Dowager Tz'u-hsi was the last strong Manchu ruler. She was not the emperor's true wife. His true wife was titled the Eastern Empress, while the one we are familiar with was titled the Western Empress. Known as "Old Buddha," she ruled by terror. Even when there were emperors ruling, she was always in charge. During the Boxer Rebellion many foreigners were killed, among them missionaries, merchants, and students. She tacitly encouraged this and later gave orders to kill all foreigners, even if they were trying to leave. She sent a message to all the provinces to "slay" all foreigners. Two kind-hearted officials changed the word to "protect." When their trick was discovered, they were summarily executed.

Reform Efforts of the Manchus—The Manchus started their reform efforts too late to save their failing empire. Some of these reforms included allowing intermarriage of Manchus and Chinese, giving up foot binding for girls, allowing sons to go abroad for education, and remodeling the examination system.

Revolutions—Why have so many revolutions occurred in the history of the world? Of course, greed is the basic cause, but discuss with your students the characteristics that lead to revolution in world history, especially noting the countries of Russia and China which you are currently studying. (Think also about the French Revolution, the American War for Independence, and the Civil War). Dissatisfaction with a poor standard of living, food shortages, and corruption and greed among the rich are some reasons revolutions happen. Sometimes dissatisfaction with laws or taxes causes the problem. Your students have seen in the previous chapter and will see in this one the revolutions caused by discontent fostered by the communists. Lack of necessary goods contributed to the discontent, and although we feel sorry for the people, we must remember that rebellion is still wrong.

Political Parties—Direct each student to create his own political party and name the party. Have each write at least ten policies for his party and compare them to other class members' party policies. Each party's policies should contain elements of religion, education, government, labor, philosophy (e.g., evolutionism vs. Creationism), and so forth. Different students will think many different things in government important, and you should receive a great variety of answers. Try not to "help" the students by giving them ideas and thereby stifling their creativity.

Mao Zedong—Born December 26, 1893, in Hunan province, Mao was the oldest of four siblings. He had two younger brothers and one sister, all of whom met violent ends for political activism. Mao's father was a Confucian capitalist who was strict to the point of meanness with his children. His mother, on the other hand, was Buddhist and was a very sweet, gentle, doting soul.

Mao attended primary school from ages 8 to 13, secondary school for a very brief period of time, and normal (teacher's) school for five years. Always an avid reader, Mao once said that although a little reading was all right, too much reading makes one an idiot. He even disdained his own education and literature-fed intellect.

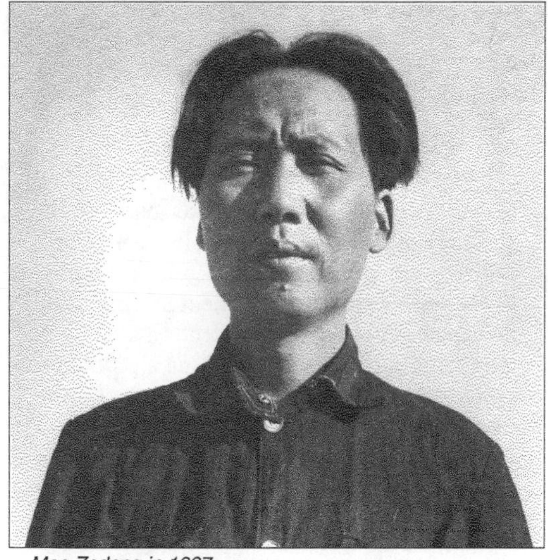

Mao Zedong in 1937

were inspired and supported by the Soviet Union, and they hoped to make China a Communist country. Chiang fought against the Communists with limited success. The Communists, led by **Mao Zedong** (MOU DZUH-DONG), made friends with the Chinese peasants by promising them a better life under Communism.

Fierce fighting took place between Chiang's Nationalist forces and Mao's Communist forces. Sometimes Chiang seemed on the verge of winning. In 1934, with the help of advisors from the German army, the Kuomintang nearly surrounded and destroyed the Communist army. However, Mao Zedong led his forces on a five-thousand-mile retreat into northern China. This retreat, known as the **Long March,** resulted in the death of eighty thousand Communist soldiers. But it preserved the nucleus of a Communist army to fight on.

Chiang's problems became worse in the 1930s when Japan attacked and conquered portions of China. (These attacks are discussed in the next section.) He tried to fight both the Communists and the Japanese but could stop

China relied heavily on the Allies for help against the Japanese. Here Chiang Kai-shek and his wife meet with Franklin Roosevelt and Winston Churchill in Cairo, Egypt (1943).

Capture the Flag—If you have an opportunity, play Capture the Flag with your students. One side should be the nationalists and the other should be the communists. You could even role-play the Chinese civil war, with the communists retreating on a "Long March" and then coming back to win.

Charting—Throughout the chapter have students keep a chart of government, leaders, and events in Japan and China. Column headings could be *Leaders, Government,* and *Major events*. Rows would be *China* and *Japan* (BLM 17-1).

The Chinese Civil War—Originally, Communists were allowed in the Kuomintang, though eventually they were expelled. Later they united their forces to fight the Japanese. This war greatly weakened the Nationalists but strengthened the Communists by allowing them to gather farmers and other peasants to their side with promises of a good life. Chiang's forces could not hold on to the country and lost strategic areas one by one. Mao took over the major cities, eventually causing Chiang and his followers to flee to Taiwan.

A Chinese sentry guards the "Flying Tigers," P-40 fighters with American pilots that provided the first American contribution to China's war against Japan.

neither. The Chinese people were in turmoil. Finally, Chiang and the Communists agreed to fight together against the Japanese.

With help from the United States, China held out against Japan. The hard fighting brought death and destruction to the land, and the Chinese were weary of the violence. When Japan was defeated at the end of World War II (1945), China regained her territory. But soon a civil war broke out as Communists sought to take over the country.

Chiang and his Nationalists fought for four more years to stop the Communists. During those years, more of the Chinese became convinced that the Communists would improve the bad conditions in their country. In 1949 Chiang and many of his followers fled to the island of Taiwan and set up the government of Nationalist China. Mao and his followers set up their rule over Communist China on the mainland. The end of Japanese oppression was about to bring a new oppression to the Chinese, this time by their own leaders.

Advisor—Each student should pretend he is an advisor to Chiang Kai-shek or Mao Zedong. What would he advise him to do in 1949 to win the civil war? What military action should he take? What propaganda should he tell the people? What is the advisor's life like? Does he follow his leader everywhere? Or does he have his own life and way of doing things? The student should write at least ten sentences describing the advisor's life.

Rupees—Rupees equal about $0.03 in American money, so the 1600 rupees paid for Gandhi's salt would equal $48.00. This amount sounds insignificant by today's standards but represented a significant amount in the 1930s.

Martin Luther King Jr.—Born on January 15, 1929, Martin Luther King Jr. grew up in a well-to-do home. His grandfather, Reverend Williams, was the first president of the NAACP (National Association for the Advancement of Colored People). After attending Morehouse College, King received a degree in theology from Crozer Theological Seminary and a Ph.D. from Boston University. His father offered him a job at his church in Atlanta, but King instead decided to pastor Dexter Avenue Baptist Church in Alabama. It was in his first year there that his political activism began.

In Montgomery, Alabama, Rosa Parks refused to give up her seat on a bus for a white man. It was the law at the time that white people were to sit at the front of the bus with black people in the back. If the bus were full, a white person could make a black person move. Since only one color could sit on a row, all black people in that row would then have to move. Rosa was arrested, and a boycott of the bus company was started among blacks, causing a great loss of money to the company. King then started his policy of nonviolence. He used this policy along with civil disobedience in many cities to aid the cause of the blacks in the South and eventually in the North.

In Alabama, public sentiment was against the blacks' cause until children started being arrested en masse and brought to jail. The conscience of the nation would not tolerate that. In Selma, the fight was centered on the right to vote. Later, in Chicago, housing was the issue.

King was outspoken against the Vietnam Conflict, and many, including some government officials, accused him of being a communist.

The last things King campaigned for were better school lunches for children in black schools and respect, better pay, and benefits (with the right to unionize) for garbage collectors.

INTERPRETATIONS

Gandhi and Indian Nonviolence

In 1947 the greatest symbol of European imperialism, Raj India, came to an end: Great Britain granted India its independence. The main leader in India's drive for independence was an unusual man named **Mohandas Gandhi.** Slender, bald, and stooped, he hardly looked like a man who could topple the British Empire.

Gandhi, often called "Mahatma" ("great soul") by his admirers, was the son of a government official. After becoming a lawyer, he dedicated himself to working for Indian independence from Britain. Drawing on his Hindu background, Gandhi announced that he would pursue independence by a policy of nonviolence instead of relying on riots or terrorism. He supported "noncooperation," for example. Gandhi simply urged Indians not to work with the British rulers. Teachers would refuse to teach. Government officials would refuse to perform their tasks or would resign their positions. Gandhi himself went on hunger strikes to attract notice to his cause.

Gandhi was famous for his policy of **civil disobedience.** He said that Indians should not obey laws they thought were unjust. By doing so, they would pressure the British to give up and leave India. The most famous example of Gandhi's civil disobedience was his protest of British salt laws. Indians had to buy government-approved salt on which they had already paid taxes. They could not gather their own salt from the seashore or salt marshes. In 1930 Gandhi led a two-hundred-mile march to the sea, where he and his followers illegally gathered salt. This simple act won Gandhi and his cause the attention of the world. Across the land Indians began to gather salt illegally in protest of British policies and British rule. The salt lump that Gandhi himself picked up from the seashore was later auctioned off for 1,600 rupees.

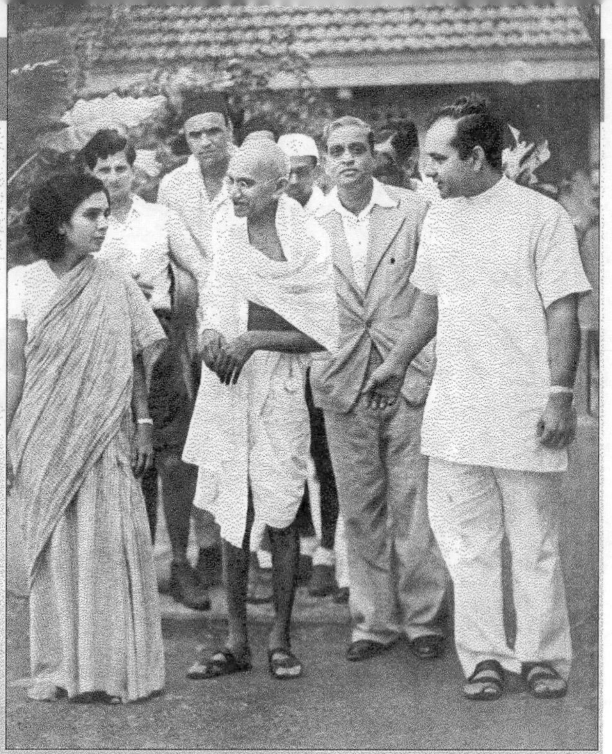

Mohandas Gandhi (center)

Gandhi actually wanted nonviolent protest to provoke a violent response from the British. Then British citizens would be revolted by the violence, he said, and the world would rally to the Indian cause. He wrote, "I want world sympathy in this battle of right against might." To a great extent, his plan worked. His success later inspired others to use his methods, such as Martin Luther King Jr. in the American civil rights movement.

Gandhi's policies worked, but they could work only against a government with some sense of morality. The British people and the British government could not bring themselves to practice the brutality needed to crush the Indian movement. Later Martin Luther King Jr. saw success with these methods by appealing to the conscience of the American people. But when a government is willing to put down any unrest with unrestrained

Laws and God's Word—Your students have just read about Mahatma Gandhi and his policy of nonviolence. Read Romans 13:1-7 with your students and discuss it with them. Have them list laws they do not like but that they need to obey because they are not against God's law (e.g., speed limit, seat belts). Ask them if they can think of any laws that would break God's law and that therefore Christians cannot obey, though we must suffer the consequences (e.g., having to hire homosexuals in Christian schools and churches). Describe the ordeal Paul went through in order to be true to his faith. He had to preach although disobeying the government; yet when he was taken to jail, he suffered his imprisonment willingly.

force, the methods do not work. South Africans who tried to use Gandhi's methods experienced only repression, violence, and death. Gandhi himself was somewhat gullible about the depth of human sinfulness. He once wrote a letter to Adolf Hitler at the height of World War II to urge the Nazi dictator to embrace nonviolence.

Christians also object to these methods. The Bible teaches that Christians may disobey the law only when the law contradicts the commands of God. Even then, the Christian must stand ready to face the consequences. When the Jewish Sanhedrin told the apostles to stop preaching about Jesus Christ, Peter told them, "We ought to obey God rather than men" (Acts 5:29; see also 4:18-20). Gandhi broke laws that he did not have to break so that he could pressure the British government to change. Christians, however, must honor the law and the government except when the government demands what belongs to God (Rom. 13:1-7).

Gandhi saw his movement crowned with success when Britain gave India its independence. But the event was not as nonviolent as Gandhi had wished. Some of the Indian resistance to Britain was very violent. Also, Britain divided the area into two nations, Hindu India and Muslim Pakistan. With independence, Hindus and Muslims clashed in fighting that left as many as one million people dead. Gandhi himself was assassinated by a fellow Hindu. Since that time India has continued to suffer religious and civil conflict. Mohandas Gandhi's philosophy of nonviolence has not spared his land from bloodshed.

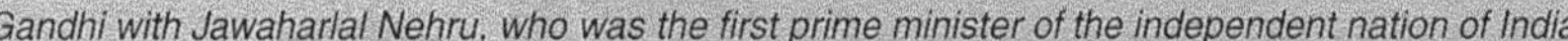

Gandhi with Jawaharlal Nehru, who was the first prime minister of the independent nation of India

Nehru—Nehru was born on November 14, 1889. He was a Hindu, from a rich, educated, and very westernized family. He spoke some Sanskrit and was fluent in Hindi, but his first language was English. He was sent to study at Harrow in England, and then he went to Trinity College in Cambridge. His father, Motilal, was soon active in the fight for Indian independence. Many times Gandhi, Motilal Nehru, and Jawaharlal Nehru would go to jail for their participation in the independence movement. Later, Nehru would be the first prime minister of a free India.

Meiji—Emperor Meiji ruled from 1868 to 1912. He was the 122nd emperor of Japan and became emperor at sixteen years of age. He led many reforms in Japan during this period. His government stated what had long been believed in Japan about the interrelationship of emperor and divinity: (1) man is a religious being and knows that gods are above men; (2) the gods have power among nations and people; (3) the government at any given time is the will of the gods; (4) the incarnation of that will is the monarch; (5) gods are eternal; so also is the imperial line; (6) therefore the nation and imperial house are one; (7) strife causes the people to search for the gods' judgment; and (8) since the two are so interrelated, the judgment of the emperor is obeyed.

Sports and Games in Japan—Many sports and games are played in Japan. Archery is an ancient sport of the Japanese along with *bajutsu* (horsemanship), *hojutsu* (gunnery), *kendo* (*kenjutsu*; sword fighting), *judo* (*jujitsu*; wrestling), *sojutsu* (spear fighting), and *sumo* wrestling.

Games that might be played include *chie-no-ita* (jigsaw puzzles), *Go* (a complicated game of checkers), badminton, marbles, hide-and-seek, *kemari* (football), *ken* (stone, paper, scissors), kites, and tops.

Japan to 1945

As we learned on page 368, over two hundred years of Japanese isolation ended in 1853. In that year Commodore Matthew Perry of the United States visited with his fleet and opened Japan to trade. In a later visit Perry brought with him several inventions that amazed the Japanese people. One was a telegraph system, which could send messages from one town to another. Another was a miniature train and railroad track. Japanese officials took turns riding around on the small train pulled by its own steam locomotive. The Japanese realized that they had much to learn if they were to catch up with the rest of the world.

Modernizing Japan

The Japanese began to trade not only with the United States but also with other countries. Soon the Japanese were **"westernizing"** their way of life (making it like that of the United States and Europe). They built factories to make new products. They sent some of their young men to the United States and Europe to learn more about new developments in industry. They began to build a large, powerful navy and army of their own.

In the midst of all this modernization, the rule of the shogun came to an end. In 1868 the emperor, Meiji (MAY jee), became the ruler of the land in reality as well as in name. He helped Japan accomplish many of the achievements listed above. At the same time, Japan developed a sort of "Dr. Jekyll and Mr. Hyde" personality. On the one side were Japanese who admired the democratic governments of the West and wanted Japan to be like them. On the other hand were militarists, warriors who wanted to use Japan's new industrial might to put all of eastern Asia under Japanese control. It soon became obvious that the samurai attitude was going to dominate Japan's future.

Militarizing Japan

When he was a student at Harvard in 1902, Franklin Roosevelt had a Japanese classmate. Roosevelt listened with interest as the young man described to him a hundred-year Japanese schedule of conquest. Starting in 1889, Roosevelt's classmate said, the Japanese were going to proceed by twelve steps to surpass China and Russia and first take over Korea; then parts of China, along with Australia and New Zealand; and finally all of the Pacific islands including Hawaii. This account impressed Roosevelt, especially when he became

Emperor Meiji and his court reflect Japan's conscious imitation of Western styles and culture.

Speaking of Samurai—Ask if any of your students have taken lessons in any of the martial arts. This would include such things as karate, judo, tae kwan do, and fencing. As time permits, encourage them to do a short demonstration for the class. Some students may be opposed to the martial arts because they stem from a culture in which the people are deeply involved in ancient Eastern traditions, also known as the New Age movement. You may want to talk about some elements of this movement at this time.

Martial Arts Session—Visit a martial arts studio to watch a session. Instruct your child to watch for other elements of Asian culture such as those from the New Age movement.

A Chinese child cries amid the wreckage resulting from Japan's brutal attack on the Chinese city of Shanghai.

president of the United States and he watched as Japan appeared to be following such a schedule of conquest.

Japan first humiliated China in a short war in 1895. As a result Japan captured the island of Formosa (Taiwan) and later took over Korea in 1910. In 1904-5, Japan took on Russia. Most countries expected Russia to crush the Japanese. Instead, Japan humiliated Russia. The Japanese navy trapped Russia's Pacific fleet in port. Russia then sent its fleet from the Baltic Sea on a ten-thousand-mile trip to the Pacific. When the Russian fleet arrived, the Japanese promptly sank it. Russia made peace on terms favorable to the Japanese. Later, in World War I, Japan sided with the Allies and seized all German colonies in the Pacific.

Japan was not driven by greed alone. The nation was suffering. Japan could not grow enough food for its people and had to import tons of rice. Even then, some Japanese were starving. To supply more raw materials for their industries and to provide more land for the growing population, the Japanese set out to control all of eastern Asia.

Japan needed land and food, Japan's military leaders said, so Japan should just take them. Like Hitler's Germany, Japan began to think that "might made right." Anyone who opposed the growing power of the military was risking his life. Between 1912 and 1945, six prime ministers were assassinated for opposing the policies of the military. Many Japanese fanatically supported the military's goals. When a group of officers was tried for the assassination of one prime minister in 1932, some Japanese wrote letters of support—in blood. Nine citizens showed their support of the assassins by cutting off their little fingers and sending them in a jar to the government.

Warrior Japan

In 1931 the Japanese attacked the northeastern section of China called **Manchuria.** The Japanese military made this attack despite the orders of the civilian government. But the campaign was so successful that no one dared question it. Japan soon became virtually a military dictatorship like that of Nazi Germany or Fascist Italy. Japan, in fact, made an alliance with Germany and Italy (as we studied in Chapter 15). Supposedly the Japanese revered their emperor and believed he was a god. Yet the emperor told the American ambassador that even he would be murdered if he

Women in Japan—Women were always below men in ancient Japan, though today there seems to be much more equality in jobs and other opportunities. There are even some women professional wrestlers in Japan today. Years ago, however, the wife always walked behind her husband. Women were not allowed to climb Mt. Fuji and several other mountains. Kimonos were traditionally worn by women and are still worn for several occasions in their culture today.

Little Fingers—This was not the only time that the Japanese cut off their little fingers. Today it is a sign of honor in the Japanese mafia to cut off your little finger if you've lost face. You may see people with one, two, or more fingers missing.

Superstitions in Japan—Like all cultures, Japan has its own peculiar superstitions. Thirteen, nineteen, thirty-three, and forty-two are considered to be unlucky ages and especially bad years in which to have children. The fifteenth and twenty-eighth days of the month are particularly lucky. The Japanese will not sleep with the head toward the north, for that is how corpses are buried; but east and south are lucky directions. The northeast is unlucky, and people will not make any openings on that side of the house.

Supposedly if one throws nail parings in a fire, the fire will come and burn down the house. Two people are required to give the news of a death because if just one goes, the spirit of the deceased will enter his body. Many restaurateurs sprinkle salt outside their establishments to ward off evil.

Interview—Interview a few students in the class by asking the following questions:

You are a Japanese person who is almost old enough to be a warrior. You know that the emperor is a god on earth, and you know that as a Japanese, you are fated to win all conflicts. At least you have so far. The Chinese cannot withstand you; the Russians are at your mercy. For such a small set of islands to conquer giant nations is no small feat. What makes you continue to fight? Why not just stop when you have enough land and food? Why go against the most powerful nation in the world, the United States? And why fight to the death for the sake of honor? Where did you get these values? And how will you pass them on? If you are still alive when Hirohito announces that he is not God and that Japan is not fated to rule the earth, what will your reaction be? Will you still pass on the heritage which has been taught to you, or will you have to adopt a new value system? How will you do this?

Did You Know?—On December 4, 1941, three days before the attack on Pearl Harbor, Frank Knox, U.S. secretary of the navy said, "Whatever happens, the U.S. Navy is not going to be caught napping."

Did America Know?—A debate goes on over whether America knew about the attack on Pearl Harbor before it happened. Henry C. Clausen, a JAG (judge advocate general) attorney for the navy, was commissioned to study this controversial issue. He has written a book about his experiences. He found out that Japan's code had been broken long before the attack and America was regularly decoding messages sent to many places, among them Washington (to the ambassadors), Honolulu, Berlin, London, Rome, and Tokyo. Many of the messages in the latter part of 1941 indicated increasing tensions between Japan and the United States, and a few even sent specific numbers and types of ships stationed at Pearl Harbor. Did we know or didn't we?

The Japanese attack on Pearl Harbor caught the United States off-guard but also brought America into the war.

stood up to the military faction. In 1937, not satisfied with Manchuria, Japan launched a war against China. Although China was bigger, the superior Japanese army seized large chunks of Chinese territory. In 1940 Japan officially entered World War II on the side of the Axis, but it had already been fighting in China for almost ten years.

The United States criticized Japanese aggression and sought ways to stop it. To prevent American interference with their conquests, the Japanese launched a surprise attack. They bombed the American naval base at **Pearl Harbor,** Hawaii, in 1941. This attack destroyed or damaged a large part of the U.S. Navy in the Pacific. In response to this attack, America entered the war.

For six months after Pearl Harbor, the Japanese enjoyed spectacular success. They took American territories, such as the Philippines, and British territories, such as Burma. Their army and navy seemed unstoppable. Soon they controlled most of China, Southeast Asia, and many islands in the Pacific Ocean. The Japanese enforced their rule with fierce cruelty. They used prisoners of war for bayonet practice and used others as slave labor for their building projects. The peoples of Asia began to rally to the Allies against the Japanese.

It took time for the United States to recover from Pearl Harbor. But finally at the **Battle of Midway Island** in 1942, the Americans defeated the Japanese fleet. The tide of war turned. The United States began to take back, one by one, the islands controlled by Japan. After three and one-half years of fighting and

The atomic blast on Hiroshima left the city a ruined shell.

World War II Review—Review Chapter 15. Discuss terms such as *kamikaze* and *shogun*. What were some things that led Japan to attack America? (*Japan thought it could not be beaten; America was anti-Japan before America's entrance into the war; the emperor of Japan was supposedly a god, and he wanted them to do so.*)

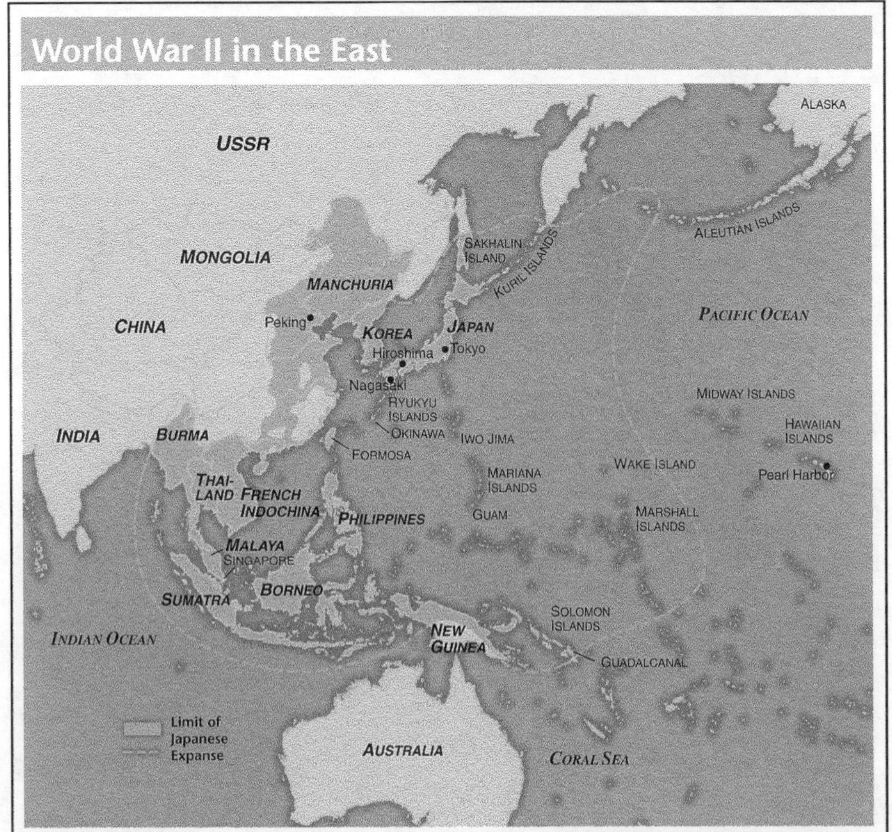

hundreds of thousands of casualties, the United States ended the war by dropping two atomic bombs in 1945. One fell on the city of Hiroshima and the other on the city of Nagasaki. Large portions of these Japanese cities were destroyed, and Japan surrendered.

Section Review

1. Name and describe each of Sun Yat-sen's Three Principles of the People.
2. Who became leader of the Kuomintang after Sun Yat-sen? Who was his main Communist opponent?
3. Where did the Nationalists establish their government after the Communist takeover in 1949?
4. What does it mean to say that a country, such as Japan, has been "westernized"?
5. What nation did Japan defeat in a war in 1895? in 1904-5?
6. What section of China did Japan attack in 1931?
7. On what two Japanese cities did the United States drop atomic bombs?

Explain why the samurai (warrior) image is a useful way to describe Japan up to the end of World War II.

For a color version of the map on this page, see page A13 in the Appendix.

The Pacific Theater—Japan was increasing its land holdings in China, much to the consternation of Britain and the United States. The Japanese decided to conquer more land in Indochina and then help Germany against Soviet Russia, another enemy. They began to do this, and Roosevelt froze all Japanese assets in the United States until Japan withdrew from Manchuria and China. The Japanese decided this could not happen and that they had better attack before the American navy could bring its forces against Japan.

The attack on Pearl Harbor was a complete surprise. After having many of the United States' planes and battleships destroyed, America had to regroup before it could be successful against Japan. Japan next attacked the Philippines and captured them.

After the Battle of Midway, the American forces took Guadalcanal and made their way across other strategic islands in a strategy called "island hopping" before finally forcing Japan to surrender by dropping the atomic bombs on Hiroshima and Nagasaki.

The Atomic Bomb—Truman knew that the Japanese would fight to the last man before surrendering. His decision to use the bomb was made to save American and Allied lives and to force Japan to surrender through this fearfully destructive and unknown weapon.

The *Enola Gay* was the plane flown to Hiroshima, piloted by Col. Paul W. Tibbetts; the bomb itself was called "Little Boy." The plane to Nagasaki was named *Bock's Car*.

Section Review Answers

1. Nationalism—that the Chinese should rule themselves; Democracy—formation of a constitutional government in which all Chinese were considered equal; Livelihood—providing every Chinese man with the means to support himself and his family
2. Chiang Kai-shek; Mao Zedong
3. Taiwan (or Formosa)
4. that it has shaped its culture in a manner similar to that of the United States and Europe
5. China; Russia
6. Manchuria
7. Hiroshima and Nagasaki

Answers will vary. The samurai is a good image for describing Japan to the end of World War II because the Japanese directed their national efforts toward military conquest.

Student Objectives

Students should be able to

1. Locate Asia on a map.
2. Analyze and create pie graphs.

Sports—Because of the mountainous regions, winter sports such as ice skating and skiing are very popular. Japan hosted the Winter Olympics in 1972 in Sapporo and in 1993 in Nagano.

Changeless Japan—The actual landscape of Japan has changed very little over the years. This is not because Japan's people have stayed the same but because the population of Japan inhabits such a small percentage of the land.

SETTINGS—Japan

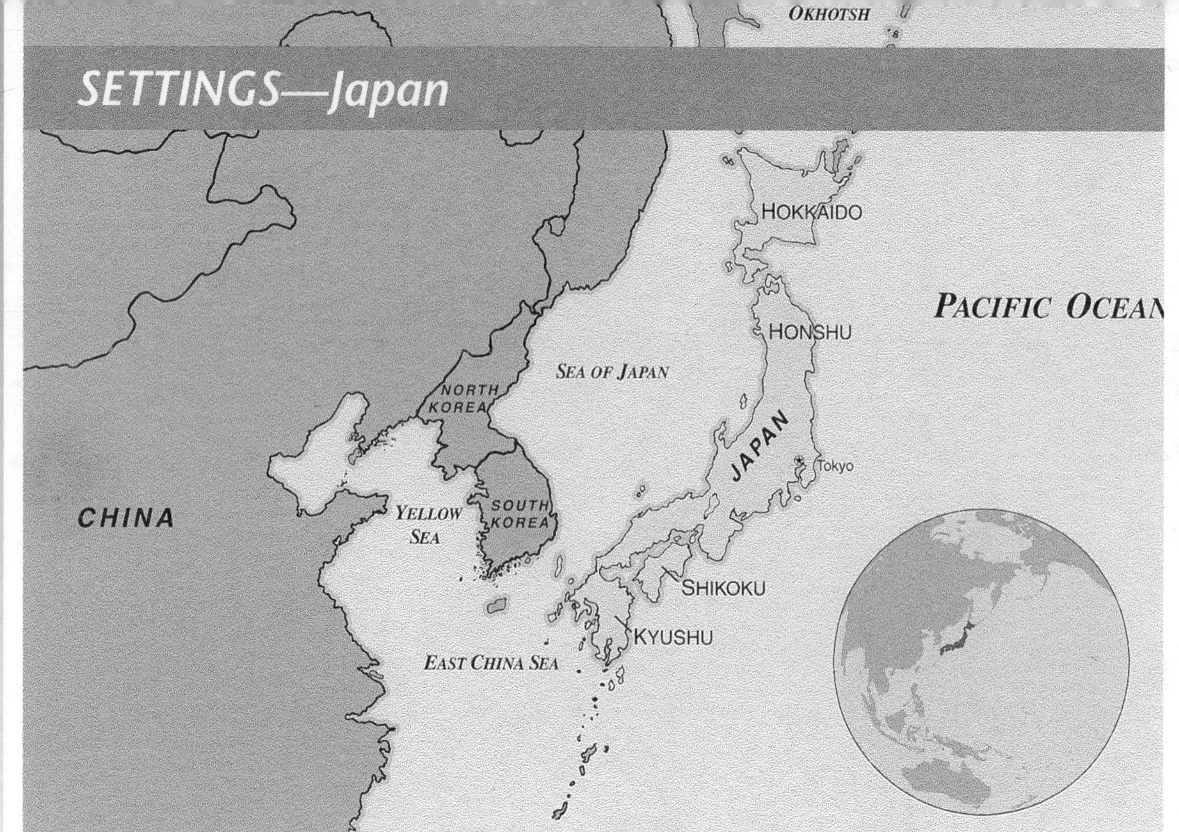

Location—Japan is a chain of islands located in the Pacific Ocean east of Russia, Korea, and China. At its closest, Japan is less than 150 miles off the Asian mainland.

Climate—The southern half of Japan has a humid subtropical climate; the northern half has a humid continental climate. Japan's temperate climate varies from north to south, much as the climate varies along the eastern coast of the United States. Average temperatures range from winter lows of 21°F in the north to summer highs of 79°F in the south. Japan receives an annual average of fifty inches of precipitation.

Topography—Japan is made up of four main islands (Hokkaido, Honshu, Shikoku, and Kyushu) and thousands of smaller islands. The Japanese islands are really the peaks of submerged mountains, and thus much of the land is mountainous. The Japanese Alps on the island of Honshu include Mt. Fuji, Japan's highest mountain (12,388 ft.). Many of the mountains are volcanoes. Some volcanoes are still active, but most, such as Mt. Fuji, are dormant.

Natural Resources—Japan has few natural resources. Its mountainous terrain leaves less than 15 percent of the land available for farming. About two-thirds of Japan is covered with forests. Small deposits of coal, zinc, copper, lead, and gold occur. The many short, swift rivers are used to provide electricity and to irrigate rice paddies.

Geography and Culture—Living on islands encouraged the Japanese people to use the sea for

486 Chapter 17

Materials

- Wall map of Asia and Japan (BLM 17-2)
- Transparencies for Chapter 17

Map Activity—Use map 17-C from the Student Activities manual to reinforce the geography lesson.

Going Beyond—Read the Settings pages and answer the questions. Use a map of South and Southeast Asia to discuss China, India, and Japan (TT 17-A).

Teach your students how to use a pie graph (TT 17-B). Have them create a pie graph of some other set of statistics, such as what types of drinks they had at lunch. *(Example: 55% had tea, 25% had a soft drink, 10% had milk, 5% had water, and 5% had nothing.)*

transportation and food. Japan's closeness to China also led to a great deal of Chinese influence on Japan's arts and religion. Japan has always faced problems because of its small size, large population, and limited resources. Sometimes this situation has caused Japan to seek to expand through military conquest. At other times, the scarce resources and large population have encouraged the Japanese to be creative and efficient.

Asia Today—Asia consists of forty-nine countries today. Located there are some of the largest countries in the world—China, India, and Asian Russia—and some of the smallest countries in the world—Bahrain, the Maldives, and Singapore (each less than three hundred square miles.

Settings Review

1. In what ocean is Japan located?
2. What are the four main islands of Japan?
3. What is Japan's tallest mountain?
4. What country greatly influenced Japan's arts and religion?

Why would Japan's small size, large population, and limited resources encourage the Japanese to be creative and efficient?

In the shadow of beautiful Mt. Fuji, the Japanese people learn to balance the old ways with the new.

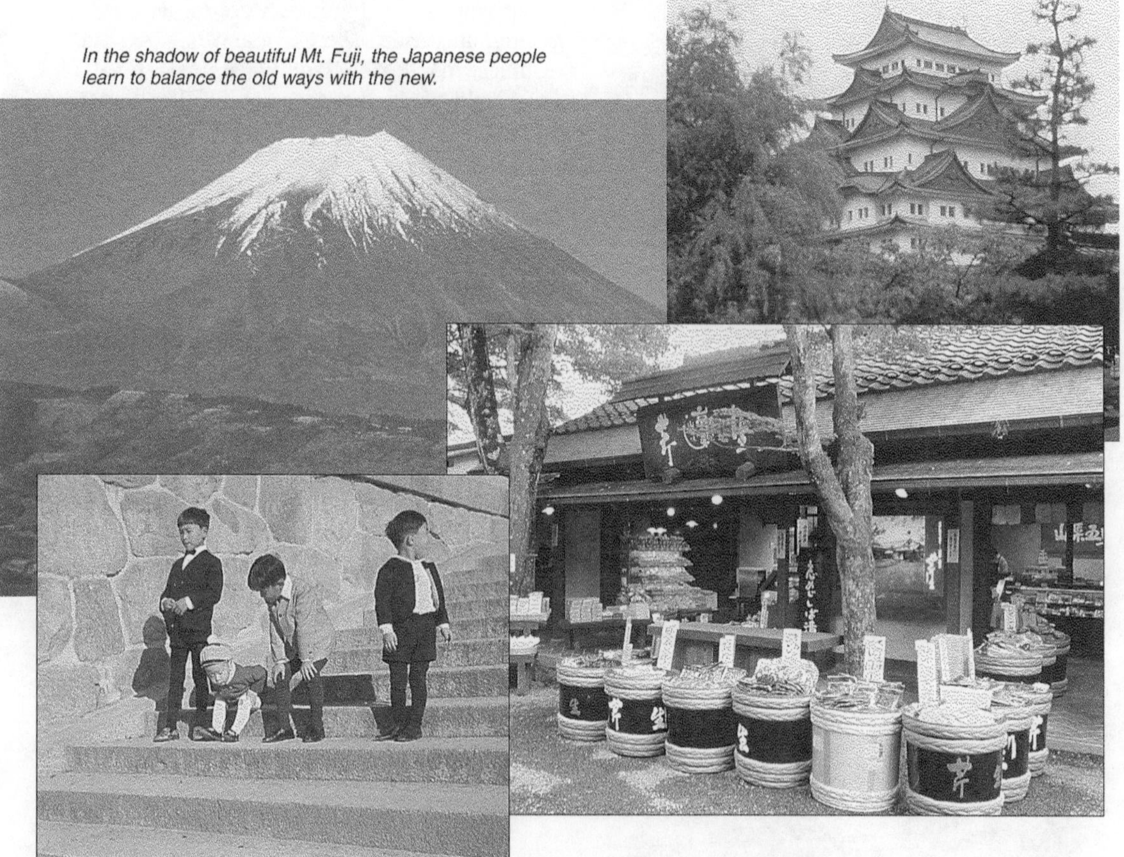

Settings Review Answers

1. Pacific
2. Hokkaido, Honshu, Shikoku, and Kyushu
3. Mt. Fuji
4. China

Answers will vary. Since the Japanese had limited resources but great needs, they learned to be efficient in what they used so that they could preserve their resources and get as much use from them as possible. They were creative because they had to find ways to get along without some resources.

SECTION 2

Student Objectives
Students should be able to

1. Recognize the proper names for the two countries of China.
2. Identify the second twentieth-century Communist leader of China.
3. Evaluate China's response to the call for democracy at Tiananmen Square.
4. Describe in their own words the problems in Korea and Vietnam.
5. Contrast Japan before and after World War II.

Taiwan—Nationalist China (Taiwan) was the accepted China in the United Nations for a few years after Chiang fled the mainland. However, the UN eventually changed its policy and allowed Communist China the status of true China. In fact, today the UN does not recognize Taiwan as an independent country. However, United States ships and others patrol the waters between Taiwan and China to guard Taiwan against the country to which it supposedly belongs.

The Communist and the Capitalist

Before World War II, the world rightly saw Japan as a dangerous aggressor and sympathized with China as the victim of outside aggression and inner disorder. After China fell to the Communists, that view changed. China became the aggressor who endangered peace and freedom in Asia. Japan, however, embraced democracy and capitalism. It became a wealthy and stable power for progress in Asia.

Chinese Communists worked diligently to bring the young into their party and indoctrinate them with Communist teachings.

Communist China

The Chinese Communists called their nation the **People's Republic of China.** It is also called Mainland China or Communist China to distinguish it from **Nationalist China** on the island of Taiwan. When the Communists took over, many Chinese rejoiced. They believed that prosperity would now come to their land. But they were dead wrong.

Living Under Communism

Many people had died during the Chinese civil war, but many more were to die under Communist rule. The Communists urged the Chinese to kill "rich" land owners and officials of the old Nationalist government. (The "rich" included those unlucky enough to own as little as thirty acres of property.) Probably two million people were killed or died in prison in the first years of Communist rule.

Those who lived suffered the loss of their freedoms. As in the Soviet Union and other Communist countries, the people could not write or speak as they thought. They could not travel to another city without permission. Of course, the atheistic Communists took away the freedom of the Chinese to worship as they wished.

The leaders of Communist China cared little for the people. Mao Zedong said he did not fear war, even nuclear war. "We may lose more than 300 million people," he said. "So what? War is war. The years will pass and we'll get to work producing more babies than ever before." In the late 1950s, Mao tried to reorganize Chinese agriculture and industry in what he called the **Great Leap Forward.** The result was a famine that killed nineteen million Chinese in 1960 alone.

SECTION 2

Materials

- Periodical articles relating to Tiananmen Square
- Pictures of Asia
- Guest speaker, a veteran of the Korean or Vietnam Conflict
- Video of China or Japan
- Nintendo (optional)

In Another's Shoes—Have each student pretend he is a Chinese nationalist who must flee mainland China for Taiwan in 1949 because of Communist oppression. He should write a one-page story about his flight. What happens on the journey? What adventures, dangerous or otherwise, does he face? What sights does he see? Whom does he meet?

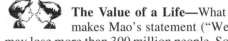

The Value of a Life—What makes Mao's statement ("We may lose more than 300 million people. So what?") so abhorrent to most Western cultures? *(Westerners have a heritage of Christianity and regard life as sacred.)* What influenced Mao to make such a statement? *(the enormous population in China, the Chinese acceptance of death and sorrow, and a disregard for the masses)* Is Mao's attitude toward the value of life still evident in China? *(yes)* How? *(in the one-child policy, which requires women to have an abortion if they become pregnant with a second child)*

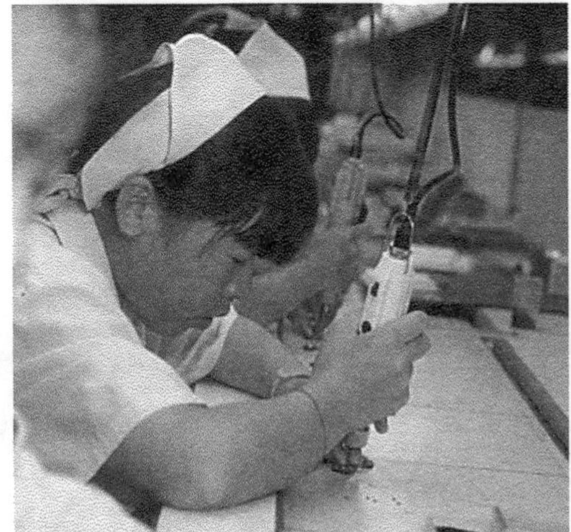

Communist China's attempts at economic reform have spurred some industrialization in that nation.

When Mao died in 1976, many Chinese hoped conditions would get better. Eventually a new ruler emerged, **Deng Xiaoping** (DUNG SHYOU-PING). He promised to reform China's economy. Deng persuaded foreign companies to invest in Chinese businesses and industries. Soon American companies such as McDonald's fast-food restaurants sprang up in Chinese cities. The government also set quotas for family farms to meet and told the farmers they could keep any extra food they produced to eat or sell for a profit. Factory workers began receiving bonuses for good work. China seemed to be turning to a form of capitalism. Deng even said in 1986, "To get rich is not a sin."

China was still a dictatorship, however. The Communist leaders needed money to survive, but they would grant no political freedom. In April of 1989, a group of students took over **Tiananmen Square** in the capital of Beijing. They called for reform of corruption and greater political freedom. As a symbol of their movement, they built a thirty-foot replica of the Statue of Liberty. The Communist authorities cracked down. Tanks rolled into Tiananmen Square and routed the students out. Two thousand people died in the putting down of the protest. The heart of Chinese Communism had not changed.

China's Wars

After it fell to Communism, China sought to spread Communism throughout Southeast Asia just as the Soviet Union was doing elsewhere in the world. Noting Churchill's description of a Communist "iron curtain" in Europe, some observers spoke of a "bamboo curtain" between freedom and Communism in Asia. China's first major battleground was Korea.

In 1950 Communist North Korea invaded South Korea, a non-Communist state since 1948. To help South Korea, the United Nations sent troops, most of them American. When it

A brave student stands up to Communist tanks at Tiananmen Square. Just after this picture was taken, he was pulled to safety.

Tiananmen Square In 1987, party leader Hu resigned. He had been too much of a reformer for the old hard-line Communists. When he died in 1989, students started many demonstrations in protest of the government opposition to Hu. When the students started these demonstrations, Deng changed his palace guard out of fear, just as Stalin used to do. The students were ordered to disband for the upcoming visit from Mikhail Gorbachev. They refused, and Gorbachev said, "I could not figure out who was in charge." Humiliated, the Chinese government geared up for military action while apparently leaving the students alone. In June 1989, soldiers opened fire on the unarmed protesters in and around Tiananmen Square. Tyranny is not dead in China.

Tiananmen Square—Find some periodicals such as *Newsweek*, *Time*, or *U.S. News and World Report* from 1989 (April-June) with information on and pictures of Tiananmen Square during the student takeover and government reaction. Encourage your students to read one of the articles or show them some of the pictures.

Internet Activity—Scan the Internet for information on Chinese civil rights.

Asia—Bring in pictures of Asia for your students to see. You may want to use pictures of the wars in China, a Japanese *kamikaze,* Hiroshima or Nagasaki after the bombs were dropped, soldiers in Korea and Vietnam, and so forth. The library usually has good picture books, such as Time-Life's books on the World Wars, relating to these events.

Conflict or War?—Remind your students that war was never actually declared by America in Korea or Vietnam, so technically each was called a conflict. However, this did not stop the soldiers from witnessing every atrocity of war, and by every other standard, it certainly was a war.

Kimchi—One interesting food that the Koreans eat is called *kimchi*. This is eaten with every meal, breakfast included. The general recipe calls for cabbage to be pickled in spices, sealed tightly, then allowed to ferment. The resulting *kimchi* is then eaten. It is usually very spicy.

American Opinion—American opinion turned radically against the war in Asia, especially in Vietnam. This was during the sixties, when peace became the all-encompassing goal. The media played a large part in shaping American opinion. The same was true in the Persian Gulf War, during which the opposite attitude toward war was greatly expressed. Everything in America—the advertising, songs, and talk—were about our great heroes in the Persian Gulf. Soldiers were welcomed home with parades, banners, ribbons, and confetti. Americans tied yellow ribbons " 'round the old oak tree" in anticipation of some friend or family member's homecoming.

looked as though the UN forces would defeat North Korea, China poured two hundred thousand soldiers into Korea to help the Communist cause. The **Korean War** dragged on until 1953 as the Chinese kept sending in men to help North Korea. Finally, the two sides signed an armistice in which neither side was the winner. North and South Korea have remained separate countries, the North Communist and the South free. China suffered one million casualties in the war.

A Korean mother and her child flee the war as an American tank rumbles by.

The spread of Communism in Asia next shifted south to Indochina and the country of Vietnam, a former French colony. During World War II the Communists had grown strong in northern Vietnam. After the war, the French tried to retake control of Vietnam, but the Communists resisted them. War broke out, and the French were unable to defeat the Communists. In 1954 the French left, and the country of Vietnam was split into North (Communist) and South (free) Vietnam.

French soldiers in Vietnam question a suspected Communist.

Other countries became interested in this **Vietnam War.** The Soviet Union and Communist China continued to support the Vietnamese Communists. Supplies for North Vietnam flowed across China's borders. The United States took up the cause of South Vietnam. In 1964 the U.S. Congress voted to send combat troops to help the South Vietnamese.

The fighting in the jungles of Vietnam was hard and bloody. Like the conflict in Korea, this war dragged on, but for even longer than in Korea. Many Americans began to protest the war. Some wanted peace, no matter what it cost, even if it left the South Vietnamese at the mercy of Communism. Finally in 1973 both sides reached an agreement for American forces to leave. The

Connections—Invite to your class a veteran from the Korean or Vietnam Conflict. Have him give a brief account of his time on the front. (These testimonials usually take longer than might be expected. Do not try to limit the speaker to five or ten minutes.) Your students will be fascinated by what they can only imagine. If possible, have the guest tell about American opinion of the war. After the speaker finishes, ask your students how they would support (or not support) an American war. What types of things would they do? What would show their patriotism best?

Picture Analysis—Look at the picture on the bottom of this page with your students. Discuss what you see in the face of the prisoner. He is also very young. Ask your students why they think most soldiers are so young. *(Some reasons include physical fitness, government drafting, and passions of the young.)*

World War II left Japan devastated.

troops withdrew, leaving South Vietnam unsupported. Two years later the Communists attacked and took over all of Vietnam and also the neighboring countries of Laos and Cambodia. The fall of China to Communism in 1949 had led to Communist enslavement throughout Southeast Asia.

Capitalist Japan

When World War II ended in 1945, the United States began to supervise the government of Japan. The Emperor **Hirohito** stunned the nation by going on the radio and announcing that he was not a god and that it was not true "that the Japanese people are superior to other races and fated to rule the world." Japan established a new republican government. The constitution called for a parliament elected by the people and a prime minister to lead the country. It prohibited Japan from rebuilding its army.

Cities were rebuilt after the destruction of warfare. Factories began to produce peacetime products. Before the war, for example, the Japanese had produced high quality lenses that were used in bombsights and other weapons. After the war, these lenses helped Japan build a profitable industry in manufacturing cameras. Trade with other nations was restored. After World War II China adopted Communism and became a harsh dictatorship. Japan adopted the capitalism of the West and became a prosperous, democratic nation.

Since World War II, Japan's economy has grown. This little island country produces everything from giant oil tanker ships to automobiles to tiny transistor radios and digital watches. Electronics has been a special strength of Japanese industry. The Japanese have produced high quality televisions, computers, stereo equipment, and other electronic items. In fact,

A Japanese officer weeps as he hears Emperor Hirohito's surrender address.

Art and Architecture—Much of Japan's artwork was influenced by ancient China. Sculpture and bronze work were usually Buddhas that the people worshiped. Paintings were usually landscapes. Other artwork included lacquer, ceramics, and *cloisonné*, an enameling process.

Architecture was simple and refined, most buildings being made of wood. These buildings were not nailed or screwed together but were held together by wooden pegs. Some buildings dating from the sixth and seventh centuries still stand today. Even before the influence of Buddhism, Shinto shrines with their *torii* gates and pagodas were common.

Media in War—Discuss with your students what effects the media have on national and world opinion. Read the information in the margin on page 490 and discuss why the media are able to wield such power. Knowing this, what could the student do to keep his opinions on national or world affairs in line with biblical teaching?

Did You Know?—In 1958 *Business Week* said, "With over 50 foreign cars already on sale here, the Japanese auto industry isn't likely to carve out a big slice of the U.S. market."

Japanese industry, destroyed by the war, rebounded and has made Japan a major industrial power.

Japan has replaced the United States as the major manufacturer for many of these items. Because Japan lacks farmland and natural resources, it imports food and raw materials. In return, it exports its manufactured goods to other countries.

The Japanese have become world leaders in producing consumer goods, such as electronics.

In addition to being well made, Japanese products often cost less than similar items made in America or Europe. The main reason is that Japanese workers usually make less money than Americans or Western Europeans. Since the labor to make Japanese products costs less, the price is lower. This does not mean, however, that Japanese workers are poorer. They also pay less for the goods they make. Most Japanese are able to buy the basic modern conveniences that Americans enjoy. They live in comfortable apartments and houses, and most families have a car.

Other nations have noted Japan's path to prosperity and have followed. After fleeing to Taiwan, Chiang Kai-shek molded that island's economy on the pattern of the West. Today, the wealth of Taiwan per person is five times greater than that of Communist China. After its destructive war with North Korea, South Korea rebuilt its economy as Japan did. Now South Korea generates twenty times more

"Home" work—Assign your students to find every item they can in their home that was made in Japan. These will probably be items like a VCR, radios, and other electronic equipment. They should make a list and bring it to school. You may also want to have them look for other Asian-made goods, such as those made in Taiwan, Hong Kong, or China.

Imports—Some people are convinced that every American should buy only American-made products so that U.S. workers will not lose jobs. Debate the advantages and disadvantages of this view and the view that Americans should be able to buy whatever product they want from wherever they want. Many imports are bought because they are less expensive. When Americans are free to buy the least expensive products, what do they usually do with their extra money? *(spend it on other products or services)* wealth each year than North Korea does. Singapore, a former British colony in Southeast Asia, also adopted a capitalist economy when it became independent in 1965. Today it has one of the highest rates of income per person in Asia. Not all of these states have been as democratic as Japan, but they do provide more liberty than Communist states. They have realized that Japan, not China, offers the better model for peace and prosperity.

Plastics—The Japanese make many plastic products, some of which house their electronics. They also make plastic clothing, helmets, shoes, and jewelry.

Singapore—Singapore, like Hong Kong, is one of the busiest ports in Southeast Asia. The per capita income is very high, partly because of Singapore's *free port* trading. No import duties are paid on goods. This makes Singapore a very desirable trading center and lowers the cost of goods.

Singapore has many strict laws to keep it running smoothly and to keep it clean. Chewing gum is forbidden in the city. Offenders can be fined.

Section Review

1. What was the name of Mao Zedong's plan to reorganize Chinese agriculture and industry? What was the result?
2. What Chinese leader after Mao introduced some capitalist practices to Communist China?
3. What two countries, both the sites of major wars, were split into northern (Communist) and southern (free) parts after World War II?
4. Name at least three products that Japan began to produce in the years after World War II.
5. What other countries in Asia followed Japan's pattern of economic development?

Why would the protesting students in China use the Statue of Liberty as their symbol?

The nation of Singapore symbolizes the western-style prosperity characterizing Asian nations that have embraced capitalist economies.

China or Japan—Show your students a video about China or Japan, including its history and present-day culture and geography.

Section Review Answers

1. Great Leap Forward; a famine that killed 19 million people in 1960 alone
2. Deng Xiaoping
3. Korea and Vietnam
4. cameras, oil tanker ships, automobiles, transistor radios, digital watches, televisions, computers, stereo equipment, video games, home entertainment systems (any three)
5. Taiwan (Nationalist China or Formosa), South Korea, Singapore

Answers will vary. The students in China used the Statue of Liberty as a symbol because it represents the liberty that they wished to have—but did not enjoy—under communist rule. Students might also mention that the protesting students saw the United States as a model for what they desired China to be.

Addiction—Another problem some have with video games is the addiction they sometimes cause. Video companies purposefully build in this feature by making games interesting with a balanced frustration level. Games must frustrate a little but not too much; they cannot be too easy or too difficult. Skill ladders are created; if the player does well, the game gets progressively harder. Though some games have methodical reinforcement (the gaining of reward the same way each time), most have random reinforcement. One never knows where the next bonus or prize will be. Auditory, visual, and emotional stimulations are added to involve more of the senses and thus draw the player in.

ANALYSIS

Nintendo: Power Through Playing

This is the story of a little card manufacturer that became one of the biggest businesses in Japan and then conquered the United States.

In 1889 the Yamauchi (yah mah OO chee) family of Kyoto, Japan, founded Nintendo Koppai as a maker of playing cards for a popular Japanese game called *hanafuda.* The company soon moved to making other kinds of cards and eventually became Japan's leading manufacturer of playing cards.

The name *Nintendo* can be translated, "Work hard, but in the end it is in heaven's hands." The story of Nintendo's success is one of hard work and good fortune. Nintendo was not hit as hard by World War II as other Japanese businesses. Part of the reason was that it was located in Kyoto, one of the few major Japanese cities not to be bombed by the Allies. When Japan's economy began to boom in the 1950s, Nintendo profited as well.

Hiroshi Yamauchi, the president of the company from 1949, realized that for his company to grow, he needed to make more than just playing cards. In 1970 Nintendo began to produce toys and games. Then in 1977 the company produced

its first video game. This was the first step in carrying Nintendo to worldwide fame.

Since the Japanese were becoming world leaders in electronics, Nintendo had the idea of using a computer to drive its games. In 1983 the company introduced its first game system: "Famicom." This computer-driven system allowed the Japanese to play electronic games on their televisions.

The idea behind Famicom was to sell the system for a relatively cheap price in order to sell many games. Nintendo made this strategy work by producing popular games. Its first big hit was *Donkey Kong* in 1981. It was sold first as an "arcade game" (one set up in places like shopping malls) and later as a home video game. The creator of the game, Shigeru Miyamoto, intended the unusual name of the game to mean something like "goofy gorilla." At any rate, it was a success. The game also introduced Mario, the short, mustached hero who fought the gorilla. Mario became Nintendo's best-known symbol.

Nintendo decided that it should next launch its home game system in the United States. This would be a challenge. When Nintendo decided to sell its system in the United States in 1985, everyone said it couldn't be done. An American company, called Atari, had launched the video game craze in 1972 and had built a huge business. But poor planning—and dull games—caused Atari to collapse in 1984. Experts said the home video-game industry was dead.

Nintendo—If you have a Nintendo system, play a game for fun. Then discuss why the Yamauchi family has been so successful with the system. Make sure that the game is not offensive or violent and that it does not have occult elements.

Undaunted, Nintendo invaded the United States. By 1985 American kids and their parents were flocking to stores to buy an NES (Nintendo Entertainment System) and the games to go with it. When Nintendo launched its SNES (Super Nintendo Entertainment System) in 1991, the units sold at the rate of one every five seconds. In 1989 Nintendo released a hand-held video-game system called "Game Boy." It sold forty thousand units the first day it was released. Nintendo's profits soared to well over a half-billion dollars a year, and "Nintendo" became a household word. During the Gulf War against Iraq in 1991, the commanding general noted all the advanced electronic technology his army was using and said that the conflict was "the first Nintendo war."

The Gulf War aside, conflict was no stranger to Nintendo. Parents worried that their children spent too much time playing the games. Others pointed with dismay to the gruesome violence and occult elements in some of the games. Competitors claimed that Nintendo was using its dominant position to pressure stores to carry only Nintendo products. The U.S. government investigated and found at least some of these charges true. Nonetheless, the Nintendo story is a remarkable example of how Japanese industry has become a major force in modern commerce.

Divisions in Modern Asia 495

Section 3

Student Objective
Students should be able to
1. Describe religion in China before and after Communism.

The Marcoses—The Marcoses fled the Philippines after a severe struggle against their dictatorship arose. Corazón Aquino then took their place. Her husband, the opposition leader, had been murdered earlier, allegedly by Marcos's supporters.

The extravagance of Imelda Marcos has been widely expressed. Her bedroom contained a double king-sized bed, a grand piano, and a Hollywood dressing room with hundreds of lights and mirrored walls. She also had many expensive French perfumes, Italian purses, and rows and rows of shoes.

Ni To-sheng—Watchman Nee was the leader of a group called the "Little Flock" in China. He was arrested along with others and served fifteen years in prison. Some rumors spread throughout China that he had been mutilated, but these were not true. He did, however, suffer from chronic illness.

Christianity in Asia

Over 250 million people in Asia are considered "Christians." That number sounds impressive, until you realize that also in Asia are over 700 million Hindus, 625 million Muslims, over 300 million Buddhists, and over 150 million atheists. Christians are a minority in Asia, and probably only a minority of those 250 million are genuine Christians. In Asia only the Philippines claims a majority of its people are Christians. Over 80 percent of Filipinos are Roman Catholic, and about 10 percent are Protestant.

There are many different kinds of Christians in Asia. India, for example, is home to the Mar Thoma ("St. Thomas") Church. This group takes its name from the legend that the apostle Thomas was the first to preach the gospel in India. Although it probably does not go back to the days of the apostles, the church's roots go back far into India's history. It is a very small group, however. Roman Catholics are the largest single Christian group, with over 100 million members.

The amount of religious freedom that Christians enjoy varies from country to country. Some countries allow as much religious freedom as the United States does. Others are very repressive. Some nations became less repressive as the twentieth century went on. Before World War II Japan was very strict in its control of religious groups. Today, Japan has perhaps the greatest religious freedom in Asia.

An Armenian church built in the tenth century typifies the many "eastern churches" (neither Roman Catholic nor Orthodox) that spread eastward across Asia during Europe's Middle Ages.

Section 3

Materials
- Prayer cards for missionaries to Asia

Missions—Using prayer cards for missionaries to Asia, have a brief prayer meeting for the missionaries. Remember that those in Communist countries are probably there as tentmakers (people who, like the apostle Paul, work a secular job in a foreign country in order to have opportunities to minister there). This may be the only way to get into the country. Today, most Asian countries gladly take English teachers as well as other skilled workers, and this is an excellent opportunity for ministry.

Ni To-sheng, known in the West as Watchman Nee

Some countries have become more repressive. For example, China allowed great freedom of religion after the 1911 revolution. The Communists, however, wanted an atheistic nation and cracked down on not only Christians but also other religious groups. The difference between China before and after the Communist revolution is seen in the career of **Ni To-sheng,** better known in the West as Watchman Nee. He was an important Christian leader during the rule of Chiang Kai-shek. Ni planted independent churches across the land and wrote popular devotional books that sold well in the West as well as in Asia. In 1952, after the Communist takeover, the government arrested Ni. He spent the rest of his life in prison and died in a prison work camp in 1972.

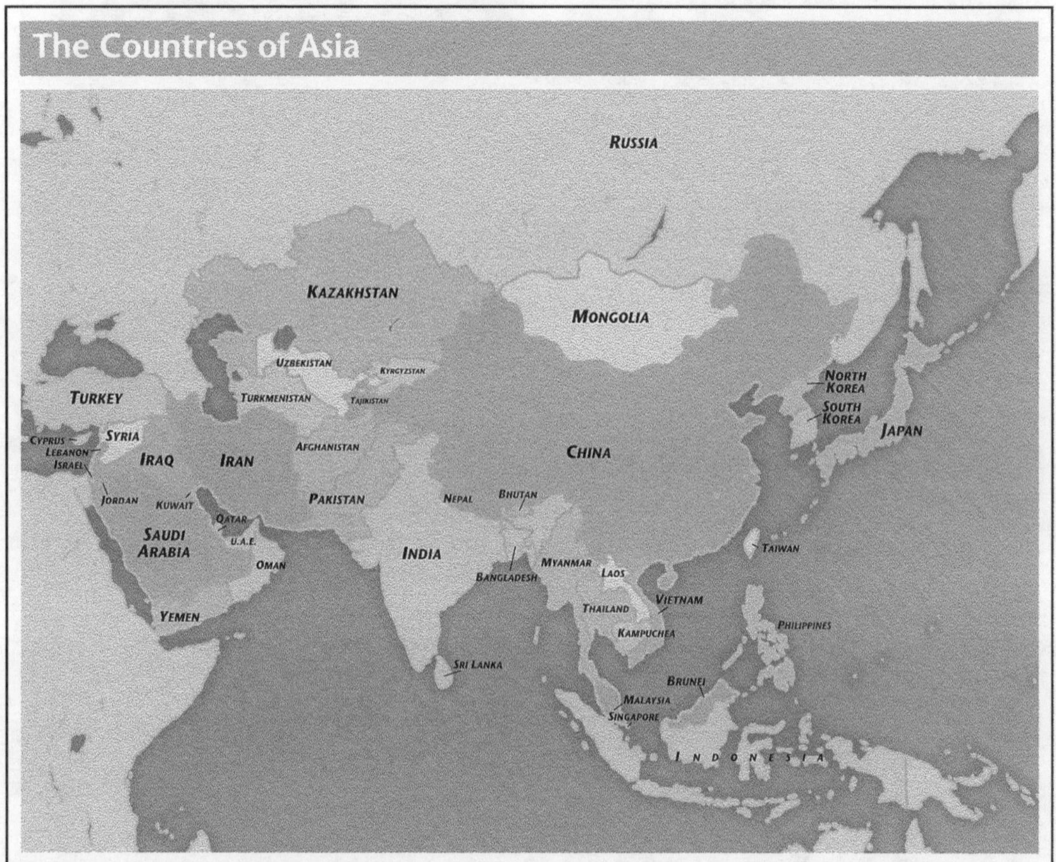

Religions in Asia—There are more than two billion people in Asia. The following chart shows the religions they represent.

Religions in Asia

Country	Religions
China	officially atheist; Buddhist, Taoist, some Muslims, some Christians
India	80% Hindu, 14% Muslim, 2% Christian, 2% Sikh
Japan	Buddhist and Shintoist shared by large majority
North Korea	activities almost nonexistent; traditionally Buddhist, Confucianist, Chondongyo
South Korea	49% Christian, 47% Buddhist
Pakistan	77% Sunni Muslim, 20% Shi'a Muslim
Philippines	83% Roman Catholic, 9% Protestant, 5% Muslim
Singapore	Buddhist, Taoist, Muslim, Christian, Hindu
Taiwan	93% mix of Buddhist, Taoist, and Confucianist; 4.5% Christian
Vietnam	mainly Buddhist and Taoist; also Roman Catholic, indigenous beliefs

Atheism—Discuss with your students why Communist nations seem to exclude God, making their religious policy one of atheism. (*If God controls the religion of the people, then the Communists have lost some control, and they do not like that. One of the reasons Communism is so bad is that God is excluded. Nothing can be run successfully that is not based on God and His Word.*)

CHARACTERIZATIONS

John Sung

Sung Shang-chieh was born in 1901 into the family of a Methodist pastor in Fukien Province in China. As a child, he claimed conversion during a revival that swept the region in which he lived. When he was eighteen, however, Sung went to the United States to study and underwent a terrible spiritual struggle.

Sung worked himself to the point of exhaustion and made a brilliant record in college. Incredibly, he finished a Ph.D. in chemistry in less than two years. But he was spiritually troubled. Sometimes Sung wondered if he were even a Christian. "The heavy burden of my soul became heavier day by day," he said, "until . . . I got to the point when I no longer had any desire to live." In the midst of this inner battle, God gave him assurance of his salvation and a conviction that he was to return to China and preach. After this, Sung took the name "John" after John the Baptist. Like John, Sung would proclaim, "Behold the Lamb of God, which taketh away the sin of the world" (John 1:29). Also like John, he would say of Christ, "He must increase, but I must decrease" (John 3:30).

Back in China, **John Sung** began an extraordinary preaching career. He preached first in his home region, then in other regions of China. A real turning point came when he preached in Nanchang in 1931. Before that meeting, Sung prayed earnestly for revival, and he saw a great awakening. At Nanchang he caught a vision for all of China, and it marked the beginning of his major evangelistic work.

Sung was a fiery, fervent preacher. An atheist once came "just to see that madman Sung jumping around the platform"; but when he heard the message, he was converted. Sung often preached for two hours at a time with breaks for the audience to sing gospel choruses. He fiercely denounced sin, especially the hypocrisy of professing Christians. His central theme was always forgiveness of sin through the cross of Jesus Christ and the shedding of His blood.

Not even crutches could keep John Sung from preaching the gospel.

To catch people's attention and drive home his point, Sung used object lessons. A missionary once decorated the platform with plants. Seeing this, Sung preached on uprooting sin in the life and uprooted all the plants one by one as he dealt with each sin. Another time he took off his outer robe as he preached and stuffed it into his shirt to represent hidden sin. Then as he talked about confessing and forsaking sin, he slowly pulled the robe out.

Preaching in China in the 1930s, Sung could not help being affected by political events. He was preaching in Manchuria in 1931 when the

Salvation Story—Using the story of John Sung, give the gospel message to your students again. Tell any who want to talk about it that you are available anytime. Do not assume that all of your students have accepted Christ as their Savior. This is rarely the case.

Japanese invaded. In fact, he preached with great effect in the city of Mukden just before the Japanese captured it. Although the Japanese allowed him to preach in areas they controlled, they would not let him go to the interior of China, which was under Nationalist control.

As the 1930s went on, Sung's crowds got bigger. Audiences numbering in the thousands crowded into auditoriums and stadiums. If nothing big enough was available, the people met in vacant lots and sat on mats to hear him. We do not know how many people found salvation in Jesus Christ through John Sung's preaching. One Christian who knew Sung studied his evangelistic campaigns from just 1933 to 1936 and estimated that one hundred thousand people professed conversion.

Because many Chinese had immigrated to Southeast Asia and the South Pacific, Sung eventually had an international impact. He made preaching tours among the 15 million Chinese living in the Philippines, Formosa (Taiwan), Thailand, Singapore, the Malay peninsula, the Dutch East Indies (modern Indonesia), Indochina, and Burma. The effects of the revivals in China, Thailand, and the Dutch East Indies helped sustain the churches through the harsh Japanese occupation of World War II.

John Sung's health was always weak. He suffered from tuberculosis and a heart condition. Finally, he developed cancer and underwent surgery late in 1940, the first of four operations. He never recovered his strength and died on August 18, 1944.

Once a liberal missionary suggested to Sung that the Chinese church could profit by the teachings of Hindu leader Mohandas Gandhi and liberal preacher Harry Emerson Fosdick. Sung replied, "China does not need the teaching of Fosdick or Gandhi. The teaching of Confucius is far better than theirs. What the Chinese need is Jesus Christ and His Cross."

Christians in a church in Singapore led by a convert from one of John Sung's campaigns are but a small part of the fruit of Sung's work in southeast Asia.

Divisions in Modern Asia 499

Religious Persecution—Legislation in China again limited freedom of religion since the government tightened up after the Beijing Massacre at Tiananmen Square. Two state council decrees prohibited any type of proselytism by foreigners and required all places of religious activity to be registered.

Freedom in America—Missionaries and Christians from other countries often marvel at Americans' freedom to worship. Simple things like singing Christian songs and hymns in church are not allowed in some countries. Remind your students of the privilege of the freedom they have.

Christians meet in house churches in Communist China.

A more recent example of repression is the treatment of **house churches** in China. Believers began meeting in private homes and formed their own congregations. The Chinese government, however, required all churches to register and considered these house churches illegal. Often Chinese officials raided house churches and arrested leaders. Some of these Christians were tortured and killed. The body of one leader was found with rope burns around his ankles that showed he had been hung in the air and beaten. One Australian evangelist arrested by the police in China said that he was told, "Too many people believe in Jesus today in China."

Korea is another example of a nation in which believers have faced persecution. In the early 1900s American Presbyterian missionaries planted thriving churches in northern Korea. A remarkable revival broke out in 1907, called by one leader the "Korean Pentecost" after the revival on the Day of Pentecost in Acts 2. But suffering followed revival. The Japanese ruled Korea from 1910 to 1945. In the worst incident of persecution, the Japanese set fire to a church and shot those who fled. Usually the Japanese simply arrested those who refused to worship at the official Shinto shrines. Many Christians died from abuse in prison. When the Communists took over North Korea after World War II, they sought to eliminate Christianity. Today South Korea has religious freedom and a large Christian population. Communist North Korea, once the site of a tremendous revival, apparently has almost no Christians.

As these incidents illustrate, God has used many different believers to spread His truth in Asia. From national Christians such as Ni To-sheng in China to the American missionaries in Korea, the heralds of the gospel came from different backgrounds. Today there are

Chinese Religious Policy—Read to your students the following paragraph from *What In The World!*, a BJUP bimonthly informational sheet to help believers know what is going on in the world today.

> Reports of widespread brutal persecution of Christians around the world continue to mount. Simple acts of worship or participation in home Bible studies often lead to threats, terrorism, imprisonment, and even death for as many as 200 million believers. . . . The government of China, in response to the growing and still illegal "house church" movement, has declared its official policy to be the "need to strangle [this] baby while it is still in the manger" (*Citizen*, March 1998).

many Christians in Asia, but there are many, many more people who need to hear the gospel of Jesus Christ. Christians around the world should pray for Asia, give to further the gospel there, and consider going themselves as missionaries. As Jesus said, "The harvest truly is great, but the labourers are few: pray ye therefore the Lord of the harvest, that he would send forth labourers into his harvest." (Luke 10:2)

Section Review

1. What is the only nation in Asia that claims a majority of its citizens are Christians?
2. According to legend, who was the first person to preach the gospel in India?
3. What is the largest Christian group in Asia?
4. By what name is Ni To-sheng better known in the West?

Why would Christians call a revival like the one in Korea in 1907 a "Pentecost"? (See Acts 2.)

Summary

Like all continents, Asia has seen triumphs and tragedies. The nation of India rejoiced in winning its independence from Great Britain in 1947. Yet the new nation suffered from poverty and violence. China established a republic in 1911. But the nation suffered from terrible civil wars until 1949 when the Communists imposed their tyranny on the land. Not satisfied with that conquest, the Communists attempted to make all of Korea Communist and succeeded in moving into Southeast Asia. Japan embraced the technology of the West and modernized their country. Then the Japanese used that technology to launch wars of conquest that ended only with the near destruction of the nation in World War II. At least in the case of Japan and a few other nations such as South Korea, the last half of the twentieth century saw a growth of democratic government and economic prosperity. Perhaps the greatest triumph for Asia was the success of both Asians and missionaries in spreading across the continent the good news of salvation through Christ.

Spanning the Ages

Controversy exists elsewhere besides Asia. Strong religious backgrounds have driven deep wedges in many parts of the Middle East. At the same time that Communism was taking over China, Israel was granted land in which to gather again as a nation. The nations around her are not friendly, and many of them have tried to rid themselves of this enemy. The next chapter focuses on the Middle East. There the conflict centers on religious rather than political beliefs.

Section Review Answers

1. the Philippines
2. the apostle Thomas
3. Roman Catholic
4. Watchman Nee

Answers will vary. The events of the Day of Pentecost in Acts 2 are an example of a great revival. Students may note specific characteristics, such as the repentance of the hearers and the many conversions.

Chapter Review Ideas

Play the Kamikaze Game. The students will be divided into two groups. Each group should line up against an opposite wall of the classroom and across the front. One student from each team comes to the middle front as opponents. You will ask a question about the chapter. The student who answers correctly first is the winner. The other one, whether he answers incorrectly, not at all, or later than the other, receives one strike. They shift to the end of the lines, and the next students in the lines do the same thing. Three strikes and you're out: the student must sit down on his third strike. This may cause the lines to be somewhat unbalanced as the game goes on; just transfer some students from the longer line to the shorter. The last two must repeat until one of them has three strikes; the other is the winner of the game.

You should encourage the students to write out the terms and their definitions on flash cards for more review. These are more convenient to study from.

Chapter Enrichment Activities

Research—For a research project, you may have your students go to the library or search the Internet to find an article about Tiananmen Square. They should write a report on their findings.

Elections—Send (or have the students send) for information on the next election's candidates and their party policies, also called their platform (the issues on which they will run). A report should be written for at least two of the candidates for any specific office.

CHAPTER REVIEW

People, Places, and Things to Know

Sun Yat-sen	Long March	People's Republic of China	Korean War
Three Principles of the People	Mohandas Gandhi	Nationalist China	Vietnam War
Kuomintang	civil disobedience	Great Leap Forward	Hirohito
warlords	"westernizing"	Deng Xiaoping	Ni To-sheng
Chiang Kai-shek	Manchuria	Tiananmen Square	John Sung
Mao Zedong	Pearl Harbor		house churches
	Battle of Midway Island		

Review Questions

Matching

Match the following terms to their definitions.

1. Kuomintang
2. westernizing
3. bamboo curtain
4. shogun
5. civil disobedience

(a) Becoming like the United States and Europe
(b) Disobeying laws that one thinks are unjust
(c) Nationalist Party in China
(d) "Great general"
(e) Imaginary line between free and Communist Asia

Matching

Match the following people to their contributions.

6. Hirohito
7. John Sung
8. Sigeru Miyamoto
9. Deng Xiaoping
10. Mohandas Gandhi
11. Chiang Kai-shek
12. Mao Zedong

(a) Led the drive for Indian independence
(b) Preached the gospel throughout China and across Southeast Asia and the South Pacific
(c) Attempted a Great Leap Forward in Chinese industry and agriculture
(d) Encouraged American companies to invest in Communist China
(e) Told the Japanese people that he was not a god
(f) Established a government on Taiwan
(g) Developed *Donkey Kong*

Chapter Review Answers

Matching

1. c
2. a
3. e
4. d
5. b
6. e

Matching

7. b
8. g
9. d
10. a
11. f
12. c

Chronology

Locate the following events in the chapter and put them in chronological order from the earliest to the latest.

13. South Vietnam falls to Communism.
14. Ni To-sheng is arrested by the government of Communist China.
15. India wins its independence from Great Britain.
16. Nintendo introduces its home game system to the United States.
17. China overthrows the Manchu dynasty.
18. Japan sinks Russia's Baltic fleet.
19. The United States drops atomic bombs on Hiroshima and Nagasaki.
20. Korean War begins.
21. Japan attacks Manchuria.
22. Students protest Communist tyranny in Tiananmen Square in Beijing.

Think About It!

How does the story of Japan in the twentieth century reveal the advantages and the dangers of modernization and westernization?

Recipe: Crab and Corn Porridge— Since Koreans live on a peninsula, much of their food comes from the ocean. This recipe combines seafood with corn.

Ingredients:
- 2½ cups basic chicken broth or 1 can condensed cream of chicken soup
- 11 oz. can corn kernels, drained
- 11 oz. can creamed corn
- 11 oz. can crabmeat, drained
- 1 egg
- 2 scallions, cut into thin rings

If using condensed soup, add two cans of mixed water and milk. Bring the broth or soup to just below the boiling point. Add the corn kernels and creamed corn to the broth. Add crabmeat and stir thoroughly. Beat the egg quickly and, holding a fork over the broth, pour the beaten egg along the back of the fork head, moving the fork in a circular motion at the same time. Remove from the heat and cover. Allow to set for about 40 seconds. Sprinkle with scallions, stir once, and serve hot.

Chronology

18. Japan sinks Russia's Baltic fleet.
17. China overthrows the Manchu dynasty.
21. Japan attacks Manchuria.
19. The United States drops atomic bombs on Hiroshima and Nagasaki.
15. India wins its independence from Great Britain.
20. Korean War begins.
14. Ni To-sheng is arrested by the government of Communist China.
13. South Vietnam falls to Communism.
16. Nintendo introduces its home game system to the United States.
22. Students protest Communist tyranny in Tiananmen Square in Beijing.

Think About It!

Answers will vary. Japan's history in the twentieth century reveals how modern, Western ways can enrich a nation; strengthen it economically, militarily, and politically; and eventually provide an avenue for democratic government. At the same time, Japan's behavior until the end of World War II shows how these benefits can be turned to evil purposes.

Canada

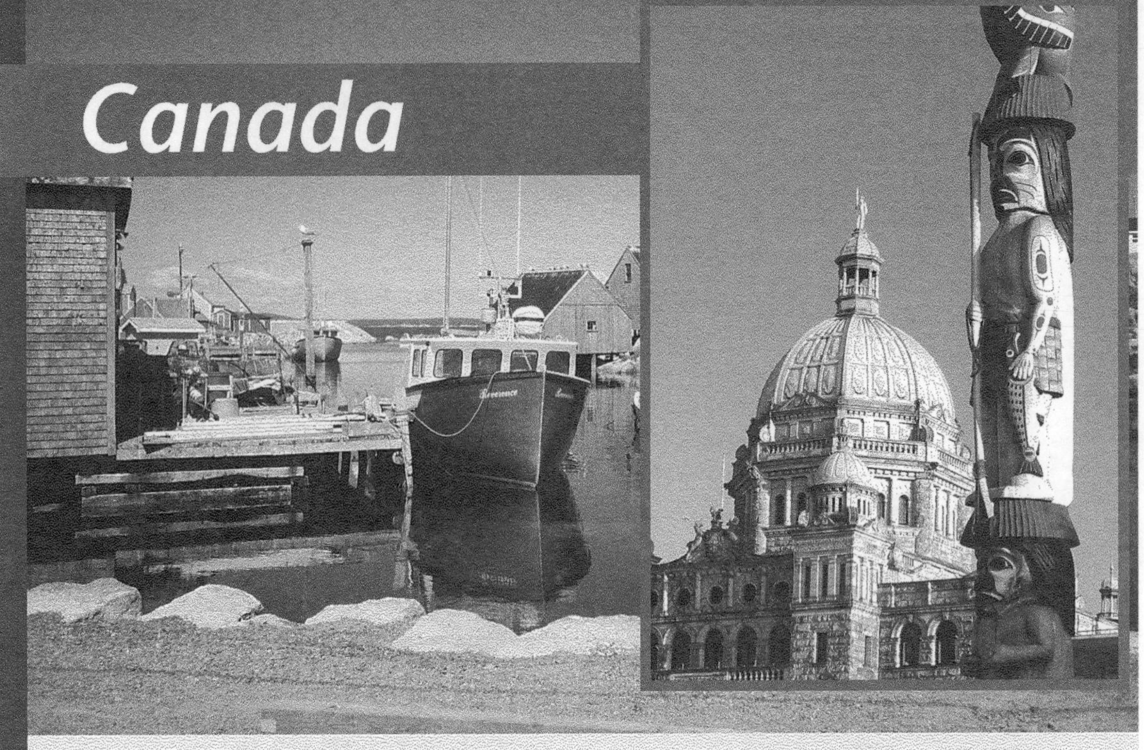

The year 1867 was the beginning of modern Canada. The British North America Act, passed in that year (see p. 215), united the different British colonies in North America into the single dominion of Canada in the British Empire. At that time, Canada began to take major steps toward filling out its borders and finally achieving full independence. Such a task was mammoth, for Canada is second only to Russia in the size of its territory.

One challenge Canada faced was uniting diverse cultures. The majority of Canadians are British Protestants. A very large and important minority are the French Catholics centered in Quebec. These two groups have often clashed over the direction Canada should go. Many Canadians, for example, served bravely in World War I and World War II. But the Canadians who supported the war most strongly were of British descent. Those of French descent preferred to stay isolated from what looked to them like two European fights.

Yet Canada's history is not one of conflict alone. Many Canadians have made contributions to both their own land and other nations. Canadian scientists Charles Best and Frederick Banting discovered insulin in 1921. Their work has aided the treatment of diabetes. Canadian author Lucy Maude Montgomery has entertained young people of many lands with her *Anne of Green Gables* and other works. Nationalities other than British and French have also enriched the land—Russian Mennonites, Germans, Ukrainians, Scandinavians, and Eastern Europeans as well as Inuits and Indians. In 1965 Canada symbolized its desire to unite these many peoples when it adopted a new flag displaying one uniquely Canadian symbol—the maple leaf.

Unit Four Feature

Poster—Divide the students into groups. Have each create posters of Canada using drawings or pictures cut from magazines. The posters should include pictures and memorabilia about the facets of Canada mentioned in this feature. These include the land, prime ministers, provinces, and religion. They may include other information as they wish. Grade for accuracy, originality, and creativity.

The Challenge of the Land

One of the first tasks facing Canada in 1867 was subduing its wild and woolly wilderness. The frozen lands of the north and the undeveloped lands of the west posed both barriers and challenges. Tying the nation together was the great transcontinental railroad, completed in 1869. Along the way, though, Indians and Métis (people of mixed Indian and French descent) resisted such settlement and development. They foresaw the destruction of their way of life of hunting and trapping, and they feared the dominance of the English-speaking Canadians. In 1885 the Métis and Indians actually rebelled, but the Canadian government put down the uprising and hanged the leader. The settlement went on. Eventually the western plains became known as one of the world's "breadbaskets," one of the largest wheat-growing regions on the planet.

The maple leaf flag of Canada replaced the British Union Jack in 1965.

A different sort of frontier struggle was the Klondike gold rush of the 1890s. In 1896 prospectors discovered gold in Bonanza Creek, near the Klondike River. Soon hordes of gold seekers flocked to the frozen north. The city of Dawson sprouted from nothing into a bustling

Canada 505

town of over 20,000 in two years. Getting to Dawson was an adventure in itself. One route was known as the "Dead Horse Trail" for its murderous effect on animals—and it was considered the *good* trail. Food was often scarce in winter, and prospectors sometimes faced near starvation. The food that was available was expensive. The price of flour in Dawson, for instance, rose from six dollars to one hundred dollars a sack. The year 1898 was the peak for individual prospectors. After that, digging for gold was so difficult that big mining companies moved in with heavy equipment to reach the deeply buried gold.

One of the last frontiers of Canada was the Northwest Passage. Since the days of the first explorers, men had sought to sail around the top of North America to reach the Far East. By the 1800s there was no longer much profit to be made in such a trip; there were cheaper ways to the East. But men stubbornly kept trying. One disastrous effort was a British expedition led by Sir John Franklin in the 1840s. His ships became trapped in the ice, and all of the crew perished. The skeletons of some were found at a place discoverers named "Starvation Point." They chose this grim name because the crewmen had resorted to cannibalism. Finally, in a difficult trip lasting from 1903 to 1906, famed arctic explorer Roald Amundsen traveled through Arctic waters from the Atlantic Ocean to the Pacific. In 1969 the oil tanker USS *Manhattan* became the first commercial ship to make the trip.

Pioneers sledding across the frozen Yukon trail in the 1890s

A more recent battle against nature was the creation of the Saint Lawrence Seaway. The Saint Lawrence River links the Great Lakes with the Atlantic Ocean. However, several stretches of shallow water and rapids near Montreal made the river impossible to navigate there. Early canals built by the Canadians were too small to permit modern cargo ships to pass. Therefore, in 1954 Canada and the United States began to build the Saint Lawrence Seaway. They enlarged the old canals and built new ones to bypass the treacherous water. When it opened in 1959, ocean-going ships were able to travel to the major cities on the Great Lakes. A resulting financial boom in shipping benefited both Canada and the United States.

506 Unit Feature

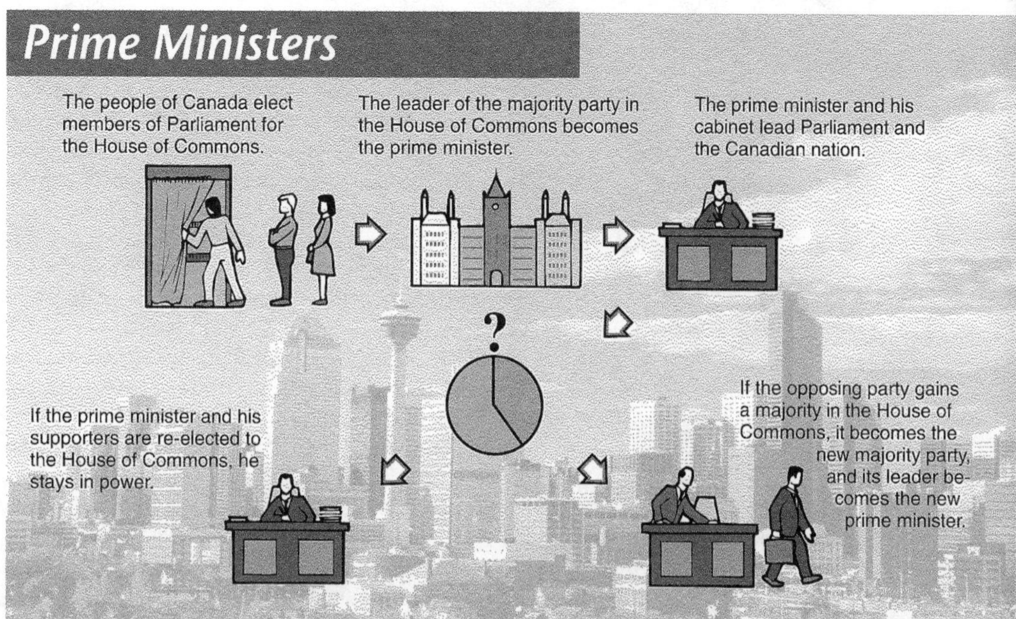

Prime Ministers
The people of Canada elect members of Parliament for the House of Commons.
The leader of the majority party in the House of Commons becomes the prime minister.
The prime minister and his cabinet lead Parliament and the Canadian nation.
?
If the prime minister and his supporters are re-elected to the House of Commons, he stays in power.
If the opposing party gains a majority in the House of Commons, it becomes the new majority party, and its leader becomes the new prime minister.

Canada has a parliamentary government, like that of Great Britain. The political party that wins the most seats in the legislature makes its leader the prime minister (the head of the government). Canada has had many prime ministers, but several have been especially notable.

The first prime minister of Canada was Sir John A. MacDonald, who served 1867-73 and 1878-91. A member of the Conservative Party (later renamed the Progressive Conservative Party), he sought to unify the new Canadian dominion. As prime minister, MacDonald pushed for the expansion of Canada and the settlement of its wilderness regions. Perhaps his greatest achievement was the construction of Canada's transcontinental railway.

Sir Wilfrid Laurier, leader of the Liberal Party, was prime minister for fifteen years (1896-1911). He was a part of Canada's French-speaking Catholic minority, but he sought to unite all Canadians. For example, a heated issue during the election of 1896 was a situation in the province of Manitoba. That province prohibited teaching in the French language in its schools. Neither could the schools offer religious instruction in Catholicism. Once in office, Laurier worked out a compromise so that French-speaking Manitobans could be taught in their own language and religion. The growth of wheat farming in the west and the Klondike gold rush helped make Laurier's term of office one of the most prosperous periods in Canadian history.

One of the most influential prime ministers in Canadian history was also a Liberal, W. L. Mackenzie King, who served a total of more than twenty years (1921-30, 1935-48). King was named for his grandfather, who had led a rebellion against the British in 1837. Like his grandfather, the prime minister promoted the idea of being Canadian instead of

Canadian prime minister Pierre Trudeau with American president Ronald Reagan

British. King helped push for the Statute of Westminster passed by the British Parliament in 1931. This legislation made Canada a completely independent nation within the British Commonwealth. Despite his desire to be independent of Europe, King threw Canada's support on the side of the Allies in World War II.

Perhaps the most important prime minister since World War II was Pierre Trudeau, who served from 1968 to 1979 and from 1980 to 1984. Like Laurier and King, he was a Liberal. A major challenge Trudeau faced was the discontent in French-speaking Quebec. Many French-speaking Canadians argued that they could defend their rights and culture only by taking Quebec out of Canada and making it an independent nation. In 1970 Quebec extremists kidnapped and murdered Pierre Laporte, Quebec's labor minister. Trudeau responded by giving the police and the army special powers to deal with the danger. But Trudeau also sought to win over Quebec. The Official Languages Act made both French and English official languages of Canada and ordered the federal government to use both.

One of Pierre Trudeau's proudest accomplishments was revising the Canadian constitution. In 1982 Canada finally won from the British Parliament the right to amend its own constitution. (Before that, the British had to approve changes.) Part of this new agreement was the Canadian Charter of Rights and Freedoms, similar to the Bill of Rights in the United States. Now the only tie remaining between Canada and Britain is that Canada recognizes the monarch of Great Britain as its official head of state.

In 1984 the Progressive Conservatives took power by winning the biggest electoral victory in Canadian history, 211 out of 282 seats in the Canadian legislature. Their leader, Brian Mulroney, became prime minister. Mulroney successfully promoted trade and cooperation with Canada's huge neighbor to the south, the United States. He failed, however, in calming Quebec. Mulroney offered a revision to the Canadian constitution that recognized Quebec as a "distinct society" with special privileges within Canada. The plan failed, though, when other provinces of Canada opposed it. They feared that the change would not protect the individual rights of English-speaking Canadians within Quebec.

Mulroney resigned in 1993. He was replaced by Kim Campbell, Canada's first female prime minister. But in 1993 the Progressive Conservatives suffered the worst defeat in Canadian history. Dismayed with the economic bad times and the failure of the constitutional reform, voters gave the Conservatives only two seats in the legislature.

508 Unit Feature

Provinces

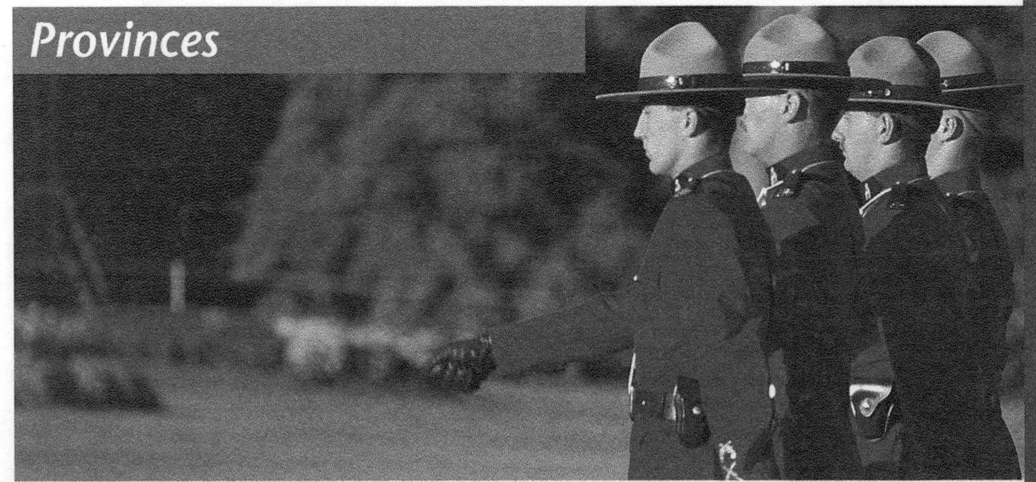

The Royal Canadian Mounted Police, or "Mounties," are one of the most familiar symbols of Canada.

As the failure of Mulroney's constitutional reform shows, provinces are extremely powerful in Canadian politics. Canada consists of ten provinces and three territories (the Yukon Territory, Nunavut, and the Northwest Territories). The federal government takes care of the three territories; the provinces take care of themselves. The provinces of Canada possess much more power over their own affairs than do the states of the United States.

E. C. Manning

Canadians group the provinces into several regions. The Maritime Provinces in the east (sometimes called the Atlantic Provinces) are New Brunswick, Nova Scotia, Prince Edward Island, and Newfoundland. The Central Provinces are Quebec and Ontario. The Western Provinces are Alberta, Saskatchewan, Manitoba, and British Columbia. (Sometimes Alberta, Saskatchewan, and Manitoba are referred to as the Plains Provinces.) The government of each province is like that of Canada as a whole. The party that controls the provincial legislature makes its leader the head of the provincial government. The chief executive of each province is known as a premier.

One of the longest serving premiers was E. C. Manning, who served as premier of Alberta from 1943 to 1968. Part of the reason for his popularity was Alberta's prosperity. The discovery of oil spurred an economic boom in the province. Hundreds of millions of dollars flowed into Alberta's treasury from oil leases and sales. Manning was able to reduce the province's debt, cut taxes, and pay dividends to citizens. Manning built roads, schools, and libraries. "When the day comes that our oil runs out," he said, "these benefits will remain."

Manning was also unashamedly a Christian. Although a layman, he often preached and broadcasted a popular religious radio program.

Canada 509

"I abhor the word *politician,*" the premier said. "I would much rather concentrate on my Bible work." He told one visitor, "People may not agree with my beliefs, but it's amazing how many respect them. . . . I believe that a whole lot of Christians get themselves into trouble by sitting on the fence instead of making their stand clear."

The great independence of the provinces has created the problem of regionalism in Canada. Each province or region (such as the Plains Provinces) can pursue its own interests without regard for other regions. The obvious example is Quebec, where some citizens talk about leaving Canada entirely. But other provinces want to maintain their independence too. Alberta has clashed with the federal government over who controls the province's rich oil resources. Newfoundland is another good example of an independent-minded province. When the Dominion of Canada was formed in the 1800s, that province refused to join. In fact, Newfoundland did not join Canada until 1949, and even then it was by a narrow vote.

Religion

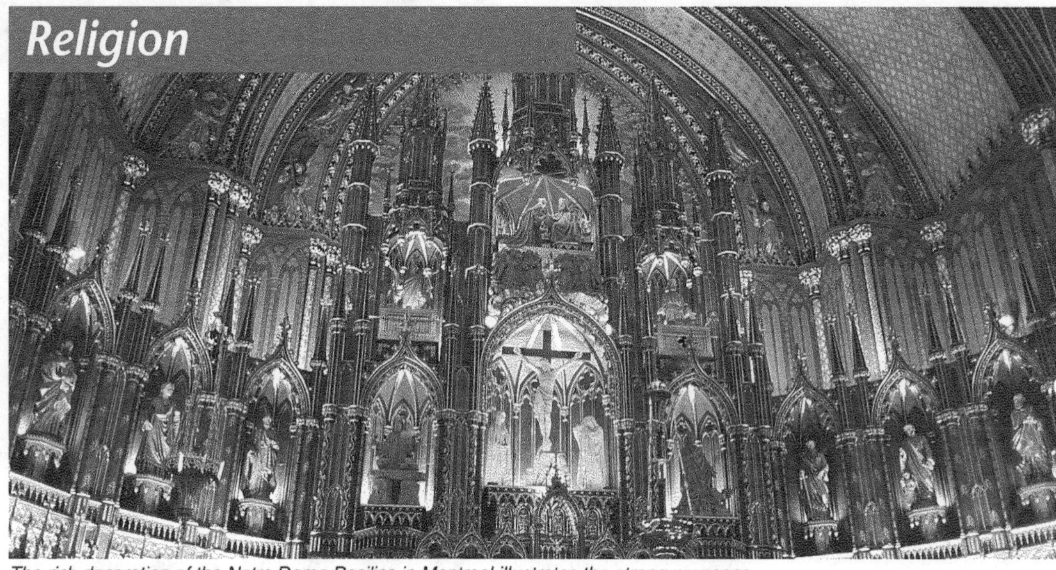

The rich decoration of the Notre Dame Basilica in Montreal illustrates the strong presence of Catholicism in Canada, especially in the province of Quebec.

The Roman Catholic Church is the largest religious group in Canada. The majority of Catholics are from the French-speaking minority, but there are many English-speaking Catholics too. Canada's British heritage has also had an influence on the nation's religion. About a tenth of the Canadian people belong to the Anglican Church of Canada, a descendant of the established church of Great Britain.

The second largest church in the nation is the United Church of Canada. This group formed in 1925 when Canadian Methodists, Presbyterians, and Congregationalists merged. To unite these different groups, the new church

510 Unit Feature

had to downplay doctrine. Therefore the United Church of Canada has tended to be liberal in its theology. A sizable minority of Presbyterians opposed the merger. They wanted to preserve their doctrine and heritage, so they stayed out of the merger and formed the Presbyterian Church in Canada.

Many evangelical Christian leaders have come from Canada. A. B. Simpson was born in Canada, where he was converted and then ordained to the ministry. He pastored churches in the United States until he formed the Christian and Missionary Alliance in 1887. This group organized churches in the United States and Canada and planted missionary churches around the world. Jonathan and Rosalind Goforth were Canadian missionaries to China who not only proclaimed the gospel in that land but also inspired others to missionary service. T. T. Shields of the Jarvis Street Baptist Church in Toronto was a leading Baptist Fundamentalist. Shields attacked growing religious liberalism in both Canada and the United States. These are but a few of the Canadian Christians who found opportunity to serve Christ at home and abroad.

Conclusion

A five-thousand-mile-long border separates Canada from the United States. Unlike national borders in many parts of the world, Canada and the United States have a large, unfortified border. Citizens of both countries may easily cross to the other side. Canada and the United States are alike in desiring peace and cooperation. Like members of the same family, these two nations share a common heritage, but Canada remains unique, "The True North, Strong and Free."

Cars line up to cross the border between Canada and the United States, symbolizing the peaceful and friendly relations that these two nations enjoy.

Canada 511

CHAPTER 18

Student Objectives
Students should be able to

1. Identify important national leaders and the country each comes from.
2. Explain the formation of Turkey from the Ottoman Empire.
3. Summarize Atatürk's modernization of Turkey.
4. Analyze the causes for the massacre of the Armenians.
5. Evaluate the movement with which the shah tried to modernize Iran.
6. Summarize the formation of Saudi Arabia.
7. Give examples of the strictness of the Wahhabi movement within Islam.
8. Explain the steps in the Zionist movement.
9. Give the year of the rebirth of the nation of Israel.
10. Interpret the aggression of Arab nations against Israel in light of biblical teaching.
11. Discuss solutions to the Palestinian conflict.
12. Distinguish the three basic varieties of Judaism.
13. Distinguish the two basic varieties of Islam.
14. Explain the connection between OPEC and world energy.
15. Describe the conflicts between Iran and Iraq and between Iraq and Kuwait.
16. Locate Lebanon on a map.
17. Analyze and create picture graphs.

Opening photo— Megiddo, also known as the Jezreel Valley

Life in the Middle East

A collage of pictures showing life in the Middle East would be interesting to your students. Put captions under each picture or group of pictures.

Another idea would be to have three columns, one for each major Middle Eastern-based religion: Judaism, Islam, and Christianity. Write facts and other information under each heading. Use different colors for each column. Or use the three headings with different colors but

The history of the Middle East in the twentieth century begins at Armageddon.

Most Christians recognize "Armageddon" as the site of the final battle between God and the forces of rebellious mankind (Rev. 16:16). But the site of Armageddon is probably a location in Palestine known as Megiddo. Some two hundred battles have taken place in that region since the days of the pharaohs and ancient Israel. (See Judg. 5:19.) In September of 1918 another fateful battle took place at Megiddo.

World War I did not just pit Germany against France and Great Britain. The Turkish Ottoman Empire sided with the Central Powers. Across the Middle East the Turks clashed with the British and Britain's Arab allies. The victorious Allies captured the ancient cities of the East: Baghdad, Mecca, and Jerusalem. General Edmund Allenby's British-Arab forces in Palestine launched the final blow on the Turks on September 18, 1918. Allied infantry cracked the Turkish front on the Mediterranean coast. Allied cavalry then swept up the Plain of Sharon, crossed behind enemy lines to Megiddo, and cut the Turks off. Shattered by the speed and strength of the blow, the Turkish forces collapsed and retreated. In less than a month, all Turkish resistance in the region was gone.

The Allied victory at Megiddo did not just end the campaign in Palestine. It also sealed the doom of the Ottoman Empire. Four hundred years of Turkish rule had ended. A new era had begun in the Middle East.

A.D. 1910 - PRESENT

World War I 1914-18

Kemal

1910

1920

Chapter 18 Lesson Plans			
Section Title	**Main Concept**	**Pages**	**Time Frame**
1. The Rise of Turkey **Interpretations: The Armenian Massacre*	At the end of World War I, the Ottoman Empire was finished, and a new nation, Turkey, was formed under Kemal Atatürk.	512-19	1 day
2. Progress and Tradition in the Middle East	Iran and Saudi Arabia represent progress and tradition in the Middle East.	520-24	1-2 days
3. The Rise of Israel **Characterizations: Golda Meir*	The re-forming of Israel in the twentieth century caused much conflict in the Middle East.	525-31	1-2 days
4. Religion in the Middle East **Center Stage: Fundamentalisms*	Judaism and Islam are the two major religions in the Middle East today.	532-37	1 day
5. Oil, Revolution, and War **Settings: Lebanon*	OPEC was formed to raise profits in oil-producing countries; Iran was brought back to tradition by Khomeini and fought Iraq; Iraq fought Kuwait in the Gulf War.	538-43	1 day
Total Suggested Days (including 1 day for review & 1 day for test)			7-9 days

Realignment in the Middle East

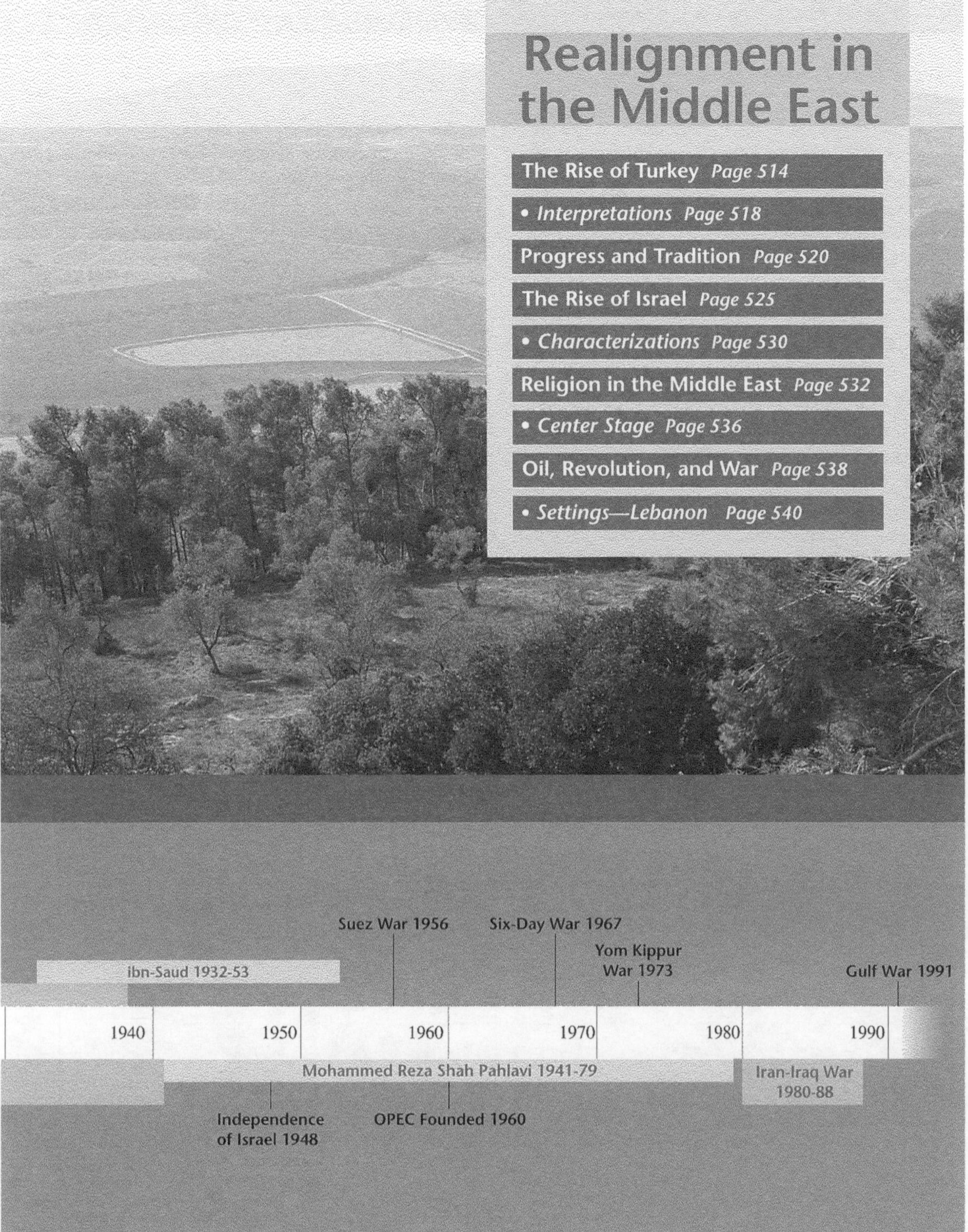

ibn-Saud 1932-53

Suez War 1956

Six-Day War 1967

Yom Kippur War 1973

Gulf War 1991

1940 | 1950 | 1960 | 1970 | 1980 | 1990

Mohammed Reza Shah Pahlavi 1941-79

Iran-Iraq War 1980-88

Independence of Israel 1948

OPEC Founded 1960

mix up the facts, using the corresponding color for each fact.

Chapter Motivator

Review with your students the beginnings of mankind in Mesopotamia. You may wish to show them maps or ask review questions such as the following. Where was Abraham living before God called him to move? *(Ur of the Chaldees)* What were the people in Phoenicia known for? *(murex, alphabet, etc.)* Ask the students for examples of experiences in the Middle East or stories about the Middle East, such as the prophecy of Armageddon (Revelation 19:17-21). This valley is the site of the final battle between God and the forces of rebellious mankind (Rev. 16:16). This battle will probably take place in what is today known as the Valley of Megiddo (pictured here), where the Allies beat the Ottomans in World War I. You may wish to have a longer discussion about Armageddon and other prophetic events.

Genesis 16:12, 17:19

Genesis 16 and 17 tell the story of the beginning of both the Arabs and the Jews. Abraham was the father of both, and the Lord promised strife between them. He also promised that the Jews would be greatly blessed. Of Ishmael God said, "And he will be a wild man; his hand will be against every man, and every man's hand against him; and he shall dwell in the presence of all his brethren" (Gen. 16:12). Of Isaac God said, "Sarah thy wife shall bear thee a son indeed; and thou shalt call his name Isaac: and I will establish my covenant with him for an everlasting covenant, and with his seed after him" (Gen. 17:19). (BLM verse 18)

Materials

- Scripture verse (BLM verse 18)
- Video on Armenia
- Bibles for Bible study
- *Arabian Nights (A Thousand and One Nights)*
- Picture book of Saudi Arabia or the whole Middle East
- Newspaper or magazine articles about the Israeli-Palestinian conflict
- Recordings of Jewish music
- Motor oil, petroleum jelly
- Guest speaker, a veteran of the Persian Gulf War
- *Teaching Transparencies* for use with *World Studies for Christian Schools* (Second Edition)
- Wall map of the Middle East (BLM 18-2)

The Rise of Turkey

Just how much did the Middle East change after World War I? To answer that question, we need only to look at **Anatolia** (Asia Minor). Before the war, the Anatolian Peninsula was the center of the decaying Ottoman Empire. After the war, it was the heart of the aggressively modern state of Turkey.

Collapse of the Ottoman Empire

Around 1300 the Ottoman Turks stormed out of a corner of northwestern Anatolia and began an incredible wave of conquest. The Ottomans swept east to Persia and south to Arabia. They subdued North Africa, all of Asia Minor, and eventually conquered the Byzantine Empire of the Greeks. By the 1500s the Ottoman Empire stretched all across the Middle East from Asia to Africa and into Europe.

But by the beginning of the twentieth century, the Ottoman Empire was tottering. Its government was corrupt, and its domains were restless under Ottoman rule. Some regions, such as the Balkans and Egypt, threw off Ottoman control. The Ottoman Empire became known as "the sick man of Europe." The leading nations of Europe looked greedily toward seizing Ottoman territory. Fortunately for the Turks, the European nations distrusted each other. They feared that if the Ottoman Empire fell apart, one nation, such as Russia,

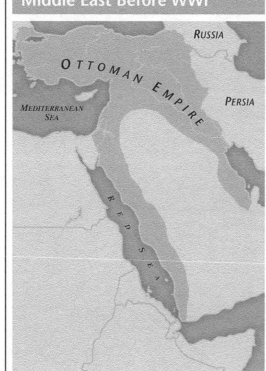

Middle East Before WWI

Middle East After WWI

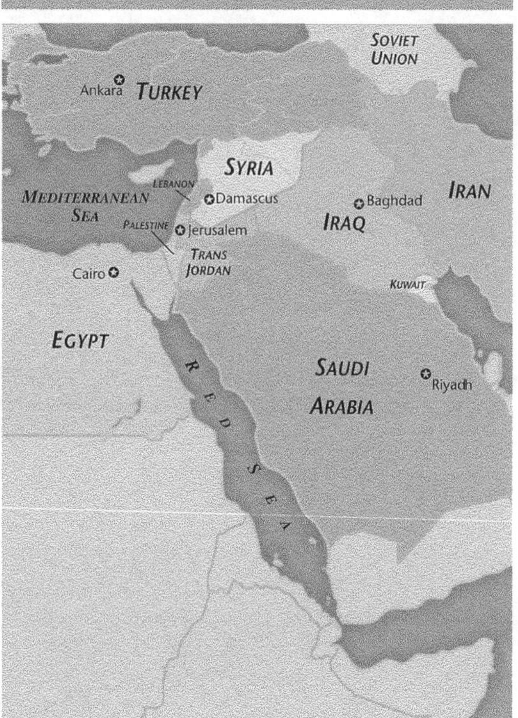

Section 1

Student Objectives
Students should be able to

1. Identify important national leaders and the country each comes from.
2. Explain the formation of Turkey from the Ottoman Empire.
3. Summarize Atatürk's modernization of Turkey.
4. Analyze the causes for the massacre of the Armenians.

Countries of the Middle East—Besides Turkey, Iran, Saudi Arabia, and Israel, the countries of the Middle East are Yemen, Oman, United Arab Emirates, Qatar, Bahrain, Kuwait, Iraq, Cyprus, Syria, Lebanon, and Egypt.

****

For a color version of the map on this page, see page A14 in the Appendix.

The Ottoman Empire and Süleyman—In 1453, Mehmed II captured Constantinople and made it the capital of his Ottoman Empire. He began a tradition of executing the brothers of any new sultan to lessen the opportunity for assassination. In fact, his grandson, Selim the Grim, killed at least sixty-five relatives along with seven of his grand viziers. He initiated his rule with the blood of forty thousand Shiites from Iran. Iran was Shiite instead of the world majority Sunni and was a bitter enemy of the Ottomans. In 1514, Selim the Grim conquered Iran and later Syria and Egypt.

Süleyman the Magnificent became the next ruler and conquered much territory, including Belgrade, Rhodes, parts of Austria, Tunis, Iraq, Hungary, and Tripoli. He is known for executing two of his own sons in Iran, the first because Süleyman was supposedly bewitched by a slave woman to have his son strangled in his presence. The second son had fought a civil war against his brother. When he was defeated, he fled to Iran, expecting the Shiites to treat him as a guest. Instead, he was held hostage. Süleyman ransomed him and immediately executed him. Even

Section 1

Materials

- Video on Armenia

Map changes—Look at the maps on the bottom of the page. Write down names, of all the countries whose names changed after World War I. *(Examples: Russia changed to the Soviet Union; Persia changed to Iran.)*

The mayor of Jerusalem prepares to surrender his city to the British during World War I as British, Arab, and Turkish troops look on.

might snatch the pieces and become too powerful. Therefore, Europe helped prop up the empire.

Then World War I broke out. Since the Russians had been mortal enemies of the Turks for centuries, the Ottoman Empire sided with Germany. The decision proved disastrous. When the Allies defeated the Central Powers, the Ottoman Empire lay helpless before the Allied armies. Arabia, Palestine, and other territories were permanently lost. Even the Turkish homeland in Asia Minor was to be divided among the victorious Allies. The Ottoman Empire was destroyed; it appeared that Turkish rule in Anatolia would soon follow.

"Father of the Turks"

The Turkish homeland was saved through the efforts of **Mustafa Kemal** (moos-TAH-fuh kuh-MAHL). An officer in the Turkish army, Mustafa Kemal had been a hero during World War I. At the end of the war, he opposed the peace settlement because he foresaw the destruction of the Turkish nation. The sultan (ruler) of the Ottoman Empire, however, was willing to go along with the Allies to try to save his throne. Mustafa Kemal began plotting to overthrow the sultan in order to save the nation. Because of riots in Asia Minor, the government gave Mustafa Kemal command of all soldiers in the interior along with broad powers to halt the violence. This was the chance he had been waiting for.

The Turkish leader launched a campaign to overthrow the sultan and halt Allied attempts to break up the Turkish homeland. His battle cry was "Independence or Death." He set up his capital in Ankara instead of Constantinople, and the Turkish people rallied to him. His main obstacle was Greece. The Allies had given Greece a section of Asia Minor surrounding the coastal

Mustafa Kemal, later known as Kemal Atatürk

for family, justice for this type of betrayal was a must.

Ottoman allies included Francis I of France and Elizabeth I of England; two enemies were Charles V of Spain and Ivan the Terrible of Russia. The Ottoman Empire lasted until World War I.

Asia Minor—Asia Minor is the ancient site of Homer's Troy. Over the years it has belonged to the Hittites, Persians, Greeks, Byzantines, Seljuk Turks, and Ottoman Turks.

Russia vs. the Turks—The Crimean War was fought between England and the Russians to determine whether the Ottoman Empire would be allowed to exist. Russia wanted control of the Black Sea and its waterways and declared war on the empire. Later in World War I, the Turks sided with the mighty military power of Germany against Russia.

Sultans—"Sultan" was the title for the ruler of the Turks, just as "king" or "emperor" is for Europeans.

Letters—Have each student decide whether he would have wanted to be on the Ottoman sultan's side or Turkish Atatürk's side. Each student should write a letter from his perspective to his family as though he were in the battle. The report should be at least one hundred words. Encourage volunteers to read their papers to the class.

Istanbul—Originally known as Byzantium, from which the Byzantine Empire got its name, Istanbul was later named Constantinople for the emperor Constantine, and then Istanbul when the Turks took over. Strange as it may seem, this historical and thriving city is located on both the European and Asian sides of the Strait of Bosporus.

Many Muslim Turkish women still wear traditional head coverings and veils during their daily activities.

city of Smyrna, which had a large Greek population. When Mustafa Kemal began his uprising, the Allies relied on Greece to put him down. But the Turkish commander rallied his forces and defeated the Greek army. In 1922 Mustafa Kemal's forces captured Smyrna and drove the Greeks entirely out of Asia Minor.

Mustafa Kemal then proceeded to reorganize the state. He abolished the office of sultan, established a legislature, and became the nation's president. He introduced sweeping changes. The new nation became known as **Turkey.** Other names changed too: Constantinople became Istanbul, and Smyrna became Izmir. The legislature gave its ruler a new name as well—**Kemal Atatürk,** "father of the Turks."

Atatürk forced the Allies to recognize his new nation. He gave up all claim to non-Turkish Ottoman possessions such as Palestine and Arabia. He wanted his state to be *Turkish,* not *Muslim* as the Ottoman Empire had been. In other words, Turkey was to be a secular state. It would not be ruled by religious law with religious leaders holding power. All religions would supposedly be equal, and the government would be religiously neutral.

Atatürk had other changes in mind. He wanted to model Turkey after the powerful Western nations of Europe and North America. He began dressing in Western-style suits. He banned the **fez,** the traditional headgear of Turkish Muslims. The ban of the fez was one example of how he sought to build a secular state. Islamic law says that a man must not wear a hat which keeps him from touching the ground with his forehead as he prays. Atatürk, however, wore billed hats and made laws to force all other men to do so too.

Atatürk also raised the status of women. He did away with the Muslim requirement that a woman always wear a veil in public. He gave women the vote and allowed them to hold office. Dismayed that less than 20 percent of the people knew how to read and write, he reformed Turkish education. He closed the Muslim schools and opened secular ones in their places. He reformed the alphabet, changing from a complex Arabic script to a simpler Western Latin alphabet.

In Another's Shoes—Encourage each student to put himself in the place of those living through Atatürk's changes in Turkey by changing the scenario to America. Imagine that we had a takeover of government by an Islamic leader who became president. He wants to change the country to an Islamic nation. He makes radical changes: cities receive Islamic names, Islam is the only religion that may be practiced, traditional Islamic clothing must be worn (fezzes for men and long robes, head coverings, and veils for women), and Arabic becomes the official language. What would the reaction in this country be? Would the people change peacefully?

Some students may suggest that Turkey changing to Western ways is better than America changing to "backward" Islamic ways. But all would agree that having conditions change rapidly, even for the better, is very hard to accept.

The Atatürk dam on the Tigris River symbolizes the modernization that Kemal Atatürk sought to bring to Turkey.

Turkey Today—The Ottoman Empire was disbanded by the Treaty of Sèvres after World War I. Atatürk took over, but after his death other problems developed. These were the Kurdish minority, lack of water, and urbanization. In 1974, the Turks invaded Cyprus, making it half Turkish. (It is still half Greek.) The population is increasing in Turkey on a larger scale than the country can accommodate, and Turkey has a general trade deficit as well. Jobs are low paying, so many people move to Germany to work.

Although he was not a tyrant like Hitler, Atatürk was a dictator. He used his authority to force these changes on sometimes unwilling citizens. He had enemies tried and executed. But he tried to move his country toward peaceful development. "The arm that wields the sword tires," he said, "but the arm that guides the plow grows stronger every day." He also hoped to move Turkey toward a more democratic government, but he was unable to accomplish this goal in his lifetime.

Atatürk died in 1938, leaving behind a nation that bore little resemblance to the creaky empire from which it had emerged. Even in death, Atatürk pushed his westernization policies. He left orders that at his funeral there was to be no traditional Turkish music. He was laid to rest to the music of Frédéric Chopin.

Section Review

1. What place in Palestine is probably the site of the Battle of Armageddon?
2. The modern-day country of Turkey is located on what peninsula?
3. Which empire joined with the Central Powers and was destroyed at the end of World War I?
4. The old city of Constantinople was renamed by Mustafa Kemal. What was its new name?
5. List at least three other changes that resulted from Kemal Atatürk's leadership of Turkish government.

Consider Atatürk's statement "The arm that wields the sword tires, but the arm that guides the plow grows stronger every day." What does this mean? Do you agree with the statement? Why or why not?

Section Review Answers

1. Megiddo
2. Asia Minor or Anatolia
3. the Ottoman Empire
4. Istanbul
5. any three of the following: abolished the office of sultan, established legislature, established secular state instead of religious, mandated Western-style clothing, raised the status of women, opened new schools, reformed the alphabet

Answers will vary. Atatürk was probably growing tired of fighting as time went on. He wanted his country to be a nation at peace and not at war. The "arm that guides the plow" speaks of the welfare of the people. The plow represents food, a basic necessity in all human life. Atatürk was saying that his people were growing stronger and that he would rather have them concerned about the important basic things in life than about the ravages of the sword. Students may agree with the statement because it emphasizes practicality and peace, or they may disagree because it does not emphasize fighting for what one believes is right.

Just like the Holocaust—Following the example of other European independence movements, the Armenians asserted their nationalism to the dismay of the sultan, for the Ottomans had given the Armenians much opportunity to better themselves and rise from the ashes of their long, downtrodden past. In retaliation the Armenian part of Istanbul was burned and looted. The massacre of over two hundred thousand Armenians in just two years was in part a response to terrorist attacks by the Armenians who wanted to gain reforms. When the Russians began invading Turkey, some Armenians were happy to see them come and later rallied to the Allied cause. After this point, over one million Armenians were slain in Turkey, very much like the Holocaust massacre of the Jews. People were terrorized and tortured. This episode again shows us man's depravity; all of mankind is depraved, not just one or two unusually wicked men such as Hitler.

INTERPRETATIONS

The Armenian Massacres

"Who still speaks today of the extermination of the Armenians?" asked Adolf Hitler. The Nazi dictator expected to get away with his deeds because, after all, no one seemed to remember the Turkish massacres of the Armenians. Hitler was mistaken in thinking he would escape, but, truly, few people recall what the Turks did to the Armenians.

The Armenians lived in a region in eastern Anatolia in the Caucasus Mountains. Mount Ararat, where Noah and the ark landed, is located there. Most of the Armenians came under control of the Ottoman Empire in the 1400s. When the empire began to decay in the 1800s, the Turks started to view the Armenians as a threat. The Armenians were Christian, whereas the Turks were Muslim. Also, many Armenians lived in nearby Russia. The Russians hoped to use the Armenians in the Ottoman Empire as a lever to pry more territory away from the Turks. When the Armenian people began asking for more self-rule, the Turks responded violently. Over one hundred thousand Armenians died in the first round of killing in the 1890s. Another round of repression in 1909 saw the deaths of over thirty thousand more. But this was nothing compared to what happened during World War I.

Homeless Armenian refugees, the result of the Turkish massacres of the Armenian people

When the war broke out, some Turkish leaders feared the Armenians might side with the enemy. Others saw an opportunity to settle "the Armenian question"—permanently. At first, there was the harassment, torture (such as nailing horseshoes to the feet of victims and making them dance), and killing of individuals. Then the Turks began rounding up and imprisoning or killing the Armenian leadership in Constantinople. Armenian soldiers in the Ottoman army were moved to "labor units." The Turks used these soldiers much as Hitler would later use slave labor in the Third Reich; members of the labor units did backbreaking jobs until they died of exhaustion. Other Armenian soldiers were simply gunned down.

Then in 1915, the real horror came. A high Turkish official wrote to one of his subordinates that "the Government has decided to exterminate entirely all the

Armenia—Your local library may have a video on the atrocities in Armenia spoken of in the Interpretations section. Your students may have a better understanding of the atrocities of this massacre while viewing a video about it. Make sure that the video is not too graphic for this young age.

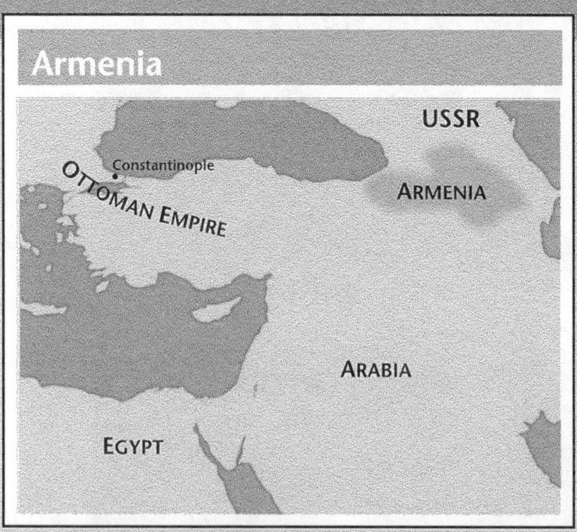

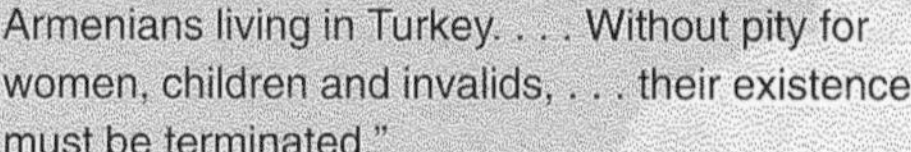

Armenians living in Turkey. . . . Without pity for women, children and invalids, . . . their existence must be terminated."

Soldiers killed Armenians freely. They shot them, bayoneted them, burned them to death in their houses. Then the Turks decided to march them two to three hundred miles to Syria and Palestine, where they would not be a "threat." In the heat of the blistering summer of 1915, the Armenians began their death march. Guards killed some on the march in order to steal their goods. Many others died of heat, exhaustion, hunger, abuse, and disease. One group that started with 18,000 finished with only 150 surviving. Those who made it to the camps were often no better off. One Turkish official kept five hundred Armenians in an outdoor pen in the summer heat without food and water until they went insane.

The U.S. ambassador complained strongly to the Turks that innocent women and children were suffering. Surely, he argued, they posed no threat. A Turkish official replied, "Those who are innocent today might be guilty tomorrow." The killing went on.

Mount Ararat, in the heart of the traditional Armenian homeland

After the war, a famine killed even more Armenians. Mustafa Kemal did not continue the policy of wiping out the Armenians. But his forces did kill many Armenians in the battles against Greece and his struggle to unite the country under his rule.

Estimates vary, but apparently 1.5 million Armenians died between 1915 and 1923. Another half-million were forced to live in exile. Not more than one hundred thousand Armenians remain in Turkey today. Most Armenians are either in the Republic of Armenia in the former Soviet Union or have moved to countries such as the United States. The nation of Turkey denies that the slaughter ever took place.

"Who still speaks today of the extermination of the Armenians?" said Hitler. The world has not forgotten Hitler's slaughter of the Jews, but, sadly, it seems to have forgotten the suffering of the Armenians.

Realignment in the Middle East 519

SECTION 2

Student Objectives
Students should be able to

1. Identify important national leaders and the country each comes from.
2. Evaluate the movement with which the shah tried to modernize Iran.
3. Summarize the formation of Saudi Arabia.
4. Give examples of the strictness of the Wahhabi movement within Islam.

Progress and Tradition in the Middle East

Turkey was not the only nation to emerge from the wreckage of the Ottoman Empire. Eventually, Syria, Lebanon, Iraq, and other countries became independent states in the Middle East. These nations, although similar in background, followed many paths of development. These different paths are illustrated by the history of two important Middle Eastern countries: Iran and Saudi Arabia.

Iran: Embracing Progress

When World War I began, there was only one other major independent power in the Middle East besides the Ottoman Empire: the ancient kingdom of Persia. After World War I, Persia's leaders imitated Kemal Atatürk in trying to build a modern, Western state.

In 1921 a cavalry officer, Reza Khan, toppled the government. He took power and in 1925 became ruler as **Reza Shah Pahlavi** (pah LAHV ee). (The word *shah* is Persian for "king.") He decided to modernize his country as Atatürk had done. Muslim custom required women to cover themselves completely except for the face or just the eyes. The shah did away with these restrictions on women's dress; in fact, the shah made it a law that women had to dress in Western styles. He expanded the nation's roads and railroads. He founded the University of Teheran to promote education. The shah even changed the name of the country. He stopped using the European *Persia* and began to use the native name, ***Iran.***

However, the shah ruled by force. Crossing his will could be dangerous. Once he took an official who displeased him and literally threw him out a window. Iranians quickly learned to obey. Once at an exhibition, the shah sampled a glass of beer and said, "This beer is not bad." A government official standing nearby quickly agreed. The shah looked at him and said, "You don't drink. How do you know it's good?" The official replied, "Your Majesty, I am not the servant of the beer, I am Your Majesty's servant. If you say it is good, then I too say it is good; if you deny it, I too shall deny it."

Mohammed Reza Shah Pahlavi

The shah fell from power by making the same mistake the Ottoman Empire had made in World War I. He threw Iran's support to Germany in World War II because he feared the Soviet Union. As a result, the British, Americans, and Soviets virtually occupied his country to keep it from helping the Axis Powers. The shah resigned, and in 1941 his son **Mohammed Reza Shah Pahlavi** became the new shah of Iran.

SECTION 2

Materials

- Bibles for Bible study
- *Arabian Nights*
- Picture book of Saudi Arabia or the whole Middle East

Review of Persia—Review with your students biblical accounts of the great empire of Persia as a preview for the section on Iran. Three books of the Bible that specifically deal with Persia are Ezra (the rebuilding of Jerusalem), Esther (the attempted extermination of the Jews), and Daniel (the lion's den). Ask the students to relate the story of each briefly. Point out Persia (Iran) on a map and explain that the modern-day country of Iran is the ancient nation of Persia. Ask your students how this might influence their perception of Iran.

The new shah followed his father's path. Because the shah staunchly opposed the Communist Soviet Union to his north, Western powers such as the United States supported him. The United States sold him millions of dollars worth of military equipment and modern technology. But the shah, like his father, ruled through terror. Relying on his secret police, the shah used torture, exile, and execution to keep his opponents in line.

Although himself a Muslim, the shah offended devout followers of Islam. Like his father, he reduced the political power of Muslim clergy. The shah shifted responsibility for education from the clergy to the state. He allowed women to divorce their husbands in violation of Islamic law. The shah even changed the Iranian calendar. Muslims number the years from the time of the prophet Muhammad. The shah, wanting to stress Persia's ancient glories, changed the basis to Cyrus the Great's founding of the Persian Empire. Thus the year 1975 (according to the Western calendar, based on the birth of Christ) became 2535 instead of the Islamic 1355.

The shah's most serious effort to transform Iran was a series of reforms he called the **"White Revolution"** in the 1960s and the 1970s. Some of the reforms he proposed were good, such as giving women the vote and improving education. Much of his reform involved difficult and expensive development of agriculture and industry. He built highways, railroads, and dams. He expanded the mining of Iran's natural resources, built new factories, and planned to construct nuclear reactors. The billions of dollars needed to finance this revolution came from Iran's enormous profits from selling oil.

But there was a harsh side to the White Revolution. The shah tried Stalin's plan to collectivize agriculture. (See p. 454.) He established huge government-run farms on which the peasants worked. In the interest of efficiency, the shah ordered over sixty thousand small rural villages combined into thirty thousand larger villages. Bulldozers leveled villages as the government forced villagers into the new settlements. In doing so, the shah shattered local ties and stirred resentment.

The shah's palace displays the luxury that caused resentment among his subjects.

Ancient Persia—The Persian Empire was huge (about the size of the continental United States), encompassing almost the entire known world of that day. The first ruler of the empire was Cyrus. He conquered the Babylonians and freed the Jews. Darius came after Cyrus's son and built great palaces in his capitals, Persepolis and Susa (called Shushan in the Bible). Darius was defeated, however, at the Battle of Marathon in Greece. His son, Xerxes (Ahasueras), Esther's husband, was also defeated by the Greeks; thus, further expansion was halted. Alexander the Great later conquered all of Persia.

Calendars—Discuss the different calendar systems available to the Iranians. The three possible systems are the Western (based on Jesus Christ), the Islamic (based on Muhammad), and the Persian (based on Cyrus the Great). Ask why each might be the favored one to use. (*because most of the world uses Western, because of strong Islamic ties, or because of strong nationalistic ties, respectively*)

The Formation of Iran—Iran is the oldest continuous political state. In the fifteenth century Shiite monks formed a state called Ardabil between the Turks and the Uzbeks (both of whom were Sunnis).

Bedouins—Bedouins travel from place to place searching for fresh water and pastureland. Like the Mongols, they live in tents and make their clothes out of animal hair and skin. They trade animal products for things they need from villages. Bedouins treasure their pride. Insulting a Bedouin's pride may lead to great feuds. Bedouins today are a dwindling group because of the lure of city life with its health care, education, and money.

Iranian revolutionaries man a bunker in front of Iran's parliament building, awaiting an attack by the shah's forces.

The shah managed to offend everyone. His outrageous spending created inflation, and the middle class turned against him as prices soared. The rural villagers resented the destruction and relocation of villages. The strict Muslims hated his casual attitude toward the teachings of Islam. The upper class had never liked either him or his father because of their "lower-class" origins. Only the army and the secret police kept him in power.

In 1978 riots broke out in protest of the shah's rule. In the violence perhaps as many as ten thousand people died. With no base of support, the shah could not reestablish order. Finally, he fled Iran in 1979, and a group of strict Muslims under the leadership of the Ayatollah Khomeini established an Islamic state. (See p. 539.) Ironically, a nation that had sought to become modern was now trying to lead the Middle East back toward tradition.

Saudi Arabia: Embracing Tradition

While Iran was trying to follow the model of Turkey and become a modern, Western nation, another major Middle Eastern nation dedicated itself to preserving tradition. The nation of Saudi Arabia was solidly traditional, even backward, in its outlook. Yet, unexpectedly, it became one of the richest, most powerful nations in the Middle East.

At the beginning of World War I, the Arabian Peninsula was divided. The Ottoman Empire controlled the northern and western sections. Several smaller Arab kingdoms existed along the seacoast and in the interior. A few regions were under European control, such as British-controlled Aden in the south. Many of the Arabian people, however, felt loyalty only to their local tribes. These were **Bedouins,** herders of sheep and goats who lived in tents and wandered from oasis to oasis to graze their flocks.

With a picture of Khomeini pinned to her dress, a child poses with a toy gun in front of the American embassy in Iran.

Pahlavi—Muhammad Reza Shah Pahlavi offended many people in many different ways. On the chalkboard write the following categories and list why each group was offended: upper class, middle class, rural villagers, and strict Muslims. *(The upper class did not like him or his father because of their lower class origins; the middle class did not like the inflation; rural villagers did not like the destruction and relocation of villages; strict Muslims did not like his casual attitude toward Islam.)*

Arabian Nights—Your students will enjoy a story or two from *Arabian Nights* (also called *A Thousand and One Nights*). Read the beginning to them about Scheherazade and the origin of the stories. (You may wish to see *FUNDAMENTALS OF LITERATURE for Christian Schools* for an example.) "Ali Baba and the Forty Thieves" or "Aladdin" are brief, well-known stories. If you have a good reader in the class, you may wish to have him read the story.

King Faud of Saudi Arabia (above) and a platform in the Persian Gulf for loading oil tankers (right)

Oil—Often when we say *oil,* we mean *petroleum*. Petroleum has been used since ancient times. Noah used pitch, a form of petroleum, to cover his ark. Egyptian mummies were also covered with pitch. King Nebuchadnezzar used pitch to build his walls and streets in Babylon. American Indians used oil for fuel and medicine. Kerosene was developed in the 1840s, but with the advent of electricity and automobiles in the early 1900s, the demand for gasoline increased. The use of oil has some drawbacks, however, such as conservation, rising cost, and environmental pollution.

Among the smaller kingdoms was the kingdom of the Nejd ("highland") in eastern Arabia, ruled by **Abdul Aziz ibn-Saud** (SAH ood). He was the descendant of a family that had fought the Ottoman Turks for over a hundred years. The Saud family were followers of the **Wahhabi** (wah HAHB ee) **movement.** This was a very strict form of Islam that arose in Arabia in the 1700s. The Wahhabis wanted to cleanse Islam of all forms of paganism and rule entirely by the Koran. They condemned dancing, music, and smoking. Part of their faith is that a Wahhabi may not leave someone alone who believes differently; the Wahhabi must make others believe as he does.

Born around 1880, ibn-Saud spent part of his childhood in exile with his family. Then in 1902 he and a band of forty handpicked men captured Riyadh, the capital of the Nejd. Slowly, he expanded his power. He first brought all of the Nejd under his control. During World War I, he captured territories controlled by the Ottoman Empire. After the war, in 1924, he captured Mecca, Islam's holy city. Finally, in 1932 he established the independent kingdom of **Saudi Arabia.** Ibn-Saud's rule was based on power. "Draw a sword in their face," he said of those he ruled, "and they will obey."

The new kingdom covered about three-fourths of the Arabian Peninsula, but its power did not lie in its physical size. In the eastern sections, near the Persian Gulf, oil was discovered in 1938. After World War II, nations needed oil to run their industries, fuel their automobiles, and warm their homes. Saudi Arabia's oil reserves became an enormous source of wealth. Saudi Arabia was earning $4 billion a year from its oil sales in 1973. That figure skyrocketed to over $100 billion by 1981. Although profits dropped after that year, the nation still enjoyed enormous wealth. During this financial boom, bankers sometimes opened their doors each morning to people lined up

Middle East—Find a picture book of Saudi Arabia or the whole Middle East. Show students pictures of typical life there. Suggestions include veiled women, camels, and the city of Riyadh. Ask the students how life is apparently different in the Middle East than in the United States. Discuss any culturalism that may be shown. (Culturalism is viewing one's own way of life as superior to another's way of life.) Explain that aspects of different cultures are not wrong if not forbidden by God's Word. Of course, Christians would disagree with many customs in Islamic countries. Make sure that any disapproval of culture stems from Christianity and not Americanism. Discuss how Christians can adapt to differing cultures but still be separated from worldly things.

Balance in Power—Though drug dealing and stealing are wrong, your students may perceive public beheading and amputation as barbaric forms of punishment. Often in Middle Eastern countries discipline is barbaric, and this severity greatly contributes to the low crime rate that most of these countries have. But a low crime rate does not necessarily stem from a good justice system. In the case of Saudi Arabia, a low crime rate means cruelty and the trampling of human rights. The fact that a system "works" does not make it viable.

Under Arabia's barren sands lies untold wealth in petroleum deposits.

waiting to deposit suitcases and garbage bags full of money.

None was more wealthy than the ruling Saud family. The family controlled the government and reaped its wealth. Because the family was so large, not all of the Sauds could be rulers. Some members of the family went into private business. Even then, the government made sure that the best business contracts went to family members. Businessmen without connection to the Saud family rightly saw this as unfair.

Saudi Arabia was a repressive state. A Saudi prince admitted in 1961, "In our country there is no law that upholds the freedom and rights of the citizen." Slavery was not abolished until 1962. The government held public beheadings for crimes such as murder and drug dealing. For a more minor crime such as stealing, authorities cut off the hand of a thief. Women chafed under the highly restrictive Islamic law. In 1990 forty-seven women drove cars into Riyadh to protest the Islamic prohibition that women not drive. The result was a near-riot. Devout Muslims held protest marches, and the government fired many of the women from their jobs for their act.

Yet there is an irony in Saudi Arabia's history. The Sauds followed one of the strictest forms of Islam. But the great wealth brought in by oil has also brought in corrupting influences. Drug abuse, for example, has become a terrible problem. A new group, called Islamic Awakening, arose to oppose the Sauds and call for a return to a purer form of Islam. The Sauds, who had sought to purify both Islam and Arabia, had become symbols of corruption in a nation increasingly marked by corruption.

Section Review

1. Give the modern name of Persia.
2. List at least three reforms of the "White Revolution."
3. How did the Ayatollah Khomeini rise to power in Iran?
4. Which one of the countries of Iran or Saudi Arabia tried to be aggressively modern? traditional?
5. What are Bedouins?
6. Describe the Wahhabi movement.
7. Describe law and punishment in Saudi Arabia.

People have clashed violently over both traditions and modernization in the Middle East as well as many other places in the world. What might make one of these more desirable than the other? What are the pros and cons of each? How would you balance them?

Section Review Answers

1. Iran
2. any three of the following: women could vote; education was improved; agriculture and industry were developed; highways, railroads, and dams were built; mining was expanded, factories were built, and nuclear reactors were planned; land was distributed, collectivized, and ruined
3. The Ayatollah Khomeini took over Iran after riots broke out that ousted the shah.
4. modern—Iran; traditional—Saudi Arabia
5. herders of sheep and goats who live in tents and wander from oasis to oasis to graze their flocks
6. a very strict form of Islam which condemns dancing, music, and smoking; Wahhabists must make others believe as they do
7. public beheadings for murder and drug dealing; cutting off the hand of a thief; greatly restricting women under the law

Answers will vary. Traditions are highly valued for ties to the past and for time-honored ways of doing things. Often traditions were started as the best way to do something. Modernization makes life easier and more comfortable and is thus desirable. Traditions can provide a sense of structure and certainty, but they can also be an obstacle to progress. Modernization can improve living conditions and encourage thought; it can also lead to corruption. A balance is needed between traditions (that are done not ritualistically but to honor the Lord and country) and modernization (for progress and not corruption).

The Rise of Israel

Among the Arab and Muslim nations of the Middle East, the Jewish nation of Israel stands out in bold contrast. Its Jewish character and its democratic form of government make Israel distinct. The unusual nature of Israel is the result of its unique heritage.

Zionism and the Founding of Israel

The beginnings of the Israeli state lie in a movement known as **Zionism.** (Zion is one of the hills on which Jerusalem is built. The word *Zion* is often used to refer to Jerusalem or to the whole Jewish nation.) **Theodor Herzl,** a German Jew, had originally dreamed of seeing the Jewish people blended into European culture. But he witnessed cruel examples in "civilized" Europe of unreasoning hatred of the Jews. The last straw for Herzl was France's court-martial of a Jewish army officer on false charges. Some French newspapers and politicians used this incident as an excuse to denounce all Jews. Herzl decided that the answer was for Jews to have their own nation. He launched an international movement to form a homeland for the Jews. This desire for the formation of a Jewish homeland became known as "Zionism."

Theodor Herzl

Originally, Herzl did not care where the Jews established their homeland. He even considered British offers of land in East Africa. But most of the Jews who embraced Zionism would accept no other site than Palestine, the Promised Land of Jewish history. Herzl himself finally concluded, "Palestine is the only land where our people can come to rest." Around the world, Jewish interest in the Zionist cause grew tremendously.

Until World War I, the Turks controlled Palestine and allowed only a few Jews to settle there. After the war, Great Britain controlled the region. During the war, Britain had tried to win Jewish support by issuing the **Balfour Declaration.** In this document, the British promised to support the formation of a Jewish homeland in Palestine. But it was not to be that easy. The Arabs who lived in Palestine did not want their land made into a Jewish homeland. The British wavered, wanting to please the Arabs. When Jews tried to enter Palestine, the British sent them back.

The Zionists did not give up. The Nazi Holocaust swayed world sympathy to the Jews. Zionist groups in Palestine began working toward a Jewish state. Unfortunately, some of the Jewish independence groups used violence. In what was perhaps the worst incident, Jewish terrorists blew up the King David Hotel in Jerusalem in 1946. Ninety-one people died,

SECTION 3

Student Objectives

Students should be able to

1. Identify important national leaders and the country each comes from.
2. Explain the steps in the Zionist movement.
3. Give the year of the rebirth of the nation of Israel.
4. Interpret the aggression of Arab nations against Israel in light of biblical teaching.
5. Discuss solutions to the Palestinian conflict.

The Dreyfus Affair—Alfred Dreyfus was a French officer who was a Jew. In 1894 he was arrested for his supposed spying for Germany. He was sentenced to life imprisonment on Devil's Island. Another officer found evidence two years later that made it seem that Dreyfus was innocent as he had claimed all along. A second trial was held, but due to the hatred of Jews in general, this one was a mockery. No favorable testimony was allowed. This time Dreyfus received a sentence of ten years, but the president pardoned him a few days later. People were up in arms about the matter. Ten years later in 1906, the highest French court reviewed the case and Dreyfus was declared innocent. He rejoined the army and was later awarded the Legion of Honor.

Reasons for and Against—Israel had a historic right to the Holy Land, but Palestine had already belonged to the Arabs for over one thousand years. Palestine was practically promised to Israel in the Balfour Declaration, but the British never consulted the Arabs. Jewish settlement constituted a democratic and progressive influence in the Middle East, but Arabs were worried that economic development was not healthy because it depended on outside subsidies. Arabs also thought that their land was being taken over by an alien minority.

The King David Hotel—The leader of the attack on the King David Hotel was Menachem Begin, later the prime minister of Israel. Although Begin claimed that the bomb was set off to destroy

SECTION 3

Materials

- Newspaper or magazine articles about the Israeli-Palestinian conflict

Zionism—Ask your students what they think about the Zionist movement. Put the situation on a real level by asking them to think about it in terms of America. Would they be happy if a nation that claimed it had rights to this land tried to create a separate country? What if some tribes of American Indians decided that Oklahoma was their rightful land and started a movement calling all other Indians of those tribes back to that land? What if Britain said that these Native Americans could have this land? The white settlers who kicked out these Indians were unfair in many cases in taking land that did not belong to them. Should the government allow the tribes to take it back? Or should it try to stop them? Remind your students that another problem facing the Jews was intense hatred by the neighboring Arabs and Muslims.

secret British records in the hotel, it was detonated during office hours. The "warning" that had been given came just two minutes before the actual explosion. Ironically, this Israeli attack foreshadowed the methods that the PLO would use later against Israel.

Destination Palestine—The British wanted to pacify the Arabs somewhat and so arrested many Jews and sent some back to their homelands. This was often a dangerous situation. In one story the ship *Exodus 1947*, formerly an American holiday ship, was bought by the Jewish resistance to bring Jews to the Holy Land. This was illegal, and the ship was attacked by five destroyers near Palestine (whether they were in or out of territorial waters is debated). Many Americans worked as crewmen on these illegal ships to Palestine. The Jews who had finally been released from Nazi concentration camps now were being herded to new ones on Cyprus, where they had no electricity or plumbing. But instead of being sent to Cyprus, the refugees from the *Exodus 1947* were sent back to Europe, to Port de Bouc in France. They would not get off the ship, however. The sun beat upon them, the rains descended upon them, but they still would not get off. Eventually they were sent back to Germany, a humiliation for the people who had been tortured under Hitler. Little by little the people escaped to Israel, and most were already there when Israel finally became a nation in 1948.

Masada—A Jewish leader named Jonathan first fortified Masada. Later, King Herod built an elaborate fortress there. In A.D. 66 a group of Jews called the Zealots took the fortress from the Romans. Four years later (A.D. 70) the Romans conquered the city of Jerusalem. The Roman army then went on a quest to rid the countryside of rebel forces. In A.D. 72 the Romans began a siege of Masada that lasted two years. Finally, when the Jews realized that defeat was imminent, they committed mass suicide rather than face capture and torture or slavery. Two women and five children survived.

including seventeen Jews. Fighting continued among Jews, Arabs, and British soldiers.

The British finally handed the whole Palestine question over to the United Nations. The UN in turn divided Palestine into Arab and Jewish sections. The Arabs refused to accept this decision; they wanted all of Palestine to be an independent Arab nation. The Israelis declared the independence of their section on May 14, 1948. The Arabs went to war, but the Jewish forces won a hard-fought victory. The modern state of Israel was born.

The Arab-Israeli Wars

The fortified hill of Masada has a special place of honor in Jewish history. A towering plateau near the Dead Sea, Masada was the site of fortifications built by Herod the Great. For seven months in A.D. 72-73, an army of Jewish Zealots had held out against a much larger Roman army. When the Romans were on the verge of finally breaking through the walls, nearly the entire garrison—960 men, women, and children—chose to commit suicide rather than surrender. Today the Israeli army brings new recruits to Masada. In the midst of the ruins and memories of Masada, with the Israeli flag snapping in the wind, the recruits vow in the words of the Hebrew poet Lamdan, "Masada shall not fall again!"

Masada, the site of Jewish resistance to the Romans in the first century, symbolizes Israel's determination to endure against the opposition of its enemies.

The Israeli **War of Independence** in 1948 was only the first of several Arab-Israeli wars that Israel had to fight for its existence. Arab states denied Israel's right to exist. One Arab leader said before the War of Independence, "This will be a war of extermination and a momentous massacre." In that conflict alone, five countries sent troops against Israel: Egypt, Jordan, Syria, Lebanon, and Iraq. Arab sympathy with the Arabs in Palestine and Muslim opposition to the Jewish presence there set the entire Middle East against Israel.

Thanks to support from countries such as the United States, Israel survived. The Israelis built an efficient military force. In 1956 Israel and Egypt fought a brief war in the Sinai Peninsula. There the Israelis dazzled the Egyptian forces with their speed and daring and captured the peninsula in one hundred hours. As part of the settlement after that war, however, Israel withdrew from Sinai.

Even more impressive was Israel's performance in the **Six-Day War** (1967).

Sinai Review—Ask your students to review what they remember about Sinai from the Bible. *(Moses received the Ten Commandments there; the Israelites wandered in the wilderness for forty years.)*

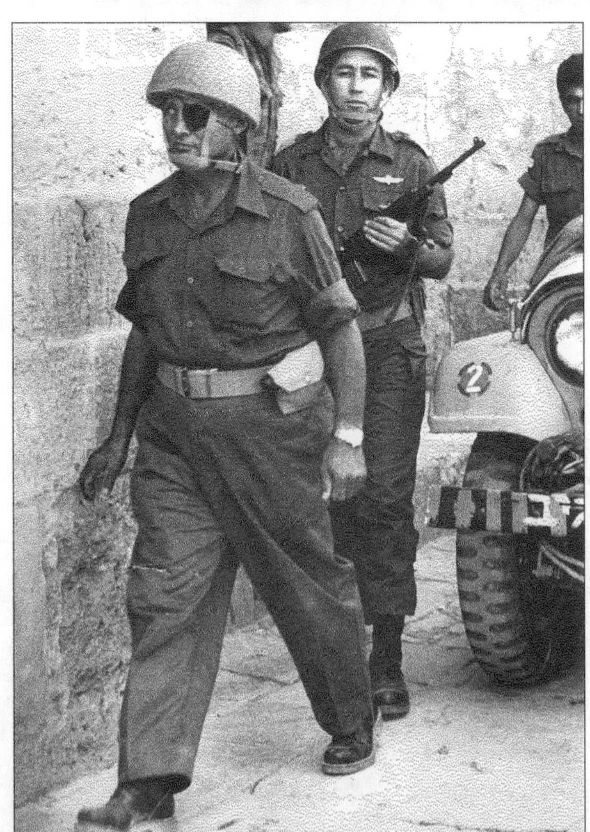

Moshe Dayan, the Israeli commander who planned the spectacularly successful campaigns in the Sinai Peninsula and the Six-Day War

Just before the war, President Gamal Nasser of Egypt said the goal would be "to exterminate the State of Israel for all time." Realizing that Egypt, Syria, and Jordan were about to attack, Israel struck first. The Israeli air force destroyed the opposing air forces while they were still on the ground. Israeli armor and infantry overwhelmed the enemy.

But in 1973 Egypt struck first. Launching an attack on Yom Kippur (October 6, the Day of Atonement, a major Jewish holiday), the Egyptians surprised the Israelis. Syria also attacked in the north. Pressed by two determined enemies, the Israelis faced the danger of defeat. Knowing they could not fight on two fronts at the same time, the Israelis turned on the Syrians first. They mauled the Syrian forces and drove them back. Then the United States began to pour arms and equipment into Israel. The Israelis fought across the Suez Canal and surrounded and trapped a portion of the Egyptian army. Both sides were exhausted, and the United Nations negotiated a cease-fire.

The **Yom Kippur War** had been a close call. But out of the war came a move for peace. Tired of unprofitable conflict, Anwar el-Sadat, the president of Egypt, astounded the world with an offer of peace between his country and Israel. With the help of the United States, Israel and Egypt made peace. Israel returned the Sinai Peninsula (which it had captured in 1967) to Egypt. Egypt in return ended the state of war and recognized Israel's right to exist. In 1994 Jordan became the second Arab nation to make peace with Israel.

Palestinian Conflict

But peace with Egypt did not solve all of Israel's problems. Other nations in the Middle East, notably Syria, remained deadly enemies of Israel. The greatest challenge facing Israel was the "Palestinian problem." In the 1967 Six-Day War, Israel had taken the **West Bank** (territory on the western side of the Jordan River, including the eastern section of Jerusalem) from Jordanian control and the Gaza Strip (territory along the Mediterranean coast) from Egyptian control. These conquests placed a large number of Arab Palestinians under Israeli rule.

The United Nations, as mentioned earlier, had originally intended to divide Palestine into Jewish and Arab sections. The Jewish state of Israel was obviously one part of that

Jewish Holidays—The High Holidays, *Rosh Hashanah* and *Yom Kippur* are the most sacred holidays in Judaism. *Rosh Hashanah* celebrates Creation and occurs on the first two days of the year. *Yom Kippur* is the Day of Atonement, the day when, according to Old Testament law, the high priest entered the Most Holy Place.

Passover reminds the Jews of their flight from Egypt. *Shavuot*, or Pentecost, reminds them of the giving of the law on Mt. Sinai. *Sukkot* is a harvest festival. *Hanukkah,* which occurs around Christmastime, is the Feast of Lights and reminds the people of their deliverance from the Syrians. This occurs around Christmastime. *Purim* reminds the people of Esther and the rescue from the plot to kill the Jews. *Tishah be-av* reminds them of the two times the temple was destroyed.

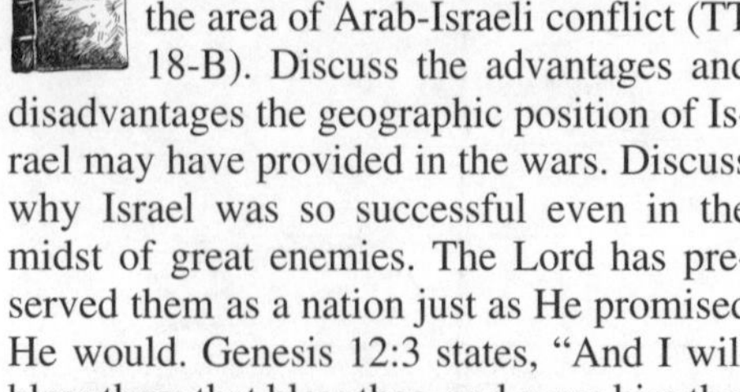

Conflict—Use a wall map to show the area of Arab-Israeli conflict (TT 18-B). Discuss the advantages and disadvantages the geographic position of Israel may have provided in the wars. Discuss why Israel was so successful even in the midst of great enemies. The Lord has preserved them as a nation just as He promised He would. Genesis 12:3 states, "And I will bless them that bless thee, and curse him that curseth thee: and in thee shall all families of the earth be blessed."

Yasir Arafat and the PLO—At forty years of age, Arafat became chairman of the PLO (Palestinian Liberation Organization). His stated goal was to work toward making the PLO the sole representative of the Palestinians by 1987. Arafat often used terrorism against Israel, but he lost many men in doing so. Arafat used Palestinians in Jordan to fight King Hussein, but with little outside aid they were forced to retreat. He appeared before the UN in 1974 claiming that he now carried "both a gun and an olive branch." As he has gotten older, Arafat has seemed to move more toward a peace process with the idea of two nations: Israel and a Palestinian homeland.

Victims of the Entebbe Rescue Operation—Lt. Col. Yonni Netanyahu, leader of the paratroopers that rescued the hostages at Entebbe, Uganda, lost his life while combing the airport for remaining terrorists. He was the older brother of Prime Minister Netanyahu.

plan. What about the Arabs? Were they to be under the control of Egypt and Jordan—as they had been until 1967? Or were they too to have their own independent state in Palestine? The idea of an independent Arab state became the goal of Arabs in Israeli-occupied Palestine.

Nearly all Arabs in the occupied areas wanted their own government, free of Israeli control. A minority resorted to violence to achieve that goal. Terrorists, notably the **Palestine Liberation Organization (PLO),** used riots, bombings, and guerrilla attacks to force the Israelis to give in to their demands.

Israel, however, feared that a new Arab state would be just one more enemy to face. Furthermore, many Israelis wanted to hold on to the occupied territories, especially the West Bank. For some, this territory would help make Israel more secure. Others, especially devout Jews, treasured the West Bank as part of God's gift of the Promised Land to the Jews. And almost no one in Israel wanted to surrender eastern Jerusalem.

At first, Israel stood firm against terrorists. In 1976 Arab terrorists hijacked a French jetliner with eighty-nine Israelis aboard. They flew to Entebbe, Uganda, and demanded the Israelis release fifty-three terrorists imprisoned in Israel. Otherwise, the hijackers would kill the passengers. The Israelis mounted a brilliant rescue operation. They landed at the airport at night, attacked the terrorists, and freed nearly all of the hostages.

But fighting back became more and more difficult. When some Palestinian terrorists began using bases in Lebanon, Israel invaded that country in 1982. World opinion condemned the act. To make matters worse, Lebanese troops working under Israeli officers went into Palestinian refugee camps and butchered over two thousand men, women, and children. Even Israeli citizens were revolted as pictures of the victims' bodies appeared on television. Incidents such as this convinced many Israeli leaders that the country must find a peaceful solution to its problems.

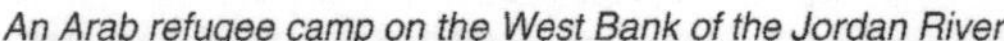

An Arab refugee camp on the West Bank of the Jordan River

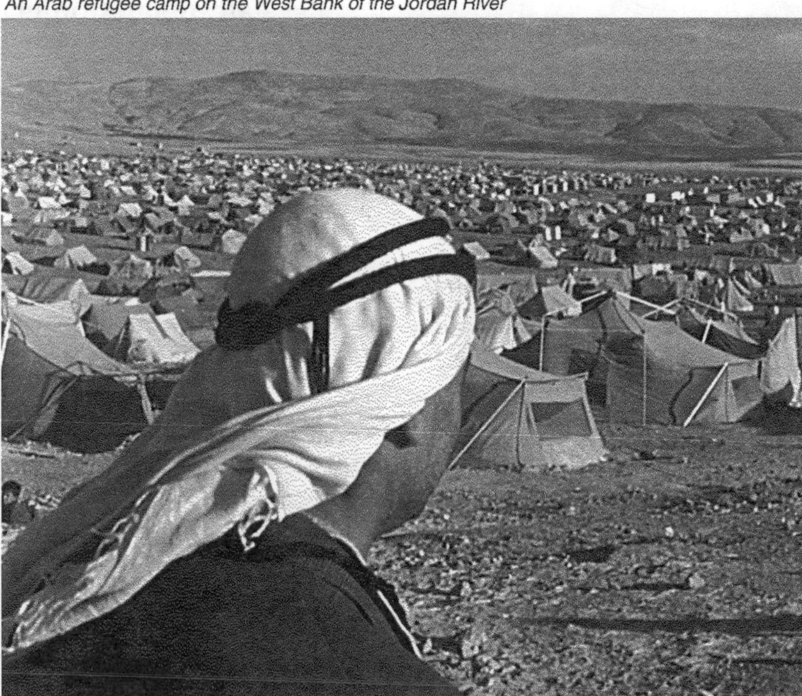

Newspaper—Have the students bring in newspaper or magazine articles concerning the Israeli-Palestinian conflict. Display them on a bulletin board throughout the duration of the chapter.

So Israel moved slowly toward meeting Arab demands. Despite more years of unrest and violence, the Israeli government and the PLO surprised the world in 1993 by announcing an agreement. It was not so much a final settlement as an agreement to work out difficulties. But under the agreement, Israel gave the Arabs some self-rule in the Gaza Strip and in selected cities and villages of the West Bank. It also left the door open for future discussions.

The government of Israel has been far from perfect. Sometimes it has mistreated Arab minorities, and its military actions, such as that in Lebanon, have caused suffering. Yet Israel remains the strongest democracy in the Middle East. With all of its flaws, Israel has remained committed to democratic ideals. The rule of law, reliance on the ballot box instead of bullets, and a commitment to justice all characterize the Jewish state. This example is very much needed in the Middle East.

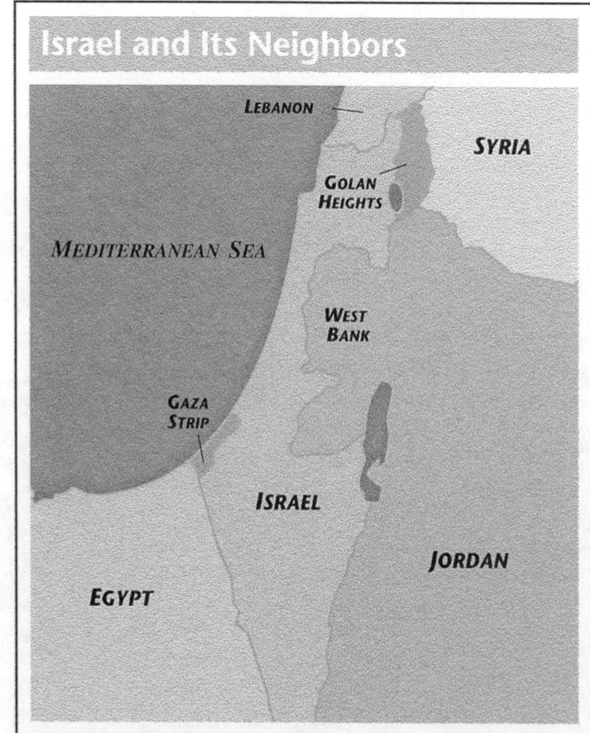

****
For a color version of the map on this page, see page A14 in the Appendix.

Occupied Territories—Three territories make up the occupied territories of Israel: the Gaza Strip, the Golan Heights, and the West Bank. The Gaza Strip was taken from Egypt in 1967 at the end of the Arab-Israeli War, and its population is mostly Palestinian, some of whom fled Israel when it became a country in 1948. Many *intifadas*, or political uprisings, began in the late 1980s. Israel and the PLO worked on an agreement in which the Gaza Strip (as well as the West Bank) would eventually gain self-rule.

Israel also occupied other territory at the end of the Arab-Israeli War. Israel took the Golan Heights from Syria, but many countries do not acknowledge that it belongs to Israel. Israel also took the West Bank from Jordan; again, many countries do not recognize the legitimacy of Israel's claim.

Assassination of Itzhak Rabin—Born on March 1, 1922, Itzhak Rabin was the first native-born prime minister of Israel. His parents were Russian immigrants. Rabin was chief of staff from 1964 to 1968, ambassador to the United States from 1968 to 1973, Knesset member in 1973, and prime minister in 1974. Rabin resigned in 1976. It was found that he had a bank account in the United States which was illegal at that time, so he withdrew from party leadership in 1977. Later he was Shimon Peres's minister of defense from 1984 to 1990, and he became prime minister again in 1992. Along with Peres and Yassir Arafat of the PLO, he received the Nobel Peace Prize in 1994 for a peace agreement reached in 1993. On November 4, 1995, Rabin was assassinated by an extremist who did not agree with the peace plans.

Benjamin Netanyahu—After Rabin was assassinated, the first direct elections took place in Israel. Benjamin Netanyahu had a very slight margin over the incumbent Peres and became the next prime minister. He was more conservative than Rabin or Peres, and the peace

Section Review

1. Who was the founder of the Zionist movement?
2. In what area was the nation of Israel reborn? In what year did Israel become an independent nation?
3. In what war did Israel destroy its enemies' planes before they could even get off the ground?
4. Where is the West Bank? the Gaza Strip?
5. What group of terrorists has attempted to regain Palestine for the Arabs by using violence against the Israelis?

Why have the Arabs been so intent on keeping Israel out of the Middle East? Look up Genesis 16 to see what the Bible has to say about the relationship between the Israelites and the Arabs; describe what you find.

Section Review Answers

1. Theodor Herzl
2. Palestine; 1948
3. Six-Day War
4. west of the Jordan River; along the Mediterranean coast
5. the Palestine Liberation Organization (PLO)

Answers will vary. The Bible promised strife between the Jews and the Arabs. Abraham's son Ishmael was the father of the Arabs, and Abraham's son Isaac was the father of the Jews. The spiritual application verses at the beginning of the chapter may help the students understand the strife between the Arabs and the world (see Gen. 16:12). However, there are also natural ethnic and religious conflicts between different groups, especially when the economic and political control of territory is involved.

process with the Palestinians became more unstable than it had been before. He stated that he did not want to give up any of the Occupied Territories to the Arabs.

Golda Meir's Husband—Golda saw her husband, Morris, as very understanding of her long absences during her fight for a Jewish homeland at the beginning of their marriage, but later her marriage began to fail as a result of her increasing absences and priorities upon politics rather than family. In fact, the couple eventually separated, although they never divorced. Golda's husband died in 1951 in Golda's house while she was away on a fundraising trip. She seemed to regret somewhat her choice that had pushed him aside.

CHARACTERIZATIONS

Golda Meir

On June 9, 1967, Golda Meir (MYE ur) stood before the Wailing Wall, all that remained of the ancient Jewish temple in Jerusalem. The Israeli army had just recaptured eastern Jerusalem. For the first time in nearly twenty years, Jews could again approach the wall. Golda Meir had never been a devout Jew, but the sight of Israeli soldiers pressing against the wall touched her. "Only a few hours earlier," she wrote, "they had fought furiously for the liberation of Jerusalem and had seen their comrades fall for its sake. Now, standing before the Wall, they wrapped themselves in prayer shawls and wept, and I, too, took a sheet of paper, wrote the word *'shalom'* (peace) on it and pushed it into a cranny of the Wall, as I had seen the Jews do so long ago." A soldier walked over, put his head on her shoulder, and wept. "I felt greatly blessed," she said, "that at that moment a young lad whom I did not know chose me to be a mother to him when he felt the need to weep on the shoulder of someone close and dear."

Golda Meir

Golda Mabovitch was born in 1898 to a Jewish family in Russia. The family fled Russia because of persecution and settled in Milwaukee, Wisconsin, in 1906. At an early age, Golda showed talents of organization and persuasion. When she was eleven years old, she found that some students in her school in Milwaukee needed money for their textbooks. She rented a hall and sent out invitations. Golda spoke to those who came about how students needed money for their texts. For the first time, Golda raised money for her cause and got her name into the newspapers.

Even while living in Russia, Golda had heard of Zionism, the desire for a Jewish homeland in Palestine. This idea became her dream too. In America she met and married Morris Meyerson in 1917. Together they moved to Palestine in 1921. Golda began working for Zionist organizations and became a leader in the movement for a Jewish homeland. The British tried to halt this movement to please the Arabs. In fact, when the British arrested many Zionist leaders in the 1940s, Golda was mildly insulted not to be arrested too.

When Israel declared its independence, Golda was one of the signers of the Israeli declaration of independence. During the War for Independence she visited the United States and raised $50 million from American Jews to help Israel. The next year she went back and raised $150 million more. She had certainly come a long way from raising money for textbooks in Milwaukee.

530 Chapter 18

Characterizations—Discuss Golda Meir's statement about the rest of the Middle East cooperating with Israel and each other. Was she being realistic? How did she help Israel?

Golda became an important official in the Israeli government. She served as ambassador to the Soviet Union (1948-49), minister of labor (1949-56), and foreign minister (1956-65). As minister of labor she faced special challenges brought on by the Law of the Return (1950). This law gave automatic citizenship to any Jew who came to live in Israel. As hundreds of thousands of Jews poured into the tiny country, she had to find housing and jobs for them. Also at this time, she, like many Israelis, took a Hebrew name. "Meyerson" became "Meir," from the Hebrew for "illuminate."

In 1969 Golda Meir became prime minister of Israel. She led Israel through some of its darkest days during the Yom Kippur War of 1973. She admitted later that the Egyptian attack caught her off guard. The prime minister realized that to lose the war would mean the destruction of the nation. She inspired and encouraged her people through the nerve-wracking days when Israel's fate hung in the balance. And she saw the nation through to final victory.

Golda Meir in 1970 described her hopes for her grandchildren: "I don't want them to live in an Israel that will always be complimented as the only democratic state here, the only developed state. I want Israel to be part of a highly developed, culturally advanced Middle East with much cooperation between its peoples. . . . Above all, I hope that Israel will become the ideal, just society of which we dreamed." She died in 1978 in Jerusalem.

Golda Meir with American civil rights leader Roy Wilkins

Working Mom—Golda Meir's political life often hurt her family life. On rare occasions when she had a headache and had to stay home, her children would sing, "Mommy's staying at home today! Mommy has a headache! Mommy's staying at home today!" She said, "It didn't help the headache any, and it hurt the heart a lot."

Realignment in the Middle East 531

SECTION 4

Student Objectives
Students should be able to
1. Distinguish the three basic varieties of Judaism.
2. Distinguish the two basic varieties of Islam.

Religions in the Middle East— Most of the Middle East is Islamic. Yet forms of Judaism and Christianity do exist. The Middle East is the birthplace of all three major monotheistic religions.

Religions in the Middle East

Country	Religions
Iran	Shi'a Muslim (89%), Sunni Muslim (10%)
Iraq	Shi'a Muslim (60-65%), Sunni Muslim (32-37%)
Kuwait	Muslim (85%)
Saudi Arabia	Muslim (100%)
Egypt	Muslim (94%), Coptic Christian and other (6%)
Israel	Jewish (82%), Muslim (14%)
Jordan	Sunni Muslim (74%), Christian (8%)
Lebanon	Muslim (70%), Christian (30%)
Syria	Sunni Muslim (74%), other Muslim (16%), Christian (10%)
Turkey	Muslim (99.8%)

Religion in the Middle East

Islam, Judaism, Christianity—all of these religions were born in the Middle East. The history of the region makes no sense to someone who does not understand the importance of religion there. In the drama of twentieth-century Middle Eastern history, Judaism and Islam have played leading roles.

Judaism

Judaism began when God called Abraham from Ur of the Chaldees. God promised him the land of Palestine (Gen. 12:1-7). From that time Abraham's descendants lived in that land, but not without interruption. From the time of Joseph (1876 B.C.) to Moses (1446 B.C.), the Hebrew people lived in Egypt. During the Babylonian captivity (586-539 B.C.), most of the Jews lived in exile. Then in A.D. 66 and again in A.D. 132 the Jews rebelled against the Roman Empire. The Romans destroyed Jerusalem and scattered the Jews all around the world. Not until the twentieth century was there a major movement of Jews back to Palestine.

During the many centuries after the Romans scattered the Jews, different forms of Judaism developed. Some of these forms are cultural and geographic. Two major groups of this kind are the **Sephardim** and the **Ashkenazim.** Sephardic Jews are those who have their roots in medieval Spain and Portugal; their traditions go back to the Jews who lived in Babylon after the exile in 586 B.C. Ashkenazic Jews have their roots in medieval northern and eastern Europe; their traditions go back to the Jews who lived in Palestine. The Ashkenazim developed the language known as **Yiddish,** a mixture of Hebrew and German. There are also other, smaller groups. Earlier we also mentioned Ethiopian Jews (p. 115). They have lived in Africa since the Middle Ages. Many of these groups are represented in modern Israel, but the Ashkenazic Jews have generally provided the leadership in that nation.

There are also different theological varieties of Judaism. The most liberal is **Reform Judaism.** It teaches that Judaism is basically

Orthodox Jews in Jerusalem

SECTION 4

Materials
- Recordings of Jewish music

Jewish music—Bring in Jewish music for the students to listen to. They may find it very different from what they are used to. You may also want to play an example of a call to prayer during one of the ritual five daily prayers of the Muslims.

Jews gather to pray at the Wailing Wall, the only surviving section of the Jewish temple of Jesus' day. The Dome of the Rock, a Muslim mosque built on the site of the temple, is clearly visible above the wall.

The Customs of Judaism—The Jews have specific laws about what they may and may not eat. They may not eat pork or shellfish, and they may not eat milk products with meat. An Orthodox Jew would never eat a cheeseburger. Many of these customs have been verified as sound medical advice. Drinking milk with meat makes meat much more difficult to digest.

concerned with principles of right and wrong. Therefore, Jews may adapt their forms of worship and manner of living to the age in which they live. Reform Jewish temples often look little different from Christian churches. Their services are conducted in the native language instead of Hebrew. Reform Jews are less concerned with traditional Jewish dietary laws, such as the ban on eating pork. They even ordain women as rabbis—a practice strongly denounced by traditional Jews.

Next is **Conservative Judaism.** This branch is similar to Reform Judaism in that it holds that Jews may adapt their manner of life to the times in which they live. Conservative Jews, however, place much more value on Jewish tradition. Congregations vary in practice; some may follow dietary laws, for example, while others do not.

Finally there is **Orthodox Judaism.** This is the general term for the strictest form of Judaism. The Orthodox believe that the Old Testament and Jewish tradition were given directly by God. Therefore, they insist on strict adherence to the law. Followers of Orthodox Judaism carefully follow all the Jewish laws concerning diet, the Sabbath, and Jewish holy days. They forbid marriage with non-Jews and wear traditional clothing. Men, for example, always wear a hat or skullcap (a *yarmulke*) to show their respect to God.

There are different forms of Orthodox Judaism. One influential group is the **Hasidim.** These are strict Jews with roots in Eastern Europe. Hasidic Jews are traditional, but much of their tradition traces back to Eastern Europe in the 1700s. They speak the language, Yiddish, that developed there. Their clothes are the style of that era: long black coats, broad-brimmed hats, and long-sleeved white shirts. The men often wear long curls of hair from their temples, their way of obeying

Branches of Religions—Discuss with students their thoughts on how different varieties and forms of a certain religion are started. Use the example of dialects in language as an analogy. Ask for examples in Protestantism, even in Fundamentalism. Talk about the Holy Spirit's leading in the Christian's life and His guidance into all truth. Discuss how He may work differently in some hearts than in others. Give and ask for examples of how this may be seen today.

Islam—See "Major Religions of the World" on page 72 for more about Islam.

The Customs of Islam—Muslims believe in five duties: (1) profession that there is no god but Allah and Muhammed is his prophet, (2) prayer five times a day toward Mecca, (3) almsgiving, (4) fasting during the month of Ramadan (they may eat at night), and (5) pilgrimage to Mecca.

Muhammed's birthday is the most important holiday; Shiites also celebrate the birth of Muhammed's daughter, Fatima, and commemorate the death of Hussain, Muhammed's grandson.

Leviticus 19:27, "Ye shall not round the corners of your heads."

Many Jews today are "nonobservant," or "secular." They do not practice any religion but think of themselves as an ethnic group. The majority of Jews in Israel are secular Jews. But the Israeli government recognizes only Orthodox Judaism as the official form of Judaism. Only the Orthodox may serve as chaplains in the Israeli armed forces, and only Orthodox rabbis may perform weddings. The Orthodox in Israel also control small political parties that hold the balance of power in the Israeli **Knesset** (legislature). Orthodox Judaism exerts more influence in modern Israel than its numbers might indicate.

A Jewish boy celebrates his bar mitzvah at the Wailing Wall.

Islam

Muslims believe in only one God, Allah, but there is more than one form of Islam. Most Muslims (90 percent of the world's Muslim population) are **Sunnite Muslims.** The Sunnis viewed the **caliphs** as the legitimate successors to Muhammad. (*Caliph* means "successor.") Starting with the first caliph, Abu-Bakr, the son-in-law of Muhammad, the caliph was the main religious leader of the Muslims. The caliph, it was believed, guarded the traditions handed down by the prophet. The Sunnis followed the caliphs of Islam until 1924, when Kemal Atatürk abolished the office. Over the years, however, the Sunnis developed a system of Islamic law called the **shari'a.** As long as Muslim governments follow the shari'a, Sunnis say today, the caliph is no longer needed.

Shiite Muslims consider the caliphs to be illegitimate successors to Muhammad. They

A gilded Muslim minaret

Religions of the Middle East—Create a chart of major Middle Eastern religions. Include Judaism, Islam, and Christianity. Categories may include *Foundings, Varieties and Forms, Rituals, Major Beliefs,* and *Important Terms.* Encourage students to use this chart as a study guide (BLM 18-1).

believe that only direct descendants of Muhammad should be leaders of Islam. The Shiites give special honor to a line of **imams** ("leaders"). Whereas the caliph was supposed to preserve tradition, the Shiite imam had special teaching authority from Allah. The twelfth imam disappeared as a child around 878. With him the office stopped, and Shiites now await the return of the twelfth imam to bring about a golden age. Scholars have always had a large role in Shiite Islam. An example of the influence of these scholars is the Ayatollah Khomeini's leadership in Iran (discussed in the next section).

Devout Muslims regularly bow in the direction of Mecca to pray.

Flags—A crescent and star together is the symbol of Islam. Today, Pakistan and Turkey include these on their flags.

The Sunnites and Shiites are often bitterly opposed to each other. Only two major countries have Shiite majorities. In Iran Shiites compose 95 percent of the population, and they make up two-thirds of the population of Iraq. (The tiny nation of Bahrain also has a Shiite majority.) Elsewhere, Sunnites are in the overwhelming majority. There are varieties even within these two groups. The Wahhabis in Saudi Arabia practice a very strict form of Sunnite Islam. (See p. 523.) The Druze are a splinter group from Shiite Islam living in Syria and Lebanon. Because the Druze do not consider Muhammad the true prophet of Allah, most Muslims consider them heretics.

In the 1970s, the strictest Islamic groups began grabbing headlines around the world. The most extreme of these groups even rebelled against governments that they thought were not purely enough Islamic. The story of the Iranian Revolution in the next section provides a chilling example of Islamic extremism in action.

Section Review

1. What language did the Ashkenazim develop?
2. List the three theological varieties of Judaism and briefly describe each.
3. Describe the Hasidic form of Orthodox Judaism.
4. Name and briefly describe the origins of the two major forms of Islam in the Middle East today.
5. What is the title of the "successor" to Muhammad that Sunnite Muslims followed? Who put an end to this office?

Compare and contrast Judaism and Islam. Is either comparable to Christianity? How? How are they different?

Section Review Answers

1. Yiddish
2. Reform Judaism—ethical form of Judaism concerned with adapting to the age in which one lives; Conservative Judaism—adapt to the age in which one lives but also preserve traditions; Orthodox Judaism—strictest form of Judaism with much emphasis on tradition
3. The Hasidim are Orthodox Jews who trace their traditions in language, clothes, and hair to the 1700s.
4. Sunni Islam—belief in the caliphs as the true successors of Islam (today the shari'a guides in place of a caliph); Shi'a Islam—belief in the direct line of Muhammad's descendants (imams) as the true successors
5. caliphs; Kemal Atatürk

Answers will vary. Both Jews and Muslims believe in one God. They both have the same father in Abraham. They trust in works to get them to heaven. However, they hate each other and have different doctrinal beliefs. Christianity also has one God, the true God, and a father in Abraham. Christianity, Islam, and Judaism are the three major monotheistic religions in the world today. Christianity's God is a God of love and peace as well as justice, while Islam's god (or Allah) is a vengeful, angry god whose main goal is to punish sin. Jews do not believe that the Messiah has come.

CENTER STAGE

Hasidic Jews represent the most conservative branch of Judaism. Their strongly traditionalist Jewish faith is sometimes mistakenly labeled "fundamentalist."

Religious "Fundamentalisms"

A group of Muslim extremists force their way into a worship service at the Holy Mosque in Mecca on November 20, 1979. For two weeks they hold this site. Finally, troops of the Saudi government force their way into the mosque and engage the rebels. Over a hundred rebels die, and another hundred are captured. The leader of the group is publicly beheaded less than a month later. Newspapers announce that the Muslim "fundamentalists" have been routed.

On April 26, 1984, Israeli officials arrest twenty-seven members of a Jewish extremist group. They had been caught wiring explosives to five buses scheduled to carry Arabs. While questioning the prisoners, the Israelis discover a plot even more shocking. This group has been planning to attack the Dome of the Rock, a Muslim holy site in Jerusalem located where the Jewish temple once stood. Members of the group armed with automatic weapons are to kill the guards, plant twenty-seven bombs, and blow the Dome to pieces. Television reports that the government has foiled this plot of these Jewish "fundamentalists."

The media and some scholars have popularized the term fundamentalist as a label for extremist religious groups. They use the term to describe certain kinds of Muslims, Jews, Buddhists, and other religious groups. Not all those labeled "fundamentalist" are as extreme as the ones described above. Even so, this use of the term *fundamentalist* is incorrect.

The term *Fundamentalist* originated in America. In the early 1900s, many Protestants in the United States opposed the growth of liberal theology. Liberals denied biblical truths such as Christ's deity, virgin birth, and resurrection. They said they wanted to make Christianity more "modern." (One form of liberalism is often called "Modernism.") In response, conservatives published a series of pamphlets called *The Fundamentals.* Articles in these pamphlets defended the teachings of God's Word against liberal attack. Then in 1920 a Baptist

Center Stage—Discuss some of the fundamentals of the Christian faith: Christ's deity, the virgin birth, and Christ's resurrection from the dead. Explain that to be a Bible-believing Christian, one must hold these to be true as stated in God's Word. They are not suggestions or symbolic pictures but literal accounts of what happened to our Lord. Explain that this is what we mean by faith: sometimes one must accept things that he cannot understand because the Lord said it is true in His Word.

newspaper editor wrote, "We suggest that those who still cling to the great fundamentals and who mean to do battle royal for the fundamentals shall be called 'Fundamentalists.' "

The Fundamentalists battled the Modernists for control of the major American denominations in the 1920s. When they lost those battles, the Fundamentalists organized their own schools, denominations, and mission boards. Because these Fundamentalists sought to defend historic Christianity, some have argued that any group that strives to maintain its traditional religious beliefs should be called "fundamentalist."

There are problems with this definition, however. Although Protestant Fundamentalists "fought for the faith," their battling was not violent. They published magazines and books, preached sermons to persuade audiences, and voted democratically in church elections as their way of standing for their faith. Non-Christian "fundamentalists," however, are commonly associated with violence. Even the many who do not commit acts of violence often support the overthrow of governments. Protestant Fundamentalists say every man should have the freedom to think and believe as he wishes. These other groups usually hold that they must force nonbelievers to accept their group's teachings.

Fundamentalism is not about *how* a person behaves but *what* he believes. Some who use the label "fundamentalist" argue that traditional Jews, Muslims, and others practice their faith in the same way as Christian Fundamentalists. But Protestant Fundamentalism is about defending the beliefs of the Christian faith. A "fundamentalist" Muslim or Jew would never accept the Bible's teaching that Jesus is God, but a Fundamentalist insists that there is no salvation apart from that belief. Historically, a Fundamentalist is not someone who holds to the "fundamentals" of just any religion; he is one who upholds the essential truths of Christianity.

The Dome of the Rock is a Muslim mosque built on the site of Solomon's temple and the rock from which Muhammad allegedly ascended to heaven. It is a point of conflict between traditionalist Jews and Muslims.

Section 5

Student Objectives
Students should be able to

1. Identify important national leaders and the country each comes from.
2. Explain the connection between OPEC and world energy.
3. Describe the conflicts between Iran and Iraq and between Iraq and Kuwait.

Oil Shortages—During the strife in Iran later that same decade, the supply of oil was again limited, causing the price of oil to rise once more. Gasoline prices were about thirty cents per gallon in the 1960s compared to current prices of about a dollar.

Oil, Revolution, and War

Jesus warned, "Take heed, and beware of covetousness: for a man's life consisteth not in the abundance of the things which he possesseth" (Luke 12:15). Sections of the Middle East enjoy great wealth through their rich resources in oil. But wealth has not brought peace to the region. Instead, it has brought competition and conflict. Some nations have used the need for the oil itself as a weapon to bend other nations to their demands. Oil has driven some nations to attack their neighbors in a frenzy of greed. Religion complicates the situation. Many of the nations fighting over oil also fight over who follows the purest form of Islam. Oil and religion are an explosive mix.

Oil

The modern world runs on oil. Anyone who drives a car or just mows his lawn relies on an oil product, gasoline. Industries use oil for fuel or for lubrication. Many homes are heated by oil or by electricity produced by oil-driven generators. Petroleum (oil and natural gas) is also an important ingredient in producing asphalt and insecticides, as well as paint, plastic, rubber, fibers, and much more.

Supertankers load oil at the Sea Island, one of Saudi Arabia's huge seacost terminals.

Two-thirds of the world's known oil deposits lie underground in the Middle East. Before World War I, only Persia (Iran) produced much oil for sale. Today, the Middle East is the center of the world's oil production. By the 1990s the Middle East produced a third of the world's oil supply; Saudi Arabia alone produced nearly half of that.

To increase their profits and power, the oil-producing nations of the Middle East formed **OPEC** in 1960. *OPEC* stands for "Organization of Petroleum-Exporting Countries." It became OPEC's goal to push oil prices as high as possible. OPEC was formed as a **cartel.** A cartel exists when the producers of an item get together to control the price of the item they produce. In this case, the members of OPEC would agree to limit how much oil they produced so that they could push the price up.

For the first few years OPEC had little success. Then when Egypt and Syria went to war against Israel in 1973, the Arab nations of OPEC refused to sell to nations that supported Israel, including the United States. They also raised the price for other countries. Oil prices shot up. A barrel of oil sold for $3 before the Arab-Israeli war began. By 1981 oil was selling for $35 a barrel.

For a few years, the OPEC nations were gorged with profits. But the oil boom did not last. As prices for oil products rose, people found ways to avoid buying Arab oil. They bought cars that used less gasoline, sought out new deposits of oil, or even turned to different

Section 5

Materials

- Motor oil, petroleum jelly
- Guest speaker, a veteran of the Persian Gulf War

Economics—Ask students why gas prices do not rise and fall unreasonably today. (*rules set down by OPEC and competition among oil companies and among oil suppliers*) Divide the students into four groups, each group having control of a single important item of trade. Have them sell to each other (you may wish to use play money), giving each group a goal of how much of each item to end up with. At first, the prices may be high because the group can charge as much as it wants, but eventually, the group will also have to buy, so they may have to spend as much money as they took in. The more the students trade with each other, the more the prices should be comparable. Explain that this would change if there were a shortage of one of these products, and act it out again. Answer questions the students may have about a balance of trade.

Oil—Bring in some motor oil and place it in a bowl. Making sure you have plenty of water and paper towels on hand, have each student dab his finger in the oil. This is not pure petroleum but refined oil. After the students have done this, let them dip a finger in petroleum jelly (Vaseline), which is also a petroleum product, to clean it off. You may need to let them wash their hands afterward.

The Ayatollah Khomeini greets a crowd of his adoring followers.

sources of fuel such as coal. As demand slackened, prices fell. Also some members of OPEC needed money and cheated the cartel by producing more oil then they said they would. This extra oil on the market helped keep prices down. The oil producers ignored a basic law of economics: the demand for an item is always related to its cost. If a producer tries to ask for too much money for his goods, he will find that demand falls as his prices rise.

Conflict in the Middle East

While oil prices were rising and falling in the 1970s and 1980s, the Middle East suffered some jolts. The first came in 1979 in Iran. As mentioned earlier, a popular uprising overthrew the shah. In his place arose a frightening figure, the **Ayatollah Ruholla Khomeini** (EYE-uh-TOH-luh roo-OH-luh koh-MAY-nee). An *ayatollah* is a respected teacher and leader among Shiite Muslims. Khomeini proceeded to establish in Iran a Muslim state of the strictest kind. He began by executing hundreds of officials from the shah's government.

Khomeini's "Islamic republic" in Iran was in many ways the exact opposite of Atatürk's secular state in Turkey. Atatürk wanted a nation in which no religion could force its will on everyone. Khomeini insisted on a state in which everyone lived according to Islamic law. Atatürk opened the door to Western ideas. Khomeini considered Western ideas corrupt and devilish. Under the Ayatollah, Iran again required women to wear the heavy veils of Islamic custom. Those who defied the law risked arrest and beatings from the Revolutionary Guards. Khomeini's fervor did not stop with Iran. He promised "to export our revolution to the four corners of the world."

Oil Fields in the Middle East

Major Producing Field
Minor Producing Field

Iran-Contra Affair—To help Iran in its war with Iraq, top officials in the Reagan administration were selling arms to Iran with the hopes of getting hostages released from Lebanon. This was done undercover, however, and Americans were not happy that this secret had been kept from them. To make matters worse, money from the sales was funneled to the Contras in Nicaragua; help to the Contras had been forbidden in a recent Congressional bill.

Iranian Leaders—Using the overhead or chalkboard, make two columns: one with the heading *Muhammad Reza Shah Pahlavi* and the other *Ayatollah Ruhollah Khomeini*. Both were leaders in Iran, but their policies were very different. List under each heading the policies for religion, place of women, and thoughts about Western ideas. Discuss how the people in Iran may have reacted to these changes.

Student Objectives

Students should be able to

1. Locate Lebanon on a map.
2. Analyze and create picture graphs.

The Middle East Today—Many people have moved from rural areas to urban areas since World War II. Urban life is generally much more technologically advanced than rural life, though rural life is slowly increasing in technology and prosperity.

The cradle of civilization, Mesopotamia (called "the land between the rivers"), is found here. The rivers are the Tigris and the Euphrates, which join into what is today called the Shatt al-Arab. This river in turn flows into the Persian Gulf.

SETTINGS—Lebanon

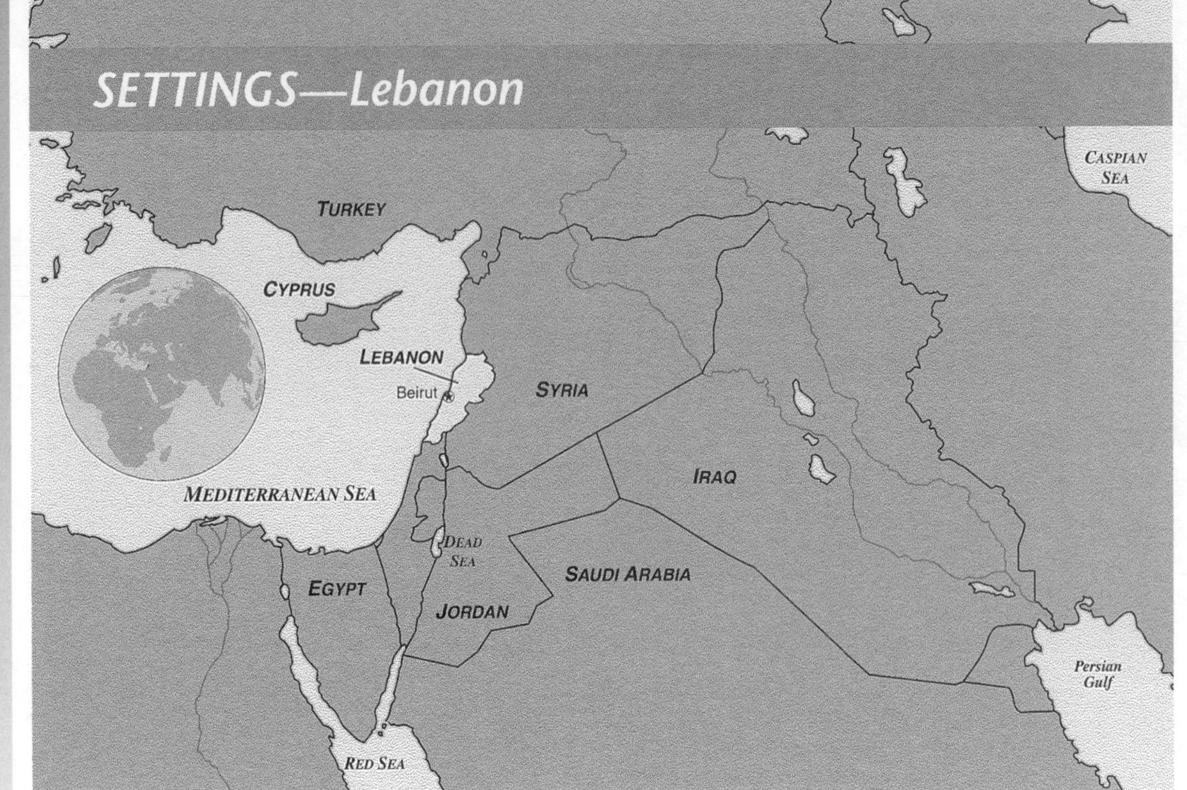

Location—Lebanon is located in the Middle East. It is bordered in the north and east by Syria and in the south by Israel. Its western border is the Mediterranean Sea.

Climate—Lebanon has a mediterranean climate with warm, dry summers and mild, wet winters. Temperatures tend to be highest along the coast while rainfall is most plentiful in the western Lebanon Mountains.

Topography—Lebanon's topography lies in four parallel strips. Along the Mediterranean Sea runs a narrow coastal plain. The backbone of the country, running north to south, is the Lebanon Mountains. To the east of the mountains lies the rich Bekaa Valley. Beyond this valley stands the Anti-Lebanon Range along the border with Syria.

Natural Resources—In ancient times Lebanon was known for the beautiful wood of its magnificent cedar trees. (See II Sam. 5:11; I Kings 5:1-12; Ezek. 27:5.) Overcutting reduced these great forests, however. Today only a limited number of cedars are available for commercial use. Instead the nation's limestone deposits make Lebanon an important producer of cement and gravel. Lebanon exports citrus fruits, apples, and tobacco. However, banking, not natural resources, is the nation's largest source of income.

Geography & Culture—Lebanon sits at a crossroads of the Middle East. Both sea trade and overland trade have enriched the region. In ancient times Lebanon was part of Phoenicia, dominated by the major trading cities of Tyre and Sidon. The richness of the region later attracted Greek and

Materials

- Transparencies for Chapter 18
- Wall map of the Middle East (BLM 18-2)

Map Activity—Use map 18-C from the Student Activities manual to reinforce the geography lesson.

Going Beyond—Read the Settings pages on the Middle East and answer the questions. Show the students a picture graph and discuss its uses (TT 18-A). Have each student create a picture graph for the number of students in class with certain physical characteristics. For example, chart the number of students with brown hair, red hair, blond hair, and so on.

then Roman conquerors. Islamic empires dominated the area from the 600s to the breakup of the Ottoman Empire after World War I. Lebanon became a nation under French oversight in the 1920s and in 1943 became completely independent.

Lebanon is also a religious crossroads. The nation is 60 to 70 percent Muslim and 30 to 40 percent Christian. An important minority of the Muslims are the Druze. (See p. 535.) Lebanon has the highest percentage of Christian citizens of any Arab country. The largest Christian group in Lebanon are the Maronites. This group is part of the Roman Catholic Church, but it maintains its own practices and customs. Unfortunately, these religious groups sometimes clash. Not only do Christians and Muslims fight each other but sometimes the Muslims fight among themselves. Lebanon is a small land, but it suffers from many conflicts.

Settings Review

1. What country lies on Lebanon's eastern border?
2. What type of climate does Lebanon have?
3. What type of wood is Lebanon known for?
4. Modern-day Lebanon was part of what kingdom in Old Testament times?

Read I Kings 5:1-12. What kind of goods did Solomon purchase from Hiram of Tyre? Why would Solomon get workers from Hiram? How might these business relationships have promoted the peace between Solomon and Hiram described in verse 12?

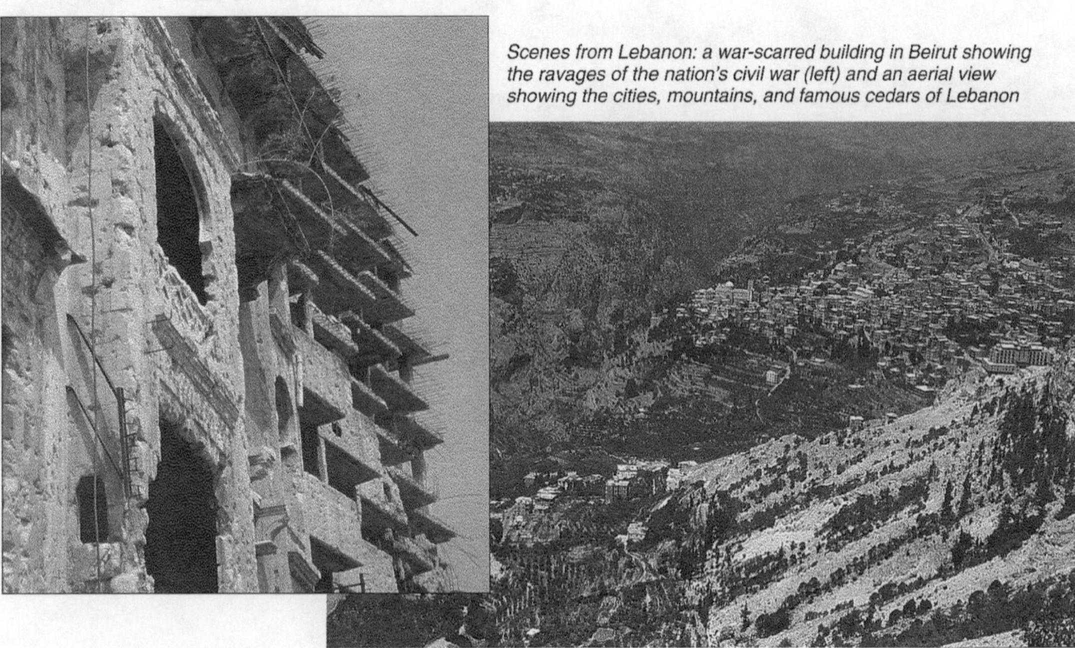

Scenes from Lebanon: a war-scarred building in Beirut showing the ravages of the nation's civil war (left) and an aerial view showing the cities, mountains, and famous cedars of Lebanon

Settings Review Answers

1. Syria
2. mediterranean
3. cedar
4. Phoenicia

Answers will vary. Solomon purchased cedar and fir (cypress) wood from Hiram. Since Tyre grew these woods, Solomon assumed Hiram's subjects were more skilled in working with the woods and thus hired them as workers. Of course, ultimately it was the Lord who gave peace between Solomon and Hiram, but humanly speaking the trade and the honest dealings between the nations helped to build trust and interdependence.

Patriot Missiles—These antimissile missiles were used mostly by Israel to repel invading Iraqi Scud missiles. Patriot missiles are reported to have approximately a 40 percent success rate, but this figure is very controversial. Different estimates range from 0 to 70 percent.

Saddam Hussein

The revolution in Iran certainly caught the attention of its next-door neighbor. Dictator **Saddam Hussein** (suh-DAHM hoo-SAYN) of Iraq saw the revolution as both a danger and an opportunity. On the one hand, he feared that his own Shiite population might get revolutionary ideas from Iran. On the other, he saw the disorder in Iran as an opportunity to seize an important waterway between the two countries.

Saddam attacked Iran on September 22, 1980. Eight years of warfare followed. The two sides blasted and bombed each other. The Iranians sent waves of fervent revolutionary soldiers streaming against Iraqi lines. Iraq in turn loosed poison gas on the Iranians. Iraqi planes bombed Iranian cities, and Iranian missiles rained down on Iraqi cities. After eight years of fighting, the two exhausted sides agreed to peace, but hatred burned on. Khomeini wished that Iran could continue until Saddam Hussein was destroyed. He said that accepting peace was "more deadly than taking poison."

Having failed in Iran, Saddam then looked for an easier victim. He found one in the small but oil-rich country of Kuwait to his south. He invaded Kuwait on August 2, 1990. If the war against Iran had been a mistake for Iraq, then the invasion of Kuwait was a disaster. The world frowned as Iraq attacked a neighbor without cause. Then the world worried as Saddam Hussein put massive forces on the border of Saudi Arabia. He threatened to seize control of a huge portion of the world's oil supply.

The United States provided the bulk of the troops used to drive Iraq out of Kuwait in the Gulf War of 1991.

Connections—Invite a veteran of the Persian Gulf War to share his experiences with the class. He may also want to share his view of American response to the war. This will be quite different from the experiences of Vietnam veterans.

Other nations saw the danger that Saddam posed. Led by the United States, the United Nations authorized military action against Iraq. The United States, European nations such as Great Britain, and Arab nations such as Saudi Arabia and Egypt sent over 250,000 troops to drive Iraq back. The **Gulf War** began on January 17, 1991, with five weeks of heavy bombing of targets in Iraq. On February 24, the anti-Iraq coalition struck. In just one hundred hours, the U.S.-led forces destroyed much of the Iraqi army and surrounded most of what was left. Kuwait had been freed and Iraq humiliated.

War rarely settles problems, however. The competition for oil wealth continued. Islamic extremism still promoted violence in the region and tried to export violence worldwide. Friction between differing ethnic groups heated into even more violence. The Middle East was the birthplace of the Prince of Peace, Jesus Christ. But the region itself is far from enjoying peace.

Spanning the Ages

The twentieth-century events we have talked about include the decolonization of India; dictatorship in Germany, Italy, Turkey, and other countries; ethnic conflict in Russia and Armenia; and conflict between Jews and Muslims. The same basic themes will be seen in our upcoming study of Africa—decolonization in Algeria, dictatorship in Ghana, racial conflict in South Africa, and tribal conflict in Rwanda.

Section Review

1. What does OPEC stand for and what was its goal?
2. What is an *ayatollah?*
3. Iran fought what country for control of an important waterway?
4. The Gulf War resulted from Iraq's invasion of which Middle Eastern country?

Why did Khomeini say that accepting peace was "more deadly than taking poison"? Do you agree? Why or why not?

Summary

The collapse of the Ottoman Empire at the end of World War I ushered in a new era of Middle Eastern history. Turkey, the heart of the old Ottoman Empire, became a modern secular state under the rule of Kemal Atatürk. Iran, under the Pahlavis, also tried to become a modern state but eventually fell under the control of Muslim extremists led by the Ayatollah Khomeini. Saudi Arabia, with its immense oil wealth, tried to be a traditionalist Muslim nation, but it found that its wealth attracted corrupting influences. Only the nation of Israel has maintained a stable democracy in the Middle East. But it has done so only in the face of Arab hostility. Religion has also been a source of conflict. Jews and Muslims have clashed not only with each other but also among themselves. Enormous wealth has not been able to forestall violence, as shown by two wars involving the nation of Iraq. Peace is not among the riches of the Middle East.

Section Review Answers

1. Organization of Petroleum Exporting Countries; to control oil prices and drive them higher
2. a respected teacher and leader among Shiite Muslims
3. Iraq
4. Kuwait

Answers will vary. Khomeini thought that leaving Saddam Hussein in power would be poisonous to the Middle East and even the whole world. According to Khomeini, Hussein was a corrupting influence that needed to be eradicated. Khomeini wanted to continue fighting until Hussein was out of power. But his country was too tired to fight on, so peace was accepted. Students may agree that Hussein should have been toppled because of his aggression, as demonstrated by the future Gulf War, or they may disagree because of convictions against fighting.

Chapter Review Idea

Play the Middle East Oil Game. Divide your class into two teams. Each team gains access to oil wells by answering review questions correctly. The first team to reach twenty oil wells wins.

Chapter Enrichment Activities

Gas Shortages—Have students ask their parents or grandparents about the gas shortages of the 1970s and write down what their parents say. They should relate this information to the class. Ask students how an oil embargo might affect the United States today.

Create a Country—Have each student create his own country. He must choose a name, symbol, flag, and motto for his country. He should draw a diagram of the country along with important cities. In about fifty words, he should explain why he is forming his own country. He should give the date of founding, the climate, the lifestyle of the people, the language, and any other relevant information. Encourage students to look up countries in the encyclopedia as examples of information needed. Discuss how difficult it would be to actually start a new country. Where would one get the land? What kind of people would already be there, and who would move there? Contrast the students' effort to create a new nation and Zionism. *(No one was fighting against the student's forming his country as was the case in Israel.)* Discuss why the Jews were allowed to have their own country and how the Israelis have managed to keep it despite all the opposition.

Research—Have students find primary sources about the Gulf War and report on their findings. These should still be available from a variety of sources, including books, magazines, newspapers, and television news reports. You may wish to share your recollections of the Gulf War with your students. The report should be at least 150 words long and should include aspects of the fighting, technology, and patriotism found in the UN or Iraqi forces in the war.

CHAPTER REVIEW

People, Places, and Things to Know

Anatolia	Abdul Aziz ibn-Saud	Palestine Liberation Organization (PLO)	caliph
Mustafa Kemal	Wahhabi movement	Sephardim	shari'a
Turkey	Saudi Arabia	Ashkenazim	Shiite Muslim
Kemal Atatürk	Zionism	Yiddish	imam
fez	Theodor Herzl	Reform Judaism	OPEC
Reza Shah Pahlavi	Balfour Declaration	Conservative Judaism	cartel
Iran	War of Independence	Orthodox Judaism	Ayatollah Ruholla Khomeini
Mohammed Reza Shah Pahlavi	Six-Day War	Hasidim	Saddam Hussein
"White Revolution"	Yom Kippur War	Knesset	Gulf War
Bedouins	West Bank	Sunnite Muslim	

Review Questions

Identify

Give the term for each definition.

1. strict form of Islam based in Arabia which wishes to make others believe as it believes
2. the movement to form an Israeli state
3. Jews whose roots are in Spain and Portugal
4. Jews whose roots are in northern and eastern Europe
5. strict Orthodox Jews with traditions from the 1700s

Matching

Match each form of religion to its definition.

(a) Conservative Judaism
(b) Orthodox Judaism
(c) Reform Judaism
(d) Shiite Muslims
(e) Sunnite Muslims

6. believe in Muhammad's descendants as the only proper leaders of Islam
7. believe in caliphs as legitimate successors to Muhammad
8. strictest form of Judaism
9. form of Judaism which stresses conformity to the age in which one lives
10. form of Judaism which conforms to the age but keeps tradition

Chapter Review Answers

Identify

1. Wahhabi movement
2. Zionist movement
3. Sephardim
4. Ashkenazim
5. Hasidim

Matching

6. d
7. e
8. b
9. c
10. a

Association

Name the country with which each of the following is associated.

11. Ayatollah Ruholla Khomeini
12. ibn-Saud
13. Kemal Atatürk
14. Mohammed Reza Shah Pahlavi
15. Mustafa Kemal
16. Reza Shah Pahlavi
17. Golda Meir

Think About It!

With your knowledge of the world today, predict the relationship of Middle Eastern countries to each other as well as to the rest of the world, especially in relation to oil and religion.

Association

11. Iran
12. Saudi Arabia
13. Turkey
14. Iran
15. Turkey
16. Iran
17. Israel

Think About It!

Answers will vary. Israel will continue to have problems with neighboring countries as it continues to determine its exact territory. Oil will become more of a bargaining tool for the Middle East as the world's resources weaken. Religion will continue to determine divisions and alliances.

Doctrines—In cooperation with the Bible teacher, if he is teaching the students about the major doctrines of the faith, have students write a few brief sentences on each major Fundamentalist doctrine. This could be in place of the discussion on the Center Stage pages.

Recipe: Shish Kebab—This recipe for broiled, skewered lamb is a common type of food eaten in Turkey.

Ingredients:

1 large onion, peeled and cut into 1/8-inch slices, separated into rings
2 Tbsp. olive oil
4 Tbsp. fresh lemon juice
2 tsp. salt
½ tsp. freshly ground black pepper
2 lbs. lean, boneless lamb, trimmed of fat and cut into 2-inch cubes
1 large tomato, cut crosswise into four slices
1 large green pepper, quartered
2 Tbsp. heavy cream

Place onion rings into deep bowl and sprinkle with olive oil, lemon juice, salt, and pepper. Add lamb and turn to coat. Marinate at room temperature for at least two hours (or in the refrigerator for four hours), turning lamb occasionally.

Remove lamb from marinade and place cubes tightly on three or four skewers. Thread tomato and green peppers alternately on another skewer. Brush the meat with cream. Grill for 10-15 minutes. The vegetables will be done before the lamb. Slide the vegetables and lamb onto a plate and serve with rice.

Student Objectives
Students should be able to

1. Locate the Democratic Republic of Congo (former Zaire).
2. Create and analyze line graphs.
3. Identify the four regions of Africa and the representative country in each.
4. Describe the course of decolonization in Algeria.
5. Evaluate the claim that Italy was "civilizing" Ethiopia by conquering it.
6. Name the major leader of the Pan-African movement.
7. Assess the goals of and the changes in the Pan-African movement.
8. Analyze the change over the years in Nkrumah's power in Ghana.
9. Define and describe the term *apartheid*.
10. Explain why one black man and one white man received the Nobel Peace Prize in South Africa.
11. Define the terms *tribalism* and *genocide*.
12. Summarize the conflict between the Tutsis and the Hutus in Rwanda.
13. Compare and contrast the major divisions of African Christianity.

Opening Photo— Tourists riding camels in Douz, Tunisia

Since I Was Born

For the last weeks of class, you may wish to create a bulletin board having to do with historical events during the lives of the students. Since students usually are least aware of what has happened in their own time (due either to apathy or lack of time to teach recent history), this will be a historical lesson in itself for the students. You may wish to use pictures of students to put next to major world events since they were born.

Another idea is to display a map of Africa and highlight the countries mentioned in the chapter by making them larger cutouts. Write facts inside each one along with current events. (For more information, see

CHAPTER 19

Africa is not a country; it is a continent. Africa is a land of deserts, jungles, and savannahs. A visitor to Africa can shiver in the snows of Mount Kilimanjaro or swelter in the humidity along the banks of the Congo River or roast in the heat of the Sahara Desert. The people of Africa are as diverse as the land—from the Muslim Berbers in North Africa to the tall Tutsi people of East Africa to the small Pygmy peoples of West Central Africa.

When we study African culture and history, it is important that we take into account this diversity. One way of studying the African continent is to study it by regions. In this chapter, we will look at four main regions: North or Saharan Africa, West (or West Central) Africa, Southern Africa, and East Africa.

But this is a history book, after all. As we look at each region, we need to understand the events that have shaped that region—and all of Africa—in the twentieth century. To accomplish this goal, we will focus on one country in each region. Then we will examine one theme of modern African history that is reflected in the history of that nation. Let us travel, then, to Algeria, Ghana, South Africa, and Rwanda to catch a glimpse of modern Africa.

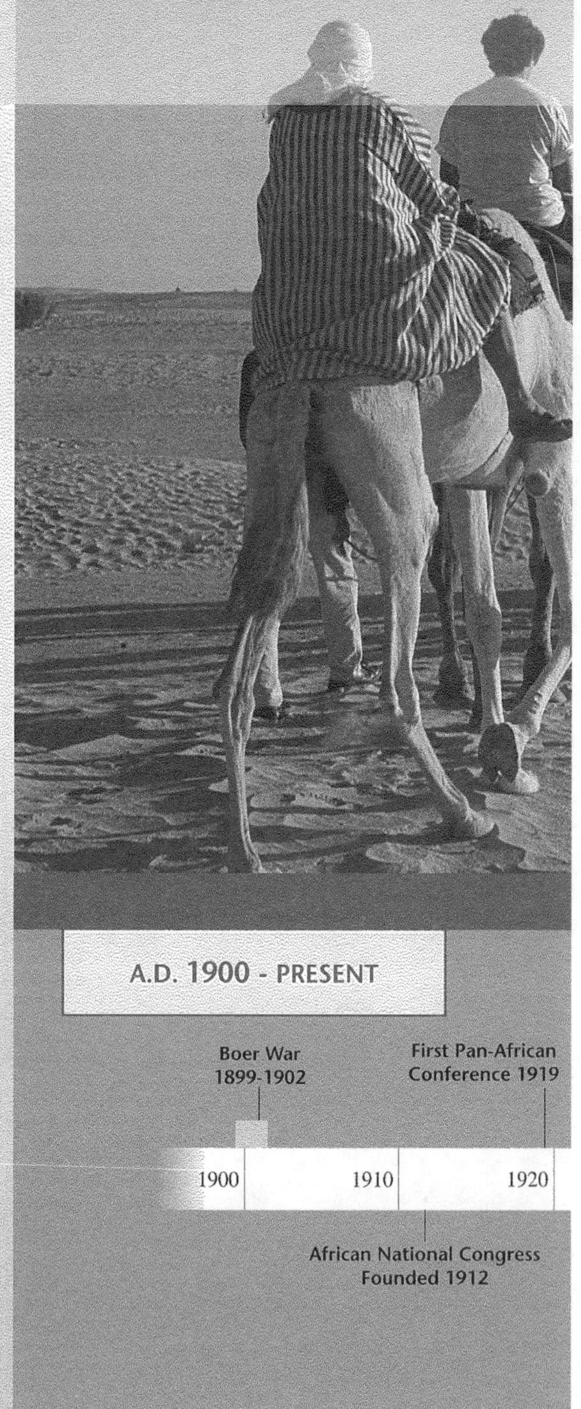

A.D. 1900 - PRESENT

Chapter 19 Lesson Plans			
Section Title	**Main Concept**	**Pages**	**Time Frame**
**Settings: Democratic Republic of Congo* *1. Saharan Africa: Algeria* **Center Stage: Italo-Ethiopian War*	Oppression and violence have been the way of life in the Saharan country of Algeria before and after independence.	546-54	2 days
2. West Africa: Ghana **Analysis: Pan-Africanism*	The idealistic leader of Ghana's independence movement became dictator and began to rule by terror.	555-60	1-2 days
3. Southern Africa: South Africa	Racism and apartheid have caused much tension in South Africa.	561-64	1 day
4. East Africa: Rwanda	The Tutsis and Hutus of Rwanda are a classic example of tribalism.	565-68	1 day
5. Christianity in Africa **Characterizations: Janani Luwum*	Religion in Africa is very diverse.	569-73	1-2 days
Total Suggested Days (including 1 day for review & 1 day for test)			8-10 days

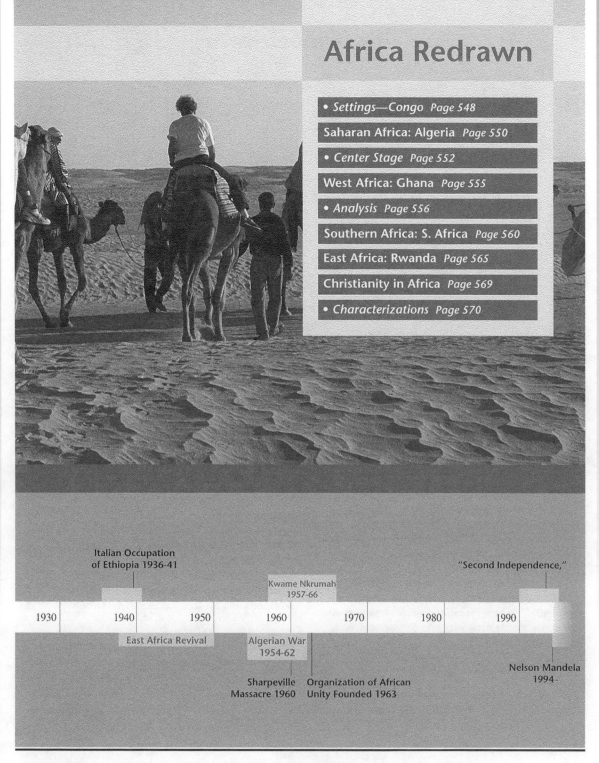

Africa Redrawn

Italian Occupation of Ethiopia 1936-41

Kwame Nkrumah 1957-66

"Second Independence,"

1930 | 1940 | 1950 | 1960 | 1970 | 1980 | 1990

East Africa Revival

Algerian War 1954-62

Sharpeville Massacre 1960

Organization of African Unity Founded 1963

Nelson Mandela 1994-

Materials

- Scripture verse (BLM verse 19)
- *Teaching Transparencies* for use with *World Studies for Christian Schools* (Second Edition)
- Wall map of Africa (BLM 19)
- Bibles for Bible study
- Video of the geographic features of Africa
- The October 1996 issue of *National Geographic*
- Recordings of African music
- Magazine and/or newspaper articles about apartheid in South Africa (See "Sources" on page A6 of the Appendix.)
- Photographs of tribal life, cities, and/or geographic features of Africa
- Letters from missionaries in Africa
- Video—*Beyond the Night* (BJUP)
- *Free Indeed: Heroes of Black Christian History* by Mark Sidwell (BJUP, 1995), pp. 47-51.

the current edition of *Current Events for Christian Schools*.)

Chapter Motivator

Review Chapters 5 and 14 for previously studied information about Africa. Remind the students of the storytellers, talking drums, masks, and so forth. Ask the following questions.

- What ancient African nation is well known for its pyramids and sphinxes? *(Egypt)*
- What famous nineteenth-century missionary dedicated his life to the people of Africa's interior? *(Livingstone)*
- What religion, started by Muhammad, spread throughout the Middle East, northern Africa, and Spain? *(Islam)*

Point to Africa on the map and show the countries that will be highlighted in this chapter: Algeria, Ghana, South Africa, and Rwanda.

James 4:7-8

There is much violence, conflict, and religious persecution in Africa. We know that man's heart is wicked and that God has said that all men can know Him. Change comes only through a personal relationship with Christ and submission to God's will. James 4:7-8 says, "Submit yourselves therefore to God. Resist the devil, and he will flee from you. Draw nigh to God, and he will draw nigh to you. Cleanse your hands, ye sinners; and purify your hearts, ye double minded." (BLM verse 19)

Student Objectives

Students should be able to

1. Locate the Democratic Republic of Congo (former Zaire).
2. Create and analyze line graphs.

Africa Today—Africa's geography is as diverse as its peoples. From sandy deserts to towering waterfalls and from tall, majestic mountains to grassy savannas, Africa is a land of beauty and diversity as well as of barrenness and monotony.

Though it has much to offer in the way of natural resources, Africa remains a poor land, bound by years of superstition and demonism. Ethnic conflict, poverty, and illiteracy cause serious problems for many Africans.

Settings—Democratic Republic of Congo

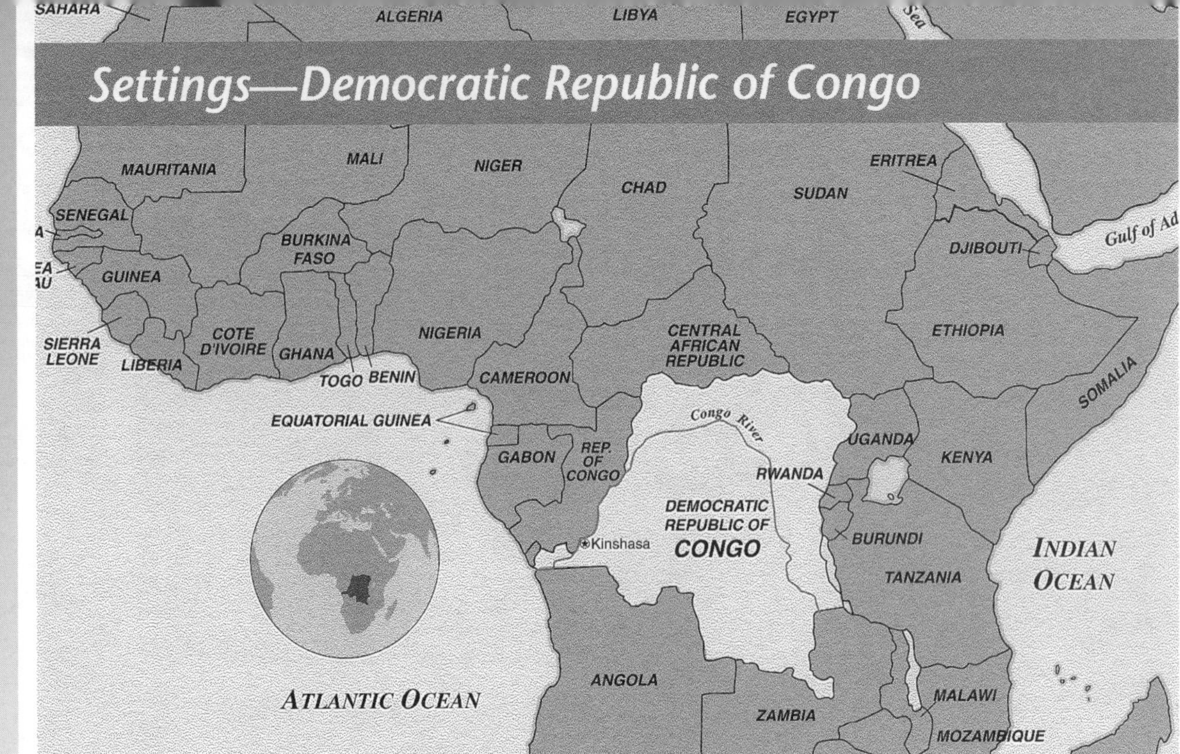

Location—The Democratic Republic of Congo is located in West Central Africa. It is mostly landlocked, with a small strip touching the Atlantic Ocean in the west. Bordering the nation are the Republic of Congo on the west (whose name is confusingly similar); the Central African Republic and Sudan to the north; Uganda, Rwanda, Burundi, and Tanzania to the east; and Angola and Zambia to the south.

Climate—Most of the northern portion of the country has a tropical wet (rain forest) climate. Most of the southern half has a tropical wet and dry (savanna) climate. Rainfall and temperatures vary with the region. The rain forest along the Congo River basin receives about seventy to eighty inches of rain each year with an average daily temperature of 90°. The savanna region receives less than 40 inches of rain each year and daily temperatures average around 75°.

Topography—At over nine hundred thousand square miles, Congo is the third largest country in Africa (after Sudan and Algeria). A major feature of the topography is the Congo River, second only to the Nile as the longest river in Africa. Above the Congo River region rise high plateaus and, in the far east, mountains.

Natural Resources—Congo has many natural resources that are thus far little developed. The country is one of the largest copper producers in the world, and it also enjoys large deposits of cobalt (nearly two-thirds of the world reserves) and diamonds. Most Congolese farmers grow crops such as bananas for their own families. But the country also exports coffee, cocoa, cotton, tea, and rubber.

Geography & Culture—The people of the Democratic Republic of Congo belong to many different tribal, or ethnic, groups. There are so many

Materials

- Transparencies for Chapter 19
- Wall map of Africa (BLM 19)

Map Activity—Complete map 19-C in the Student Activities manual to reinforce the geography lesson.

Going Beyond—Read the Settings pages on the Democratic Republic of Congo with your students and answer the questions. Use a political map of Africa to discuss Congo's location and neighboring countries (TT 19-B).

Show the students a line graph (TT 19-A). Analyze the information on the graph. Have each student create his own line graph using statistics from gym classes, such as how many times he played each sport or how many minutes he spent on each activity.

local languages that the government uses French as the official language since it is more commonly understood. About three-fourths of the Congolese claim to be Christian. The majority of these are Catholic, but about 10 percent of the population belong to the Kimbanguist Church. (See p. 572.)

Several early African kingdoms flourished in this area. The most important of these was probably the Kongo kingdom, which in the 1400s covered much of what is today Congo and Angola. Europeans took control of the region when Belgium's King Leopold established the Congo Free State in 1885 as his own personal colony. Leopold's rule was so cruel that the Belgian government took control in 1908 and renamed the colony the Belgian Congo.

In 1960 the region became the independent nation of Congo. (The country went by the name *Zaire* from 1971 to 1997). The southeastern section of the country, called the Katanga Province, tried to become independent in 1960. It was brought back in 1963 with help from troops from the United Nations. During most of its history since independence, Congo has been ruled by military dictatorship.

Settings Review

1. Describe the two types of climates in Congo.
2. What is the second longest river in Africa?
3. List five natural resources of Congo that are commonly used today.
4. What is the official language of Congo?
5. Who established this area as his personal colony in 1885?

Why might a person or nation want territory in a land such as Africa? Discuss the resources available and the prestige of obtaining land.

Dominated by the Congo River and lush jungles, the Democratic Republic of Congo lies in the heart of Africa.

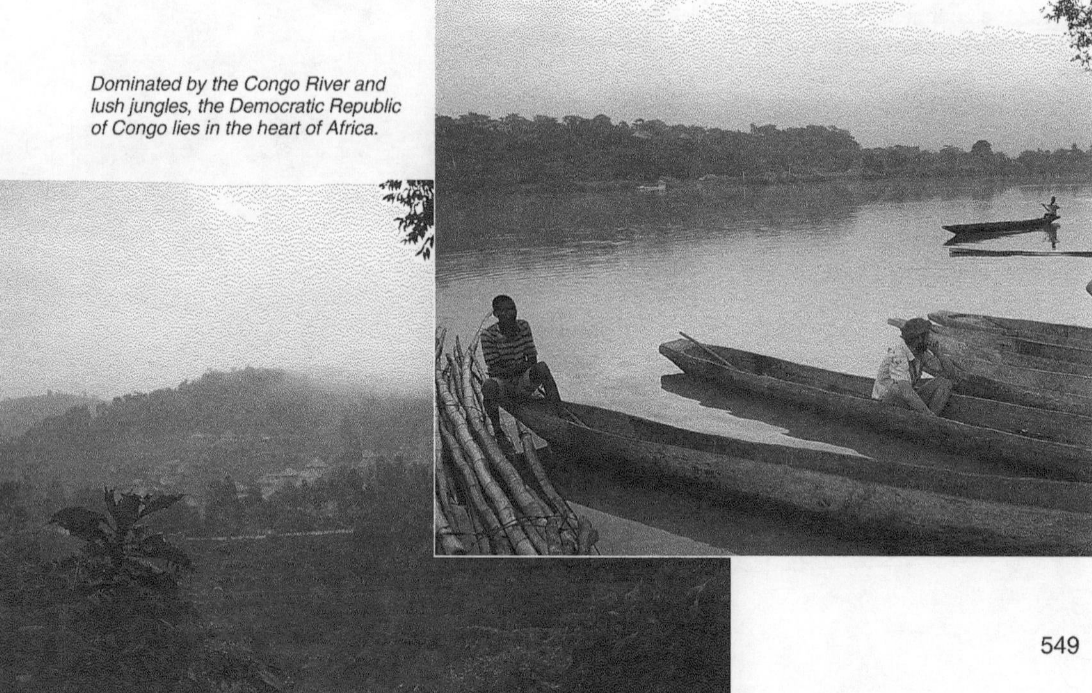

Settings Review Answers

1. Tropical Wet—Rain forest; Tropical Wet and Dry—Savanna
2. Congo River
3. copper, diamonds, bananas, coffee, cocoa, cotton, tea, rubber, and cobalt (any five)
4. French
5. King Leopold of Belgium

Answers will vary. New territory may bring new wealth for one's self or one's country. Finding new cultures, acquiring slaves, and having influence in the lives of many people were pressing reasons for imperialism.

SECTION 1

Student Objectives
Students should be able to

1. Identify the Saharan region of Africa and its representative country.
2. Describe the course of decolonization in Algeria.
3. Evaluate the claim that Italy was "civilizing" Ethiopia by conquering it.

Saharan Africa—Besides Algeria, the countries of the Saharan region are Egypt, the Sudan, Libya, Tunisia, Morocco, Mauritania, Mali, Niger, and Chad.

Life on the Sahara—About two million people live in this large desert. Moors, a mix of Arab and Berber bloods, along with the Tuareg and Toubou make up most of this population. Most of the people are nomads, moving about from oasis to oasis. Rarely does one find more than two thousand people at one oasis. Although camels are still the chief mode of transportation, one can find paved (and unpaved) roads on which to drive a car. Planes also make regular trips to the larger Saharan cities.

There are few plants. Some plants have very short life spans, from six to eight weeks. Other long-lasting plants have long roots or the ability to absorb water from the air through their leaves.

A few animals live in the Sahara. White gazelles, addax (a type of antelope), fennecs (small foxes), snakes, lizards, and gerbils need little water. The smaller animals usually go out at night and hibernate underground during the day.

The Maghreb—Northern Africa is often referred to as the Maghreb, meaning the western arm of the Middle East, because of the Islamic influence there.

Saharan Africa: Algeria and Decolonization

Imagine a place almost as large as the United States (including Alaska). Imagine that in this place there are fewer than one hundred villages and no cities. Imagine that between those villages lie hundreds of miles of sand and rock. Imagine temperatures climbing above 100°F in the day and then falling to near freezing at night. Years may pass in parts of this land before a drop of rain falls. When rain does come to this parched place, the water rolls quickly over the sand and rock. Soon, however, the scorching heat licks up the moisture, and the land is hot and dry once more.

The place you have just imagined is the largest desert in the world, the **Sahara.** It stretches for three thousand miles across northern Africa from the Atlantic Ocean to the Red Sea. It reaches southward from the Mediterranean coast or nearby mountains for over one thousand miles. So vast is the Sahara Desert that writers often divide the continent into Saharan Africa (the northern section dominated by the desert) and sub-Saharan Africa (that part that lies south of the Sahara).

Decolonization and Assimilation

We learned in Chapter 14 that the European nations in the late 1800s began dividing up Africa among themselves. France, Great Britain, and even Spain, Portugal, and tiny Belgium began to build enormous empires for themselves in Africa. Arab North Africa was likewise divided up by the European powers.

After World War II, these European empires in Africa began to break up. We sometimes call this process the **decolonization** of Africa. In 1960 alone fourteen former colonies became independent nations. Sometimes the transition to independence was peaceful. Tanganyika (later called Tanzania) in East Africa won its independence peacefully from Britain in 1961. Sometimes the coming of independence was violent. In no country was decolonization any bloodier or more destructive than in the North African nation of Algeria.

France took control of the major coastal city of Algiers in 1830 and by degrees extended its control over all of Algeria. France pursued a policy of the **assimilation** of Algeria.

Algeria

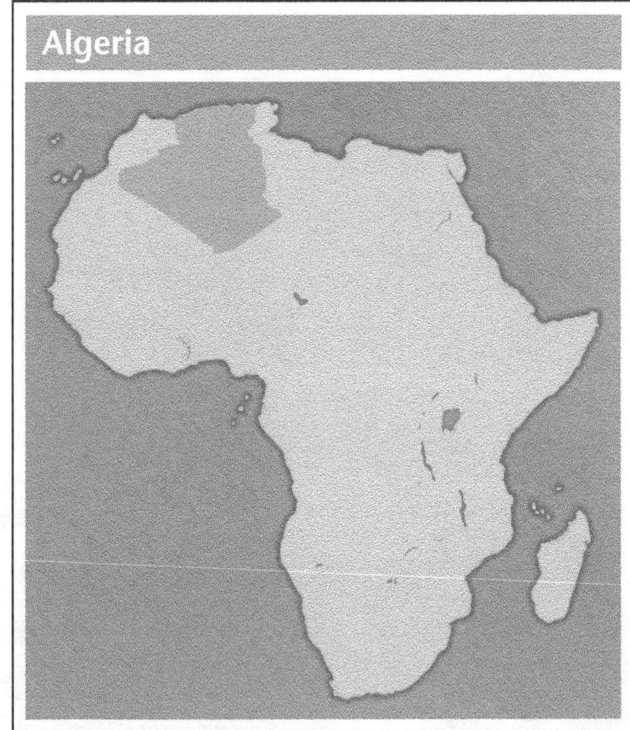

SECTION 1

Materials

- Bibles for Bible study

Desert—If you live near the Painted Desert or another very dry area, compare your region with the Saharan region. Discuss what life forms (if any) live in each region, as well as what types of climate, vegetation, and scenery are found.

Charles de Gaulle greets Muslim soldiers in Algeria. He took power in France in part to find a solution to the Algerian crisis.

In other words, the French hoped to make Algeria a province of France—a real part of the French nation.

The French, however, were slow to grant full political rights to all Algerians until they thought the people ready for such rights. Instead they gave full rights to the many Europeans who settled there and to a small number of Algerian Muslims who embraced French culture. Most Algerians, however, received none of these benefits and furthermore had no desire to be French.

War in Algeria

In 1954 war broke out in Algeria. The **Front for National Liberation** (*Front de libération nationale,* or FLN) was a native Muslim Algerian group that dedicated itself to winning Algerian independence. Eight years of warfare followed. The FLN used terror to advance its cause, and the French responded with fierce repression.

The FLN at first killed only Muslims who cooperated with the French. "Take their children and kill them," said one leader of how to treat the pro-French Algerians. "Kill all those who pay taxes and those who collect them." Then the FLN decided to spread the terror further by slaughtering European civilians. They sought international attention for their cause, and as one Algerian terrorist said, "One corpse in a suit is always worth more than twenty in uniform." In an attack on Philippeville in 1955, FLN terrorists murdered over one hundred people—men, women, and children, Algerian and European.

The French responded firmly, even harshly. As many as 500,000 French troops came to Algeria to restore order. When some rebels began setting up bases in neighboring Tunisia and Morocco, the French closed the borders. They did so by an elaborate system of defenses, including an electric fence two hundred miles long. To get information and frighten the FLN, the French began to torture prisoners.

The French found themselves forced to hold on to Algeria by a military occupation almost as harsh as that the Nazis had imposed on France during World War II. The government began to lose control of the army. The French army bombed a village in Tunisia to get at rebel bases, without even bothering to get government approval. Army officers threatened to bring down the whole French government if France tried to abandon Algeria.

Casablanca—One of the famous cities in northern Africa is Casablanca, the sight of the meeting of Roosevelt and Churchill during World War II to decide the course of the war. A classic movie is named after the city as well. The name of this largest city in Morocco means "white house" in Spanish and refers to the whitewashed houses the Spanish merchants found there. The Portuguese founded the city in 1575 where an old fishing village had been and rebuilt it after an earthquake in 1755.

Independence—Was it right for the Algerians to strive for independence in the way that they did? Was it right for the French to try to suppress them so brutally? Discuss opposing viewpoints. Group the students according to viewpoint, and ask each group to find at least two Scripture verses that support its viewpoint. Why were the French so insistent on keeping Algeria? Why were the Algerians so insistent on independence? Of course, Algeria still has major problems with violence. How did the struggle for independence contribute to this trend? What future do your students see for Algeria?

CENTER STAGE

The Italo-Ethiopian War

To Africans, perhaps no state has been as symbolically important as Ethiopia. At the beginning of World War I, Ethiopia (sometimes called Abyssinia) was the only major area of Africa not under European control. (The tiny nation of Liberia in West Africa was also independent.) The nation's history of independence went back all the way to the days of the Roman Empire. The area had embraced Christianity in the 300s, and an independent Ethiopian Orthodox Church had existed from that time. During the Middle Ages, Ethiopia's highlands and mountains had enabled the nation to defend itself against Muslim conquest. Later these same features had helped Ethiopia resist European dominance.

Ethiopia's independence was not the result of being ignored by Europe. In 1896 Italy invaded Ethiopia to make the nation part of the growing Italian empire in Africa. The Ethiopians stunned the world by defeating the Italians at the Battle of Adowa. Ethiopia was safe, but Italy burned for revenge.

In the 1930s the Fascist dictator Benito Mussolini determined to avenge Adowa as a step in building a new Roman Empire. Italy controlled colonies bordering on Ethiopia (Eritrea and Italian Somaliland) and had been arguing with Ethiopia over the boundary. On December 5, 1934, the two sides clashed at Walwal, an oasis in the desert just inside the Ethiopian border. This clash gave Mussolini the excuse he needed for war.

It took months for the Italians to prepare for the campaign, and the invasion began on October 10, 1935. The Ethiopians knew the land well, and in small clashes their troops fought with brave ferocity. But technology favored the Italians. Ethiopia did not have enough guns for every man to have one, and its air force had only twelve planes. The Italians had hundreds of planes, heavy artillery, tanks, and poison gas. Italian engineers skillfully built roads and bridges over the rough Ethiopian countryside.

Air power was probably the Italians' main advantage. Their bombing of Ethiopia was a foretaste of what Europe would experience in World War II a few years later. Mussolini's son was one of the pilots in the Ethiopian campaign, and he described what he called the "beauty" of dropping bombs on tribesmen and seeing them spread out "just like a flowering rose."

During a visit to Italy's African colonies, Mussolini waves a "sword of Islam" given to him by his Muslim subjects.

Center Stage—Discuss with your students reasons that the world would not help Ethiopia against Italy. *(Some reasons could include that Ethiopia was not thought of as an important country and that the world was keeping its distance from aggressors at this time, as shown by the policy of appeasement toward Hitler.)*

As the Italians advanced, foreigners and Ethiopian leaders prepared to flee. A group of Swedish officers who had been advising the Ethiopian army were met by the cadets they had been training. The young Ethiopians wept and said, "This is the end of Ethiopia. . . . Go, God bless you. Save yourselves." The Italians occupied Addis Ababa, the capital, on May 5, 1936.

The emperor of Ethiopia, **Haile Selassie** (HYE-lee seh-LAS-ee), managed to get out of the country. He went to Geneva to appeal to the League of Nations (an international organization much like today's United Nations). Before representatives of the nations of the world he said, "I assert that the problem submitted to the Assembly today . . . is not merely a settlement of Italian aggression. . . . In a word, it is international morality that is at stake. . . . It is us today. It will be you tomorrow."

At the conclusion of his speech, Haile Selassie said, "What reply shall I have to take back to my people?" The reply was silence. The nations of Europe were not willing to go to war over Ethiopia. Mussolini announced that "civilization has triumphed over barbarism" and established a new colony, Italian East Africa. At times, however, Italian rule looked more barbaric than civilized. After an attempt to assassinate the colonial governor, vengeful Italian troops killed over three thousand Ethiopians and executed many Ethiopian nobles. The Italians even attacked a monastery accused of being disloyal to Mussolini and killed over three hundred monks

When World War II broke out, however, Italian forces in Africa found themselves cut off. A force led by British and African troops liberated Ethiopia, and Emperor Haile Selassie reentered Addis Ababa May 5, 1941, exactly five years after the Italians had captured it. The leading free state in Africa was free once more.

Emperor Haile Selassie of Ethiopia vainly entreats the League of Nations to intervene on behalf of his nation against the Italians.

Africa Redrawn 553

Religious Conflicts—Algeria continued to have many problems in many realms, not the least of which was religion. The militant Muslim political group, the Islamic Salvation Front (FIS), was banned on the basis of their overwhelming victory in 1991. The FIS would not stand for this and incited rebellion and riots throughout the country, led mostly by an even more radical group, the GIA (Armed Islamic Group). Religious leaders as well as many journalists were the victims of bombings and other assassinations. Sixty thousand people have died in the fighting since the strife began in 1992. In 1994, the GIA threatened any foreigners in Algeria, giving them one month to get out of the country or face death. In December, the GIA attacked a hydroelectric company and brutally killed twelve Christians. Eight Bosnians were allowed to live because they were Muslims. In the first two weeks of 1998, over one thousand deaths were reported by the extremists, possibly the worst record yet in Algerian history.

Qadhafi and Libya—His name can be spelled in many ways: Gadhafi, Qadhafi, Kaddafi, and Qaddafi. He became the military leader of Libya in 1969 after overthrowing the monarchy. He is generally thought to aid terrorists in the mission of spreading Islam throughout the world. During Reagan's presidency, America decided to show its support of antiterrorism by bombing Libyan military buildings. Sanctions against Libya were imposed when the country refused to give up a suspected terrorist for trial.

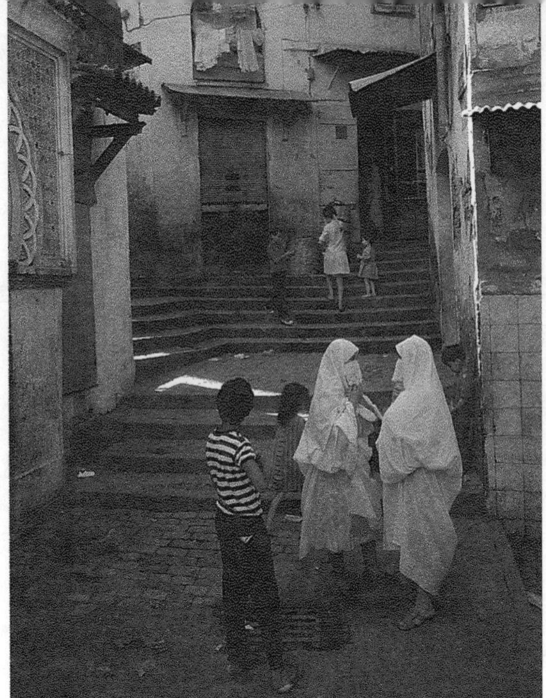

Veiled Muslim women converse in the Casbah section of Algiers, Algeria.

DeGaulle Seeks Peace

Under pressure from the armed forces, the government reorganized. **Charles de Gaulle,** a former general and World War II hero, became the new president of France. But de Gaulle quickly realized that France could not hold Algeria. To the anger of the generals, President de Gaulle dedicated himself to decolonizing Algeria.

The furious soldiers reacted violently. They attempted to assassinate de Gaulle. Then in 1961 the army and European settlers in Algeria arose in rebellion against the French government. When that uprising was crushed, a small secret organization of former French army officers launched a terrorist campaign as bloody as that of the FLN.

But de Gaulle persevered. In 1962 Algeria became an independent nation. Virtually all settlers of European descent fled Algeria at independence. Their numbers went from over a million to only about 30,000 by the end of 1962. A Muslim official told de Gaulle that the pro-French Algerians would suffer when the French pulled out. De Gaulle replied, "Oh, well, you will suffer." Many Muslims who had cooperated with the French were slaughtered by the new government.

But independence did not bring peace to Algeria. Within three years the Algerian army had toppled the government and set up a military dictatorship. By the 1990s Algeria experienced a new wave of terrorism from Muslim extremists inspired by the revolution in Iran. (See p. 522.) The FLN still held power long after Algeria had won independence from France. But it held on against terrorist attacks as fierce as those it had launched against the French. And the FLN maintained power by means as harsh as those France had used in ruling the region. In some ways, independence had not changed the situation in Algeria.

Section Review

1. List the four main regions of Africa.
2. What is the largest desert in the world?
3. What country wanted to assimilate Algeria into its nation?
4. What group fought against the French for independence?
5. Which French president tried to decolonize Algeria?

How could the decolonization of the African empires have been done more easily? Why would a nation have wanted to be assimilated or decolonized during this period? Explain your answer.

Section Review Answers

1. Northern or Saharan Africa, Western or West Central Africa, East Africa, and Southern Africa
2. Sahara
3. France
4. Front for National Liberation (FLN)
5. Charles de Gaulle

Answers will vary. Decolonization would have proceeded more smoothly if the "mother country" had helped the colony become independent. A nation may have wanted to be assimilated to enjoy the benefits of a stable economy and government. (Students may remember Canada's relationship to England.) A nation may want to be decolonized to be truly independent after years of imperialistic control.

West Africa: Ghana and Dictatorship

When many non-Africans try to picture Africa, they often imagine steaming jungles and hordes of wild animals. West (sometimes called West Central) Africa probably comes as close to this image as any section of the continent. Although the Sahara Desert lies only a few hundred miles to the north, most of West Africa receives abundant rainfall. Rain forests and thick jungles dominate the landscape. Meandering through this lush undergrowth are the Niger and Congo Rivers. Wild animals such as hippopotamuses, crocodiles, pythons, and colorful tropical birds roam the region.

The lush jungle vegetation of Ghana

West Africa is the home of many nations, large and small, that gained independence after World War II. But many African peoples had little experience in self-government, except on a local level. As a result, many African nations began as democracies with several political parties but soon became dictatorships ruled by one party which was led by one powerful leader. There are several examples of cruel dictatorships in Africa, such as the bloody rule of Idi Amin Dada in Uganda in the 1970s. But rulers such as Amin were never anything but thugs. What is even sadder is the story of well-intentioned, idealistic rulers who nonetheless took their nations into dictatorship. Such is the story of Kwame Nkrumah (uhn KROO muh) of Ghana.

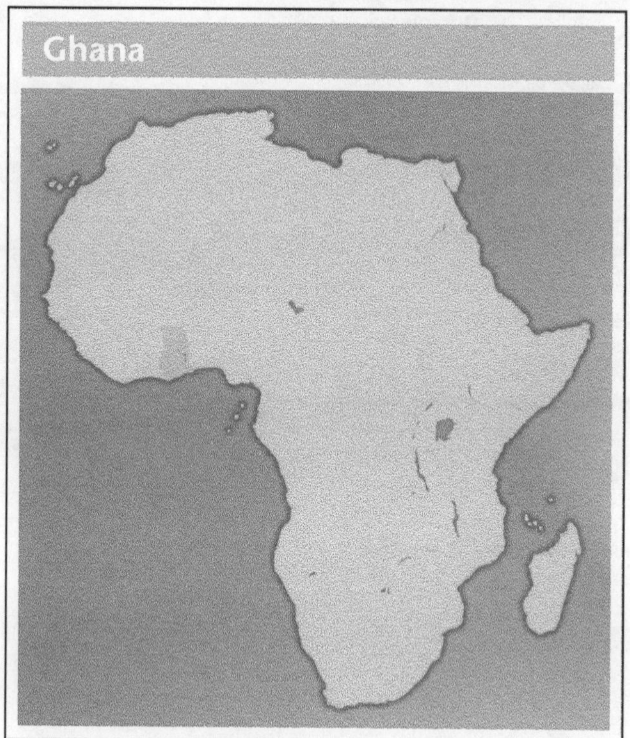

SECTION 2

Student Objectives
Students should be able to

1. Identify the western region of Africa and its representative country.
2. Name the major leader of the Pan-African movement.
3. Assess the goals and changes in the Pan-African movement.
4. Analyze the change over the years in Nkrumah's power in Ghana.

Countries of West Africa—Besides Ghana, other countries of West Africa are Senegal, Gambia, Guinea, Guinea-Bissau, Sierra Leone, Liberia, Côte d'Ivoire, Ghana, Burkina Faso, Togo, Benin, and Nigeria.

Idi Amin Dada—Amin exiled many Asians living in Uganda when he came to power and killed many Ugandans who opposed him.

Before coming to power, Amin had been heavyweight boxing champion in Uganda for nine years.

SECTION 2

Materials

- Video of the geographic features of Africa
- The October 1996 issue of *National Geographic*
- Recordings of African music

Africa—Show a video on the geographic features of Africa: desert, jungle, savannah, and so forth. This may also include animals and plant life as well as culture. This type of video should be easily found at your local library or video store or through a video catalog. (If the video contains any evolutionary viewpoints, discuss these in the light of Scripture.)

Pan-Africanism—Though Pan-Africanism is difficult to define, we can give it some boundaries. It includes intellectual and political movements, encourages racial solidarity, and promotes the view of Africa as the true homeland of Africans. It strives for cultural unity and political independence. Its aim is the political unity or close collaboration of all Africa.

Of course, Pan-Africanism is a result of slavery and abolition. America tried to give blacks the right to emigrate to Africa by creating the country of Liberia, but sometimes slave owners and others forced them back.

Another famous Pan-Africanist was Marcus Garvey, an imperialist from Jamaica.

ANALYSIS

Pan-Africanism

At the dawn of the twentieth century, most of Africa lay under European rule. Despite that fact—or perhaps because of it—African hopes for the future found expression in a new movement. **"Pan-Africanism,"** as it became known, is not an easy term to define. Originally, the movement was a call for fair treatment of all people of black African descent regardless of where they lived. It presented Africa as the fatherland to all blacks, who would look to the continent for inspiration and who would offer it their help in its struggles. Many early spokesmen for Pan-Africanism were African Americans who were as concerned with the situation of blacks in the United States as with those in Africa. An idea dear to all Pan-Africanists, though, was the liberation of Africa from colonial control.

American **W. E. B. Du Bois** was a major leader. In 1919, while the powers of Europe were holding the Versailles Peace Conference at the end of World War I, Du Bois held a Pan-African Congress in Paris. Du Bois and the other leaders sought to give a united voice for blacks around the world. They urged the victorious Allies to grant equality to the land of Africa and to all people of African descent. The congress saw few victories. It did at least, however, persuade the European powers not to divide Germany's African colonies among the victors of World War I. Instead, the colonies became mandates supervised by European nations under the guidance of the League of Nations. The supervising nations would theoretically prepare these mandates for independence.

Future Pan-African Congresses did not accomplish even this much. Some black African leaders opposed what they saw as overly harsh criticism of colonialism by Du Bois. Blaise Diagne of Senegal argued that black Africans must work with the colonial powers. "To isolate the black race and to let it work out its own evolution is ridiculous," he said. "The evolution of our race . . . requires the cooperation of everybody." Discouraged, Du Bois eventually moved to Ghana in 1961 shortly before his death. There, at least, he could live under the rule of a leader, Kwame Nkrumah, who was a Pan-African Marxist like himself.

W. E. B. Du Bois

The fighting and suffering caused by Nigeria's Biafran War severely tested the Organization of African Unity and its attempts to deal with Africa's problems.

As new nations in Africa emerged after World War II, the Pan-African spirit showed new vigor. Along with Nkrumah of Ghana, other new African leaders such as Kenneth Kaunda of Zambia embraced the idea. They asserted the unity of all the peoples of Africa and said how they must all work together to solve the problems of the continent. There was some shift in the meaning of Pan-Africanism. It became less racial ("black") and more geographical ("African") as Arab North African states became part of the Pan-African movement.

The most visible expression of Pan-Africanism was the founding of the Organization of African Unity (OAU) in 1963. The OAU sought to defend Africa from exploitation and to promote cooperation. Still existing today, it is a forum for nations to discuss their problems, much like the United Nations. Like the UN, the OAU has enjoyed some successes and many failures. The organization settled border disputes between Somalia and Kenya and between Somalia and Ethiopia. But it proved unable to stop the bloody Biafran civil war in Nigeria in the late 1960s.

The problem for the OAU and the whole Pan-African movement is that neither Africa nor Africans have one set of problems or one set of enemies. Instead, different groups with conflicting goals usually compete to accomplish their own individual goals. Only as a movement succeeds in creating a common purpose can it achieve unity.

Movements That Have Worked—The Pan-African movement has been unsuccessful in many of its goals because of disunity. Discuss some movements that have been more successful in forwarding their agenda. *(Examples include the Civil Rights Movement, the homosexual movement, the Pro-life movement, and the Pro-choice movement.)* How do these groups attain their goals?

The Gold Coast—Since the 1300s, the Asante tribe of Ghana (Gold Coast) and the Adioukrou of Côte d'Ivoire have done gold working, usually melting down old gold and forming it into new objects of beauty. The amount of gold they possess is astounding. Natives sometimes wear so much that they can barely move.

From Gold Coast to Ghana

The nation of Ghana on the western coast of Africa was originally the British colony of Gold Coast. As its colonial name suggests, the land was rich in gold. In addition, the region has supplies of diamonds, and it is a large supplier of cocoa, the main ingredient in producing chocolate. Gold Coast was in fact one of the most prosperous colonies in Africa.

But the people of Gold Coast desired to be free of British rule. One of the leaders of the drive for independence was **Kwame Nkrumah.** Born in Gold Coast in 1909, Nkrumah went to study in the United States and Great Britain. There he adopted the views of Karl Marx, joined the Communist Party, and became a leading opponent of British imperialism in Africa. In 1947 he returned to Gold Coast as secretary for a group seeking independence from Britain.

Kwame Nkrumah (in center on dais) is sworn in as the first prime minister of Ghana.

Ghana possessed rich resources that seemed to promise future prosperity for the nation after it gained independence.

Nkrumah soon seized control of the independence movement by his spellbinding personality and political shrewdness. The British first imprisoned him. Then, when Nkrumah still proved popular, the British made him prime minister of the colony. He ruled well and helped convince the British that Gold Coast, with him as the leader, could make the transition from colony to nation.

A new nation was born in 1957 with Nkrumah as its prime minister. It took the name *Ghana* after the African empire that had covered western Africa in the Middle Ages. Nkrumah embraced the idea of Pan-Africanism (see pp. 558-59) and dreamed that Ghana would become the leader of an independent African continent. "Our independence is meaningless," he said, "unless it is linked with the total liberation of the African continent."

From Democracy to Dictatorship

Circumstances looked promising for the young nation. Its parting from Great Britain had been friendly. Its economic resources gave

Cocoa—Since the Gold Coast is such a large supplier of cocoa (the main ingredient in chocolate), have a cocoa day. The students should bring in cocoa or chocolate (not white chocolate since it has no cocoa) to eat or drink.

How Much Gold?—The October 1996 issue of *National Geographic* has an article about the gold of the Asante tribe. If possible, bring a copy of the magazine to show pictures to your students.

the nation great potential for prosperity. And its new leader was idealistic and full of hope.

But things did not go well in Ghana. Nkrumah's government began to spend the nation's wealth on wasteful building projects. He built a major highway from the capital to the seacoast, although there were few vehicles to use it. He built huge silos to store cocoa, but they were so poorly constructed that they proved useless. While Nkrumah built, the standard of living for unskilled workers fell to its lowest level since before World War II.

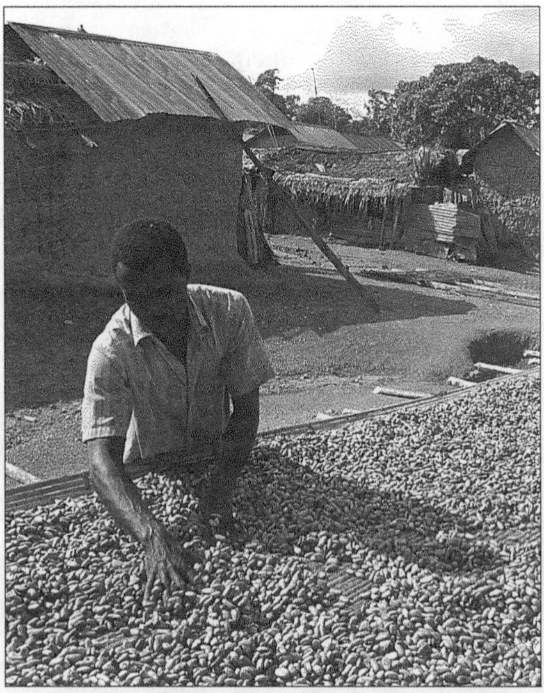

Nkrumah began to crack down on his opponents as he ruled by terror. He outlawed all political parties but his own and had himself declared president for life. He had some of his former associates tried for treason. When the judge declared them innocent, Nkrumah overturned the verdict. He had the men retried and convicted this time. He not only fired the judge but threw him into jail, where he died two years later.

Nkrumah began to organize special security forces to enforce his rule and to protect him from assassination. He portrayed himself to the people of Ghana as a sort of messiah. A loyal newspaper said, "When our history is recorded, the man Kwame Nkrumah will be written of as the liberator, the Messiah, the Christ of our day." Groups of young people paraded through the streets carrying signs that said "Nkrumah never dies" and "Nkrumah is the new Messiah." Nkrumah took all of this praise seriously. He said in 1961, "All Africans know that I represent Africa and that I speak in her name. Therefore no African can have an opinion that differs from mine."

His government became increasingly corrupt as his officials enriched themselves by

Farmers in Ghana split the cocoa pods (right) and spread the seeds out to dry (left). Cocoa has long been one of Ghana's main sources of wealth.

African music—Bring in a recording of African music to play for your class. Some African music would not be appropriate, but appropriate cultural pieces do exist. You may wish to check your local library or music store.

Second Independence Movements—Tracking the second period of African independence in the 1990s is a somewhat uncertain task. Many of the new democracies were unstable, and not all ruled as justly and fairly as one might like. However, those hopeful about the progress of stable democracy in Africa could point to the independence of Namibia and Eritrea as well as the following remarkable record from the 1990s.

- Benin ended Marxist rule and held its first free presidential elections in 1991.
- Burkina Faso became a multiparty democracy in the early 1990s after years of military rule.
- The Central African Republic elected a civilian government in 1993 after a dozen years of military rule.
- The Republic of Congo repudiated Marxism in 1990 and held free elections in 1992.
- Cote d'Ivoire held multiparty elections in 1990.
- Ethiopia held its first multiparty elections in 1995.
- Guinea-Bissau held multiparty elections in 1994 after years of dictatorship.
- Lesotho restored constitutional rule in 1994.
- Madagascar in 1990 allowed multiparty politics.
- Malawi adopted a new constitution and allowed multiparty elections in 1994 after thirty years of one-party rule.
- Mauritania adopted a new constitution and allowed opposition parties in 1991.
- Niger in 1993 held its first free elections ever, but a military coup followed in 1996.
- Togo in 1994 held its first multiparty elections, although these were marred by violence.
- Zambia ended one-party rule in 1991.

Eritrea—Eritrea began as an Italian colony in 1890. When the Italian forces in East Africa collapsed during World War II, the colony came under British control. It was then made part of Ethiopia, which ruled the region until Eritrea voted for independence in 1993.

The African coast near Accra, Ghana

taking bribes. Finally, in 1966, while Nkrumah was visiting Communist China, the army overthrew him. Nkrumah died six years later in exile. But the end of Nkrumah's rule brought no peace to Ghana. The nation went through alternating periods of multiparty democracy and military rule. Ghana experienced four uprisings between 1972 and 1981.

In the 1990s, however, the continent of Africa went through what some writers have called a **"second independence."** Some fifteen nations, in varying degrees, turned their backs on one-party dictatorship. Some adopted new constitutions, and nearly all held new elections in which several parties could participate. Two entirely new nations won their independence (Namibia in 1990 and Eritrea in 1993). Ghana shared in this new birth of freedom. The nation approved a new constitution in 1992 that allowed for multiparty politics.

The future for these struggling democracies is still uncertain. The road to stable democracy in Africa has not been an easy one. But at least there are signs that the dreams of independence that followed World War II might yet become a reality.

Section Review

1. What was Ghana originally named by the British and why?
2. Who led the drive for independence in Ghana?
3. Explain one result of Nkrumah's belief in himself as a kind of messiah.
4. In the "second independence" of the African continent in the 1990s, what two new nations gained independence?

Why do you think Kwame Nkrumah became a dictator after his original attraction to Marxism? Do you know of other examples of those who promoted Communism and then turned toward dictatorship?

Independence—Ask the students how they would promote a "second independence movement." Would they create their own country or modify an existing one? What would be the pros and cons of each? *(Pros for creating one's own country: The country might be named after you, use your laws, and be run your way. Cons for creating one's own country: Much work is required to start a new country; people would have to be attracted to the area and would have to be willing to conform to your wishes.) (Pros for modifying an existing country: Leadership may already be in place, existing geographic boundaries, and national loyalty. Cons for modifying an existing country: The people may resist; decisions would require more than one person.)*

Section Review Answers

1. the Gold Coast because of rich resources in gold
2. Kwame Nkrumah
3. loyalty from his people seen in newspapers and parades, egotism as seen in his statement about his opinion being the only correct one
4. Namibia in 1990 and Eritrea in 1993

Answers will vary. Students should see that though there are *theoretically* many good points in Marxism, it takes a perfect society with perfect people to run a real Communist government. When this utopia does not exist, a dictatorship or aristocracy (such as the Politburo of the former USSR) must rule to enforce such "goodwill to men." Nkrumah spent money extravagantly, not practically. He feared opponents so much that he ruled by terror. In a sinful society, power often leads to corruption. Romania, China, and Cuba are other Communist countries turning toward dictatorship.

Southern Africa: South Africa & Racial Conflict

Southern Africa is roughly the area explored by the famous British missionary David Livingstone. It is an area rich in diamonds and gold and somewhat drier and cooler than the rest of Africa (although not as dry, of course, as the Sahara Desert). Much of the land consists of plateaus and highlands. Pleasant savannas (grasslands) also cover much of the region. Along rivers such as the Zambezi you can also find jungles like those in West Africa (although smaller).

Southern Africa was the first part of sub-Saharan Africa to be settled by white Europeans in large numbers. (See Chapter 14.) Historically, it has been the site of the fiercest racial conflict between blacks and whites. Racial conflict in Africa is not always black vs. white. Jews have often suffered persecution from African governments, particularly those with Muslim rulers. Israel helped resettle within its borders many Jews from Ethiopia to protect them from oppression. Uganda in the 1970s expelled nearly all of its Asian citizens and seized their wealth. Still, the black-white conflict, especially that in South Africa, has been the most prominent racial clash on the continent.

Afrikaners and Apartheid

As we noted in Chapter 14, after the Boer War (1899-1902) the sections of Southern Africa settled by the Dutch (called Boers and later **Afrikaners**) were joined to the sections settled by the English in the Union of South Africa. At that time, whites made up only a

South Africa

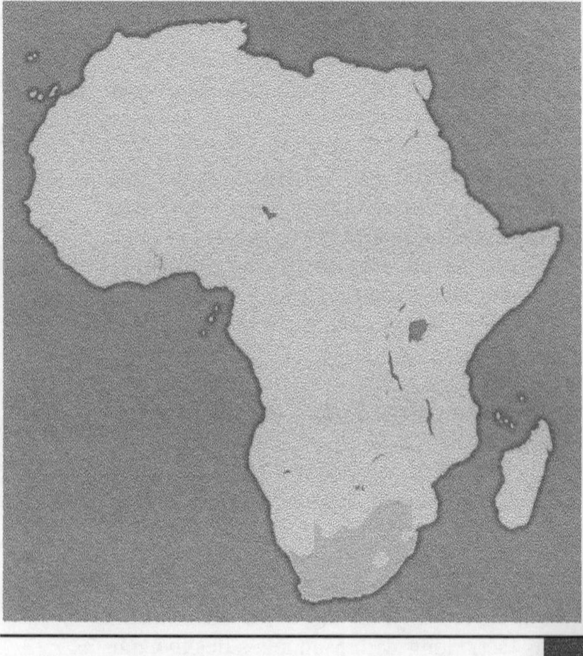

The breathtaking landscape of South Africa

Section 3

Student Objectives

Students should be able to

1. Identify the southern region of Africa and its representative country.
2. Define and describe the term *apartheid*.
3. Explain why one black man and one white man received the Nobel Peace Prize in South Africa.

Countries of Southern Africa— Besides South Africa, the countries in Southern Africa are Angola, Zambia, Malawi, Namibia, Botswana, Zimbabwe, Mozambique, Lesotho, Swaziland, Madagascar, Comoros, and the Seychelles.

Afrikaners—The two major groups of whites who live in South Africa are the Afrikaners (Dutch descent) and whites of British descent. The people of Dutch descent are often called the "white tribe of Africa." The term *Afrikaners* refers to these colonists born on African soil. Since Britain had taken control by 1806, some of the Afrikaners took the "Great Trek" into the interior, which was Zulu land. In the battle at Blood River, over ten thousand Zulus were defeated by only five hundred Afrikaners (then called Boers). This battle of spears against guns was taken as a sign from God. The Boers formed two republics: the Orange Free State and the Transvaal. When the Boers found diamonds and gold, the British flooded into the Boer territories. The Boer War resulted, eventually ending with the formation of the Union of South Africa.

Section 3

Materials

- Magazine and/or newspaper articles about apartheid in South Africa (See "Sources" on page A6 of the Appendix.)

Apartheid—The people of South Africa are still segregated in many areas of life, and the healing process may be long. One of the major reasons that South Africa ended its policy of apartheid was that many nations were boycotting economic trade with the country.

Today black factions are fighting against each other, specifically the Inkatha Freedom Party and the African National Congress. These infightings seem to be a remnant of apartheid violence as well as tribal conflicts.

Mandela—Nelson Mandela's father was a tribal chief in South Africa. Mandela became a lawyer and then a radical protester in the 1950s. After his prison term and release, he worked with F. W. de Klerk to bring change for blacks in his country. In 1992, he separated from his wife after she was convicted of kidnapping while helping the Mandela United Football Club.

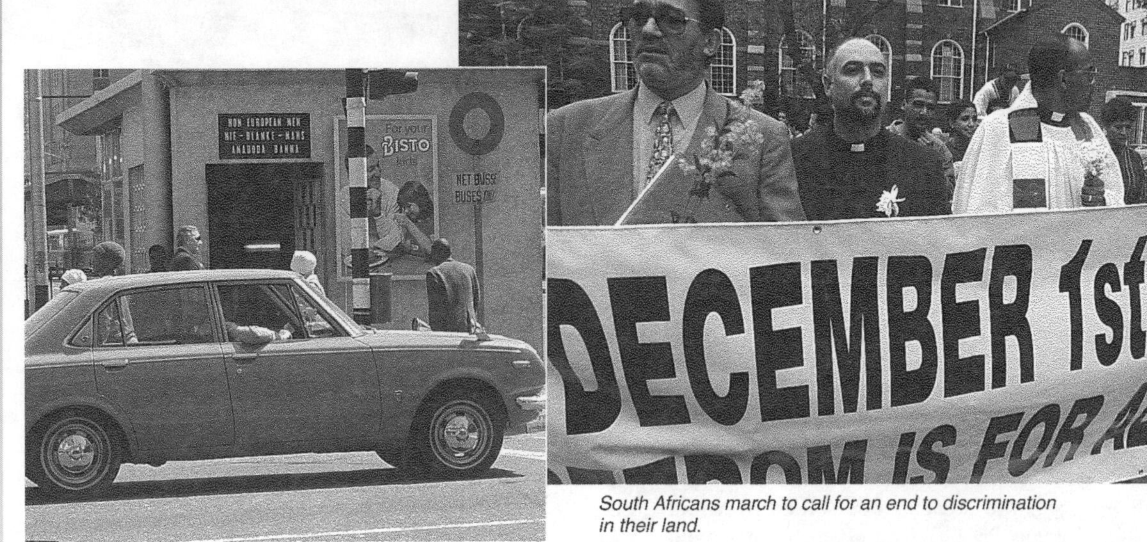

The South African policy of apartheid called for almost total separation of the races, even to the point of separate entrances to buildings.

South Africans march to call for an end to discrimination in their land.

little under a third of the population, but the white minority—both Dutch and English—refused to share power with the black majority.

Until World War II the English-speaking whites led the government. After the war the Afrikaners took power. The English had already established a pattern of legal racial separation, but the Afrikaners made the distinction firmer. They instituted a policy called **apartheid** (from an Afrikaans word meaning "separate"). In theory, apartheid provided for the separate development of the ethnic groups in South Africa. In addition to blacks and whites, South Africa is home to Asians and **"coloureds"**—those of mixed racial heritage. In practice, apartheid preserved white economic and political dominance.

Apartheid laws rigidly separated the races. The government marked areas in which each race could live and forcibly moved those who did not conform. Invariably it was the blacks or coloureds who were moved, not whites. The Afrikaner government mandated complete racial segregation in education, marriage, and even churches. The government took control of all education and effectively shut down schools run by missionaries. The government even determined the kinds of jobs blacks could hold (reserving certain occupations for whites) and how much they could be paid. The South African government ruthlessly crushed dissent.

But there was dissent nonetheless. Black resentment of apartheid led to protests and riots. The leading opposition group was the **African National Congress (ANC),** founded in 1912. Its early leaders supported peaceful demonstrations and boycotts. The situation changed drastically on February 3, 1960. On that day, in what became known as the **Sharpeville massacre,** the police opened fire on a group of unarmed demonstrators, killing sixty-nine and wounding eighty-six. Thereafter, many protest leaders rejected peaceful means of change. One leader, **Nelson Mandela,** formed a radical branch of the ANC called *Umkonto we Sizwe* ("Spear of the Nation").

Mandela advocated violence and called for the overthrow of the white government. This fact, along with Mandela's ties to Com-

Apartheid—Bring in articles from magazines or newspapers and have students read them and write about apartheid in South Africa. In at least seventy-five words, the student should describe the causes, effects, fall, or future of apartheid.

Equality in God's Eyes—Read and discuss James 2:1-9 about respect of persons. The Bible clearly states that this is a sin, whether purposeful or not. Many times our Western culture teaches us to regard rich people as more important than poor people. Unfortunately, discrimination sometimes extends to color, ethnicity, and other factors. Teach the students that any lingering prejudices should be changed to God's perspective: all men are sinners and need the blood of Christ to cleanse them of their sins.

Nelson Mandela

munism, led to his arrest in 1962 and his imprisonment for twenty-seven years. But even in prison he proved to be a powerful symbol of resistance.

Winds of Change

Other nations inside and outside Africa began pressuring South Africa to reform and allow majority rule. The white minority dug in and tried to hold on to power. Rich resources in diamonds, gold, chromium, and other materials at first gave the nation the economic strength to resist this pressure. But a growing economic boycott by other nations and internal violence weakened the minority's resolve. Finally, an Afrikaner prime minister, **F. W. de Klerk,** began to reform the state. He led the repeal of apartheid laws and released Mandela from prison. In a special vote, two-thirds of the whites in South Africa approved of his efforts to draft a new constitution.

Finally, the opposing sides agreed on a transition from minority rule to majority rule. In a 1994 election Mandela and the African National Congress won handily. Mandela himself received over 60 percent of the vote for president against several candidates, while de Klerk was a distant second with 20 percent. The two candidates also shared a great honor. They both received the Nobel Peace Prize for their work in trying to heal the divisions in South Africa.

South Africa had finally moved from minority to majority rule, but violence did not end. White and black extremists opposed the agreement. Even some of Mandela's supporters argued among themselves. Yet the evil of apartheid had ended, and all South Africans held their future in their hands through the ballot. They could hope only in the vision that Nelson Mandela had offered twice—once at his trial in 1964 and again during his election

The cell in Robben Island Prison in which South African authorities imprisoned Mandela for eighteen years

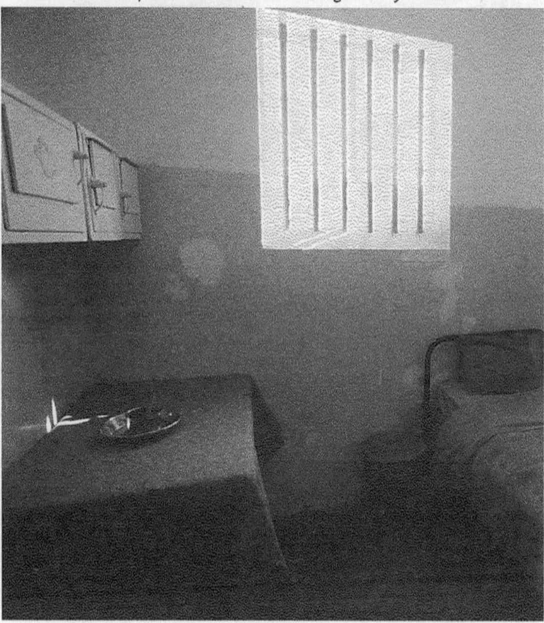

De Klerk—De Klerk was a lawyer after he graduated from college. His political career began in the House of Assembly (1972-89). He was a member of the former prime minister's cabinet starting in 1978. He was responsible for repealing many of the laws regarding apartheid.

Phrases—As in Australia, South Africa has its own English phrases which other English-speaking countries might not understand. This is true in all English-speaking countries (Great Britain, the United States, and others). Think of some uniquely American English phrases that other English-speaking cultures might not understand. *(Example: In America, "under the weather" means to be sick; in Australia it means to be drunk.)*

campaign in 1994. He said, "I have fought against white domination, I have fought against black domination. I have cherished the ideal of a democratic and free society in which all people live together in harmony and with equal opportunities." If the leaders of South Africa can attain that vision, then perhaps all races in the region can live together peaceably. But any leader who would rule well must always acknowledge the problem of man's natural sinfulness. There is no true and lasting harmony apart from Jesus Christ.

Section Review

1. Name at least two sets of conflicting groups in Southern Africa.
2. List two other names for the Dutch-descended people of Southern Africa.
3. What does apartheid mean?
4. What group led the protest against apartheid?
5. What powerful leader of the ANC was jailed but later became president?
6. Who was the prime minister of South Africa who worked for reform and won the Nobel Peace Prize with Nelson Mandela?

What causes one person to think of another as inferior to himself? What steps would be needed to correct the problem in thinking? Use Bible verses to support your reasons. Possible verses include I Samuel 16:7, I Corinthians 12:1-27, and James 2:1-9.

Nelson Mandela receives an award in Philadelphia as F. W. de Klerk and President Clinton of the United States congratulate him.

Section Review Answers

1. Some conflicting groups are Afrikaners and blacks, Asians, and "coloureds" in South Africa; Muslims and Jews; blacks and Asians in Uganda.
2. Boers, Afrikaners
3. to separate
4. African National Congress (ANC)
5. Nelson Mandela
6. F. W. de Klerk

Answers will vary. Pride, culture, training, and experience give man his view of himself in relation to others. Sometimes a person thinks that he is better than someone else because of some talent or skill that the Lord has given him. In South Africa, many of the Dutch were taught since birth that they were "better" than others. The only way to correct this type of wrong thinking is to get a biblical view of man as seen by God. First Samuel 16:7 says not to look at a person on the outside to judge him, because God looks at a person's heart even though man looks at his appearance. First Corinthians 12:1-27 says that all who are saved are part of the body of Christ and that the body needs every part. James 2:1-9 talks about the rich and the poor and says that it is a sin to have respect of persons.

East Africa: Rwanda and Tribal Conflict

The landscape of East Africa is incredibly diverse. From low coastal plains, the land soars to plateaus and mountains. **Mount Kilimanjaro,** the highest mountain in Africa, lies in this region. Scorching deserts lie in areas bordering the Red Sea. Running through East Africa is a deep valley, the massive **Great Rift Valley.** Africa's largest lakes—**Lake Victoria, Lake Tanganyika,** and **Lake Nyasa**—lie in the region.

Many people in East Africa speak Swahili, a language whose roots date back to the Middle Ages. But the widespread use of this language partially masks a division common among African societies. Racial conflict, as in South Africa, is not the only conflict in Africa. Even older is the historic African conflict between tribes. A tribe, you will recall from Chapter 5, is a group of people who share a common language, beliefs, and customs. When the European nations divided Africa and later allowed their colonies to become nations, they often drew national boundaries without caring where the different tribes lived. As a result, some peoples were divided by artificial boundaries. In other cases, tribes that had been enemies for years became citizens of the same country.

This conflict between African peoples is called **tribalism** or sometimes regionalism. There are many painful examples of such conflict in Africa. From 1967 to 1970 Nigeria underwent a bloody civil war between the Ibo people on the one side and the Yoruba and Hausa on the other. Estimates are that as many as one million people died in the Nigerian war. Likewise the racial conflict in South Africa was complicated by strife between the Xhosa and Zulu tribes.

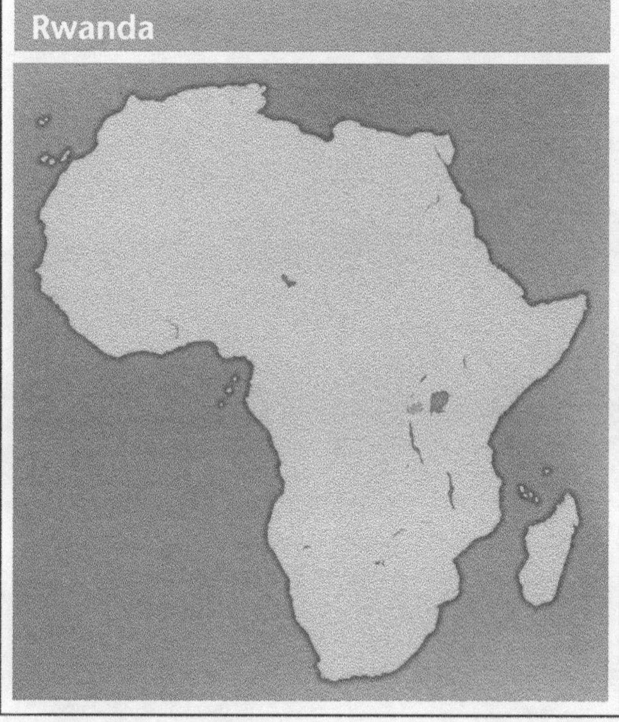

Tutsi vs. Hutu

Small African nations are not immune to this sort of conflict. The tiny nation of Rwanda is an example. Long before Europe colonized Africa, this area in East Africa had seen conflict between the remarkably tall **Tutsi** people and the more numerous **Hutu** people. The Tutsi had maintained control by ruling as an aristocracy, like that which existed in

Section 4

Student Objectives
Students should be able to

1. Identify the eastern region of Africa and its representative country.
2. Define the terms *tribalism* and *genocide*.
3. Summarize the conflict between the Tutsis and the Hutus in Rwanda.

Countries of East Africa—The other countries in East Africa are Ethiopia, Eritrea, Djibouti, Somalia, Kenya, Tanzania, Uganda, and Burundi.

Ibo vs. Hausa—In Nigeria in the 1960s, the Hausa were powerful. The Ibos resented this and seized power in a bloody civil war. This made the Hausa riot for fear of Ibo control. In 1967 a military leader took over, and the eastern region declared itself an independent republic named Biafra; the civil war to reclaim the eastern region lasted three years.

Section 4

Materials

- Photographs of tribal life, cities, and/or geographic features of Africa

Tribal Life—Bring in photos of the geographic features, tribal life, and cities of Africa. Discuss these in class with the students. Ask how each feature may or may not contribute to tribalism.

Africa Redrawn 565

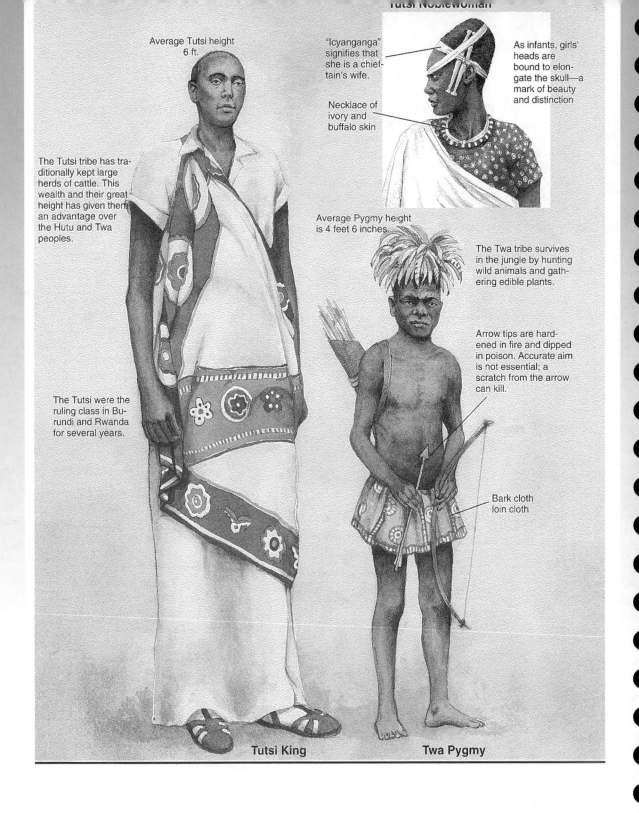

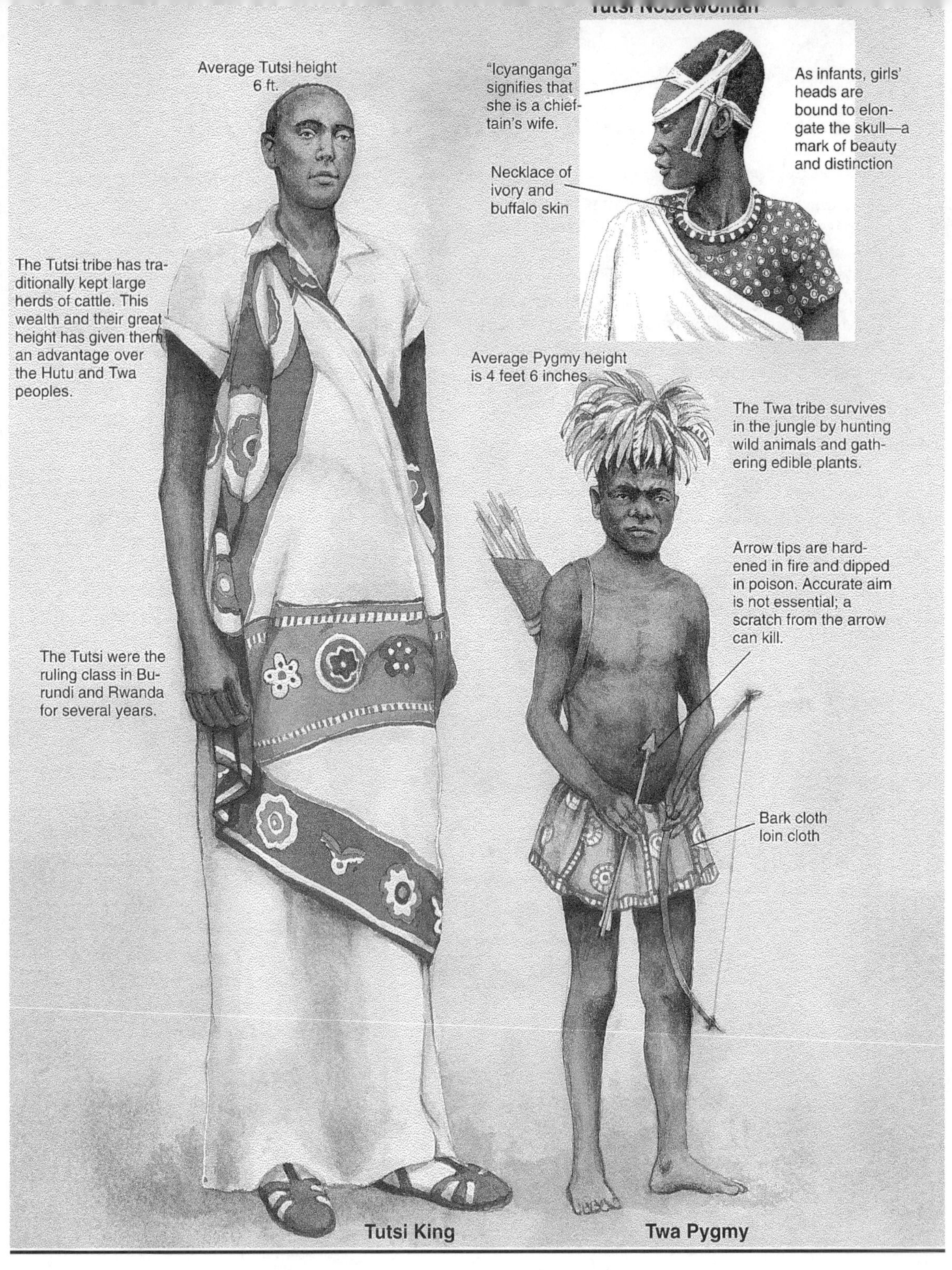
Tutsi Noblewoman
Average Tutsi height
6 ft.
"Icyanganga" signifies that she is a chieftain's wife.
As infants, girls' heads are bound to elongate the skull—a mark of beauty and distinction
Necklace of ivory and buffalo skin
The Tutsi tribe has traditionally kept large herds of cattle. This wealth and their great height has given them an advantage over the Hutu and Twa peoples.
Average Pygmy height is 4 feet 6 inches.
The Twa tribe survives in the jungle by hunting wild animals and gathering edible plants.
Arrow tips are hardened in fire and dipped in poison. Accurate aim is not essential; a scratch from the arrow can kill.
The Tutsi were the ruling class in Burundi and Rwanda for several years.
Bark cloth loin cloth
Tutsi King
Twa Pygmy

Tutsi refugees, young and old, flee Hutu massacres in Rwanda.

France before the French Revolution. When first the Germans and then the Belgians controlled the region, they worked through the Tutsi leaders.

But the Hutus saw no reason that they should serve the less numerous Tutsis. Just before independence, the Hutus of Rwanda threw off the Tutsis. About 150,000 Rwandans died in this fighting. When the Republic of Rwanda was born in 1962, it was under Hutu control. Many Tutsis became **refugees** (people fleeing war, persecution, or other dangers) and lived across Rwanda's borders in Congo, Uganda, Tanzania, and Burundi. There they built refugee camps that became centers of opposition to the Hutus.

The Tutsis did not give up without a fight. From their bases in neighboring countries, Tutsi forces sometimes attacked Rwanda. Tutsi invaders, called "cockroaches" by their opponents, invaded Rwanda several times after independence. Each time the invaders were driven out with great bloodshed on both sides. Inside Rwanda's borders were constant clashes between the tribes.

Other factors worsened the tribal conflict. The economy of the tiny, overcrowded country was weak, depending chiefly on a few exports such as coffee and tin. Rwanda is completely landlocked and must ship its goods through other countries. But conflicts with those countries, notably Uganda, sometimes closed the borders. Economic suffering resulted as Rwanda could not get its goods out to markets. Also the government of Rwanda was dictatorial and corrupt. Therefore, even some Hutus sided with the Tutsis working for reform.

Rwandan Patriotic Front

Refugees in Uganda eventually formed the **Rwandan Patriotic Front (RPF)** to overthrow the government. Led mainly by the Tutsis, the RPF called for political and economic reform. On October 1, 1990, the RPF invaded Rwanda from Uganda. The rebels

Burundi—The neighboring country of Burundi had a situation similar to Rwanda's. It has the same proportion of Tutsis and Hutus in its population, and it became an independent nation about the same time. The Tutsis in Burundi, however, held power (and protected themselves) by making the army 95 percent Tutsi.

Rwanda's Problems—Have each student list five problems in present-day Rwanda in a column on the left side of a piece of paper. He should then trade his paper with another student. Each student should then try to fill in on the right side of the page a solution to each problem, whether biblical, economic, political, or otherwise.

Refugee Camps—Most of the refugee camps were in Uganda, and most were made up of Tutsis. Over 200,000 refugees were in Tanzania, and others were in Burundi, Kenya, and the Democratic Republic of Congo (formerly Zaire). The refugees in Uganda were given voting rights in 1980 (they had been there since the sixties) but were still looked upon as foreigners. The refugees formed what is called the Rwandese Patriotic Front (RPF) to invade Rwanda periodically.

Conflict Between Ethiopia and Somalia—Somalia is unique in Africa because its people share a common history, language, culture, and religion (Islam). Border conflicts began with Ethiopia, and skirmishes were fought off and on for years. The Ogaden War was fought for control of the borders and is usually viewed as a war of Somali aggression. Haile Selassie of Ethiopia had wanted integration of these smaller territories (including Djibouti and Burundi), but so far Ethiopia has not been able to accomplish these goals.

won a number of victories but could not take the whole country. Finally, in August of 1993, the two sides agreed to a peace treaty. President Juvénal Habyamira, although himself a Hutu, promised to rule in a manner fair to all sides.

But the peace was shattered in April 1994. Hutu extremists, angered at Habyamira's compromise with the Tutsis, shot down his plane and killed him. Civil war broke out again as the RPF renewed its campaign. The RPF took control of the country in July 1994. But before they did so, Hutu forces began slaughtering Tutsis. Probably five hundred thousand died in this attempt at **genocide** (the destruction of a whole racial, ethnic, or political group).

The Tutsi-led Rwandan Patriotic Front fought the Hutu-led government of Rwanda and eventually won control of the nation.

The RPF now had power but still had trouble. The country was devastated by the fighting. The economy was ruined. It now became the Hutus' turn to be refugees as some two million fled the country. The refugee camps became centers of death by disease as well as bases for raids by Hutu forces on Rwanda. The new government began trying to bring the mass murderers of the Tutsis to justice. But it found that the court system was so ravaged by violence that it had ceased to function. The United Nations had to step in to restore order.

There are no easy answers to such tribal conflict. Years of hatred and conflict cannot be solved by a small dose of goodwill on the part of a few. The Christian realizes that only as men's natures are changed by Christ can they really make peace with one another (II Cor. 5:17-21).

Section Review

1. Name Africa's highest mountain. Name its three largest lakes.
2. Give two examples of tribal conflict in Africa.
3. Name the two major tribes in Rwanda and describe each.
4. What is genocide?

Why is tribalism such a problem in Africa? Compare this tribalism to tribes in the Americas.

Section Review Answers

1. Mount Kilimanjaro; Lake Victoria, Lake Tanganyika, Lake Nyasa
2. Tutsis against the Hutus; Xhosa against the Zulu; Ibo against the Yoruba and Hausa (any two)
3. Tutsi—tall, aristocratic, originally dominated; Hutu—more numerous, average height
4. the destruction of a whole racial, ethnic, or political group

Answers will vary. African tribes are diverse in culture, language, and background. In the past there was relatively little interaction among the tribes, and they knew each other mainly through warfare. In America, the Native Americans sometimes fought among themselves in very bloody warfare. We know that the Aztecs and Mayas of ancient Latin America frequently needed human sacrifices, and they often found their "volunteers" among other tribes.

Christianity in Modern Africa

Christianity has existed in Africa for centuries. The Bible records the conversion of the "Ethiopian eunuch" (Acts 8:26-40) in the first century. Some churches in Africa have a history tracing back to the era of the Roman Empire. Members of the **Coptic Church** in Egypt number around five million. The Copts, however, often suffer severe persecution and even violence from the Muslim majority. The **Ethiopian Orthodox Church** in Ethiopia is almost as old as the Coptic. It is in fact very close to the Coptic Church in teaching and practice. Until 1959 the *abuna* (head of the Ethiopian Church) was appointed by the Coptic Church. Today, the Ethiopian Church is independent. Roman Catholics have been present in Africa since the 1400s. The largest numbers of Catholics in Africa today are in those countries that were once colonies of Catholic nations, such as Belgium and France.

The Church of St. Barbara in Cairo is part of Egypt's Coptic Church, one of the oldest Christian groups in Africa.

Some of the most notable Christian growth in Africa in the twentieth century has come among Protestant and independent groups. Often these churches are connected to denominations in Europe and North America. Many of these churches resulted from the work of American and European missionaries. Today, national pastors (pastors native to Africa) are taking more and more of the burden from missionaries—but there are still great needs.

African Independent Churches

The growing importance of African Christian workers is also seen in what are known as the **African Independent Churches.** These are churches, denominations, and other groups that are controlled entirely by Africans. According to estimates, there are over five thousand different groups that can be classified as independent. There are two major kinds of African Independent Churches: Ethiopian churches and Zionist churches.

Members of the Ethiopian Orthodox Church join in a Christmas celebration at the rock-hewn Bet Marian Church.

Section 5

Student Objectives
Students should be able to

1. Compare and contrast the major divisions of African Christianity.

Religion in Africa—Widely diverse, Africa is probably one of the first places Western Christians think of when they think of missions.

Religions in Africa

Country	Religions
Algeria	Sunni Muslim 99%
Libya	Sunni Muslim 97%
Ghana	indigenous 38%, Muslim 30%, Christian 24%
Liberia	traditional beliefs 70%, Muslim 20%, Christian 10%
Democratic Republic of Congo	Christian 50%, indigenous 48%, Muslim 2%
Ethiopia	Muslim 50%, Ethiopian Orthodox 40%, animist 10%
Rwanda	Christian 74%, indigenous 25%, Muslim 1%
Uganda	Christian 66%, indigenous 18%, Muslim 16%
South Africa	mainly Christian; Hindu and Muslim minorities

Section 5

Materials

- Letters from missionaries in Africa
- Video—*Beyond the Night* (BJUP)
- *Free Indeed: Heroes of Black Christian History* by Mark Sidwell (BJUP, 1995), pp. 47-51.

Missionary Letter—Bring in (or have students bring in) letters from missionaries in Africa. (You may be able to photocopy prayer letters that missionaries have sent to their supporting churches.) Read brief portions of the letters in class and write the prayer requests on the board. Take time in class to pray for the missionaries. As time allows, have the students choose a missionary to write a letter to. Collect the letters and send them.

CHARACTERIZATIONS

Janani Luwum

Janani Luwum

Three hundred thousand Ugandans died under the rule of cruel dictator Idi Amin Dada of Uganda. But no death was more publicized than that of Janani Luwum. The future martyr was born in 1922 in northern Uganda. Although reared in a Christian home, Luwum was not converted until 1948. At that time he became one of the *balokole* ("saved ones") as a result of the East Africa Revival. In his first public testimony he said, "Today I have become a leader in Christ's army. I am prepared to die in the army of Jesus. As Jesus shed His blood for the people, if it is God's will, I will do the same."

Luwum eventually decided to become a minister of the Anglican Church in Uganda. He studied in both his own country and England. He pastored small scattered churches across rugged northern Uganda, and he also worked with a college. His church made him bishop of northern Uganda in 1969.

Luwum was made an archbishop in 1974. On his election, he said, "Many people have learned about Christ as an academic exercise. The church must help such people to transfer Christ from their heads into their hearts. I had Christ in my head and not my heart before I was converted. In 1948 I was 'born again' and Christ became the controller of my life. My sense of direction and values changed. Even now I am still growing in Him."

Archbishop Janani Luwum was human and had his failings. In some ways he was undiscerning. Despite his knowledge of the need for conversion, he tended to accept everyone as "Christian" who claimed the term, no matter what a person might teach or how he might live. But the archbishop showed great courage in the face of evil.

From 1971 to 1979 Uganda suffered under the rule of General Idi Amin Dada. To call Amin cruel would be an understatement. He ruthlessly slaughtered not only opponents but also friends and family members. His security forces delighted in torture. A man accused of theft, for example, was taken to a stadium and tied down. Then soldiers drove motorcycles over his body until he was dead. Amin himself was said to practice cannibalism. A Muslim, the dictator hoped to change Uganda from a predominantly Christian country to an Islamic one.

The archbishop tried vainly to work with Amin and cooperate with the government. The violence only got worse. Finally, in August 1976 Luwum held a meeting of religious leaders of Uganda. They asked for an end to the killings and illegal arrests. Amin was furious and was especially angry at Luwum, who had called the meeting and whose signature was first on the protest. A few months later Luwum said, "I live as though there will be no tomorrow. I face daily being picked up by the soldiers. While the opportunity is there, I preach the gospel with all my might, and my conscience

Beyond the Night*—*Beyond the Night is a video offered by Bob Jones University Press. It is the story of modern medical missionaries to Africa. This is a true story about their struggles with the African country's government.

***Free Indeed*—**Read with your students about Christianity among blacks in *Free Indeed* by Mark Sidwell, available from BJUP. The stories are mostly about Americans, but the story about Samuel Morris focuses on a native African.

is clear before God. . . . Whenever I have the opportunity I have told the President the things the churches disapprove of. God is my witness."

On February 16, 1977, Amin called a number of religious leaders to a meeting. There an official read charges accusing the archbishop of plotting to overthrow the government. As this was being read, Luwum whispered to a bishop standing by him, "They are going to kill me. I am not afraid." The officials dismissed the group but held Luwum back because Amin wanted to see him. As his friends left, the archbishop said, "I can see the hand of the Lord in this."

It is not known exactly what happened next. Some accounts say that Amin tried to force Luwum into signing a confession that he had committed treason. When Luwum began to pray, Amin told his guards to shut him up, and they shot him in the mouth, then twice in the chest. The government refused to release the body and announced that the archbishop was killed in a car accident.

Luwum's death took place on the one hundredth anniversary of the coming of Christianity to Uganda. At a service following the archbishop's martyrdom, the congregation sang a hymn originally sung by the first Ugandan martyrs nearly a century before:

> Grant, O Lord, our eyes be open
> Here to see our Saviour King,
> And our hearts be ever eager
> Him to hear, His praise to sing.

Two years later, the Amin regime ended, but the church of Jesus Christ continues forward.

Ugandan dictator Idi Amin Dada, persecutor of Christians and slayer of Janani Luwum

Ethiopian groups—It is important to distinguish between the Ethiopian Orthodox Church, a religious group closely akin to the Coptic Church of Egypt, and the Ethiopian churches, a branch of the African Independent Churches.

Kimbangu—Kimbangu was born in 1889 and claimed to have received a call similar to that of Samuel's in the Old Testament. He is said to have healed many people, including a woman who was in critical condition, the deaf, the blind, and the crippled. The government began to believe that he was gathering people to foster rebellion, and Kimbangu fled on the first arrest attempt. Three months later, he voluntarily turned himself in. He was sentenced to 120 lashes with a whip and death, but his sentence was changed to life imprisonment later. His followers continued to tell the legends of their founder's greatness during his imprisonment and after his death.

An African church service

Ethiopian churches take their name from Psalm 68:31—"Ethiopia shall soon stretch out her hands unto God." Because Ethiopia never came under European control, Africans see that land as a symbol of independence. Psalm 68:31 also expresses the hope of many African Christians that the entire continent will come under the influence of the gospel of Christ. Ethiopian churches are often much like European or North American churches in practice and doctrine. Their main distinguishing characteristic is their total independence from non-African control. Many of these Ethiopian churches are also involved in politics as a way to solve Africa's problems.

Zionist churches are also independent of non-African control, but they are even more independent in their teaching and practice. The Zionist churches often blend Christianity with traditional African culture. Zionist churches, for example, may permit polygamy (the marriage of a man to more than one wife) despite the Bible's teaching against it. Often Zionist groups will borrow ceremonies from traditional pagan African religions or incorporate elements of witchcraft. Zionist churches also usually look to one outstanding leader who is treated as a kind of prophet.

The Kimbanguist Church, centered in Congo, is a good example of a Zionist church. The founder was Simon Kimbangu (1889-1951), a popular Baptist preacher and healer. Such large crowds began to gather to hear him that authorities in the Belgian Congo (today the Democratic Republic of Congo) arrested him in 1921 and sentenced him to death. The sentence was changed to life imprisonment, and he remained jailed until his death. Even with Kimbangu in prison, the church grew. After his death, Kimbanguists sang hymns claiming that Kimbangu had been raised from the dead in some manner and continued to work among men. The importance of Kimbangu to the church as a prophet is reflected by its official name, "The Church of Jesus Christ on Earth Through the Prophet Simon Kimbangu."

East Africa Revival

One of the most dramatic events in modern African church history was the **East Africa Revival,** which centered in Tanzania, Uganda, and Kenya. It began among Anglican evangelicals in the 1930s and profoundly affected the Protestant churches of the region. Its effects continued through at least the 1950s, and many major religious leaders of Africa were converted in the revival, such as Archbishop Janani Luwum of Uganda (see pp. 570-71).

Write A Quiz—Have each student write a What Am I? quiz for one of the religious groups mentioned in this chapter. It should include 5-10 clues about the religion.

What Am I?

1. I take my name from Psalm 68:31.
2. I am totally independent of any non-African control.
3. I am often involved in politics.
4. I hope for my entire continent to come under the influence of the gospel of Christ.
5. I am one major type of African Independent Church.

I am the ___________. *(Ethiopian church)*

African Food—Have each student try some traditional African food or drink. Kenyan coffee might be easy and palatable. Look in ethnic cookbooks for other examples.

The revival stressed the confession of sin and the need to preach the gospel to the unsaved. The importance of Christ's atonement for sin through the shedding of His blood became an important theme. A favorite gospel song of the revival was "What can wash away my sin? Nothing but the blood of Jesus." One Christian converted in the revival described the effects of the awakening:

> Conviction of sin came upon people. The Word of God became real and alive. The church was packed and the atmosphere was charged with the power of the Spirit. . . . People were rejoicing and talking from experience and singing praises to God. Jesus was so close, they talked about him while shopping. They talked about him when they drew water. People were even converted at the watering places for cattle—cattlemen speaking to cattlemen. It was wonderful! This was like what happened in the New Testament.

In short, the religious life of African Christians is probably as diverse as it is in any continent. But events such as the East Africa Revival reveal that God is working among Africans as He is among all peoples of the world. As the apostle Peter said, "Of a truth I perceive that God is no respecter of persons: but in every nation he that feareth him, and worketh righteousness, is accepted with him" (Acts 10:34-35).

Spanning the Ages

Throughout the twentieth century, conflicts have risen from the same roots: extreme nationalism, hunger for power, and pride. These causes have led to wars, independence movements, dictatorships, and racial tensions. But the same Lord is over all and can heal anyone who trusts in Him.

Section Review

1. In what country is the Coptic Church found? the Ethiopian Orthodox Church?
2. Name the two major kinds of African Independent Churches.
3. Describe the East Africa Revival.

How did European and American religions spread to Africa? Describe the effects that those cultures had on Africans.

Summary

African history and culture in the twentieth century has been just as diverse as the continent's landscape. The modern age has presented Africa with many challenges: decolonization (as illustrated by Algeria), dictatorships (as illustrated by Ghana), racial conflict (as illustrated by South Africa), and tribal conflict (as illustrated by Rwanda). But in addition there has been hope on the continent, especially the hope of the gospel found in Christianity. God moves among the Africans as He moves among all the peoples of the world.

Section Review Answers

1. Egypt; Ethiopia
2. Ethiopian churches, Zionist churches
3. Anglican evangelicals and other Protestants experienced a revival in which many significant African leaders were converted. This revival was centered in Tanzania, Uganda, and Kenya. Despite the many native religions in Africa, Christianity is taking a strong foothold there as a result of missionaries and native witnesses.

Answers will vary. Missionaries, traders, and explorer/adventurers brought both culture and religion to Africa. These influences have greatly affected Africa in almost all areas, including education, entertainment, family life, communication, and religion. If the opposite had happened and African native religion had been transported to Europe, the Western world might have adopted pagan practices which would have kept it in spiritual darkness.

Chapter Review Idea

Use the pyramid game to review the chapter. You will have to create questions in advance. Divide the class into two groups. Each student will choose a triangle in the pyramid (triangles are worth different amounts, depending on the difficulty of the question), and if a student answers the question correctly, he will receive the number of points for that spot. The student must answer independently. No help may be given by his teammates. The team with the most points at the end of the game wins.

Chapter Enrichment Activities

Comparison—Look at the challenges in Africa presented in each section: decolonization, dictatorship, racial conflict, tribal conflict, and Christianity. If possible, compare each to a facet of American history.

CHAPTER REVIEW

People, Places, and Things to Know

Sahara
decolonization
assimilation
Front for National Liberation (FLN)
Haile Selassie
Charles de Gaulle
"Pan-Africanism"
W. E. B. Du Bois
Kwame Nkrumah
"second independence"
Afrikaners
apartheid
"coloureds"
African National Congress (ANC)
Sharpeville massacre
Nelson Mandela
F. W. de Klerk
Mount Kilimanjaro
Great Rift Valley
tribalism
Tutsi
Hutu
refugees
Rwandan Patriotic Front (RPF)
genocide
Coptic Church
Ethiopian Orthodox Church
African Independent Churches
Ethiopian churches
Zionist churches
East Africa Revival

Review Questions

Matching

Match each section of Africa with the country used to characterize it.

1. Saharan Africa
2. West Africa
3. Southern Africa
4. East Africa

(a) Algeria
(b) Ghana
(c) Rwanda
(d) South Africa

Fill-in-the-Blank

5. Egypt has about five million members in the _____ Church.
6. The _____ Church in Ethiopia is led by the *abuna*.
7. Churches that are similar to non-African churches but are distinguished by their independence from outside control are known as _____ churches.
8. The _____ churches combine Christianity with traditional African culture.

Connections

Write a sentence describing the relationship between the following pairs of terms.

9. decolonization / assimilation
10. Nelson Mandela / F. W. de Klerk
11. "Pan-Africanism" / W. E. B. Du Bois

Chapter Review Answers

Matching

1. a
2. b
3. d
4. c

Fill-in-the-Blank

5. Coptic
6. Ethiopian Orthodox
7. Ethiopian
8. Zionist

Connections

9. In the process of assimilation, European countries tried to bring colonies into the mother country; When they failed, they made their colonies independent in a process called decolonization.
10. Nelson Mandela and F. W. de Klerk both received the Nobel Peace Prize for their efforts to initiate democratic majority rule in South Africa.
11. W. E. B. Du Bois, a leader in the "Pan-Africanism" movement, called for the world to treat blacks fairly and equally. He wanted independence for African colonies, an end to exploitation, and a means for cooperation.

Matching

Match each term with the country it represents.

12. Front for National Liberation (FLN)
13. Tutsi
14. Gold Coast
15. apartheid
16. tribalism
17. Belgian Congo
18. African National Congress
19. Afrikaners
20. Hutu
21. Charles de Gaulle
22. Haile Selassie
23. Kwame Nkrumah
24. King Leopold
25. Mussolini

(a) Algeria
(b) Ethiopia
(c) Ghana
(d) Rwanda
(e) South Africa
(f) Democratic Republic of Congo

Think About It!

What are some other examples of planned or practiced genocide? What might man's reasoning be to use genocide? Can genocide ever be justified?

Recipe: Stewed Sweet Potatoes— This is a common vegetable dish in South Africa.

Ingredients:
1/4 c. light brown sugar
1 Tbsp. flour
1 tsp. salt
2 lbs. sweet potatoes, peeled and sliced into 1/2-inch rounds
3 Tbsp. butter, cut into 1/4-inch pieces
3 one-inch pieces stick cinnamon
1/2 c. water

Combine sugar, flour, and salt. Place one third of the sweet potatoes in a 3- to 4-quart sauce pan, completely covering the bottom of the pan. Sprinkle with one third of the sugar mixture and dot with one third of the butter. Repeat this sequence two times. Tuck cinnamon under top layer of potatoes and pour water down the side of the pan. Bring to a boil over high heat, cover tightly and reduce to low heat. Slide pan occasionally to keep bottom layer from scorching and simmer for 45 minutes or until soft. Using a slotted spoon, transfer potatoes to a bowl and moisten with 1/2 cup of the cooking liquid. Serve hot.

Matching

12. a
13. d
14. c
15. e
16. d
17. f
18. e
19. e
20. d
21. a
22. b
23. c
24. f
25. b

Think About It!

Answers will vary. Hitler's mass destruction of the Jews is an example of both planned and practiced genocide. Thankfully, he could not find them all. In many African nations during the 1950s-1970s, Christians and other political enemies were killed on a grand scale. Man may think he is ridding the world of unwanted groups (by methods such as abortion or euthanasia), or he may just have a bent toward the sin of murder. Maybe a certain group has caused him great problems in the past, and he wishes to retaliate or "save face." Genesis 9:6 says that "whoso sheddeth man's blood, by man shall his blood be shed." The Bible condones capital punishment and war in certain situations, but murder is a sin against a holy God.

Student Objectives
Students should be able to

1. Identify Diaz, Huerta, Zapata, Carranza, and Villa as leaders of Mexico.
2. Design a small mural about modern-day society.
3. Explain the effects of the PRI on Mexico.
4. Label Mexico, Brazil, Argentina, and Costa Rica on a map of Latin America.
5. Review types of graphs and geographic features of the world.
6. Summarize the political situation in Argentina since World War II.
7. Analyze the Peróns' ability to stay in power.
8. Describe the Falklands War.
9. List factors that have made Costa Rica successful.
10. Compare and contrast religions in Latin America.

Opening Photo— View of Rio de Janeiro from Sugarloaf Mountain

Counting the Cost

Place pictures of the missionaries to the Auca Indians on the board with the quotation "He is no fool who gives what he cannot keep to gain what he cannot lose." Attach pictures of worldly treasures and heavenly treasures. Your students may be a source of ideas for these treasures.

Another idea is to place a map of Central and South America on the board. Highlight Mexico, Argentina, and Costa Rica. Attach pictures or information about the country next to each country.

CHAPTER 20

Even at this point in the school year, you probably remember that Chapters 6 and 7 discussed the early history of Latin America. We saw there how the Spanish moved first into Central America and the Caribbean and how they shared the settlement of South America with Portugal. Today over five hundred million people live in Latin America. These millions of inhabitants represent several cultural heritages—Spanish, Portuguese, Indian, African, and other nationalities. How can anyone survey the history of a people so numerous and so diverse in just a single chapter?

Actually, we can learn the basic themes of Latin American history by studying selected countries in the region. By looking at Mexico, Argentina, and Costa Rica, we can get some idea of the course of Latin American history. In addition, the Characterizations, Settings, and other special features in the chapter allow us to take a few "detours" to sample Latin American history—just as you might sample Latin American food at a feast by tasting a little bit of everything. Of course, you will not learn *everything* about Latin American history in just a few pages. But you will discover some of the forces and personalities that have shaped the region.

A.D. 1910 - PRESENT

Mexican Revolution 1910-20

1910 1920

Chapter 20 Lesson Plans			
Section Title	**Main Concept**	**Pages**	**Time Frame**
1. Mexico: Preserving a Revolution **Settings: Brazil*	The Mexican Revolution resulted in the one-party system of today.	576-83	2 days
2. Argentina: **Backgrounds: The Falklands War*	Juan and Eva Perón ruled Argentina amid much change.	584-89	1 day
3. Costa Rica: Success Story **Characterizations: Heitor Villa-Lobos*	Costa Rica's efforts to maintain democracy have made it one of the best-governed countries in Latin America.	590-95	1 day
4. Christianity in Latin America **Center Stage: Mission to the Aucas*	Although mostly Roman Catholic, Latin America is seeing growth in Protestant groups such as Charismatics and Pentecostals.	596-99	1-2 days
Total suggested days (including 1 day for review & 1 day for test)			7-8 days

The Changing Face of Latin America

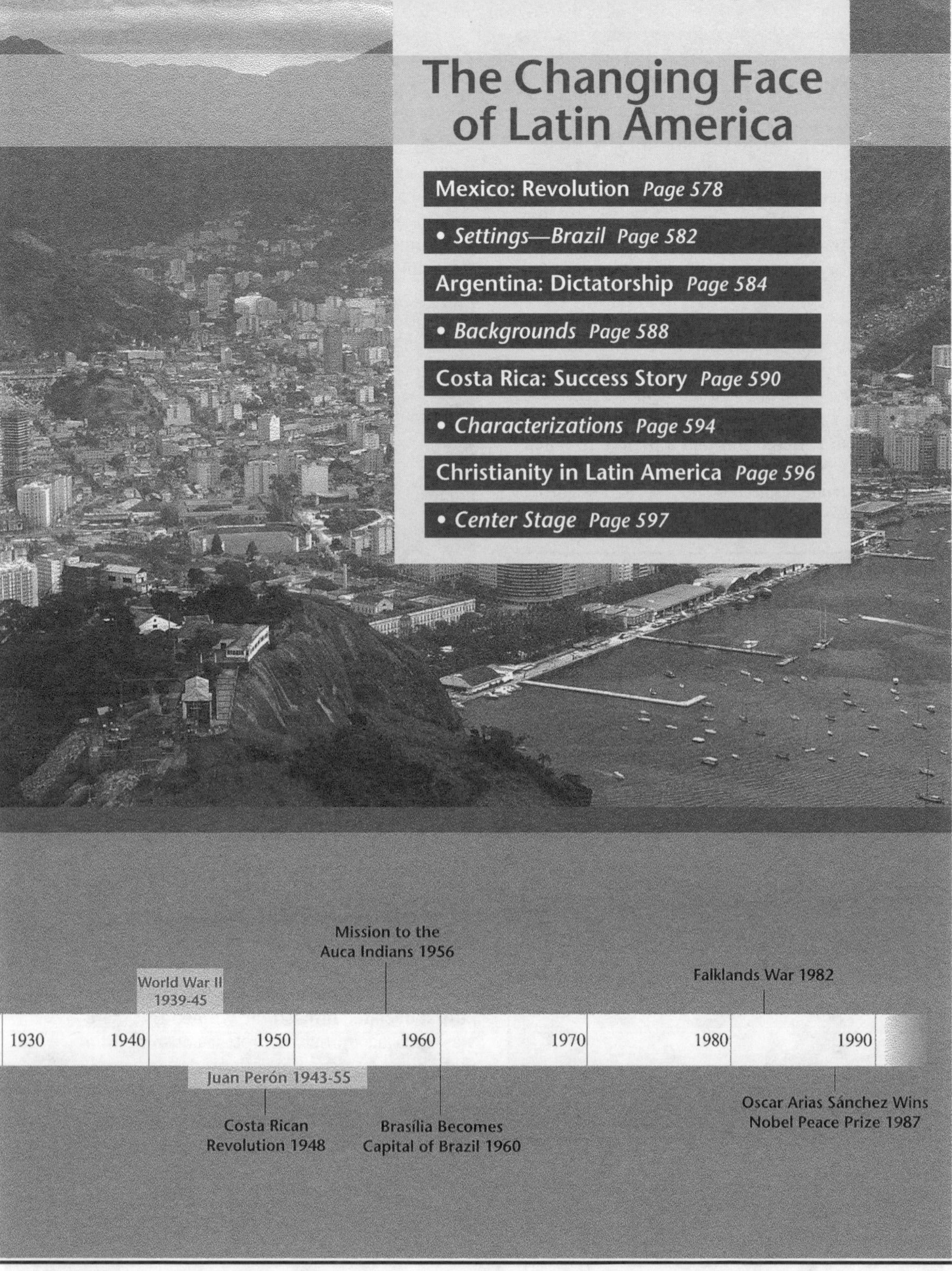

Chapter Motivator

Review what your students already know about Latin America from Chapters 6 and 7. Ask them the following questions.

- Based on what you know about the rest of the world in modern times, can you predict what might be happening in Latin America as well? *(political or religious divisions, a trend toward democracy, more international interdependence, etc.)*
- How many Latin American countries can you name? *(Use a map or globe as a visual of countries the students name or those they cannot remember.)*

Give each student a map of Latin America (BLM 6-2, 7-2). Have the students fill in the countries to review their locations.

Ask the students what they think the representative countries of Latin America might be. Direct them toward the divisions in this chapter: Mexico, Argentina, and Costa Rica. (You may also wish to mention Brazil, which is covered in the settings pages and the pages on Heitor Villa-Lobos.)

Colossians 1:16

Different forms of government are abundant in the world today, and Latin America is one area of vast diversity. Remind your students that God sets up all governments in His will and way. Colossians 1:16 says, "For by him were all things created, that are in heaven, and that are in earth, visible and invisible, whether they be thrones, or dominions, or principalities, or powers: all things were created by him, and for him." (BLM verse 20)

Materials

- Scripture verse (BLM verse 20)
- Latin American food
- Souvenirs from Latin American countries
- Large roll of paper for mural
- *Teaching Transparencies* for use with *WORLD STUDIES for Christian Schools* (Second Edition)
- Wall map of Central and South America (BLM 20-1)
- Video of Latin America or the Rain Forest
- Coffee and bananas
- Recording of the music of Heitor Villa-Lobos
- *Through Gates of Splendor* by Elisabeth Elliot
- Guest speaker, a native Latin American

SECTION 1

Student Objectives
Student should be able to

1. Identify Diaz, Huerta, Zapata, Carranza, and Villa as leaders of Mexico.
2. Design a small mural about modern-day society.
3. Explain the effects of the PRI on Mexico.

Northern Latin America—Mexico is the northernmost Latin American country and is the only Latin American country in North America.

Napoleon III—Napoleon III was Napoleon I's nephew. He was born in Paris in 1808, but his family was kicked out of France after Napoleon's defeat. He then lived in Italy, Germany, and Switzerland. He tried revolutionary activities and was imprisoned in France in 1840 but escaped to England six years later. France again became a republic, and Napoleon III was elected to the assembly. Later he was made president, but he seized power and became emperor.

Napoleon III helped to modernize many things in France, but he still had trouble on many sides. He meddled in other countries' affairs, one example of which was his making Maximilian emperor of Mexico. Maximilian's reign ended when he had to surrender to the Prussians. Napoleon III lost power, and a new republic was formed in France.

Mexico: Preserving a Revolution

Mexico is one of the largest Latin American countries. Originally home to the Mayan and Aztec civilizations, Mexico fell under Spanish control. From the conquest of the Aztecs by Cortés in the 1500s, Mexico was a colony of Spain until it gained independence in the 1820s.

In the 1800s, after independence, Mexico went through periods in which it was an empire, a republic, and a dictatorship. A disastrous war with the United States (1846-48) cost the nation half of its territory. The Mexicans also suffered through a period in which Emperor Napoleon III of France tried to force an Austrian nobleman on the nation as its emperor.

Mexico achieved some stability in 1877 when General **Porfirio Díaz** (por-FEER-ee-oh DEE-ahs) became dictator. He encouraged foreign investment and reorganized the Mexican government. By stern rule, Díaz kept order in the country.

Porfirio Díaz

Revolution

But after more than thirty years of Díaz's rule, many leaders were tiring of his sometimes harsh control. They wondered who would succeed the aging dictator. In 1910 Francisco Madero challenged Díaz in a presidential election. The dictator tried to fix the election and at first declared himself the winner. But there was such an uproar of protest and rebellion that Díaz's dictatorship collapsed.

But the end of Díaz did not mean relief for the Mexican people. The nation was soon suf-

SECTION 1

Materials

- Latin American food
- Souvenirs from Latin American countries
- Large roll of paper for mural
- Transparencies for Chapter 20

Taste Test—For a change of pace, have students bring food to make a Latin American lunch. Foods might include tacos, enchiladas, burritos, tortilla chips, salsa, and fruit juice (especially lime, lemon, strawberry, or pineapple). Before you eat, discuss the significance of each food item to Latin Americans.

Souvenirs—Bring in (or have students bring in) souvenirs from Mexico or another Latin American country. Many students will have something that fits in this category. Sombreros, music makers, beads, and jewelry are common souvenirs from Latin America.

Pancho Villa on horseback

In northern Mexico, Francisco **"Pancho" Villa** (VEE-uh) was a bandit who supported Madero. A skilled soldier, he helped the revolutionary forces win major victories in the north. Villa at first supported Carranza but soon broke with him and joined forces with Zapata. When the United States supported Carranza, the angry Villa murdered sixteen American engineers working in Santa Isabel and then crossed the U.S. border to attack Columbus, New Mexico. Angered by these actions, President Wilson sent a U.S. Army force under General **John Pershing** into Mexico to track down Villa. But American soldiers could never pin down the wily Villa, and they eventually withdrew.

suffering through a bloody period that has become known as the **Mexican Revolution.** Madero tried to rule, but he was quickly overthrown and executed by General **Victoriano Huerta** (WHER ta), who became dictator.

But Huerta could not establish order either. Other revolts flared up across the country, and the United States opposed Huerta. President Woodrow Wilson called him "that scoundrel" and a "desperate brute." Huerta's government fell, and rival armies began contending for control of Mexico.

In southern Mexico, **Emiliano Zapata** led an uprising of peasants who wanted to break up the large estates and provide land for the small farmers. They took the slogan "Land and Liberty!" Zapata was able to gather as many as twenty-five thousand men into his forces. He virtually ruled the south of the country.

In central Mexico, **Venustiano Carranza** had been a supporter of the slain Madero. Carranza rallied the opposition to Huerta but was unable to hold his forces together after Huerta was gone. He eventually presented himself as the legitimate leader of Mexico and won the support of the United States.

Emiliano Zapata

Emiliano Zapata—Zapata and Villa allied against Carranza. When Villa asked Zapata if he would like to sit in the presidential chair, Zapata said, "It would be better to burn it, for I have seen that everybody who has sat in this chair has become an enemy of the people."

Venustiano Carranza—Carranza was the president or "First Chief" of Mexico and the leader supported by the United States. He called a convention, but when it ended up being in Villa-controlled northern Mexico, he boycotted the convention. It was held anyway, and the convention ousted him. He refused to step down, instead fighting the resistance led by Zapata and Villa. In the end his forces were victorious.

Mexican Leaders—Divide your class into three groups. Have each group create a diary chronicling at least five days in the life of one of the three leaders of Mexico after Huerta. Make sure each includes the following categories: social life, religious life, political issues, tactical (battle) strategies, and personal concerns. Try to help students see that these were real people with real lives and not just storybook characters. Have a spokesperson from each group read the diary aloud to the rest of the class. You may wish to grade these for participation, creativity, originality, and so forth.

The Mexican War—Look back at the map of United States Expansion in the text (page 211 or TT 8-B). Remind the students of the amount of territory the United States claimed at the end of the war. Discuss the pros and cons of the United States's claiming that territory. *(The U.S. felt it was part of Manifest Destiny; U.S. citizens lived in the territory. Mexicans believed it was theirs by virtue of territorial sovereignty and their Spanish heritage.)*

Muralists—Murals have been around for a very long time. Cave drawings are murals, and ancient Egyptians painted murals in many places, including the pyramids. Greeks and Romans decorated walls with murals. The Renaissance painter Giotto created murals of Bible scenes. Other Italian muralists were Andrea Mantegna, Masaccio, Piero della Francesca, Raphael, and of course Michelangelo. Famous muralists at the end of the nineteenth century were Puvis de Chavannes from France and John La Farge from America. David Siqueiros was a famous Mexican muralist.

All three revolutionary leaders died violently. Zapata was killed in 1919 in an ambush by Carranza's forces. Villa retired to his ranch in 1920 but was gunned down in 1923 under mysterious circumstances. Carranza seemed to be the victor when he became president of Mexico in 1917. Moreover, he presided over the adopting of the Constitution of 1917, the constitution by which Mexico is still governed today. But in 1920 he tried to arrange for one of his supporters to succeed him as president. The army rebelled, and Carranza was killed as he attempted to flee Mexico City.

Search for Stability

This violence, bloodshed, and unrest convinced Mexico's leaders that they must find a better way to rule the country. Violence continued in the 1920s, but Mexico began to build a stable system. They finally decided that the solution was to move away from personal rule. In other words, the government would no longer be centered on the popularity of a single leader. The cry of politics became "No reelection." With reelection forbidden, Mexican presidents would find it harder to increase their power by winning (or sometimes stealing) election after election. After one six-year term, the president had to step down.

Mexican leaders decided to preserve the revolution by replacing personal rule with party rule. In 1928 what became known as the **Institutional Revolutionary Party** *(Partido Revolucionario Institucional,* or **PRI**) was established. The PRI virtually became the government of Mexico. The president and most of the high officials belonged to the party. Under the PRI's guidance, Mexico escaped revolutionary violence. Although still a poor nation in many ways, Mexico began to industrialize and change itself into a more urban country. Under the rule of the PRI, Mexico found stability.

As its name indicates, one of the goals of the PRI was to "institutionalize" the revolution. The party's leaders wanted to preserve all the gains of the Mexican Revolution and carry forward its principles of reform and democracy. The government demonstrated this concern in many ways. One of the most visible ways (literally) was Mexico's support of the **muralists.** Painters such as **Diego Rivera** and José Clemente Orozco painted great murals on the walls of public buildings. In a deceptively simple style, these murals celebrate Mexico's history and feature the common

Distribution of Arms, *a mural by Diego Rivera celebrating the Mexican Revolution*

Art—Have students create a mural using a large piece of paper as their "wall." Encourage them to depict life in their own society. Display the finished work.

Worth a Thousand Words—Use the following questions to direct a discussion about the picture on this page.

- What type of people are receiving weapons? *(workers)*
- Do they look rich? *(no)*
- What do the hammer and sickle in the background represent? *(Communism)*
- What other things do you see in the mural that tell you about the situation it depicts? *(Answers will vary.)*

people, not the rich elites that the muralists despised. Rivera said, "For the first time in the history of art, Mexican mural painting made the masses the hero of monumental art."

A scenic view of Monterrey, Mexico, illustrates how far the nation has come since the revolution in the early twentieth century.

The PRI—The original name of the PRI was the National Revolutionary Party (PRN); it was changed during the presidency of Miguel Alemán (1946-52) in order to stress the goal of preserving the gains of the revolution.

The poet who referred to the Mexican government under the PRI as a "philanthropic ogre" was Octavio Paz.

But there was a cost to stability. The PRI allowed Mexicans to participate in the rule of their country—but they usually had to do so through the PRI. The party manipulated elections so that it won most of them. Although other parties could usually win a few offices, power remained in the hands of the PRI. Not until 1997 did the Mexican legislature start a session without a majority of its members belonging to the PRI. As a result, Mexico has a government that is sensitive to the people's wishes but that also devotes its energies to maintaining power. A Mexican poet described government under the PRI as a "philanthropic ogre." In other words, the government of Mexico is well-meaning in its attempt to rule justly and provide for the needs of its people. But it is an "ogre," a monster, in that it is controlled by just one faction that will use even corrupt means to stay in power.

The one-party rule of Mexico has served the country better than the multiple governments and revolutions of the 1800s. Also, thanks to the nation's natural resources—notably oil—the nation has even enjoyed some prosperity. But Mexico still suffers from debt and economic depression, especially when oil prices drop. The corruption sometimes characterizing the PRI's rule has led other parties to seek an end to PRI domination. A few radical groups have even taken up arms against the government. Mexico has enjoyed some peace and prosperity, but it has yet to enjoy a truly open democracy.

Section Review

1. To whom did Mexico lose half of its territory in the middle of the 1800s?
2. Whom did Victoriano Huerta overthrow to become president of Mexico?
3. Name the three leaders of Mexico who vied for control in the 1910s and tell from which section each came.
4. What is the major political party in Mexican politics?
5. Name two well-known muralists from this time period.

Give other examples of government being a "philanthropic ogre." What evidences do we see in the Mexican government to support this? How would one balance philanthropy and big government?

The PRI—Discuss with your students the effects of the PRI on Mexico. These include bringing stability to the nation, supporting muralists, and trying to remain in power through many means (the idea of the "philanthropic ogre").

Section Review Answers

1. the United States
2. Porfirio Diaz
3. Emiliano Zapata—southern; Venustiano Carranza—central; "Pancho" Villa—northern
4. Institutional Revolutionary Party (PRI)
5. Diego Rivera; José Clemente Orozco

Answers will vary. Sweden, Canada, and the United States are prime examples of "philanthropic ogres." They try to aid the poor but, in doing so, propagate a way of life that is neither practical nor biblical. There are, of course, legitimate needs that the government has seen fit to fill, but to balance this philanthropy and the potential for big government to become corrupt, one needs to take the biblical philosophy that one who does not work should not eat. At the same time, legitimate needs (such as some health care insurance and unemployment compensation due to layoffs, etc.) could be taken care of as long as the government is authorized by the people and feels responsible to take care of its citizens in that way.

Student Objectives

Students should be able to

1. Label Mexico, Brazil, Argentina, and Costa Rica on a map of Latin America.
2. Review types of graphs and geographic features of the world.

Latin America Today—Latin America is widely diverse. Some of its current social issues are of worldwide concern. Drugs and violence have skyrocketed in Colombia. The political struggles between factions in Nicaragua (such as the Contras and the Sandinistas) have led to much violence and chaos. Slums in Mexico City grow faster than the government's ability to provide sanitation, so thousands of people live and work in the garbage dumps. In Peru the center of everyone's conversation is inflation and the value of the currency. Argentina has problems with its government. Brazil has experienced a great influx of all kinds of sects and cults. Often traditional African and Native American religions are mixed with new ones. In Bolivia and Panama (as well as other countries) cocaine production and trade are an important way of life.

Brasília—The capital of Brazil, Brasília, is a forward capital. This means that the government is trying to get people to move inland from more heavily populated coastal cities.

SETTINGS—Brazil

Location—The largest country in South America, Brazil dominates the continent. On its eastern side are thousands of miles of coastline along the shore of the Atlantic Ocean. On its western side, Brazil touches at some point every other Southern American country, except Chile and Ecuador. The equator falls across the northern part of the country.

Climate—The northern part of Brazil, along the Amazon River Basin, has a tropical wet (rain forest) climate. This region receives over eighty inches of rain per year. The climate of the southern plateau and the highlands is chiefly tropical wet and dry (savanna). Rainfall here is only forty to sixty inches per year.

Topography—Dominating the northern half of the country is the Amazon River Basin. The future of the rain forest along this river has become a source of international concern. Brazil has been clearing away the rain forest to provide land for farming and industry. Some scientists worry that this policy will harm the ecology of not just Brazil but also the rest of the world. The rest of the nation outside the Amazon region is mostly plateau and highlands.

Natural Resources—Brazil enjoys some mineral wealth. Its most profitable mineral products are iron and manganese, although Brazil lacks the coal it needs to turn the iron to steel. Brazil, like many Latin American countries, has tended to rely on one major crop for export. Originally, sugar was Brazil's main cash crop and later rubber was an important export. Today, Brazil's main crop is coffee, and the country is the world's largest coffee grower. The problem with one-crop economies is that national prosperity goes up and down as the crop's value goes up and down. Brazil has learned this fact to its sorrow and now tries to diversify its exports.

582 Chapter 20

Materials

- Transparencies for Chapter 20
- Wall map of Central and South America (BLM 20-1)
- Video of Latin America or the Rain Forest

Map Activity—Use map 20-C from the Student Activities manual to reinforce the geography lesson.

Going Beyond—Read the Settings pages with your students. Review different types of graphs and show examples of each: bar, pie, picture, and line (TT 16-B, 17-B, 18-A, 19-A).

Use a map of the world to review geographic features learned throughout the book or to review countries.

Geography & Culture—Brazil differs from the rest of Latin America in that its culture is Portuguese instead of Spanish. Its major cities include Rio de Janeiro (day zhuh-NEHR-oh; the original capital) on the Atlantic coast and São Paolo (its largest city).

Brazil's capital, **Brasília,** has an unusual history. Most of Brazil's major cities are on the coast. To encourage development of the interior, in 1957 the Brazilian government began building a new capital city some five hundred miles inland. Starting from virtual wilderness, the thoroughly modern city of Brasilia rose above that wilderness and was dedicated as the capital in 1960. Today the former wilderness is home to over a million inhabitants.

After winning independence from Portugal, Brazil was an empire for many years. (See pp. 182-83.) The country was a republic from 1889 to 1930. Since that time Brazil has alternated between military dictatorships and democratic governments. In 1985 military rule finally gave way to a democratic civilian government.

Settings Review

1. What is another name for tropical wet climate? tropical wet and dry?
2. What area of Brazil is a source of international ecological concern?
3. What is Brazil's major export today?
4. What is the main language in Brazil?
5. Name two major cities in Brazil.

What are the pros and cons of ecological conservation? Should we do anything to take care of God's creation, or should we allow nature to take care of itself?

Three faces of Brazil (left to right): the modernizing nation, the rain forest, and an immigrant to a newly settled area

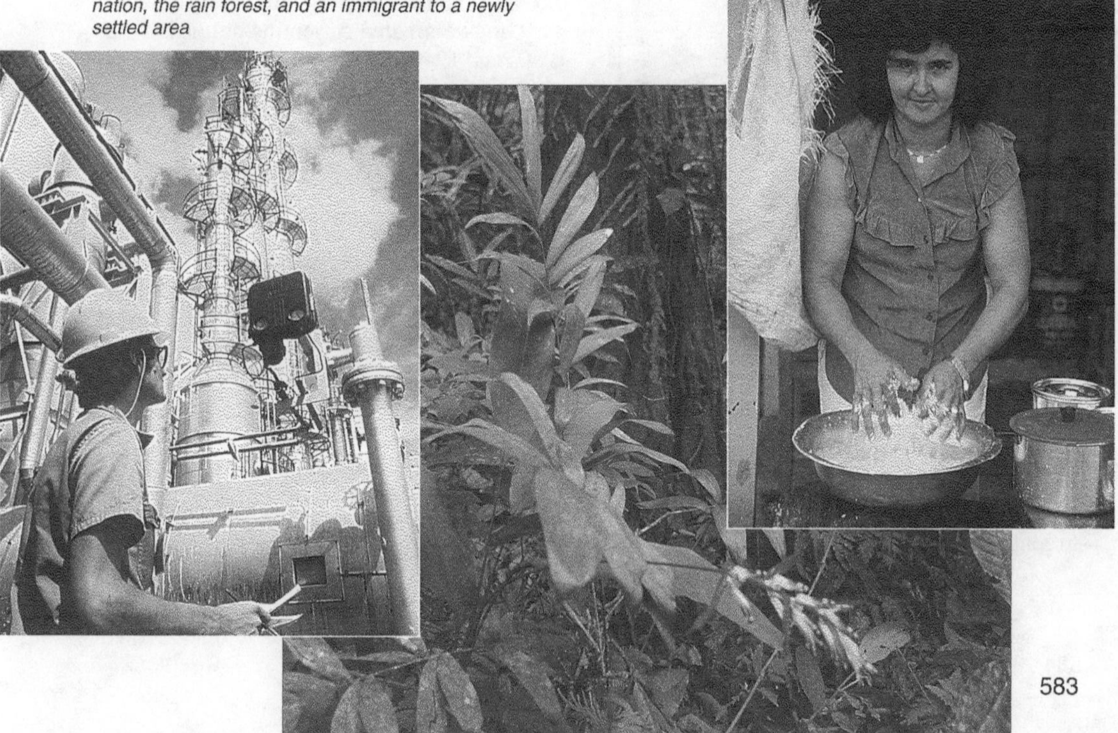

Latin America—Show a video to your students depicting life in Latin America. You will probably find that most videos about Latin America are about the Amazon Rain Forest. The science teacher may also have a video from which you may want to show parts.

Settings Review Answers

1. Rain Forest; Savanna
2. the Amazon River basin
3. coffee
4. Portuguese
5. Rio de Janeiro, São Paolo, Brasilia (any two)

Answers will vary. Some ecological conservation is good. The Bible says that Christians should take care of the earth. Keeping natural surroundings helps rid the air of impurities; our natural environment is also very beautiful. Conserving nature is a good goal as long as it is kept in perspective. The Bible says that we are to subdue nature for our purposes. We should do what we can to make sure that God's gift is preserved but also used in a way that will give glory to Him.

SECTION 2

Student Objectives
Students should be able to

1. Summarize the political situation in Argentina since World War II.
2. Analyze the Peróns' ability to stay in power.
3. Describe the Falklands War.

South America—Besides Argentina, the South American countries are Colombia, Venezuela, Ecuador, Peru, Bolivia, Chile, Uruguay, Paraguay, Brazil, Guyana, Suriname, and French Guiana.

Argentina: From Dictatorship to Democracy

At the beginning of the twentieth century, Argentina was one of the richest nations in Latin America. Its exports of grain and beef built a strong trading relationship with other nations, especially Great Britain. Argentina prided itself on being European in its culture and tastes.

This situation began to change from the time of World War I to the beginning of the Great Depression in 1929. Argentina found that its farm exports no longer brought in enough money to maintain prosperity. Although Argentina was not harmed by the Great Depression as much as some other Latin American countries, the economic downturn led to changes.

One distinct change throughout Latin America and in Argentina was the end of the hacienda as a major economic force. In the 1800s the haciendas dominated the economic life of the region. Much of life outside the cities centered on the hacienda. (See p. 178.) But when the profits began to fall, the system began to fall apart. Many hacienda workers went to the cities to find better-paying jobs in factories. The hacienda owners exercised less and less influence on the government.

Dictatorship

A more drastic change in Argentina was in government. The earlier period of prosperity brought stable democracy to Argentina. But democracy was one of the first victims of hard times. In 1930 the military toppled the government and dominated Argentine politics in the 1930s and 1940s. Many Western democracies were worried by Argentina's open sympathy with the Fascist states of Germany and Italy. Argentina, in fact, remained neutral in World War II until it was obvious that the Axis powers would lose.

In 1943 the army again brought down the government, but a leader in this rebellion would soon transform Argentine politics. **Juan Perón** (puh ROHN) was a leading military officer. Like many in the army, he was sympathetic to Germany under the Nazis. He also spent time as a representative for the Argentine government in Italy in the 1930s, where he developed an admiration for Mussolini's Fascist state.

When the army installed a new government in 1943, Perón became secretary of the army and secretary of labor. By winning the

---

SECTION 2

Opinion—Have students discuss their opinions on politics in Argentina. Why was Argentina fascinated with fascist states? *(Fascist countries were run in a highly efficient, though often vicious, way.)* Why did the military keep toppling the government? *(They were not happy with its rule and wanted things their way.)* What made the Peróns so popular? *(They were supported at first by both the military and the workers. When the military turned against them, the workers turned against the military, for not only did the Peróns help the workers, but they were from the working class themselves.)*

Juan Perón and his wife Eva wave to cheering crowds of Argentine workers.

The tomb of Eva Perón in Buenos Aires is still honored by her admirers years after her death.

Word Origin—The term *descamisados* originated in Spain in the 1820s. It was a term for the poor peasants or working classes that indicated their poverty.

support of both the army and the workers, Perón built a base of support unlike the previous governments. The army gave him military support; the workers gave him widespread popular support.

One worker said of Perón, "He had the virtue of leaving his audience satisfied without promising them anything." But Perón did keep some of his promises. He supported the large meatpackers' union in its conflicts with management. As secretary of labor, he gave the workers a minimum wage and paid holidays. His wife, former actress **Eva Duarte Perón** (known as "Evita"), increased his appeal. Evita was beautiful and at least as magnetic in personality as her husband. She had risen from poverty herself and sympathized with the poor. The Peróns identified themselves with the ***descamisados*** (DAYS-kah-mee-SAH-thohs; "shirtless ones"), the poor factory workers who crowded into Argentina's cities.

The support of the *descamisados* paid off for Perón. The army, fearing his labor reforms, forced him out of office and arrested him. But on October 17, 1945, the workers marched on the capital chanting, "There is no work without Perón." Frightened by the unity of the workers, the government freed Perón. In February of 1946, Perón was easily elected president of Argentina.

President Perón continued his program of social reform. His wife led the Eva Perón Foundation, which distributed money, food, and medicines to the poor. (She raised the money by telling businesses that they might find the government more cooperative if they gave to her foundation.) Income began to rise, and Perón gave women the vote in 1947. A

The Peróns—Have your students list at least five ways the Peróns went against traditional democratic ideas in running the Argentine government. *(sympathizing with Nazi Germany under Hitler, sympathizing with Fascist Italy under Mussolini, bribing businesses to raise money, spending all surpluses in socialistic practices, and ruling harshly after Evita died)* Discuss why they were able to keep power. *(They greatly appealed to the working class.)*

Perón—After Evita died, Perón came into increasing conflict with the church. The church excommunicated him in 1955. He fled later that year, living in many Spanish countries and eventually settling in Madrid.

The plaza of modern Buenos Aires, Argentina

popular slogan was *"Perón cumple"* ("Perón delivers"). He was easily elected to a second term in 1952. At a huge rally that year, Evita thrilled the crowds with her oratory:

> It is the working people, the little people of the nation, who here and throughout the country are on their feet, ready to follow Perón, the Leader of the people, the Leader of humanity, because he has raised high the banner of salvation and justice for the masses; ready to follow him against the oppression of traitors within and without, traitors who in the darkness of the night would like to inject their snake venom into the soul and body of Perón, which is the soul and body of the Nation. But they won't succeed, any more than toads in their jealousy can succeed in silencing the nightingale's song or snakes succeed in halting the flight of the condor. They won't succeed, my General, because we—the men and women of the People—we are here to guard your dreams and watch over your life . . . and we would never forgive ourselves if we hadn't protected a man as fine as General Perón, who nurtured the dreams of all Argentines, particularly the dreams of the working people.

But after his reelection, Perón's regime began to fall apart. Shortly after giving this speech, Evita—so enormously popular among the poor—died of cancer. More harmful to Perón was the downturn of the economy. By remaining neutral for most of World War II, Argentina had traded with both sides and built a huge financial surplus. Perón, however, spent this surplus to keep his followers happy, and by the early 1950s, the surplus was gone. As an admirer of Fascism, Perón had never much respected basic freedoms such as freedom of the press. When discontent began to grow, he became even harsher in his rule. The dictator became increasingly unpopular. Finally, in 1955, the military ended his rule just as Perón himself had helped topple the government in 1943. He fled the country.

Persuasive Speeches—Encourage students to write a short speech to introduce someone famous from the chapter. Have a few volunteers give their speeches in front of the class. Tell the speakers to deliver their speeches persuasively.

From Disorder to Democracy

But the exile of Perón brought no peace to Argentina. In the nearly twenty years that followed his departure, not a single president of the nation finished out his term of office. Each time, the armed forces forced the president out of office. Finally Perón himself returned to Argentina and was elected president in 1973. His second wife, Isabel, was elected vice president. The aged dictator died less than a year after taking office. Isabel Perón tried to rule for two years after her husband's death, but the military eventually toppled her as it had her husband and so many other presidents.

Argentina became an undisguised military dictatorship. The military began to crack down on all opponents. In what became known as the **"dirty war"** against opposition, the government began arresting citizens suspected of treasonous views. Those arrested simply vanished, never to be seen again by their friends and family. Economically, Argentina suffered from staggering inflation. Prices rose as much as 600 percent a year.

Increasingly unpopular, the military rulers tried a desperate gamble to increase their support among the people. Argentina and Great Britain had for years been arguing over who should control the **Falkland Islands** in the south Atlantic. (See pp. 588-89.) Argentina's rulers stunned the British by sending troops to seize the Falklands in April of 1982. The Argentine rulers hoped that the British would do nothing. Instead, Great Britain recaptured the islands and humiliated the Argentine armed forces. The discredited dictators were forced out of power.

In 1983 free elections were again held in Argentina—and this time the president was allowed to finish out his term. The new government brought members of the old dictatorship to trial and punished them for their abuses of power. In 1989 Argentina elected a member of the Perónist party as president, and reelected him in 1995. Now even the Perónists were committed to democratic government. Many obstacles lie ahead, but Argentina appears to be on its way to establishing stable democracy.

Isabel Perón—Isabel Perón was the first female vice-president and president in Latin America. When her husband died, she gained the support of most Perónists with the pledge to keep the status quo. Many problems followed, however. Violence escalated, leaders resigned, and labor unions tightened their hold on laborers. Mrs. Perón created a more conservative Cabinet and banned two new leftist newspapers. Terrorism and assassinations increased so much that she declared a state of siege, suspending constitutional rights. Droughts and floods also became a problem. In 1975 she took a one-month leave of absence for health reasons but came back only to be removed from office.

Section Review

1. What were two major changes in Argentina after the Great Depression?
2. Who was sympathetic to Nazism and Fascism while he served as secretary of labor and later became president?
3. Who were the *descamisados?*
4. Describe government in Argentina after Perón was ousted from power.
5. Whom did Argentina fight for control of the Falkland Islands?

Why might such a popular leader as Perón have been ousted from office? Explain the influence his wife had on his success in government. Why was he allowed back?

Section Review Answers

1. the end of the hacienda as a major economic force; governmental instability
2. Juan Perón
3. "shirtless ones"; the poor factory workers
4. No president stayed in office for an entire term; each was toppled by the military.
5. Great Britain

Perón's very popular wife died, and the people lost a role model (though not a very good one). The plunging economy had a negative effect in many countries. Perón also spent the surplus money from World War II foolishly, and he became more and more a dictator. Eva Perón was very much a part of Juan's success in office because of her relationship with the poor as well as her experience as an actress. After a period of exile, Perón was permitted to return to try to fix the government, which could not keep a president in office.

Falkland Feuds—Shortly after Bougainville's settlement, the British set up residence in the Falklands. However, Spanish troops expelled the settlers in 1770. On the verge of war, Spain finally backed down and returned the port and fort to the British.

The British maintained the settlement until 1774, when a poor economy forced them to abandon it. The Spanish also kept a settlement among the islands until 1816. In that year there was an uprising in Buenos Aires over Spanish authority. Spain gave up its claim to the islands.

By 1816, Argentina had established its own settlers in the Falklands. However, the British believed an Argentinian claim was as bad as a Spanish one. They reasserted their own claim in 1833, expelling the Argentine settlers. By 1892 the islands were granted the status of a colony of the British Empire.

The next major conflict surrounding the islands took place offshore during World War I. The British navy engaged, and ultimately defeated, the German navy. This victory foreshadowed Britain's success in the Falklands War, although that victory would not come as quickly or as easily.

BACKGROUNDS

The Falklands War

The Falklands are a group of islands in the south Atlantic, about three hundred miles off the coast of Argentina. There are two main islands—East Falkland and West Falkland—and many smaller ones. The islands have few natural resources, an average temperature range of 35° in winter to 49° in summer, sparse vegetation, and only around two thousand inhabitants—although there are about five million penguins. Yet the Falklands have been a point of contention between Europe and Latin America.

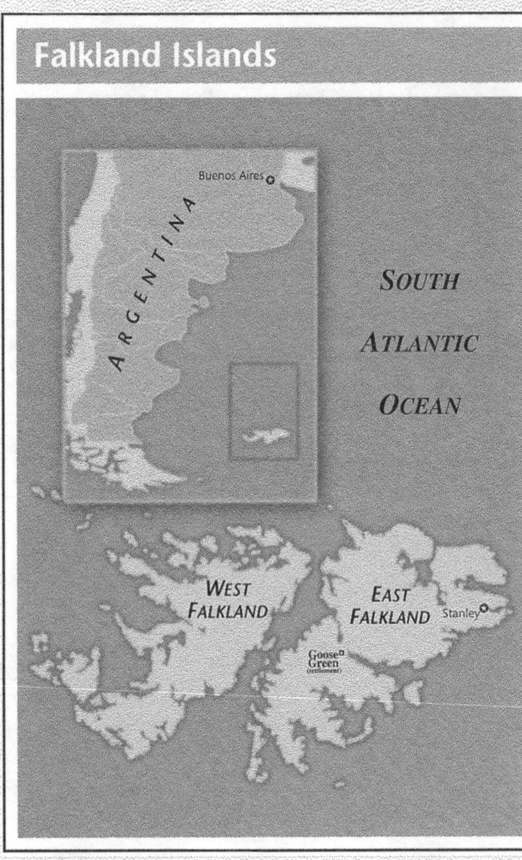

Beginning in the mid-1700s, Britain, France, and Spain all tried to settle the then-uninhabited Falklands. Each of these early settlements failed, but the British finally established a permanent colony there in 1833. The settlers all came from Britain and were fiercely loyal to their native country. The Falklands became a British colony, and the colonists devoted themselves to making a living on the islands. They concentrated on farming, especially the raising of sheep. (There are over three hundred sheep for every human being on the Falklands.) The small seaport of Stanley (population about one thousand) became the capital.

However, Argentina also claimed the Falklands, which it called the Islas Malvinas. The Argentines said that the early Spanish claims on the islands—which Argentina said it inherited—and the closeness of the Falklands to their nation made them part of Argentina. They demanded that Britain leave. Great Britain refused to surrender the Falklands, especially since the people of the Falklands wished to remain British.

Years of negotiation over the islands seemed to accomplish nothing, so in 1982 Argentina invaded the Falklands. The Argentine forces easily overwhelmed the small garrison of British marines and claimed the islands. Angrily, Great Britain sent a fleet of warships to retake the Falklands. The war lasted less than three months, but it drew worldwide attention.

Britain's armed forces proved superior to those of Argentina. British bombers destroyed the airstrip near Stanley so that the Argentines could not use it. A British submarine sank the cruiser *General Belgrano,* causing Argentina to pull back its warships for fear of losing even more. (Ironically, Argentina had bought the *General Belgrano* from the United States, where the ship had survived the Japanese attack on Pearl Harbor in 1941.) Argentina's air force then took on the burden of the fighting and did very well,

588 Chapter 20

History of the Falklands—Review with your students Bougainville's trip to the Falklands. (See Chapter 10, page 264.)

The Falklands War: The British warship HMS Fearless *patrols the Falklands coast with an Argentine Mirage III-E fighter just visible between its masts (above), and the HMS* Sheffield *burns after being struck by a missile fired by an Argentine aircraft (left).*

sinking some British ships and downing several enemy planes.

In the end the superior discipline of the British army won out. Landing on the west side of East Falkland, the British troops spread out rapidly and pushed back the inexperienced Argentines. In the battle for the town of Goose Green, for example, fewer than five hundred British paratroopers defeated and captured over fifteen hundred Argentine soldiers. Eventually the Argentines surrendered and left the island. The war did not settle the question, however, for Argentina still claimed the islands, and the British had to commit forces to the Falklands to protect them from further attack.

The Changing Face of Latin America 589

SECTION 3

Student Objectives
Students should be able to

1. List factors that have made Costa Rica successful.

Central America—Often called Middle America, these countries include (besides Costa Rica) Guatemala, Belize, El Salvador, Honduras, Nicaragua, and Panama.

Costa Rica: Latin American Success Story

A Chinese curse says, "May you always live in interesting times." The reason that this bland statement is a curse is that wars, floods, and famines are what makes an era "interesting." By comparison, peace and prosperity seem dull.

Sometimes it is easy to focus on the "interesting" in Latin American history and miss the less dramatic success stories. The Central American republic of Costa Rica is rarely in newspaper headlines. Although located between the troubled nations of Nicaragua and Panama, the nation is never involved in wars. It does not even have an army. The story of Costa Rica is a quiet story of successful democracy.

A Moderate History

Costa Rica is Spanish for "rich coast." It was discovered in 1502 and named by Christopher Columbus, who thought it might be a land rich with gold. However, Costa Rica has no great mineral wealth. It does have rich soil and a moderate climate, though. Other Latin American nations suffered exploitation from outside the region. Some nations developed societies split by class conflict between rich and poor. But Costa Rica developed an agricultural economy made up of numerous small farmers. There was not great wealth, but what there was was spread evenly.

Costa Rica continued its unusual development after it separated from Spain in 1821. It was the first Latin American country to abolish

The volcanic activity in Costa Rica is in sharp contrast to the relative peace of that nation's history.

SECTION 3

Materials

- Coffee and bananas
- Recording of the music of Heitor Villa-Lobos

"Interesting" Times—Sometimes we call "interesting" things acts of God; these may refer to floods, tornadoes, hurricanes, and so forth. Ask your students what other things in life are "interesting." *(breaking a bone, failing a test, etc.)* Ask them how something that the Chinese considered a curse could be perceived as a blessing. Does God work through difficult times?

Jose Maria Figueres Ferrer

slavery. In 1869 Costa Rica established a free public school system. (Its first president, in fact, was a schoolteacher.) In 1889 the little nation held what is considered to be the first free election in Latin America.

Conditions were not perfect, of course. In the 1930s, for example, the nation had a leader with pro-Nazi sympathies. Political corruption also troubled the land on occasion. A stolen election, in fact, sparked a remarkable revolution and reform that were uniquely Costa Rican.

In 1948 the government, after losing an election, tried to hold on to power illegally. A Costa Rican coffee planter, **Jose Maria Figueres Ferrer** (fee GAYR ays; fondly called "Don Pepe"), put together an army to challenge the corrupt government. Figueres's small army defeated the government forces, losing only sixty men to the two thousand of his opponents. But Figueres did not establish a dictatorship. After reorganizing the government, he peacefully handed over power to the winner of the 1948 election. Figueres said, "The health of democracy in Latin America demands that men who have seized power by force go home when normalcy is restored. We restored normalcy and went home." Grateful Costa Ricans later elected Figueres to full terms as president in 1953 and 1970.

Don Pepe's Costa Rica—Costa Rica has fewer than three million people, but it is the most democratic state of Central America. It has many national parks, varied ecosystems, and no army. Its people live the longest (74 years) and have the lowest infant mortality rate (19 per 1,000). They eat the most calories (2,800 per day) and have the highest literacy (93%). Wealth is distributed relatively evenly. Costa Rica was the first Latin American nation to prohibit slavery and to enforce free education.

Perched near a Costa Rican river, an egret surveys the scene.

Figueres—Ask the students to put themselves in Figueres's shoes. Would they have kicked out the bad government and then just peacefully gone away? Would they have stayed to make sure a new government went smoothly? Would they have taken control themselves? Or would they have done nothing at all? Discuss the consequences of each decision.

Humility—God greatly commends humility in His Word. One of the reasons Costa Rica has been able to have a peaceful democracy is the humility of some of its leaders. Figueres could have taken dictatorial control but did not for the good of his country. Proverbs 22:4 states, "By humility and the fear of the Lord are riches, and honour, and life." Paul mentions in Acts 20:19 his own attitude in ministering to the Ephesians. Other related verses include Romans 12:3, Philippians 2:3-4, and I Peter 5:5-6.

The OAS—The Organization of American States' principles include belief in international law, social justice, economic cooperation, and equality for all people. Another principle states that if any member nation of the OAS is attacked, then all members will consider themselves attacked. Though still a member, Cuba is not allowed to be actively involved in the OAS while under communism.

Quakers—The true name of Quakers is the Society of Friends. They are generally pacifists and strive to end war and human injustices. They follow an "inner light" which guides them toward the truth and the Holy Spirit. They have no pastor, but at meetings they have silence until someone breaks it with a message from God. William Penn was probably the most famous Quaker. He was given Pennsylvania as a grant from the king of England, and many Quakers settled there.

Oscar Arias Sánchez

Safeguards for Democracy

The new government under Figueres enacted several reforms to protect Costa Rican democracy. As in Mexico, the president could no longer succeed himself. This reform made it impossible for a leader to entrench himself by holding on to power for a long time. To guarantee free and honest elections, the **Supreme Electoral Tribunal** became a separate branch of government, like the legislature and the courts. This independent body watches over the election process to guard against abuses. The tribunal even takes control of the police during elections to make sure that no other government department uses the police to influence the outcome of the election.

The most important reform of Figueres was to abolish the army. Since 1948 only a police force of over ten thousand men exists to maintain order. Costa Rica relies on international organizations such as the Organization of American States to protect itself against foreign threats. Twice, in 1948 and 1955, the OAS helped Costa Rica against invasions from Nicaragua. The absence of an army is certainly unusual and has even attracted settlers. The lack of an army, for example, drew a group of North American Quakers (who do not believe in fighting in wars) to Costa Rica. There they developed a profitable cheese-manufacturing business.

Costa Rica's heritage of democracy has enabled it to play a leading role in the affairs of Central America. In the 1980s, for example, the region was torn by conflicts in Nicaragua, El Salvador, and elsewhere. In 1987 Costa Rica's President **Oscar Arias Sánchez** put forth a plan to bring peace to the region. The Arias plan called for a cease-fire in all Central American conflicts between governments and rebels. It also demanded an end to the flow of military supplies from outside the region and free elections in all nations. Under the Arias plan, all the conflicting sides would sit down and discuss their differences.

Eventually, the Central American nations agreed to the proposals. Although peace did not suddenly come to the region, the Arias plan was a first step toward solving some of the area's problems. In recognition of his peace plan, Arias was awarded the Nobel Peace Prize for 1987. When asked whether the award had made a difference in his life, Arias replied, "Yes, people no longer introduce me as the president of Puerto Rico."

There are still problems in Costa Rica. Its economy, based on the export of coffee and

Economics—Ask the students to bring in items that they would like to trade. Bring in coffee and bananas and try to trade these with the students for the items they brought in. Some will trade with you, but most probably will not. (This could change depending on how close it is to lunch time.) Explain to the students that a one- or two-export system (as opposed to a multi-export system) is subject to the whims of the buyers and will go up and down based on changing demand. Discuss why the production of illegal drugs is so profitable in Latin American countries.

bananas, is subject to ups and downs according to how well those products are selling around the world. Costa Rica has also sometimes found itself in the crossfire of the ugly drug trade that thrives in some parts of Latin America. Some drug smugglers have used the country as a secret supply point for the drug trade. But on the whole, Costa Rica endures as a model of how democracy can work in the region of Latin America.

Drug Trade—Latin America is known for its production and illegal transport of drugs. The drug trade rose and fell over the last two decades. Illegal drugs include marijuana, cocaine, and heroin. The United States uses much money and manpower trying to combat this fierce system.

Did You Know?—Coca-Cola's unusual name came from the cocaine used when it was originally produced. Cocaine was not illegal at that time.

Section Review

1. *Costa Rica* is the Spanish term for what?
2. What type of economy did Costa Rica have that was able to spread wealth more easily than in other Latin American countries?
3. What is Jose Maria Figueres Ferrer known for?
4. What organization has helped Costa Rica against Nicaraguan threats?
5. Name two problems that exist in Costa Rica.

Why has Costa Rica been able to establish a democratic government? What factors in its government enable it to stay democratic? What other groups of people might be expected to move to an army-free nation? Explain your answer.

Although a small land, Costa Rica is blessed with beautiful scenery.

Section Review Answers

1. rich coast
2. agricultural
3. He formed an army to kick out the illegal government, then stepped aside.
4. Organization of American States (OAS)
5. economic—it has only a one- or two-crop economy; drug trafficking

Instead of extreme wealth and poverty, the Costa Ricans have an agricultural economy in which wealth is relatively evenly shared. In the case of Figueres, power was not hoarded; the government was allowed to evolve democratically. Costa Rica has a tribunal to check elections. In other countries, elections are known to be very corrupt. Costa Rica also does not get involved in wars since it has no army. Pacifist groups such as the Amish and the Quakers may be expected to move to an army-free country so that they do not have to trouble their consciences with thoughts of war.

Villa-Lobos—Of *Bachianas brasileiras* Villa-Lobos said, "This is a special kind of musical composition based on an intimate knowledge of the great works of J. S. Bach and also on the composer's affinity with the harmonic, contrapuntal, and melodic folklore of northeastern Brazil."

CHARACTERIZATIONS

Heitor Villa-Lobos

Heitor Villa-Lobos (VEE-luh-LOH-bohs) was born in Rio de Janeiro in 1887; he died in Rio de Janeiro in 1959. Although his life began and ended in the same city, in between he traveled the world and built a reputation far beyond the city limits of Rio. He became not simply Brazil's greatest musician but one of the world's leading composers.

Heitor Villa-Lobos

Villa-Lobos had little formal musical training and was really self-taught. He mastered the cello (with lessons from his father, a librarian and amateur musician) and guitar. As a young man, Villa-Lobos listened to the popular musicians of Brazil and played along with them. He traveled to the Brazilian interior and even to Barbados to study native music. (He later spun a tale of how he was once captured by cannibals and persuaded them to spare him because of his talents as a musician.) He began to write music based on what he heard.

In 1919 Villa-Lobos met the famed pianist Arthur Rubinstein, who was touring Brazil, and showed the pianist samples of his compositions. Deeply impressed by the young man's work, Rubinstein successfully urged the Brazilian government to support Villa-Lobos.

With this government help, Villa-Lobos was able to study in Paris from 1923 to 1930. The composer, however, claimed he was more interested in making Brazilian music known than in learning French styles. He told a French interviewer, "Did you think I came here to absorb your ideas? I came here to show you what I've done. If you don't like what I do, I'm going away."

He returned to Brazil in 1930, where the government made him Director of Music Education. Villa-Lobos promoted the teaching of music in Rio de Janeiro's public schools and established a conservatory for Brazilian musicians. In 1945 he founded the Brazilian Academy of Music. The composer also found time to tour the United States and become popular there through his concerts.

Villa-Lobos wrote perhaps two thousand works in his lifetime. (He would often leave the manuscripts of his works lying around the house, and souvenir hunters would carry them off.) Like other classical composers, he wrote symphonies, concertos, and string quartets. But he also wrote classical pieces based on Brazilian folk music. For example, as a young man he heard street musicians play a *choro,* a kind of dance music. Inspired by this music, Villa-Lobos wrote fourteen *Chôros* (1920-29).

There was always a strong Brazilian flavor to his music. Since drums were so dominant in Brazilian folk music, he used a lot of percussion in his compositions. Villa-Lobos incorporated the sound of the bird calls of the jungles in pieces

Heitor Villa-Lobos—Find a recording of the music of Heitor Villa-Lobos to play for your class. Check your public library or music store.

such as *Cancão da Terra* ("Song of the Earth"). He even used some lyrics written in the native tongues of Indians of Brazil and used Indian myths as his themes.

Perhaps the best example of the composer's blending of styles was his *Bachianas brasileiras*. As the name suggests, these nine suites combined elements of the music of both Johann Sebastian Bach and Brazil. Villa-Lobos noticed some similarities between Bach's style and that of some Brazilian folk music. He then composed the *Bachianas brasileiras*, which are perhaps more inspired by Bach than an actual copy of Bach's music. Villa-Lobos even named the segments of the suites with both classical terminology (e.g., Aria, Toccata) and Brazilian terms (e.g., *Picapao,* after a woodpecker-like bird whose sound the music suggests). These suites are among his finest works.

The music of Heitor Villa-Lobos embodies the spirit of Brazil. The composer himself said, "I study the history, the country, the speech, the customs, the background of the people. I have always done this, and it is from these sources, spiritual as well as practical, that I have drawn my art."

Villa-Lobos was a prolific composer, writing numerous classical pieces of astonishing variety.

The Changing Face of Latin America 595

SECTION 4

Student Objective
Students should be able to

1. Compare and contrast religions in Latin America.

Religions in Latin America— Though Roman Catholicism is the dominant religion in Latin America today, Protestantism is gaining a small foothold.

Religions in Latin America

Country	Religions
Mexico	Roman Catholic 89%, Protestant 6%
Costa Rica	Roman Catholic 95%
Argentina	Roman Catholic 90%
Brazil	Roman Catholic 70%

Christianity in Latin America

Ever since the colonization of Latin America by Spain and Portugal, Roman Catholicism has been Latin America's main religion. About four hundred million Latin Americans (over 80 percent of the population) are Catholics.

A Catholic church in Hermosillo, Mexico

Catholicism

The Catholic Church has long exercised great political and economic power in the region. Since the church often used that power on behalf of sometimes repressive governments, many Latin American reformers sought to curb the church's power. Beginning in the 1800s, many Latin American nations began taking away Catholicism's official government support. These reformers believed that only as Catholicism was limited could democracy flourish. During the debates over the Mexican Constitution of 1917, Francisco Múgica said,

> I am an enemy of the clergy because I consider it the most baleful and perverse enemy of our country. . . . What ideas can the clergy bring to the soul of the Mexican masses, or to the middle class, or to the wealthy? Only the most absurd ideas—tremendous hate for democratic institutions, the deepest hate for the principles of equity, equality and fraternity.

By the 1960s, however, some Catholic priests and theologians had become reformers themselves. But these Catholic reformers, known as **liberation theologians,** did not address the root of man's problems: sin. (See Matt. 12:35; Mark 7:21; James 4:1.) Instead, they borrowed concepts from Karl Marx. They saw the struggle between rich and poor as the root of society's problems, not as a symptom of human sinfulness. Some even preached liberation through violence.

The great majority of Catholics, though, follow traditional Catholic teaching. They heed the teaching of the church and obey their priests. When Pope John Paul II visited Latin America in the 1980s, crowds of traditionalist Catholics warmly greeted him.

SECTION 4

Materials

- *Through Gates of Splendor* by Elisabeth Elliot
- Guest speaker, a Latin American native

Religion graph—Instruct the students to use what they have learned about graphs to create a graph on the religions in Latin America (BLM 20-2).

Liberation Theology—Have the students list advantages and disadvantages of liberation theology. Some disadvantages are already in the text, such as no spiritual relief. Some advantages may be physical and emotional relief. Discuss how a person could incorporate the good points of liberation theology into true missions while steering clear of the bad points.

Center Stage

Mission to the Aucas

"He is no fool who gives what he cannot keep to gain what he cannot lose." This was the testimony of Jim Elliot, a missionary who literally gave his life for Jesus Christ. In 1956 Elliot and four other men—Nate Saint, Roger Youderian, Ed McCully, and Pete Fleming—became twentieth-century martyrs for Christ.

These men believed that God wanted them to go to the mission field and to preach to a people who had never before heard the gospel, the **Auca Indians** of Ecuador. The Aucas were a fierce, primitive people. Every other contact between the Aucas and whites had ended in violence. In the 1800s the Aucas had clashed with rubber hunters in the Amazon. Only a little more than ten years before the missionaries arrived, the Aucas had killed eleven employees of Shell Oil who were working in Ecuador. When Elliot's wife mentioned the danger, he replied, "Well, if that's the way God wants it to be, I'm ready to die for the salvation of the Aucas."

The missionaries began planning their effort. They worked first among a group of friendly Indians to become familiar with the land and the work. They talked with one Auca woman who had fled the tribe. She helped them learn a little of the Auca language, but warned of the Aucas: "Never, never trust them. They may appear friendly and then they will turn around and kill."

In January 1956 the missionaries began their outreach by flying over an Auca village. As Nate Saint, the pilot, flew the plane over the village, they dropped presents to attract the Indians to the base. They called out in Auca, "I like you" and "I want to be your friend." They set up a base on a riverbank near the village. After a few days, three Aucas visited the missionaries. The missionaries talked to them in the Auca language and tried to win their friendship. The Indians left after a few hours, but the next day Saint flew over the village and saw a group of Aucas moving toward the base. He radioed to his wife, "Pray for us. This is the day! Will contact you next at four-thirty."

Three of the "Ecuadorian martyrs," missionaries who gave their lives in carrying the gospel to the Auca Indians: Ed McCully, Pete Fleming, and Jim Elliot

The four-thirty call never came.

When no word came from the base by the next morning, the missionaries' wives notified the authorities. A group of missionaries and Ecuadorian soldiers journeyed through the jungles to the base. There they found that the Aucas had attacked and killed all five missionaries. The would-be rescuers buried the bodies near the landing strip that the five missionaries had used as their base.

Their deaths, however, did not end the story of the Auca mission. Inspired by the Ecuadorian martyrs, others dedicated themselves to missionary service to Ecuador and other nations. The widows of the martyrs continued to work among the Aucas. Even some of the Indians who had killed the missionaries came to Christ through this work. Out of the deaths of Jim Elliot, Nate Saint, Roger Youderian, Ed McCully, and Pete Fleming, God brought triumph.

Through Gates of Splendor—After her husband's death, Elisabeth Elliot wrote a book about the work among the Aucas. Read portions of *Through Gates of Splendor* to your students and discuss the willingness it takes to do the will of God. Though it may seem dangerous, the will of God is the safest place to be.

Tongues—First Corinthians 12:15-18 reminds us that the body is not all one part such as an eye or foot. That would be a huge problem! In I Corinthians 14:22 we read that tongues were a sign to unbelievers. At Pentecost, tongues were used to witness. The apostles preached in actual spoken languages of the day. Some people present at Pentecost could understand only their native language. Tongues was one of many gifts that a believer might be given upon salvation. If there was no interpreter, the gift was false. Speaking in tongues is a gift that is not needed today.

Charismatics—Charismatics place the highest priority on glorifying the Holy Spirit rather than Christ. John 15:26 says the opposite: "But when the Comforter [Holy Spirit] is come, whom I will send unto you from the Father, even the Spirit of truth, which proceedeth from the Father, he shall testify of me." The Holy Spirit's goal is always to give glory to Christ or the Father, not to Himself.

Some Charismatics go so far as to say that one is not a complete Christian until he has experienced tongues. This leads to pride. It also exalts experience over the solid foundation of the Word of God. Another problem is ecumenism, a bringing together of groups not all in line with doctrine. Some Catholics are Charismatic, and Protestant Charismatics are often willing to associate with them, despite the Bible's warnings against having fellowship with those who bring a false doctrine (II John 9-11).

A Protestant church service in Latin America

Protestantism

One surprising characteristic of religious life in Latin America has been the growth of Protestantism since World War II. Violence has sometimes greeted such growth. In the 1950s, for example, Catholic mobs in Colombia killed over a hundred Protestants and destroyed over fifty churches.

Although their numbers are not nearly as large as those of the Roman Catholics, Protestants have grown from only a tiny fraction of the population in the 1800s to perhaps a tenth today. Some ethnic minorities have been even quicker to embrace Protestantism. The Quichua (KEE-choo-ah) Indians in Ecuador and the Miskito Indians in Central America are examples of groups that turned to Protestantism in large numbers. Some experts estimate that by early in the twenty-first century a nation such as Guatemala may become the first predominantly Catholic country to become predominantly Protestant.

Most of these converts to Protestantism are known as **Pentecostals** or Charismatics. These two groups actually overlap. The name Pentecostal derives from the biblical Day of Pentecost. On the Day of Pentecost the apostles "began to speak with other tongues, as the Spirit gave them utterance" (Acts 2:4). Pentecostals believe that when a Christian is baptized by the Holy Spirit, he will speak in tongues as a sign of the Holy Spirit's presence. Pentecostals also believe in the practice of other miraculous gifts such as healing the sick and exorcising demons.

The **Charismatics** are closely related to Pentecostals. In fact, many Pentecostals would claim to be Charismatics. The name *Charismatic* comes from the Greek word for "gift" *(charisma)* because Charismatics also claim to practice spiritual gifts such as tongues-speaking. One difference between Pentecostals and Charismatics is their denominational association. Pentecostals usually belong to groups that have the word "Pentecostal" in their name (such as the Pentecostal Missionary Church) or that describe themselves as Pentecostal in teaching (such as the Assemblies of God). Charismatics, on the other hand, can belong to nearly any denomination—Baptist, Presbyterian, Episcopalian. Even some Roman Catholics claim to be Charismatic.

The Pentecostals and Charismatics have grown in influence as their numbers have grown. Guatemala even had a dictator (1982-83), Mario Enrique Ríos Montt, who belonged to a leading Charismatic church in that country. Many Pentecostal and Charismatic leaders, however, warn their followers against becoming so involved in politics that they neglect spiritual concerns.

Connections—Invite a native Latin American to speak to your class. Your guest may want to teach the students a few Spanish (or Portuguese) phrases and tell about life in his country, especially religious life. If he was formerly a Catholic, have him tell about his conversion.

In evaluating any group, the Christian should not look just at outward signs—large numbers of followers or apparent miracles. A person or group that is truly Christian will also display "the fruit of the Spirit" (Gal. 5:22-23). This fruit, the apostle Paul says, includes "love, joy, peace, longsuffering, gentleness, goodness, faith, meekness, temperance." Where this fruit is present, a Christian has reason to believe that the Holy Spirit is truly present.

Section Review

1. What percentage of Latin Americans are Roman Catholic?
2. What problem do liberation theologians not address?
3. Compare and contrast Pentecostals and Charismatics.

Why might Protestantism be gaining ground in Latin America? What effects might Pentecostalism or Charismaticism have on formerly dominantly Roman Catholic nations? Would you support these groups based on what you know about them and Roman Catholicism?

Summary

Modern historian Edwin Williamson has noted of Latin America that "in the mid-1970s only Colombia, Venezuela and Costa Rica had elected governments." Yet, by the 1990s, he pointed out, only a handful of Latin American nations did *not* have elected governments. With all of the challenges the region has faced, democracy has grown. Sometimes that growth stopped short of full democracy (as in Mexico). Sometimes that growth has been through violence and unrest (as in Argentina). And sometimes that growth has been so quiet as to be almost unobserved (as in Costa Rica). We can only hope that the trend toward stable, honest, peaceful democracy at the close of the twentieth century will continue to be the trend of the future in Latin America.

Spanning the Ages

Before, during, and after World War I, Mexico's leaders fought for control of the country. Two years before the end of World War II, Perón became president of Argentina. And during this whole time, Costa Rica was becoming a peaceful democracy. The events of Chapters 15-20 all happened in the twentieth century. What will happen in the twenty-first?

Section Review Answers

1. 80%
2. sin as the root of man's problems
3. Both Pentecostals and Charismatics believe in gifts, especially tongues; Pentecostals tend to be from a church with the word *Pentecostal* in its name, while Charismatics are from many denominations, including the Roman Catholic Church.

Answers will vary. Latin America has had contact with the rest of the world and thus with the truth in the 1900s. Religions may become mixed as in many predominantly Roman Catholic countries; Roman Catholicism is blended with the traditional native religion. Pentecostalism and/or Charismaticism may surpass Catholicism and become dominant. The students may or may not support the groups based on what they know about them and Roman Catholicism. They should give clear explanations for their reasons.

Chapter Review Idea

Divide your class into three teams. Each team will represent one of the countries featured in this chapter: Mexico, Argentina, or Costa Rica. Each student must answer a review question from the chapter, then bounce (or roll) a kickball (playground ball) into a box. If he successfully accomplishes this, he gains a point for his team. The first team to earn ten points is the country that wins a democratic government through legal elections.

Chapter Enrichment Activities

***Through Gates of Splendor*—** Encourage students to read the entire book *Through Gates of Splendor*. They may write a report to be submitted for a grade or extra credit.

CHAPTER REVIEW

People, Places, and Things to Know

Porfirio Díaz	Institutional Revolutionary Party (PRI)	*descamisados*	Oscar Arias Sánchez
Mexican Revolution	muralists	"dirty war"	Heitor Villa-Lobos
Victoriano Huerta	Diego Rivera	Falkland Islands	liberation theologians
Emiliano Zapata	Brasília	Jose Maria Figueres Ferrer	Auca Indians
Venustiano Carranza	Juan Perón	Supreme Electoral Tribunal	Pentecostals
"Pancho" Villa	Eva Duarte Perón		Charismatics
John Pershing			

Review Questions

Completion

Argentina — Brazil
Costa Rica — Mexico

1. General Porfirio Diaz became dictator of _____ and reorganized government.
2. _____ set up the Supreme Electoral Tribunal to oversee elections.
3. Juan and Evita Perón were extremely popular leaders of _____ .
4. Brasilia is the capital of _____ .
5. A group of Quakers moved to _____ because it has no army.
6. The old capital of _____ was Rio de Janeiro.
7. John Pershing was sent to find Pancho Villa, a bandit in _____ .
8. _____ fought the British for control of the Falkland Islands.
9. Villa-Lobos was a famous composer from _____ .

Matching

(a) liberation theologians
(b) Pentecostals
(c) Charismatics

10. believe in speaking in tongues
11. generally Catholic
12. belong to many denominations
13. concentrate on the struggle between rich and poor
14. take their name from Acts 2:4
15. comes from a word meaning "gift"

Chapter Review Answers

Completion

1. Mexico
2. Costa Rica
3. Argentina
4. Brazil
5. Costa Rica
6. Brazil
7. Mexico
8. Argentina
9. Brazil

Matching

10. b or c
11. a
12. c
13. a
14. b
15. c

Multiple Choice

Choose the letter of the answer that correctly finishes the statement.

16. When the United States gave support to another Mexican revolutionary, ______ crossed the border into New Mexico and murdered sixteen U.S. citizens.
    (a) Victoriano Huerta
    (b) Emiliano Zapata
    (c) Venustiano Carranza
    (d) "Pancho" Villa
17. Diego Rivera and José Clemente Orozco were ______ who represented the concerns of the common people.
    (a) priests
    (b) muralists
    (c) politicians
    (d) military leaders
18. The control of the Falkland Islands was at the center of an international fight between ______ and Great Britain.
    (a) Argentina
    (b) Mexico
    (c) Brazil
    (d) Chile

Think About It!

Based on our study of Latin America, what causes the government of a nation to succeed or to experience problems? Give examples in Latin America of both a successful government and a government that experienced problems.

Recipe: Tortillas— Latin Americans eat these as the basis for almost every meal. Corn tortillas are more popular than flour tortillas.

Ingredients:
2 1/4 c. instant corn flour
1 tsp. salt
1 1/3 c. cold water

Combine corn flour and salt. Gradually pour in one cup of water, stirring constantly. Knead with your hands, adding a tablespoon of water at a time, until the dough becomes firm and no longer sticks to your fingers. Roll out with a rolling pin to 1/16-inch thickness (you may need to do this in three or four batches). Using a plate as a pattern, cut with a knife or pastry wheel into five-inch rounds.

Cook tortillas one at a time on a griddle or frying pan over medium heat. Cook for two minutes on each side until it turns a delicate brown.

Multiple Choice
16. d
17. b
18. a

Think About It!

Answers will vary. Students should realize that pride and greed cause governments to crumble or experience radical change. When the people of a nation try to work together and place checks and balances on themselves, the government tends to be much more successful. Costa Rica is an example of a successful government; Argentina and Mexico are more problematic.

EPILOGUE

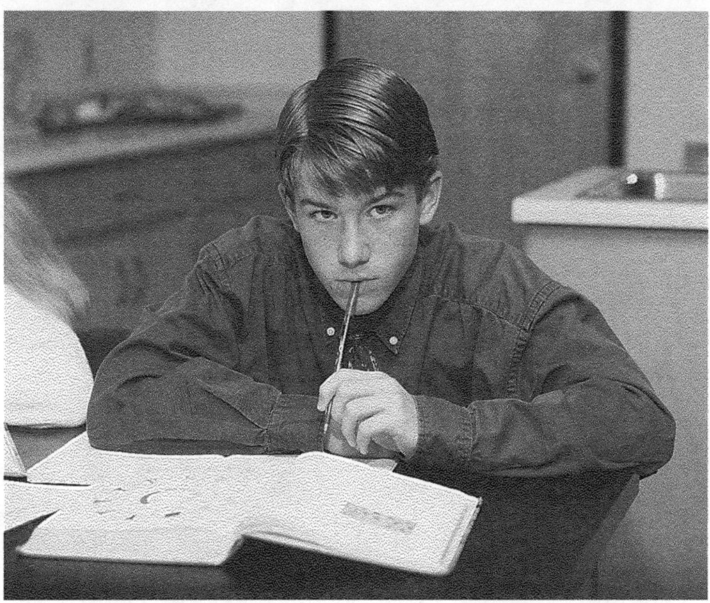

"Proving what is acceptable unto the Lord." (Eph. 5:10)

We have traveled a long way this year in World Studies. We have toured distant lands, met unfamiliar people, and seen thousands of events. And now we are at the end. Or are we? In many ways the end of this book is only a beginning. Yes, history will continue until the decree of God ends it. But more than that, this is a beginning for you. You have studied many things this year, and now you must answer the question, "What will I do with what I have learned?"

By now you are very familiar with the three elements of world studies: geography, history, and culture. In studying *geography,* we have learned about the place that God provided for man to live in, the earth. We have seen that where one lives affects how he acts and thinks. For example, the ancient Chinese believed that they were at the center of the world because so many natural barriers surrounded them. Medieval towns were built near rivers for transportation. Because geography does affect people's ways of life, a knowledge of geography is important to help you understand people around the world.

The *history* we have studied has given us a framework in which to see the working of God in time. It has also given us many examples for living, both positive and negative. In many cases we have learned good and bad from the same people. In the life of Genghis Khan, we may admire his leadership abilities but must reject his brutality and wickedness. The key to judging between a good and a bad example in history is discernment learned from the truth of God's Word. The Lord promises

602 Epilogue

that the Holy Spirit will guide the Christian into truth (John 16:13) so that he can discern good from evil in all he does.

However, while geography tells us where people lived and history tells us when people lived, the focus in World Studies has been on *how* people have lived, that is, their *culture*. We have divided culture into six elements: government, economics, thought and learning, arts and crafts, society, and religion. Each of these elements characterizes not only the lives of people living in the past or in different places, but also your own life.

At the beginning of this book, you were asked to look at your own culture, or way of life. As you have read this book, you have learned more about your culture by comparing it with other cultures. You have also had many opportunities to compare your way of life with what the Bible says about living. In these last few paragraphs, apply that information to these six areas in your own life. It is now up to you to decide what to do with the truth.

Government All your life you have had people in authority over you. Your parents, teachers, pastors, coaches—each of these people contributes to the governing of your life. They have a responsibility to make and enforce rules that will help you become a godly person. Your response to their rule will carry over to your eventual response to governmental authority. In reacting to any authority you should follow the guidelines set down in Scripture. "Let every soul be subject unto the higher powers. For there is no power but of God: the powers that be are ordained of God" (Rom. 13:1). However, the Christian's highest authority is God. Our obedience to Him and His Word comes before obedience to any person on earth. As Peter said in Acts 5:29, "We ought to obey God rather than men."

Economics Although you do not have a full-time job yet, you may have some work responsibilities—babysitting, delivering papers, or doing odd jobs. Each of us works for different reasons, but nearly everyone who works does so to support himself or his family. Even now you need to be developing principles to determine how you earn and spend money. In studying World Studies this year, you have met many industrious traders, merchants, manufacturers, and businessmen who were successful—at least in the world's eyes—because they gained great wealth. You have also learned about many pastors, missionaries, and other godly men and women who attained great spiritual success without much financial gain. A Christian should make sure that his first priority is spiritual wealth, not earthly wealth. "Lay not up for yourselves treasures upon earth, where moth and rust doth corrupt, and where thieves break through and steal: but lay up for yourselves treasures in heaven, where neither moth nor rust doth corrupt, and where thieves do not break through nor steal: for where your treasure is, there will your heart be also" (Matt. 6:19-21). All we have comes from God and should be returned to Him with grateful hearts and sincere service.

Thoughts and Learning Right now you are probably thinking more about your vacation and summer plans than about schoolwork. And yet, learning does not stop—not even in the summertime. God has given each of us a brain with the ability to think and to learn. With that gift comes the responsibility

Epilogue 603

to use it to glorify Him. One way to do that is by using your mind wisely and diligently in learning all that you can about God's Word and then applying that knowledge to all other areas of learning. As God gave Daniel, Shadrach, Meshach, and Abednego "knowledge and skill in all learning and wisdom" (Dan. 1:17), He can give you the ability to master the subjects you will encounter. God desires for us to learn as much as we can so that we will be well equipped to reach others with the gospel.

Arts and Crafts You may or may not have any artistic talent. Perhaps you can play the piano, the flute, or the trombone. Perhaps you can paint or draw. These talents are special gifts from God. He desires for you to use them to honor and glorify Him. That means you must be diligent in developing them. It also means that you must follow scriptural principles in your use of them. For example, the music you play or the pictures you draw must not offend His holiness. We usually judge a work of art by its beauty; and, although individuals may have different opinions about what is beautiful, it is interesting to note the use of beauty in Scripture. Several times in the Old Testament we read the phrase "the beauty of holiness," which tells us that God often measures beauty in spiritual terms. If as Christians we desire to create or appreciate true beauty, then our standard must be God's Word, which reveals the nature of His holiness.

Society We all have families and friends. Beyond our families and friends we each have neighbors, live in communities, and are citizens of a nation. The relationships we have with others in these groups are the social part of our lives. God created us to enjoy fellowship, first with Him and then with others; the people we know or will someday know are a part of His plan for our lives. From your own experience you know that they influence you and that you influence them through your words and actions. Scripture has much to say about our social relationships and our testimony before others. Galatians 6:10 gives us clear guidance for a Christian's behavior toward others: "As we have therefore opportunity, let us do good unto all men, especially unto them who are of the household of faith." In doing good to others, we show God's love to them and influence them for the gospel. In the same way, if we do evil to others, we will turn them away from the gospel and the message of God's love. Sometimes a Christian's actions and attitudes are all that others will know of God's message. What a great responsibility we have to make every part of our relationships with others pleasing to God!

Religion The most important relationship you will ever have is your relationship with Jesus Christ. Your human relationships, your abilities, your knowledge—all will be worthless unless you have eternal life by accepting Christ as your Savior. Throughout this study of the world, we have talked about man's religions. The word *religion* comes from the same Latin root as the word *rely.* Whatever a person relies on for the safety of his eternal soul is his religion. Some people rely on idols made of stone or wood, and some rely on their ancestors. Others rely on evil spirits or rituals, while others trust in their own intellectual

604 Epilogue

understanding. These "religions" are all false religions that cannot give their followers peace in this life or in the next. The only true religion is complete reliance on the Lord Jesus Christ for salvation through His blood.

If you do not know that you are relying on God for your salvation, examine your life to see whether you have confessed your sins to God and asked Christ to save you. God has promised us that "whosoever believeth in him should not perish, but have everlasting life" (John 3:16). This is the most important decision you will ever make and one that no one else can make for you.

If you are trusting in Christ for salvation, are you relying on Him each day for guidance and strength? The familiar verses Proverbs 3:5-6 tell us how we should live: "Trust in the Lord with all thine heart; and lean not unto thine own understanding. In all thy ways acknowledge him, and he shall direct thy paths." At this point of beginning, the rest of your life stretches before you: *What will you do with what you have learned?*

"Be ye doers of the word, and not hearers only." (James 1:22)

Epilogue 605

Atlas: World Political

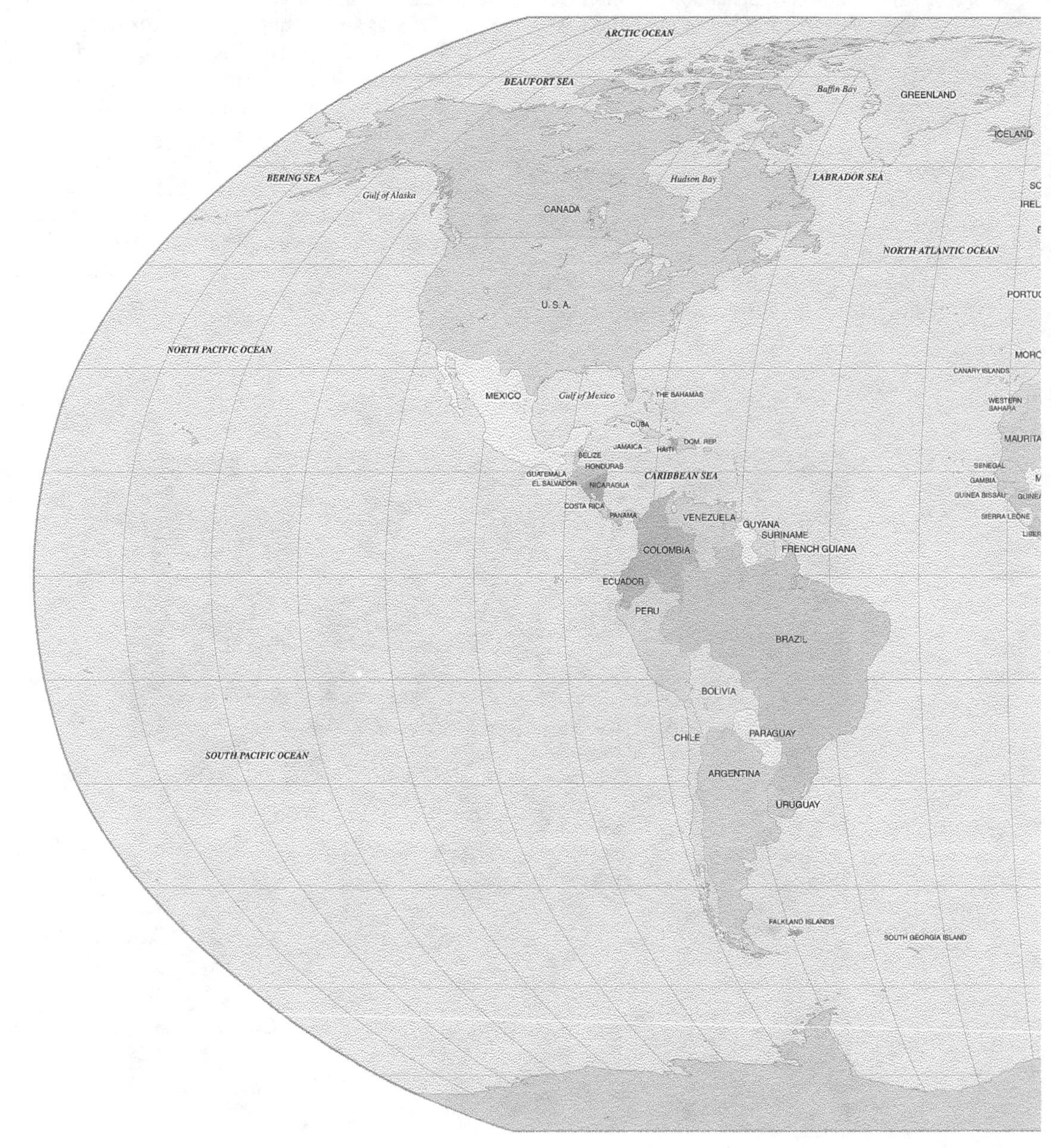

SWEDEN
FINLAND
RUSSIA
ESTONIA
LATVIA
LITHUANIA
POLAND
BELARUS
UKRAINE
CZECH
SLOVAKIA
AUSTRIA
HUNGARY
MOLDOVA
SLOVENIA
CROATIA
ROMANIA
BOSNIA
SERBIA
MONTENEGRO
BULGARIA
ITALY
MACEDONIA
ALBANIA
GREECE
BLACK SEA
GEORGIA
ARMENIA
AZERBAIJAN
TURKEY
CASPIAN SEA
ARAL SEA
KAZAKHSTAN
UZBEKISTAN
KYRGYZSTAN
TURKMENISTAN
TAJIKISTAN
MONGOLIA
SEA OF OKHOTSK
SEA OF JAPAN
NORTH KOREA
SOUTH KOREA
JAPAN
TUNISIA
MEDITERRANEAN SEA
CYPRUS
LEBANON
ISRAEL
SYRIA
IRAQ
IRAN
AFGHANISTAN
CHINA
EAST CHINA SEA
JORDAN
PAKISTAN
KUWAIT
NEPAL
BHUTAN
NORTH PACIFIC OCEAN
LIBYA
EGYPT
QATAR
U.A.E.
Gulf of Oman
SAUDI ARABIA
INDIA
TAIWAN
RED SEA
OMAN
ARABIAN SEA
MYANMAR
LAOS
BANGLADESH
Bay of Bengal
SOUTH CHINA SEA
PHILIPPINE SEA
CHAD
ERITREA
YEMEN
THAILAND
PHILIPPINES
SUDAN
Gulf of Aden
KAMPUCHEA
VIETNAM
DJIBOUTI
SOMALIA
ANDAMAN SEA
Gulf of Thailand
SRI LANKA
CENTRAL AFRICAN REPUBLIC
ETHIOPIA
CAMEROON
BRUNEI
MALAYSIA
UGANDA
KENYA
SINGAPORE
GABON
RWANDA
CONGO
DEMOCRATIC REPUBLIC OF CONGO
BURUNDI
TANZANIA
JAVA SEA
INDONESIA
PAPUA NEW GUINEA
ANGOLA
INDIAN OCEAN
ARAFURA SEA
TIMOR SEA
Gulf of Carpentaria
ZAMBIA
CORAL SEA
ZIMBABWE
MALAWI
FIJI
NAMIBIA
BOTSWANA
MOZAMBIQUE
MADAGASCAR
NEW CALEDONIA
AUSTRALIA
SWAZILAND
SOUTH AFRICA
LESOTHO
Great Australian Bight
TASMAN SEA
NEW ZEALAND
ANTARCTICA

Atlas: Climates of the World

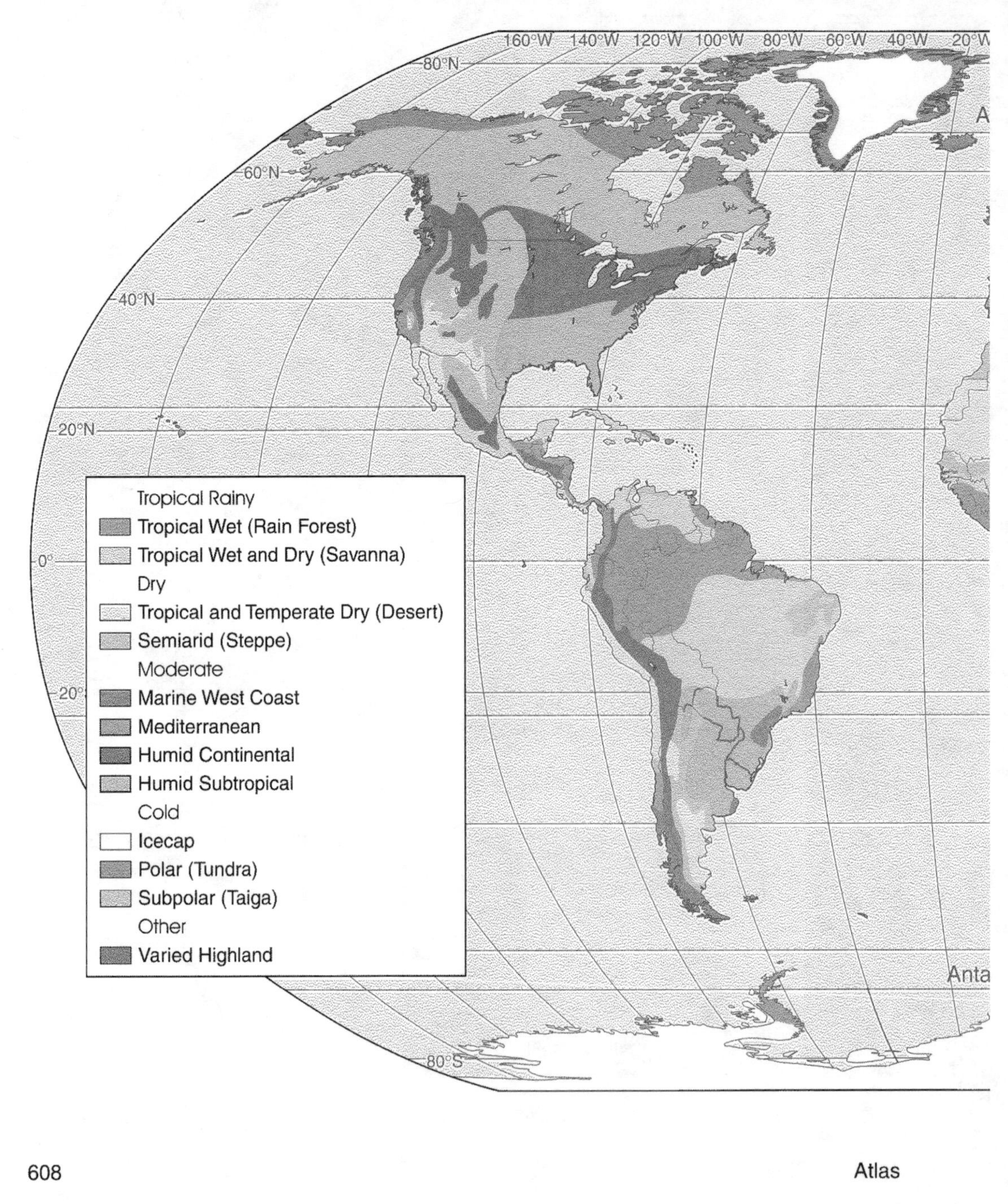
160°W
140°W
120°W
100°W
80°W
60°W
40°W
20°W
80°N
60°N
40°N
20°N
0°
20°
80°S
Anta
Tropical Rainy
Tropical Wet (Rain Forest)
Tropical Wet and Dry (Savanna)
Dry
Tropical and Temperate Dry (Desert)
Semiarid (Steppe)
Moderate
Marine West Coast
Mediterranean
Humid Continental
Humid Subtropical
Cold
Icecap
Polar (Tundra)
Subpolar (Taiga)
Other
Varied Highland

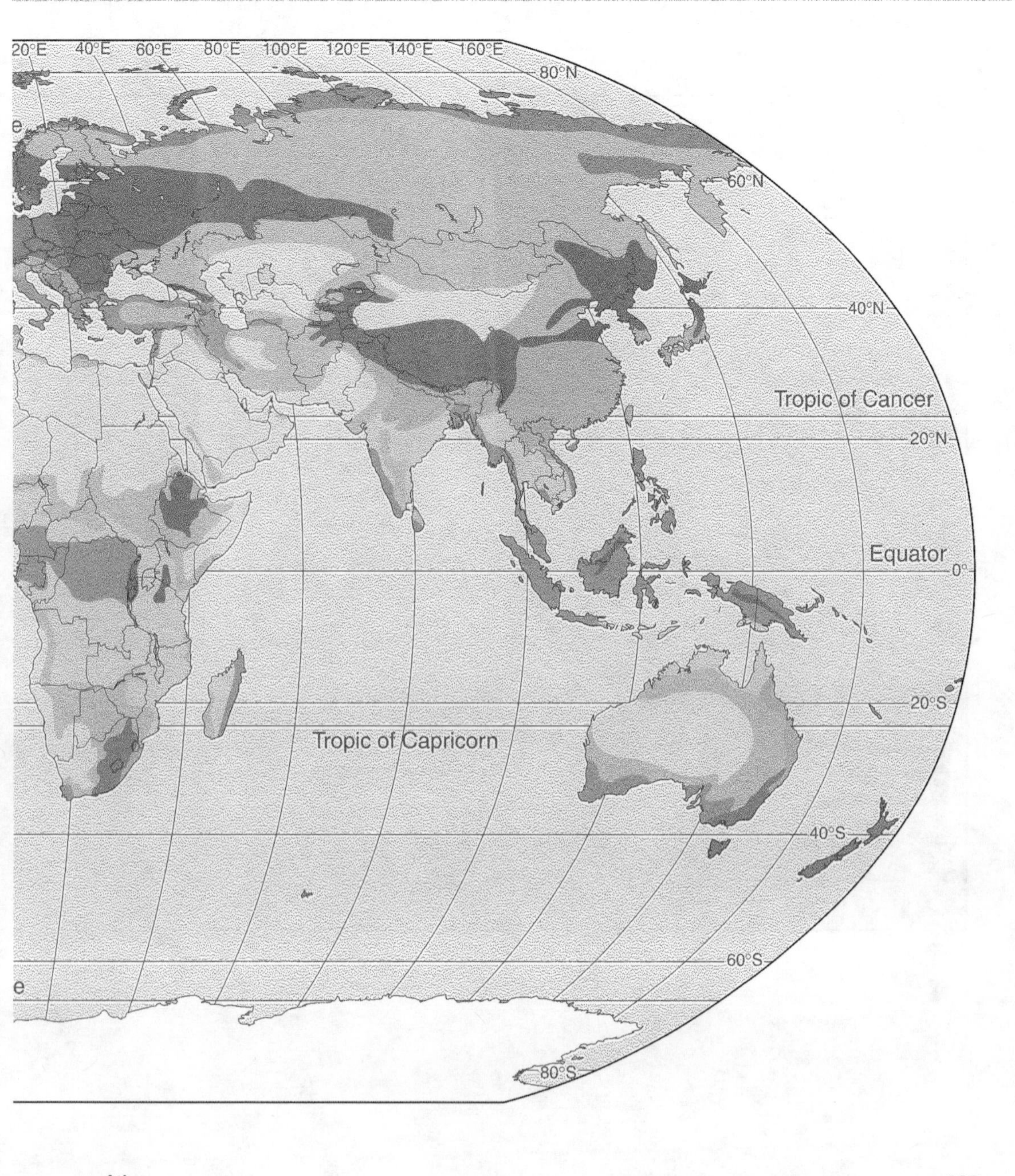
20°E
40°E
60°E
80°E
100°E
120°E
140°E
160°E
80°N
60°N
40°N
Tropic of Cancer
20°N
Equator
0°
20°S
Tropic of Capricorn
40°S
60°S
80°S

Atlas: Europe

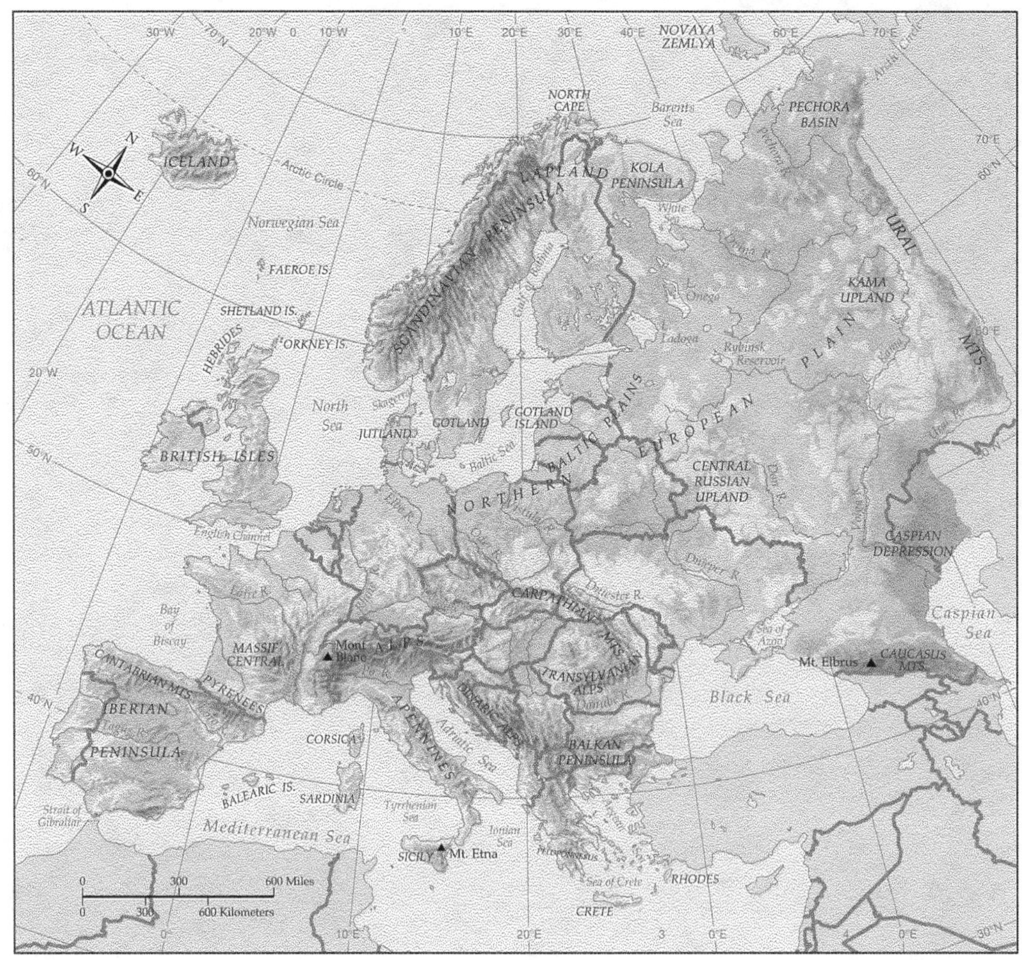

Atlas: Asia

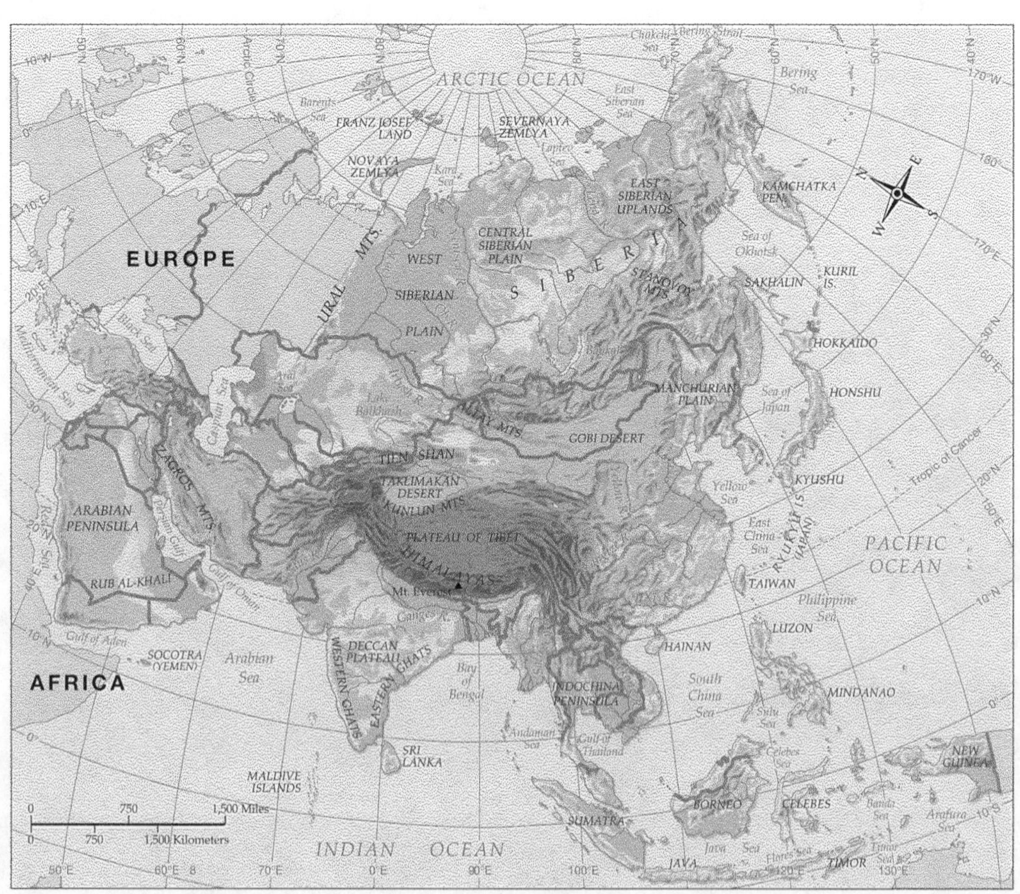

ARCTIC OCEAN
FRANZ JOSEF LAND
SEVERNAYA ZEMLYA
NOVAYA ZEMLYA
EUROPE
URAL MTS.
WEST SIBERIAN PLAIN
CENTRAL SIBERIAN PLAIN
SIBERIA
EAST SIBERIAN UPLANDS
KAMCHATKA PEN.
Sea of Okhotsk
SAKHALIN
KURIL IS.
HOKKAIDO
HONSHU
KYUSHU
MANCHURIAN PLAIN
Sea of Japan
GOBI DESERT
ALTAI MTS.
TIEN SHAN
TAKLIMAKAN DESERT
KUNLUN MTS.
PLATEAU OF TIBET
HIMALAYAS
Mt. Everest
ZAGROS MTS.
ARABIAN PENINSULA
RUB AL-KHALI
Black Sea
Caspian Sea
Aral Sea
Lake Balkhash
Yellow Sea
East China Sea
PACIFIC OCEAN
TAIWAN
Philippine Sea
LUZON
HAINAN
South China Sea
MINDANAO
Sulu Sea
INDOCHINA PENINSULA
DECCAN PLATEAU
WESTERN GHATS
EASTERN GHATS
Bay of Bengal
Arabian Sea
SOCOTRA (YEMEN)
Gulf of Aden
AFRICA
SRI LANKA
MALDIVE ISLANDS
Andaman Sea
Gulf of Thailand
SUMATRA
BORNEO
CELEBES
Celebes Sea
Banda Sea
NEW GUINEA
Arafura Sea
Java Sea
JAVA
Flores Sea
TIMOR
Timor Sea
INDIAN OCEAN
Bering Sea
Bering Strait
Barents Sea
Kara Sea
Laptev Sea
East Siberian Sea
Tropic of Cancer
Arctic Circle
0 750 1,500 Miles
0 750 1,500 Kilometers

Atlas: Africa

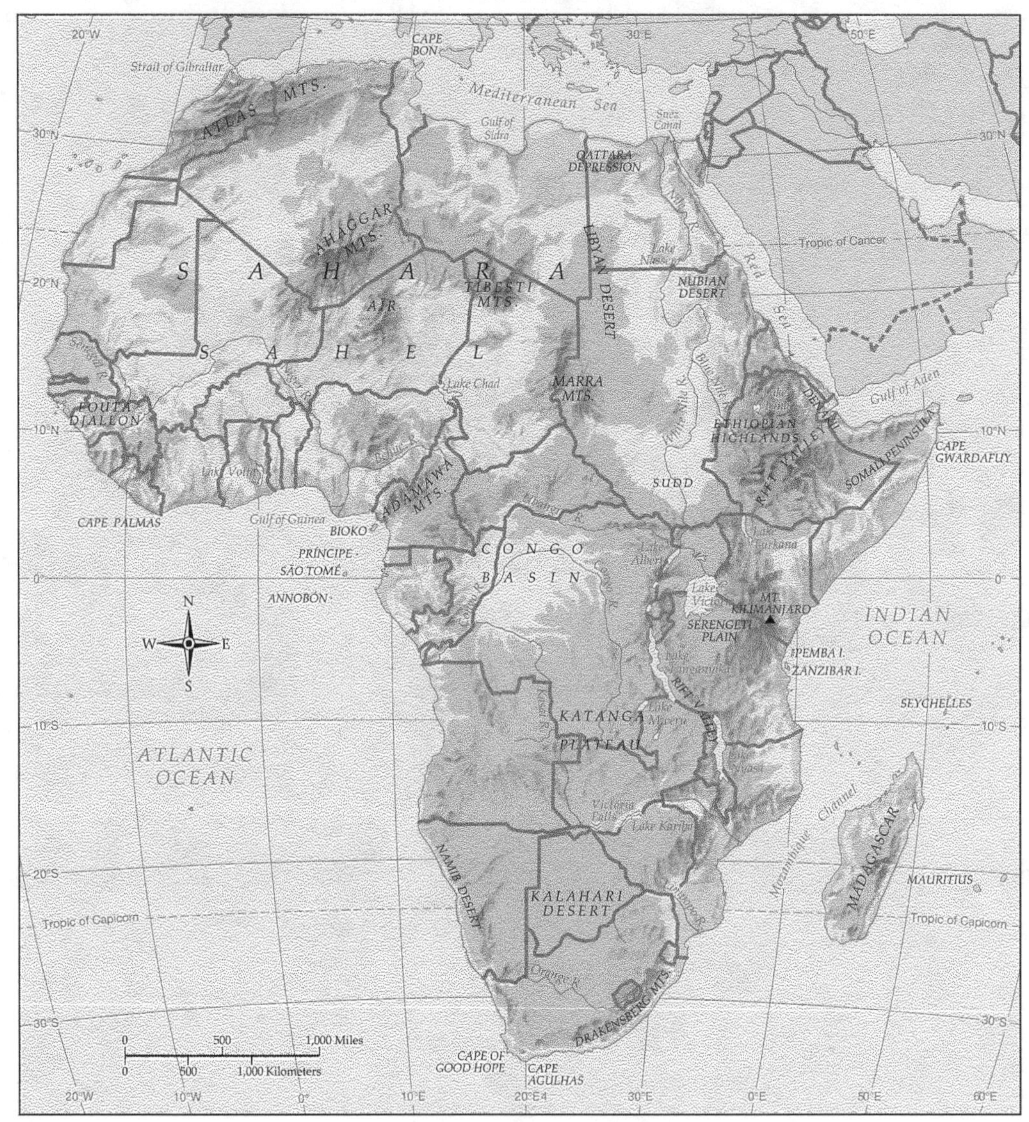

Atlas: South America

Atlas: North America

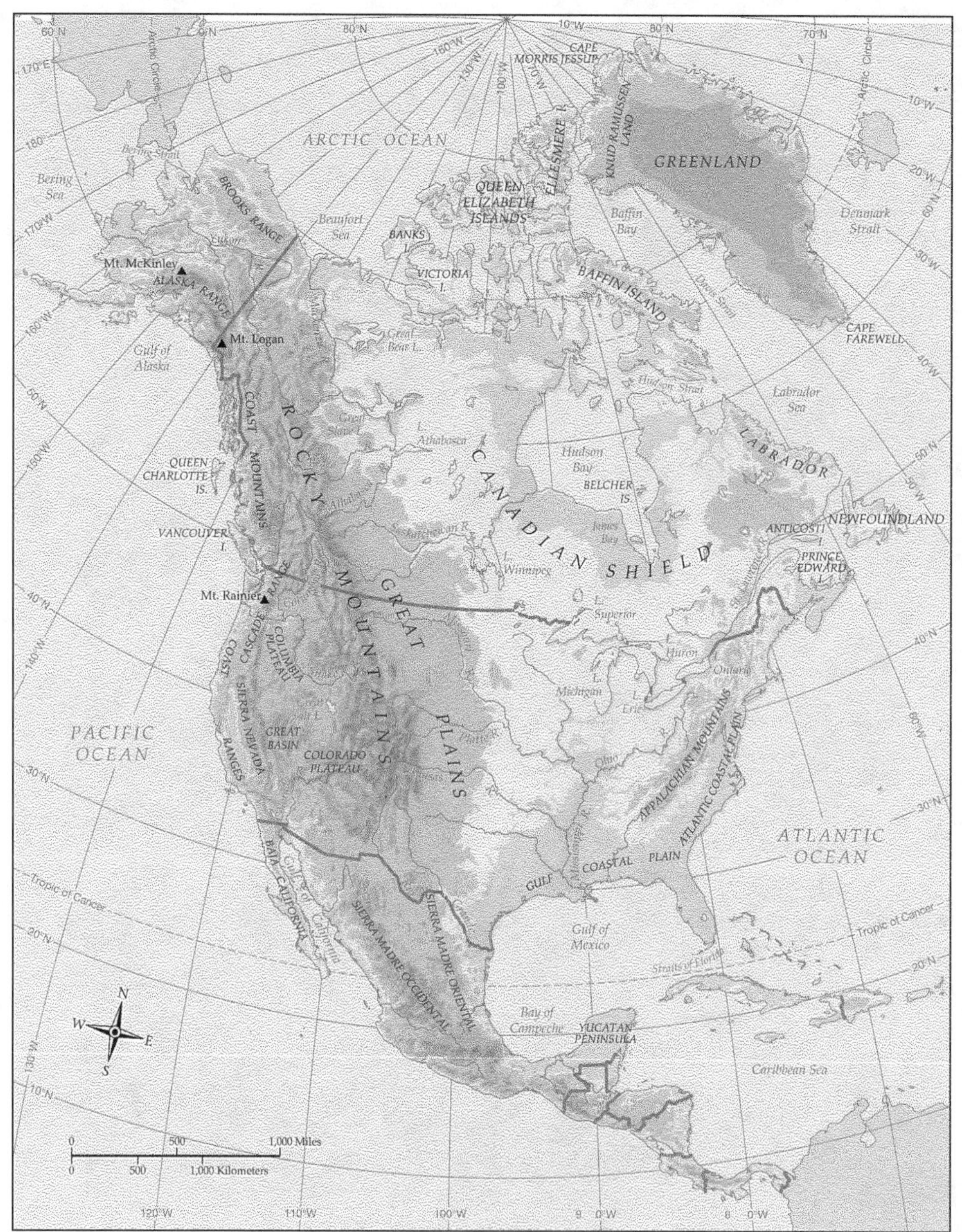

Index

Photo Credits

The following agencies and individuals have furnished materials to meet the photographic needs of this textbook. We wish to express our gratitude to them for their important contribution

APN Photo
Carl Abrams
Jeffrey Alford
American Heritage Company
Ward Andersen
J. B. Anderson
Aramco World Magazine
John Armstrong
Tony Arruza
Artists Rights Society, New York (ARS)
Asia Access
Astronomy Charted
Australian Creation Research Society
Australian Tourism Commission (ATC)
Austrian Press and Information Service
Gary Balius
David Barnett
David Batchelor
J. Bean
The Bettmann Archive
Bob Jones University Archives
Bob Jones University Press Photo Collection
Mr. Emery Bopp
The British Library
The British Museum
Rose Brouhard
Michele Burgess
Geremy Butler Photography
Lewis Carl
Jimmy Carter Library
Kay Chernush
Christie's Images
George R. Collins
Jeanne Conte
Corbis-Bettmann
Corel Corporation
The Corning Museum of Glass
Creation Science Foundation
D. Donne Bryant Stock Photography
Larry Daughters
Bill Davis
The Detroit Institute of Arts
Digital Stock
Dover Publications
Evan Drake
Naomi Duguid
W. E. Dutton
Eastman Kodak Company
Egyptian Tourist Authority
Victor Englebert
Bill Fitzpatrick
Giuseppe Franchini
J. A. Franklin
Winston Fraser
Dr. Kenneth Frederick
Free China Review
Carson Fremont
GeoSystems Global Corporation
German Information Center
Rajan Gill
Mary Goldenberg
Gospel Fellowship Association (GFA)
Mr. Leslie H. Green
Greenville County Library
Greenville County Museum of Art
Yosef Hadar
Grace C. Hargis
Peggy Beth Hargis
The Havemeyer Collection
Michael Heuer
Robert Holmes
Edwin G. Huffman
The Huntington Library
Imperial War Museum
Albert Isaak family
Israel Ministry of Tourism
Italian Cultural Institute
Japan National Tourist Organization
Dr. Tim Keesee
Stephen Kirkpatrick
David Koontz
Joyce Landis
José Lara
Jason Lauré
Venet C. Lefteroff, Sr.
Robert Lehman Collection
Library of Congress
Rob Loach
Lufthansa German Airlines
Fred Mang, Jr.
Jaime Martin-Escobal
Mary Evans Picture Library
Ivan Massar
Brian McGilloway
Metropolitan Museum of Art
Colonel Kemp Moore
Moscow Images and Reporting (MIR)
Museum of Modern Art
National Aeronautics and Space Administration (NASA)
National Archives
National Library of Australia
National Library of Medicine
National Park Service
National Portrait Gallery, London
National Tourism Promotion Agency, Poland
Nelson-Atkins Museum of Art
New York Public Library
Nintendo of America, Inc.
Richard Nixon Library
Novosti Press Agency
Pana-Vue Slide
Panos Pictures
Embassy of Papua New Guinea
Parke-Davis
Alan Patterson
Tony Payne
Walter Persegati
Photo Disc, Inc.
James Pickerell
Planet Art
J. Norman Powell
Precision Graphics
Promotion Australia
John Pruden
Rakow Research Library
Ronald Reagan Library
Reuters/Corbis-Bettmann
George Rogier
Esther Root
The Roving Tortoise
Gina Santi
Ken Scheer
Eugene Schulz
Tomas Sennett
Kay Shaw
John Springer
Cecil W. Stoughton
Randy Studdard
Sword of the Lord
Tea Council of the U.S.A., Inc.
Ricardo Teles
Gustavo Tomsich
Underwood & Underwood
Unicorn Stock Photos
Union Pacific Railroad
United States Army
United States Department of Agriculture (USDA)
United States Government
University of London
Unusual Films
UPI/Corbis-Bettmann
David Utter
Mrs. Marj Van der Puy
Georgi P. Vins
Baldwin H. Ward
Warner-Lambert Company
Kay Washer
Dawn L. Watkins
Dr. Christian Wei
Nik Wheeler
The White House
Ray Witlin
John Wolsieffer
World Bank
World Wide Photos
Worldwide Slides
Yale University Library

COVER:
Photo Disc, Inc. (all)

TITLE PAGES:
Photo Disc, Inc. (all)

CONTENTS PAGES: Greenville County Library v (top); Christie's Images vi (top); Corbis-Bettmann v (bottom), vi (bottom)

PROLOGUE: Unusual Films ix, x; Corel Corporation xi (top); World Bank, by Ray Witlin xi (middle); World Bank, by Yosef Hadar xi (bottom); Gary Balius xii (top); Astronomy Charted, courtesy of David Batchelor xii (middle); ATC/Tandanya xii (bottom); NASA xiii; Lufthansa German Airlines xv; Japan National Tourist Organization xvi; BJU Press Photo Collection xvii

UNIT I OPENER: Greenville County Library xviii-1

CHAPTER 1: Photo Disc, Inc. 2-3, 14, 17 (left), 19; Tea Council of the U.S.A., Inc. 7 (background); David Barnett 9 (left); Corel Corporation 9 (top right), 15, 17 (right); Rob Loach 9 (bottom right); Dover Publications 12; George R. Collins 16 (background); Evan Drake 18

CHAPTER 2: Planet Art 22-23, 39 (left), 40 (left); Metropolitan Museum of Art, bequest of Mrs. H. O. Havemeyer, 1929, The Havemeyer Collection (29.100.16) Photograph ©1990 The Metropolitan Museum of Art 24; Corbis-Bettmann 27; Library of Congress 28; Gustavo Tomsich/Corbis-Bettmann 29; Unusual Films 30 (left, background), 31, 34 (bottom), 38 (all), 42 (left); Digital Stock 32 (left); Walter Persegati 32 (right); German Information Center 34 (top); Dawn L. Watkins 35 (left); GFA, Bill Davis 35 (right); BJU Press Photo Collection 37 (top); George R. Collins 37 (bottom); Christie's Images 39 (right); Lewis Carl 40 (right); Italian Cultural Institute, N.Y. 41; MIR 42 (right); Photo Disc, Inc. 43

CHAPTER 3: Photo Disc, Inc. 46-47, 63 (left); German Information Center 48, 49, 51 (both), 61; Michael Heuer 50; GFA 53 (left); Esther Root 53 (middle); George R. Collins 53 (right); Library of Congress 54, 59, 67 (bottom); The British Museum 57; Corel Corporation 61 (background); Unusual Films 62, 64-65 (background), 66 (bottom), 67 (top); Astronomy Charted, courtesy of David Batchelor 63 (right); Metropolitan Museum of Art, Robert Lehman Collection, 1975. (1975.1.146) Photograph ©1980 The Metropolitan Museum of Art 66 (top); Gift of Mr. Leslie H. Green, Photograph ©1998 The Detroit Institute of Arts 68

RELIGIONS OF THE WORLD: Japan National Tourist Organization 72 (top); Robert Holmes 72 (middle); Photo Disc, Inc. 72 (bottom), 73, 74, 75, 77; Aramco World Magazine 72 (background), 78; World Bank, by Yosef Hadar 76; Unusual Films 79

CHAPTER 4: Nik Wheeler 80-81, 91, 93 (bottom); Photo Disc, Inc. 87 (left, right), 99, 101; Gary Balius 87 (middle), 89 (left); Aramco World Magazine 89 (right); Unusual Films 92, 93 (top series); National Park Service/W. E. Dutton 98

CHAPTER 5: World Bank, by Yosef Hadar 104-5, 108 (right), 121; Carl Abrams 106; J. A. Franklin 107; World Bank, by James Pickerell 108 (left); GFA, Randy Studdard 108 (middle), 120; World Bank, by Kay Chernush 111 (top left); World Bank, by Ray Witlin 111 (bottom left), 113-14 (background); Kay Washer 111 (right), 112, 117 (both); Photo Disc, Inc. 113 (left), 118 (both); Robert Holmes 113 (right); Victor Englebert 114 (both), 115, 116, 119, 122 (top, background); George R. Collins 120 (background); The British Library 124

UNIT II OPENER: Nowitz: Richard/Corbis 128-29

CHAPTER 6: Photo Disc, Inc. 130-31, 149 (middle, right); Aramco World Magazine 132 (top); Library of Congress 132 (bottom), 146; Tony Arruza 133; Winston Fraser 140-41 (background); Eugene Schulz 141; Asia Access/by Naomi Duguid 145 (top); Unusual Films 145 (bottom); Corel Corporation 149 (left); Michele Burgess 151 (left, middle), 153 (both); World Bank, by Guiseppe Franchini 151 (right); Digital Stock 152; American Heritage Company, courtesy of New York Public Library 154

CHAPTER 7: Photo Disc, Inc. 158-59; Corbis-Bettmann 161, 171, 179; World Bank, by Edwin G. Huffman 163, 165 (middle right, bottom right), 167 (right); John Wolsieffer 164, 165 (center), 167 (left), 170, 175; World Bank 165 (top left); World Bank, by Jaime Martin-Escobal 165 (top right), 176; World Bank, by Larry Daughters 165 (middle left); World Bank, by Tomas Sennett 165 (bottom left); Planet Art 173 (left); Dr. Kenneth Frederick 173 (right); Unusual Films 174 (right, background); Ricardo Teles/D. Donne Bryant Stock Photography 177 (left); Gina Santi 177 (right); Kay Shaw 178 (bottom, background)

CHAPTER 8: Photo Disc, Inc. 186-87, 189 (left), 196 (both), 205 (top left, bottom left), 217 (left); Corel Corporation 189 (right), 214 (bottom), 217 (middle); Corbis-Bettmann 190, 198 (top), 204, 213, 214 (top left); BJU Press Collection 194 (top); J. Norman Powell 195; Library of Congress 198 (bottom), 199 (right), 207, 212; Parke-Davis, Division of Warner-Lambert Company 199 (left); National Portrait Gallery, London 200; George R. Collins 201 (both), 210; David Koontz 202-3 (background); National Park Service/Fred Mang, Jr. 205 (right); Yale University Library 209 (both); Unusual Films 214 (top right); Joyce Landis 217 (right); National Park Service/Cecil W. Stoughton 218 (top); Union Pacific Railroad 218 (bottom)

CHAPTER 9: Grace C. Hargis 222-23, 224 (right), 226; Christie's Images 224 (left); Library of Congress 225, 228 (right), 230, 236 (bottom), 238 (left), 239, 246 (left); Austrian Press and Information Service, NY 228 (left); German Information Center 229 (left); Corbis-Bettmann 229 (right), 238 (right), 244-45 (background), 245; National Library of Medicine 233; Courtesy: National Tourism Promotion Agency, Poland 235 (left, top right); Photo Disc, Inc. 235 (bottom right); Worldwide Slides 236 (top left); George R. Collins 236 (top middle); Pana-Vue Slide 236 (top right); Corel Corporation 242; Venet C. Lefteroff, Sr./Corbis-Bettmann 246 (right)

FULFILLING THE GREAT COMMISSION: GFA, Randy Studdard 250 (background); GFA 250 (left); GFA, David Utter 250 (right); Unusual Films 251; Mary Evans Picture Library 252; Library of Congress 253; National Portrait Gallery, London 254; John Pruden 257

CHAPTER 10: National Library of Australia 258-59, 262, 263, 266, 272 (right), 274; Corbis-Bettmann 261, 275; Photo Disc, Inc. 265 (left), 280, 281, 282, 283 (bottom); National Portrait Gallery, London 265 (right), 272 (left); ATC/J. B. Anderson 269 (left); Australian Creation Research Society/J. Bean 269 (top right), 271 (right); Australian Creation Research Society 269 (bottom right), 279 (both); Promotion Australia 270 (left); ATC/John Armstrong 270 (right), 271 (left); Kay Shaw 273 (left); ATC 276 (bottom), 276-77 (background); Creation Science Foundation 277 (left); ATC/Tandanya 277 (right); USDA 278; Unusual Films 283 (top); University of London School of Oriental & African Studies/Geremy Butler Photography 284; Robert Holmes 284-85 (background); Library of Congress 286 (top); The Roving Tortoise 286-87 (background); Embassy of Papua New Guinea 288

UNIT III OPENER: Christie's Images 292-93

CHAPTER 11: Collection of the Juliette K. and Leonard S. Rakow Research Library of The Corning Museum of Glass 294-95; BJU Press Photo Collection 296 (left); Library of Congress 296 (right), 297, 302, 307 (right), 308 (top), 318 (top); GFA, courtesy of Ken Scheer 299 (all); Corbis-Bettmann 300, 301, 303; Eastman Kodak Company 307 (left); Photo Disc, Inc. 308 (bottom); Collection of Mr. Emery Bopp 312; National Library of Medicine 313; Sword of the Lord 314; Planet Art 316 (top), 318 (bottom); The Metropolitan

Museum of Art, Gift of Mary Goldenberg, 1899. (99.11.3) Photograph ©1978 The Metropolitan Museum of Art 316 (bottom)

CHAPTER 12: Photo Disc, Inc. 322-23, 333 (top); Corbis-Bettmann 324, 337 (bottom), 338; Library of Congress 325, 339; National Portrait Gallery, London 327 (top); Corbis 327 (bottom); World Bank 329 (top left); World Bank, by Tomas Sennett 329 (right), 335, 343; World Bank, by Ray Witlin 329(bottom left), 333(bottom); Underwood & Underwood/Corbis-Bettmann 330; John Springer/Corbis-Bettmann 334 (top); Asia Access/Naomi Duguid 334 (bottom), 337 (top); Nelson-Atkins Museum of Art 340 (top); Robert Holmes 340 (bottom); Peggy Beth Hargis 341, 344 (top); Asia Access/Jeffery Alford 344 (bottom)

CHAPTER 13: Photo Disc, Inc. 348-49, 355 (both), 356 (both); Library of Congress 350; Brian McGilloway 351 (both); Asia Access/Jeffery Alford 353, 361 (bottom left); The Bettmann Archive 357; Asia Access/Rajan Gill 361 (right); World Bank, by Yosef Hadar 361 (top left); Carson Fremont 362 (background); Dr. Christian Wei 365; UPI/Corbis-Bettmann 366; Digital Stock 368 (top); The British Museum 368 (bottom); New York Public Library 369; National Archives 371, 374

CHAPTER 14: Photo Disc, Inc. 378-79; Library of Congress 380, 381, 396 (top); Panos Pictures 382 (both), 383; Corbis-Bettmann 384, 401 (bottom); GFA, Tony Payne 384-85 (background), 386 (bottom right) 391 (left); National Portrait Gallery, London 385 (left), 397; Egyptian Tourist Authority 385 (right); Kay Washer 386 (left); J. A. Franklin 386 (top right); BJU Press Photo Collection 391 (middle); World Bank, by Ivan Massar 391 (right); University of London School of Oriental and African Studies/Geremy Butler Photography, 392, 393, 396 (bottom); Jason Lauré 400; Aramco World Magazine 400-401 (background); Corbis 402

MUSIC AND ART IN HISTORY: Planet Art 406 (inset), 407, 408, 411; Unusual Films 406 (background), 409; Greenville County Museum of Art, Greenville, SC 413

UNIT IV: UPI/Corbis-Bettmann 414-15

CHAPTER 15: U.S. Government 416-17, 439; Library of Congress 418, 435; Corbis-Bettmann 419, 429; National Archives 420 (both), 424, 425, 426, 432 (both), 433; Dr. Tim Keesee 423 (top left), 438 (both); Aramco World Magazine 423 (bottom left); World Bank, by Yosef Hadar 423 (right); Courtesy of the Museum of Modern Art, NY and ©1998 Estate of Pablo Picasso/ARS, New York 427 (top); Planet Art 427 (bottom); National Portrait Gallery 428; World Wide Photos 434; Reuters/Corbis-Bettmann 436; Corel Corporation 440; Imperial War Museum 442; Joyce Landis 442 (background)

CHAPTER 16: Photo Disc, Inc. 446-47, 451 (left), 453 (left, top right); The Bettmann Archive 448; MIR 449 (top), 451 (right), 455 (all), 456, 461 (both), 462, 471; National Archives 449 (bottom), 460 (top both); Corel Corporation 453 (bottom right); Library of Congress 454, 459 (right), 469; UPI/Corbis-Bettmann 457, 459 (left); Courtesy of Richard Nixon Library 460 (bottom); Novosti Press Agency 463; APN Photo 464 (top); Unusual Films 464 (bottom), 465; Courtesy of Albert Isaak family 466; Courtesy of Georgi Vins 467; The White House, by Bill Fitzpatrick 468

CHAPTER 17: Photo Disc, Inc. 474-75, 476 (left), 492 (top); Library of Congress 477, 478 (bottom), 480; UPI/Corbis-Bettmann 478 (top), 481, 484 (bottom); National Archives 479, 483, 484 (top) 490 (both), 491 (both); Robert Holmes 480-81 (background), 492 (bottom); Corbis-Bettmann 482; Japan National Tourist Organization 487 (top left, bottom right); Rose Brouhard 487 (bottom left); GFA, Alan Patterson 487 (top right); Brian McGilloway 488, 498-99 (background); Free China Review 489 (top); Reuters/Corbis-Bettman 489 (bottom); World Bank, by Edwin G. Huffman 493; Nintendo of America, Inc. 494 (both), 495 (all); Asia Access/Jeffrey Alford 496; University of London School of African and Asian Studies/Geremy Butler Photography 497, 498 (top); Dr. Christian Wei 499 (bottom), 500 (both)

CANADA: Joyce Landis 504 (background); Photo Disc, Inc. 504 (inset), 511; Baldwin H. Ward/Corbis-Bettmann 506; Courtesy: Ronald Reagan Library 508; Robert Holmes 509 (top), 510; Bob Jones University Archives 509 (bottom)

CHAPTER 18: Jeanne Conte 512-13; Corbis-Bettmann 515 (top), 525; Col. Kemp Moore 516 (top); World Bank, by Yosef Hadar 516 (bottom); Asia Access/Jeffrey Alford 517, 518-19 (background), 519 (right); UPI/Corbis-Bettmann 518 (left), 522 (both), 527, 530, 539; Courtesy: Jimmy Carter Library 520; Unusual Films 521, 526, 530-31 (background); Aramco World Magazine 523 (both) 524, 528, 538; Library of Congress 531; Israel Ministry of Tourism 532, 533 (right); Ward Andersen 533 (left), 534 (right); Robert Holmes 534 (left), 536; Photo Disc, Inc. 535, 537, 541 (left); Asia Access/Rajan Gill 541 (right); Reuters/Corbis-Bettmann 542 (top); U.S. Army 542 (bottom)

CHAPTER 19: Michele Burgess 546-47; Jason Lauré 549 (both), 562 (both), 563 (bottom), 564, 572; UPI/Corbis-Bettmann 551, 557 (both), 571; National Archives 552; Library of Congress 553, 558 (bottom); Victor Englebert 554, 555, 558 (top), 559 (both), 569 (bottom); Corel Corporation 560; Photo Disc, Inc. 561, 569 (top); Reuters/Corbis-Bettmann 563 (top); Unicorn Stock Photos 567 (both), 568

CHAPTER 20: Photo Disc, Inc. 576-77, 583 (middle), 585 (right), 586, 590 (bottom); Library of Congress 578, 579 (bottom); Corbis-Bettmann 579 (top), 585 (left), 594, 595; Planet Art 580; Kay Shaw 581, 591, 593; World Bank, by James Pickerell 583 (left); World Bank, by Yosef Hadar 583 (right); Imperial War Museum 589 (both); Reuters/Corbis-Bettmann 592; Robert Holmes 594-95 (background); George Rogier 596; Used by permission of Mrs. Marj Van der Puy 597; Stephen Kirkpatrick 597 (background); José Lara 598

EPILOGUE: Unusual Films 602, 605

MAP SECTION: Precision Graphics 608-9; Copyright 1998 GeoSystems Global Corporation 610-15

Appendix

Chapter Eleven

TIME LINE NOTATIONS

- Rosetta Stone found—1799
- Waltzing appears in ballrooms—1813
- Congress of Vienna—1814-15
- Queen Victoria's reign—1838-1901
- First women obtain university degrees in America—1841
- Knickerbocker Baseball Club codifies rules of baseball—1845
- Great Exhibition—1851
- Roller skating comes to America—1863
- "In God We Trust" printed on U.S. coins—1864
- First woman professor (Vassar College)—1865
- P. T. Barnum starts circus called "The Greatest Show on Earth"—1871
- King C. Gillette invents a new razor with safety features—1895

SOURCES

Burchell, S. C. *Age of Progress.* New York: Time Incorporated, 1966.

Clark, Robert E. *Darwin: Before and After.* London: The Paternoster Press, 1950.

Cunliffe, Marcus. *The Age of Expansion 1848-1917.* Springfield, Mass.: G & C Merriman Co., 1974.

Hart, Roger. *English Life in the Nineteenth Century.* New York: G. P. Putnam's Sons, 1971.

Lewis, John. *The Life and Teaching of Karl Marx.* New York: International Publishers, 1965.

Lichten, Frances. *Decorative Art of Victoria's Era.* New York: Charles Scribner's Sons, 1950.

Osborne, John. *Britain.* New York: Time Inc., 1961.

Perry, George, and Nicholas Mason. *The Victorians: A World Built to Last.* New York: The Viking Press, 1974.

Reader, W. J. *Victorian England.* New York: G. P. Putnam's Sons, 1973.

Rudé, George. *Revolutionary Europe 1783-1815.* New York: Harper & Row, 1964.

Walvin, James. *English Urban Life 1776-1851.* London: Hutchinson & Co., 1984.

Williams, Raymond. *The English Novel From Dickens to Lawrence.* New York: Oxford University Press, 1970.

Chapter Twelve

TIME LINE NOTATIONS

- Hard rubber caoutchouc ("India rubber") comes to England—1736
- Robert Clive arrives in Madras as a clerk with the East India Company—1744
- 120 British soldiers are imprisoned and die in India ("The Black Hole of Calcutta")—1756
- Lord Hastings, Governor General of India, declares war on the Gurkhas (Nepal)—1814
- The great cholera pandemic begins in India—1826
- Suttee outlawed in British India—1829
- British take control of India from the East India Company—1858
- Rudyard Kipling publishes *The Jungle Book*—1894
- Famine in India—1897
- Railroad completed—1900

SOURCES

Andrews, H. V. *India's Girls and Women.* Harrisburg, Pa.: Christian Alliance Publishing Company, 1923.

Brown, Joe David. *India.* New York: Time Incorporated, 1961.

Caine, W. S. *Picturesque India.* New York: George Routledge and Sons Ltd., 1890.

Compton, Herbert. *Indian Life in Town and Country.* New York: G. P. Putnam's Sons, 1904.

Dyer, Helen S. *Pandita Ramabai.* London: Pickering and Inglis, 1923.

India. Amsterdam: Time-Life Books, 1986.

India's Sunny Plains. Scotland: John Ritchie, Ltd., [1920-56?]

Keay, John. *The Honourable Company.* New York: Macmillan Publishing Company, 1991.

Kennedy, Jean. *Here Is India.* New York: Charles Scribner's Sons, 1945.

Mueller, J. Theodore. *Great Missionaries to India.* Grand Rapids: Zondervan, 1952.

Watson, Francis. *A Concise History of India.* New York: Charles Scribner's Sons, 1975.

Wolpert, Stanley. *A New History of India.* New York: Oxford University Press, 1997.

Chapter Thirteen

TIME LINE NOTATIONS

- St. Francis Xavier arrives in Asia as a Catholic missionary—1542
- Portugal founds the colony of Macao on the coast of China—1557
- Tea from China is shipped for the first time to Europe by the Dutch East India Company—1609
- Japan closes its doors to all Europeans—1639
- The English Civil War ends with the surrender of Oxford to the Roundheads—1646
- The Napoleonic Wars sweep across Europe—1803-15
- The first bicycle is constructed by Scottish inventor Kirkpatrick Macmillian—1834
- Britain takes Hong Kong—1841
- France annexes the three eastern provinces of Cochin China—1862
- Aspirin is marketed—1897

SOURCES

Broomhall, Marshall, ed. *Martyred Missionaries of the China Inland Mission.* London: Morgan and Scott, 1901.

Bueno de Mequita, Bruce, David Newman, and Alvin Rabushka. *Red Flag over Hong Kong.* Chatham, N.J.: Chatham House Publishers, 1996.

China. Amsterdam: Time-Life Books, 1984.

Doolittle, Justus. *Social Life of the Chinese.* New York: Harper, 1876.

Goforth, Rosalind. *Climbing.* Grand Rapids: Zondervan, 1945.

Goforth, Rosalind. *How I Know God Answers Prayer.* New York: The Sunday School Times Co., 1921.

Haldane, Charlotte. *The Last Great Empress of China.* Indianapolis: Bobbs-Merrill Company, 1965.

Haw, Stephen G. *A Traveller's History of China.* New York: Interlink Books, 1995.

Hefley, James, and Marti Hefley. *China! Christian Martyrs of the 20th Century.* Milford, Mich.: Mott Media, 1978.

Holt, Edgar. *The Opium Wars in China.* London: Putnam and Company, 1964.

MacFarquhar, Roderick, et al. *The Forbidden City.* New York: Newsweek, [1972].

Nutting, Anthony. *Gordon: Martyr and Misfit.* London: The Reprint Society, 1966.

O'Connor, Richard. *The Spirit Soldiers.* New York: G. P. Putnam's Sons, 1973.

Selby, John. *The Paper Dragon.* New York: Frederick A. Praeger Publishers, 1968.

Scott, J. M. *The White Poppy: A History of Opium.* New York: Funk and Wagnalls, 1969.

Schiffer, Herbert. *Chinese Export Porcelain.* Exton, Pa.: Schiffer Publishing Ltd., 1975.

Schurmann, Franz, and Orville Schell. *Imperial China: The Decline of the Last Dynasty and the Origins of Modern China.* Vol. 1 of *The China Reader.* New York: Random House, 1967.

Warner, Marina. *The Dragon Empress.* New York: Macmillan Company, 1972.

Chapter Fourteen

TIME LINE NOTATIONS

- Benjamin Franklin invents the lightning conductor—1752
- The African slave trade begins to attract criticism— 1762
- James Bruce traces the Blue Nile to its confluence with the White Nile—1772
- Davy Crockett is killed at the Alamo—1836
- Close to three thousand Zulus are killed by the Boers in the Battle of Blood River—1838
- Charles Dickens publishes "A Christmas Carol"—1843
- The American Civil War begins—1861
- Stanley finds Livingston at Ujiji—1871
- Gold is discovered in the Transvaal—1884
- The Lake Victoria railway is completed—1901

SOURCES

Beyan, Amos J. *The American Colonization Society and the Creation of the Liberian State.* Lanham, Md.: University Press of America, 1991.

Blaikie, W. Garden. *The Personal Life of David Livingstone.* New York: Fleming H. Revell, n.d.

Curtin, Philip D. *Africa Remembered: Narratives by West Africans from the Era of the Slave Trade.* Madison, Wis.: University of Wisconsin Press, 1977.

Davidson, Basil. *Africa in History.* New York: Simon and Schuster, 1996.

Huxley, Elspeth. *The Challenge of Africa.* London: Aldus Books Ltd., 1971.

Kinross, Lord. *Between Two Seas: The Creation of the Suez Canal.* New York: William Morrow and Company, Inc., 1969.

Lee, Emanoel. *To the Bitter End.* New York: Penguin Books, 1986.

Lloyd, B. W., ed. *Livingstone.* Cape Town: C. Struik (Pty) Ltd., 1973.

Longgood, William F. *Suez Story: Key to the Middle East.* New York: Greenberg Publisher, 1957.

McLynn, Frank. *Stanley: The Making of an African Explorer.* Chelsea, Mich.: Scarborough House/ Publishers, 1990.

Mountfield, David. *A History of African Exploration.* Northbrook, Ill.: Domus Books, 1976.

Nielsen, Lewis T. "Mosquitoes, the Mighty Killers." *National Geographic* 156 (November 1979): 426.

Northcott, Cecil. *Robert Moffat: Pioneer in Africa 1817-1870.* New York: Harper Brothers, 1961.

Pakenham, Thomas. *The Scramble for Africa 1876-1912.* New York: Random House, 1991.

Tomes, Jacqueline. *The Story of Mary Slessor.* New York: William Morrow, 1964.

Warwick, Peter, ed. *The South African War.* London: Trewin Copplestone Books Ltd., 1980.

Wiley, Bell I., ed. *Slaves No More: Letters from Liberia.* Lexington, Ky.: University Press of Kentucky, 1980.

Chapter Fifteen

TIME LINE NOTATIONS

- Winston Churchill—1871-1947
- Arnold Schoenberg—1874-1951
- Pablo Picasso—1881-1973
- Igor Stravinsky—1882-1971
- T. S. Eliot—1888-1965
- Erich Maria Remarque—1898-1970
- Ernest Hemingway—1899-1961
- Salvador Dali—1904-89
- China abolishes slavery—1910
- Halley's comet observed—1910
- *Titanic* sinks on maiden voyage—1912
- First Charlie Chaplin film—1913
- Charles Lindbergh flies his plane "Spirit of St. Louis" from New York to Paris—1927
- Stock Market Crash—October 29, 1929
- Amelia Earhart disappears over the Pacific Ocean—1937
- Disney's *Snow White and the Seven Dwarfs* is released—1937
- Color television's first appearance—1951

SOURCES

Bayliss, Gwyn M. *Bibliographic Guide to the Two World Wars: An Annotated Survey of English-language Reference Materials.* London: Bowker, 1977.

Bloomberg, Marty, and Hans H. Weber. *World War II and its Origins: A Select Annotated Bibliography of Books in English.* Littleton, Colo.: Libraries Unlimited, 1975.

Henley, Wallace. *Europe at the Crossroads: A Reporter Looks at Europe's Spiritual Crisis.* Westchester, Ill.: Good News Publishers, 1978.

Hersey, John. *A Bell for Adano.* Garden City, N.Y.: Sun Dial Press, 1945.

Higgins, Jack. *Storm Warning, a Novel.* New York: Holt, Rinehart and Winston, 1976.

Hope, Bob. *I Never Left Home.* New York: Simon and Schuster, 1944.

Hickman, Tom. *What Did You Do in the War, Auntie?* London: BBC Books, 1995.

Life Goes to War: A Picture History of World War II. Boston: Little, Brown, 1977. (Time-Life book)

McLeod, Hugh. *Religion and the People of Western Europe.* New York: Oxford University Press, 1981.

Walters, Philip, ed. *World Christianity: Eastern Europe.* Monrovia, Calif.: MARC, 1988.

Chapter Sixteen

TIME LINE NOTATIONS

- The Trans-Siberian railway is completed—1917
- The Chinese Communist Party is founded—1921
- Disney introduces the first Mickey Mouse films—1928
- Sergei Prokofiev composes "Peter and the Wolf"—1936
- The Russians defeat the German army at the battle of Stalingrad—1942
- The USSR launches Sputnik I and II, first earth satellites—1957
- An American U2 spy plane is shot down in the USSR—1960
- Yuri Gagarin becomes the first man in space—1961
- The Berlin Wall is constructed—1961
- There is a major nuclear power plant disaster at Chernobyl, Ukraine—1986

SOURCES

Crowley, Joan Frances, and Dan Vaillancourt. *Lenin to Gorbachev: Three generations of Soviet Communists.* Arlington, Ill: Harlan Davidson, Inc., 1989.

Lands and Peoples, Special Edition: The Changing Face of Europe. Grolier, Inc., 1996.

Monks, Alfred L. *The Soviet Intervention in Afghanistan.* Washington, D.C.: American Enterprise Institute for Public Policy Research, 1981.

Orlov, Alexander. *The Secret History of Stalin's Crimes.* New York: Random House, 1953.

Testimony from Prison

(Nikolai, a man from Minsk, Belarus) I lived quietly until 1939 when Christianity began to be trodden down. The most active, intelligent people were put in prison. The youth rose up in revolt, but it did not last long. Many were sent away from their homes in the Ukraine, including me. The conditions in [Siberia] were severe. We survived by foraging for food, or else we died. Some militiamen were very cruel. I had two fingers banged in the door and three teeth broken. It was worse for those who hung out in bars or smoking houses. I worked in a coal mine; wet ones were so cold they made people die. I was in a dry one. If a person coming back from work was too weak, the patrol would shoot him unless the people carried him in the middle. They were said to have tried to escape. They stacked people to freeze outside when dead in the winter—naked until the spring came when they dug mass graves. Foxes were seen carrying body parts from these stacks into the woods. They had some radishes for cattle that they made soup from for the prisoners. On Passover, some were shot for trying to eat it before it was made soup. Some were taken to the forest as a punishment. Escapees could be seen among the short trees or they would freeze on the ground. As punishment, they had to lie for three days in front of the barracks.

Until 1948, the death toll was very high. Just to make sure the corpses were dead, their heads were smashed with a hammer. In 1948, sheets and other stuff began to be provided more because even [the Communists] thought the death rate rather high. I am amazed that man, the crown of creation, could be so cruel. My brother, after fighting in the war, was brought to court because I was in jail. My mom was taken to Siberia and came back. Then they knocked all her teeth out. I was a political prisoner for fourteen years and seven months.

In our camp there were 9,000 prisoners, one of whom was a czar's attendant. Outsiders who tried to bring food to prisoners received ten-year sentences themselves. We had fellowships every two months and discussed different ideas, beliefs, and religion. The czar's attendant was humble and a Christian and told me of it.

Usually, prisoners had a little bread in their shirt to save them in case of near death. I thought one was dead, but as I went to take his bread he said, "I am still alive." That scared me, and I never did again. He died before morning. In the hospitals, if someone died, others would eat his bread by lifting the dead man's hand. If found out, the thief was beaten.

Khruschev came and made amnesty, and I was set free at age 36.

Chapter Seventeen

TIME LINE NOTATIONS

- Japan annexes Korea—1910
- The Chinese Communist Party is founded—1921
- Hirohito succeeds his father as Emperor of Japan—1926
- Gandhi leads the Salt March in India—1930
- The Empire State Building is constructed in New York—1930-31
- The Japanese bomb Pearl Harbor—1941
- Gandhi is assassinated—1948
- Elizabeth II becomes queen—1952
- Japan and China become the fourth and fifth nations to launch satellites into space—1970
- Four students die in a Vietnam War protest at Kent State University in Ohio—1970

SOURCES

Bush, Lewis. *Japan Dictionary*. New York: Philosophical Library, 1956.

Giles, Herbert Alan. *China and the Manchus*. New York: G. P. Putnam's Sons, 1912.

Say, Allen. *The Bicycle Man*. Boston: Houghton Mifflin, 1982.

Takeshita, Jiro. *Food in Japan*. Vero Beach, Fla.: Rourke Publications, 1989.

Yoshiko, Uchida. *A Jar of Dreams*. New York: Simon and Schuster, 1981.

Chapter Eighteen

TIME LINE NOTATIONS

- Ottoman Empire—c. 1300-1918
- Turkey becomes a nation—1922
- Mustafa Kemal Atatürk abolishes office of caliph—1924
- Saudi Arabia formed—1932
- Oil discovered in Saudi Arabia—1938
- First oil embargo—1973
- "White Revolution" in Iran—1960s and 1970s
- Ayatollah Khomeini comes to power in Iran—1979
- Israel invades Lebanon—1982
- PLO-Israeli agreement—1993

SOURCES

Churchill, Randolph S. *The Six-Day War*. Boston: Houghton Mifflin, 1967.

Cottrell, Alvin J., ed. *The Persian Gulf States: A General Survey*. Baltimore: Johns Hopkins University Press, 1980.

Eban, Abba S. *Promised Land*. Nashville: T. Nelson, 1978.

Elazar, Daniel J. *The Other Jews: The Sephardim Today*. New York: Basic Books, 1989.

Friedman, Morman. *Desert Victory*. Annapolis, Md.: Naval Institute Press, 1992.

Heller, Mark. *A Palestinian State: The Implications for Israel*. Cambridge, Mass.: Harvard University Press, 1983.

Hyamson, Albert M. *Palestine Under the Mandate 1920-1948*. Westport, Conn.: Greenwood Press, 1976.

Karsh, Efraim. *Saddam Hussein: A Political Biography*. New York: Free Press, 1991.

Lesch, Ann M., and Dan Tschirgi. *Origins and Development of the Arab-Israeli Conflict*. Westport, Conn.: Greenwood Press, 1998.

London Sunday Times. *The Yom Kippur War*. Garden City, N.Y.: Doubleday, 1994.

Meir, Golda. *My Life*. New York: Putnam, 1975.

Rozenman, Eric, and Jeff Rubin, eds. *Myths and Facts 1989: A Concise Record of the Arab-Israeli Conflict*. Washington, D.C.: Near East Report, 1988.

Sygma photographers. *In the Eye of Desert Storm: Photographers of the Gulf War*. New York: H. N. Abrams, 1991.

Webster, Donald E. *The Turkey of Atatürk: Social Progress in the Turkish Reformation*. New York: AMS Press, 1973.

Chapter Nineteen

TIME LINE NOTATIONS

- France controls Algiers—1830
- W. E. B. Du Bois—1868-1963
- Charles de Gaulle—1890-1970
- Haile Selassie—1892-1975
- Boer War—1899-1902
- Nelson Mandela—1918-
- F. W. de Klerk—1936-
- Gold Coast becomes Ghana—1957
- Congo's independence (Zaire/Republic of Congo) from Britain—1960
- Rwanda becomes a nation—1962
- Mickey Mouse's 40th birthday—1968
- First man on the moon—1969
- Namibia's independence—1990
- Eritrea's independence—1993
- Attempted genocide of Tutsis by Hutus—1994
- Mandela becomes president of South Africa—1994

SOURCES

Abercrombie, Thomas J. "Algeria: Learning to Live with Independence." *National Geographic*. 144 (August 1973): 200-33.

Beckwith, Carol, and Angela Fisher. "Royal Gold of the Asante Empire." *National Geographic*. 190 (October 1996): 36-47.

Brink, André. "The Afrikaners." *National Geographic*. 174 (October 1988): 56-85.

Cobb, Charles E., Jr. "Eritrea Wins the Peace." *National Geographic*. 189 (June 1996): 82-105.

———. "The Twilight of Apartheid." *National Geographic*. 183 (February 1993): 66-93.

Countries of the World and Their Leaders Yearbook. Detroit, Mich.: Gale Research Co., 1980.

Dorsey, Learthen. *Historical Dictionary of Rwanda*. Metuchen, N.J.: Scarecrow Press, 1994.

Flint, John E. *Nigeria and Ghana*. Englewood Cliffs, N.J.: Prentice-Hall, 1966.

Moodie, T. *The Rise of Afrikanerdom*. Berkeley: University of California Press, 1975.

Ruedy, John. *Modern Algeria: The Origins and Development of a Nation*. Bloomington: Indiana University Press, 1992.

Ward, William Ernest Frank. *A History of Ghana*. London: Allen and Unwin, 1958.

Chapter Twenty

TIME LINE NOTATIONS

- Christopher Columbus discovers Costa Rica—1502
- Mexican-American War—1846-48
- First free election in Latin America is held in Costa Rica—1889
- Mexican Constitution written—1917
- PRI established in Mexico—1928
- Perón becomes president of Argentina for the first time—1946

SOURCES

Atkin, Ronald. *Mexico: Revolution 1910-20*. New York: J. Day Co., 1969.

Barnes, John. *Evita, First Lady: A Biography of Eva Perón*. New York: Grove Press, 1978.

Freedman, Lawrence. *Signals of War: The Falkland Conflict of 1982*. Princeton, N.J.: Princeton University Press, 1991.

Hastings, Max. *The Battle for the Falklands*. New York: Norton, 1983.

Krauze, Enrique. *Mexico: A Biography of Power*. New York: HarperCollins Publishers, 1997.

London Sunday Times. *War in the Falklands*. New York: Harper and Row, 1982.

Meyor, Michael C. *The Course of Mexican History*. New York: Oxford University Press, 1979.

New Countries in the 1800s
NETHERLANDS
GERMANY
POLAND
BELGIUM
FRANCE
SWITZ.
AUSTRIA
ITALY
GREECE

Chapter 11, page 306

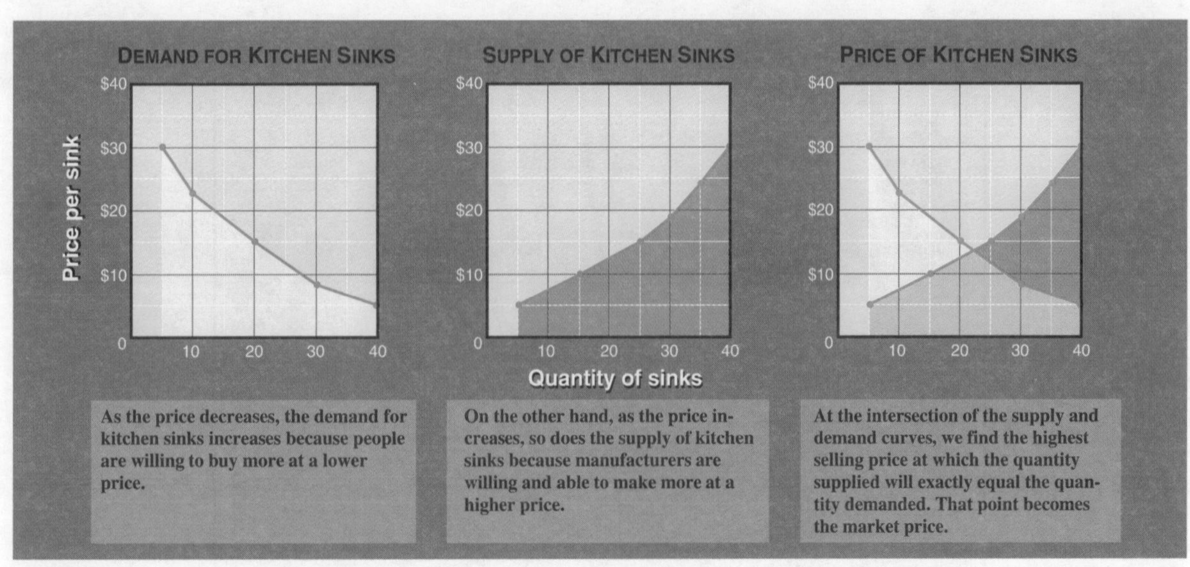
DEMAND FOR KITCHEN SINKS
SUPPLY OF KITCHEN SINKS
PRICE OF KITCHEN SINKS
Price per sink
$40
$30
$20
$10
0
10
20
30
40
Quantity of sinks
As the price decreases, the demand for kitchen sinks increases because people are willing to buy more at a lower price.
On the other hand, as the price increases, so does the supply of kitchen sinks because manufacturers are willing and able to make more at a higher price.
At the intersection of the supply and demand curves, we find the highest selling price at which the quantity supplied will exactly equal the quantity demanded. That point becomes the market price.

Chapter 11, page 310

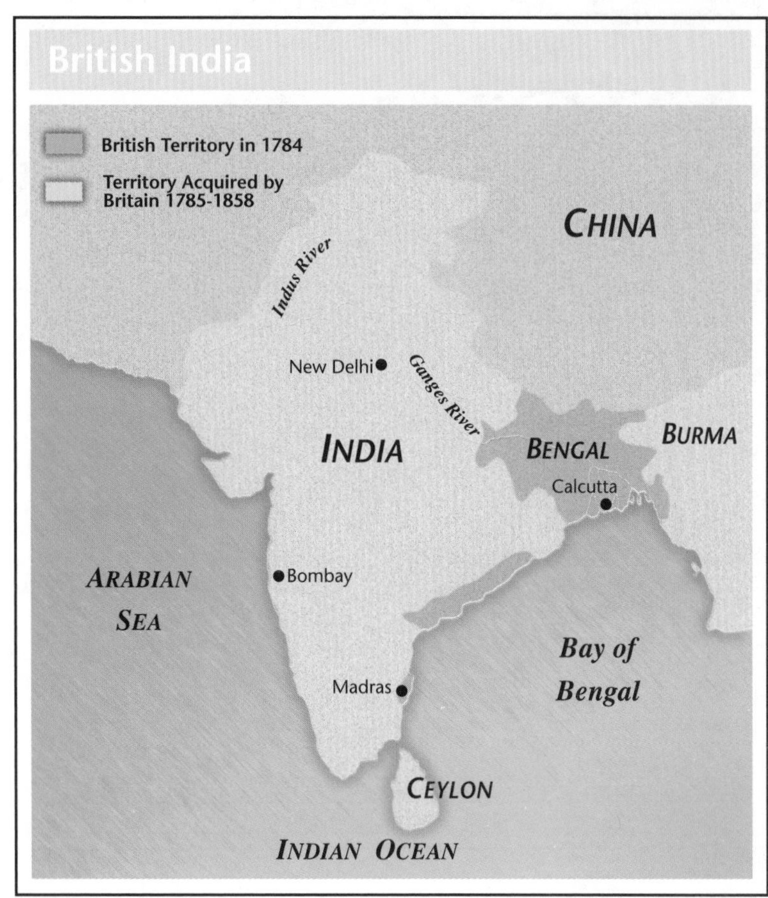
British India
British Territory in 1784
Territory Acquired by Britain 1785-1858
CHINA
Indus River
New Delhi
Ganges River
INDIA
BENGAL
BURMA
Calcutta
ARABIAN SEA
Bombay
Bay of Bengal
Madras
CEYLON
INDIAN OCEAN
Chapter 12, page 326

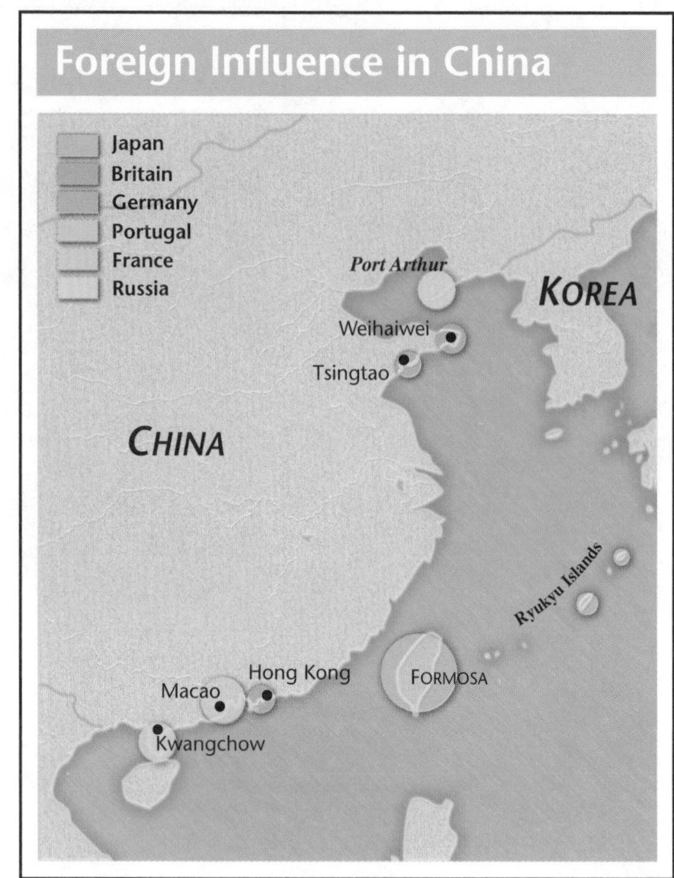
Foreign Influence in China
Japan
Britain
Germany
Portugal
France
Russia
Port Arthur
KOREA
Weihaiwei
Tsingtao
CHINA
Ryukyu Islands
Hong Kong
FORMOSA
Macao
Kwangchow
Chapter 13, page 369

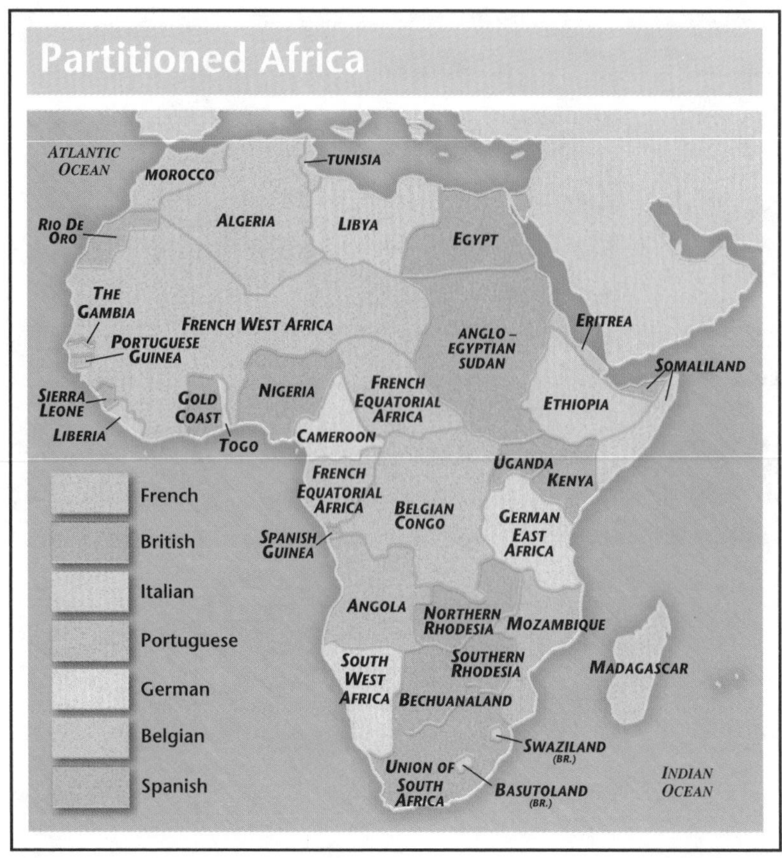
Partitioned Africa
ATLANTIC OCEAN
TUNISIA
MOROCCO
RIO DE ORO
ALGERIA
LIBYA
EGYPT
THE GAMBIA
FRENCH WEST AFRICA
PORTUGUESE GUINEA
ANGLO-EGYPTIAN SUDAN
ERITREA
SOMALILAND
SIERRA LEONE
GOLD COAST
NIGERIA
FRENCH EQUATORIAL AFRICA
ETHIOPIA
LIBERIA
TOGO
CAMEROON
UGANDA
KENYA
FRENCH EQUATORIAL AFRICA
BELGIAN CONGO
GERMAN EAST AFRICA
SPANISH GUINEA
ANGOLA
NORTHERN RHODESIA
MOZAMBIQUE
SOUTH WEST AFRICA
SOUTHERN RHODESIA
MADAGASCAR
BECHUANALAND
SWAZILAND (BR.)
UNION OF SOUTH AFRICA
BASUTOLAND (BR.)
INDIAN OCEAN
French
British
Italian
Portuguese
German
Belgian
Spanish
Chapter 14, page 399

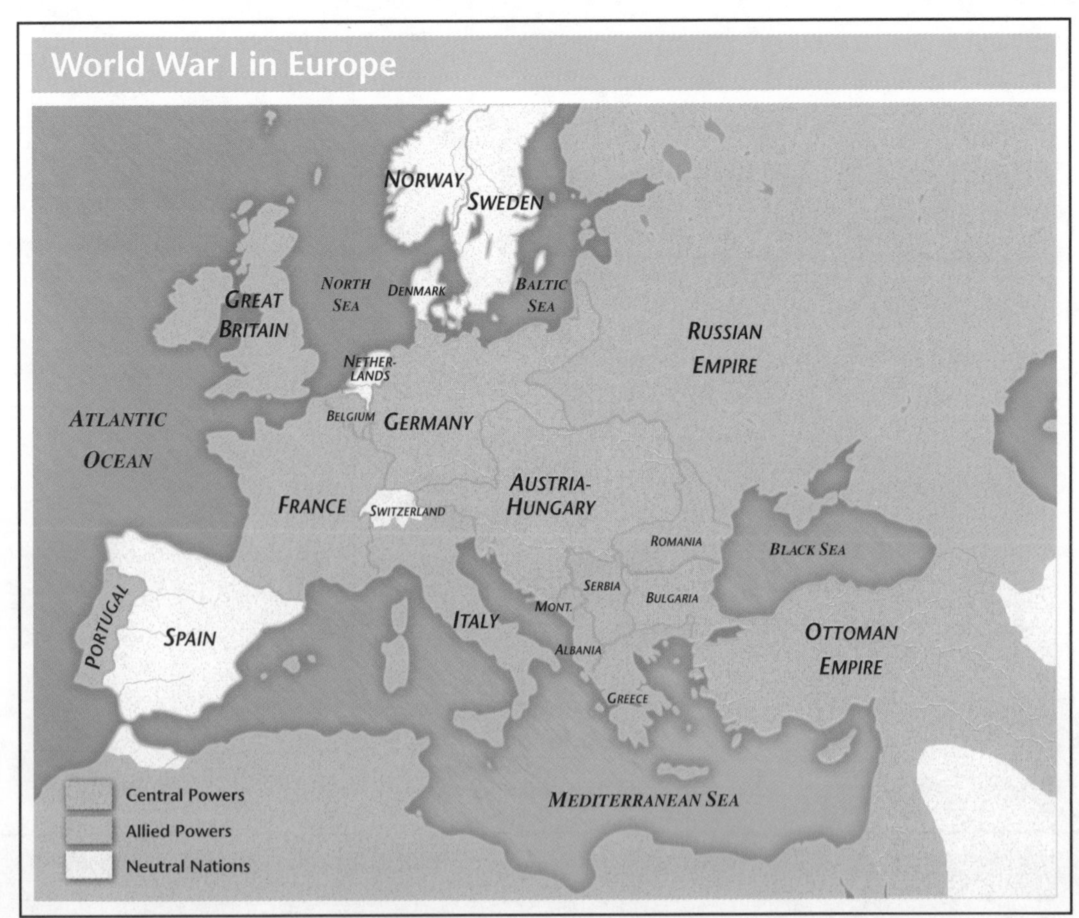
World War I in Europe
Norway
Sweden
North Sea
Denmark
Baltic Sea
Great Britain
Russian Empire
Nether-lands
Atlantic Ocean
Belgium
Germany
Austria-Hungary
France
Switzerland
Romania
Black Sea
Serbia
Bulgaria
Portugal
Spain
Mont.
Italy
Albania
Ottoman Empire
Greece
Mediterranean Sea
Central Powers
Allied Powers
Neutral Nations

Chapter 15, page 421

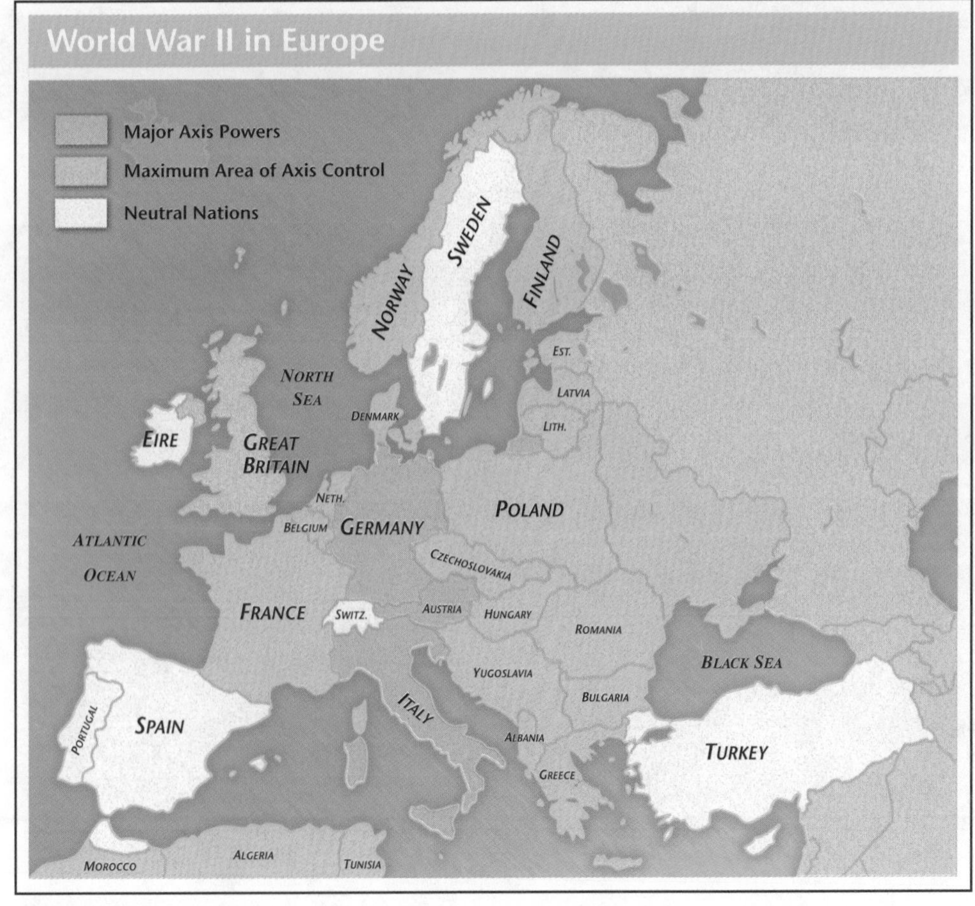
World War II in Europe
Major Axis Powers
Maximum Area of Axis Control
Neutral Nations
Sweden
Norway
Finland
Est.
North Sea
Latvia
Denmark
Lith.
Eire
Great Britain
Neth.
Poland
Belgium
Germany
Atlantic Ocean
Czechoslovakia
France
Switz.
Austria
Hungary
Romania
Yugoslavia
Black Sea
Italy
Bulgaria
Portugal
Spain
Albania
Turkey
Greece
Morocco
Algeria
Tunisia

Chapter 15, page 431

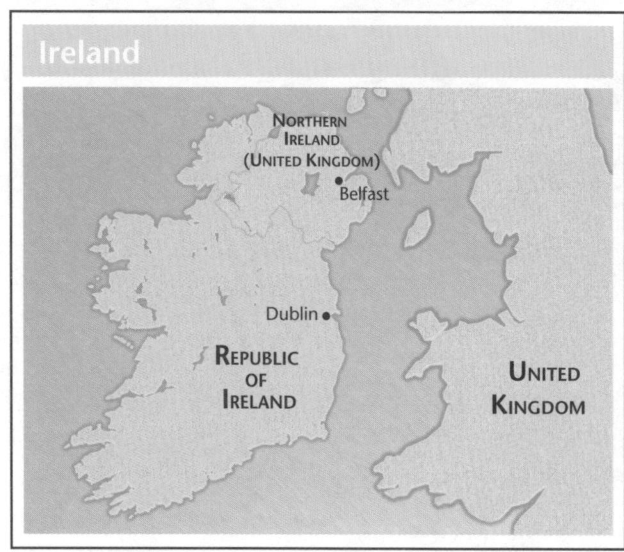

Chapter 15, page 441

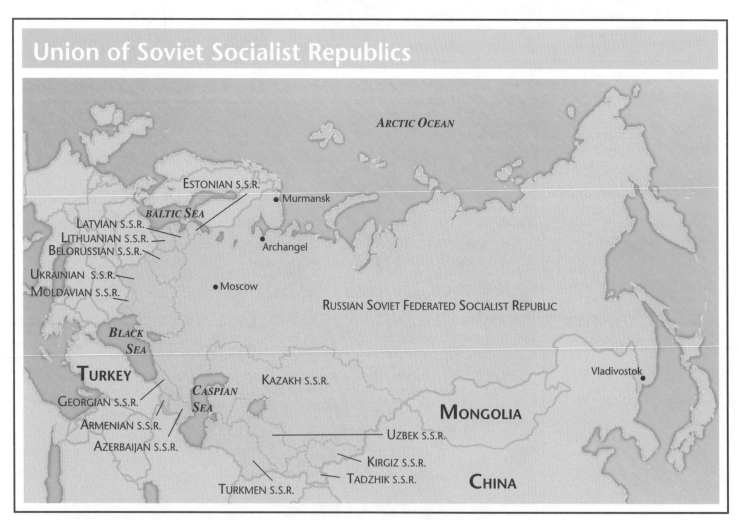

Union of Soviet Socialist Republics

Arctic Ocean
Estonian S.S.R.
Murmansk
Baltic Sea
Latvian S.S.R.
Lithuanian S.S.R.
Belorussian S.S.R.
Archangel
Ukrainian S.S.R.
Moscow
Moldavian S.S.R.
Russian Soviet Federated Socialist Republic
Black Sea
Turkey
Kazakh S.S.R.
Vladivostok
Caspian Sea
Georgian S.S.R.
Armenian S.S.R.
Mongolia
Azerbaijan S.S.R.
Uzbek S.S.R.
Kirgiz S.S.R.
Tadzhik S.S.R.
Turkmen S.S.R.
China

Chapter 16, page 450

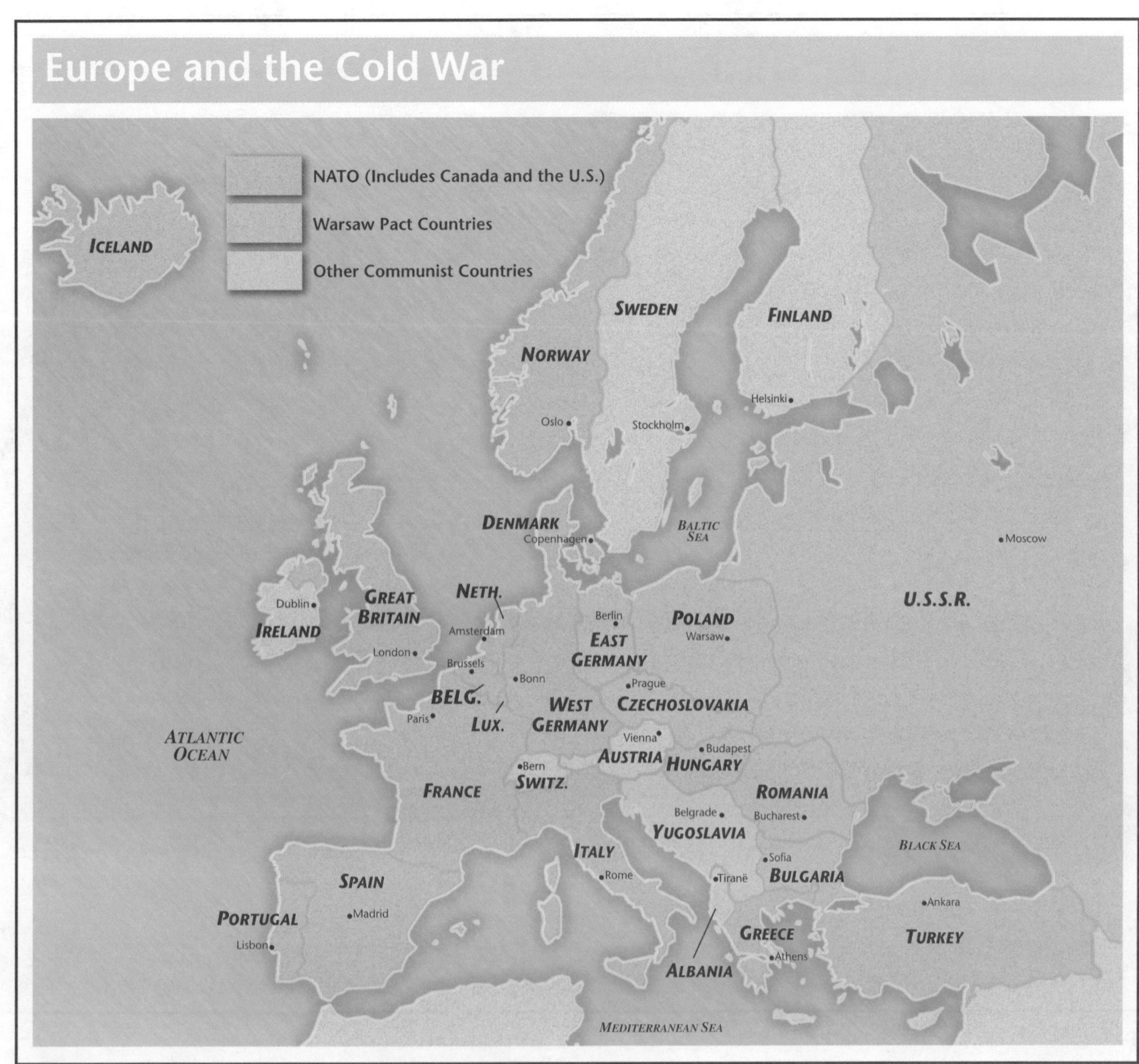
Europe and the Cold War
NATO (Includes Canada and the U.S.)
Warsaw Pact Countries
Other Communist Countries
ICELAND
NORWAY
SWEDEN
FINLAND
Oslo
Stockholm
Helsinki
DENMARK
Copenhagen
BALTIC SEA
Moscow
U.S.S.R.
IRELAND
Dublin
GREAT BRITAIN
London
NETH.
Amsterdam
Brussels
BELG.
LUX.
Paris
Bonn
Berlin
EAST GERMANY
POLAND
Warsaw
Prague
WEST GERMANY
CZECHOSLOVAKIA
Vienna
AUSTRIA
Budapest
HUNGARY
ATLANTIC OCEAN
FRANCE
Bern
SWITZ.
ROMANIA
Bucharest
Belgrade
YUGOSLAVIA
ITALY
Rome
Sofia
BULGARIA
Tiranë
BLACK SEA
Ankara
TURKEY
SPAIN
Madrid
PORTUGAL
Lisbon
GREECE
Athens
ALBANIA
MEDITERRANEAN SEA

Chapter 16, page 458

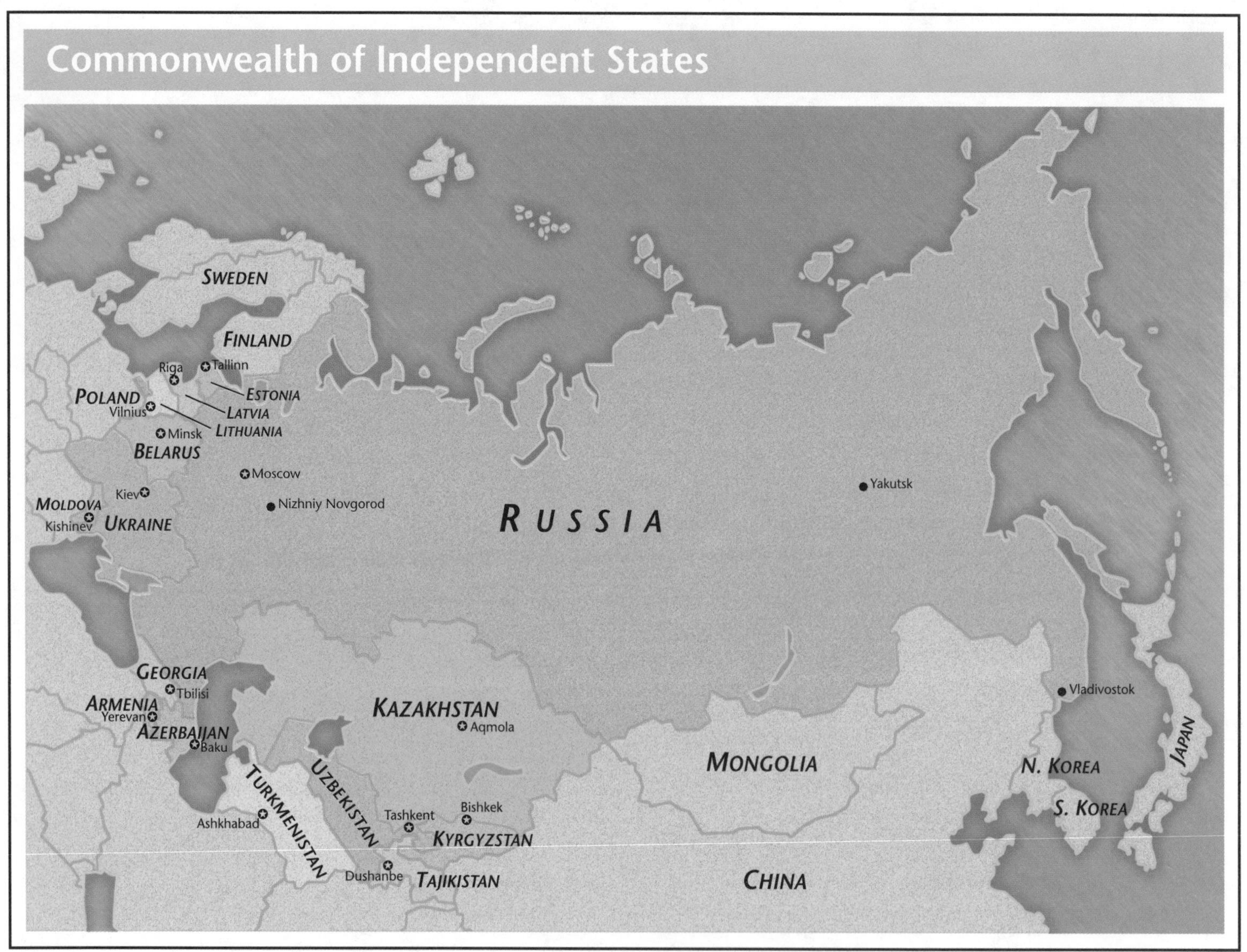

Chapter 16, page 470

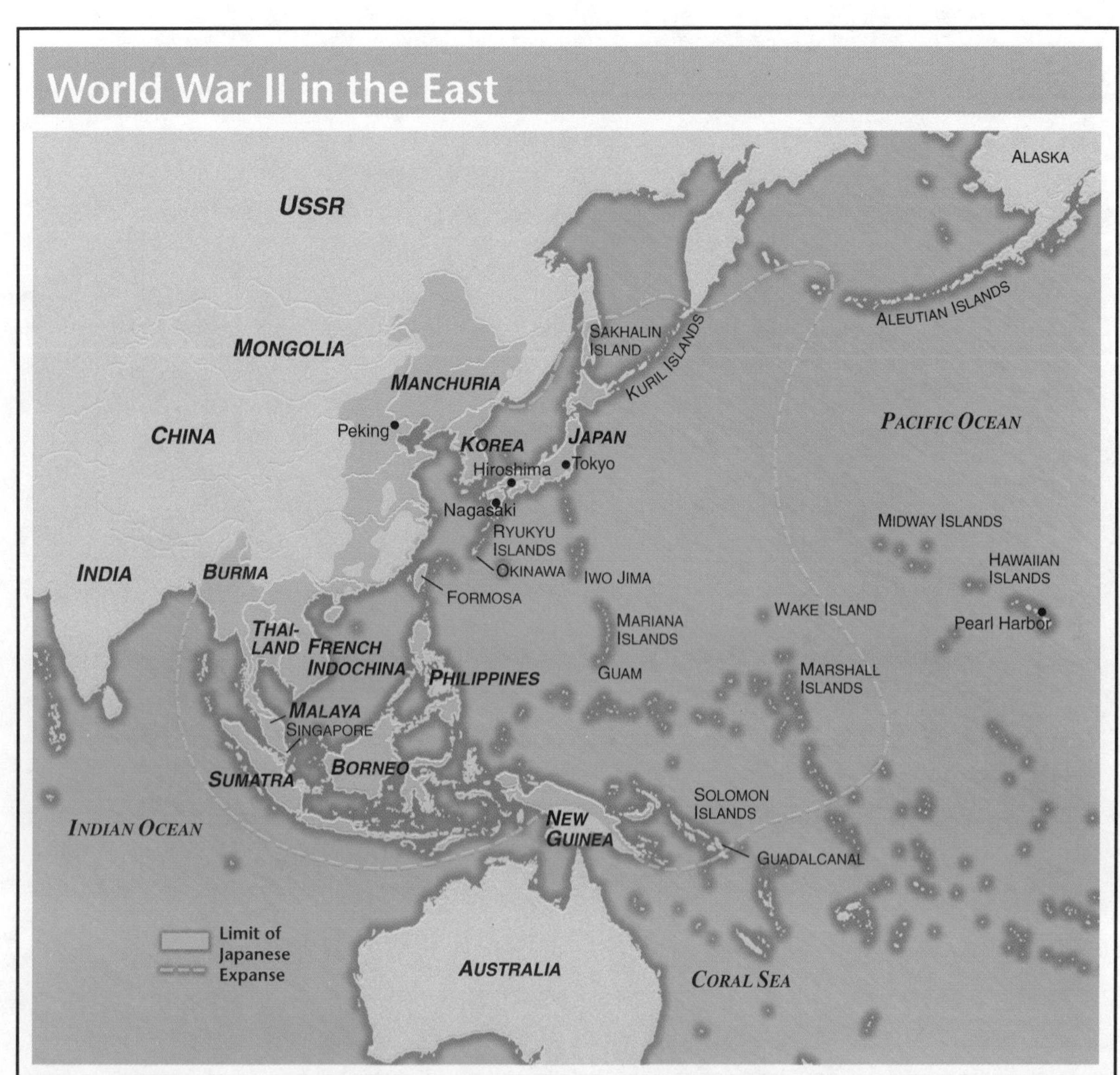
World War II in the East
USSR
ALASKA
ALEUTIAN ISLANDS
SAKHALIN ISLAND
KURIL ISLANDS
MONGOLIA
MANCHURIA
CHINA
Peking
KOREA
JAPAN
Tokyo
Hiroshima
Nagasaki
PACIFIC OCEAN
RYUKYU ISLANDS
OKINAWA
IWO JIMA
MIDWAY ISLANDS
HAWAIIAN ISLANDS
Pearl Harbor
INDIA
BURMA
FORMOSA
WAKE ISLAND
MARIANA ISLANDS
THAI-LAND
FRENCH INDOCHINA
PHILIPPINES
GUAM
MARSHALL ISLANDS
MALAYA
SINGAPORE
SUMATRA
BORNEO
SOLOMON ISLANDS
INDIAN OCEAN
NEW GUINEA
GUADALCANAL
Limit of Japanese Expanse
AUSTRALIA
CORAL SEA

Chapter 17, page 485

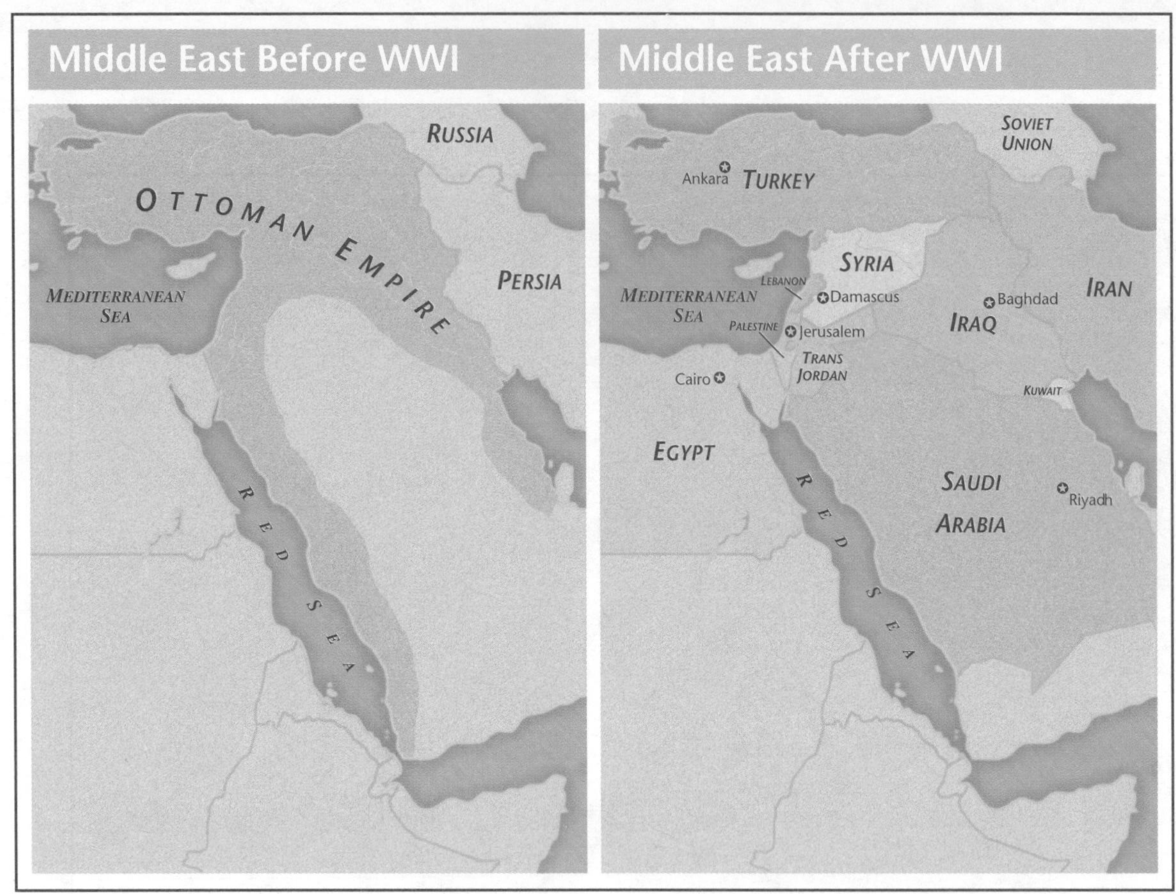
Middle East Before WWI
Russia
Ottoman Empire
Persia
Mediterranean Sea
Red Sea
Middle East After WWI
Soviet Union
Ankara
Turkey
Syria
Lebanon
Damascus
Iran
Baghdad
Mediterranean Sea
Palestine
Jerusalem
Iraq
Trans Jordan
Cairo
Kuwait
Egypt
Saudi Arabia
Riyadh
Red Sea

Chapter 18, page 514

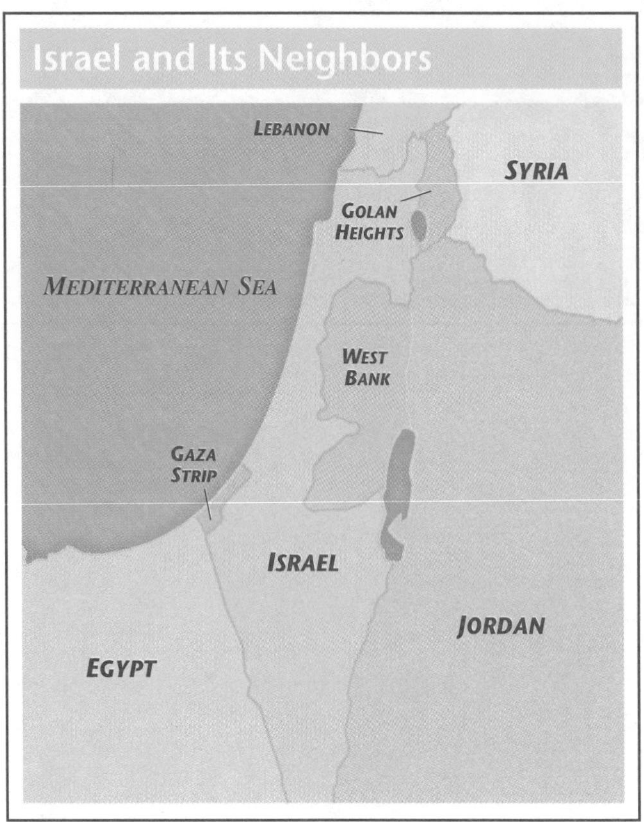
Israel and Its Neighbors
Lebanon
Syria
Golan Heights
Mediterranean Sea
West Bank
Gaza Strip
Israel
Jordan
Egypt

Chapter 18, page 529

Working Together

Whether you have been teaching for many years or are just getting started, your comments are vital in helping us maintain our standard of excellence. In fact, most of the improvements in our materials started with good advice from consumers. So after you have put our products to the test, please give us your thoughtful comments and honest assessment.

And thanks for your valuable help!

Book Title ______________________ **Grade level** __________

Material was ☐ used in classroom. ☐ used in home school. ☐ examined only.

How did you hear about us?

____

I liked

____

I'd like it better if

____

How did our material compare with other publishers' materials?

____

Other comments?

____

(OPTIONAL)

☐ Dr. ☐ Miss ☐ Mrs. ☐ Mr. ______________________

School ______________________

Street ______________________

City __________ State ______ ZIP ______

Phone( ) ______________________

E-mail ______________________

Fold and tape. DO NOT STAPLE.
Mailing address on the other side.

BJU PRESS
Greenville, SC 29614

Return address:

TAPE SHUT—DO NOT STAPLE

NO POSTAGE
NECESSARY IF
MAILED IN THE
UNITED STATES

BUSINESS REPLY MAIL
FIRST-CLASS MAIL PERMIT NO. 344 GREENVILLE, SC

POSTAGE WILL BE PAID BY ADDRESSEE

BJU PRESS
TEXTBOOK DIVISION
1700 WADE HAMPTON BLVD.
GREENVILLE, SC 29609-9971

------ Fold here ------

------ Fold here ------